SAINT THOMAS AQUINAS

OPUSCULA I
TREATISES

COMPENDIUM OF THEOLOGY
ON THE PRINCIPLES OF NATURE
ON BEING AND ESSENCE
ON SEPARATE SUBSTANCES
ON KINGSHIP

OPUSCULA

Volume 55
Latin/English Edition of the Works of St. Thomas Aquinas

AQUINAS INSTITUTE | EMMAUS ACADEMIC
GREEN BAY, WI | STEUBENVILLE, OH

This printing was funded in part by donations made in memory of:
Marcus Berquist, Rose Johanna Trumbull, John and Mary Deignan,
Thomas and Eleanor Sullivan, Ann C. Arcidi, and Fr. John T. Feeney and his sister Mary

This printing was also made possible by donations from Kevin Bergdorf, Patricia Lynch, Josh and Holly Harnisch,
and by donations made in honor of the Studentate Community of the Dominican Province of St. Albert the Great, USA,
Fr. Brian McMaster, Dr. Brian Cutter, and in gratitude to the Very Rev. Romanus Cessario, OP, STM

Published with the ecclesiastical approval of
The Most Reverend David L. Ricken, DD, JCL
Bishop of Green Bay
Given on July 16, 2016

PUBLISHER'S CATALOGING-IN-PUBLICATION DATA

Thomas Aquinas, St., 1225–1274
  Opuscula I / Saint Thomas Aquinas; edited by The Aquinas Institute;
  translated by Cyril Vollert, SJ, Robert T. Miller, R. A. Kocourek, Francis J. Lescoe, and Gerald B. Phelan
  p. 424 cm.
  ISBN 978-1-62340-055-2

Thomas, Aquinas, Saint, 1225-1274--Philosophy

B765.T52 E5
189´.4   2017937384

Notes on the Text

Latin Text of St. Thomas

The Leonine Edition is the source for all the Latin texts used in this volume: the texts of the *Compendium Theologiae* and the *de Regno* are taken from vol. 42 (1979); the *de Principiis Naturae* and the *de Ente et Essentia* are taken from vol. 43 (1976); and the *de Angelis, seu de Substantiis Separatis* is taken from vol. 40D (1968). The orthography of the later volumes of the Leonine Edition has been adapted to standard Ecclesiastical Latin.

English Translation of St. Thomas

The translation of the *Compendium of Theology* is based on the public domain translation of Cyril Vollert, SJ (St. Louis: Herder, 1947). It has been edited by Michael Bolin, Jeremy Holmes, Peter Kwasniewski, and John Mortensen. The remaining translations have been edited by John P. Joy.

The translation of *On the Principles of Nature* is based on the public domain translation of Roman A. Kocourek (St. Paul, MN: North Central Publishing, 1951).

The translation of *On Being and Essence* was prepared by Robert T. Miller. Translation © 1997, revised 2017 by Robert T. Miller. All persons are licensed to reproduce this translation and the footnotes hereto for personal or educational purposes, provided that the notice of copyright set forth above and this notice are included in their respective entireties in all copies. This license includes reproduction by a commercial entity engaged in the business of providing copying services if such reproduction is made pursuant to an agreement the other party to which would be licensed under the preceding sentence to reproduce this translation for personal or educational purposes.

The translation of *On Angels, or On Separate Substances* is based on the public domain translation of Francis J. Lescoe (West Hartford, CT: St. Joseph College, 1962).

The translation of *On Kingship* is based on the public domain translation of Gerald B. Phelan, revised by Ignatius T. Eschmann, OP (Toronto: Pontifical Institute of Medieval Studies, 1949).

The Aquinas Institute requests your assistance in the continued perfection of these texts.
If you discover any errors, please send us a note by email: editor@theaquinasinstitute.org

DEDICATED WITH LOVE TO
OUR LADY OF MT. CARMEL

Contents

COMPENDIUM OF THEOLOGY

BOOK II – ON HOPE

ON THE PRINCIPLES OF NATURE

ON BEING AND ESSENCE

ON SEPARATE SUBSTANCES

On Kingship

COMPENDIUM OF THEOLOGY

BOOK I

ON FAITH

CHAPTER 1

First, the intention of the work is set down

Aeterni Patris Verbum sua immensitate universa comprehendens, ut hominem per peccata minoratum in celsitudinem divinae gloriae revocaret, breve fieri voluit nostra brevitate assumpta, non sua deposita maiestate. Et ut a caelestis Verbi capessenda doctrina nullus excusabilis redderetur, quod propter studiosos diffuse et dilucide per diversa Sacrae Scripturae volumina tradiderat, propter occupatos sub brevi summa humanae salutis doctrinam conclusit.

Consistit enim humana salus in veritatis cognitione, ne per diversos errores intellectus obscuretur humanus; in debiti finis intentione, ne indebitos fines sectando a vera felicitate deficiat; in iustitiae observatione, ne per vitia diversa sordescat.

Cognitionem autem veritatis humanae saluti necessariam in brevibus et paucis fidei articulis comprehendit; hinc est quod Apostolus ad Romanos dicit: *Verbum abbreviatum faciet Dominus super terram*, et *Hoc quidem est verbum fidei quod praedicamus*. Intentionem humanam brevi oratione rectificavit, in quo dum orare nos docuit, quo nostra intentio et spes tendere debeat ostendit. Humanam iustitiam quae in legis observatione consistit, uno praecepto caritatis consummavit: *plenitudo enim legis est dilectio*.

Unde Apostolus ad Corinthios in fide, spe et caritate, quasi in quibusdam salutis nostrae compendiosis capitulis, totam praesentis vitae perfectionem consistere docuit, dicens: *Nunc autem manent fides, spes et caritas*. Unde haec tria sunt, ut beatus Augustinus dicit, quibus colitur Deus.

Ut igitur tibi, fili carissime Reginalde, compendiosam doctrinam de Christiana religione tradam, quam semper prae oculis possis habere, circa haec tria in praesenti opere tota nostra versatur intentio. Ac primum de fide, secundo de spe, tertio vero de caritate agemus; hoc enim et Apostolicus ordo habet, et ratio recta requirit. Non enim amor rectus esse potest nisi primo debitus finis spei statuatur, nec hoc esse potest si veritatis cog-

The Word of the eternal Father, containing all things by his immensity, willed to become small in order to recall man, laid low by sin, to the height of divine glory. This he did not by putting aside his majesty, but by taking to himself our littleness. Lest anyone be excused from grasping the teaching of the heavenly Word, which he handed down clearly and at great length through the various volumes of Sacred Scripture for those who have leisure to study, he has compressed his teaching about human salvation into a brief summary for those who have little time.

Man's salvation consists in knowing the truth, so that the human mind may not be confused by various errors; in aiming for the right goal, so that man may not fall away from true happiness by pursuing the wrong ends; and in carrying out the law of justice, so that he may not besmirch himself with various vices.

He encompassed the knowledge of the truth necessary for man's salvation within a few brief articles of faith. This is what the Apostle says in Romans 9:28: *The Lord shall make a shortened word upon the earth*; and later he adds: *This is the word of faith, which we preach* (Rom 10:8). He straightened out man's aim with a short prayer in which, while he taught us to pray, he showed us where our aim and hope should point. In a single precept of charity he summed up that human justice which consists in observing the law: *Therefore, love is the fulfilling of the law* (Rom 13:10).

Hence the Apostle, in 1 Corinthians 13:13, taught that the whole perfection of this present life consists in faith, hope, and charity, as in certain brief headings outlining our salvation: *so faith, hope, and charity abide*. These are the three virtues, as St. Augustine says, by which God is worshiped.

Wherefore, my dearest son Reginald, so that I may hand on to you a compendious teaching about the Christian religion, which you can keep continually before your eyes, my entire aim in the present work revolves around these three virtues. I shall treat first of faith, then of hope, and lastly of charity, both because the Apostle's order has this sequence and because right reason demands it. Love cannot be rightly ordered unless the proper goal of our hope is

nitio desit. Primo igitur necessaria est fides, per quam veritatem cognoscas; secundo spes, per quam in debito fine tua intentio collocetur; tertio necessaria est caritas, per quam tuus affectus totaliter ordinetur.

established; nor can this happen if knowledge of the truth is lacking. Therefore, the first thing necessary is faith, by which you may come to a knowledge of the truth. Second, hope, that your aim may be fixed on the right end. Third, love is necessary, that your affections may be perfectly put in order.

CHAPTER 2

Order of topics concerning faith

Fides autem praelibatio quaedam est illius cognitionis quae nos in futuro beatos faciet. Unde et Apostolus dicit quod est *substantia sperandarum rerum*, quasi iam in nobis res sperandas, id est futuram beatitudinem, per modum cuiusdam inchoationis subsistere faciens. Illam autem beatificantem cognitionem circa duo cognita Dominus consistere docuit, scilicet circa divinitatem Trinitatis et humanitatem Christi; unde ad Patrem loquens dicit: *Haec est vita aeterna ut cognoscant te verum Deum*, etc.

Circa haec ergo duo tota fidei cognitio versatur, scilicet circa divinitatem Trinitatis et circa humanitatem Christi: nec mirum, quia Christi humanitas via est qua ad divinitatem pervenitur. Oportet igitur et in via viam cognoscere per quam possit pervenire ad finem; et in patria Deo gratiarum actio sufficiens non esset, nisi viae per quam salvati sunt cognitionem haberent. Hinc est quod Dominus discipulis dixit: *Et quo ego vado scitis, et viam scitis.*

Circa divinitatem vero tria cognosci oportet, primo quidem essentiae unitatem, secundo personarum Trinitatem, tertio divinitatis effectus.

Faith is a certain foretaste of that knowledge which is to make us happy in the life to come. The Apostle says, in Hebrews 11:1, that faith is *the substance of things to be hoped for*, as though implying that faith is already, in some preliminary way, making in us the things that are to be hoped for (which is future beatitude). Our Lord has taught us that this beatific knowledge has to do with two truths: namely, the divinity of the Trinity and the humanity of Christ. That is why, addressing the Father, he says: *This is eternal life, that they know thee the only true God, and Jesus Christ whom thou hast sent* (John 17:3).

All the knowledge imparted by faith revolves around these two points, the divinity of the Trinity and the humanity of Christ. This should cause us no surprise, for the humanity of Christ is the way by which we come to the divinity. Therefore, while we are still wayfarers, we ought to know the way leading to our goal. In the heavenly fatherland adequate thanks would not be rendered to God if men had no knowledge of the way by which they are saved. This is the meaning of our Lord's words to his disciples: *Where I am going you know, and the way you know* (John 14:4).

Now three truths must be known about the divinity: first, the unity of the divine essence; second, the Trinity of persons; third, the effects wrought by the divinity.

CHAPTER 3

That God exists

Circa essentiae quidem divinae unitatem, primo quidem tenendum est Deum esse; quod ratione conspicuum est. Videmus enim omnia quae moventur ab aliis moveri: inferiora quidem per superiora, sicut elementa per corpora caelestia; et in elementis quod fortius est movet id quod debilius est; et in corporibus etiam caelestibus inferiora a superiori aguntur. Hoc in infinitum procedere impossibile est. Cum enim omne quod movetur ab aliquo sit quasi instrumentum quoddam primi moventis, si primum movens non sit, quaecumque movent instrumenta erunt. Oportet autem, si in infinitum procedatur in moventibus et motis, primum movens non esse; omnia igitur infinita moventia et mota erunt instrumenta. Ridiculum est autem, etiam apud indoctos, ponere instrumenta moveri, nisi ab aliquo principali agente: simile enim est hoc ac si aliquis circa constitutionem arcae vel lecti ponat serram vel securim absque carpentario operante. Oportet igitur primum movens esse quod sit omnibus supremum; et hoc dicimus Deum.

Regarding the unity of the divine essence, we must first believe that God exists. This is a truth clearly known by reason. For we observe that all things that move are moved by other things. Lower things are moved by higher things, as the elements are moved by heavenly bodies; and among the elements themselves, the stronger moves the weaker; and even among the heavenly bodies, the lower are driven by the higher. This cannot go on to infinity. For since everything that is moved by another is a sort of instrument of the first mover, if a first mover is lacking, then all things that move will be instruments. Now if one goes on to infinity with movers and things moved, there can be no first mover. In such a case, these infinitely many movers and moved things will all be instruments. But even the unlearned perceive how ridiculous it is to suppose that instruments are moved without some principal agent. This would be like fancying that, when a chest or a bed is being built, the saw or the hatchet performs its functions without the carpenter. Accordingly, there must be a first mover that is above everything else; and this we call God.

CHAPTER 4

That God is immovable

Ex hoc autem apparet quod necesse est Deum omnino immobilem esse. Cum enim sit primum movens, si moveretur, necesse esset se ipsum vel a se ipso vel ab alio moveri. Ab alio quidem moveri non potest: oporteret enim esse aliud movens prius eo, quod est contra rationem primi moventis.

A se ipso autem si movetur, hoc potest esse dupliciter: aut quod secundum idem sit movens et motum, aut ita quod secundum aliquid sui sit movens et secundum aliquid motum. Horum quidem primum esse non potest. Cum enim omne quod movetur, inquantum huiusmodi, sit in potentia, quod autem movet sit in actu, si secundum idem esset movens et motum, oporteret quod secundum idem esset in potentia et actu: quod est impossibile. Secundum etiam esse non potest. Si enim esset aliud movens et alterum motum, non esset ipsum secundum se primum movens, sed ratione partis quae

From this it is clear that God must be immovable. For, since he is the first mover, if he were moved he would have to be moved either by himself or by another. He cannot indeed be moved by another, for then there would have to be another mover prior to him, which is against the very idea of a first mover.

If he is moved by himself, this can be conceived in two ways: either that he is mover and moved according to the same respect, or that he is a mover according to one aspect of him and is moved according to another aspect. Now the first of these alternatives is impossible. For since everything that is moved is, to that extent, in potency, and whatever moves is in act, if God were both mover and moved according to the same respect then he would have to be in potency and in act according to the same respect, which is impossible. The second alternative is also impossible. If one part were moving and another were moved, he would

movet. Quod autem est per se, est prius eo quod non est secundum se; non potest igitur esse primum movens, si ratione suae partis hoc ei conveniat. Oportet igitur primum movens omnino immobile esse.

Ex his etiam quae moventur et movent hoc ipsum considerari potest. Omnis enim motus videtur ab aliquo immobili procedere, quod scilicet non movetur secundum illam speciem motus: sicut videmus quod alterationes et generationes et corruptiones, quae sunt in istis inferioribus, reducuntur sicut in primum movens in corpus caeleste, quod secundum hanc speciem motus omnino non movetur, cum sit ingenerabile et incorruptibile et inalterabile. Illud ergo quod est primum principium omnis motus, oportet esse immobile.

not be the first mover essentially, but by reason of that part of him which moves. But what is essential is prior to that which is not essential. Hence there cannot be a first mover at all, if being the first mover belongs to him by reason of one of his parts. Accordingly, the first mover must be altogether immovable.

The same thing can be investigated based on things that move and are moved. For every motion is observed to proceed from something immobile, namely, from something that is not moved according to that species of motion. Thus we see that alterations and generations and corruptions occurring in lower bodies are traced back (as to a first mover) to a heavenly body that is in no way moved according to this species of motion, since it is incapable of being generated, corrupted, or altered. Therefore, the first principle of all motion must be immoveable.

CHAPTER 5

That God is eternal

Ex hoc autem apparet ulterius Deum esse aeternum. Omne enim quod incipit esse vel desinit, per motum vel per mutationem hoc patitur; ostensum est autem quod Deus est omnino immobilis: est ergo aeternus.

From this, it is furthermore evident that God is eternal. For everything that begins to be or that ceases to be undergoes this through motion or change. But we have just shown that God is absolutely immoveable. Therefore, he is eternal.

CHAPTER 6

That God's existence is necessary in itself

Per hoc autem ostenditur quod Deum esse est necessarium. Omne enim quod possibile est esse et non esse, est mutabile; sed Deus est omnino immutabilis, ut ostensum est: ergo Deum non est possibile esse et non esse. Omne autem quod est, et non est possibile ipsum non esse, necesse est ipsum esse, quia necesse esse et non possibile non esse idem significant: ergo Deum esse est necesse.

Item, omne quod est possibile esse et non esse, indiget aliquo alio quod faciat ipsum esse, quia quantum est in se, se habet ad utrumque. Quod autem facit aliquid esse, est prius eo; omni igitur eo quod est possibile esse et non esse, est aliquid prius. Deo autem non est aliquid prius; ergo non est possibile ipsum esse et non esse, sed necesse est eum esse. Et quia aliqua necessaria sunt

The same line of reasoning shows that it is necessary for God to exist. For everything that has the possibility of existing and not existing is mutable. But God is absolutely immutable, as has been demonstrated. Therefore, God does not have the possibility of existing and not existing. But anything that exists, and does not have the possibility of not existing, exists necessarily, since to exist necessarily and to be unable not to exist mean the same thing. Therefore, it is necessary for God to exist.

Moreover, everything that has the possibility of existing and of not existing needs something else to make it exist, for in itself it stands indifferently toward either alternative. But that which causes another thing to exist is prior to that thing. Hence there is something prior to anything that has the possibility of existing and of not existing. However, nothing is prior to God. Therefore, he does not have

quae suae necessitatis causam habent, quam oportet eis esse priorem, Deus qui est omnium primum non habet causam suae necessitatis; unde Deum esse per se ipsum est necesse.

the possibility of existing and of not existing, but he must necessarily exist. And since there are some necessary things that have a cause of their necessity, which cause must be prior to them, God, who is the first of all, has no cause of his own necessity. Hence God's existence is necessary by his very nature.

CHAPTER 7

That God always is

Ex his autem manifestum est quod Deus est semper. Omne enim quod est necesse esse, est semper, quia quod non possibile est non esse impossibile est non esse, et ita numquam non est; sed necesse est Deum esse, ut ostensum est: ergo Deus semper est.

Adhuc, nihil incipit esse aut desinit nisi per motum vel mutationem; Deus autem est omnino immutabilis, ut probatum est: impossibile est igitur quod esse inceperit vel quod esse desinat.

Item, omne quod non semper fuit, si esse incipiat, indiget aliquo quod sit ei causa essendi; nihil enim se ipsum educit de potentia in actum vel de non esse in esse. Deo autem nulla potest esse causa essendi, cum sit primum ens; causa enim prior est causato. Necesse est igitur Deum semper fuisse.

Amplius, quod convenit alicui non ex aliqua causa extrinseca, convenit ei per se ipsum; esse autem Deo non convenit ex aliqua causa extrinseca, quia illa causa esset eo prior; Deus igitur habet esse per se ipsum. Sed ea quae per se sunt, semper sunt, et ex necessitate; igitur Deus semper est.

From all this it is evident that God exists always. For whatever necessarily exists, always exists, because it is impossible for a thing that has no possibility of not being, not to be. Hence it never does not exist. But it is necessary for God to exist, as has been shown. Therefore, God exists always.

Again, nothing begins to be or ceases to be except through motion or change. But God is entirely immutable, as has been proved. Therefore, it is impossible for him ever to have begun to be or to cease to be.

Likewise, anything that has not always existed, if it begins to exist, needs some cause for its existence. For nothing brings itself forth from potency to act or from non-being to being. But God can have no cause of his being, since he is the first being, for a cause is prior to what is caused. Of necessity, therefore, God must always have existed.

Furthermore, whatever pertains to anyone not from an external cause, pertains to him of himself, essentially. But existence does not come to God from any external cause, since such a cause would have to be prior to him. Therefore, God has existence of himself, essentially. But what exists of itself exists always and necessarily. Therefore, God exists always.

CHAPTER 8

That there is no succession in God

Successio enim non invenitur nisi in illis quae sunt aliqualiter motui subiecta; prius enim et posterius in motu causant temporis successionem. Deus autem nullo modo est motui subiectus, ut ostensum est; non igitur est in eo aliqua successio, sed eius esse est totum simul.

Item, si alicuius esse non est totum simul, oportet quod ei aliquid deperire possit et aliquid advenire; deperit enim ei illud quod transit, et advenire ei potest illud quod in futurum expectatur. Deo autem nihil deperit

Succession is only found in things that are in some way subject to motion; for prior and posterior in motion cause the succession of time. God, however, is in no sense subject to motion, as has been shown. Accordingly, there is no succession in God, but his existence is simultaneously whole.

Again, if a being's existence is not simultaneously whole, something can be lost to it and something can accrue to it. For that which passes is lost, and what is expected in the future can be acquired. But nothing is lost to God or ac-

nec accrescit, quia immobilis est; igitur eius esse est totum simul.

Ex his autem duobus apparet quod proprie est aeternus; illud enim proprie est aeternum quod semper est et eius esse totum est simul, secundum quod Boetius dicit quod *aeternitas est interminabilis vitae tota simul et perfecta possessio.*

crues to him, since he is immutable. Therefore, his existence is simultaneously whole.

From these two observations the proper meaning of eternity emerges. That is properly eternal which always exists and whose existence is simultaneously whole, in accord with what Boethius says: *Eternity is the simultaneously whole and perfect possession of endless life.*[1]

CHAPTER 9

That God is simple

Inde etiam apparet quod oportet primum movens simplex esse. Nam in omni compositione oportet esse duo quae ad invicem se habeant sicut potentia ad actum; in primo autem movente, si est omnino immobile, impossibile est esse potentiam cum actu, nam unumquodque ex hoc quod est in potentia mobile est: impossibile est igitur primum movens compositum esse.

Adhuc, omni composito necesse est esse aliquid prius, nam componentia naturaliter sunt priora composito; illud igitur quod est omnium entium primum, impossibile est esse compositum. Videmus etiam in ordine eorum quae sunt, supra composita simplicia esse: nam elementa naturaliter sunt priora corporibus mixtis; inter ipsa etiam elementa primum est ignis, quod est subtilissimum; omnibus autem elementis prius est caeleste corpus, quod in maiori simplicitate constitutum est, cum ab omni contrarietate sit purum. Relinquitur igitur quod primum entium oportet omnino simplex esse.

Hence it is also clear that the first mover must be simple. For any composite being must contain two factors that are related to each other as potency to act. But in the first mover, which is altogether unmoveable, all combination of potency and act is impossible, because whatever is in potency is, by that very fact, movable. Accordingly, the first mover cannot be composite.

Moreover, something has to exist prior to any composite, since composing elements are naturally prior to a composite. Hence the first of all beings cannot be composite. We also observe that, in the order of things that exist, simpler things are before composite things. Thus elements are naturally prior to mixed bodies. Likewise, among the elements themselves, the first is fire, which is the simplest of all. Prior to all elements is the heavenly body, which has a even simpler construction since it is free from all contrariety. Hence the truth remains that the first of beings must be absolutely simple.

CHAPTER 10

That God is his own essence

Sequitur autem ulterius quod Deus sit sua essentia. Essentia enim uniuscuiusque rei est illud quod significat definitio eius. Hoc autem est idem cum re cuius est definitio, nisi per accidens, inquantum scilicet definito accidit aliquid quod est praeter definitionem ipsius: sicut homini accidit album praeter id quod est animal rationale et mortale, unde animal rationale et mortale est idem homini, sed non idem homini albo inquantum est album. In quocumque igitur non est invenire duo quorum unum est per se et aliud per accidens, oportet quod essentia eius sit omnino idem cum eo. In Deo autem,

The further conclusion follows that God is his own essence. The essence of anything is that which its definition signifies. This is identical with the thing of which it is the definition, except accidentally, namely, insofar as something is added to the thing defined over and above its definition. Thus whiteness is added to man, over and above the fact that he is a rational and mortal animal. Hence 'rational and mortal animal' is the same as man, but not the same as a white man, insofar as he is white. In any being, therefore, in which there are not found two factors, of which one is essential and the other accidental, its essence must

---

1. Boethius, *The Consolation of Philosphy*, Book V, Prosa 6.

cum sit simplex, ut ostensum est, non est invenire duo quorum unum sit per se et aliud per accidens; oportet igitur quod essentia eius sit omnino idem quod ipse.

Item, in quibuscumque essentia non est omnino idem cum re cuius est essentia, est invenire aliquid per modum potentiae et aliquid per modum actus; nam essentia formaliter se habet ad rem cuius est essentia, sicut humanitas ad hominem. In Deo autem non est invenire potentiam et actum, sed est actus purus; est igitur ipse sua essentia.

be altogether identical with it. In God, however, since he is simple (as has been shown), there are not found two factors whereof one is essential and the other accidental. Therefore, his essence must be absolutely the same as he himself.

Moreover, whenever an essence is not absolutely identical with the thing of which it is the essence, something is found in that thing by way of potency and something else by way of act. For an essence is formally related to the thing of which it is the essence as humanity is related to a man. In God, however, one does not find potency and act: he is pure act. Therefore, he is his essence.

CHAPTER 11

That God's essence is not other than his existence

Ulterius autem necesse est quod Dei essentia non sit aliud quam esse ipsius. In quocumque enim aliud est essentia et aliud esse eius, oportet quod illud alio sit et alio aliquid sit; nam per esse suum de quolibet dicitur quod est, per essentiam vero suam de quolibet dicitur quid sit: unde et definitio significans essentiam demonstrat quid est res. In Deo autem non est aliud quo est et aliud quo aliquid est, cum non sit in eo compositio, ut ostensum est; non est igitur in eo aliud eius essentia et suum esse.

Item, ostensum est quod Deus est actus purus absque alicuius potentialitatis permixtione; oportet igitur quod eius essentia sit ultimus actus, nam omnis actus qui est citra ultimum est in potentia ad ultimum actum. Ultimus autem actus est ipsum esse. Cum enim omnis motus sit exitus de potentia in actum, oportet illud esse ultimum actum in quem tendit omnis motus; et cum motus naturalis in hoc tendat quod est naturaliter desideratum, oportet hoc esse ultimum actum quod omnia desiderant: hoc autem est esse. Oportet igitur quod essentia divina, quae est actus purus et ultimus, sit ipsum esse.

Furthermore, God's essence cannot be other than his existence. In any being whose essence is distinct from its existence, the being must be by one thing and be something by another thing. For in virtue of a thing's existence we say that it is, and in virtue of its essence we say what it is. This is why a definition that signifies an essence manifests what a thing is. In God, however, there is not one thing by which he exists, and another by which he is something, since there is no composition in him, as has been shown. Therefore, God's essence is nothing else than his existence.

Again, we have proved that God is pure act without any admixture of potentiality. Accordingly, his essence must be ultimate act; for any act that is short of the ultimate act is in potency to that ultimate act. But the ultimate act is being itself. For, since all motion is an issuing forth from potency to act, the ultimate act must be that toward which all motion tends; and since natural motion tends to what is naturally desired, the ultimate act must be that which all desire. This is being. Consequently, the divine essence, which is pure and ultimate act, must be being itself.

CHAPTER 12

That God is not in a genus

Hinc autem apparet quod Deus non est in aliquo genere sicut species. Nam differentia addita generi constituit speciem, igitur cuiuslibet speciei essentia habet aliquid additum supra genus; sed ipsum esse, quod est essentia Dei, nihil in se continet quod sit alteri additum: Deus igitur non est species alicuius generis.

Item, cum genus contineat differentias potestate, in omni constituto ex genere et differentiis est actus permixtus potentiae. Ostensum est autem in Deo esse purum actum absque permixtione potentiae; non est igitur eius essentia constituta ex genere et differentiis, et ita non est in genere.

We infer from the above that God is not contained within any genus as a species. For a specific difference added to a genus constitutes a species. Hence the essence of any species possesses something over and above its genus. But being itself, which is God's essence, does not contain within itself anything that is added to something else. Accordingly, God is not a species of any genus.

Furthermore, since genus contains specific differences potentially, in every being composed of genus and differences, act is commingled with potency. But we have shown that God is pure act without any commingling of potency. Therefore, his essence is not composed of genus and differences; and so he is not in any genus.

CHAPTER 13

That God is not a genus

Ulterius autem ostendendum est quod neque possibile est Deum esse genus. Ex genere enim habetur quid est res, non autem rem esse; nam per differentias specificas constituitur res in proprio esse. Sed hoc quod Deus est, est ipsum esse; impossibile est ergo quod sit genus.

Item, omne genus differentiis aliquibus dividitur; ipsius autem esse non est accipere aliquas differentias, differentiae enim non participant genus nisi per accidens, inquantum species constitutae per differentias genus participant. Non potest autem esse aliqua differentia quae non participat esse, quia non ens nullius est differentia; impossibile est igitur quod Deus sit genus de multis speciebus praedicatum.

Furthermore, it is to be shown that God cannot be a genus, either. What a thing is comes from its genus, but not that it is; for the thing is established in its proper existence through specific differences. But that which God is, is very existence itself. Therefore, he cannot be a genus.

Moreover, every genus is divided by some differences. But no specific differences can be found for being itself. For differences do not share in genus except indirectly, insofar as the species that are constituted by differences share in a genus. But there cannot be any difference that does not share in being, since non-being is not a specific difference of anything. Accordingly, God cannot be a genus predicated of several species.

CHAPTER 14

That God is not a species said of many individuals

Neque etiam est possibile quod sit sicut una species de multis individuis praedicata. Individua enim diversa quae conveniunt in una essentia speciei distinguuntur per aliqua quae sunt praeter essentiam speciei; sicut homines conveniunt in humanitate, sed distinguuntur ab invicem per id quod est praeter rationem humanitatis. Hoc autem in Deo non potest accidere, nam ipse Deus est sua essentia, ut ostensum est; impossibile est igitur quod Deus sit species quae de pluribus individuis praedicetur.

Item, plura individua sub una specie contenta differunt secundum esse, et tantum conveniunt in una essentia speciei. Ubicumque igitur sunt plura individua sub una specie, oportet quod aliud sit esse et aliud essentia speciei; in Deo autem idem est esse et essentia, ut ostensum est: impossibile est igitur quod Deus sit sicut quaedam species de pluribus praedicata.

Nor can God be, as it were, a single species predicated of many individuals. Various individuals that come together in one essence of a species are distinguished by factors that lie outside the essence of the species. For example, men are alike in their common humanity but differ from one another in virtue of something that is outside the notion of humanity. This cannot occur in God, for God himself is his essence, as has been shown. Therefore, God cannot be a species that is predicated of several individuals.

Again, a number of individuals comprised under one species differ in their existence, and yet are alike in their one essence. Accordingly, whenever a number of individuals are under one species, their existence must be different from the essence of the species. But in God existence and essence are identical, as has been demonstrated. Therefore, God cannot be a sort of species predicated of many individuals.

CHAPTER 15

That it is necessary for God to be one

Hinc etiam apparet quod necesse est unum solum Deum esse. Nam si sint multi dii, aut aequivoce aut univoce dicentur dii. Si aequivoce, hoc non est ad propositum: nihil enim prohibet quod nos appellamus lapidem, alios appellare Deum. Si autem univoce, oportet quod conveniant vel in genere vel in specie; ostensum est autem quod Deus neque potest esse genus, neque species plura sub se continens: impossibile est igitur esse plures deos.

Item, illud quo essentia communis individuatur, impossibile est pluribus convenire: unde licet possint esse plures homines, impossibile tamen est hunc hominem esse nisi unum tantum. Si igitur essentia per se ipsam individuetur et non per aliquid aliud, impossibile est quod pluribus conveniat; sed essentia divina per se ipsam individuatur, quia in Deo non est aliud essentia et quod est, cum ostensum sit quod Deus sit sua essentia: impossibile est ergo quod sit Deus nisi unus tantum.

Item, duplex est modus quo aliqua forma potest multiplicari: unus per differentias, sicut forma generalis, ut color in diversas species coloris; alius per subiecta, sicut albedo. Omnis ergo forma quae non potest multiplicari

Hence the conclusion is also evident that there can only be one God. If there were many gods, they would be called gods either equivocally or univocally. If they are called gods equivocally, this is not relevant to our topic: there is nothing to prevent other peoples from applying the name 'god' to what we call a stone. If they are called gods univocally, they must agree either in genus or in species. But we have just shown that God can be neither a genus nor a species comprising many individuals under itself. Accordingly, a multiplicity of gods is impossible.

Again, that whereby a common essence is individuated cannot pertain to many. Although there can be many men, it is impossible for this particular man to be more than one only. So if an essence is individuated by itself, and not by something else, it cannot pertain to many. But the divine essence is individuated by itself, since God's essence is not distinct from his existence; for we have shown that God is his essence. Hence God cannot be more than one only.

Again, a form can be multiplied in two ways: first, by specific differences, as in the case of a generic form; this is how color is differentiated into the various species of color. Second, by the subjects in which it inheres, as whiteness is

per differentias, si non sit forma in subiecto existens, impossibile est quod multiplicetur; sicut albedo si subsisteret sine substantia, non esset nisi una tantum. Essentia autem divina est ipsum esse, cuius non est accipere differentias, ut ostensum est; cum igitur ipsum esse divinum sit quasi forma per se subsistens, eo quod Deus est suum esse, impossibile est quod essentia divina sit nisi una tantum. Impossibile est igitur esse plures deos.

multiplied. Therefore, any form incapable of being multiplied by specific differences, if it is a form that does not exist in a subject, cannot be multiplied at all. Thus whiteness, if it were to subsist without a subject, would not be more than one. But the divine essence is being itself, which does not admit of specific differences, as we have shown. Since, therefore, the divine existence is like a form subsisting by itself (for God is his existence), the divine essence cannot be more than one. Accordingly, a plurality of gods is impossible.

CHAPTER 16

That it is impossible for God to be a body

Patet autem ulterius quod impossibile est ipsum Deum esse corpus. Nam in omni corpore compositio aliqua invenitur, omne enim corpus est partes habens; id igitur quod est omnino simplex, corpus esse non potest.

Item, nullum corpus invenitur movere nisi per hoc quod ipsum movetur, ut per omnia inducenti apparet; si ergo primum movens est omnino immobile, impossibile est ipsum esse corpus.

It is evident, further, that God himself cannot be a body. For in every body some composition is found, since every body has parts. Hence that which is absolutely simple cannot be a body.

Moreover, we find that a body only moves something else by being moved itself, as is clear to one whose considers all the cases. So if the first mover is absolutely immovable, he cannot be a body.

CHAPTER 17

That it is impossible for him to be the form of a body

Neque etiam est possibile ipsum esse formam corporis aut aliquam virtutem in corpore. Cum enim omne corpus mobile inveniatur, oportet corpore moto, ea quae sunt in corpore moveri, saltem per accidens; primum autem movens non potest nec per se nec per accidens moveri, cum oporteat ipsum esse omnino immobile, ut ostensum est: impossibile est igitur quod sit forma vel virtus in corpore.

Item, oportet movens ad hoc quod moveat dominium supra rem quae movetur habere: videmus enim quod quanto magis virtus moventis excedit virtutem mobilis, tanto sit velocior motus. Illud igitur quod est omnium moventium primum, oportet maxime dominari supra res motas; hoc autem esse non posset si esset mobili aliquo modo obligatum, quod esse oporteret si esset forma eius vel virtus: oportet igitur primum movens neque corpus esse, neque virtutem in corpore, neque formam in corpore. Hinc est quod Anaxagoras posuit intellectum immixtum, ad hoc quod imperet et omnia moveat.

Nor is it possible for God to be the form of a body or any kind of power existing in a body. For, since all bodies are found to be mobile, whatever is present in a body must be moved, at least incidentally, if the body itself is moved. The first mover, however, cannot be moved either of itself or incidentally, for it must be absolutely immobile, as has been shown. Therefore, it is impossible that God be a form or a power in a body.

Again, in order to move an object, every mover must have dominion over the thing that is moved. For we observe that motion is more rapid in proportion as the mover's power exceeds the power of the mobile object. Therefore, that which is the very first among all movers must have the greatest dominion over all the things moved. But this would be impossible if the mover were in any way attached to the mobile object, as it would have to be if it were the body's form or power. Consequently, the first mover cannot be a body, or a power in a body, or a form in a body. This is why Anaxagoras postulated an intelligence unmixed with matter, that it might rule and move all things.

CHAPTER 18

That God is infinite according to essence

Hinc etiam considerari potest ipsum esse infinitum, non quidem privative secundum quod infinitum est passio quantitatis, prout scilicet infinitum dicitur quod est natum habere finem ratione sui generis, sed non habet; sed negative, prout infinitum dicitur quod nullo modo finitur. Nullus enim actus invenitur finiri nisi per potentiam quae est eius receptiva: invenimus enim formas limitari secundum potentiam materiae. Si igitur primum movens est actus absque potentiae permixtione, quia non est forma alicuius corporis neque virtus in corpore, necessarium est ipsum infinitum esse.

Hoc etiam ipse ordo qui in rebus invenitur demonstrat: nam quanto aliqua in entibus sunt sublimiora, tanto suo modo maiora inveniuntur. Inter elementa enim quae sunt superiora, maiora in quantitate inveniuntur, sicut et in simplicitate: quod eorum generatio demonstrat, cum in multiplicata proportione ignis ex aere generetur, aer ex aqua, aqua autem ex terra; corpus autem caeleste manifeste apparet totam quantitatem elementorum excedere. Oportet igitur id quod inter omnia entia primum est, et eo non potest esse aliud prius, infinitae quantitatis suo modo existere.

Nec mirum, si id quod est simplex et corporea quantitate caret, infinitum ponatur, et sua immensitate omnem corporis quantitatem excedere; cum intellectus noster, qui est incorporeus et simplex, omnium corporum quantitatem vi suae cogitationis excedat, et omnia circumplectatur. Multo igitur magis id quod est omnium primum sua immensitate universa excedit, omnia circumplectens.

This leads to the consideration of God's infinity. God is not infinite by way of privation, according to which infinity is a passion of quantity: in this sense something is called 'infinite' which naturally would have a limit by reason of its genus, but does not. Rather, God is infinite negatively, as a thing is called 'infinite' that is in no way limited. For no act is found to be limited except by a potency that is receptive of the act; thus we observe that forms are limited in accordance with the potency of matter. Hence, if the first mover is an act without any admixture of potency, since it is not the form of any body or a force inhering in a body, it must be infinite.

The very order perceived in things is also a proof of this. For the higher the position occupied in the scale of being, the greater are things found to be in their own way. Among the elements, nobler things are found to be greater in quantity, as also in simplicity. Their generation demonstrates this, since fire is generated from air in a multiplied proportion, and air from water, and water from earth; and the heavenly body clearly exceeds the entire quantity of the elements. Necessarily, therefore, that which is the first among all beings, and which can have nothing prior to it, must be of infinite quantity in its own mode.

Nor is there anything to wonder at if what is simple and lacks bodily quantity is said to be infinite and to exceed in its immensity all quantity of body. For our own intellect, which is non-bodily and simple, exceeds the quantity of all bodies by the strength of its knowledge, and embraces all things. Much more, then, that which is the very first of all exceeds the universe in its immensity, and embraces everything.

CHAPTER 19

That God is of infinite power

Hinc etiam apparet Deum infinitae virtutis esse. Virtus enim consequitur essentiam rei, nam unumquodque secundum modum quo est agere potest; si igitur Deus secundum essentiam suam infinitus est, oportet quod eius virtus sit infinita.

Hoc etiam apparet, si quis rerum ordinem diligenter inspiciat. Nam unumquodque secundum quod est in potentia, secundum hoc habet virtutem receptivam vel passivam; secundum vero quod actu est, habet virtutem activam. Quod igitur est in potentia tantum, scilicet ma-

From this it is also apparent that God is infinite in power. For power is consequent upon a thing's essence; for anything whatever is able to act according to the manner in which it exists. Therefore, if God is infinite in his essence, his power must be infinite.

This is also clear if we diligently consider the order of things. For any given thing has a receptive or passive power according as it is in potency, but it has an active power according as it is in act. Hence what is exclusively in potency (namely, prime matter) has an unlimited power of recep-

teria prima, habet virtutem infinitam ad recipiendum, nihil de virtute activa participans; et supra ipsam quanto aliquid formalius est, tanto illud abundat in virtute agendi: propter quod ignis inter omnia elementa est maxime activum. Deus igitur, qui est actus purus, nihil potentialitatis permixtum habens, in infinitum abundat in virtute activa super alia.

tivity, but has no part in active power. And in the scale of being above matter, the more a thing has of form, the more it abounds in the power of acting. This is why fire is the most active of all the elements. Therefore, God, who is pure act without any admixture of potency, infinitely abounds in active power above all others.

CHAPTER 20

That the infinite in God does not convey imperfection

Quamvis autem infinitum quod in quantitatibus invenitur imperfectum sit, tamen quod Deus infinitus dicitur summam perfectionem in ipso demonstrat. Infinitum enim quod est in quantitatibus ad materiam pertinet, prout fine privatur; imperfectio autem accidit rei secundum quod materia sub privatione invenitur; perfectio autem omnis ex forma est. Cum igitur Deus ex hoc infinitus sit quia tantum forma vel actus, nullam materiae vel potentialitatis cuiusque permixtionem habens, sua infinitas ad summam perfectionem ipsius pertinet.

Hoc etiam ex rebus aliis considerari potest. Nam licet in uno et eodem quod de imperfecto ad perfectum producitur, prius sit tempore aliquid imperfectum quam perfectum, sicut prius puer quam vir; tamen oportet quod omne imperfectum a perfecto tradat originem: non enim oritur puer nisi ex viro, nec semen nisi ex animali vel planta. Illud igitur quod est naturaliter omnibus prius, omnia movens, oportet omnibus perfectius esse.

Although the infinity found in quantities is imperfect, the infinity predicated of God indicates supreme perfection in him. The infinity that is in quantities pertains to matter insofar as it lacks limits; but imperfection occurs in a thing according as matter is found in a state of privation. But every perfection comes from form. Consequently, since God is infinite because he is exclusively form or act, and has no admixture of matter or potentiality, his infinity pertains to his supreme perfection.

This can also be gathered from a consideration of other things. Although something imperfect precedes the perfect in one and the same being which is led from imperfect to perfect—as, for example, the boy is prior to the man—nevertheless everything imperfect must derive its origin from what is perfect. The child is not begotten except by a man, and the seed does not receive existence except from an animal or a plant. Accordingly, that which is by nature prior to all other things, and moves them all, must be more perfect than them all.

CHAPTER 21

That every sort of perfection found in things is more eminently in God

Inde etiam apparet quod omnes perfectiones in quibuscumque rebus inventas, necesse est originaliter et superabundanter in Deo esse. Nam omne quod movet aliquid ad perfectionem, prehabet in se perfectionem quam aliis confert; sicut doctor prehabet in se doctrinam quam aliis tradit. Si igitur Deus, cum sit primum movens, omnia alia moveat in suas perfectiones, necesse est omnes perfectiones rerum in ipso praeexistere superabundanter.

Item, omne quod habet aliquam perfectionem, si alia perfectio ei desit, est limitatum sub aliquo genere vel specie: nam per formam, quae est perfectio rei, quaelibet

The further inference clearly follows that all perfections found in anything at all must originally and superabundantly be present in God. For whatever moves something toward perfection must first possess in itself the perfection it confers on others, as a teacher has in his own mind the knowledge he hands on to others. Therefore, since God is the first mover, and moves all other beings toward their perfections, all perfections found in things must preexist in him superabundantly.

Again, whatever has a particular perfection but lacks another perfection is contained under some genus or species. For each thing is classed under a genus or a species by

res in genere et specie collocatur. Quod autem est sub genere et specie constitutum non potest esse infinitae essentiae: nam oportet quod ultima differentia per quam in specie ponitur, terminet eius essentiam; unde et ratio speciem notificans definitio vel finis dicitur. Si igitur divina essentia infinita est, impossibile est quod alicuius tantum generis vel speciei perfectionem habeat, et aliis privetur; sed oportet quod omnium generum et specierum perfectiones in ipso existant.

its form, which is the thing's perfection. But what is placed under species and genus cannot be infinite in essence; for the ultimate difference whereby it is placed in a species is necessarily the boundary of its essence. Hence the account that makes a species known is called its definition or end.[2] Therefore, if the divine essence is infinite, it cannot possess merely the perfection of some genus or species and be lacking in other perfections; but the perfections of all genera or species must exist in God.

CHAPTER 22

That in God all perfections are one

Si autem colligamus ea quae superius dicta sunt, manifestum est quod omnes perfectiones in Deo sunt unum secundum rem. Ostensum est enim supra Deum simplicem esse; ubi autem est simplicitas, diversitas eorum quae insunt esse non potest. Si ergo in Deo sunt omnium perfectiones, impossibile est quod sint diversae in ipso; relinquitur ergo quod omnes sint unum in eo.

Hoc autem manifestum fit consideranti in virtutibus cognoscitivis. Nam superior vis secundum unum et idem est cognoscitiva omnium quae ab inferioribus viribus secundum diversa cognoscuntur: omnia enim quae visus, auditus et ceteri sensus percipiunt, intellectus una et simplici virtute diiudicat. Simile etiam apparet in scientiis: nam, cum inferiores scientiae secundum diversa genera rerum, circa quae versatur earum intentio, multiplicentur, una tamen scientia, quae est eis superior, est ad omnia se habens: quae dicitur philosophia prima. Apparet etiam idem in potestatibus: nam in regia potestate, cum sit una, includitur omnis potestas quae per diversa officia sub dominio regis distribuitur. Sic igitur et perfectiones quae in inferioribus rebus secundum diversitatem rerum multiplicantur, oportet quod in ipso rerum vertice, scilicet Deo, uniantur.

If we gather together the various points established thus far, we perceive that all perfections in God are in reality one. For we have shown above that God is simple. But where there is simplicity, there can be no difference between the things that are present. Hence, if the perfections of all things are in God, they cannot be different in him. Therefore, we are left with the conclusion that they are all one in him.

This is made clear by considering the cognitive powers. For a higher power knows by one and the same knowledge all that is known by lower powers through different knowledges, for all that the sight, the hearing, and the other senses perceive, the intellect judges with a power that is one and simple. Something similar is clear in the sciences: the lower sciences are multiplied in accord with the various classes of beings that constitute their objects, yet one science that is higher than them concerns itself with everything; this is called first philosophy. The same situation is observed in civil power: in the royal power, which is one, are included all the powers which are distributed through various offices within the jurisdiction of the kingdom. In the same way perfections, which in lower things are multiplied according to the diversity of these things, must be united in the pinnacle of being, that is, in God.

---

2. This argument rests upon the etymological likeness of the Latin words *infinitus*, *definitio*, and *finis*.

CHAPTER 23

That no accident is found in God

Inde etiam apparet quod in Deo nullum accidens esse potest. Si enim in eo omnes perfectiones sunt unum, ad perfectionem autem pertinet esse, posse, agere et omnia huiusmodi, necesse est omnia in eo idem esse quod eius essentia; nullum igitur eorum in eo est accidens.

Item, impossibile est infinitum esse perfectione, cuius perfectioni aliquid adiici potest; si autem aliquid est cuius aliqua perfectio sit accidens, cum omne accidens superaddatur essentiae, oportet quod eius essentiae aliqua perfectio adiici possit: non igitur invenitur in eius essentia perfectio infinita. Ostensum est autem Deum secundum suam essentiam infinitae perfectionis esse; nulla igitur in eo perfectio accidentalis esse potest, sed quidquid in eo est, substantia eius est.

Hoc etiam facile est concludere ex summa simplicitate ipsius, ex hoc quod est actus purus, et ex hoc quod est primum in entibus. Est enim aliquis compositionis modus accidentis ad subiectum; id etiam quod subiectum est non potest esse actus purus, cum accidens sit quaedam forma subiecti; semper etiam quod est per se, est prius eo quod est per accidens: ex quibus omnibus secundum supradicta haberi potest quod in Deo nihil secundum accidens dicatur.

It is also clear that there can be no accident in God. For if all perfections are one in him, and if existence, power, action, and all such attributes pertain to perfection, they are necessarily all identical with his essence. Therefore, none of these perfections is an accident in God.

Furthermore, a being to whose perfection something can be added cannot be infinite in perfection. But if a being has some perfection that is an accident, a perfection can be added to its essence, since every accident is added to an essence. Hence infinite perfection will not be found in its essence. But, as we have shown, God is of infinite perfection according to essence. Consequently, there can be in him no accidental perfection; but whatever is in him is his substance.

The same truth can be easily inferred from God's supreme simplicity, from the fact that he is pure act, and from the fact that he is the first among beings. For some sort of composition obtains between an accident and its subject. Likewise, that which is a subject of this kind cannot be pure act, since an accident is a kind of form of the subject. Similarly, what is essential is always prior to what is accidental. From all this we can infer, in keeping with what was said above, that nothing can be predicated of God as an accident.

CHAPTER 24

That the many names applied to God do not remove his simplicity

Per hoc autem apparet ratio multitudinis nominum quae de Deo dicuntur, licet ipse in se sit omnino simplex. Cum enim intellectus noster essentiam eius in se ipsa capere non sufficiat, in eius cognitionem consurgit ex rebus quae apud nos sunt, in quibus inveniuntur diversae perfectiones quarum omnium radix et origo in Deo una est, ut ostensum est. Et quia non possumus aliquid nominare nisi secundum quod intelligimus, sunt enim nomina intellectuum signa, Deum non possumus nominare nisi ex perfectionibus in aliis rebus inventis, quarum origo in ipso est; et quia haec in rebus istis multiplices sunt, oportuit multa nomina Deo imponere. Si autem essentiam eius in se ipsa videremus, non requireretur nominum multitudo, sed esset simplex notitia eius sicut est et simplex essentia; et hoc in die nostrae gloriae expectamus, secundum illud Zach.: *In illa die erit Dominus unus, et nomen eius unum.*

This enables us to perceive the reason for the many names that are applied to God, even though in himself he is absolutely simple. Since our intellect is unable to grasp his essence as it is in itself, we rise to a knowledge of that essence from the things that surround us. In these things, we discern various perfections, all of whose root and origin is one in God, as has been shown. Since we cannot name an object except as we understand it, seeing as names are signs of things understood, we cannot give names to God except from perfections perceived in other things that have their origin in him. And since these perfections are multiple in such things, we must assign many names to God. If we saw his essence as it is in itself, a multiplicity of names would not be required: our knowledge of it would be simple, just as his essence is simple. And we await this vision in the day of our glory, in accord with Zachariah 14:9: *On that day the Lord will be one and his name one.*

CHAPTER 25

That although different names are said of God, nevertheless they are not synonyms

Ex his autem tria possumus considerare, quorum primum est quod diversa nomina, licet idem secundum rem in Deo significent, non tamen sunt synonima. Ad hoc enim quod nomina aliqua sint synonima, oportet quod significent eandem rem, et eandem intellectus conceptionem repraesentent. Ubi vero significatur eadem res secundum diversas rationes, id est apprehensiones quas habet intellectus de re illa, non sunt nomina synonima, quia non est penitus significatio eadem, cum nomina immediate significent conceptiones intellectus quae sunt rerum similitudines. Et ideo, cum diversa nomina dicta de Deo significent diversas conceptiones quas intellectus noster habet de ipso, non sunt synonima, licet omnino eandem rem significent.

In this connection three observations are in order. The first is that the various names applied to God are not synonyms, even though they signify what is in reality the same thing in God. In order to be synonyms, names must signify the same thing and represent the same intellectual conception. But when the same object is signified according to diverse notions, that is, diverse understandings which the mind forms of that object, the names are not synonymous. For then the meaning is not entirely the same, since names directly signify intellectual conceptions, which are likenesses of things. Therefore, since the various names predicated of God signify the various conceptions our mind forms of him, they are not synonymous, even though they signify absolutely the same reality.

CHAPTER 26

That by the definitions of these names one cannot define that which is in God

Secundum est quod, cum intellectus noster secundum nullam harum conceptionum quas nomina dicta de Deo significant, divinam essentiam perfecte capiat, impossibile est quod per definitiones horum nominum definiatur id quod est in Deo: sicut quod definitio potentiae sit definitio potentiae divinae, et similiter in aliis.

Quod etiam alio modo est manifestum. Omnis enim definitio ex genere et differentia constat; id etiam quod proprie definitur species est: ostensum est autem quod divina essentia non concluditur sub aliquo genere nec sub aliqua specie, unde non potest eius esse aliqua definitio.

A second point is this: since our intellect does not perfectly grasp the divine essence in any of the conceptions which the names applied to God signify, the definitions of these names cannot define what is in God, such that the definition of 'power' would be a definition of the divine power, and so on regarding other attributes.

The same is clear for another reason. Every definition is made up of genus and specific difference, and what is properly defined is a species. But we have shown that the divine essence is not included under any genus or species. Consequently, there can be no definition of it.

CHAPTER 27

*That names given to God and creatures are not said
altogether univocally nor altogether equivocally*

Tertium est quod nomina de Deo et aliis rebus nec omnino univoce nec omnino aequivoce dicuntur. Univoce namque dici non possunt, cum definitio eius quod de creatura dicitur non sit definitio eius quod dicitur de Deo; oportet autem univoce dictorum eandem definitionem esse.

Similiter autem neque omnino aequivoce: in his enim quae sunt a casu aequivoca, idem nomen imponitur uni rei nullo habito respectu ad rem aliam, unde per unum non potest ratiocinari de alio. Haec autem nomina quae dicuntur de Deo et de aliis rebus, attribuuntur Deo secundum aliquem ordinem quem habet ad istas res in quibus intellectus significata eorum considerat, unde et per alias res ratiocinari de Deo possumus; non igitur omnino aequivoce dicuntur ista de Deo et aliis rebus, sicut ea quae sunt a casu aequivoca.

Dicuntur igitur secundum analogiam, id est secundum proportionem ad unum. Ex eo enim quod alias res comparamus ad Deum sicut ad suam primam originem, huiusmodi nomina quae significant perfectiones aliarum rerum Deo attribuimus. Ex quo patet quod, licet quantum ad nominis impositionem huiusmodi nomina per prius de creaturis dicantur, eo quod ex creaturis intellectus nomina imponens ascendit in Deum, tamen secundum rem significatam per nomen per prius dicuntur de Deo, a quo perfectiones descendunt in alias res.

The third point is that names applied to God and to other beings are not predicated either altogether univocally or altogether equivocally. They cannot be predicated univocally, because the definition of what is said of a creature is not a definition of what is said of God. But things predicated univocally must have the same definition.

Nor are these names altogether equivocal. For in the case of a chance equivocation, the same name is attached to one object with no regard to the other object. Hence through the one we cannot reason about the other. But the names predicated of God and of other things are attributed to God according to some relation he has to those things in which the intellect considers the names' significations. This is why we can reason about God through other things. Therefore, such terms are not predicated altogether equivocally about God and about other things, as happens in a chance equivocation.

Consequently they are predicated according to analogy; that is, according to their proportion to one thing. For we attribute to God such names as signify perfections in other things based on the fact that we compare other things to God as to their first origin. This clearly brings out the truth that, as regards the assigning of the names, such names are primarily predicated of creatures, inasmuch as the intellect that assigns the names ascends from creatures to God. But as regards the thing signified by the name, they are primarily predicated of God, from whom the perfections descend to other beings.

CHAPTER 28

That God must be intelligent

Ulterius autem ostendendum est quod Deus est intelligens. Ostensum est enim quod in ipso praeexistunt omnes perfectiones quorumlibet entium superabundanter; inter omnes autem perfectiones entium ipsum intelligere praecellere videtur, cum res intellectuales sint omnibus aliis potiores: oportet igitur Deum esse intelligentem.

Item, ostensum est supra quod Deus est actus purus absque potentialitatis permixtione; materia autem est ens in potentia: oportet igitur Deum esse omnino immunem a materia. Immunitas autem a materia est causa intellectualitatis, cuius signum est quod formae

We must go on to demonstrate that God is intelligent. We have already proved that all perfections of all beings whatsoever preexist in God superabundantly. Now, among all the perfections found in beings, intelligence is seen to possess a special preeminence, since intellectual beings are more powerful than all others. Therefore, God must be intelligent.

Moreover, we pointed out above that God is pure act without any admixture of potentiality. But matter is a being in potency. Therefore, God must be utterly free from matter. But freedom from matter is the cause of intellectuality. An indication of this is that material forms are rendered

materiales efficiuntur intelligibiles actu per hoc quod abstrahuntur a materia et a materialibus conditionibus: est igitur Deus intelligens.

Item, ostensum est Deum esse primum movens; hoc autem videtur esse proprium intellectus, nam intellectus omnibus aliis videtur uti quasi instrumentis ad motum: unde et homo suo intellectu utitur quasi instrumentis et animalibus et plantis et rebus inanimatis. Oportet igitur Deum, qui est primum movens, esse intelligentem.

intelligible in act by being abstracted from matter and from material conditions. Therefore, God is intelligent.

We proved, further, that God is the first mover. This very perfection appears to be a property of intellect, for we observe that the intellect uses all other things as instruments, so to speak, for movement. Thus man, by his intellect, uses animals and plants and inanimate objects as instruments of a sort. Consequently, God, the first mover, must be intelligent.

CHAPTER 29

That in God there is understanding neither in potency nor in habit, but in act

Cum autem in Deo non sit aliquid in potentia sed in actu tantum, ut ostensum est, oportet quod Deus non sit intelligens neque in potentia aut habitu, sed actu tantum. Ex quo patet quod nullam in intelligendo patitur successionem aut vicissitudinem. Cum enim aliquis intellectus successive multa intelligit, oportet quod, dum unum intelligit actu, alterum intelligat in potentia; si igitur Deus nihil intelligit in potentia, absque omni successione est eius intelligentia. Unde sequitur quod omnia quaecumque intelligit simul intelligat, inter ea enim quae simul sunt non est aliqua successio; et iterum quod nihil de novo intelligat, intellectus enim de novo aliquid intelligens prius fuit intelligens in potentia.

Inde etiam patet quod intellectus eius non est discursivus, ut ex uno in cognitionem alterius deveniat, sicut intellectus noster in ratiocinando patitur: discursus enim talis in intellectu nostro est, dum ex noto pervenimus in cognitionem ignoti vel eius quod prius actu non considerabamus: quae in intellectu divino accidere non possunt.

Since in God nothing is in potency but all is in act, as has been shown, God cannot be intelligent either potentially or habitually but only actually. An evident consequence of this is that he undergoes no succession or change in understanding. For the intellect that understands many things successively must understand one thing actually while understanding another only potentially. So if God understands nothing in potency, his understanding is free from all succession. Accordingly, whatever he understands, he understands simultaneously, for among things that are simultaneous there is no succession. It also follows that he does not begin to understand anything. For the intellect that begins to understand something was previously in potency to understanding.

It is likewise evident that God's intellect does not understand discursively, proceeding from one truth to the knowledge of another, as is the case with our intellect in reasoning. A discursive process of this sort takes place in our intellect when we advance from the known to a knowledge of the unknown, or of what we had not actually thought of before. Such processes cannot occur in the divine intellect.

CHAPTER 30

That God understands through no other species than his own essence

Patet etiam ex praedictis quod Deus non intelligit per aliam speciem quam per essentiam suam. Omnis enim intellectus intelligens per speciem aliam a se, comparatur ad illam speciem intelligibilem sicut potentia ad actum, cum species intelligibilis sit perfectio eius faciens ipsum intelligentem actu; si igitur in Deo nihil est in potentia sed est actus purus, oportet quod non per aliam speciem sed per essentiam suam intelligat. Et inde sequitur quod directe et principaliter se ipsum intelligat. Essentia enim rei non ducit proprie et directe in cognitionem alicuius nisi eius cuius est essentia: nam per definitionem hominis proprie cognoscitur homo, et per definitionem equi equus. Si igitur Deus est per essentiam suam intelligens, oportet quod id quod est intellectum ab eo directe et principaliter sit ipse Deus; et cum ipse sit sua essentia, sequitur quod in eo intellectus et quo intelligit et intellectum sit omnino idem.

The foregoing exposition makes it clear that God understands through no other species than through his essence. For any intellect that understands through a species other than itself is related to that intelligible species as potency to act, since an intelligible species is a perfection of the intellect that causes it to understand in act. Therefore, if nothing in God is in potency, but he is pure act, he must understand through his own essence, and not through any other kind of species. From this it follows that he directly and principally understands himself. For the essence of a thing does not properly and directly lead to the knowledge of anything else than of that being whose essence it is. Thus what is properly known through the definition of man is man, and what is properly known through the definition of horse is horse. Therefore, if God understands through his essence, that which is directly and principally understood by him must be God himself. And, since God is his own essence, it follows that, in him, understanding and that whereby he understands and that which is understood are absolutely identical.

CHAPTER 31

That God is his own act of understanding

Oportet etiam quod ipse Deus sit suum intelligere. Cum enim 'intelligere' sit actus secundus ut considerare, primus enim actus est intellectus vel scientia, omnis intellectus qui non est suum intelligere comparatur ad suum intelligere sicut potentia ad actum; nam semper in ordine potentiarum et actuum quod est prius est potentiale respectu sequentis, et ultimum est completivum, loquendo in uno et eodem, licet in diversis sit e converso: nam movens et agens comparatur ad motum et actum sicut agens ad potentiam. In Deo autem, cum sit actus purus, non est aliquid quod comparetur ad alterum sicut potentia ad actum; oportet ergo quod ipse Deus sit suum intelligere.

Item, eodem modo comparantur intellectus ad intelligere et essentia ad esse; sed Deus est intelligens per essentiam suam, essentia autem sua est suum esse: ergo eius intellectus est suum intelligere. Et sic per hoc quod est intelligens nulla compositio in eo ponitur, cum in eo non sit aliud intellectus, intelligere et species intelligibilis; et haec non sunt aliud quam eius essentia.

God must also be his own act of understanding. Since 'to understand' is second act (as, for example 'to consider'), whereas the corresponding first act is intellect or knowledge, any intellect that is not its own understanding is related to its understanding as potency to act. For in the order of potencies and acts, what is first is always potential with respect to what follows, and what is last is perfective. This is true only with reference to one and the same being, for among different beings the converse obtains; thus a mover and an agent are related to the thing moved and actuated as act to potency. In God, however, since he is pure act, there is nothing that is related to anything else as potency to act. Accordingly, God must be his own act of understanding.

Furthermore, the intellect is related to its act of understanding as essence is related to existence. But God understands through his essence, and his essence is his existence. Therefore, his intellect is his act of understanding. And thus the fact that God is intelligent implies no composition in him, since in him intellect and act of understanding and intelligible species are not distinct; and these in turn are nothing else than his essence.

CHAPTER 32

That there must be will in God

Ulterius autem manifestum est quod necesse est Deum esse volentem. Ipse enim se ipsum intelligit qui est bonum perfectum, ut ex dictis patet; bonum autem intellectum ex necessitate diligitur, hoc autem fit per voluntatem: necesse est igitur Deum volentem esse.

Item, ostensum est supra quod Deus est primum movens per intellectum; intellectus autem non movet nisi mediante appetitu, appetitus autem sequens intellectum est voluntas: oportet igitur Deum esse volentem.

We perceive, further, that God must have will. For he understands himself, who is perfect good, as is clear from what has been said. But the good apprehended is necessarily loved, and this happens through the will. Consequently, God must have will.

Moreover, we showed above that God is the first mover through intellect. But the intellect only moves through the intermediary of appetite, and the appetite that follows intellectual apprehension is the will. Therefore, God must have will.

CHAPTER 33

That the very will of God must be nothing other than his intellect

Patet autem quod oportet ipsam Dei voluntatem nihil aliud esse quam eius intellectum. Bonum enim intellectum, cum sit obiectum voluntatis, movet voluntatem et est actus et perfectio eius; in Deo autem non differt movens et motum, actus et potentia, perfectio et perfectibile, ut ex superioribus patet: oportet igitur voluntatem divinam esse ipsum bonum intellectum. Hoc autem est intellectus divinus et essentia divina; voluntas igitur Dei non est aliud quam intellectus divinus et essentia eius.

Item, inter alias perfectiones rerum praecipuae sunt intellectus et voluntas, cuius signum est quod inveniuntur in rebus nobilioribus; perfectiones autem omnium rerum sunt in Deo unum quod est eius essentia, ut supra ostensum est: intellectus igitur et voluntas sunt in Deo idem quod essentia.

Moreover, it is clear that God's will cannot be anything other than his intellect. For a good apprehended by the intellect, since it is the object of the will, moves the will and is the will's act and perfection. In God, however, there is no distinction between mover and moved, act and potency, perfection and perfectible, as is clear from the foregoing. Therefore, it is necessary that the divine will be the good apprehended by the intellect. But this is the divine intellect and the divine essence. Therefore, the will of God is not other than the divine intellect and God's essence.

Again, among the various perfections of things, the chief are intellect and will. A sign of this is that they are found in the nobler beings. But the perfections of all things are one in God, and this is his essence, as we showed above. In God, therefore, intellect and will are identical with his essence.

CHAPTER 34

That God's will and willing are the same

Hinc etiam apparet quod voluntas divina est ipsum velle Dei. Ostensum enim est quod voluntas in Deo est idem quod bonum volitum ab ipso; hoc autem esse non posset nisi velle esset idem quod voluntas, cum velle sit voluntati ex volito: est igitur Dei voluntas suum velle.

Item, voluntas Dei est idem quod eius intellectus et eius essentia; intellectus autem Dei est suum intelligere, et essentia est suum esse: ergo oportet quod voluntas sit suum velle. Et sic patet quod voluntas Dei simplicitati non repugnat.

Hence it is also clear that the divine will is the very act of willing in God. As has been shown, God's will is identical with the good willed by him. But this would be impossible if his willing were not the same as his will; for willing is in the will because of the object willed. Accordingly, God's will is his willing.

Again, God's will is the same as his intellect and his essence. But God's intellect is his act of understanding, and his essence is his existence. Therefore, his will must be his act of willing. And so we see clearly that God's will is not opposed to his simplicity.

CHAPTER 35

That all the aforesaid truths are gathered into one article of faith

Ex his autem omnibus quae supra dicta sunt, colligere possumus quod Deus est unus, simplex, perfectus, infinitus, intelligens et volens. Quae quidem omnia in Symbolo Fidei brevi articulo comprehenduntur, cum nos profitemur credere *in Deum unum omnipotentem*. Cum enim hoc nomen *Deus* a nomine Graeco quod dicitur *theos* dictum videatur, quod quidem a *theaste* dicitur, quod est 'videre' vel 'considerare', in ipso nomine Dei manifestatur quod sit intelligens, et per consequens volens. In hoc autem quod dicimus eum *unum*, excluditur deorum pluralitas et omnis compositio: non enim est simpliciter unum nisi quod est simplex. Per hoc autem quod dicimus *omnipotentem*, ostenditur quod sit infinitae virtutis cui nihil subtrahi possit; in quo etiam includitur quod sit infinitus et perfectus, nam virtus rei perfectionem essentiae eius consequitur.

From everything that has been said above, we can gather that God is one, simple, perfect, infinite, intelligent, and has will. All these truths are assembled in a brief article of our Creed, wherein we profess to believe *in one God, almighty*. For, since this name *God (Deus)*, is apparently derived from the Greek name *Theos*, which comes from *theasthai*, meaning 'to see' or 'to consider', the very name of God indicates that he is intelligent and consequently that he wills. In proclaiming that he is *one*, we exclude a plurality of gods, and also all composition; for a thing is not simply one unless it is simple. The fact that we say *almighty* shows that he possesses infinite power, from which nothing can be taken away. And this includes the further truth that he is infinite and perfect; for the power of a thing follows on the perfection of its essence.

CHAPTER 36

That all these things were laid down by the philosophers

Haec quidem quae in superioribus de Deo sunt tradita, a pluribus etiam gentilium philosophis subtiliter considerata sunt, quamvis nonnulli eorum circa praedicta erraverunt; et qui in his verum dixerunt, post longam et laboriosam inquisitionem ad veritatem praedictam pervenire vix potuerunt. Sunt alia nobis de Deo tradita in doctrina Christianae religionis ad quae pervenire non potuerunt, circa quae per Christianam fidem ultra humanum sensum instruimur. Est autem hoc quod, cum sit Deus unus et simplex, ut ostensum est, est tamen Deus Pater, Deus Filius et Deus Spiritus Sanctus, et hi tres non tres dii sed unus Deus est. Quod quidem quantum possibile nobis est, considerare intendimus.

The truths about God thus far proposed have been subtly discussed by a number even of the pagan philosophers, although many of them erred concerning these matters. And those who propounded the truth regarding these matters were scarcely able to arrive at such truths even after long and painstaking investigation. There are other truths about God, handed down to us in the teaching of the Christian religion which were beyond the reach of the philosophers. These are truths about which we are instructed through Christian faith in a way that exceeds human perception. The teaching is this: although God is one and simple, as has been shown, he is nevertheless God the Father, God the Son, and God the Holy Spirit; and these three are not three gods, but are one God. We now turn to a consideration of this truth, so far as is possible to us.

CHAPTER 37

How a Word is attributed to God

Accipiendum est autem ex his quae supra dicta sunt quod Deus se ipsum intelligit et diligit; item quod intelligere in ipso et velle non sit aliud quam eius esse. Quia ergo Deus se ipsum intelligit, omne autem intellectum in intelligente est, oportet Deum in se ipso esse sicut intellectum in intelligente. Intellectum autem prout est in intelligente, est verbum quoddam intellectus; hoc enim exteriori verbo significamus quod interius intellectu comprehendimus: sunt enim, secundum Philosophum, voces signa intellectuum. Oportet igitur in Deo ponere Verbum ipsius.

We take from the things said above that God understands and loves himself; likewise, that understanding and willing in him are not something other than his being. Since God understands himself, and since everything understood is in the one understanding, it is necessary that God be in himself as the thing understood in the one understanding. But the thing understood, so far as it is in the one understanding, is a certain word of the intellect; for we signify by an exterior word what we comprehend interiorly in our intellect. For words, according to the Philosopher, are signs of things understood. Hence we must posit in God his Word.

CHAPTER 38

That Word in God is called a conception

Id autem quod in intellectu continetur, ut interius verbum, etiam communi usu loquendi conceptio intellectus dicitur. Nam corporaliter aliquid concipi dicitur quod in utero animalis viventis vivifica virtute formatur, mare agente et femina patiente in qua fit conceptio, ita quod ipsum conceptum pertinet ad naturam utriusque, quasi secundum speciem conforme.

What is contained in the intellect, as an interior word, is by common usage also said to be a concept or conception of the intellect. For something is said to be conceived in a bodily way if it is formed in the womb of a living animal by a life-giving power, in virtue of the active function of the male and the passive function of the female, in whom the conception takes place. The being thus conceived shares in the nature of both parents and conforms to them in appearance.

Quod autem intellectus comprehendit in intellectu formatur, intelligibili quasi agente et intellectu quasi patiente. Et ipsum quod intellectu comprehenditur, intra intellectum existens, conforme est et intelligibili moventi, cuius quaedam similitudo est, et intellectui quasi patienti secundum quod esse intelligibile habet. Unde id quod intellectu comprehenditur non immerito conceptio intellectus vocatur.

Now, what the intellect comprehends is formed in the intellect, with the intelligible object being, as it were, the active principle, and the intellect the passive principle. That which is thus comprehended by the intellect, existing within the intellect, is conformed both to the moving intelligible object of which it is a certain likeness, and to the intellect as the passive principle, so to speak, in accord with which it has intelligible existence. Hence what is comprehended by the intellect is not unfittingly called the conception of the intellect.

CHAPTER 39

How the Word stands to the Father

In hoc autem consideranda est differentia. Nam cum id quod in intellectu concipitur sit similitudo rei intellectae, eius speciem repraesentans, quaedam proles ipsius esse videtur. Quando igitur intellectus intelligit aliud a se, res intellecta est sicut pater verbi in intellectu concepti; ipse autem intellectus magis gerit similitudinem matris, cuius est ut in ea fiat conceptio. Quando vero intellectus intelligit se ipsum, verbum conceptum comparatur ad intelligentem sicut proles ad patrem; cum igitur de Verbo loquamur secundum quod Deus se ipsum intelligit, oportet quod ipsum Verbum comparetur ad Deum, cuius est Verbum, sicut filius ad patrem.

But here a point of difference must be considered. For since that which is conceived in the intellect is a likeness of the thing understood, representing its species, it seems to be a certain offspring of the intellect itself. Therefore, when the intellect understands something other than itself, the thing understood is, so to speak, the father of the word conceived; while the intellect itself resembles a mother, to whom it belongs that conception should take place in her. But when the intellect understands itself, the word conceived is related to the one understanding as offspring to father. Since, therefore, we are speaking of the Word according as God understands himself, it is necessary that this Word must be compared to God, whose Word it is, as son to father.

CHAPTER 40

How generation in God is understood

Hinc est quod in regula Catholicae fidei Patrem et Filium in divinis confiteri docemur, cum dicitur: *Credo in Deum Patrem et Filium eius.* Et ne aliquis, audiens nomen Patris et Filii, carnalem generationem suspicaretur secundum quam apud nos pater dicitur et filius, evangelista Iohannes, cui revelata sunt secreta caelestia, loco *Filii Verbum* posuit ut generationem intelligibilem agnoscamus.

Hence in the rule of Catholic faith we are taught to profess belief in the Father and Son in God by saying: *I believe in God the Father, and in his Son.* And lest anyone, hearing Father and Son mentioned, should have any notion of carnal generation, according to which father and son receive their designation among us, John the Evangelist, to whom were revealed heavenly mysteries, substitutes *Word* for *Son* (John 1:14), so that we may understand that the generation is intellectual.

CHAPTER 41

That the Word, which is the Son, has the same existence and essence as the Father

Considerandum est autem quod, cum in nobis aliud sit esse naturale et intelligere, oportet quod verbum in nostro intellectu conceptum, quod habet esse intelligibile tantum, alterius naturae et essentiae sit quam intellectus noster, qui habet esse naturale. In Deo autem idem est esse et intelligere. Verbum igitur Dei, quod in Deo cuius est Verbum secundum esse intelligibile, idem esse habet cum Deo cuius est Verbum; et per hoc oportet quod sit eiusdem essentiae et naturae cum ipso, et omnia quaecumque de Deo dicuntur Verbo Dei conveniant.

It must be considered that, since in us natural being and the act of understanding are distinct, it is necessary that the word conceived in our intellect, which has intelligible being only, differ in nature and essence from our intellect, which has natural existence. In God, however, to be and to understand are the same. Therefore, the Word of God, which is in God (whose Word he is according to intellectual existence), has the same being as God, whose Word he is. And because of this, it is necessary that he be of the same essence and nature as God himself, and everything whatsoever that is said of God must belong also to the Word of God.

CHAPTER 42

That the Catholic faith teaches this

Et inde est quod in regula Catholicae fidei docemur confiteri Filium *consubstantialem Patri*, per quod duo excluduntur: primo quidem ut non intelligatur Pater et Filius secundum carnalem generationem quae fit per aliquam decisionem substantiae filii a patre, ut sic oporteat Filium non esse Patri consubstantialem; secundo ut etiam non intelligamus Patrem et Filium secundum generationem intelligibilem prout verbum in mente nostra concipitur, quasi accidentaliter superveniens intellectui et non de essentia eius existens.

Hence we are instructed in the rule of Catholic faith to profess that the Son is *consubstantial with the Father*, a phrase that excludes two things. First, the Father and the Son may not be thought of according to bodily generation, which is effected by a separation of the son's substance from the father, such that the the Son could not be consubstantial with the Father. Second, so that we do not think of the Father and the Son according to intellectual generation in the way that a word is conceived in our mind: as a thing coming to the intellect as an accident and not existing from its essence.

CHAPTER 43

That in God the Word differs from the Father neither in time, nor in species, nor in nature

Eorum autem quae secundum essentiam non differunt, impossibile est esse differentiam secundum tempus, speciem aut naturam; quia ergo Verbum Patri est consubstantiale, necesse est ut secundum nihil dictorum a Patre differat.

Et quidem secundum tempus differre non potest. Cum enim secundum hoc Verbum in Deo ponatur quod Deus se ipsum intelligit sui Verbum intelligibiliter concipiendo, oportet quod, si aliquando Dei Verbum non fuit, quod tunc Deus se ipsum non intellexerit; semper autem quandocumque Deus fuit se intellexit, quia suum intelligere est suum esse: semper igitur et Verbum ipsius fuit. Et ideo in regula Catholicae fidei dicimus Dei Filium *ex Patre natum ante omnia saecula*.

Secundum speciem etiam impossibile est Verbum Dei a Deo quasi minoratum differre, cum Deus se ipsum non minus intelligat quam quod est; Verbum autem perfectam speciem habet ex hoc quod id cuius est Verbum perfecte intelligitur. Oportet igitur Dei Verbum omnino perfectum secundum speciem divinitatis esse.

Inveniuntur autem quae ex aliis procedunt eorum ex quibus procedunt perfectam speciem non consequi. Uno modo sicut in generationibus aequivocis: a sole enim non generatur sol sed quoddam animal; ut igitur talis imperfectio a generatione divina excludatur, confitemur natum *Deum de Deo*.

Alio modo quod generatur vel quod procedit ex aliquo, deficit ab eo a quo procedit propter defectum

Among things that are not different in essence, there can be no difference according to time, species, or nature. Therefore, since the Word is consubstantial with the Father, he cannot differ from the Father in any of these respects.

There can be no difference according to time. For the divine Word is present in God because God understands himself by conceiving his intelligible Word. Hence, it is necessary that if at any time there were no Word of God, during that time God would not understand himself. But God always understood himself during his whole existence, for his understanding is his existence. Therefore, his Word also existed always. And so in the rule of the Catholic faith we say that the Son of God is *born of the Father before all ages*.

According to species, too, it is impossible for the Word of God to differ from God, as though he were inferior; for God does not understand himself as less than he is. The Word has a perfect likeness to the Father, because that of which he is the Word is perfectly understood. Therefore, the Word of God must be absolutely perfect according to the species of divinity.

Some beings, it is true, that proceed from others are found not to inherit the perfect species of those from whom they proceed. One way in which this can happen is in equivocal generations: for the sun does not generate a sun, but an animal of some kind. To exclude imperfection of this sort from divine generation, we confess that the Word is born *God from God*.

What is generated or proceeds from another can fall short of it in another way due to a defect in purity, namely,

puritatis, dum scilicet ab eo quod est in se simplex et purum, per applicationem ad extraneam materiam aliquid proceditur a prima specie deficiens: sicut ex domo quae est in mente artificis fit domus quae est in materia, a lumine recepto in corpore terminato fit color, ex igne adiuncto aliis elementis fit corpus mixtum, ex radio per oppositionem corporis opaci fit umbra; ut hoc igitur a divina generatione excludatur, additur: *Lumen de Lumine.*

Tertio, quod ex aliquo procedit non consequitur speciem eius propter defectum veritatis, quia scilicet non vere recipit naturam eius sed quandam eius similitudinem tantum, sicut imago hominis in speculo vel in pictura aut in sculptura aliqua, aut etiam similitudo rei in intellectu vel sensu nostro; non enim imago hominis dicitur homo verus sed hominis similitudo, *neque lapis est in anima*, ut Philosophus dicit, *sed species* lapidis: ut igitur hoc a divina generatione excludatur, additur: *Deum verum de Deo vero.*

Secundum naturam etiam impossibile est Verbum a Deo cuius est Verbum differre, cum hoc sit Deo naturale quod se ipsum intelligat. Habet enim omnis intellectus aliqua quae naturaliter intelligit, sicut intellectus noster naturaliter intelligit prima principia; multo igitur magis Deus, cuius intelligere est suum esse, se ipsum naturaliter intelligit. Verbum igitur ipsius naturaliter ex ipso est, non sicut ea quae praeter naturalem originem procedunt, ut a nobis procedunt res artificiales quas facere dicimur; quae vero naturaliter a nobis procedunt dicimur generare, ut filius. Ne igitur Dei Verbum non naturaliter a Deo procedere intelligatur, sed secundum potestatem suae voluntatis, additur: *genitum, non factum.*

when from what is simple and pure in itself something proceeds through an application to extraneous matter, and so turns out to be inferior to the original species. Thus, from a house that is in the architect's mind, a house is fashioned in various materials; and from light received in the surface of a body, color results; and from fire, by adding other elements, a mixed body arises; and from a beam of light, by interposing an opaque body, a shadow is caused. To exclude any imperfection of this kind from divine generation, we add: *Light from Light.*

In yet a third way, what proceeds from another can fail to equal the latter's species due to a deficiency in truth. That is, it does not truly receive the nature of its original, but only a certain likeness thereof: for example, the image of a man in a mirror or in a picture or in a statue, or even the likeness of a thing in the intellect or in one of our senses. For the image of a man is not said to be a true man, but is a likeness of a man; *and a stone is not in the soul*, as the Philosopher notes, *but a likeness* of the stone. To exclude this from the divine generation, we add: *true God from true God.*

Lastly, it is impossible for the Word to differ from God according to nature, since it is natural for God to understand himself. Every intellect has some things which it naturally understands, as our intellect naturally understands first principles. Much more does God, whose act of understanding is his existence, naturally understand himself. Therefore, his Word proceeds from him naturally, not in the way that things proceed otherwise than by natural origin; that is, not in the way that the artificial objects we are said to make proceed from us. What proceeds from us naturally, such as a son, we are said to generate. Accordingly, lest it be thought that the Word of God proceeds by the power of his will and not naturally, the phrase is added: *begotten, not made.*

CHAPTER 44

Conclusion from the foregoing

Quia ergo, ut ex praemissis patet, omnes praedictae divinae generationis conditiones ad hoc pertinent quod Filius est Patri consubstantialis, ideo post omnia subiungitur quasi summa universorum: *consubstantialem Patri.*

Since, therefore, as is evident from the foregoing, all the characteristics of divine generation we have been discussing pertain to the fact that the Son is consubstantial with the Father, by way of summing up all these points it is added: *consubstantial with the Father.*

CHAPTER 45

That God is in himself as beloved in lover

Sicut autem intellectum in intelligente est inquantum intelligitur, ita et amatum esse oportet in amante inquantum amatur; movetur enim quodammodo amans ab amato quadam intrinseca motione: unde cum movens contingat id quod movetur, necesse est amatum intrinsecum amanti esse. Deus autem sicut intelligit se ipsum, ita necesse est quod se ipsum amet: bonum enim intellectum secundum se amabile est. Est igitur Deus in se ipso tanquam amatum in amante.

As the object known is in the knower, insofar as it is known, so the beloved must be in the lover, insofar as it is loved. The lover is, in some way, moved by the beloved with a certain intrinsic motion. Therefore, since a mover is in contact with the object moved, the beloved must be intrinsic to the lover. But God, just as he understands himself, must likewise love himself; for a good understood is in itself lovable. Consequently, God is in himself as the beloved in the lover.

CHAPTER 46

That love in God is called the Spirit

Cum autem intellectum in intelligente sit, et amatum in amante, diversa ratio eius quod est esse in aliquo utrobique consideranda est. Cum enim intelligere fiat per assimilationem aliquam intelligentis ad id quod intelligitur, necesse est id quod intelligitur in intelligente esse secundum quod eius similitudo in eo existit. Amatio autem fit secundum quandam motionem amantis ab amato, amatum enim trahit ad se ipsum amantem. Non igitur perficitur amatio in similitudine amati sicut perficitur intelligere in similitudine intellecti, sed perficitur in attractione amantis ad ipsum amatum.

Since the object known is in the knower, and the beloved is in the lover, the different ways of existing in something must be considered in both cases before us. Since the act of understanding takes place by a certain assimilation of the knower to the object known, the object known must be in the knower according as a likeness of it is present in him. But the act of loving takes place through the lover's being moved in a certain way by the beloved, for the beloved draws the lover to himself. Accordingly, the act of loving does not reach its perfection in a likeness of the beloved, as the act of understanding reaches perfection in a likeness of the object understood, but rather reaches its perfection in a drawing of the lover to the beloved himself.

Traductio autem similitudinis principaliter fit per generationem univocam, secundum quam in rebus viventibus generans pater et generatus filius nominatur; in eisdem etiam prima motio fit secundum spiritum. Sicut igitur in divinis modus ille quo Deus est in Deo ut intellectum in intelligente exprimitur per hoc quod dicimus Filium qui est Verbum Dei, ita modum quo Deus est in Deo sicut amatum in amante exprimimus per hoc quod ponimus ibi Spiritum qui est amor Dei. Et ideo secundum regulam Catholicae fidei credere in Spiritum iubemur.

The bestowal of a likeness is principally effected by univocal generation, in accord with which, among living beings, the begetter is called father and the begotten is called son. Among such things, the first motion occurs according to a spirit. Therefore, as within the Godhead the way whereby God is in God as the known in the knower is expressed by our calling the Word of God 'Son', so we express the way by which God is in God as the beloved is in the lover by acknowledging a Spirit in God, who is the love of God. And this is why, according to the rule of Catholic faith, we are directed to believe in the Spirit.

CHAPTER 47

That the Spirit, which is in God, is holy

Considerandum autem est quod cum bonum amatum habeat rationem finis, ex fine autem motus voluntarius bonus vel malus reddatur, necesse est ut amor quo ipsum summum bonum amatur, quod Deus est, eminentem quandam optineat bonitatem, quae nomine sanctitatis exprimitur, sive dicatur 'sanctum' quasi 'purum' secundum Graecos, quia in Deo est purissima bonitas ab omni defectu immunis, sive dicatur 'sanctum,' id est 'firmum,' secundum Latinos, quia in Deo est immutabilis bonitas: propter quod et omnia quae ad Deum ordinantur sancta dicuntur, sicut templum et vasa templi et omnia divino cultui mancipata. Convenienter igitur Spiritus quo nobis insinuatur amor quo Deus Deum amat, Spiritus Sanctus nominatur; unde et regula Catholicae fidei praedictum Spiritum Sanctum nominat, cum dicitur: *Credo in Spiritum Sanctum.*

It must also be considered that since the good that is loved has the character of an end, and since the motion of the will is rendered good or evil by the end it pursues, the love whereby the supreme good that is God is loved must possess the supereminent goodness that goes by the name of holiness. This is true whether 'holy' is taken as equivalent to 'pure,' in accord with the Greeks (since in God there is most pure goodness free from all defect), or whether 'holy' is taken to mean 'firm,' in accord with the Latins (since in God there is unchangeable goodness). In either case, everything dedicated to God is called holy, such as a temple, and the vessels of the temple, and all objects consecrated to divine service. Rightly, then, the Spirit, who represents to us the love whereby God loves himself, is called the Holy Spirit. For this reason the rule of Catholic faith names the Spirit 'Holy,' when it says, *I believe in the Holy Spirit.*

CHAPTER 48

That love in God is not accidental

Sicut autem intelligere Dei est suum esse, ita et eius amare est suum esse; non igitur Deus amat se ipsum secundum aliquid suae essentiae superveniens, sed secundum essentiam suam. Cum igitur amet se ipsum secundum hoc quod ipse in se ipso est ut amatum in amante, non est Deus amatus in Deo amante per modum accidentalem, sicut res amatae sunt in nobis amantibus accidentaliter, sed Deus est in se ipso ut amatum in amante substantialiter. Ipse igitur Spiritus Sanctus, quo nobis insinuatur divinus amor, non est aliquid accidentale in Deo, sed est res subsistens in essentia divina sicut Pater et Filius; et ideo regula Catholicae fidei ostenditur: *coadorandus et simul glorificandus cum Patre et Filio.*

Just as God's act of understanding is his existence, so also his act of loving is his existence. Therefore, God does not love himself through something that comes to his essence from outside it, but he loves himself through his very essence. When, therefore, God loves himself according as he is in himself as the beloved in the lover, God the beloved is not in God the lover in an accidental way, as the objects of our love are accidentally in us who love them. Rather, God is substantially in himself as beloved in lover. Therefore, the Holy Spirit, who represents the divine love to us, is not something accidental in God, but is a thing subsisting in the divine essence like the Father and the Son. And so in the rule of Catholic faith he is shown *to be adored and glorified together with the Father and the Son.*

CHAPTER 49

That the Holy Spirit proceeds from the Father and the Son

Est etiam considerandum quod ipsum intelligere ex virtute intellectiva intellectus procedit; secundum autem quod intellectus actu intelligit, est in ipso id quod intelligitur: hoc igitur quod est intellectum esse in intelligente procedit ex virtute intellectiva intelligentis, et hoc est verbum ipsius, ut supra dictum est. Similiter etiam id quod amatur est in amante secundum quod actu amatur; quod autem aliquid actu ametur, procedit et ex virtute amativa amantis et ex bono amabili actu intellecto: hoc igitur quod est amatum esse in amante ex duobus procedit, scilicet ex principio amativo et ex intelligibili apprehenso quod est verbum conceptum de ipso amabili. Cum igitur in Deo se ipsum intelligente et amante Verbum sit Filius, is autem cuius est Verbum sit Verbi Pater, ut ex dictis patet, necesse est quod Spiritus Sanctus, qui pertinet ad amorem secundum quod Deus in se ipso est ut amatum in amante, ex Patre procedat et Filio: unde et in Symbolo dicitur: *qui ex Patre Filioque procedit.*

We should recall that the act of understanding proceeds from the intellectual power of the intellect. Now the object known is present in the one knowing according as the intellect understands in act. Therefore, the presence of the object known in the knower proceeds from the intellectual power of the one knowing, and this is its word, as we said above. Likewise, what is loved is in the lover when it is actually loved. And the fact that an object is actually loved proceeds from the lover's power to love and from the lovable good as actually understood. Therefore, the presence of the beloved in the lover proceeds from two things: the loving principle and the intelligible object as apprehended, which is the word conceived about the lovable object. Therefore, since in God knowing and loving himself the Word is the Son, and the one whose Word he is, is the Father of the Word, as is clear from the things said, it is necessary that the Holy Spirit, who pertains to the love whereby God is in himself as beloved in lover, proceeds from the Father and the Son. And so we say in the Creed: *who proceeds from the Father and the Son.*

CHAPTER 50

That a Trinity of persons in God is not opposed to unity of essence

Ex omnibus autem quae dicta sunt colligere oportet quod in divinitate quendam ternarium ponimus, qui tamen unitati et simplicitati divinae essentiae non repugnat. Oportet enim concedi Deum esse et existentem in sua natura, et intellectum et amatum a se ipso.

Aliter autem hoc accidit in Deo et in nobis. Quia enim homo in sua natura substantia est, intelligere autem et amare ipsius non sunt eius substantia, homo quidem secundum quod in natura sua consideratur quaedam res subsistens est; secundum autem quod est in suo intellectu, non est res subsistens sed intentio quaedam rei subsistentis, et similiter secundum quod est in se ipso ut amatum in amante. Etsi ergo in homine tria quaedam considerari possunt, id est homo in natura sua existens et homo in intellectu existens et homo in amore existens, tamen hi tres non sunt unum quia intelligere eius non est eius esse, similiter autem et amare; et horum trium unus solus est res quaedam subsistens, scilicet homo in natura sua existens.

In Deo autem idem est esse, intelligere et amare; Deus ergo in esse suo naturali existens et Deus existens in intellectu suo et Deus existens in amore suo unum sunt, et tamen unusquisque eorum est subsistens. Et quia res subsistentes in intellectuali natura *personas* Latini nominare consueverunt, Graeci vero *hypostases*, propter hoc in divinis Latini dicunt tres personas, Graeci vero tres hypostases, Patrem scilicet et Filium et Spiritum Sanctum.

From all that has been said we must gather that we hold there to be a kind of three in the Godhead, which nevertheless is not opposed to the unity and simplicity of the divine essence. For we must acknowledge that God exists both in his nature and as known and loved by himself.

But this occurs otherwise in God than in us. For man is a substance in his nature, but his actions of knowing and loving are not his substance. Considered in his nature, man is indeed a subsisting thing; as he exists in his mind, however, he is not a subsisting thing, but a certain representation of a subsisting thing; and similarly with regard to his existence in himself as beloved in lover. Therefore, even though a kind of three can be considered in man—that is, man existing in his nature, man existing in his intellect, and man existing in his love—yet these three are not one, for man's knowing is not his existence, and the same is true of his loving. Only one of these three is a subsisting thing: namely, man existing in his nature.

In God, on the contrary, to be, to know, and to love are identical. Therefore, God existing in his natural being and God existing in the divine intellect and God existing in the divine love are one thing. Yet each of them is subsistent. And, because Latins are accustomed to call things subsisting in intellectual nature *persons*, while Greeks call them *hypostases*, consequently the Latins say that there are three persons in God, and the Greeks say that there are three hypostases, namely, the Father, the Son, and the Holy Spirit.

CHAPTER 51

How a Trinity of persons in God seems to be a contradiction

Videtur autem ex praedictis repugnantia quaedam suboriri. Si enim in Deo ternarius aliquis ponitur, cum omnis numerus divisionem aliquam consequatur, oportebit in Deo aliquam differentiam ponere per quam tres ab invicem distinguantur; et ita non erit in Deo summa simplicitas. Nam si in aliquo tres conveniunt et in alio differunt, necesse est ibi esse compositionem, quod superioribus repugnat.

Rursus, si necesse est esse unum solum Deum, ut supra ostensum est, nulla autem res una oritur vel procedit a se ipsa, impossibile videtur quod sit Deus genitus vel Deus procedens; falso igitur in divinis ponitur nomen Patris et Filii et Spiritus procedentis.

But a certain contradiction seems to arise from what has been said. For if some kind of three is asserted in God, then, since number always follows on some division, some division will have to be acknowledged in God, whereby the three may be distinguished from one another. Thus supreme simplicity will be lacking in God. For, if three agree in some respect and differ in another, composition must be present; which is contrary to what was set forth above.

Again, if there can be only one God, as was shown above, and if one and the same thing cannot originate or proceed from itself, it seems impossible for God to be begotten or to proceed. Wrongly, therefore, are the names of Father and of Son and of proceeding Spirit posited in the Godhead.

CHAPTER 52

Solution of the difficulty: in God there is no distinction except according to relation

Principium autem ad dissolvendum hanc dubitationem hinc sumere oportet, quod secundum diversitatem naturarum est in diversis rebus diversus modus aliquid exoriendi vel procedendi. In rebus enim vita carentibus, quia non sunt se ipsa moventia sed solum extrinseca movere possunt, oritur ex uno aliud quasi exterius alteratum et immutatum, sicut ab igne generatur ignis et ab aere aer.

In rebus vero viventibus, quarum proprietas est ut se ipsa moveant, generatur aliquid in ipso generante, sicut fetus animalium et fructus plantarum. In viventibus autem est considerare diversum modum processionis secundum diversas vires et operationes earundem. Sunt enim quaedam vires in eis quarum operationes non se extendunt nisi ad corpora secundum quod materialia sunt, sicut patet de viribus animae vegetabilis, quae sunt nutritiva et augmentativa et generativa; et secundum hoc genus virium animae non procedit nisi aliquid corporale corporaliter distinctum, et tamen aliquo modo coniunctum in viventibus ei a quo procedit.

Sunt autem quaedam vires quarum operationes, etsi corpora non transcendant, tamen se extendunt ad species corporum sine materia eas recipiendo, sicut est in omnibus viribus animae sensitivae: est enim sensus susceptivus specierum sine materia, ut Philosophus dicit.

The principle for solving this difficulty must be derived from this fact: namely, that there are different ways something can originate or proceed among different kinds of things. Among lifeless beings, which do not move themselves but can only be moved from outside, one thing arises from another by being, as it were, outwardly altered and changed. In this way fire is generated from fire and air from air.

But among living beings, whose characteristic property is that they move themselves, something is generated within the one generating; for example, the fetuses of animals and the fruits of plants. Moreover, one must notice different ways of proceeding among living beings according to their different powers and operations. For there are certain powers in them whose operations extend only to bodies according as they are material; this is clear with regard to the powers of the vegetative soul, which serve nutrition, growth, and generation. In virtue of this class of the soul's powers, there proceeds only what is bodily and bodily distinct, although in the case of living beings what proceeds is joined in some way to that from which it proceeds.

There are other powers whose operations, although they do not go beyond bodies, nonetheless extend to the species of bodies by receiving them without their accompanying matter. This is the case with all the powers of the sensitive soul. For sense is capable of receiving species without

Huiusmodi autem vires, licet quodammodo immaterialiter formas rerum suscipiant, non tamen eas suscipiunt absque organo corporali. Si qua igitur processio in huiusmodi viribus animae inveniatur, quod procedit non erit aliquod corporale, vel corporaliter distinctum aut coniunctum ei a quo procedit, sed incorporaliter et immaterialiter quodammodo, licet non omnino absque adminiculo organi corporalis. Sic enim procedunt in animalibus formationes rerum imaginatarum, quae quidem sunt in imaginatione non sicut corpus in corpore sed quodam spirituali modo: unde et ab Augustino imaginaria visio spiritualis nominatur.

Si autem secundum operationem imaginationis procedit aliquid non per modum corporalem, multo fortius hoc accidet per operationem partis intellectivae, quae nec etiam in sui operatione indiget organo corporali, sed omnino eius operatio immaterialis est. Procedit enim verbum secundum operationem intellectus ut in ipso intellectu dicentis existens, non quasi localiter in eo contentum nec corporaliter ab eo separatum, sed in ipso quidem existens secundum potestatem naturalis operationis, ab eo vero distinctum secundum ordinem originis; et eadem ratio est de processione quae attenditur secundum operationem voluntatis, prout res amata existit in amante, ut supra dictum est.

Licet autem vires intellectivae et sensitivae secundum propriam rationem sint nobiliores viribus animae vegetabilis, non tamen in hominibus aut in aliis animalibus secundum processionem imaginativae partis aut sensitivae procedit aliquid subsistens in natura speciei eiusdem, sed hoc solum accidit per processionem quae fit secundum operationem animae vegetabilis; et hoc ideo est quia in omnibus compositis ex materia et forma, multiplicatio individuorum in eadem specie fit secundum materiae divisionem. Unde in hominibus et aliis animalibus, cum ex forma et materia componantur, secundum corporalem divisionem quae invenitur in processione quae est secundum operationem animae vegetabilis, et non in aliis operationibus animae, multiplicantur individua in eandem speciem. In rebus vero quae non sunt ex materia et forma compositae, non potest esse nisi distinctio formalis tantum; sed si forma secundum quam attenditur distinctio sit substantia rei, oportet quod illa distinctio sit rerum subsistentium quarundam, non autem si forma illa non sit rei substantia.

Est igitur commune in omni intellectu, ut ex dictis patet, quod oportet id quod intellectu concipitur, ab intelligente quodammodo procedere inquantum intelligens est, et sua processione quodammodo ab ipso distingui, sicut conceptio intellectus quae est intentio intellecta distinguitur ab intellectu intelligente; et similiter oportet quod affectio amantis, per quam amatum est in amante, procedat a voluntate amantis inquantum est amans. Sed hoc proprium habet intellectus divinus

matter, as the Philosopher says. But such faculties, although they are receptive of the forms of things in a sort of immaterial way, do not receive them without a bodily organ. If procession takes place within these powers of the soul, that which proceeds will not be something bodily, nor will it be distinct from or joined to that faculty whence it proceeds in a bodily way, but in a certain non-bodily and immaterial way (although not entirely without the help of a bodily organ). This is how, in animals, the representations of things imagined proceed, which exist in the imagination not as a body in a body, but in a certain spiritual way. This is why Augustine calls imaginary vision spiritual.

But if something proceeds in a way that is not bodily when the imagination operates, this will be the case much more in the operation of the intellectual faculty, which does not need a bodily organ in its operation, but whose operation is entirely immaterial. For in an intellectual operation a word proceeds in such a way that it exists in the very intellect of the speaker: not as locally contained there, nor as bodily separated, but as existing in it according to the power of the natural operation while distinct from it according to the order of origin. The same is true in that procession which is observed to take place in the operation of the will, so far as the beloved exists in the lover, as was said above.

However, although the intellectual and sensitive powers are nobler in character than the powers of the vegetative soul, nothing that subsists in the nature of the same species proceeds either in men or in other animals according to the procession of the imaginative or sensitive faculties. This occurs only in that procession which takes place through the operation of the vegetative soul. The reason for this is that in all beings composed of matter and form, the multiplication of individuals in the same species is effected by a division of matter. Hence among men and other animals, composed as they are of form and matter, individuals are multiplied in the same species by the bodily division which ensues in the procession that is proper to the operation of the vegetative soul, but that does not take place in other operations of the soul. In beings that are not composed of matter and form, there can only be formal distinction. But if the form that is the reason for the distinction is a thing's substance, then the distinction must be between subsistent things. (Of course, this is not the case if the form in question is not the substance of the thing.)

As is clear from what has been said, every intellect has this in common: what is conceived in the intellect must in some way proceed from the knower, so far as he is knowing; and it must be in some way distinguished from him by its procession, just as the conception of the intellect, which is the intellectual likeness, is distinguished from the knowing intellect. Similarly, the affection of the lover, whereby the beloved is in the lover, must proceed from the will of the lover insofar as he is loving. But the divine intellect has

quod, cum intelligere eius sit esse ipsius, oportet quod conceptio intellectus, quae est intentio intellecta, sit substantia eius; et similiter est de affectione in ipso Deo amante. Relinquitur igitur quod intentio intellectus divini, quae est Verbum ipsius, non distinguitur a producente ipsum in hoc quod est esse substantiam, sed solum secundum relationem processionis unius ex alio; et similiter est de affectione amoris in Deo amante, quae ad Spiritum Sanctum pertinet.

Sic igitur patet quod nihil prohibet Verbum Dei, quod est Filius, esse unum cum Patre secundum substantiam, et tamen distingui ab eo secundum relationem processionis, ut dictum est. Unde et manifestum est quod eadem res non oritur neque procedit a se ipsa, quia Filius secundum quod a Patre procedit ab eo distinguitur; et eadem ratio est de Spiritu Sancto per comparationem ad Patrem et Filium.

this unique to itself: since God's understanding is his existence, his intellectual conception (which is the intelligible likeness) must be his substance; and the case is similar with affection in God's loving. Consequently, the representation in the divine intellect, which is God's Word, is not distinguished from him who produces the Word as regards substantial existence, but only according to the relation of procession of one from the other. The case is similar concerning the affection of love in God loving, which pertains to the Holy Spirit.

Thus it is plain that nothing prevents God's Word, who is the Son, from being one with the Father in substance, and that, nevertheless, the Word is distinct from the Father according to the relation of procession, as we have said. Hence it is also evident that the same thing does not arise or proceed from itself; for the Son, as proceeding from the Father, is distinct from him. And the same observation holds true of the Holy Spirit, relative to the Father and the Son.

CHAPTER 53

That the relations whereby Father, Son, and Holy Spirit are distinguished are real, and not merely rational

Istae autem relationes quibus Pater et Filius et Spiritus Sanctus ab invicem distinguuntur sunt relationes reales et non rationis tantum. Illae enim relationes sunt rationis tantum quae non consequuntur ad aliquid quod est in rerum natura, sed ad aliquid quod est in apprehensione tantum, sicut dextrum et sinistrum in lapide non sunt relationes reales sed rationis tantum, quia non consequuntur aliquam virtutem realem in lapide existentem, sed solum acceptionem apprehendentis lapidem ut sinistrum quia est alicui animali ad sinistrum; sed in animali dextrum et sinistrum sunt relationes reales, quia consequuntur virtutes quasdam in determinatis partibus animalis inventas. Cum igitur relationes praedictae, quibus Pater et Filius et Spiritus Sanctus distinguuntur, sint realiter in Deo existentes, oportet quod relationes praedictae sint relationes reales et non rationis tantum.

The relations by which the Father, the Son, and the Holy Spirit are distinguished from one another are real relations, and not merely rational. Those relations are purely rational which do not follow from anything found in the nature of things, but follow from intellectual apprehension alone. Thus right and left in a stone are not real relations, but only rational relations; they do not follow from any real disposition present in the stone, but only from the perception of one who apprehends the stone as left because it is to the left of some animal. On the other hand, left and right in an animal are real relations, because they follow on certain dispositions found in definite parts of the animal. Accordingly, since the relations whereby the Father and the Son and the Holy Spirit are distinguished really exist in God, the aforesaid relations must be real relations, and are not merely relations of reason.

CHAPTER 54

That such relations do not inhere accidentally

Non est etiam possibile quod sint accidentaliter inhaerentes, tum quia operationes ad quas consequuntur dictae relationes sunt ipsa Dei substantia, tum etiam quia supra ostensum est quod in Deo nullum accidens esse potest. Unde si relationes praedictae realiter sint in Deo, oportet quod non sint accidentaliter inhaerentes sed subsistentes. Quomodo autem id quod est in aliis rebus accidens in Deo substantialiter esse possit, ex praemissis manifestum est.

These relations cannot inhere in God accidentally, both because the operations on which the relations follow are the very substance of God, and also because, as was shown above, there can be no accident in God. Hence, if the relations are really in God, they cannot be accidentally inherent, but must be subsistent. How it is that what is an accident in other things can exist substantially in God, is clear from what has been previously set forth.

CHAPTER 55

That the personal distinction is constituted through the aforesaid relations in God

Quia ergo in divinis distinctio est per relationes quae non sunt accidentes sed subsistentes, rerum autem subsistentium in natura quacumque intellectuali est distinctio personalis, necesse est quod per praedictas relationes in Deo personalis distinctio constituatur. Pater igitur et Filius et Spiritus Sanctus sunt tres personae, et similiter tres hypostases, quia 'hypostasis' significat aliquid subsistens completum.

Since distinction in the Godhead is by relations that are not accidental, but subsistent, and since among beings subsisting in an intellectual nature there is personal distinction, it necessarily follows that personal distinction in God is constituted by the aforesaid relations. Therefore, the Father and the Son and the Holy Spirit are three persons, and similarly three hypostases, since 'hypostasis' means something that is subsistent and complete.

CHAPTER 56

That it is impossible for there to be more than three persons in God

Plures autem personas tribus esse in divinis impossibile est, cum non sit possibile divinas personas multiplicari per substantiae divisionem, sed solum per alicuius processionis relationem, nec cuiuscumque processionis, sed talis quae non terminetur ad aliquod extrinsecum: nam si terminaretur ad aliquod extrinsecum, non haberet naturam divinam, et sic non posset esse persona aut hypostasis divina. Processio autem in Deo ad exterius non terminata non potest accipi nisi aut secundum operationem intellectus, prout procedit Verbum, aut secundum operationem voluntatis, prout procedit amor, ut ex dictis patet. Non igitur potest esse aliqua persona divina procedens nisi vel ut Verbum quod dicimus Filium, vel ut amor quod dicimus Spiritum.

Rursus, cum Deus omnia uno intuitu per suum intellectum comprehendat, et similiter uno actu voluntatis

There cannot be more than three persons in God, for the divine persons cannot be multiplied by a division of their substance, but solely by the relation of some procession; and not by any sort of procession, but only by such as does not have its term in something outside of God. If the relation had something external as its term, this would not possess the divine nature, and so could not be a divine person or hypostasis. But procession in God that does not terminate outside of God must be either according to the operation of the intellect, whereby the Word proceeds, or according to the operation of the will, whereby love proceeds, as is clear from the things said. Therefore, no divine person can proceed unless he proceeds as the Word, whom we call the Son, or as love, whom we call the Holy Spirit.

Moreover, since God comprehends everything in his intellect by a single gaze, and similarly loves everything by a

omnia diligat, impossibile est in Deo esse plura verba aut plures amores; si igitur Filius procedit ut Verbum, vel Spiritus Sanctus procedit ut amor, impossibile est in Deo esse plures Filios aut plures Spiritus Sanctos.

Item, perfectum est extra quod nihil est; quod igitur extra se aliquid sui generis patitur non est simpliciter perfectum, propter quod et ea quae sunt simpliciter in suis naturis perfecta numero non multiplicantur, sicut Deus, sol et luna, et alia huiusmodi. Oportet autem tam Filium quam Spiritum Sanctum esse simpliciter perfectos, cum uterque eorum sit Deus, ut ostensum est; impossibile est igitur esse plures Filios aut plures Spiritus Sanctos.

Praeterea, illud per quod aliquid subsistens est hoc ab aliis distinctum, impossibile est quod numero multiplicetur, eo quod individuum de pluribus praedicari non potest; sed filiatione Filius est haec persona divina in se subsistens et ab aliis distincta, sicut per principia individuantia Socrates est haec persona humana. Sicut igitur principia individuantia quibus Socrates est hic homo non possunt convenire nisi uni, ita etiam filiatio in divinis non potest nisi uni convenire; et simile est de relatione Patris et Spiritus Sancti: impossibile est igitur in divinis esse plures Patres aut plures Filios aut plures Spiritus Sanctos.

Adhuc, ea quae sunt unum secundum formam non multiplicantur numero nisi per materiam, sicut multiplicatur albedo per hoc quod est in pluribus subiectis; in divinis autem non est materia, quidquid igitur est unum specie et forma in divinis impossibile est multiplicari secundum numerum: huiusmodi autem sunt paternitas et filiatio et Spiritus Sancti processio, impossibile est igitur in divinis esse plures patres aut filios vel spiritus sanctos.

single act of his will, there cannot be several words or several loves in God. If, then, the Son proceeds as Word, and if the Holy Spirit proceeds as love, there cannot be several Sons or several Holy Spirits in God.

Again, the perfect is that beyond which there is nothing. Hence a being that tolerates anything of its own kind outside itself is not absolutely perfect. This is why things that are simply perfect in their natures are not numerically multiplied, such as God, the sun, the moon, and so on. But both the Son and the Holy Spirit must be simply perfect, since each of them is God, as we have shown. Therefore, several Sons or several Holy Spirits are impossible.

Besides, that by which a subsistent thing is this particular thing (distinct from other things) cannot be numerically multiplied, because an individual cannot be predicated of many. But it is by sonship that the Son is this divine person, subsisting in himself and distinct from the other divine persons, just as Socrates is constituted as this human person by individuating principles. Accordingly, as the individuating principles whereby Socrates is this man cannot pertain to more than one man, so sonship in the Godhead cannot pertain to more than one divine person. And it is similar with the relation of the Father and the Holy Spirit. Hence there cannot be several Fathers in God or several Sons or several Holy Spirits.

Further, things that are one according to form are not numerically multiplied except through matter; thus whiteness is multiplied by existing in many subjects. But there is no matter in God. Consequently, whatever is one in species and form in the Godhead cannot be numerically multiplied. Such are paternity and filiation and the procession of the Holy Spirit. And thus there cannot be several Fathers or Sons or Holy Spirits in God.

CHAPTER 57

Of the properties or notions in God, and how many are enumerated in the Father

Huiusmodi autem existente numero personarum in divinis, necesse est et personarum proprietates quibus ad invicem distinguuntur in aliquo numero esse. Quarum tres oportet Patri convenire: una qua distinguatur a Filio solo, et haec est paternitas; alia qua distinguatur a duobus, scilicet Filio et Spiritu Sancto, et haec est innascibilitas quia Pater non est Deus procedens ab alio, Filius autem et Spiritus Sanctus ab alio procedunt; tertia est qua ipse Pater simul cum Filio distinguuntur a Spiritu

Now, this being the number of persons in God, the properties whereby the persons are distinguished from one another must be of some definite number. Three properties are characteristic of the Father. The first is that whereby he is distinguished from the Son alone. This is paternity. The second is that whereby the Father is distinguished from the other two persons, namely, the Son and the Holy Spirit. And this is innascibility; for the Father is not God as proceeding from another person, whereas the Son and the

Sancto, et haec dicitur communis spiratio. Proprietatem autem qua Pater differat a solo Spiritu Sancto non est assignare, eo quod Pater et Filius sunt unum principium Spiritus Sancti, ut ostensum est.

Holy Spirit do proceed from another person. The third property is that whereby the Father along with the Son is distinguished from the Holy Spirit. This is called their common spiration. But a property whereby the Father may be distinguished from the Holy Spirit alone is not to be assigned, for the reason that the Father and the Son are a single principle of the Holy Spirit, as has been shown.

Chapter 58

Of the properties of the Son and the Holy Spirit, what they are and how many

Filio autem necesse est duas convenire: unam scilicet qua distinguatur a Patre, et haec est filiatio; aliam qua simul cum Patre distinguatur a Spiritu Sancto, quae iterum est communis spiratio. Non est autem assignare proprietatem qua distinguatur a solo Spiritu Sancto quia, ut iam dictum est, Filius et Pater sunt unum principium Spiritus Sancti. Similiter etiam non est assignare proprietatem unam qua Spiritus Sanctus et Filius simul distinguantur a Patre; Pater enim ab eis distinguitur una proprietate, scilicet innascibilitate, inquantum est non procedens. Sed quia Filius et Spiritus Sanctus non una processione procedunt sed pluribus, duabus proprietatibus a Patre distinguuntur. Spiritus autem Sanctus habet unam proprietatem tantum, qua distinguitur simul a Patre et Filio, et dicitur processio. Quod autem non possit esse aliqua proprietas qua Spiritus Sanctus distinguatur a Filio solo vel Patre solo, ex dictis patet.

Sunt igitur quinque quae personis attribuuntur, scilicet innascibilitas, paternitas, filiatio, communis spiratio et processio.

Two properties must pertain to the Son: one whereby he is distinguished from the Father, and this is filiation; another whereby, along with the Father, he is distinguished from the Holy Spirit; and this is their common spiration. But no property is to be assigned whereby the Son is distinguished from the Holy Spirit alone, because as we said above, the Son and the Father are a single principle of the Holy Spirit. Similarly, no single property is to be assigned whereby the Holy Spirit and the Son together are distinguished from the Father. For the Father is distinguished from them by one property, namely, innascibility, inasmuch as he does not proceed. However, since the Son and the Holy Spirit proceed not by one procession, but by several, they are distinguished from the Father by two properties. The Holy Spirit has only one property by which he is distinguished from the Father and the Son, and this is called procession. That there cannot be any property by which the Holy Spirit may be distinguished from the Son alone or from the Father alone is evident from this whole discussion.

Accordingly, five properties in all are attributed to the divine persons: innascibility, paternity, filiation, spiration, and procession.

Chapter 59

Why these properties are called notions

Hae autem quinque 'notiones' personarum dici possunt eo quod per eas nobis innotescit in divinis distinctio personarum; non tamen haec quinque possunt dici proprietates, si hoc in proprietatis ratione observetur ut proprium esse dicatur quod convenit uni soli, nam communis spiratio Patri et Filio convenit. Sed secundum illum modum quo aliquid dicitur 'proprium' aliquibus per respectum ad aliud, sicut bipes homini et avi per

These five properties can be called 'notions' of the persons, for the reason that the distinction between the persons in God is brought to our notice through them. On the other hand, they cannot be called properties if the root meaning of a property is insisted on, so that a property is taken to mean a characteristic pertaining to one individual alone: for common spiration pertains to the Father and the Son. But if the word 'property' is employed in the sense

respectum ad quadrupedia, nihil prohibet etiam communem spirationem proprietatem dici.

Quia vero in divinis personae solis relationibus distinguuntur, notiones autem sunt quibus divinarum personarum distinctio innotescit, necesse est omnes notiones aliqualiter ad relationem pertinere. Sed earum quatuor verae relationes sunt quibus personae divinae ad invicem referuntur; quinta vero notio, scilicet innascibilitas, ad relationem quidem pertinet sicut relationis negatio, nam negationes ad genus affirmationum reducuntur et privationes ad genus habituum, sicut 'non homo' ad genus hominis et 'non album' ad genus albedinis.

Sciendum tamen quod relationum quibus personae ad invicem referuntur, quaedam quidem nominatae sunt, ut paternitas et filiatio quae proprie relationem significant; quaedam vero innominatae sunt, relationes scilicet illae quibus Pater et Filius ad Spiritum Sanctum referuntur et Spiritus Sanctus ad eos; sed loco relationum utimur nominibus originum. Manifestum est enim quod communis spiratio et processio originem significant, non autem relationes originem consequentes: quod potest perpendi ex relationibus Patris et Filii. Generatio enim significat activam originem, quam consequitur paternitatis relatio; nativitas vero significat passivam originem Filii, quam consequitur relatio filiationis. Similiter igitur ad communem spirationem sequitur aliqua relatio, et etiam ad processionem; sed quia relationes innominatae sunt, utimur nominibus actuum pro nominibus relationum.

of an attribute that is proper to some individuals as setting them off from others, in the way that two-footed, for example, is proper to man and bird as distinguished from quadrupeds, there is nothing to prevent even common spiration from being called a property.

Since, however, the persons in God are distinguished solely by relations, and distinction among the divine persons is manifested by the notions, the notions must in some sense pertain to relationship. But only four of the notions are real relations, whereby the divine persons are related to one another. The fifth notion, innascibility, pertains to relation as being the denial of relation; for negations are reduced to the genus of affirmations, and privations are reduced to the genus of habits, as, for example, 'not man' is reduced to the genus of man, and 'not white' is reduced to the genus of whiteness.

We should note that some of the relations by which the divine persons are related to one another have definite names, such as paternity and filiation, which properly signify relationship. But others lack a definite name, namely, those whereby the Father and the Son are related to the Holy Spirit, and the Holy Spirit is related to them. So for these we use names of origin in place of relative names. We perceive clearly that common spiration and procession signify origin, but not relations that follow origin. This can be brought out in the case of the relations between the Father and the Son. Generation denotes active origin, and is followed by the relation of paternity; nativity signifies the passive generation of the Son, and is followed by the relation of filiation. In like manner, some relation follows common spiration, and the same is true of procession. But as these relations lack definite names, we use the names of the actions instead of relative names.

CHAPTER 60

*That although there are four relations subsisting in
God, nevertheless there are but three persons*

Considerandum autem quod, quamvis relationes subsistentes in divinis sint ipsae personae divinae, ut supra dictum est, non tamen oportet esse quinque aut quatuor personas secundum numerum relationum. Numerus enim distinctionem aliquam consequitur; sicut enim unum est indivisibile vel indivisum, ita pluralitas est divisibile vel divisum. Ad pluralitatem igitur personarum requiritur quod relationes vim distinctivam habeant ratione oppositionis, nam formalis distinctio non est nisi per oppositionem.

Si igitur praedictae relationes inspiciantur, paternitas et filiatio oppositionem ad invicem habent relativam,

We must realize that, although the relations subsisting in the Godhead are the divine persons themselves, as was stated above, we are not to conclude that there are four or five persons corresponding to the number of relations. For number follows distinction of some sort. Just as unity is indivisible or undivided, so is plurality divisible or divided. For a plurality of persons requires that relations have power to distinguish by reason of opposition, since formal distinction necessarily entails opposition.

If, then, the relations in question are closely examined, paternity and filiation will be seen to have relative oppo-

unde non se compatiuntur in eodem supposito; propter quod oportet quod paternitas et filiatio sint duae personae subsistentes. Innascibilitas autem opponitur quidem filiationi, paternitati autem non opponitur; unde paternitas et innascibilitas possunt uni et eidem personae convenire. Similiter communis spiratio non opponitur neque paternitati neque filiationi, neque etiam innascibilitati; unde nihil prohibet communem spirationem inesse et personae Patris et personae Filii, propter quod communis spiratio non est persona subsistens seorsum a persona Patris et Filii. Processio autem oppositionem relativam habet ad communem spirationem; unde, cum communis spiratio conveniat Patri et Filio, oportet quod processio subsistens sit alia persona a persona Patris et Filii.

Hinc autem patet quare Deus non dicitur quinus propter quinarium notionum, sed dicitur trinus propter Trinarium personarum; quinque enim notiones non sunt quinque res subsistentes, sed tres personae sunt tres res subsistentes.

Licet autem uni personae plures notiones aut proprietates conveniant, una tamen sola est quae personam constituit; non enim sic constituitur persona proprietatibus quasi ex pluribus composita, sed eo quod ipsa proprietas relativa subsistens persona est. Si igitur intelligerentur plures proprietates ut seorsum per se subsistentes, essent iam plures personae et non una. Oportet igitur intelligi quod plurium proprietatum seu notionum uni personae convenientium, illa quae praecedit ordine naturae personam constituit; aliae vero intelliguntur ut personae iam constitutae inhaerentes.

Manifestum est autem quod innascibilitas non potest esse prima notio Patris quae personam eius constituat, tum quia nihil negatione constituitur, tum quia naturaliter affirmatio negationem praecedit. Communis autem spiratio ordine naturae praesupponit paternitatem et filiationem, sicut processio amoris processionem Verbi; unde nec communis spiratio potest esse prima notio Patris, sed neque Filii: relinquitur quod prima notio Patris sit paternitas, Filii autem filiatio, Spiritus autem Sancti sola processio notio est.

Relinquitur igitur quod tres sunt notiones constituentes personas, scilicet paternitas, filiatio et processio; et has quidem notiones necesse est proprietates esse: id enim quod personam constituit oportet soli illi personae convenire, principia enim individuantia non possunt pluribus convenire. Dicuntur igitur praedictae tres notiones proprietates personales, quasi constituentes personas modo praedicto. Aliae vero duae dicuntur proprietates seu notiones personarum, non autem personales quia personam non constituunt.

sition to each other; hence they are incompatible in the same suppositum. Consequently, paternity and filiation in God must be two subsistent persons. Innascibility, on the other hand, although opposed to filiation, is not opposed to paternity. Hence paternity and innascibility can pertain to one and the same person. Similarly, common spiration is not opposed either to paternity or to filiation, nor to innascibility. Thus nothing prevents common spiration from being in both the person of the Father and the person of the Son. Accordingly, common spiration is not a subsisting person distinct from the persons of the Father and the Son. But procession has a relation of opposition to common spiration. Therefore, since common spiration pertains to the Father and the Son, procession must be a person distinct from the persons of the Father and the Son.

Accordingly, the reason is clear why God is not called quiune on account of the notions, which are five in number, but is called triune, on account of the Trinity of persons. The five notions are not five subsisting things, but the three persons are three subsisting things.

Although several notions or properties may pertain to a single person, only one of them constitutes the person. For a divine person is constituted by the properties, not in the sense that he is constituted by several of them, but in the sense that the relative, subsisting property itself is a person. If several properties were understood as subsisting in themselves apart, they would be several persons, and not one person. Hence we must understand that, of the several properties or notions belonging to a single person, the one that precedes according to the order of nature constitutes the person; the others are understood as inhering in the person already constituted.

Thus it is evident that innascibility cannot be the first notion of the Father, constituting his person, because nothing is constituted by a negation, and also because affirmation naturally precedes negation. Further, common spiration presupposes paternity and filiation in the order of nature, just as the procession of love presupposes the procession of the Word. Hence common spiration cannot be the first notion of the Father, nor of the Son. The first notion of the Father is paternity, and the first notion of the Son is filiation, whereas procession alone is the notion of the Holy Spirit.

Accordingly, the notions constituting persons are three in number: paternity, filiation, and procession. And these notions must be strict properties. For that which constitutes a person must pertain to that person alone: individuating principles cannot belong to several individuals. For this reason the three notions in question are called personal properties, in the sense that they constitute the three persons in the manner described. The remaining notions are called properties or notions of the persons, but not personal properties or notions, because they do not constitute a person.

CHAPTER 61

That the hypostases would not remain if the personal properties were removed by the intellect

Ex hoc autem apparet quod remotis per intellectum proprietatibus personalibus, non remanent hypostases. In resolutione enim quae fit per intellectum, remota forma, remanet subiectum formae, sicut remota albedine remanet superficies, qua remota remanet substantia, cuius forma remota remanet materia prima; sed remoto subiecto nihil remanet. Proprietates autem personales sunt ipsae personae ut subsistentes, nec constituunt personas quasi praeexistentibus suppositis advenientes, quia nihil in divinis potest esse distinctum quod absolute dicitur, sed solum quod relativum est. Relinquitur igitur quod proprietatibus personalibus remotis per intellectum, non remanent aliquae hypostases; sed remotis notionibus non personalibus, remanent hypostases distinctae.

This makes it clear that if we were to remove the personal properties by intellectual abstraction, the hypostases could not remain. If a form is removed by intellectual abstraction, the subject of the form remains. Thus if whiteness is removed, the surface remains; if the surface is removed, the substance remains; if the form of the substance is removed, prime matter remains. But if the subject is removed, nothing remains. In the case of God, the personal properties are the subsisting persons themselves. They do not constitute the persons in the sense that they are added to preexisting supposita, for in the Godhead nothing that is predicated absolutely, but only what is relative, can be distinct. Therefore, if the personal properties are removed by intellectual abstraction, no distinct hypostases remain. But if non-personal notions are thus removed, distinct hypostases do remain.

CHAPTER 62

How the divine essence would remain if personal properties were removed by an act of intellect

Si quis autem quaerat utrum, remotis per intellectum proprietatibus personalibus, remaneat essentia divina, dicendum est quod quodam modo remanet, quodam vero modo non. Est enim duplex resolutio quae fit per intellectum. Una quidem secundum abstractionem formae a materia, in qua quidem proceditur ab eo quod formalius est ad id quod est materialius: nam id quod est primum subiectum ultimo remanet, ultima vero forma primo removetur. Alia vero resolutio est secundum abstractionem universalis a particulari, quae quodammodo contrario ordine se habet: nam prius removentur conditiones materiales individuantes, ut accipiatur quod commune est.

Quamvis autem in divinis non sit materia et forma neque universale et particulare, est tamen in divinis commune et proprium, et suppositum naturae communi; personae enim comparantur ad essentiam divinam, secundum modum intelligendi, sicut supposita propria ad naturam communem. Secundum igitur primum modum resolutionis qui fit per intellectum, remotis proprietatibus personalibus quae sunt ipsae personae subsistentes, non remanet natura communis; modo autem secundo remanet.

If someone were to ask whether, in consequence of the personal properties' removal by intellectual abstraction, the divine essence would remain, the answer is that in one respect it would remain, but in another it would not. Intellectual abstraction can take place in two ways. The first is by abstracting form from matter. In this abstraction, the mind proceeds from the more formal to the more material; the first subject remains until the end, and the ultimate form is removed first. The second way of abstracting is by the abstraction of the universal from the particular, and this proceeds according to an order that is, in a sense, the opposite; the individuating material conditions are first removed, so that what is common may be retained.

In God, of course, there are neither matter and form, nor universal and particular. Nevertheless, there is in the Godhead something that is common and something that is proper and supposes the common nature: for, in our human way of thinking, the divine persons are to the divine essence what individual supposita are to a common nature. According to the first type of intellectual abstraction, therefore, if we remove the personal properties, which are the subsisting persons themselves, the common nature does not remain. But in the second type of abstraction it does remain.

CHAPTER 63

Of the order of personal acts to personal properties

Potest etiam ex dictis manifestum esse qualis sit ordo secundum intellectum actuum personalium ad proprietates personales. Proprietates enim personales sunt subsistentes personae; persona autem subsistens in quacumque natura agit communicando suam naturam virtute suae naturae, nam forma speciei est principium generandi simile secundum speciem. Cum igitur actus personales ad communicationem naturae divinae pertineant, oportet quod persona subsistens communicet naturam communem virtute ipsius naturae.

Et ex hoc duo possunt concludi, quorum unum est quod potentia generativa in Patre sit ipsa natura divina: nam potentia quaecumque agendi est principium cuius virtute aliquid agitur; aliud est quod actus personalis, scilicet generatio, secundum modum intelligendi praesupponit et naturam divinam et proprietatem personalem Patris, quae est ipsa hypostasis Patris, licet huiusmodi proprietas inquantum relatio est ex actu consequatur. Unde si in Patre attendatur quod subsistens persona est, dici potest quod quia Pater est generat; si autem attendatur quod relationis est, e converso dicendum videtur quod quia generat Pater est.

We can perceive from this discussion the nature of the order between the personal acts and the personal properties. The personal properties are subsistent persons. But a person subsisting in any nature whatsoever acts in virtue of his nature when he communicates his nature; for the form of a species is the principle for generating a product of like species. Consequently, since personal acts in God have to do with communicating the divine nature, a subsisting person must communicate the common nature in virtue of the nature itself.

Two conclusions follow from this. The first is, that the generative power of the Father is the divine nature itself; for the power of performing any action is the principle in virtue of which a thing acts. The second conclusion is that, according to our way of conceiving, the personal act of generation presupposes both the divine nature and the personal property of the Father, which is the very hypostasis of the Father. This is true even though such property, regarded as a relation, follows from the act. Thus, in speaking of the Father, if we attend to the fact that he is a subsistent person, we can say that he generates because he is the Father. But if we are thinking of what pertains to relationship, it seems we should say, contrariwise, that he is the Father because he generates.

CHAPTER 64

How generation must be taken with respect to the Father and with respect to the Son

Sciendum tamen quod alio modo oportet accipere ordinem generationis activae ad paternitatem, alio vero modo generationis passivae sive nativitatis ad filiationem. Generatio enim activa praesupponit ordine naturae personam generantis; sed generatio passiva sive nativitas ordine naturae praecedit personam genitam, quia persona genita nativitate sua habet ut sit. Sic igitur generatio activa secundum modum intelligendi praesupponit paternitatem, secundum quod est constitutiva personae Patris; nativitas autem non praesupponit filiationem secundum quod est constitutiva personae Filii, sed secundum intelligendi modum praecedit eam utroque modo, scilicet et secundum quod est constitutiva personae et secundum quod est relatio. Et similiter intelligendum est de his quae pertinent ad processionem Spiritus Sancti.

However, we should understand that the order of active generation, with reference to paternity, is to be taken in one way, and that the order of passive generation, or nativity, with reference to filiation, is to be taken in another way. In the order of nature, active generation presupposes the person of the begetter. But in the same order of nature, passive generation, or nativity, precedes the begotten person, for the begotten person owes his existence to his birth. Hence active generation, according to our manner of understanding, presupposes paternity (understood as constituting the person of the Father). Nativity, however, does not presuppose filiation understood as constituting the person of the Son, but, according to our manner of conceiving, precedes it in both respects, that is, both as being constitutive of the person and as being a relation. And whatever pertains to the procession of the Holy Spirit is to be understood in a similar way.

CHAPTER 65

How notional acts do not differ from persons except according to reason

Ex ordine autem assignato inter actus notionales et proprietates notionales, non intendimus quod actus notionales secundum rem a proprietatibus personalibus differant, sed solum secundum modum intelligendi; sicut enim intelligere Dei est ipse Deus intelligens, ita et generatio Patris est ipse Pater generans, licet alio modo significetur. Similiter etiam licet una persona plures notiones habeat, non tamen in ea est aliqua compositio; innascibilitas enim cum sit proprietas negativa, nullam compositionem facere potest. Duae vero relationes quae sunt in persona Patris, scilicet paternitas et communis spiratio, sunt quidem idem secundum rem prout comparantur ad personam Patris: sicut enim paternitas est ipse Pater, ita et communis spiratio in Patre est Pater, et in Filio est Filius. Differunt autem secundum ea ad quae referuntur: nam paternitate Pater refertur ad Filium, communi spiratione ad Spiritum Sanctum; et similiter Filius filiatione quidem ad Patrem, communi vero spiratione ad Spiritum Sanctum.

In thus indicating the order between the notional acts and the notional properties, we do not mean to imply that the notional acts differ from the personal properties in reality, for they are distinct only according to our manner of understanding. Just as God's act of understanding is God himself understanding, so the Father's act of begetting is the begetting Father, although the modes of signifying are different. Likewise, although one divine person may have several notions, there is no composition in him. Innascibility cannot cause any composition, since it is a negative property. And the two relations in the person of the Father (namely, paternity and common spiration) are in reality identical as referring to the person of the Father; for, as the paternity is the Father, so common spiration in the Father is the Father, and in the Son is the Son. But these two properties differ according to the terms to which they refer; for by paternity the Father is related to the Son, and by common spiration he is related to the Holy Spirit. Similarly, the Son is related to the Father by filiation, and to the Holy Spirit by common spiration.

CHAPTER 66

That relative properties are the divine essence itself

Oportet etiam quod ipsae proprietates relativae sint ipsa divina essentia. Proprietates enim relativae sunt ipsae personae subsistentes; persona autem subsistens in divinis non potest esse aliud quam essentia divina, essentia enim divina est ipse Deus, ut supra ostensum est: unde relinquitur quod proprietates relativae sint secundum rem idem quod divina essentia.

Item, quidquid est in aliquo praeter essentiam eius, inest ei accidentaliter; in Deo autem nullum accidens esse potest, ut supra ostensum est: proprietates igitur relativae non sunt aliud ab essentia divina secundum rem.

The relative properties must be the divine essence itself. For the relative properties are precisely the subsistent persons. But a person subsisting in the Godhead cannot be something other than the divine essence; and the divine essence is God himself, as was shown above. Therefore, the relative properties are in reality identical with the divine essence.

Moreover, whatever is in a being besides its essence is in it accidentally. But there cannot be any accidents in God, as was pointed out above. Accordingly, the relative properties are not really distinct from the divine essence.

Chapter 67

That relations are not externally affixed, as Gilbert de la Porrée said

Non autem dici potest quod proprietates praedictae non sint in personis sed exterius ad eas se habeant, ut Porretani dixerunt. Relationes enim reales oportet esse in rebus relatis, quod quidem in creaturis manifestum est: sunt enim relationes reales in eis sicut accidentia in subiectis. Relationes autem istae quibus personae distinguuntur in divinis sunt relationes reales, ut supra ostensum est; oportet igitur quod sint in personis divinis, non quidem sicut accidentia: nam et alia quae in creaturis sunt accidentia ad Deum translata a ratione accidentium cadunt, ut sapientia et iustitia et alia huiusmodi, ut supra ostensum est.

Praeterea, in divinis non potest esse distinctio nisi per relationes, nam quaecumque absolute dicuntur communia sunt. Si igitur relationes exterius se habeant ad personas, nulla in ipsis personis distinctio remanebit. Sunt igitur proprietates relativae in personis, ita tamen quod sunt ipsae personae et etiam ipsa essentia divina, sicut sapientia et bonitas dicuntur esse in Deo et sunt ipse Deus et essentia divina, ut supra ostensum est.

The view proposed by Gilbert de la Porrée and some of his followers, that the properties under discussion are not in the persons, but are external to them, cannot be defended. Real relations must be in the things that are related. This is evident in the case of creatures, for real relations are in them as accidents in their subjects. But the relations whereby the persons are distinguished within the Godhead are real relations, as was demonstrated above. Hence they must be in the divine persons; but not, of course, as accidents. Other perfections, too, which in creatures are accidents, cease to be accidents when transferred to God, as was shown above.

Besides, there can be no distinction in God except through the relations, because all perfections that are predicated absolutely are common. Therefore, if the relations were external to the persons, no distinction would remain among the persons themselves. And so there are relative properties in the persons; but they are the persons themselves, and also the divine essence itself. In the same way wisdom and goodness are said to be in God, and are God himself and the divine essence, as was said above.

CHAPTER 68

Of the effects of divinity, and first, of being

His igitur consideratis quae ad unitatem essentiae divinae pertinent et ad personarum Trinitatem, restat de effectibus divinitatis considerandum. Primus autem effectus Dei in rebus est ipsum esse, quod omnes alii effectus praesupponunt et super ipsum fundantur. Necesse est autem omne quod quolibet modo est a Deo esse. In omnibus enim ordinatis hoc communiter invenitur quod id quod est primum et perfectissimum in aliquo ordine, est causa eorum quae sunt post in ordine illo, sicut ignis qui est maxime calidus est causa caliditatis in reliquis corporibus calidis: semper enim imperfecta a perfectis inveniuntur habere originem, sicut semina ab animalibus et plantis. Ostensum est autem supra quod Deus est primum et perfectissimum ens; necesse est igitur ipsum esse causam essendi omnibus quae esse habent.

Adhuc, omne quod habet aliquid per participationem reducitur in id quod habet illud per essentiam sicut in principium et causam, sicut ferrum ignitum participat igneitatem ab eo quod est ignis per essentiam suam. Ostensum est autem supra quod Deus est ipsum suum esse; unde esse convenit ei per suam essentiam, omnibus autem aliis convenit per participationem: non enim alicuius alterius essentia est eius esse, quia esse absolutum et per se subsistens non potest esse nisi unum, ut supra ostensum est. Necesse est igitur Deum esse causam essendi omnibus quae sunt.

After considering the truths which pertain to the unity of the divine essence and to the Trinity of persons, we turn to a study of the effects of the divinity. Now, the first effect wrought by God in things is existence itself, which all other effects presuppose, and on which they are based. Anything that exists in any way must necessarily have its origin from God. For in all things that are arranged in orderly fashion, we find universally that what is first and most perfect in any order is the cause of whatever follows in that order. Thus fire, which is hot in the highest degree, is the cause of heat in all other heated bodies. For imperfect things are always found to have their origin from perfect things; seeds, for instance, come from animals and plants. But, as we showed above, God is the first and most perfect being. Therefore, he must be the cause of being in all things that have being.

Again, whatever has some perfection by participation is traced back, as to its principle and cause, to what possesses that perfection essentially. Thus molten iron participates in fireness from that which is fire by its essence. We showed above that God is existence itself; hence existence belongs to him in virtue of his essence, but pertains to all other things by way of participation. For there is no other thing whose essence is its existence, since being that is absolute and subsistent essentially cannot but be one, as was shown above. Therefore, God must be the cause of existence of all things that are.

CHAPTER 69

That God in creating things does not presuppose matter

Per hoc autem ostenditur quod Deus in creando res non praeexigit materiam ex qua operetur. Nullum enim agens praeexiget ad suam actionem id quod per suam actionem producitur: aedificator enim lapides et ligna ad suam actionem praeexigit quia ea sua actione producere non potest, domum autem producit agendo sed non praesupponit. Necesse est autem materiam produci per actionem Dei, cum ostensum sit quod omne quod quoli-

This makes it clear that, in creating, God has no need of preexisting matter from which to fashion things. No agent needs prior to his action what he produces by his action. The builder requires stones and lumber before he can set to work, because he is unable to produce these materials by his action. On the other hand, he does not presuppose a house, but produces it by his activity. But matter must be produced by God's action since, as has just been proved,

bet modo est Deum habeat causam essendi. Relinquitur igitur quod Deus in agendo materiam non praesupponit.

Adhuc, actus naturaliter prior est potentia, unde et per prius competit sibi ratio principii; omne autem principium quod in causando aliud principium praesupponit, per posterius habet rationem principii: cum igitur Deus sit principium rerum sicut actus primus, materia autem sicut ens in potentia, inconveniens est quod Deus in agendo materiam praesupponat.

Item, quanto aliqua causa est magis universalis, tanto effectus eius est universalior: nam causae particulares effectus universalium causarum ad aliquid determinatum appropriant, quae quidem determinatio ad effectum universalem comparatur sicut actus ad potentiam; omnis igitur causa quae facit aliquid esse in actu, praesupposito eo quod est in potentia ad actum illum, est causa particularis respectu alicuius universalioris causae. Hoc autem Deo non competit, cum ipse sit causa prima, ut supra ostensum est; non igitur praeexigit materiam ad suam actionem. Ipsius igitur est producere res in esse ex nihilo, quod est creare; et inde est quod fides Catholica eum Creatorem confitetur.

everything that exists in any way at all has God as the cause of its existence. Therefore, the conclusion follows that God does not presuppose matter in his activity.

Moreover, act is naturally prior to potency, and hence the notion of principle primarily belongs to act. But any principle that in creating would presuppose some other principle has the notion of principle only in a secondary way. Accordingly, since God is the principle of things as first act, whereas matter is a principle of things as being-in-potency, it is unfitting that God, in acting, should presuppose matter.

Furthermore, the more universal a cause is, the more universal its effect is. For particular causes make use of the effects of universal causes for something determinate; and such determination is related to a universal effect as act to potency. Hence any cause that causes something to be in act, utilizing preexisting material that is in potency to that act, is a particular cause with respect to some more universal cause. But this sort of procedure cannot pertain to God, since he is the first cause, as we showed above. Consequently, God does not need matter as a prerequisite to his action. Therefore, he has the power to bring things into existence from nothing or, in other words, to create. This is why the Catholic faith professes that he is the Creator.

CHAPTER 70

That to create belongs to God alone

Hoc etiam apparet quod soli Deo competit esse Creatorem. Nam creare illi causae convenit quae aliam universaliorem non praesupponit, ut ex dictis patet; hoc autem soli Deo competit: solus igitur ipse est Creator.

Item, quanto potentia est magis remota ab actu, tanto necesse est esse maiorem virtutem per quam reducatur in actum. Sed quantacumque distantia potentiae ad actum detur, semper remanet maior distantia si ipsa potentia subtrahatur; creare igitur aliquid ex nihilo requirit infinitam virtutem. Sed solus Deus est infinitae virtutis, cum ipse solus sit infinitae essentiae; solus igitur Deus potest creare.

From this it appears, further, that God alone can be Creator. For to create is the prerogative of that cause which does not presuppose another cause that is more universal, as we saw in the preceding chapter. But this pertains to God alone. He alone, therefore, is Creator.

Again, the more remote a potency is from act, the greater must be the power that reduces it to act. But whatever distance may be imagined between potency and act, the distance will ever be still greater if the very potency itself is withdrawn. To create from nothing, then, requires infinite power. But God alone is infinite in power, since he alone is infinite in essence. Consequently, God alone can create.

CHAPTER 71

That diversity of matter is not the cause of diversity in things

Manifestum est autem ex praeostensis quod causa diversitatis in rebus non est materiae diversitas. Ostensum est enim quod materia non praesupponitur actioni divinae qua res in esse producit; causa autem diversitatis rerum non est ex materia nisi secundum quod materia ad rerum productionem praeexigitur, ut scilicet secundum diversitatem materiae diversae inducantur formae: non igitur causa diversitatis in rebus a Deo productis est materia.

Adhuc, secundum quod res habent esse, ita habent unitatem et pluralitatem, nam unumquodque secundum quod est ens est etiam unum. Non autem habent esse formae propter materias, sed magis materiae propter formas; nam actus melior est potentia, id autem propter quod aliquid est oportet melius esse. Neque igitur formae ideo sunt diversae quia sunt materiae diversae, sed magis materiae institutae sunt diversae ut competant formis diversis.

The foregoing exposition shows clearly that the cause of diversity in things is not diversity on the part of matter. For, as we have proved, the divine action which brings things into being does not suppose the preexistence of matter. The cause of diversity in things could not be on the side of matter unless matter were needed prior to the production of things, so that the various forms induced would follow diversity in the matter. Therefore, the cause of diversity in the things produced by God is not matter.

Again, things have unity and plurality according as they have being, for a given thing, inasmuch as it is a being, is also one. But forms do not possess existence for the sake of matter; rather, matter receives existence for the sake of form. For act is better than potency; and that for the sake of which something exists must be better than it. Therefore, neither are forms diverse in order that they may befit various types of matter, but rather diverse matters were established so that they might befit diverse forms.

CHAPTER 72

The cause of diversity in things

Si autem hoc modo se habeant res ad unitatem et multitudinem sicut se habent ad esse, totum autem esse rerum dependet a Deo, ut ostensum est, necesse est pluralitatis rerum causam ex Deo esse. Quod quidem qualiter sit, considerandum est.

Necesse est enim quod omne agens agat sibi simile secundum quod possibile est. Non autem erat possibile quod similitudinem divinae bonitatis res a Deo productae consequerentur in illa simplicitate secundum quam invenitur in Deo; unde oportuit ut id quod in Deo est unum et simplex, repraesentaretur in rebus creatis diversimode et dissimiliter: necesse igitur fuit diversitatem esse in rebus a Deo productis, ut divinam perfectionem rerum diversitas secundum suum modum imitaretur.

Item, unumquodque creatum finitum est, solius enim Dei est essentia infinita, ut supra ostensum est; quodlibet autem finitum per additionem alterius redditur maius: melius igitur fuit diversitatem in rebus creatis esse ut sic plura bona essent, quam quod esset unum tantum genus rerum a Deo productum. Optimi autem est optima adducere; conveniens igitur fuit Deo quod in rebus diversitatem produceret quam patitur esse creatum.

If things relate to unity and multiplicity as they relate to being, and if the entire being of things depends on God, as has been shown to be the case, the cause of plurality in things must be sought in God. We must now examine how this is the case.

Every agent cause necessarily produces something like itself, so far as this is possible. Now, the things produced by God could not be endowed with a likeness of the divine goodness in the simplicity in which that goodness is found in God. Hence what is one and simple in God had to be represented in created things in various and dissimilar ways. Consequently, there had to be diversity in the things produced by God, in order that the diversity found in things might in its own way imitate the divine perfection.

Furthermore, whatever is caused is finite, since only God's essence is infinite, as was demonstrated above. And any finite thing is made better by the addition of something else. Hence it was better to have diversity in created things, and thus to have multiple good things, than to have but one kind of thing produced by God. Now, the best cause appropriately produces the best effects. Therefore, it was fitting for God to produce in things the diversity that created being permits.

44

CHAPTER 73

Of the diversity, gradation, and order of things

Oportuit autem diversitatem in rebus cum ordine quodam constitui, ut scilicet quaedam aliis essent potiora. Hoc enim ad abundantiam divinae bonitatis pertinet, ut suae bonitatis similitudinem rebus creatis communicet quantum possibile est; Deus autem non solum in se bonus est, sed etiam alia in bonitate excellit et ea ad bonitatem adducit. Ut igitur perfectior esset rerum creatarum similitudo ad Deum, necessarium fuit ut quaedam res aliis constituerentur meliores, et ut quaedam in alia agerent ea ad perfectionem inducendo.

Praeterea, diversitas rerum principaliter in diversitate formarum consistit. Formalis autem diversitas secundum contrarietatem est, dividitur enim genus in diversas species contrariis differentiis; in contrarietate autem ordinem necesse est esse, nam semper alterum contrariorum perfectius est: oportet igitur rerum diversitatem cum quodam ordine a Deo esse institutam, ut scilicet quaedam sint aliis potiora.

Moreover, diversity among things was rightly established according to a definite order, so that some things might be more excellent than others. For this pertains to the lavishness of the divine goodness, that God should communicate a likeness of his goodness to created things as far as possible. Now, God is not only good in himself, but exceeds other beings in goodness, and guides them toward goodness. Consequently, so that the likeness which created beings bear to God might be heightened, it was necessary for some things to be made better than others, and for some to act upon others by leading them toward perfection.

Further, the diversity among things consists chiefly in diversity of forms. Formal diversity is achieved by way of contrariety; for a genus is divided into various species by contrary differences. But order is necessarily found in contrariety, for of two contraries one is always better than the other. Therefore, diversity among things had to be established by God with a particular order, such that some beings are more excellent than others.

CHAPTER 74

How certain created things have more potency and less actuality, and certain others the reverse

Quia vero unumquodque intantum nobile et perfectum est inquantum ad divinam similitudinem accedit, Deus autem est actus purus absque potentiae permixtione, necesse est ea quae sunt suprema in entibus magis esse in actu et minus de potentia habere, quae autem inferiora sunt magis in potentia esse. Hoc autem qualiter sit, considerandum est.

Cum enim Deus sit sempiternus et incommutabilis in suo esse, illa sunt in rebus infima, utpote de similitudine divini esse minus habentia, quae sunt generationi et corruptioni subiecta, quae quandoque sunt et quandoque non sunt. Et quia esse sequitur formam rei, sunt quidem huiusmodi quando formam habent, desinunt autem esse quando forma privantur.

Oportet igitur in eis esse aliquid quod possit quandoque formam habere, quandoque vero forma privari, quod dicimus materiam. Huiusmodi igitur quae sunt in rebus infima oportet esse ex materia et forma composita.

Illa vero quae sunt suprema in entibus creatis ad similitudinem divini esse maxime accedunt, nec est in

A being is noble and perfect in the measure that it approaches likeness to God, who is pure act without any admixture of potency. Therefore, those things that are highest among beings must be more in act and must have less of potency, whereas inferior beings are more in potency. We must now examine how this is the case.

Since God is eternal and immutable in his being, those things are lowest in the scale of beings, as possessing less likeness to God, which are subject to generation and corruption. Such beings exist for a time, and then cease to be. And, since existence follows the form of a thing, beings of this kind exist while they have their form, but cease to exist when deprived of their form.

Hence there must be something in them that can retain a form for a time, and can then be deprived of the form. This is what we call matter. Therefore, such beings as are lowest in the scale of beings must be composed of matter and form.

But beings that are supreme among created entities approach most closely to likeness with God. They have no

eis potentia ad esse et non esse, sed a Deo per creationem sempiternum esse adepta sunt. Cum autem materia hoc ipsum quod est sit potentia ad esse quod est per formam, huiusmodi entia in quibus non est potentia ad esse et non esse, non sunt composita ex materia et forma, sed sunt formae tantum subsistentes in suo esse quod acceperunt a Deo. Necesse est autem huiusmodi substantias incorruptibiles esse; in omnibus enim corruptibilibus est potentia ad non esse, in his autem non est, ut dictum est: sunt igitur incorruptibiles.

Item, nihil corrumpitur nisi per separationem formae ab ipso, nam esse semper consequitur formam; huiusmodi autem substantiae, cum sint formae subsistentes, non possunt separari a suis formis et ita esse amittere non possunt: ergo sunt incorruptibiles.

Sunt autem inter utraque praedictorum quaedam media, in quibus etsi non sit potentia ad esse et non esse, est tamen in eis potentia ad ubi. Huiusmodi autem sunt corpora caelestia, quae generationi et corruptioni non subiiciuntur quia in his contrarietas non invenitur, et tamen sunt mutabilia secundum locum; sic autem invenitur in aliquibus materia sicut et motus, est enim motus actus existentis in potentia. Habent igitur huiusmodi corpora materiam non subiectam generationi et corruptioni, sed solum loci mutationi.

potency with regard to existence and non-existence, but they have received everlasting existence from God through creation. Since matter, by the very fact that it is what it is, is a potency for that existence which is imparted through form, those beings which have no potency for existence and nonexistence are not composed of matter and form, but are forms only, subsisting in their being which they have received from God. Such non-bodily substances must be incorruptible. For all corruptible beings have a potency for non-existence; but these beings have no such potency, as we said. Hence they are incorruptible.

Furthermore, nothing is corrupted unless its form is separated from it, for existence always follows form. Since the substances in question are subsisting forms, they cannot be separated from their forms, and so cannot lose existence. Therefore, they are incorruptible.

Between the extremes mentioned, there are certain intermediate beings which have no potency for existence and nonexistence, but which have a potency for place. Such are the heavenly bodies, which are not subject to generation and corruption, since there are no contraries in them. However, they are changeable according to place. Thus in some there is found matter as well as motion, for motion is the act of a being in potency. Accordingly, such bodies have matter that is not subject to generation and corruption, but is subject only to change of place.

CHAPTER 75

That certain ones are intellectual substances, which are called immaterial

Praedictas autem substantias quas immateriales diximus, necesse est etiam intellectuales esse. Ex hoc enim aliquid intellectuale est quod immune a materia est, quod ex ipso intelligibili percipi potest. Intelligibile enim in actu et intellectus in actu sunt unum; manifestum est autem aliquid esse actu intelligibile per hoc quod est a materia separatum, nam et de rebus materialibus intellectualem cognitionem habere non possumus nisi per abstractionem a materia: unde oportet idem iudicium de intellectu esse, ut scilicet quae sunt immaterialia sint intellectualia.

Item, substantiae immateriales sunt primae et supremae in entibus, nam actus naturaliter est prior potentia; omnibus autem rebus apparet intellectus esse superior, intellectus enim utitur corporalibus quasi instrumentis: oportet igitur substantias immateriales intellectuales esse.

Adhuc, quanto aliqua sunt superiora in entibus, tanto magis pertingunt ad similitudinem divinam. Videmus enim res quasdam infimi gradus participare divinam similitudinem quantum ad esse tantum, velut inanimata; quaedam autem quantum ad esse et vivere, ut plantae; quaedam autem etiam quantum ad cognoscere, ut animalia; supremus autem modus cognitionis est per intellectum, et maxime Deo conveniens. Supremae igitur creaturae sunt intellectuales; et quia inter ceteras creaturas magis ad Dei similitudinem accedunt, propter hoc dicuntur *ad imaginem Dei* constitutae.

The substances mentioned above, which are called immaterial, must also be intellectual. A being is intellectual for the reason that it is free from matter. This can be perceived from the very way it understands. The intelligible in act and the intellect in act are the same thing. But it is clear that a thing is intelligible in act because it is separated from matter; for we cannot have intellectual knowledge of material things except by abstracting from matter. Accordingly, we must pronounce the same judgment regarding the intellect; that is, whatever is immaterial, is intellectual.

Furthermore, immaterial substances hold the first place and are supreme among beings; for act is naturally prior to potency. But the intellect is clearly above all other beings; for the intellect uses bodily things as instruments. Therefore, immaterial substances must be intellectual.

Moreover, the higher a thing is among beings, the closer it draws to the divine likeness. Thus we observe that some things, those pertaining to the lowest degree (such as lifeless beings), share in the divine likeness with respect to existence only; others, for example, plants, share in the divine likeness with respect to existence and life; yet others, such as animals, with respect to knowledge. But the highest way of knowing, and the one most befitting God, is through intellect. Consequently, the highest creatures are intellectual. And because they among all creatures approach most closely to the likeness of God, they are said to be made *in God's image.*

CHAPTER 76

How such substances have free will

Per hoc autem ostenditur quod sunt arbitrio liberae. Intelligens enim non agit aut appetit absque iudicio sicut inanimata; neque etiam iudicium intellectus est ex naturali impetu sicut in brutis, sed est ex propria apprehensione, quia intellectus et finem cognoscit et id quod est ad finem et habitudinem unius ad alterum; et ideo ipse sui iudicii causa esse potest quo appetat et agat aliquid propter finem. Liberum autem dicimus quod sui causa est. Appetit igitur et agit omne intelligens libero iudicio, quod est esse liberum arbitrio. Supremae igitur substantiae sunt arbitrio liberae.

Adhuc, liberum est quod non est obligatum ad aliquid unum determinatum. Appetitus autem substantiae intellectivae non est obligatus ad aliquod unum determinatum bonum; sequitur enim apprehensionem intellectus, quae est de bono universaliter. Est igitur appetitus substantiae intelligentis liber, utpote communiter se habens ad quodcumque bonum.

This fact shows that such beings have freedom of choice. The intellect does not act or desire without forming a judgment, as lifeless beings do, nor is the judgment of the intellect the product of natural impulse, as in brutes, but results from its own apprehension. For the intellect perceives the end, the means leading to the end, and the bearing of one on the other. Hence the intellect can be the cause of its own judgment, whereby it desires a good and performs an action for the sake of an end. But what is a cause unto itself is precisely what we call free. Accordingly, the intellect desires and acts in virtue of a free judgment, which is the same as having freedom of choice. Therefore, the highest substances enjoy freedom of choice.

Furthermore, that is free which is not tied down to any one definite course. But the appetite of an intellectual substance is not tied down any one definite good, for it follows intellectual apprehension, which embraces good universally. Therefore, the appetite of an intelligent substance is free as having a common stance toward any given good.

CHAPTER 77

That in them there is order and gradation according to perfection of nature

Sicut autem hae substantiae intelligentes quodam gradu aliis substantiis superponuntur, ita etiam ipsas substantias necesse est aliquibus gradibus ab invicem distare. Non enim ab invicem possunt differre materiali differentia, cum materia careant: unde si in eis est pluralitas, necesse est eam per distinctionem formalem causari, quae diversitatem speciei constituit. In quibuscumque autem est speciei diversitas, necesse est in eis gradum quendam et ordinem considerare; cuius ratio est quod, sicut in numeris additio vel subtractio unitatis speciem variat, ita per additionem et subtractionem differentiarum res naturales specie differre inveniuntur; sicut quod est animatum tantum ab eo quod est animatum et sensibile, et quod est animatum et sensibile tantum ab eo quod est animatum, sensibile et rationale. Necesse est igitur praedictas immateriales substantias secundum quosdam gradus et ordines esse distinctas.

As intellectual substances occupy a higher place in the scale of perfection than other substances, so these same substances must also occupy difference places than each other. For they cannot differ from one another by material differentiation, since they lack matter; hence if any plurality is found among them, it must be caused by formal distinction, which establishes diversity of species. And among beings that differ in species, one must note a certain gradation and order. The reason is that just as addition or subtraction of a unit causes variation of species in numbers, so natural things are found to vary in species by the addition or subtraction of differences. For instance, what is merely alive differs from what is both alive and endowed with sense perception; and what is endowed only with life and sensation differs from what is alive, endowed with sense, and rational. Therefore, the immaterial substances under discussion must be distinct according to various degrees and orders.

CHAPTER 78

How there is order and gradation of understanding in them

Et quia secundum modum substantiae rei est modus operationis ipsius, necesse est quod superiores earum nobilius intelligant, utpote formas intelligibiles et virtutes magis universales et magis unitas habentes; inferiores autem esse debiliores in intelligendo et habere formas magis multiplicatas et minus universales.

Since the nature of a being's activity is in keeping with its substance, the higher intellectual substances must understand in a more perfect way, inasmuch as they have intelligible species and powers that are more universal and are more unified. On the other hand, intellectual substances that are less perfect must be weaker in intelligence, and must have species that are more numerous and less universal.

CHAPTER 79

That the substance through which man understands is the
lowest in the genus of intellectual substances

Cum autem non sit in rebus in infinitum procedere, sicut est invenire supremam in praedictis substantiis quae propinquissime accedit ad Deum, ita necesse est inveniri infimam quae maxime appropinquat materiae corporali. Et hoc quidem aliter potest esse manifestum. Intelligere enim homini supra alia animalia convenit; manifestum est enim quod homo solus universalia considerat, et habitudines rerum et res immateriales: quae solum intelligendo percipiuntur. Intelligere autem impossibile est quod sit actus exercitus per organum corporale, sicut visio exercetur per oculum. Necesse est enim quod omne instrumentum virtutis cognoscitivae careat illo genere rerum quod per ipsum cognoscitur, sicut pupilla caret coloribus ex sua natura, sic enim cognoscuntur colores inquantum colorum species recipiuntur in pupilla; recipiens autem oportet esse denudatum ab eo quod recipit. Intellectus autem cognoscitivus est omnium naturarum sensibilium; si igitur cognosceret per organum corporale, oporteret illud organum esse denudatum ab omni natura sensibili: quod est impossibile.

Item, omnis ratio cognoscitiva eo modo cognoscit quo species cogniti est apud ipsam, nam haec est sibi principium cognoscendi. Intellectus autem cognoscit res immaterialiter, etiam eas quae in sua natura sunt materiales, abstrahendo formam universalem a materialibus conditionibus individuantibus; impossibile est ergo quod species rei cognitae sit in intellectu materialiter: ergo non recipitur in organo corporali, nam omne organum corporale materiale est.

Idem etiam apparet ex hoc quod sensus debilitatur et corrumpitur excellentibus sensibilibus, sicut auditus a magnis sonis et visus a rebus valde fulgidis, quod

Infinite progression is impossible in any series. Among intellectual substances, one must ultimately be found to be supreme: namely, the one which approaches most closely to God. Likewise, one must be found to be the lowest, and this will be the one most intimately associated with bodily matter. This can be explained in the following way. Understanding is proper to man beyond all the other animals. Evidently, man alone comprehends universals, and the relations between things, and immaterial things, which are perceptible only to the intelligence. Understanding cannot be an act performed by a bodily organ, in the way that vision is exercised by the eye. For no faculty endowed with cognitive power can belong to the genus of things known through its agency: thus the pupil of the eye lacks color by its very nature. Colors are recognized to the extent that the species of colors are received into the pupil; but a recipient must lack what it receives. Now, the intellect is capable of knowing all sensible natures. Therefore, if it knew through the medium of a bodily organ, that organ would have to be entirely lacking in sensible nature; but this is impossible.

Moreover, every cognitive faculty knows according to the way the species of the object known is in it, for this is its principle of knowing. But the intellect knows things immaterially, even those things that are by nature material, by abstracting a universal form from its individuating material conditions. Therefore, the species of the object known cannot exist in the intellect materially; and so it is not received into a bodily organ, seeing that every bodily organ is material.

The same is clear from the fact that a sense is weakened and injured by excessively strong sensible objects. Thus the ear is impaired by excessively loud sounds, and

accidit quia solvitur organi harmonia. Intellectus autem magis roboratur ex excellentia intelligibilium; nam qui intelligit altiora intelligibilium, non minus potest intelligere alia sed magis. Sic igitur, cum homo inveniatur intelligens et intelligere hominis non sit per organum corporale, oportet quod sit aliqua substantia incorporea per quam homo intelligat; nam quod per se potest operationem habere sine corpore, etiam eius subsistentia non dependet a corpore. Omnes enim virtutes et formae quae per se subsistere non possunt sine corpore, operationem sine corpore habere non possunt: non enim calor per se calefacit, sed corpus per calorem. Haec igitur substantia incorporea per quam homo intelligit, est infima in genere substantiarum intellectualium et maxime materiae propinqua.

the eye by excessively bright lights, because the harmony within the organ is shattered. The intellect, on the contrary, is perfected by the excellence of intelligible objects; he who understands the higher objects of intelligence is able to understand other objects more, rather than less, perfectly. Consequently, if man is found to be intelligent, and if man's understanding is not through a bodily organ, there must be some non-bodily substance whereby man exercises the act of understanding. For the substance of a being that can perform an action by itself, without the aid of a body, is not dependent on a body. But all powers and forms that are unable to subsist by themselves without a body cannot exercise any activity without a body. Thus heat does not cause warmth by itself; rather, a body causes warmth by the heat that is in it. Accordingly, this non-bodily substance whereby man understands occupies the lowest place in the genus of intellectual substances, and is the closest to matter.

Chapter 80

Of the difference of intellects in understanding

Cum autem esse intelligibile sit supra esse sensibile sicut intellectus supra sensum, ea autem quae sunt inferiora in entibus imitantur ut possint superiora, sicut corpora generabilia et corruptibilia imitantur aliquo modo circulationem caelestium corporum: necesse est et sensibilia intelligibilibus suo modo assimilari, et sic ex similitudine sensibilium utcumque possumus in intelligibilium notitiam devenire.

Est autem in sensibilibus aliquid quasi supremum quod est actus, scilicet forma, et aliquid infimum quod est in potentia tantum, scilicet materia prima, et aliquid medium, scilicet compositum ex materia et forma. Sic etiam et in esse intelligibili considerandum est: nam supremum intelligibile quod est Deus est actus purus; substantiae vero intellectuales aliae sunt habentes aliquid de actu et de potentia secundum esse intelligibile; infima vero intellectualium substantiarum, per quam homo intelligit, est quasi in potentia tantum in esse intelligibili. Huic etiam attestatur quod homo invenitur a principio potentia tantum intelligens, et postmodum paulatim reducitur in actum; et inde est quod id quo homo intelligit vocatur intellectus possibilis.

Since intellectual being is superior to sensible being just as intellect is superior to sense, and since lower beings imitate higher beings as best they may (as bodies subject to generation and corruption imitate in some fashion the circulatory motion of heavenly bodies), it follows that sensible beings resemble, in their own way, intellectual beings. Thus from the resemblance of sense to intellect we can mount to some knowledge of intellectual beings.

In sensible beings a certain factor is found to be the highest: this is act, or form. Another factor is found to be the lowest, for it is pure potency: this is matter. Midway between the two is the composite of matter and form. We expect to find something similar in the intellectual world. The supreme intellectual being, God, is pure act. Other intellectual substances have something of act and of potency, but in a way that befits intellectual being. And the lowest among intellectual substances, through which man understands, has, so to speak, intellectual being only in potency. This is borne out by the fact that man is at first found to be only potentially intelligent, and this potency is gradually reduced to act in the course of time. And this is why the faculty whereby man understands is called the possible intellect.

Chapter 81

That the possible intellect receives intelligible forms from sensible things

Quia vero, ut dictum est, quanto substantia intellectualis est altior, tanto formas intelligibiles universaliores habet, consequens est ut intellectus humanus quem possibilem diximus, inter alias intellectuales substantias formas habeat minus universales; et inde est quod formas intelligibiles a rebus sensibilibus accipit.

Hoc etiam aliter consideranti manifestum esse potest. Oportet enim formam esse proportionatam susceptibili; sicut igitur intellectus possibilis humanus inter omnes substantias intellectuales propinquior invenitur materiae corporali, ita necesse est quod eius formae intelligibiles rebus materialibus sint maxime propinquae.

As was stated above, the higher an intellectual substance is in perfection, the more universal are the intelligible forms it possesses. Of all the intellectual substances, consequently, the human intellect, which we have called possible, has forms of the least universality. This is the reason it receives its intelligible forms from sensible things.

This can be made clear from another point of view. A form must have some proportion to the potency which receives it. Therefore, since of all intellectual substances man's possible intellect is found to be the closest to bodily matter, its intelligible forms must, likewise, be most closely allied to material things.

Chapter 82

That man needs sense powers in order to understand

Considerandum autem quod formae in rebus corporeis particulares sunt et materiale esse habentes, in intellectu vero universales sunt et immateriales: quod quidem demonstrat intelligendi modus. Intelligimus enim res universaliter et immaterialiter; modus autem intelligendi speciebus intelligibilibus quibus intelligimus, necesse est ut correspondeat: oportet igitur quod, cum de extremo ad extremum non perveniatur nisi per medium, quod formae a rebus corporeis ad intellectum perveniant per aliqua media.

Huiusmodi autem sunt potentiae sensitivae, quae formas rerum materialium recipiunt quidem sine materia, fit enim in oculo species lapidis sed non materia; recipiuntur tamen in potentiis sensitivis formae rerum particulariter, nam potentiis sensitivis non nisi particularia cognoscimus. Necesse igitur fuit hominem ad hoc quod intelligat etiam sensus habere. Huius autem signum est quod cui deficit unus sensus, deficit scientia sensibilium quae illo sensu apprehenduntur, sicut caecus natus de coloribus scientiam habere non potest.

However, we must realize that forms in bodily things are particular, and have a material existence. But in the intellect they are universal and immaterial. Our manner of understanding brings this out. That is, we apprehend things universally and immaterially. This way of understanding must conform to the intelligible species whereby we understand. Consequently, since it is impossible to pass from one extreme to another without traversing what lies between, forms reaching the intellect from bodily objects must pass through certain media.

These are the sense faculties, which receive the forms of material things without their matter; what lodges in the eye is the species of the stone, but not its matter. However, the forms of things received into the sense faculties are particular; for we know only particular objects with our sense faculties. Hence man must be endowed with senses as a prerequisite to understanding. A proof of this is the fact that if a man is lacking in one of the senses, he has no knowledge of sensible objects that are apprehended by that sense. Thus a person born blind can have no knowledge of colors.

CHAPTER 83

That it is necessary to posit an agent intellect

Inde autem manifestum fit quod scientia rerum in intellectu nostro non causatur per participationem aut influxum aliquarum formarum actu intelligibilium per se subsistentium, sicut Platonici posuerunt et alii quidam ipsos sequentes, sed intellectus acquirit eam a rebus sensibilibus mediantibus sensibus.

Sed cum in potentiis sensitivis formae rerum sint particulares, ut dictum est, non sunt intelligibiles actu sed potentia tantum: intellectus enim non nisi universalia intelligit. Quod autem est in potentia non reducitur in actum nisi ab aliquo agente; oportet igitur quod sit aliquod agens quod species in potentiis sensitivis existentes faciat intelligibiles actu. Hoc autem non potest facere intellectus possibilis, ipse enim magis est in potentia ad intelligibilia quam intelligibilium activus; necesse est igitur ponere alium intellectum qui species intelligibiles in potentia faciat intelligibiles actu, sicut lumen facit colores visibiles potentia esse visibiles actu: et hunc dicimus intellectum agentem, quem ponere non esset necesse si formae rerum essent intelligibiles actu, sicut Platonici posuerunt.

Sic igitur ad intelligendum primo necessarius est nobis intellectus possibilis, qui est receptivus specierum intelligibilium; secundo intellectus agens qui facit intelligibilia actu. Cum autem intellectus possibilis iam fuerit per species intelligibiles perfectus, vocatur intellectus in habitu, cum species intelligibiles sic iam habet quod possit eis uti cum voluerit, medio quodam modo inter potentiam puram et actum completum; cum vero praedictas species in actu completo habuerit, vocatur intellectus in actu: sic enim actu intelligit res, cum species rei facta fuerit forma possibilis intellectus; propter quod dicitur quod intellectus in actu est intellectum in actu.

This discussion brings out the truth that knowledge of things in our intellect is not caused by any participation or influence of forms that are intelligible in act and that subsist by themselves, as was taught by the Platonists and certain other philosophers who followed them in this doctrine. Rather, the intellect acquires such knowledge from sensible objects through the intermediacy of the senses.

However, since the forms of objects in the sense faculties are particular, as we just said, they are intelligible not in act, but only in potency. For the intellect understands nothing but universals. But what is in potency is not reduced to act except by some agent. Hence there must be some agent that causes the species existing in the sense faculties to be intelligible in act. The possible intellect cannot perform this service, for it is in potency with respect to intelligible objects rather than active in rendering them intelligible. Therefore, we must posit some other intellect, which will cause species that are intelligible in potency to become intelligible in act, just as light causes colors that are potentially visible to be actually visible. This faculty we call the agent intellect, which we would not have to postulate if the forms of things were intelligible in act, as the Platonists held.

To understand, therefore, we have need, first, of the possible intellect which receives intelligible species, and second, of the agent intellect which renders things intelligible in act. Once the possible intellect has been perfected by the intelligible species, it is called the habitual intellect, for then it possesses intelligible species in such a way that it can use them at will; in other words, it possesses them in a fashion that is midway between pure potency and complete act. But when it has these species in full actuality, it is called the intellect in act. That is, the intellect actually understands a thing when the species of the thing is made the form of the possible intellect. This is why we say that the intellect in act is the object actually understood.

CHAPTER 84

That the human soul is incorruptible

Necesse est autem secundum praemissa, intellectum quo homo intelligit incorruptibilem esse. Unumquodque enim sic operatur secundum quod habet esse; intellectus autem habet operationem in qua non communicat sibi corpus, ut ostensum est, ex quo patet quod est operans per se ipsum: ergo est substantia subsistens in suo esse. Ostensum est autem supra quod substantiae intellectuales sunt incorruptibiles; ergo intellectus quo homo intelligit est incorruptibilis.

Adhuc, proprium subiectum generationis et corruptionis est materia. Intantum igitur unumquodque a corruptione recedit inquantum recedit a materia: ea enim quae sunt composita ex materia et forma sunt per se corruptibilia; formae autem materiales sunt corruptibiles per accidens et non per se; formae autem immateriales, quae materiae proportionem excedunt, sunt incorruptibiles omnino. Intellectus autem omnino secundum suam naturam supra materiam elevatur: quod eius operatio ostendit, non enim intelligimus aliqua nisi per hoc quod ipsa a materia separamus. Est igitur intellectus secundum suam naturam incorruptibilis.

Item, corruptio absque contrarietate esse non potest, nihil enim corrumpitur nisi a suo contrario; unde corpora caelestia, in quibus non est contrarietas, sunt incorruptibilia. Sed contrarietas longe est a natura intellectus, in tantum quod ea quae secundum se sunt contraria, in intellectu contraria non sunt: est enim contrariorum ratio intelligibilis una, quia per unum intelligitur aliud. Impossibile est igitur quod intellectus sit corruptibilis.

A necessary consequence of the foregoing doctrine is that the intellect whereby man understands is incorruptible. Every being acts in a way that is conformable to its existence. The intellect has an activity which it does not share with the body, as we have proved. This shows that it can act by itself. Hence it is a substance subsisting in its own being. But, as was pointed out above, intellectual substances are incorruptible. Accordingly, the intellect whereby man understands is incorruptible.

Again, the proper subject of generation and corruption is matter. Hence a thing is immune to corruption to the extent that it is free from matter. Things composed of matter and form are essentially corruptible; material forms are corruptible accidentally, though not essentially. Immaterial forms, which are above material conditions, are wholly incorruptible. The intellect by its very nature is elevated completely beyond matter, as its activity shows: we do not understand anything unless we separate it from matter. Consequently, the intellect is by nature incorruptible.

Moreover, corruption cannot take place without contrariety; for nothing is corrupted except by its contrary. This is why the heavenly bodies, which do not admit of contrariety, are incorruptible. But all contrariety is far removed from the nature of the intellect, so much so that things which are contraries in themselves are not contraries in the intellect. The intelligible aspect of contraries is one, inasmuch as one thing is understood in terms of another. Thus it is impossible for the intellect to be corruptible.

CHAPTER 85

That there is not one possible intellect in all men

Forte autem aliquis dicet quod intellectus quidem incorruptibilis est, sed est unus in omnibus hominibus, et sic quod post corruptionem omnium hominum remanet non est nisi unum. Quod autem sit unus tantum intellectus in omnibus, multipliciter astrui potest.

Primo quidem ex parte intelligibilia quia, si est alius intellectus in me et alius in te, oportebit quod sit alia species intelligibilia in me et alia, in te, et per consequens aliud intellectum quod ego intelligo et aliud quod tu. Erit ergo intentio intellecta multiplicata secundum

An objector may say: the intellect is indeed incorruptible, but there is only one intellect in all men; and so what remains after the corruption of all men is but one. That there is only one intellect for all men, the objector may continue, can be established on many grounds.

First, on the part of the intelligible species. If I have one intellect and you have another, there will have to be one intelligible species in me and another in you, and consequently there will be one object that I understand and another that you understand. Hence the intelligible species

numerum individuorum, et ita non erit universalis sed individualis. Ex quo videtur sequi quod non sit intellecta in actu, sed in potentia tantum, nam intentiones individuales sunt intellecta in potentia, non in actu.

Deinde quia, cum ostensum sit quod intellectus est substantia subsistens in suo esse, substantiae autem intellectuales plures numero non sint in una specie, ut supra etiam ostensum est, sequitur si alius est intellectus in me et alius in te secundum numerum, quod sit etiam alius specie; et sic ego et tu non sumus eiusdem speciei.

Item, cum in natura speciei omnia individua communicent, oportet poni aliquid praeter naturam speciei secundum quod ab invicem individua distinguantur. Si igitur in omnibus hominibus est unus intellectus secundum speciem, plures autem secundum numerum, oportet ponere aliquid quod faciat numero differre unum intellectum ab alio; hoc autem non potest esse aliquid quod sit de substantia intellectus, cum intellectus non sit compositus ex materia et forma. Ex quo sequitur quod omnis differentia quae accipi posset secundum id quod est de substantia intellectus, sit differentia formalis et diversificans speciem. Relinquitur ergo quod intellectus unius hominis non possit esse alius numero ab intellectu alterius, nisi propter diversitatem corporum; corruptis igitur corporibus diversis, videtur quod non remaneant plures intellectus sed unus tantum.

Hoc autem quod impossibile sit, evidenter apparet. Ad quod ostendendum, procedendum est sicut proceditur contra negantes principia, ut ponamus aliquid quod omnino negari non potest. Ponamus igitur quod hic homo, puta Socrates vel Plato, intelligit: quod negare non posset respondens nisi intelligeret esse negandum; negando igitur ponit, nam affirmare et negare intelligentis est. Si autem hic homo intelligit, oportet quod id quo formaliter intelligit sit forma eius, quia nihil agit nisi secundum quod est actu, illud ergo quo agit agens est actus eius, sicut calor quo calidum calefacit est forma eius; intellectus igitur quo homo intelligit est forma huius hominis, et eadem ratione illius. Impossibile est autem quod forma eadem numero sit diversorum secundum numerum, quia diversorum secundum numerum non est idem esse; unumquodque autem habet esse per suam formam: impossibile est igitur quod intellectus quo homo intelligit sit unus in omnibus.

Huius autem rationis difficultatem aliqui cognoscentes, conati sunt invenire viam evadendi. Dicunt enim quod intellectus possibilis, de quo supra est habitum, recipit species intelligibiles quibus fit in actu. Species autem intelligibiles sunt quodammodo in phantasmatibus.

will be multiplied according to the number of individuals, and so it will not be universal but individual. The conclusion would then seem to follow that it is understood not in act, but only in potency; for individual species are intelligible in potency, not in act.

Moreover, since the intellect, as we have seen, is a substance subsisting in its own being, and since intellectual substances that are numerically many do not belong to one species, as we have also seen, it follows that if I have one intellect and you have another that is numerically different, the two must differ specifically. And so you and I would not belong to the same species.

Furthermore, since all individuals share in one specific nature, there must be something besides specific nature whereby individuals may be distinguished from one another. Accordingly, if there is one specific intellect in all men, but many intellects that are numerically distinct, something must be found that will make one intellect differ numerically from another. This cannot be anything pertaining to the substance of the intellect, since the intellect is not composed of matter and form. Consequently, any difference that might be admitted on the part of the substance of the intellect would be a formal difference that would cause diversity in the species. The only possibility left is that the intellect of one man cannot differ numerically from the intellect of another man except by reason of the diversity of their bodies. Therefore, when the various bodies are destroyed, it seems that only one intellect, and not a plurality of intellects, would remain.

The absurdity of this whole position is easily perceived. To make this clear, let us proceed as one would proceed against those who deny fundamental principles. That is, let us establish a truth that simply cannot be denied. Let us suppose that this man, for example, Socrates or Plato, understands. Our adversary could not deny that the man understands, unless he knew that it ought to be denied. By denying he affirms, for affirmation and denial are intelligent actions. If, then, the man in question understands, that whereby he formally understands must be his form, since nothing acts unless it is in act. Hence that whereby an agent acts is his act; just as the heat by which a heated body causes warmth is its act. Therefore, the intellect whereby a man understands is the form of this man, and the same is true of another man. But the same numerical form cannot belong to numerically different individuals, for numerically different individuals do not possess the same existence; and yet everything has existence by reason of its form. Accordingly, the intellect whereby a man understands cannot be but one in all men.

Perceiving the force of this difficulty, some endeavor to find a way of escaping it. They say that the possible intellect, of which there was question above, receives the intelligible species by which it is reduced to act. These intelligible species are, in some way, in the phantasms. Hence the possi-

Inquantum igitur species intelligibilis est in intellectu possibili et in phantasmatibus quae sunt in nobis, intantum intellectus possibilis continuatur et unitur nobiscum, ut sic per ipsum intelligere possumus.

Sed haec responsio omnino nulla est. Primo quidem quia species intelligibilis secundum quod est in phantasmatibus est intellecta in potentia tantum, secundum autem quod est in intellectu possibili est intellecta in actu; secundum igitur quod est in intellectu possibili non est in phantasmatibus, sed magis a phantasmatibus abstracta. Nulla ergo remanet unio intellectus possibilis ad nos. Deinde, dato quod sit aliqua unio, non tamen sufficeret ad hoc quod faceret nos intelligentes. Per hoc enim quod species alicuius est in intellectu, non sequitur quod ipsum intelligat sed quod intelligatur: non enim lapis intelligit, et si eius species sit in intellectu. Neque igitur per hoc quod species phantasmatum quae sunt in nobis sunt in intellectu possibili, sequitur quod nos sumus intelligentes, sed magis quod nos sumus intellecti, vel potius phantasmata quae sunt in nobis.

Hoc autem evidentius apparet si quis consideret comparationem quam facit Aristoteles in III *de Anima*, dicens quod intellectus se habet ad phantasmata sicut visus ad colores. Manifestum est autem quod per hoc quod species colorum qui sunt in pariete fiunt in visu, non habet paries quod videat, sed quod videatur; neque igitur ex hoc quod species phantasmatum quae sunt in nobis fiunt in intellectu, sequitur quod nos simus intelligentes, sed solum quod simus intellecti.

Amplius, si nos per intellectum formaliter intelligimus, oportet quod ipsum intelligere intellectus sit intelligere hominis, sicut eadem est calefactio ignis et caloris. Si igitur idem est numero intellectus in me et in te, sequetur de necessitate quod respectu eiusdem intelligibilis sit idem numero intelligere meum et tuum, dum scilicet simul aliquid idem intelligimus; quod est impossibile: non enim diversorum operantium potest esse una et eadem operatio numero. Impossibile est igitur quod sit unus intellectus in omnibus. Sequitur igitur quod, si intellectus est incorruptibilis ut ostensum est, quod destructis corporibus remaneant plures intellectus secundum numerum hominum.

Ea vero quae in contrarium obiiciuntur facile est solvere.

Prima enim ratio multipliciter deficit primo quidem quia concedimus idem esse intellectum ab omnibus hominibus, dico autem intellectum id quod est intellectus obiectum; obiectum autem intellectus non est species intelligibilis, sed quidditas rei: non enim scientiae intellectuales omnes sunt de speciebus intelligibilibus, sed sunt de naturis rerum, sicut etiam obiectum visus est color, non species coloris quae est in oculo. Quamvis igitur sint plures intellectus diversorum hominum, non tamen

ble intellect is continuous and is joined to us so far as the intelligible species is both in the possible intellect and in the phantasms that are in us. It is thus that we are able to understand through the agency of the possible intellect.

But this response is completely worthless. In the first place, the intelligible species, as it exists in the phantasms, is a concept only in potency; and as it exists in the possible intellect, it is a concept in act. As existing in the possible intellect, it is not in the phantasms, but rather is abstracted from the phantasms. Hence no union of the possible intellect with us remains. Second, even granting that there may be some sort of union, this would not suffice to enable us to understand. The presence of the species of some object in the intellect does not mean that the object understands itself, but only that it is understood; a stone does not understand, even though a species of it may be in the possible intellect. Hence, from the fact that species of phantasms present in us are in the possible intellect, it does not follow that we therefore understand. It only follows that we ourselves, or rather the phantasms in us, are understood.

This will appear more clearly if we examine the comparison proposed by Aristotle in Book III of *de Anima*, where he says that the intellect is to phantasm what sight is to color. Manifestly, the fact that the species of colors on a wall are in our vision does not cause the wall to see, but to be seen. Likewise, the fact that the species of the phantasms in us come to be in the intellect does not cause us to understand, but to be understood.

Further, if we understand formally through the intellect, the intellectual action of the intellect must be the intellectual action of the man, just as the heating action of fire and of heat are the same. Therefore, if intellect is numerically the same in me and in you, it follows that, with respect to the same intelligible object, my action of understanding must be the same as yours, provided, of course, both of us understand the same thing at the same time. But this is impossible, for different agents cannot perform one and the same numerical operation. Therefore, it is impossible for all men to have but a single intellect. Consequently, if the intellect is incorruptible, as has been demonstrated, many intellects, corresponding to the number of men, will survive the destruction of their bodies.

The arguments advanced to support the contrary view are easily answered.

The first argument has many defects. First of all, we concede that the same thing may be understood by all. By the thing understood I mean that which is the object of the intellect. However, the object of the intellect is not the intelligible species, but the essence of the thing. The intellectual sciences are all concerned with the natures of things, not with intelligible species; just as the object of sight is color, not the species of color in the eye. Hence, although there may be many intellects belonging to different men,

est nisi unum intellectum apud omnes, sicut unum coloratum est quod a diversis inspicientibus videtur. Secundo, quia non est necessarium, si aliquid est individuum, quod sit intellectum in potentia et non in actu, sed hoc est verum in illis tantum quae individuantur per materiam: oportet enim illud quod est intellectum in actu esse immateriale; unde substantiae immateriales, licet sint quaedam individua per se existentia, sunt tamen intellecta in actu. Unde et species intelligibiles quia sunt immateriales, licet sint aliae numero in me et in te, non propter hoc perdunt quin sint intelligibiles actu; sed intellectus intelligens per eas suum obiectum reflectitur supra se ipsum, intelligendo ipsum suum intelligere et speciem qua intelligit.

Deinde considerandum est quod, etiam si ponatur unus intellectus omnium hominum, adhuc eadem remanet difficultas, quia adhuc remanet multitudo intellectuum, cum sint plures substantiae separatae intelligentes; et ita sequeretur secundum eorum rationem quod intellecta essent diversa secundum numerum, et per consequens individualia et non intellecta in actu. Patet igitur quod praemissa ratio, si aliquid necessitatis haberet, auferret pluralitatem intellectuum simpliciter et non solum in hominibus; unde cum haec conclusio sit falsa, manifestum est quod ratio non ex necessitate concludit.

Secunda etiam ratio facile solvitur, si quis consideret differentiam intellectualis animae ad substantias separatas. Anima enim intellectiva ex natura suae speciei hoc habet ut uniatur alicui corpori ut forma, unde et in definitione animae cadit corpus; et propter hoc secundum habitudinem ad diversa corpora diversificatur secundum numerum, quod non est in substantiis separatis.

Ex quo etiam patet qualiter tertia ratio sit solvenda. Non enim anima intellectiva ex natura suae speciei habet corpus partem sui, sed unibilitatem ad ipsum; unde per hoc quod est unibilis diversis corporibus diversificatur secundum numerum, quod etiam manet in animabus corporibus destructis: sunt enim unibiles corporibus diversis, licet non actu unitae.

the thing understood by all may be but one; just as a colored object which many look at is but one. Second, the consequence does not necessarily follow that, if a thing is individual, it is understood in potency and not in act. This is true only of things that are individuated by matter. Of course, what is understood in act must be immaterial. Accordingly, immaterial substances, even though they may be individuals existing by themselves, are understood in act. The same holds for intelligible species, which are immaterial; although they differ numerically in me and in you, they do not on that account lose their property of being intelligible in act. The intellect that understands its objects by means of them reflects upon itself, thereby understanding its very action of understanding as well as the species whereby it understands.

Moreover, we should realize that, even if we admit but one intellect for all men, the difficulty is still the same. There would still remain many intellects, because there are many separate substances endowed with intelligence. And so it would follow, pursuing our adversaries' line of reasoning, that the objects understood would be numerically different—hence individual and not understood in first act. Obviously, therefore, if the objection under discussion were necessary at all, it would do away with a plurality of intellects simply as such, and not merely in men. Since this conclusion is false, it is obvious that the argument does not follow from necessity.

The second argument is readily answered, if we but consider the difference between an intellectual soul and separate substances. In virtue of its specific nature, the intellectual soul is meant to be united to some body as the latter's form; the body even enters into the definition of the soul. For this reason, souls are numerically differentiated according to the relation they have to different bodies; which is not the case with separate substances.

This also indicates how the third argument is to be answered. In virtue of its specific nature, the intellectual soul does not possess the body as a part of itself, but has only an aptitude for union with the body. Therefore, it is numerically differentiated by its capacity for union with different bodies. And this remains the case with souls even after their bodies have been destroyed: they retain a capacity for union with different bodies even when they are not actually united to their respective bodies.

CHAPTER 86

That the agent intellect is not one in all men

Fuerunt autem quidam qui, licet concederent intellectum possibilem diversificari in hominibus, posuerunt tamen intellectum agentem unum respectu omnium esse. Quae quidem opinio, licet sit tolerabilior quam praemissa, similibus tamen rationibus confutari potest.

Est enim actio intellectus possibilis recipere intellecta et intelligere ea, actio autem intellectus agentis facere intellecta in actu abstrahendo ipsa; utrumque autem horum huic homini convenit, nam hic homo, ut Socrates vel Plato, et recipit intellecta et abstrahit et intelligit abstracta. Oportet igitur quod tam intellectus possibilis quam intellectus agens uniatur huic homini ut forma, et sic oportet quod uterque multiplicetur numero secundum numerum hominum.

Item, agens et patiens oportet esse ad invicem proportionata sicut et materia et forma, nam materia fit in actu ab agente; et inde est quod cuilibet potentiae passivae respondet potentia activa sui generis, actus enim et potentia unius generis sunt. Intellectus autem agens comparatur ad possibilem sicut potentia activa ad passivam, ut ex praedictis patet; oportet igitur utrumque esse unius generis. Cum igitur intellectus possibilis non sit secundum esse separatus a nobis sed uniatur nobis ut forma, et multiplicetur secundum multitudinem hominum, ut ostensum est, necesse est quod intellectus agens sit aliquid unitum nobis formaliter, et multiplicetur secundum numerum hominum.

There were also some philosophers who argued that, even granting the diversification of the possible intellect in men, at any rate the agent intellect was but one for all. This view, while less objectionable than the theory discussed in the preceding chapter, can be refuted by similar considerations.

The action of the possible intellect consists in receiving the objects understood and in understanding them. And the action of the agent intellect consists in causing things to be actually understood by abstracting species. But both these functions pertain to one particular man. This man, such as Socrates or Plato, receives the objects understood, abstracts the species, and understands what is abstracted. Hence the possible intellect as well as the agent intellect must be united to this man as a form. And so both must be numerically multiplied in accord with the number of men concerned.

Moreover, agent and patient must be proportionate to each other. Examples are matter and form, for matter is reduced to act by an agent. This is why an active potency of the same genus corresponds to every passive potency; for act and potency pertain to one genus. But the agent intellect is to the possible intellect what active potency is to passive potency, as is clear from this discussion. Hence they must both pertain to one genus. Therefore, since the possible intellect has no separate existence apart from us, but is united to us as a form and is multiplied according to the number of men, as we have shown, the agent intellect must likewise be something that is united to us as a form, and must be multiplied according to the number of men.

CHAPTER 87

That the possible intellect and agent intellect are founded in the soul's essence

Cum autem tam intellectus possibilis quam agens nobis formaliter uniatur, necesse est dicere quod in eadem essentia animae conveniant. Omina enim quod alicui unitur formaliter, aut unitur ei per modum formae substantialis, aut per modum formae accidentalis. Si igitur intellectus possibilis et agens uniantur homini per modum formae substantialis, cum unius rei non sit nisi una forma substantialis, necesse est dicere quod intellectus possibilis et agens conveniant in una essentia formae, quae est anima. Si vero uniantur homini per modum formae accidentalis, manifestum est quod

Since the agent intellect and the possible intellect are formally united to us, we must acknowledge that they pertain to the same essence of the soul. Whatever is formally united to another thing is united to it either in the manner of a substantial form or in the manner of an accidental form. If the possible intellect and the agent intellect were united to man after the fashion of a substantial form, we would have to hold that they share in the one essence of that form which is the soul, since one thing cannot have more than one substantial form. On the other hand, if they are united to man after the fashion of an accidental form,

neutrum eorum potest esse accidens corpori, ex hoc quod operationes eorum sunt absque organo corporali, ut supra ostensum est; sequitur quod uterque eorum sit accidens animae. Non est autem in uno homine nisi anima una; oportet igitur quod intellectus agens et possibilis in una essentia animae conveniant.

Item, omnis actio quae est propria alicui speciei, est a principiis consequentibus formam quae dat speciem; intelligere autem est operatio propria humanae speciei: oportet igitur quod intellectus agens et possibilis, qui sunt principia huius operationis sicut ostensum est, consequantur animam humanam a qua homo speciem habet. Non autem sic consequuntur eam quasi ab ipsa procedentia in corpus, quia, ut ostensum est, praedicta operatio est sine organo corporali; cuius autem est potentia, et actio: relinquitur igitur quod intellectus possibilis et agens conveniant in una essentia animae.

neither of them, evidently, can be an accident of the body. Besides, the fact that their operations are performed without a bodily organ, as we proved above, shows that each of them is an accident of the soul. But there is only one soul in one man. Therefore, the agent intellect and the possible intellect must belong to the one essence of the soul.

Furthermore, every action that is proper to a species is from principles consequent upon the form which confers the species. But the action of understanding is an operation proper to the human species. Therefore, the agent intellect and the possible intellect, which are principles of this action, as has been shown, are consequent upon the human soul, whence man has his species. However, they do not issue from the soul in such a way as to extend to the body, because, as we have said, the operation in question takes place independently of a bodily organ. Since, therefore, action pertains to the same subject as does potency, the possible intellect and the agent intellect belong to the one essence of the soul.

CHAPTER 88

In what way these two powers come together in one essence of the soul

Considerandum autem relinquitur quomodo hoc possit esse. Videtur enim circa hoc aliqua difficultas suboriri. Intellectus enim possibilis est in potentia ad omnia intelligibilia; intellectus autem agens facit intelligibilia in actu, et sic oportet ut comparetur ad ea sicut actus ad potentiam. Non videtur autem possibile quod idem respectu eiusdem sit in potentia et in actu; sic igitur impossibile videtur quod in una substantia animae conveniant intellectus possibilis et agens.

Haec autem dubitatio de facili solvitur, si quis consideret qualiter intellectus possibilis sit in potentia respectu intelligibilium, et qualiter intellectus agens faciat ea in actu. Est enim intellectus possibilis in potentia ad intelligibilia secundum quod non habet in sui natura aliquam determinatam formam rerum sensibilium, sicut pupilla est in potentia ad colores. Inquantum ergo phantasmata a rebus sensibilibus abstracta sunt similitudines determinatarum naturarum sensibilium, comparantur ad intellectum possibilem sicut actus ad potentiam; sed tamen phantasmata sunt in potentia ad aliquid quod anima intellectiva habet in actu, scilicet esse abstractum a materialibus conditionibus, et quantum ad hoc anima intellectiva comparatur ad ipsa ut actus ad potentiam. Non est autem inconveniens quod aliquid respectu eiusdem sit in actu et in potentia secundum diversa: propter hoc enim naturalia corpora agunt et patiuntur

We have still to consider how this union is possible. Some difficulty may seem to arise in this matter. The possible intellect is in potency with respect to all that is intelligible, whereas the agent intellect causes what is intelligible in potency to be intelligible in act, and so must be related to what is intelligible as act to potency. But the same thing, seemingly, cannot be both in potency and in act with respect to the same object. Thus it would appear that the possible intellect and the agent intellect cannot be united in the same substance of the soul.

This doubt is easily resolved if we examine how the possible intellect is in potency with respect to intelligible objects, and how the agent intellect renders them actually intelligible. The possible intellect is in potency with regard to intelligible objects in the sense that it does not contain within its nature any determinate form of sensible things, as in the same way the pupil of the eye is in potency with regard to all colors. To the extent, then, that phantasms abstracted from sensible things are likenesses of definite sensible things, they are related to the possible intellect as act to potency. Nevertheless, the phantasms are in potency with regard to something that the intellectual soul possesses in act, namely being, as abstracted from material conditions. And in this respect the intellectual soul is related to the phantasms as act to potency. No contradiction is involved if a thing is in act and potency with regard to the same object according to different points of view. Thus natural bodies

ad invicem, quia utrumque est in potentia respectu alterius. Sic igitur non est inconveniens quod eadem anima intellectiva sit et in potentia respectu ad omnia intelligibilia, prout ponitur in ea intellectus possibilis, et comparetur ad ea ut actus prout ponitur in ea intellectus agens.

Et hoc quidem manifestius apparebit ex modo quo intellectus facit intelligibilia in actu. Non enim sic facit intelligibilia in actu quasi ab ipso effluant in intellectum possibilem, sic enim non indigeremus phantasmatibus et sensu ad intelligendum; sed facit intelligibilia in actu abstrahendo ea a phantasmatibus, sicut lumen facit quodammodo colores in actu, non quasi habeat eos apud se, sed inquantum dat eis quodammodo visibilitatem. Sic igitur aestimandum est unam esse animam intellectivam, quae caret naturis sensibilium et potest eas recipere per modum intelligibilem, et quae phantasmata facit intelligibilia in actu, abstrahendo scilicet ab eis species intelligibiles. Unde potentia eius secundum quam est receptiva intelligibilium specierum vocatur intellectus possibilis; potentia autem eius secundum quam abstrahit species intelligibiles a phantasmatibus vocatur intellectus agens, qui est quasi quoddam lumen intelligibile quod anima intellectiva participat ad imitationem superiorum substantiarum intellectualium.

act upon each other and are acted upon by each other, for each is in potency with respect to the other. The same intellectual soul, therefore, can be in potency with regard to all intelligible objects and nevertheless, without any contradiction, can be related to them as act, if both a possible intellect and an agent intellect are acknowledged in the soul.

This will be seen more clearly from the way the intellect renders objects actually intelligible. The agent intellect does not render objects actually intelligible in the sense that the latter flow from it into the possible intellect. If this were the case, we would have no need of phantasms and sense in order to understand. No, the agent intellect renders things actually intelligible by abstracting them from phantasms (just as light, in a certain sense, renders colors actual not as though it contained the colors within itself, but so far as it confers visibility on them). In the same way we are to judge that there is a single intellectual soul that lacks the natures of sensible things but can receive them in an intelligible manner, and that renders phantasms actually intelligible by abstracting intelligible species from them. The power whereby the soul is able to receive intelligible species is called the possible intellect, and the power whereby it abstracts intelligible species from phantasms is called the agent intellect. The latter is a sort of intelligible light communicated to the intellectual soul, in imitation of what takes place among the higher intellectual substances.

CHAPTER 89

That all powers are rooted in the soul's essence

Non solum autem intellectus agens et possibilis in una essentia animae humanae conveniunt, sed etiam omnes aliae potentiae quae sunt principia operationum animae. Omnes enim huiusmodi potentiae quodammodo in anima radicantur: quaedam quidem, sicut potentiae vegetativae et sensitivae partis, in anima sicut in principio, in coniuncto autem sicut in subiecto, quia earum operationes coniuncti sunt et non solum animae: cuius enim est actio, eius est potentia; quaedam vero in anima sicut in principio et in subiecto, quia earum operationes sunt animae absque organo corporali, et huiusmodi sunt potentiae intellectivae partis. Non est autem possibile esse plures animas in homine; oportet igitur quod omnes potentiae ad eandem animam pertineant.

Not only the agent intellect and the possible intellect, but also all the other powers that are principles of the soul's operations are united in the essence of the soul. All such powers are somehow rooted in the soul. Some of them, indeed, such as the powers of the vegetative and sensitive parts, are in the soul as in their principle, but in the composite as in their subject, because their activities pertain to the composite, not to the soul alone; for power and action belong to the same subject. Some of them, on the other hand, are in the soul both as principle and as subject, for their operations pertain to the soul apart from any bodily organ. These are the powers of the intellectual part. But a man cannot have several souls. Accordingly, all the powers must pertain to the same soul.

CHAPTER 90

That there is one soul in one body

Quod autem impossibile sit esse plures animas in uno corpore, sic probatur. Manifestum est enim animam esse formam substantialem habentis animam, ex hoc quod animatum per animam genus et speciem sortitur. Impossibile est autem plures formas substantiales unius et eiusdem rei esse. Forma enim substantialis in hoc differt ab accidentali quod forma substantialis facit esse hoc aliquid simpliciter; forma autem accidentalis advenit ei quod iam est hoc aliquid et facit ipsum esse quale vel quantum aut aliqualiter se habens. Si igitur plures formae sint unius et eiusdem rei, aut prima earum facit hoc aliquid, aut non: si non facit hoc aliquid, non est forma substantialis; si autem facit hoc aliquid, ergo omnes formae consequentes adveniunt ei quod iam est hoc aliquid: nulla igitur consequentium erit forma substantialis, sed accidentalis. Sic igitur patet quod impossibile est formas substantiales esse plures unius et eiusdem rei; neque igitur possibile est plures animas in uno et eodem esse.

Adhuc, manifestum est quod homo dicitur vivens secundum quod habet animam vegetabilem, animal autem secundum quod habet animam sensitivam, homo autem secundum quod habet animam intellectivam. Si igitur sint tres animae in homine, scilicet vegetabilis, sensibilis et rationalis, sequetur quod homo secundum aliam animam ponatur in genere et secundum aliam speciem sortiatur. Hoc autem est impossibile: sic enim ex genere et differentia non fieret unum simpliciter, sed unum per accidens vel quasi congregatum, sicut musicum et album, quod non est esse unum simpliciter. Necesse est igitur in homine unam tantum animam esse.

That there cannot be several souls in one body is proved as follows. The soul is clearly the substantial form of any being possessing a soul, because a living being is constituted in genus and species by its soul. But the same thing cannot have several substantial forms. A substantial form differs from an accidental form in this: a substantial form causes a particular thing simply to be, whereas an accidental form is added to a particular being already constituted as such, and determines its quality or quantity or its mode of being. Hence, if several substantial forms belong to one and the same thing, either the first of them causes it to be this particular thing or it does not. If it does not, the form is not substantial; if it does, then all the subsequent forms accrue to what is already this particular thing. Therefore, none of the subsequent forms will be the substantial form, but only some accidental form. Clearly, therefore, one and the same thing cannot have several substantial forms; and so one and the same person cannot have several souls.

Furthermore, it is evident that a man is said to be living because he has a vegetative soul, that he is called an animal because he has a sensitive soul, and that he is a man because he has an intellectual soul. Consequently, if there were three souls in man, namely, vegetative, sensitive, and rational, man would be placed in a genus because of one of his souls, and in a species because of another. But this is impossible. For thus genus and specific difference would constitute, not what is simply one, but what is one accidentally, or a sort of conglomeration, such as musical and white; but such is not a being that is simply one. Accordingly, a man can have only one soul.

CHAPTER 91

Arguments that seem to prove that in man there are many souls

Videntur autem quaedam huic sententiae adversari. Primo quidem quia differentia comparatur ad genus ut forma ad materiam; animal autem est genus hominis, rationale autem est differentia constitutiva eius. Cum igitur animal sit corpus animatum anima sensitiva, videtur quod corpus animatum anima sensitiva adhuc sit in potentia respectu animae rationalis, et sic anima rationalis erit anima alia ab anima sensitiva.

Item, intellectus non habet organum corporale, sensitivae autem potentiae et nutritivae habent organum

Certain considerations seem opposed to our doctrine. In the first place, specific difference is to genus what form is to matter; but animal is the genus of man, and rational is the difference that makes man what he is. Accordingly, since animal is a body animated by a sensitive soul, it seems that a body animated by a sensitive soul is still in potency with respect to the rational soul. Thus the rational soul would be distinct from the sensitive soul.

Moreover, the intellect does not possess a bodily organ. But the sensitive and nutritive powers do possess bod-

corporale; impossibile igitur videtur quod eadem anima sit et intellectiva et sensitiva, quia non potest esse idem separatum et non separatum.

Adhuc, anima rationalis est incorruptibilis, ut supra ostensum est; vegetabilis autem anima et sensibilis sunt corruptibiles, sunt enim actus corruptibilium organorum: non igitur eadem anima est vegetabilis et sensibilis et rationalis, cum impossibile sit idem esse corruptibile et incorruptibile.

Praeterea, in generatione hominis apparet vita quae est per animam vegetabilem antequam conceptum appareat esse animal per sensum et motum, et prius demonstratur animal esse per sensum et motum quam habeat intellectum. Si igitur est eadem anima per quam conceptum primo vivit vita plantae, secundo vita animalis et tertio vita hominis, sequetur quod vel vegetabilis, sensibilis et rationalis sint ab exteriori principio, vel etiam quod intellectiva sit ex virtute quae est in semine. Utrumque autem horum videtur inconveniens quia, cum operationes animae vegetabilis et sensibilis non sint sine corpore, nec earum principia sine corpore esse possunt; operatio autem animae intellectivae est sine corpore: et sic impossibile videtur quod aliqua virtus in corpore sit eius causa. Impossibile igitur videtur quod eadem anima sit vegetabilis, sensibilis et rationalis.

ily organs. Hence it seems impossible for the same soul to be both intellectual and sensitive, because the same thing cannot both be separated and not separated from another thing.

Furthermore, the rational soul is incorruptible, as was shown above. On the other hand, the vegetative and the sensitive souls are corruptible, as they are acts of corruptible organs. Therefore, the rational soul is not the same as the vegetative and the sensitive souls, for the same thing cannot be both corruptible and incorruptible.

Besides, in the generation of man the life conferred by the vegetative soul appears before the fetus is observed to be an animal through its sense activity and motion; and this same being is discerned to be an animal through its sense activity and movement before it has an intellect. Therefore, if the soul by which the fetus first lives the life of a plant, then the life of an animal, and third the life of a man, is the same, it would follow that the vegetative, sensitive, and rational principles come from an outside source, or else that the intellectual soul arises from the energy in the semen. Both of these alternatives are inadmissible. On the one hand, since the operations of the vegetative and sensitive soul are not exercised apart from the body, their principles cannot be without a body. On the other hand, the operation of the intellectual soul is exercised without a body: and so, apparently, no bodily energy can be its cause. Therefore, the same soul cannot be vegetative, sensitive, and rational.

CHAPTER 92

Refutation of the preceding arguments

Ad huiusmodi igitur dubitationes tollendas considerandum est quod, sicut in numeris species diversificantur per hoc quod una earum super alteram addit, ita etiam in rebus naturalibus una species aliam in perfectione excedit. Quod enim perfectionis est in corporibus inanimatis, hoc habent plantae et adhuc amplius; et rursum quod habent plantae, habent animalia et aliquid plus; et sic quousque perveniatur ad hominem, qui est perfectissimus inter corporeas creaturas. Omne autem quod est imperfectum se habet ut materia respectu perfectioris, et hoc quidem in diversis manifestum est.

Nam elementa sunt materia corporum similium partium, et rursus corpora similium partium sunt materialia respectu animalium. Et similiter in uno et eodem considerandum est. Quod enim in rebus naturalibus ad altiorem gradum perfectionis attingit, per suam formam habet quidquid perfectionis convenit inferiori naturae, et per eandem habet id quod ei de perfectione super alia

To set aside such doubts, we should reflect that, in material things, one species surpasses another in perfection, in the way that, in numbers, species are diversified by adding one to another. Whatever perfection is found in lifeless bodies, plants also possess, and more besides. Again, whatever plants have, animals have too, and something else in addition. And thus we proceed until we come to man, the most perfect of bodily creatures. All that is imperfect is related as matter to what is more perfect. This is clear in the various classes of beings.

The elements constitute the matter of bodies that are composed of similar parts; and again, bodies having similar parts are matter with respect to animals. And this is likewise to be observed in one and the same being. Among natural things, that which is endowed with a higher degree of perfection has, in virtue of its form, whatever perfection is found in lower nature, and in virtue of the same form

additur: sicut planta per suam animam habet quod sit substantia, et quod sit substantia corporea, et ulterius quod sit animatum corpus. Animal autem per suam animam habet haec omnia, et adhuc quod sit sentiens; homo autem super haec omnia per suam animam habet quod sit intelligens. Si igitur in re aliqua consideretur id quod ad inferioris gradus perfectionem pertinet, erit materiale respectu eius quod pertinet ad perfectionem superioris gradus, puta si consideretur in animali quod habet vitam plantae, hoc est quodammodo materiale respectu eius quod pertinet ad vitam sensitivam quae est propria animali.

Genus autem non est materia, non enim praedicaretur de toto, sed est aliquid a materia sumptum: denominatio enim rei ab eo quod est materiale in ipsa est genus eius; et per eundem modum differentia sumitur a forma. Et propter hoc corpus vivum seu animatum est genus animalis, sensibile autem differentia constitutiva ipsius; et similiter animal genus hominis, et rationale differentia constitutiva eius. Quia igitur forma superioris gradus habet in se ipsa omnes perfectiones inferioris gradus, non est alia forma secundum rem a qua sumitur genus et a qua sumitur differentia; sed ab eadem forma secundum quod habet inferioris gradus perfectionem sumitur genus, secundum vero quod habet perfectionem superioris gradus sumitur ab ea differentia. Et sic patet quod, quamvis animal sit genus hominis et rationale sit differentia constitutiva, non tamen oportet quod sit in homine alia anima sensitiva et alia intellectiva, ut prima ratio obiiciebat.

Per eadem autem apparet solutio secundae rationis. Dictum est enim quod forma superioris speciei comprehendit in se omnes inferiorum graduum perfectiones. Considerandum est autem quod tanto species naturalis est altior, quanto magis fuerit materia formae subiecta, et sic oportet quod quanto aliqua forma est nobilior, tanto magis super materiam elevetur; unde anima humana, quae est nobilissima naturalium formarum, ad summum elevationis gradum pertingit, ut scilicet habeat operationem absque communicatione materiae corporalis. Quia tamen eadem anima inferiorum graduum perfectiones comprehendit, habet nihilominus et operationes in quibus communicat materia corporalis. Manifestum est autem quod operatio procedit a re secundum eius virtutem. Oportet igitur quod anima humana habeat aliquas vires sive potentias quae sint principia operationum quae exercentur per corpus, et has oportet esse actus aliquarum partium corporis, et huiusmodi sunt potentiae vegetativae et sensitivae partis; habeat etiam aliquas potentias quae sint principia operationum quae sine corpore exercentur, et huiusmodi sunt intellectivae partis potentiae quae non sunt actus aliquo-

has, besides, its own added perfection. Through its soul, the plant is a substance, and is bodily, and besides is an animated body. Through its soul, an animal has all these perfections, and moreover is sentient. In addition to all this, man is intelligent through his soul. Thus, in any object, if we consider what pertains to the perfection of a lower grade of being, this will be material when compared with what pertains to the perfection of a higher grade. For example, if we observe that an animal has the life of a plant, this life is in some fashion material with respect to what pertains to sensitive life, which is characteristic of an animal.

Genus, of course, is not matter, for then it would not be predicated of the whole. But it is something derived from matter; for the designation attaching to a thing, in terms of what is material in it, is its genus. Specific difference is derived from the form of a thing in the same way. This is the reason why living or animated body is the genus of animal, and sensitive is the specific difference that constitutes it. Similarly, animal is the genus of man, and rational is the difference that constitutes him. Therefore, since the form of a higher grade of being comprises within itself all the perfections of a lower grade, there is not, in reality, one form from which genus is derived, and another from which specific difference is derived. Rather, genus is derived from a form so far as it has a perfection of lower degree, and specific difference is derived from the same form so far as it has a perfection of higher degree. Thus, although animal is the genus of man and rational is the specific difference constituting him, there need not be in man a sensitive soul distinct from the intellectual soul, as was urged in the first argument.

This indicates the solution of the second difficulty. As we have pointed out, the form of a higher species comprises within itself all the perfections of lower classes of being. We must note, however, that the species of a material being is higher in proportion as it is less subject to matter. And so the nobler a form is, the more it must be elevated above matter. Hence the human soul, which is the noblest of all forms of matter, attains to the highest level of elevation, where it enjoys an activity that is independent of the concurrence of bodily matter. Yet, since the same soul includes the perfection of lower levels, it also has activities in which bodily matter shares. However, activity proceeds from a thing according to its power. Therefore, the human soul must have some powers or potentialities that are principles of activities exercised through the body, and these must be actions of certain parts of the body. Such are the powers of the vegetative and sensitive parts. The soul has also certain powers that are the principles of activities exercised without the body. Such are the powers of the intellectual part, whose actions are not performed by any organs. For this reason both the possible intellect and the agent intellect are said to be separate; they have no organs as principles of their

rum organorum. Et ideo intellectus tam possibilis quam agens dicitur separatus, quia non habent organa quorum sint actus, sicut visus et auditus; sed tamen fundantur in anima quae est corporis forma, unde non oportet propter hoc quod intellectus dicitur separatus et caret organo corporali, non autem sensus, quod alia sit anima sensitiva et intellectiva in homine.

Ex quo etiam patet quod nec ex hoc cogimur ponere aliam animam intellectivam et aliam sensitivam in homine quia anima sensitiva est corruptibilis, intellectiva vero incorruptibilis, ut tertia ratio procedebat. Esse enim incorruptibile competit intellectivae parti inquantum est separata; sicut igitur in eadem essentia animae fundantur potentiae quae sunt separatae et non separatae, ut dictum est, ita nihil prohibet quasdam potentiarum animae simul cum corpore deficere, quasdam autem incorruptibiles esse.

Secundum praedicta patet etiam solutio quartae obiectionis. Nam omnis motus naturalis paulatim ex imperfecto ad perfectum procedit, quod tamen aliter accidit in alteratione et generatione. Nam eadem qualitas suscipit magis et minus; et ideo alteratio quae est motus in qualitate, una et continua existens, de potentia ad actum procedit de imperfecto ad perfectum. Forma vero substantialis non recipit magis et minus, quia esse substantiale unicuique est unum et indivisibiliter se habens; unde una generatio non procedit continue per multa media de imperfecto ad perfectum, sed oportet esse ad singulos gradus perfectionis novam generationem et corruptionem. Sic igitur in generatione hominis conceptum quidem primo vivit vita plantae per animam vegetabilem; deinde remota hac forma per corruptionem, acquirit quadam alia generatione animam sensibilem et vivit vita animalis; deinde remota hac anima per corruptionem, introducitur forma ultima et completa quae est anima rationalis, comprehendens in se quidquid perfectionis in praecedentibus formis erat.

actions, such as sight and hearing have, but inhere in the soul alone, which is the form of the body. Hence we need not conclude, from the fact that the intellect is said to be separate and lacks a bodily organ, whereas neither of these is true of the senses, that the intellectual soul is distinct from the sensitive soul in man.

This also makes it clear that we are not forced to admit an intellectual soul distinct from the sensitive soul in man on the ground that the sensitive soul is corruptible whereas the intellectual soul is incorruptible, as the third objection set out to prove. Incorruptibility pertains to the intellectual part so far as it is separate. Therefore, as powers that are separate, in the sense mentioned above, and powers that are not separate, are all rooted in the same essence of the soul, there is nothing to prevent some of the powers of the soul from lapsing when the body perishes, while others remain incorruptible.

The points already made lead to a solution of the fourth objection. All natural movement gradually advances from imperfect to perfect. The same quality is receptive of greater and less; hence alteration, which is movement in quality, being unified and continuous in its progress from potency to act, advances from imperfect to perfect. But substantial form is not receptive of greater and less, for the substantial nature of each being exists indivisibly. Therefore, natural generation does not proceed continuously through many intermediate stages from imperfect to perfect, but at each level of perfection a new generation and corruption must take place. Thus in the generation of a man the fetus first lives the life of a plant through the vegetative soul; next, when this form is removed by corruption it acquires, by a sort of new generation, a sensitive soul and lives the life of an animal; finally, when this soul is in turn removed by corruption, the ultimate and complete form is introduced. This is the rational soul, which comprises within itself whatever perfection was found in the previous forms.

CHAPTER 93

Of the production of the rational soul, which is not by natural transmission

Haec autem ultima et completa forma, scilicet anima rationalis, non educitur in esse a virtute quae est in semine, sed a superiori agente. Virtus enim quae est in semine est virtus corporis cuiusdam; anima autem rationalis excedit omnem corporis naturam et virtutem, cum ad eius intellectualem operationem nullum corpus pertingere possit. Cum igitur nihil agat ultra suam speciem, eo quod agens est nobilius patiente et faciens facto, impossibile est quod virtus alicuius corporis causet animam rationalem, neque igitur virtus quae est in semine.

Adhuc, secundum quod unumquodque habet esse de novo, sic competit ei fieri; eius enim est fieri cuius est et esse, ad hoc enim aliquid fit ut sit. Eis igitur quae secundum se habent esse secundum se competit fieri, sicut rebus subsistentibus; eis autem quae secundum se non habent esse, non competit per se fieri, sicut accidentibus et formis materialibus. Anima autem rationalis secundum se habet esse, quia secundum se habet operationem, ut ex supra dictis patet. Animae igitur rationali secundum se competit fieri. Cum igitur non sit composita ex materia et forma, ut supra ostensum est, sequitur quod non possit educi in esse nisi per creationem. Solius autem Dei creare est, ut supra ostensum est. A solo igitur Deo anima rationalis in esse producitur.

Hoc etiam rationabiliter accidit. Videmus enim in artibus ad invicem ordinatis quod suprema ars inducit ultimam formam, artes vero inferiores disponunt materiam ad ultimam formam. Manifestum est autem quod anima rationalis est ultima et perfectissima forma quam potest consequi materia generabilium et corruptibilium. Convenienter igitur naturalia agentia inferiora causant praecedentes dispositiones et formas; supremum vero agens, scilicet Deus, causat ultimam formam quae est anima rationalis.

This ultimate and complete form, the rational soul, is brought into existence, not by the power that is in the semen, but by a higher cause. For the power that is in the semen is a bodily power. But the rational soul exceeds the whole nature and power of the body, since no body can rise to the heights of the soul's intellectual activity. Nothing can act in a way that surmounts its species, because the agent is nobler than the patient, and the maker excels his product. Hence the power possessed by a body cannot produce the rational soul, nor, consequently, can the energy inherent in the semen do so.

Moreover, a thing that has new existence must also have a new becoming; for that which is, must first become, since a thing becomes in order that it may be. Thus things which have being in their own right must have becoming in their own right, such as subsistent beings. But things that do not possess being in their own right do not properly have a becoming, such as accidents and material forms. The rational soul has being in its own right because it has its own operation, as is clear from our previous discussion. Therefore, becoming is properly predicated of the rational soul. Since the soul is not composed of matter and form, as was shown above, it cannot be brought into being except by creation. But God alone can create, as we said above. Consequently, the rational soul is produced by God alone.

We can readily understand why this should be so. For we see in arts ordered to one another that the highest art induces the ultimate form, whereas the lower arts dispose matter for the reception of the ultimate form. The rational soul, evidently, is the ultimate and most perfect form that the matter of beings subject to generation and corruption can achieve. Therefore, natural agents, which operate on lower levels, appropriately cause preliminary dispositions and forms, whereas the supreme agent, God, causes the ultimate form, which is the rational soul.

CHAPTER 94

That the rational soul is not of the substance of God

Non tamen credendum est animam rationalem esse de substantia Dei, secundum quorundam errorem. Ostensum est enim supra quod Deus simplex et indivisibilis est; non igitur animam rationalem corpori unit quasi eam a sua substantia separando.

Item, ostensum est supra quod impossibile est Deum esse formam alicuius corporis; anima autem rationalis unitur corpori ut forma: non igitur est de substantia Dei.

Adhuc, ostensum est supra quod Deus non movetur neque per se neque per accidens, cuius contrarium in anima rationali manifeste apparet: mutatur enim de ignorantia ad scientiam et de vitio ad virtutes; non est igitur de substantia Dei.

However, we are not to imagine that the rational soul is derived from the substance of God, as some have erroneously thought. We demonstrated above that God is simple and indivisible. Therefore, he does not join the rational soul to a body as though he had first severed it from his own substance.

Furthermore, we pointed out above that God cannot be the form of any body. But the rational soul is united to the body as the latter's form. Hence it is not derived from the substance of God.

Besides, we showed above that God is not moved either in himself or by reason of some other thing that is moved. But the contrary of this is observed to take place in the rational soul, which is moved from ignorance to knowledge, from vice to virtue. Accordingly, the soul is not of the substance of God.

CHAPTER 95

That God creates things immediately

Ex his autem quae supra ostensa sunt, ex necessitate concluditur quod illa quae non possunt produci in esse nisi per creationem sunt immediate a Deo. Manifestum est autem quod corpora caelestia non possunt produci in esse nisi per creationem. Non enim potest dici quod ex materia aliqua praeiacenti sunt facta, quia sic essent generabilia et corruptibilia et contrarietati subiecta; quod eis non competit, ut motus eorum declarat: moventur enim circulariter, motus autem circularis non habet contrarium. Relinquitur igitur quod corpora caelestia sint immediate a Deo in esse producta.

Similiter etiam elementa secundum se tota non fiunt ex aliqua materia praeiacenti, quia illud quod praeexisteret haberet aliquam formam; et sic oporteret quod aliquod aliud corpus ab elementis esset prius eis in ordine causae materialis, si materia praeexistens elementis haberet formam aliam ab elementis; vel oporteret quod unum eorum esset aliis prius in eodem ordine, si materia praeexistens formam elementi haberet. Oportet igitur ipsa elementa immediate esse a Deo producta.

Multo autem magis impossibile est substantias incorporeas et invisibiles ab aliquo alio creari, omnes enim huiusmodi substantiae immateriales sunt. Non enim potest esse materia nisi dimensioni subiecta, secundum

The doctrine established above necessarily leads to the conclusion that things that cannot be brought into existence except by creation come immediately from God. Thus the heavenly bodies, as is manifest, cannot be produced except by creation. They cannot be said to be made from some preexisting matter, for then they would be capable of generation and corruption, and would also be subject to contrariety. But they are not, as their motion proves. For they move in circles, and circular motion has no contrary. Consequently, the heavenly bodies were produced immediately by God.

Similarly the elements, regarded as complete units, do not come from any preexisting matter. Anything that would thus preexist would have some form. And thus some body, other than the elements, would exist prior to them in the order of material cause. But if the matter existing prior to the elements had a distinct form, one of the elements would have to be prior to the others in the same order, supposing that the preexisting matter had the form of an element. Therefore, the very elements must have been produced immediately by God.

It is even more impossible for non-bodily and invisible substances to be created by someone else, for all such substances are immaterial. Matter cannot exist unless it is subject to dimension, whereby it is capable of being marked

quam materia dividitur ut ex una materia plura fieri possunt; unde impossibile est quod ex materia praeiacenti causentur. Relinquitur igitur quod per creationem solum a Deo producuntur in esse; et propter hoc fides Catholica confitetur Deum esse *Creatorem caeli et terrae*, et *omnium visibilium*, necnon et *invisibilium*.

off, so that many things can be made from the same matter. Hence immaterial substances cannot be made from preexisting matter. Consequently, they can be produced only by God through creation. For this reason the Catholic faith professes that God is the *Creator of heaven and earth*, and *of all things visible*, and also *of all things invisible*.

CHAPTER 96

That God brings things into existence not by natural necessity but by will

Ex hoc autem ostenditur quod Deus res in esse producit non naturali necessitate sed voluntate. Ab uno enim naturaliter agente non est immediate nisi unum; agens autem voluntarium diversa producere potest, quod ideo est quia omne agens agit per suam formam; forma autem naturalis per quam aliquid naturaliter agit unius una est, formae autem intellectae per quas aliquid voluntarie agit sunt plures. Cum igitur a Deo immediate plura producantur in esse, ut iam ostensum est, manifestum est quod Deus res in esse producit voluntate, et non naturali necessitate.

Adhuc, agens per intellectum et voluntatem est prius in ordine agentium agente per necessitatem naturae: nam agens per voluntatem praestituit sibi finem propter quem agit, agens autem naturale agit propter finem sibi ab alio praestitutum. Manifestum est autem ex praemissis Deum esse primum agens; est igitur agens per voluntatem et non per necessitatem naturae.

Item, ostensum est in superioribus Deum esse infinitae virtutis; non igitur determinatur ad hunc effectum vel illum, sed indeterminate se habet ad omnes. Quod autem indeterminate se habet ad diversos effectus determinatur ad unum producendum per desiderium, sicut homo qui potest ambulare et non ambulare, quando vult ambulat; oportet igitur quod effectus a Deo procedant secundum determinationem voluntatis: non igitur agit per necessitatem naturae sed per voluntatem. Inde est quod fides Catholica Deum omnipotentem non solum 'Creatorem' sed etiam 'Factorem' nominat, nam facere proprie est artificis qui per voluntatem operatur. Et quia omne agens voluntarium per conceptionem sui intellectus agit, quae verbum ipsius dicitur, ut supra dictum est, Verbum autem Dei Filius est, ideo etiam fides Catholica confitetur de Filio quod per eum *omnia facta sunt*.

From this it is clear that God has brought things into existence not through any necessity of his nature but by his will. Of one natural agent there is immediately but one effect, whereas a voluntary agent can produce a variety of effects. The reason for this is that every agent acts in virtue of its form. The natural form, whereby a cause operates naturally, is limited to one for each agent. But the forms in the understanding, whereby an agent operates through his will, are many. Therefore, since many things are immediately produced by God, as we have just shown, God evidently produces things by his will, and not by natural necessity.

Further, in the order of causes, an agent operating through intellect and will is prior to an agent operating by the necessity of its nature. For an agent operating through his will predetermines for himself the end for the sake of which he acts, whereas a natural cause operates on account of an end predetermined for it by another. But, as is clear from all that has gone before, God is the first agent. Hence he acts through his will, and not by a necessity of his nature.

Moreover, it was shown above that God is infinite in power. Consequently, he is not determined to this or that effect, but is undetermined with regard to all effects. But desire determines what is undetermined regarding various effects to produce one of them. Thus a man, who is free to walk or not to walk, walks when he wills. Hence effects proceed from God according to the determination of his will. And so he acts, not by a necessity of his nature, but by his will. This is why the Catholic faith calls the omnipotent God not only 'Creator,' but also 'Maker.' For making is properly the action of an artificer who operates by his will. And since every voluntary agent acts in virtue of the conception of his intellect, which is called his word, as we said above, and since the Word of God is his Son, the Catholic faith professes that *all things were made* through the Son.

CHAPTER 97

That God is unchangeable in his action

Ex hoc autem quod voluntate res in esse producit, manifestum est quod absque sui mutatione res de novo in esse producere potest. Haec est enim differentia inter agens naturale et agens voluntarium, quod agens naturale eodem modo agit quandiu eodem modo se habet, eo quod quale est talia facit; agens autem voluntarium agit qualia vult. Potest autem contingere absque eius mutatione quod velit nunc agere et prius non agere; nihil enim prohibet adesse alicui voluntatem de operando in posterum, etiam quando non operatur. Potest igitur absque Dei mutatione contingere quod Deus, quamvis sit aeternus, res in esse produxerit non ab aeterno.

The fact that God produces things by his will clearly shows that he can produce new things without any change in himself. The difference between a natural agent and a voluntary agent is this: a natural agent acts in the same manner as long as it is in the same condition. Such as it is, thus does it act. But a voluntary agent acts as he wills. Accordingly, it may well be that, without any change in himself, he wishes to act now and not previously. For there is nothing to prevent a person from willing to perform an action later, even though he is not doing it now. Thus it can happen, without any change in God, that God, although he is eternal, did not bring things into existence from eternity.

CHAPTER 98

An argument proving motion to have been from eternity, and its refutation

Videtur autem quod etsi Deus voluntate aeterna et immutabili novum effectum producere possit, quod tamen oporteat quod novum effectum aliquis motus praecedat. Non enim videmus quod voluntas illud quod vult facere retardet, nisi propter aliquid quod vel nunc est et cessat in posterum, vel non est et expectatur futurum; sicut homo in aestate habet voluntatem ut induat se aliquo indumento, quod tamen ad praesens induere non vult sed in futurum, quia nunc est calor qui cessabit frigore adveniente in posterum.

Si igitur Deus ab aeterno voluit aliquem effectum producere et non ab aeterno produxit, videtur quod vel aliquid expectaretur futurum quod nondum erat, vel aliquid esset auferendum quod tunc erat; utrumque autem horum sine motu contingere non potest: videtur igitur quod a voluntate praecedente non posset effectus aliquis produci in posterum nisi aliquo motu praecedente. Et sic si voluntas Dei fuit aeterna de rerum productione et res non sunt ab aeterno productae, oportet quod earum productionem praecedat motus, et per consequens mobilia: quae si a Deo producta sunt et non ab aeterno, iterum oportet praeexistere alios motus et mobilia usque in infinitum.

Huius autem obiectionis solutio facile potest perpendi, si quis differentiam consideret universalis et particularis agentis. Nam agens particulare habet actio-

We might imagine that, although God can produce a new effect by his eternal and immutable will, some sort of motion would have to precede the newly produced effect. For we observe that the will does not delay doing what it wishes to do unless because of some motive that is operative now but will cease later, or because of some motive that is inoperative now but is expected to become operative in the future. In summer a man has the will to clothe himself with a warm garment, yet he does not wish to wear it now but in the future, for now the weather is hot, but will cease to be so when a cold front comes along later in the year.

Accordingly, if God wished from eternity to produce some effect, but did not produce it from eternity, it seems either that something was expected to happen in the future that had not yet occurred, or else that some obstacle had to be removed that was then present. Neither of these alternatives can take place without motion. Thus, it seems that a subsequent effect cannot be produced by a preceding will unless some motion previously occurs. And so, if God's will relative to the production of things was eternal, and nevertheless things were not produced from eternity, their production must have been preceded by motion, and consequently by mobile objects. And if the latter were produced by God, but not from eternity, yet other motions and mobile objects must have preceded, and so on, in infinite recession.

The solution to this objection readily comes to mind if we but attend to the difference between a universal and a particular agent. A particular agent has an activity that con-

nem proportionatam regulae et mensurae quam agens universale praestituit; quod quidem in civilibus apparet, nam legislator proponit legem quasi regulam et mensuram secundum quam iudicari oportet ab aliquo particulari iudice. Tempus autem est mensura actionum quae fiunt in tempore. Agens enim particulare habet actionem tempori proportionatam, ut scilicet nunc et non prius agat propter aliquam determinatam rationem. Agens autem universale quod Deus est huiusmodi mensuram quae tempus est instituit, et secundum suam voluntatem; inter res igitur productas a Deo etiam tempus est. Sicut igitur talis est uniuscuiusque rei quantitas et mensura qualem Deus ei tribuere voluit, ita etiam talis est quantitas temporis qualem ei Deus dare voluit, ut scilicet tempus et ea quae in tempore sunt tunc inciperent quando Deus ea esse voluit.

Obiectio autem praemissa procedit quasi de agente quod praesupponit tempus et agit in tempore, non autem instituit tempus. Quaestio enim qua quaeritur quare *voluntas aeterna producit effectum nunc et non prius* praesupponit tempus praeexistens, nam nunc et prius partes sunt temporis. Circa universalem igitur rerum productionem, inter quas etiam tempus consideratur, non est quaerendum *quare nunc et non prius*, sed *quare huius temporis voluit esse mensuram*: quod ex divina voluntate dependet, cui indifferens est hanc quantitatem vel aliam tempori assignare.

Quod quidem et circa quantitatem dimensivam mundi considerari potest. Non enim quaeritur quare Deus corporalem mundum in tali situ constituit, et non supra vel subtus vel secundum aliquam positionis differentiam, quia non est locus extra mundum; sed hoc ex divina voluntate provenit quod talem quantitatem mundo corporali tribueret, ut nihil eius esset extra hunc situm secundum quamcumque positionis differentiam.

Licet autem ante mundum tempus non fuerit, nec extra mundum sit locus, utimur tamen tali modo loquendi, ut dicamus quod antequam mundus esset nihil erat nisi Deus, et quod extra mundum non est aliquod corpus, non intelligentes per 'ante' et 'extra' tempus aut locum nisi secundum imaginationem tantum.

forms to a norm and measure prescribed by the universal agent. This is clear even in civil government. The legislator enacts a law which is to serve as a norm and measure. Any particular judge must base his decisions on this law. Now, time is the measure of actions which occur in time. A particular agent is endowed with activity regulated by time, so that he acts for some definite reason now, and not before. But the universal agent, God, instituted this measure, which is time, and he did so in accord with his will. Hence time also is to be numbered among the things produced by God. Therefore, just as the quantity and measure of each object are such as God wishes to assign to it, so the quantity of time is such as God wished to mete out; that is, time and the things existing in time began just when God wished them to begin.

The objection we are dealing with argues from the standpoint of an agent that presupposes time and acts in time, but did not institute time. Hence the question: *Why does God's eternal will produces an effect now and not earlier?* presupposes that time exists; for 'now' and 'earlier' are segments of time. With regard to the universal production of things, among which time is also to be counted, we should not ask: *Why now and not earlier?* Rather we should ask: *Why did God wish the measure of this time?* And this depends on the divine will, which is perfectly free to assign this or any other quantity to time.

The same may be noted with respect to the dimensional quantity of the world. No one asks why God located the material world in such and such a place rather than higher up or lower down or in some other position; for there is no place outside the world. The fact that God portioned out so much quantity to the world that nothing of it would be outside this place according to any difference of position depends on the divine will.

However, although there was no time prior to the world and no place outside the world, we speak as if there were. Thus we say that before the world existed there was nothing except God, and that there is no body lying outside the world. But in thus speaking of 'before' and 'outside,' we have in mind nothing but time and place as they exist in our imagination.

CHAPTER 99

*Arguments showing that from eternity matter must have preceded the
creation of the world, and their refutations*

Videtur autem quod etsi rerum perfectarum produc-tio ab aeterno non fuerit, quod materiam necesse sit ab aeterno fuisse. Omne enim quod habet esse post non esse mutatur de non esse ad esse. Si igitur res creatae, ut puta caelum et terra et alia huiusmodi, ab aeterno non fuerunt sed inceperunt esse postquam non fuerant, necesse est dicere eas mutatas esse de non esse ad es-se. Omnis autem mutatio et motus subiectum aliquod habent, est enim motus actus existentis in potentia; su-biectum autem mutationis per quam aliqua res in esse producitur non est ipsa res producta, haec enim est terminus motus; non est autem idem motus terminus et subiectum, sed subiectum praedictae mutationis est id ex quo res producitur, quod materia dicitur. Videtur igitur quod, si res in esse productae sint postquam non fuerant, quod oporteat materiam eis praeextitisse; quae, si iterum producta est postquam non fuerat, oportet quod habeat aliam materiam praecedentem. Non est autem procedere in infinitum: relinquitur igitur quod oporteat devenire ad aliquam materiam aeternam quae non sit producta postquam non fuerat.

Item, si mundus incepit esse postquam non fuerat, antequam mundus esset, aut erat possibile mundum esse vel fieri, aut non. Si non possibile erat esse vel fieri, ergo ab aequipollenti impossibile erat mundum esse vel fieri; quod autem impossibile est fieri, necesse est non fieri: necesse est igitur mundum non esse factum. Quod cum manifeste sit falsum, necesse est dicere quod, si mundus incepit esse postquam non fuerat, quod possibile erat antequam esset ipsum esse vel fieri; erat igitur aliquid in potentia ad fieri et esse mundi. Quod autem est in potentia ad fieri et esse alicuius est materia eius, sicut lignum se habet ad scamnum; sic igitur videtur quod necesse est materiam semper fuisse, etiam si mundus semper non fuit.

Sed cum ostensum sit supra quod etiam materia non est nisi a Deo, pari ratione fides Catholica non confitetur materiam esse aeternam, sicut neque mundum aeter-num. Oportuit enim hoc modo exprimi in ipsis rebus causalitatem divinam, ut res ab eo producte inciperent

However, even though finished products were not in ex-istence from eternity, it may seem that matter had to ex-ist from eternity. For everything that has being subsequent to non-being is changed from non-being to being. There-fore, if created things, such as heaven and earth and the like, did not exist from eternity, but began to be after they had not been, we must admit that they were changed from non-being to being. But all change and motion have some sort of subject; for motion is the act of a thing existing in potency. However, the subject of the change whereby a thing is brought into existence is not the thing itself that is produced, because this thing is the terminus of the mo-tion, and the terminus and subject of motion are not the same. Rather, the subject of the change is that from which the thing is produced, and this is called matter. Accord-ingly, if things are brought into being after a state of non-being, it seems that matter had to exist prior to them. And if this matter is, in turn, produced subsequent to a period of non-existence, it had to come from some other, preexisting matter. But infinite procession along these lines is impossi-ble. Therefore, we must eventually come to eternal matter, which was not produced subsequent to a period of non-existence.

Again, if the world began to exist after it had first not existed, then, before the world actually existed, it was either possible for the world to be or become, or it was not pos-sible. It is the same to say that it was not possible for the world to be or to become as that it was impossible for the world to be or to become. But if it is impossible for a thing to become, it is necessary for that thing not to become. In that case we must conclude that the world was not made. Since this conclusion is patently false, we are forced to ad-mit that if the world began to be after it had first not been, it was possible for it to be or to become before it actually existed. Accordingly, there was something in potency with regard to the becoming and being of the world. But what is thus in potency to the becoming and existence of some-thing is the matter of that thing, as wood is to a bench. Ap-parently, therefore, matter must have existed always, even if the world did not exist always.

But since it was shown above that the very matter of the world has no existence except from God, the Catholic faith does not admit that matter is eternal for the same reason that it does not admit that the world is eternal. We have no other way of expressing the divine causality in things

postquam non fuerant: hoc enim evidenter et manifeste ostendit eas non a se ipsis esse, sed ab aeterno Auctore.

Non autem praemissis rationibus artamur ad ponendum aeternitatem materiae. Non enim universalis rerum productio proprie 'mutatio' dici potest: in nulla enim mutatione subiectum mutationis per mutationem producitur, quia non est idem subiectum mutationis et terminus, ut dictum est. Cum igitur universalis productio rerum a Deo, quae creatio dicitur, se extendat ad omnia quae sunt in re, huiusmodi productio rationem mutationis proprie habere non potest, etiam si res creatae producantur in esse postquam non fuerant. Esse enim post non esse non sufficit ad veram rationem mutationis, nisi subiectum supponatur quod nunc sit sub privatione, nunc autem sub forma: unde in quibusdam invenitur hoc post illud in quibus proprie ratio motus aut mutationis non est, sicut cum dicitur quod ex die fit nox. Sic igitur etsi mundus esse inceperit postquam non fuerat, non oportet quod hoc per aliquam mutationem sit factum, sed per creationem; quae vere mutatio non est, sed quaedam relatio rei creatae a Creatore secundum suum esse dependentis, cum ordine ad non esse praecedens. In omni enim mutatione oportet esse aliquid idem aliter et aliter se habens, utpote quod nunc sit sub uno extremo et postmodum sub alio: quod quidem in creatione secundum rei veritatem non invenitur sed solum secundum imaginationem, prout imaginamur unam et eandem rem prius non fuisse et postmodum esse; et sic secundum quandam similitudinem creatio mutatio dici potest.

Similiter etiam secunda obiectio non cogit. Etsi enim verum sit dicere quod antequam mundus esset, possibile erat mundum esse vel fieri, non tamen oportet hoc secundum aliquam potentiam dici. Dicitur enim possibile in enuntiabilibus quod significat aliquem modum veritatis, quod scilicet neque est necessarium neque impossibile; et huiusmodi possibile non secundum aliquam potentiam dicitur, ut Philosophus docet in V *Methaphisice*. Si autem secundum aliquam potentiam dicitur, non est necessarium quod dicatur secundum potentiam passivam, sed secundum potentiam activam; ut quod dicitur, quod mundum possibile fuit esse antequam esset, sic intelligatur quia Deus potuit mundum in esse producere antequam produceret unde non cogimur ponere

themselves than by saying that things produced by God began to exist after they had previously not existed. This way of speaking evidently and clearly brings out the truth that they have existence not of themselves, but from the eternal Author.

The arguments just reviewed do not compel us to postulate the eternity of matter, for the total production of things cannot properly be called 'change.' In no change is the subject of the change produced by the change, for the reason rightly alleged by the objector, namely, that the subject of change and the terminus of the change are not identical. Consequently, since the total production of things by God, which is known as creation, extends to all the reality that is found in a thing, production of this kind cannot properly have the character of change, even though the things created are brought into existence subsequently to non-existence. Being that succeeds to non-being does not suffice to constitute real change unless we suppose that a subject is first in a state of privation, and later under its proper form. Hence, 'this' is found coming after 'that' in certain things in which motion or change do not really occur, as when we say that day turns into night. Accordingly, even though the world began to exist after having not existed, this is not necessarily the result of some change. In fact, it is the result of creation, which is not a true change, but is rather a certain relation of the created thing—namely, the relation of depending upon the Creator for its very being—with succession to previous non-existence. In every change there must be something that remains the same although it undergoes alteration in its manner of being, in the sense that at first it is under one extreme and subsequently under another. In creation this does not take place in objective reality, but only in our imagination. That is, we imagine that one and the same thing previously did not exist, and later existed. And so creation can be called change, because it has some resemblance to change.

The second objection, too, lacks force. Although we can truly say that before the world was, it was possible for the world to be or to become, this possibility need not be taken to mean potentiality. In propositions, that which signifies a certain modality of truth—namely, that which is neither necessary nor impossible—is said to be possible. What is possible in this sense does not involve any potentiality, as the Philosopher teaches in Book V of his *Metaphysics*. However, if anyone insists on saying that it was possible for the world to exist according to some potency, we reply that this need not mean a passive potency, but can mean active potency; and so if we say that it was possible for the world to be before it actually was, we should understand this to mean that God could have brought the world into existence

materiam praeextitisse mundo. Sic ergo fides Catholica nihil Deo coaeternum ponit, et propter hoc eum *Creatorem* et *Factorem omnium visibilium et invisibilium* confitetur.

before he actually produced it. Hence we are not forced to postulate that matter existed before the world. Thus the Catholic faith acknowledges nothing to be coeternal with God, and for this reason professes that he is the *Creator* and *Maker of all things visible and invisible*.

CHAPTER 100

That God effects all things on account of an end

Quoniam autem supra ostensum est quod Deus res in esse produxit non per necessitatem naturae sed per intellectum et voluntatem, omne autem agens per intellectum et voluntatem agit propter finem, operativi enim intellectus finis principium est: necesse est omnia quae a Deo sunt facta propter finem esse.

Adhuc, productio rerum a Deo optime facta est, optimi enim est optime facere unumquodque; melius est autem fieri aliquid propter finem quam absque finis intentione, ex fine enim est ratio boni in his quae fiunt: sunt igitur res a Deo factae propter finem.

Huius etiam signum apparet in his quae natura aguntur, quorum nihil in vanum est sed propter finem unumquodque. Inconveniens autem est dicere ordinatiora esse quae fiunt a natura quam ipsa institutio naturae a primo agente, cum totus ordo naturae exinde derivetur; manifestum est igitur res a Deo productas esse propter finem.

We showed above that God has brought things into existence, not through any necessity of his nature, but by his intellect and will. Any agent that works in this way acts for an end, for the end is the principle of the operative intellect. Accordingly, everything that is made by God necessarily exists for the sake of an end.

Moreover, things were produced by God in the best way; for it belongs to the best being to do everything in the best way. But it is better for a thing to be made for an end than to be made without the intention of an end; for in things that are made, the character of goodness in them comes from their end. Therefore, things were made by God for an end.

An indication of this is also seen in effects produced by nature. None of them is in vain; rather, all are for an end. But it is absurd to say that things produced by nature are better ordered than is the very constituting of nature by the first agent, since the entire order of nature is derived from the latter. Clearly, therefore, things produced by God exist for an end.

CHAPTER 101

That the ultimate end of all things is the divine goodness

Oportet autem ultimum finem rerum divinam bonitatem esse. Rerum enim factarum ab aliquo per voluntatem agente ultimus finis est quod est primo et per se volitum ab agente, nam propter hoc agit agens omne quod agit; primum autem volitum divinae voluntatis est eius bonitas, ut ex superioribus patet: necesse est igitur omnium rerum factarum a Deo ultimum finem divinam bonitatem esse.

Item, finis generationis uniuscuiusque rei generatae est forma eiusdem, hac enim adepta generatio quiescit. Unumquodque autem generatum, sive per artem sive per naturam, secundum suam formam similatur aliquo modo agenti, nam omne agens agit aliqualiter sibi simile: domus enim quae est in materia procedit a domo quae est in mente artificis, in naturalibus etiam homo generat hominem; et si aliquid sit genitum vel factum secundum naturam quod non sit simile generanti secundum spe-

The ultimate end of things is necessarily the divine goodness. For the ultimate end of things produced by one who works through his will is that which willed by the agent first and for its own sake. It is for this that the agent does all that he does. But the first object willed by the divine will is God's goodness, as is clear from what we have said previously. Hence the ultimate end of all things made by God must necessarily be the divine goodness.

Furthermore, the end of the generation of anything generated is its form. Once this is achieved, generation ceases. Moreover, everything that is generated, whether by art or by nature, is in some way rendered similar to the agent in virtue of its form, since every agent produces an effect that has some resemblance to the agent himself. Thus the house that is in matter proceeds from the house existing in the mind of the architect. In the realm of nature, likewise, man begets man. And if anything that is generated or effected by

ciem, similatur tamen suis agentibus sicut imperfectum perfecto.

Ex hoc enim contingit quod generanti secundum speciem non similantur, quia ad eius perfectam similitudinem pervenire non possunt, sed aliqualiter eam imperfecte participant, sicut animalia et plantae quae generantur ex virtute solis. Omnium igitur quae fiunt finis generationis sive factionis est forma facientis vel generantis, ut scilicet ad eius similitudinem perveniatur. Forma autem primi agentis, scilicet Dei, non est aliud quam eius bonitas; propter hoc igitur omnia facta sunt ut divinae bonitati assimilentur.

natural processes is not like its generating cause according to species, it is at any rate likened to its efficient causes as imperfect to perfect.

The fact that a generated product is not assimilated to its generating cause according to species is explained by its inability to rise to perfect likeness with its cause; but it does participate in that cause to some extent, however imperfectly. This occurs, for example, in animals and plants that are generated by the power of the sun. Hence in all things that are made, the end of their generation or production is the form of their maker or generator, in the sense that they are to achieve a likeness of that form. But the form of the first agent, God, is nothing else than his goodness. This, then, is the reason why all things were made: that they might be made like the divine goodness.

CHAPTER 102

That assimilation to the divine is the cause of diversity in things

Ex hoc igitur fine accipienda est ratio diversitatis et distinctionis in rebus. Quia enim divinam bonitatem perfecte repraesentari ab uno impossibile fuit propter distantiam uniuscuiusque creaturae a Deo, necessarium fuit ut repraesentaretur per multa, ut sic quod deest ex uno suppleretur ex alio: nam et in conclusionibus syllogisticis quando per unum medium non sufficienter demonstratur conclusio, oportet media multiplicari ad conclusionis manifestationem, ut in syllogismis dyalecticis accidit. Nec tamen tota universitas creaturarum perfecte divinam bonitatem repraesentat per aequiparantiam, sed secundum perfectionem possibilem creaturae.

Item, illud quod est in causa universali simpliciter et unite, invenitur in effectibus multipliciter et distincte: nobilius est enim aliquid in causa quam in effectibus. Divina autem bonitas una et simplex principium est et radix totius bonitatis quae in creaturis invenitur; necesse est igitur sic creaturas divinae bonitati assimilari sicut multa et distincta assimilantur uni et simplici. Sic igitur multitudo et distinctio provenit in rebus non casualiter aut fortuito, sicut nec rerum productio est a casu aut fortuna, sed propter finem: ex eodem enim principio est esse et unitas et multitudo in rebus. Neque etiam distinctio rerum causatur ex materia: nam prima rerum institutio est per creationem, quae materiam non requirit; similiter quae solum ex necessitate materiae proveniunt casualia esse videntur.

The reason for the diversity and distinction in things must be understood in light of this end. Since the divine goodness could not be adequately represented by one creature alone, on account of the distance that separates each creature from God, it had to be represented by many creatures, so that what is lacking to one might be supplied by another. Even in syllogistic conclusions, when the conclusion is not sufficiently demonstrated by one means of proof, the means must be multiplied in order to make the conclusion clear, as happens in dialectical syllogisms. Nevertheless, not even the entire universe of creatures perfectly represents the divine goodness by setting it forth adequately, but represents it only in the measure of perfection possible to creatures.

Moreover, a perfection existing in a universal cause simply and in a unified manner is found to exist in the effects of that cause as multiple distinct perfections. For a perfection has a nobler existence in a cause than in its effects. But the divine goodness is one, and is the simple principle and root of all the goodness found in creatures. Hence creatures must be made like the divine goodness in the way that many and distinct things are assimilated to what is one and simple. Therefore, multiplicity and distinction occur in things not by chance or fortune but for an end, just as the production of things is not the result of chance or fortune, but is for an end. For existence, unity, and multiplicity in things all come from the same principle. The distinction among things is not caused by matter; for things were originally constituted in being by creation, which does not require any matter. Moreover, things which issue purely from the necessity of matter seem to be chance events.

Similiter autem neque multitudo in rebus causatur propter ordinem mediorum agentium, puta quod ab uno primo simplici procedere immediate non potuerit nisi unum, distans tamen a primo in simplicitate ita quod ex eo iam procedere potuerit multitudo; et sic deinceps quanto magis a primo simplici receditur tanto numerosior multitudo invenitur, ut aliqui posuerunt. Iam enim supra ostensum est quod plura sunt quae in esse prodire non potuerunt nisi per creationem, quod solius Dei est, ut supra ostensum est; unde relinquitur quod ab ipso Deo sunt plura immediate creata.

Manifestum est etiam quod secundum hanc positionem rerum multitudo et distinctio casualis esset, quasi non intenta a primo agente. Est autem rerum multitudo et distinctio ab intellectu divino excogitata et instituta in rebus ad hoc quod diversimode divina bonitas a rebus creatis repraesentaretur, et eam secundum diversos gradus diversa participarent; ut sic ex ipso diversarum rerum ordine quaedam pulchritudo reluceret in rebus, quae divinam sapientiam commendaret.

Furthermore, multiplicity in things is not explained by the order of intermediate agents, as though from one, simple first being there could proceed directly only one thing, which nonetheless would be far removed from the first being in simplicity, so that a multitude could issue from it, and thus, as the distance from the first, simple being increased, the more numerous a multitude would be discerned. Some have suggested this explanation. But we have shown that there are many things that could not have come into being except by creation, which is exclusively the work of God, as has been proved. Hence we conclude that many things have been created directly by God himself.

It is likewise evident that, according to that view, the multiplicity and distinction among things would be fortuitous, as not being intended by the first agent. But the multiplicity and distinction existing among things were devised by the divine intellect and established in things so that the divine goodness might be represented by created things in various ways, and that different things might participate in the divine goodness in varying degree. All this was so that a certain beauty might shine forth from the very order existing among diverse things, a beauty which would direct the mind to the divine wisdom.

CHAPTER 103

That the divine goodness is the cause not only of things, but also of all motion and activity

Non solum autem institutionis rerum finis est divina bonitas, sed etiam omnis operationis et motus creaturae cuiuslibet necesse est divinam bonitatem finem esse. Unumquodque enim quale est talia agit, sicut calidum calefacit; quaelibet autem res creata secundum suam formam similitudinem quandam participat divinae bonitatis, ut ostensum est: igitur et omnis actio et motus creaturae cuiuslibet in divinam bonitatem ordinatur sicut in finem.

Praeterea, omnis motus et operatio rei cuiuslibet in aliquod perfectum tendere videtur. Perfectum autem habet rationem boni, perfectio enim cuiuslibet est bonitas sua; omnis igitur motus et actio rei cuiuslibet ad bonum tendit. Bonum autem quodlibet est similitudo quaedam summi boni, sicut et esse quodlibet est similitudo primi entis; igitur motus et actio cuiuslibet rei tendit in assimilationem bonitatis divinae.

Praeterea, si sint multa agentia ordinata, necesse est quod omnium agentium actiones et motus ordinentur in bonum primi agentis: sicut in ultimum finem. Cum enim a superiori agente inferiora agentia moveantur, et omne movens moveat ad finem proprium, oportet

The divine goodness is not only the end of the creation of things; it must also be the end of every operation and movement of any creature whatever. For each thing acts according to the way it is: for example, what is hot causes heat. But every created thing has, in keeping with its form, some participated likeness to the divine goodness, as we have pointed out. Therefore, too, all actions and movements of every creature are directed to the divine goodness as their end.

Further, every movement and operation of every thing are seen to tend toward something perfect. Now, the perfect has the character of the good, since the perfection of any given thing is its goodness. Hence every movement and action of anything whatever tend toward good. But any given good is a certain likeness of the supreme Good, just as all being is a likeness of the first Being. Therefore, the movement and action of any given thing tends toward taking on a likeness to the divine goodness.

Moreover, if there are many agents arranged in order, the actions and movements of all the agents must be directed to the good of the first agent as to their ultimate end. For since lower agents are moved by the higher agent, and every mover moves toward its proper end, consequently the

quod actiones et motus inferiorum agentium tendant in finem primi agentis: sicut in exercitu omnium ordinum actiones ordinantur sicut in ultimum ad victoriam quae est finis ducis. Ostensum est autem supra quod primum movens et agens est Deus, finis autem eius non est aliud quam sua bonitas, ut etiam supra ostensum est; necesse est igitur quod omnes actiones et motus quarumcumque creaturarum sint propter divinam bonitatem, non quidem causandam neque augendam sed suo modo acquirendam, participando siquidem aliquam similitudinem eius.

Divinae autem bonitatis similitudinem res creatae per suas operationes diversimode consequuntur, sicut et diversimode secundum suum esse ipsam repraesentant: unumquodque enim operatur secundum quod est. Quia igitur omnibus creaturis commune est ut divinam bonitatem repraesentent inquantum sunt, omnibus etiam commune est ut per operationes suas consequantur divinam similitudinem in conservatione sui esse et communicatione sui esse ad alterum. Unaquaeque enim creatura sua operatione primo quidem se in esse perfecto secundum quod ei possibile est conservare nititur, in quo suo modo tendit in similitudinem divinae perpetuitatis; secundo vero per suam operationem unaquaeque creatura suum esse perfectum alteri communicare conatur secundum suum modum, et per hoc tendit in similitudinem divinae causalitatis.

Sed creatura rationalis per suam operationem tendit in divinam similitudinem singulari quodam modo prae ceteris, sicut et prae ceteris creaturis nobilius esse habet. Esse enim ceterarum creaturarum sic per materiam constrictum est et finitum, ut infinitatem non habeat nec actu nec potentia; omnis vero natura rationalis infinitatem habet vel potentia vel actu, secundum quod intellectus continet in se intelligibilia. In nobis igitur intellectualis natura in suo primo esse considerata est in potentia sua intelligibilia, quae cum sint infinita, infinitatem quandam in potentia habet; unde intellectus est species specierum, quia non tantum habet speciem determinatam ad unum, ut lapis, sed speciem omnium specierum capacem. Natura vero intellectualis in Deo est infinita in actu, utpote in se praehabens totius entis perfectionem, ut supra ostensum est; creaturae vero intellectuales alio medio modo se habent inter potentiam et actum. Tendit igitur intellectualis creatura per suam operationem in divinam similitudinem, non solum in hoc quod se in esse conservet vel suum esse quodammodo communicando multiplicet, sed ut in se actu habeat quod per naturam in potentia habet. Est igitur finis intellectualis creaturae, quem per suam operationem consequitur, ut intellectus eius totaliter efficiatur in actu secundum omnia intelligibilia quae in potentia habet: secundum hoc enim maxime Deo similis erit.

actions and movements of lower agents must tend toward the end of the first agent. Thus in an army the actions of all the subordinate units are ultimately directed to victory, which is the end intended by the commander-in-chief. But we showed above that the first mover and agent is God, and that his end is nothing else than his goodness. Therefore, all the actions and movements of all creatures exist on account of the divine goodness, not, of course, in the sense that they are to cause or increase it, but in the sense that they are to acquire it in their own way, by sharing to some extent in a likeness of it.

Now, created things attain to the likeness of the divine goodness by their operations in different ways, as they also represent it in different ways conformably to their being. For each of them acts according as it is. Therefore, as all creatures in common represent the divine goodness inasmuch as they exist, so by their actions they all in common attain to the divine likeness in the conservation of their being and in the communication of their being to others. For every creature endeavors, by its activity, first of all to keep itself in perfect being, so far as this is possible. In such endeavor it tends, in its own way, to an imitation of the divine permanence. Second, every creature strives, by its activity, to communicate its own perfect being, in its own fashion, to another; and in this it tends toward an imitation of the divine causality.

But the rational creature tends toward the divine likeness by its activity in a special way beyond all other creatures, as it also has a nobler existence than all other creatures. The existence of other creatures is finite, since it is hemmed in by matter, and so lacks infinity both in act and in potency. But every rational nature has infinity either in act or in potency, according to the way its intellect contains intelligibles. Thus our intellectual nature, considered in its first state, is in potency to its intelligibles; since these are infinite, our intellect has a certain infinity in potency—this is why intellect is the species of species, because it has a species that is not determined to one thing alone, like a stone, but has a capacity for all species. Now, the intellectual nature of God is infinite in act, because it precontains within itself the perfection of all being, as was shown above. And other intellectual creatures occupy a middle position between potency and act. By its activity, therefore, the intellectual creature tends toward the divine likeness, not only in the sense that it preserves itself in existence, or that it multiplies its existence, in a way, by communicating it; it also has as its end the possession in act of what by nature it possesses in potency. Consequently, the end of the intellectual creature, to be achieved by its activity, is the complete actuation of its intellect by all the intelligibles for which it has a potency. In this respect it will become most like to God.

Chapter 104

That the ultimate end of the intellectual creature is to see God in his essence

Est autem aliquid in potentia dupliciter: uno modo naturaliter, respectu eorum scilicet quae per agens connaturale possunt reduci in actum; alio modo respectu eorum quae reduci non possunt in actum per agens connaturale, sed per aliquod aliud agens. Quod quidem in rebus corporalibus apparet; quod enim ex puero fiat vir est in potentia naturali, vel quod ex semine fiat animal; sed quod ex ligno fiat scamnum vel ex caeco fiat videns, non est in potentia naturali.

Sic autem et circa intellectum nostrum accidit. Est enim intellectus noster in potentia naturali respectu quorundam intelligibilium, quae scilicet reduci possunt in actum per intellectum agentem, qui est principium innatum nobis ut per ipsum efficiamur intelligentes in actu. Est autem impossibile nos ultimum finem consequi per hoc quod intellectus noster sic reducatur in actum; nam virtus intellectus agentis est ut phantasmata quae sunt intelligibilia in potentia fiant intelligibilia in actu, ut ex superioribus patet. Phantasmata autem sunt accepta per sensum; per intellectum igitur agentem intellectus noster in actum reducitur respectu horum intelligibilium tantum in quorum notitiam per sensibilia possumus devenire.

Impossibile autem est in tali cognitione ultimum hominis finem consistere: nam ultimo fine adepto desiderium naturale quiescit; quantumcumque autem aliquis proficiat in intelligendo secundum praedictum modum cognitionis quo a sensu scientiam percipimus, adhuc remanet naturale desiderium ad alia cognoscenda. Multa enim sunt ad quae sensus pertingere non potest, de quibus per sensibilia non nisi modicam notitiam accipere possumus, ut forte sciamus de eis quod sint, non autem quid sint, eo quod substantiarum immaterialium quidditates alterius generis sunt a quidditatibus rerum sensibilium et eas quasi improportionabiliter transcendentes.

Circa ea etiam quae sub sensu cadunt, multa sunt quorum rationem cognoscere per certitudinem non possumus, sed quorundam quidem nullo modo, quorundam vero debiliter; unde semper remanet naturale desiderium respectu perfectioris cognitionis. Impossibile est autem naturale desiderium esse vanum.

Consequimur igitur ultimum finem in hoc quod intellectus noster fiat in actu aliquo sublimiori agente quam sit agens nobis connaturale, quod quiescere faciat desiderium quod nobis inest naturaliter ad sciendum. Tale est autem in nobis sciendi desiderium, ut cognoscentes effectum desideremus cognoscere causam; et in quacumque re cognitis quibuscumque eius circumstan-

A thing may be in potency in two ways: either naturally, that is, with respect to perfections that can be reduced to act by a connatural agent; or else with respect to perfections that cannot be reduced to act by a connatural agent but require some other agent. This is seen to take place even in bodily beings. That a boy should grow up to be a man or a spermatozoon develop into an animal is the realization of a natural potency. But that lumber should become a bench or a blind man receive sight is not from a natural potency.

The same is the case with our minds. Our intellect has a natural potency with regard to certain intelligible objects, namely, those that can be reduced to act by the agent intellect. We possess this faculty as an innate principle so that through it we may understand in actuality. However, we cannot attain our ultimate end by the actuation of our intellect through the agent intellect. For the agent intellect's function is to render actually intelligible the phantasms that of themselves are only potentially intelligible. This was explained above. These phantasms are received through the senses. Consequently, the agent intellect actuates our intellect only with respect to those intelligible objects that we can come to know through sensible things.

However, man's last end cannot consist in this kind of knowledge. For once the ultimate end has been reached, natural desire ceases. But no matter how much we may advance in this kind of understanding, whereby we derive knowledge from the senses, there still remains a natural desire to know other things. For there are many things beyond the reach of the senses. About such things we can gain only a slight knowledge through sensible things: we may come to know that they exist, but we cannot know what they are, for the essences of immaterial substances belong to a different genus than the essences of sensible things, and they excel them, so to speak, beyond all proportion.

Moreover, even as regards things that do fall under the senses, there are many whose nature we cannot know with any certainty. The nature of some we do not grasp in any way; of others, we know the nature only weakly. Hence our natural desire for more perfect knowledge ever remains. But a natural desire cannot be in vain.

Accordingly, we reach our last end when our intellect is actualized by some higher agent than an agent connatural to us, that makes our inborn desire for knowledge rest. Now, the desire for knowledge within us is such that, once we apprehend an effect, we wish to know its cause. Moreover, after we have gained some circumstantial knowledge of any given thing, our desire is not satisfied until we pene-

tiis, non quiescit nostrum desiderium quousque eius essentiam cognoscamus. Non igitur naturale sciendi desiderium potest quietari in nobis quousque primam causam cognoscamus, non quocumque modo sed per eius essentiam; prima autem causa Deus est, ut ex superioribus patet; est igitur finis ultimus intellectualis creaturae Deum per essentiam videre.

trate to its essence. Therefore, our natural desire for knowledge cannot come to rest within us until we know the first cause, and that not in just any way, but in its very essence. Now, the first cause is God, as is clear from what has been said above. Consequently, the ultimate end of an intellectual creature is the vision of God in his essence.

CHAPTER 105

How the created intellect can see the divine essence

Hoc autem quomodo possibile sit considerandum est. Manifestum est autem quod, cum intellectus noster nihil cognoscat nisi per aliquam speciem eius, impossibile est quod per speciem unius rei cognoscat essentiam alterius; et quanto magis species per quam cognoscit intellectus plus distat a re cognita, tanto intellectus noster imperfectiorem cognitionem habet de essentia rei illius. Puta, si cognosceret bovem per speciem asini, cognosceret eius essentiam imperfecte, scilicet quantum ad genus tantum; magis autem imperfecte si cognosceret per lapidem, quia cognosceret per genus magis remotum; si autem cognosceret per speciem alicuius rei quae nullo bovi communicaret in genere, nullo modo essentiam bovis cognosceret.

Manifestum est autem ex superioribus quod nullum creatum communicat cum Deo in genere; per quamcumque igitur speciem creatam, non solum sensibilem sed intelligibilem, Deus per essentiam cognosci non potest. Ad hoc igitur quod Deus per essentiam cognoscatur, necesse est quod ipse Deus fiat forma intellectus ipsum sic cognoscentis et coniungatur ei, coniungatur inquam non ad unam naturam constituendam sed sicut species intelligibilis intelligenti; ipse enim sicut est suum esse, ita est sua veritas, quae est forma intellectus.

Necesse est autem quod omne quod consequitur aliquam formam, consequatur dispositionem aliquam ad formam illam. Intellectus autem noster non est ex ipsa sua natura in ultima dispositione existens respectu formae illius quae est veritas, quia a principio ipsam assequeretur; oportet igitur quod, cum eam consequitur, aliqua dispositione de novo addita elevetur: quod dicimus gloriae lumen, quo quidem intellectus noster a Deo perfunditur qui solus secundum suam naturam hanc formam propriam habet, sicut nec dispositio caloris ad formam ignis potest esse nisi ab igne. Et de hoc lumine dicitur in Psalmo *in lumine tuo videbimus lumen.*

We must now consider how this is possible. Manifestly, since our intellect knows nothing except through an intelligible species of the thing known, the species of one thing cannot disclose the essence of another thing. The more distant the species through which the intellect knows is from the thing known, the less perfect knowlege our intellect has of that thing's essence. For example, if we should know an ox by the species of an ass, we would have an imperfect knowledge of the essence of the ox: indeed, it would only be of the genus. Our knowledge would be still more defective if we were to know the ox through the medium of a stone, because then we would know it by a more remote genus. And if our knowledge were gained through the species of a thing that did not agree with the ox in any genus, we could not know the essence of the ox at all.

It is clear from the previous discussion that no creature shares a genus with God. Hence the essence of God cannot be known through any created species whatever, whether sensible or intelligible. Accordingly, if God is to be known as he is, in his essence, God himself must become the form of the intellect knowing him and must be joined to that intellect, not indeed so as to constitute a single nature with it, but in the way an intelligible species is joined to the intelligence. For God, who is his own being, is also his own truth, and truth is the form of the intellect.

Whatever receives a form must first acquire a disposition to that form. Our intellect does not by its very nature have the last disposition toward that form which is truth; otherwise it would be in possession of that truth from the beginning. Consequently, when it does attain to truth, it must be elevated by some disposition newly conferred on it. And this we call the light of glory, with which God fills our intellect, who alone by his very nature has this form properly as his own, even as heat, which is the disposition toward the form of fire, can come from fire alone. This is the light spoken of in Psalm 36 [35]:9: *In thy light we shall see light.*

Chapter 106

How natural desire comes to rest in the vision of God
in his essence, in which beatitude consists

Hoc autem fine adepto, necesse est naturale desiderium quietari, quia essentia divina, quae modo praedicto coniungetur intellectui Deum videntis, est sufficiens principium omnia cognoscendi et fons totius bonitatis, ut nihil restare possit ad desiderandum. Et hic etiam est perfectissimus modus divinam similitudinem consequendi, ut scilicet ipsum cognoscamus eo modo quo se ipse cognoscit, scilicet per essentiam suam, licet non comprehendamus ipsum sicut ipse se comprehendit: non quod aliquam partem eius ignoremus, cum partem non habeat, sed quia non ita perfecte ipsum cognoscemus sicut cognoscibilis est, cum virtus intellectus nostri in intelligendo non possit adaequari veritati ipsius secundum quod cognoscibilis est, cum eius claritas seu veritas sit infinita, intellectus autem noster finitus. Intellectus autem eius infinitus est sicut et veritas eius, et ideo ipse tantum se cognoscit quantum cognoscibilis est: sicut conclusionem demonstrabilem ille comprehendit qui eam per demonstrationem cognoscit, non autem qui cognoscit eam imperfectiori modo, scilicet per probabilem rationem.

Et quia ultimum finem hominis dicimus 'beatitudinem,' in hoc consistit hominis felicitas sive beatitudo quod Deum videat per essentiam; licet in perfectione beatitudinis multum distet a Deo, cum hanc beatitudinem Deus per suam naturam habeat, homo vero eam consequatur per divini luminis participationem, ut supra dictum est.

Once this end is reached, natural desire must come to rest. For the divine essence, thus united to the intellect of the one who sees God, is the adequate principle for knowing everything and is the wellspring of all goodness, so that nothing can remain to be desired. This, too, is the most perfect way of attaining likeness with God: to know God in the way he knows himself, by his own essence. Of course, we shall never comprehend him as he comprehends himself. This does not mean that we shall be unaware of some part of him, for he has no parts. Rather, it means that we shall not know him as perfectly as he can be known, since the capacity of our intellect for knowing cannot be brought to a level with the knowability of his truth: God's clarity or truth is infinite, whereas our intellect is finite. But his intellect is infinite, just as his truth is; and so he alone knows himself to the full extent that he is knowable; just as a person comprehends a demonstrable conclusion if he knows it through demonstration, but not if he knows it only in an imperfect way, by a probable proof.

And since we call man's ultimate end 'beatitude,' man's happiness or beatitude consists in the fact that he sees God in his essence; although man is far below God in the perfection of his beatitude, since God has this beatitude by his very nature, whereas man attains beatitude by participation in the divine light, as was said above.

Chapter 107

That motion toward God for the acquiring of beatitude is like natural motion

Considerandum autem est quod, cum procedere de potentia in actum vel sit motus vel simile motui, circa processum huius beatitudinis consequendae similiter se habet sicut in motu vel in mutatione naturali. In motu enim naturali primo quidem consideratur aliqua proprietas per quam proportionatur vel inclinatur mobile ad talem finem, sicut gravitas in terra ad hoc quod feratur deorsum: non enim moveretur aliquid naturaliter ad certum finem nisi haberet proportionem ad illum; secundo autem consideratur ipse motus ad finem; tertio autem ipsa forma vel locus; quarto autem quies in forma vel in loco.

We should note that, since advance from potency to act is motion, or at least is similar to motion, the process of arriving at beatitude has points of resemblance with natural motion or change. In natural motion we may consider, first, a certain property by which the mobile object has a proportion to such and such an end, or is inclined in its direction, as heaviness in earth is inclined to being borne downward. No object would move naturally toward a definite end unless it had a proportion to that end. Second, we may consider the motion itself toward its end. Third, the form or place toward which there is motion. Fourth, the repose in the form attained or in the place reached.

Sic igitur in intellectuali motu ad finem, primum quidem est amor inclinans in finem; secundum autem est desiderium, quod est quasi motus in finem, et operationes ex tali desiderio provenientes; tertium autem est ipsa forma quam intellectus consequitur; quartum autem est delectatio consequens, quae nihil est aliud quam quietatio voluntatis in fine adepto.

Sicut igitur generationis naturalis finis est forma et motus localis locus, non autem quies in forma vel loco, sed hoc est consequens finem, et multo minus motus est finis vel proportio ad finem: ita ultimus finis creaturae intellectualis est videre Deum, non autem delectari in ipso, sed hoc est concomitans finem et quasi perficiens ipsum; et multo minus desiderium vel amor possunt esse ultimus finis, cum etiam haec ante finem habeantur.

Thus, therefore, in an intellectual movement toward an end, there is first the love inclining toward the end; second, the desire which is like a motion toward the end, and the actions issuing from such desire; third, the form which the intellect receives; and fourth, the resulting delight, which is nothing else than the repose of the will in the end reached.

Just as, therefore, the end of natural generation is a form and the end of local motion is a place, yet the end is not rest in form or place, but this rest follows upon the attainment of the end (and much less does the end consist in motion or in proportion to the end), even so the ultimate end of an intellectual creature is seeing God, not delighting in God; but such delight accompanies attainment of the end and, as it were, perfects it. Much less can desire or love be the ultimate end, because they are present even before the end is reached.

CHAPTER 108

Of the error of seeking happiness in creatures

Manifestum est ergo quod felicitas falso a quibusdam quaeritur, in quibuscumque praeter Deum quaeratur, sive in voluptatibus corporalibus, quae sunt homini et brutis communes; sive in divitiis, quae ad conservationem habentium proprie ordinantur, quae est communis finis omnis entis creati; sive in potestatibus, quae ordinantur ad communicandum perfectionem suam aliis, quod etiam diximus omnibus esse commune; sive in honoribus vel fama, quae alicui debentur secundum quod finem iam habet vel ad finem bene dispositus est; seu in cognitione quarumcumque rerum etiam supra hominem existentium, cum in sola divina cognitione desiderium hominis quietetur.

Clearly, therefore, they are in error who seek happiness in various things outside of God. Some seek it in carnal pleasures, which are common to man and brute animals. Others in wealth, which is rightly directed to the sustenance of those who have such possessions, and is an end common to every created being. Others look to power, which is ordained to the communication of one's own perfection to others; this, too, we said, is common to all beings. Yet others seek it in honors or reputation, which are due to a person because of the end he has already reached, or because of the noble dispositions which equip him to reach an end. Nor is it the knowledge of any created things whatever, even though they may be far above man; for man's desire comes to rest in the knowledge of God alone.

CHAPTER 109

That God alone is good by essence, whereas the creature is good by participation

Ex praemissis igitur apparet quod diversimode se habent ad bonitatem Deus et creaturae secundum duplicem modum bonitatis qui in creaturis considerari potest. Cum enim bonum habeat rationem perfectionis et finis, secundum duplicem perfectionem et finem creaturae attenditur duplex eius bonitas. Attenditur enim quaedam creaturae perfectio secundum quod in sua natura persistit, et haec est finis generationis aut factionis ipsius; alia vero perfectio ipsius attenditur quam consequitur per suum motum vel operationem, et haec est finis motus vel operationis ipsius.

Secundum utramque vero creatura deficit a bonitate divina nam cum forma et esse rei sit bonum et perfectio ipsius secundum quod in sua natura consideratur, substantia composita neque est sua forma neque suum esse; substantia vero simplex creata, etsi sit ipsa forma, non tamen est suum esse. Deus vero est sua essentia et suum esse, ut supra ostensum est.

Similiter etiam omnes creaturae consequuntur perfectam bonitatem ex fine extrinseco: perfectio enim bonitatis consistit in adeptione ultimi finis; finis autem ultimus cuiuslibet creaturae est extra ipsam, quod est divina bonitas, quae quidem non ordinatur ad ulteriorem finem. Relinquitur igitur quod Deus modis omnibus est sua bonitas et est essentialiter bonus; creaturae vero simplices non omnino sunt sua bonitas, tum quia non sunt suum esse, tum quia ordinantur ad aliquid extrinsecum sicut ad ultimum finem; in substantiis vero compositis manifestum est quod nullo modo sunt sua bonitas. Solus igitur Deus est pura bonitas et essentialiter bonus, alia vero dicuntur bona secundum participationem aliquam ipsius.

All this brings to light the different relationship that God and creatures have to goodness. We may examine this difference from the standpoint of the two kinds of goodness discerned in creatures. Since the good has the nature of perfection and of end, the twofold perfection and end of the creature disclose its twofold goodness. For a certain perfection is observed in the creature inasmuch as it persists in its nature, and this perfection is the end of its generation or formation. The creature has a further perfection which it reaches by its motion or activity, and this perfection is the end of its movement or operation.

In both kinds of perfection the creature falls short of the divine goodness. For the form and existence of a thing are its good and perfection when considered from the standpoint of the thing's nature. But a composite substance is neither its own form nor its own existence; and a simple created substance, although it is its own form, is not its own existence. God, however, is his own essence and his own existence, as was shown above.

Likewise, all creatures receive their perfect goodness from an end extrinsic to them. For the perfection of goodness consists in attainment of the ultimate end. But the ultimate end of any creature is outside the creature. This end is the divine goodness, which is not ordained to any ulterior end. Consequently, God is his own goodness in every way and is essentially good. But simple creatures are not entirely their own goodness, because they are not their own existence, and also because they are ordained to something external as to their ultimate end. As for composite substances, clearly they are not their own goodness in any way. Hence God alone is his own goodness, and he alone is essentially good. All other beings are said to be good according to some participation in him.

CHAPTER 110

That God cannot lose his own goodness

Per hoc autem apparet quod Deus nullo modo potest deficere a bonitate. Quod enim alicui essentialiter inest non potest ei abesse, sicut animal non potest ab homine removeri; neque igitur Deum possibile est non esse bonum. Et ut magis proprio utatur exemplo, sicut non potest esse quod homo non sit homo, ita non potest esse quod Deus non sit perfecte bonus.

The foregoing clearly shows that God cannot in any way be deficient in goodness. For what is essential to a being cannot be lacking from it; for instance, 'animal' cannot be removed from 'man.' Neither is it possible for God not to be good. And to use an even more appropriate example: just as it is impossible for a man not to be a man, so it is impossible for God not to be perfectly good.

CHAPTER 111

That the creature can fall away from its goodness

In creaturis autem considerandum est qualiter possit esse bonitatis defectus. Manifestum est enim quod duobus modis aliqua bonitas inseparabiliter creaturae inest: uno modo ex hoc quod ipsa bonitas est de essentia eius, alio modo ex hoc quod est determinata ad unum. Primo igitur modo, in substantiis simplicibus ipsa bonitas quae est forma inseparabiliter se habet ad ipsas, cum ipsae essentialiter sint formae. Secundo autem modo, bonum quod est esse amittere non possunt: non enim forma est sicut materia, quae se habet ad esse et non esse, sed forma consequitur esse, etsi etiam non sit ipsum esse.

Unde patet quod substantiae simplices bonum naturae in qua subsistunt amittere non possunt, sed immutabiliter se habent in illo. Substantiae vero compositae, quia non sunt suae formae nec suum esse, bonum naturae amissibiliter habent, nisi in illis in quibus potentia materiae non se habet ad diversas formas, neque ad esse et non esse, sicut in corporibus caelestibus patet.

However, we must consider how there can be a lack of goodness in creatures. In two respects goodness is clearly inseparable from the creature: first, from the fact that goodness pertains to the creature's very essence; second, from the fact that the creature is determined to one thing. As regards the first point of view, the goodness which is the form of simple substances is inseparable from them, since they are forms in essence. As regards the second point of view, such substances cannot lose the good which is existence. For form is not like matter, which is indifferent to existence and nonexistence. Rather, form follows upon existence, even though it is not existence itself.

Therefore, simple substances clearly cannot lose the good of nature wherein they subsist, but are immutably established in that good. But composite substances, which are neither their own forms nor their own existence, possess the good of nature in such a way that they can lose it. This is not true, however, of those things whose matter is not in potency to various forms or to being and non-being, such as is clear in the case of heavenly bodies.

CHAPTER 112

How creatures may fall away from goodness in their activities

Sed quia bonitas creaturae non solum consideratur secundum quod in sua natura subsistit, sed perfectio bonitatis ipsius est in hoc quod ordinatur ad finem, ad finem autem ordinatur per suam operationem, restat considerare quomodo creaturae deficiant a bonitate secundum suas operationes, quibus ordinantur ad finem.

Ubi primo considerandum est quod de operationibus naturalibus idem est iudicium sicut ei de natura quae est earum principium: unde quorum natura defectum pati non potest, nec in operationibus eorum naturalibus defectus accidere potest; quorum autem natura defectum pati potest, et operationes eorum deficere contingit.

Unde in substantiis incorruptibilibus, sive corporeis sive incorporeis, nullus defectus naturalis actionis contingere potest: in angelis enim semper virtus naturalis

But a creature's goodness is not only considered inasmuch as it subsists in its nature, but the perfection of its goodness is found in its ordering toward the end. And since creatures are ordered toward their end by their activity, we have still to inquire how creatures may be lacking in goodness from the point of view of their actions, whereby they are oriented toward their end.

In this connection we should first note that a judgment concerning natural operations is equivalent to a judgment concerning the nature which is the principle of these operations. Therefore, in beings whose nature cannot suffer defect, no defect in natural operations can arise; but in beings whose nature can admit of defect, a defect in activity can occur.

Hence in incorruptible substances, whether non-bodily or bodily, no defect in natural activity can take place. Thus angels forever retain their natural power of exercising their

manet potens ad suas operationes exercendas; similiter motus corporum caelestium numquam exorbitare invenitur. In corporibus vero inferioribus multi defectus naturalium actionum contingunt propter corruptiones et defectus in naturis eorum accidentes: ex defectu enim alicuius naturalis principii contingit plantarum sterilitas, monstruositas in generatione animalium et aliae huiusmodi inordinationes.

proper activity. Likewise, the movements of heavenly bodies are found never to leave their appointed orbits. But in lower bodies many defects in natural activity result from the corruptions and defects incidental to their natures. Thus from a defect in some natural principle come the sterility of plants, monstrosities in the generation of animals, and other such disorders.

CHAPTER 113

Of the twofold principle of action, and in which one there can be defect

Sunt autem quaedam actiones quarum principium non est natura sed voluntas, cuius obiectum est bonum, finis quidem principaliter, secundario autem quod est ad finem. Sic igitur se habet operatio voluntaria ad bonum sicut se habet naturalis operatio ad formam per quam res agit. Sicut igitur defectus naturalium actionum accidere non potest in illis quae non patiuntur defectum secundum suas formas, sed solum in corruptibilibus quorum formae deficere possunt: ita voluntariae actiones deficere quidem possunt in illis in quibus voluntas potest a fine deficere; sicubi autem non potest voluntas a fine deficere, manifestum est quod ibi defectus voluntariae actionis esse non potest.

Voluntas autem deficere non potest respectu boni quod est ipsius volentis natura: quaelibet enim res suo modo appetit suum esse perfectum, quod est bonum uniuscuiusque; respectu vero boni exterioris deficere potest bono sibi connaturali contenta. Cuius igitur volentis natura est ultimus finis voluntatis ipsius, in hoc defectus voluntariae actionis contingere non potest.

Hoc autem solus Deus est, nam sua bonitas, quae est ultimus finis rerum, est sua natura. Aliorum autem volentium natura non est ultimus finis voluntatis ipsorum; unde potest in eis defectus voluntariae actionis contingere per hoc quod voluntas remaneat fixa in proprio bono, non tendendo ulterius in summum bonum quod est ultimus finis. In omnibus igitur substantiis intellectualibus creatis potest defectus voluntariae actionis contingere.

There are certain actions whose principle is not nature but the will. The object of the will is the good, which consists primarily in the end, secondarily in whatever leads to the end. Therefore, voluntary action is related to the good as natural action is related to the form by which a thing acts. Consequently, just as a defect in natural activity cannot ensue in things that do not admit of defect in their forms, but can occur only in corruptible things whose forms are defectible, so voluntary actions can be deficient only in beings whose will can deflect from their proper end. Hence, if the will cannot deflect from its proper end, deficiency in voluntary action is clearly impossible.

Now, the will cannot be deficient with regard to the good which is the nature of the very being that wills; for every being in its own way seeks its perfect being, which is each thing's good. But as regards an external good the will can be deficient, by resting content with a good connatural to it. Therefore, if the nature of the being that wills is the ultimate end of its will, no deficiency in voluntary action can arise.

Such is the case with God alone. For his goodness, which is the ultimate end of things, is his very nature. But the nature of other beings endowed with will is not the ultimate end of their will. Hence a defect in voluntary action can occur in them, if their will remains fixed on their individual good and does not push on to the supreme good, which is the last end. Therefore, in all created intellectual substances a deficiency in voluntary action is possible.

Chapter 114

What is understood in things by the name good or bad

Est autem hic considerandum quod, sicut nomine boni intelligitur esse perfectum, ita nomine mali nihil aliud esse intelligitur quam privatio esse perfecti. Quia vero privatio proprie accepta est eius quod natum est et quando natum est et quomodo natum est haberi, manifestum est quod ex hoc aliquid dicitur malum quod caret perfectione quam debet habere. Unde homo si visu careat malum est ei, non autem malum est lapidi quia non est natus visum habere.

Here we must consider that, as the term 'good' signifies perfect being, so the term 'evil' signifies nothing else than privation of perfect being. For privation is properly taken as of that which is made to be possessed, and at a certain time in a certain way. Evidently, therefore, a thing is called 'evil' if it lacks a perfection it ought to have. Thus if a man lacks the sense of sight, this is an evil for him. But the same lack is not an evil for a stone, for the stone is not by nature such as to have the faculty of sight.

Chapter 115

That it is impossible for evil to be a nature

Impossibile est autem malum esse aliquam naturam. Nam omnis natura vel est actus vel potentia aut compositum ex utroque. Quod autem actus est, perfectio est et boni optinet rationem, cum id quod est in potentia appetat naturaliter esse actu; bonum vero est quod omnia appetunt. Unde et compositum ex actu et potentia, inquantum participat actum participat bonitatem. Potentia etiam inquantum ordinatur ad actum bonitatem habet, cuius signum est quod quanto potentia est capacior actus et perfectionis, tanto magis commendatur. Relinquitur igitur quod nulla secundum se sit malum.

Item, unumquodque secundum hoc completur quod fit in actu, nam actus est perfectio rei. Nullum autem oppositorum completur per admixtionem alterius, sed magis destruitur vel minuitur, et sic neque malum completur per participationem boni. Omnis autem natura completur per hoc quod habet esse in actu, et sic cum esse sit bonum ab omnibus appetibile, omnis natura completur per participationem boni; nulla igitur natura est malum.

Adhuc, quaelibet natura appetit conservationem sui esse et fugit destructionem quantum potest. Cum igitur bonum sit quod omnia appetunt, malum vero e contrario quod omnia fugiunt, necesse est dicere quod esse unamquamque naturam secundum se sit bonum, non esse vero malum. Esse autem malum non est bonum, sed magis non esse malum sub boni comprehenditur ratione; nulla igitur natura est malum.

It is impossible for evil to be a nature. Every nature is either act or potency or a composite of the two. Whatever is act is a perfection, and has the character of the good, since what is in potency has a natural appetite to be in act, and what all beings desire is the good. Therefore, too, what is composed of act and potency participates in goodness to the extent that it participates in act. Potency also possesses goodness inasmuch as it is ordained to act; an indication of this is the fact that potency is esteemed in proportion to its capacity for act and perfection. Consequently, no nature is of itself an evil.

Again, every being achieves its fulfillment according as it comes to be in act, for act is the perfection of a thing. However, neither of a pair of opposites achieves fulfillment by being mixed with the other, but is rather destroyed or weakened thereby; therefore, evil does not realize its full capacity by sharing in good. But every nature realizes its full capacity by having existence in act; and so, since existence is the good desirable to all things, a nature achieves fulfillment by participating in good. Therefore, no nature is an evil.

Moreover, any nature whatever desires the preservation of its being, and shuns destruction to the extent that it can. Consequently, since good is that which all desire, and evil, on the contrary, is that which all shun, we must conclude to be a given nature is in itself good, while not to be is evil. To be evil, however, is not good; in fact, not to be evil is included in the notion of good. Therefore, no nature is an evil.

CHAPTER 116

In what way good and evil are differences of being, contraries, and genera of contraries

Considerandum igitur restat quomodo bonum et malum dicantur contraria et contrariorum genera, et differentiae aliquas species, scilicet habitus morales, constituentes. Contrariorum enim utrumque est natura aliqua; non ens etiam non potest esse neque genus neque differentia, cum genus praedicetur de re in eo quod quid, differentia vero in eo quod quale quid.

Sciendum est igitur quod, sicut naturalia consequuntur speciem a forma, ita moralia a fine qui est voluntatis obiectum, a qua omnia moralia dependent. Sicut autem in naturalibus uni formae adiungitur privatio alterius, puta formae ignis privatio formae aeris vel ligni, ita in moralibus uni fini adiungitur privatio alterius. Cum igitur privatio perfectionis debitae sit malum, et in naturalibus formam accipere cui adiungitur privatio formae debitae malum est, non propter formam sed propter privationem ei adiunctam, sicut ignis malum est ligno.

Et in moralibus etiam inhaerere fini cui adiungitur privatio finis debiti malum est, non propter finem sed propter privationem adiunctam. Et sic duae actiones morales quae ad contrarios fines ordinantur secundum bonum et malum differunt, et per consequens contrarii habitus, quasi bono et malo differentiis existentibus et contrarietatem ad invicem habentibus, non propter privationem ex qua dicitur malum, sed propter finem cui privatio adiungitur.

Per hunc etiam modum quidam intelligunt ab Aristotele dictum quod bonum et malum sunt genera aliorum contrariorum, scilicet moralium; sed si recte attendatur, bonum et malum in genere moralium magis sunt ut differentiae quam ut species. Unde melius videtur dicendum quod bonum et malum dicuntur genera secundum positionem Pictagoris, qui omnia reduxit ad bonum et malum sicut ad prima genera: quae quidem positio habet aliquid veritatis inquantum omnium contrariorum unum est perfectum et alterum diminutum, ut patet in albo et nigro, dulci et amaro, et sic de aliis; semper autem quod perfectum est pertinet ad rationem boni, quod autem diminutum ad rationem mali.

We have next to inquire how good and evil may be regarded as contraries and genera of contraries and differences constituting species of a sort, namely, moral habits. Each member of a pair of contraries is some kind of nature. For non-being can be neither genus nor specific difference, since genus is predicated of a thing according to what it is and difference according to what sort of thing it is.

One must know therefore that, as physical entities receive their species from their form, so moral entities receive their species from the end which is the object of the will and on which all morality depends. Now, in physical entities the presence of one form entails the privation of another, as, for instance, the form of fire entails the privation of the form of air or wood. In moral entities, similarly, one end involves the privation of another end. Since the privation of a due perfection is an evil, in physical things the reception of a form which implies the privation of the form that ought to be possessed is an evil; not, indeed, because of the form itself, but because of the privation its presence involves. For example, to be on fire is an evil for wood.

Similarly, in moral actions the pursuit of an end that entails the privation of the right end is an evil, not on account of the end itself, but because of the privation necessarily implied. It is in this way that two moral actions directed to contrary ends—and consequently the contrary habits as well—differ as good and evil, as though they differed by good and evil as specific differences contrary to one another. But this is so not on account of the privation from which evil receives its designation, but on account of the end that involves the privation.

This is the sense in which some philosophers understand Aristotle's assertion that good and evil are genera of other contraries, namely, of moral contraries. But if we examine the matter closely, we shall find that in the sphere of morals, good and evil are differences rather than species. Hence it seems better to say that good and evil are called genera according to the opinion of Pythagoras, who reduced everything to good and evil as to supreme genera. This position does, indeed, contain some truth, in the sense that in all contraries one member is perfect, whereas the other is deficient, as is clear in the case of white and black, sweet and bitter, and so on. And what is perfect always relates to the notion of good, while what is deficient relates to the notion evil.

CHAPTER 117

That nothing can be essentially or supremely evil, but evil is the corruption of some good

Habito igitur quod malum est privatio perfectionis debitae, iam manifestum fit qualiter malum corrumpit bonum, inquantum scilicet est eius privatio, sicut et caecitas dicitur corrumpere visum quia est ipsa visus privatio. Nec tamen totum bonum corrumpit, quia supra dictum est quod non solum forma est bonum sed etiam potentia ad formam, quae quidem potentia est subiectum privationis sicut et formae. Unde oportet quod subiectum mali sit bonum, non quidem quod est oppositum malo, sed quod est potentia ad ipsum.

Ex quo etiam patet quod non quodlibet bonum potest esse subiectum mali, sed solum bonum quod est in potentia respectu alicuius perfectionis qua potest privari; unde in his quae solum actus sunt, vel in quibus actus a potentia separari non potest, quantum ad hoc non potest esse malum.

Patet etiam ex hoc quod non potest esse aliquid quod sit essentialiter malum, cum semper oporteat malum in aliquo subiecto bono fundari; ac per hoc nihil potest esse summe malum, sicut est summe bonum quod est essentialiter bonum.

Secundum eadem etiam patet quod malum non potest esse desideratum, neque aliquid agere nisi virtute boni adiuncti. Desiderabile enim est perfectio et finis, principium vero actionis est forma. Quia vero uni perfectioni vel formae adiungitur privatio alterius perfectionis aut formae, contingit per accidens quod privatio seu malum desideratur et est alicuius actionis principium, non inquantum est malum sed propter bonum adiunctum, sicut musicus aedificat non inquantum musicus, sed inquantum aedificator.

Ex quo etiam patet quod impossibile est malum esse primum principium, eo quod principium per accidens est posterius eo quod est per se.

Knowing that evil is the privation of a due perfection, now we can easily see how evil corrupts good; it does so inasmuch as it is the privation of good, as, for example, blindness is said to corrupt sight because it is the privation of sight. However, evil does not completely corrupt good, because, as we remarked above, not only form, but also potency to form, is good; and potency is the subject of privation as well as of form. Therefore, the subject of evil must be good, not in the sense that it is the opposite of evil, but in the sense that it is a potency to the opposite.

This also brings out the fact that not every good can be the subject of evil, but only such a good as is in potency with respect to some perfection of which it can be deprived. Hence in beings which are exclusively act, or in which act cannot be separated from potency, there can, to this extent, be no evil.

And this makes it clear that nothing can be essentially evil, since evil must always have as its foundation some subject that is good. And so there cannot be a supreme evil in the way that there is a supreme good which is essentially good.

The same consideration also makes it clear that evil cannot be desired, and that it can only do something in virtue of the good connected with it. For only perfection and end are desirable; and the principle of action is form. However, since a particular perfection or form involves the privation of some other perfection or form, it can happen accidentally that privation or evil is desired and is the principle of some action—not insofar as it is evil, but because of the good connected with it, like a musician who constructs a house not insofar as he is a musician, but insofar as he is a builder.

From this we may also infer that evil cannot be a first principle, for an accidental principle is subsequent to a principle that is such essentially.

CHAPTER 118

That evil is grounded in the good as in a subject

Si quis autem contra praedicta obiicere velit quod bonum non potest esse subiectum mali, eo quod unum oppositorum non sit subiectum alterius nec umquam in aliis oppositis invenitur quod sint simul, considerare debet quod alia opposita sunt alicuius generis determinati, bonum autem et malum communia sunt. Nam omne ens inquantum huiusmodi bonum est, omnis autem privatio inquantum talis est mala. Unde sicut subiectum privationis oportet esse ens, ita et bonum; non autem subiectum privationis oportet esse album aut dulce aut videns, quia haec non dicuntur de ente inquantum huiusmodi. Et ideo nigrum non est in albo nec caecum in vidente, sed malum est in bono sicut et caecitas est in subiecto visus; sed quod subiectum visus non dicatur videns, hoc est quia videns non est commune omni enti.

But someone may want to object against the aforesaid that good cannot be the substratum of evil, for one of a pair of opposites cannot be the substratum of the other, nor do extremes ever exist together in other kinds of opposites. But they should reflect that other kinds of opposition belong to some definite genus, whereas good and evil are common to all genera. For every being, as such, is good; and every privation, as such, is evil. Consequently, the subject of a privation must be a being, and so a good. But the subject of a privation need not be white or sweet or endowed with sight, because none of these predicates belongs to being as such. And so black is not in white, nor blindness in the person who sees; but evil is in the good, just as blindness is in the subject of sight. The reason why the subject of sight is not called 'seeing' is that seeing is not a predicate common to every being.

CHAPTER 119

Of the two kinds of evil

Quia igitur malum est privatio et defectus, defectus autem, ut ex dictis patet, potest contingere in re aliqua non solum secundum quod in natura sua consideratur, sed etiam secundum quod per actionem ordinatur ad finem: consequens est ut malum utroque modo dicatur, scilicet secundum defectum in ipsa re, prout caecitas est quoddam malum animalis, et secundum defectum in actione, prout claudicatio significat actionem cum defectu. Malum igitur actionis ad aliquem finem ordinatae ad quem non debito modo se habet peccatum dicitur, tam in voluntariis quam in naturalibus. Peccat enim medicus in actione sua dum non operatur convenienter ad sanitatem; et natura etiam peccat in sua operatione dum non ad debitam dispositionem et formam rem generatam producit, sicut cum accidunt monstra in natura.

Since evil is privation and defect, and since defect, as is clear from what we said above, can occur in a thing both as regarded in its nature and as it is ordered to an end by its action, we may speak of evil in both senses: that is, by reason of a defect in the thing itself (as blindness is a certain evil in an animal), and by reason of a defect in a creature's action (as limping is an action with a defect). Evil in an action that is directed to an end in such a way that it is not rightly related to the end is called fault both in voluntary agents and in natural agents. A physician is faulty in his action when he does not proceed in such a way as to procure health. Nature, too, is faulty in its activity when it fails to generate a thing with its proper disposition and form; this is why monsters occur in nature.

CHAPTER 120

Of three kinds of action, and of the evil of sin

Sed sciendum quod actio aliquando est in potestate agentis, ut sunt omnes voluntariae actiones: voluntariam autem actionem dico cuius principium est in agente sciente ea in quibus actus consistit. Aliquando vero actiones non sunt voluntariae, cuiusmodi sunt actiones violentae, quarum principium est extra, et actiones naturales vel quae per ignorantiam aguntur, quia non procedunt a cognitivo principio. Si igitur in actionibus non voluntariis ordinatis ad finem defectus accidat, peccatum tantum dicitur; si autem accidat in actionibus voluntariis, dicitur non solum peccatum sed culpa, eo quod agens, cum sit dominus suae actionis, vituperio dignus est et poena. Si quae vero actiones sunt mixtae, habentes scilicet aliquid de voluntario et aliquid de involuntario, tanto minoratur culpa quanto plus ibi de involuntario admiscetur.

Quia vero naturalis actio rei naturam sequitur, manifestum est quod in rebus incorruptibilibus, quarum natura transmutari non potest, naturalis actionis peccatum accidere non potest. Voluntas autem cuiuslibet intellectualis creaturae defectum pati potest in voluntaria actione, ut supra ostensum est. Unde relinquitur quod, licet carere malo naturae omnibus incorruptibilibus sit commune, carere tamen ex necessitate suae naturae malo culpae, cuius sola rationalis natura est capax, solius Dei proprium invenitur.

We should observe that sometimes action is in the power of the agent. Such are all voluntary actions. By voluntary action I mean an action that has its principle in an agent who is conscious of the various factors constituting his action. Sometimes actions are not voluntary. In this class are violent actions, whose principle is outside the agent, and natural actions and actions performed in ignorance as well, since they do not proceed from a conscious principle. If a defect occurs in non-voluntary actions that are directed to an end, it is called simply a fault. But if such a defect occurs in voluntary actions, it is called not only fault, but sin. For in this case the agent, being master of his own action, deserves blame and punishment. If actions are mixed, that is, are partly voluntary and partly involuntary, the sin is diminished in proportion to the admixture of the involuntary.

Since natural action follows the nature of a being, a fault in natural activity clearly cannot occur in incorruptible things, for their nature is incapable of change. But the will of any intellectual creature can suffer defect in voluntary action, as was shown above. Consequently, freedom from evil in nature is common to all incorruptible things. But to be free by natural necessity from the evil of sin, of which rational nature alone is capable, is found to be an exclusive property of God.

CHAPTER 121

That some evil has the nature of punishment, and not of fault

Sicut autem defectus actionis voluntariae constituit rationem peccati et culpae, ita defectus cuiuslibet boni pro culpa illatus contra voluntatem eius cui infertur poenae optinet rationem. Poena enim infertur ut medicina culpae et ut ordinativa ipsius. Ut medicina quidem inquantum homo propter poenam retrahitur a culpa, dum ne patiatur quod est suae contrarium voluntati, dimittit agere inordinatam actionem quae suae foret placita voluntati. Est etiam ordinativa ipsius, quia per culpam homo transgreditur metas ordinis naturalis, plus suae voluntati tribuens quam oportet; unde ad ordinem iu-

Just as a defect in voluntary action constitutes the notion of fault and sin, so any lack of good inflicted on account of sin against the will of him on whom the lack is inflicted has the notion of punishment. Punishment is inflicted as a medicine for sin, and also as restoring it to right order. Punishment functions as a medicine inasmuch as fear of punishment deters a man from sinning; that is, a person refrains from doing an inordinate action, which would be pleasing to his will, lest he have to suffer what is opposed to his will. Punishment also restores right order, because by sinning a man exceeds the limits of the natural order,

stitiae fit reductio per poenam per quam subtrahitur aliquid voluntati. Unde patet quod conveniens poena pro culpa non redditur, nisi plus contrarietur voluntati poena quam placeat culpa.

bestowing upon his will more than is right. Hence a return to the order of justice is effected by punishment, whereby some good is withdrawn from the sinner's will. So clearly a suitable punishment is not assigned for the sin unless the punishment is more contrary to the will than the sin was attractive to it.

CHAPTER 122

That not all punishment is contrary to the will in the same way

Non eodem autem modo omnis poena est contra voluntatem. Quaedam enim poena est contra id quod homo actu vult, et haec poena maxime sentitur; quaedam vero non contrariatur voluntati in actu sed in habitu, sicut cum aliquis privatur re aliqua, puta filio vel possessione, eo ignorante: unde per hoc non agitur actu aliquid contra eius voluntatem, esset autem contrarium voluntati si sciret. Quandoque vero poena contrariatur voluntati secundum naturam ipsius potentiae. Voluntas enim naturaliter ordinatur ad bonum. Unde si aliquis privetur virtute, quandoque quidem non est contra actualem voluntatem eius, quia forte virtutem contemnit; neque contra habitualem, quia forte est dispositus secundum habitum ad volendum contraria virtuti; est tamen contra naturalem rectitudinem voluntatis qua homo naturaliter appetit virtutem.

Ex quo etiam patet quod gradus poenarum dupliciter mensurari possunt: uno modo secundum quantitatem boni quod per poenam privatur; alio modo secundum quod magis vel minus est contrarium voluntati: quandoque enim minus est contrarium voluntati maiori bono privari quam privari minori.

Not all punishment is opposed to the will in the same way. Some punishments are opposed to what man actually wills; and this kind of punishment is felt most keenly. Some punishments are opposed not to the act of the will but to the habitual tendency of the will, as when a person is deprived of something, for instance, his son or his property, without his knowledge. In this case, nothing actually thwarts his will; but the withdrawal of the good would be against his will if he were aware of what was happening. At times a punishment is opposed to the will according to the very nature of that faculty. For the will is naturally ordered to what is good. Thus if a person is lacking in a virtue, this is not always opposed to his actual will, for he may, perhaps, despise this virtue; nor need it be against his habitual will, for he may, perhaps, have a habitual disposition of will toward what is contrary to the virtue. Nevertheless, such a privation is opposed to the natural rectitude of the will, whereby man naturally desires virtue.

Consequently, as is evident, the degrees of punishment may be measured by two standards: first, by the quantity of the good of which a man is deprived by his punishment; second, by the greater or less opposition it arouses in the will. For sometimes it is less contrary to the will to be deprived of a greater good than to be deprived of a lesser.

CHAPTER 123

That all things are ruled by divine providence

Ex praedictis autem manifestum esse potest quod omnia divina providentia gubernantur. Quaecumque enim ordinantur ad finem alicuius agentis ab illo agente diriguntur in finem sicut omnes qui sunt in exercitu ordinantur ad finem ducis qui est victoria, et ab ipso diriguntur in finem. Supra autem ostensum est quod omnia suis actionibus tendunt in finem divinae bonitatis; ab ipso igitur Deo, cuius hic finis proprius est, omnia diriguntur in finem. Hoc autem est providentia alicuius regi et gubernari; omnia igitur divina providentia reguntur.

Adhuc, ea quae deficere possunt et non semper eodem modo se habent, ordinari inveniuntur ab his quae semper eodem modo se habent, sicut omnes motus corporum inferiorum, qui defectibiles sunt, ordinem habent secundum invariabilem motum caelestis corporis. Omnes vero creaturae mutabiles aut defectibiles sunt. Nam in creaturis intellectualibus, quantum ex eorum natura est, defectus voluntariae actionis inveniri potest; creaturae vero aliae motu participant vel secundum generationem et corruptionem, vel secundum locum tantum: solus autem Deus est in quem nullus defectus cadere potest. Relinquitur igitur quod omnia alia ordinantur ab ipso.

Item, ea quae sunt per participationem reducuntur in id quod est per essentiam sicut in causam: omnia enim ignita suae ignitionis ignem causam habent aliquo modo. Cum igitur solus Deus per essentiam sit bonus, cetera vero omnia per quandam participationem complementum optineant bonitatis, necesse est quod omnia ad complementum bonitatis perducantur a Deo. Hoc autem est regi et gubernari; secundum hoc enim aliqua gubernantur vel reguntur quod in ordine boni statuuntur. Omnia igitur gubernantur et reguntur a Deo.

We can see from the foregoing that all things are governed by divine providence. For whatever is ordered to the end of a certain agent is directed toward that end by that agent. For example, all the soldiers in an army are ordered to the end intended by the commander, which is victory, and are directed by him to that end. Now, we showed above that all things tend by their actions to the divine goodness as their end. Hence all things are directed to this end by God himself, to whom this end properly belongs. To be thus directed is the same as to be ruled and governed by providence. Therefore, all things are ruled by divine providence.

Moreover, things that can fail, and that do not always remain constant, are found to be under the direction of beings that do remain constant. Thus all the movements of lower bodies, being defectible, are regulated in accordance with the undeviating movement of a heavenly body. But all creatures are changeable or defectible. As regards intellectual creatures, their very nature is such that deficiency in voluntary action can arise in them. Other creatures have some part in movement, either by way of generation and corruption, or at least according to place. God himself is the only being in whom no defect can arise. Consequently, all creatures are set in order by him.

Furthermore, whatever is by participation is traced back, as to its cause, to that which is by essence; for example, what is burning has fire in some way as the cause that ignited it. Since God alone is good by his very essence, and all other things obtain their full measure of goodness by some sort of participation, all beings must be brought to their full measure of goodness by God. But this is what it means to be ruled and governed; for things are governed or ruled by being established in the order of good. And so all things are governed and ruled by God.

CHAPTER 124

That God rules lower creatures by higher ones

Secundum hoc autem oportet quod inferiores creaturae a Deo per superiores regantur. Secundum hoc enim aliquae creaturae superiores dicuntur quod in bonitate perfectiores existunt; ordinem autem boni creaturae consequuntur a Deo inquantum reguntur ab ipso: sic igitur superiores creaturae plus participant de ordine divinae gubernationis quam inferiores. Quod autem magis participat quamcumque perfectionem, comparatur ad id quod minus ipsam participat, sicut actus ad potentiam et agens ad patiens; superiores igitur creaturae comparantur ad inferiores in ordine divinae providentiae sicut agentes ad patientes: per superiores igitur inferiores creature gubernantur.

Item, ad divinam bonitatem pertinet ut suam similitudinem communicet creaturis; sic enim propter suam bonitatem Deus omnia dicitur fecisse, ut ex supradictis patet. Ad perfectionem autem divinae bonitatis pertinet, et quod in se bonus sit et quod alia ad bonitatem inducat; utrumque igitur creaturae communicat, et quod in se bona sit et quod una aliam ad bonum inducat. Sic igitur per quasdam creaturas alias ad bonum ducit. Has autem oportet esse superiores creaturas: nam quod participat ab aliquo agente similitudinem formae ipsius et actionis, perfectius est eo quod participat similitudinem formae et non actionis, sicut luna perfectius recipit lumen a sole, quae non solum fit lucida sed etiam illuminat, quam corpora opaca quae illuminantur tantum et non illuminant. Deus igitur per creaturas superiores inferiores gubernat.

Adhuc, bonum multorum melius est quam bonum unius tantum, et per consequens est magis divinae bonitatis repraesentativum quae est bonum totius universi. Si autem creatura superior, quae abundantiorem bonitatem a Deo participat, non cooperaretur ad bonum inferiorum creaturarum, illa abundantia bonitatis esset unius tantum; per hoc autem fit communis multorum quod ad bonum multorum cooperatur: pertinet igitur hoc ad divinam bonitatem ut Deus per superiores creaturas inferiores regat.

We can see from this that lower creatures must be ruled by God through the agency of higher creatures. Some creatures are said to be higher in virtue of the fact that they are more perfect in goodness; but creatures obtain the order of the good from God inasmuch as they are governed by him. Consequently, higher creatures have a greater share in the order of divine government than lower creatures. But what has a greater share in any perfection is related to what has a smaller share in that perfection, as act is related to potency, and agent to patient. Therefore, higher creatures are related to lower creatures in the order of divine providence as agents are related to patients. Accordingly, lower creatures are governed through higher creatures.

Again, divine goodness communicates a likeness of itself to creatures. This is the sense in which God is said to have made all things for the sake of his goodness, as is clear from a previous chapter. To the perfection of divine goodness belongs both that God is good in himself, and that he leads other beings to goodness. Therefore, he shares both with creatures: they are good in themselves, and some lead others to goodness. In this way God brings some creatures to goodness through other creatures. Now, the latter must be higher creatures; for what receives a likeness of both form and action from some agent is more perfect than what receives a likeness of form but not of action. Thus the moon, which not only glows with light, but also illuminates other bodies, receives light from the sun more perfectly than do dark bodies, which are merely illuminated but do not illuminate. Therefore, God governs lower creatures by higher creatures.

Likewise, the good of many is better than the good of an individual, and so is more representative of the divine goodness, which is the good of the whole universe. If a higher creature, which receives more abundant goodness from God, did not cooperate in procuring the good of lower creatures, that abundance of goodness would be merely the good of an individual. But it becomes common to many by the fact that the more richly endowed creature cooperates in procuring the good of many. Hence the divine goodness requires that God should rule lower creatures by higher creatures.

Chapter 125

That lower intellectual substances are ruled by higher ones

Quia igitur intellectuales creaturae ceteris creaturis sunt superiores, ut ex praemissis patet, manifestum est quod per creaturas intellectuales omnes aliae creaturae gubernantur a Deo. Item, cum inter ipsas creaturas intellectuales quaedam aliis sint superiores, per superiores inferiores reguntur a Deo. Unde fit ut homines, qui infimum locum secundum naturae ordinem in substantiis intellectualibus tenent, gubernentur per superiores spiritus, qui eo quod divina hominibus annuntiant angeli vocantur, id est nuntii; ipsorum etiam angelorum inferiores per superiores reguntur, secundum quod in ipsis diversae hierarchiae, id est sacri principatus, et in singulis hierarchiis diversi ordines distinguuntur.

Since intellectual creatures excel other creatures, as is clear from what was said above, we can readily understand that God governs all other creatures through the agency of intellectual creatures. Likewise, since among intellectual creatures themselves some are higher than others, God rules the lower through the higher. Accordingly, the higher spirits govern men, who occupy the lowest place in the order of nature among intellectual substances. These are called angels, that is, 'messengers,' because they announce divine things to men. Among angels, too, the lower are directed by the higher. For they are distributed among various hierarchies, or sacred principalities; and each hierarchy is divided into different orders.

Chapter 126

Of the ranks and order of the angels

Et quia omnis substantiae intellectualis operatio inquantum huiusmodi ab intellectu procedit, oportet ut secundum diversum intelligentiae modum diversitas operationis et praelationis et ordinis in substantiis intellectualibus inveniatur. Intellectus autem quanto est sublimior seu dignior, tanto magis in altiori et universaliori causa rationes effectuum considerare potest. Superius etiam dictum est quod superior intellectus species intelligibiles universaliores habet.

Primus igitur intelligendi modus substantiis intellectualibus conveniens est ut in ipsa prima causa, scilicet Deo, effectuum rationes percipiant, et per consequens suorum operum, cum per eas Deus inferiores effectus dispensat. Et hoc est proprium primae hierarchiae, quae in tres ordines dividitur secundum tria quae in qualibet operativa arte considerantur quorum primum est finis ex quo rationes operum sumuntur, secundum est rationes operum in mente artificis existentes, tertium est applicationes rationum ad effectus. Primi igitur ordinis est in ipso summo bono, prout est ultimus finis rerum, de effectibus edoceri: unde ab ardore amoris seraphim vocantur, quasi ardentes vel incendentes, amoris enim obiectum est bonum. Secundi vero ordinis est effectus Dei in ipsis rationibus intelligibilibus contemplari, prout sunt in Deo: unde cherubin dicuntur a plenitudine scientiae. Tertii vero ordinis est considerare in ipso Deo quomodo a creaturis participetur rationibus intelligibili-

Since every action of an intellectual substance, as such, proceeds from the intellect, diversity of operation, of rank, and of order among intellectual substances follows diversity in their manner of understanding. In proportion to its eminence or dignity, the intellect can contemplate the natures of effects in their higher and more universal cause. Also, as we remarked above, the intelligible species of a higher intellect are more universal.

The first way of understanding suitable to intellectual substances is the knowledge imparted to them of effects, and hence of their own works, in the first cause itself, namely, in God; for it is through them that God carries out lower effects. This knowledge is proper to the first hierarchy, which is divided into three orders corresponding to the three characteristics discerned in any operative art. The first of these is the end from which the exemplars of the works are derived; the second is the exemplars of the works as existing in the mind of the artificer; the third is the application of the exemplars to the effects. Consequently, the first order has the privilege of being instructed about the effects of things in the supreme Good itself, regarded as the last end. For this reason angels of the first order are called seraphim from the ardor of love, as though they were aflame or on fire; for the object of love is the good. The second order has the function of contemplating God's effects in their intelligible exemplars as they exist in God. Hence

bus ad effectus applicatis: unde ab habendo in se Deum insidentem throni sunt dicti.

Secundus autem intelligendi modus est rationes effectuum prout sunt in causis universalibus considerare, et hoc est proprium secundae hierarchiae; quae iterum in tres ordines dividitur secundum tria quae ad universales causas, et maxime secundum intellectum agentes, pertinent. Quorum primum est praeordinare quae agenda sunt, unde in artificialibus supremae artes praeceptivae sunt, quae architectonicae dicuntur: et ex hoc primus ordo huius hierarchiae dominationes vocatur, domini enim est praecipere et praeordinare. Secundum vero quod in causis universalibus invenitur est aliquid primo movens ad opus, quasi principatum executionis habens: et ex hoc secundus ordo huius hierarchiae principatus vocatur secundum Gregorium, vel virtutes secundum Dionysium, ut virtutes intelligantur ex eo quod primo operari maxime est virtuosum. Tertium autem quod in causis universalibus reperitur est aliquid impedimenta executionis removens: unde et tertius ordo huius hierarchiae est potestatum, quarum officium est omne quod posset obviare executioni divini imperii cohercere; unde et daemones arcere dicuntur.

Tertius vero intelligendi modus est rationes effectuum in ipsis effectibus considerare, et hoc est proprium tertiae hierarchiae; quae immediate nobis praeficitur qui ex effectibus cognitionem de ipsis effectibus accipimus. Quae etiam tres ordines habet, quorum infimus angeli nominantur ex eo quod hominibus annuntiant ea quae ad eorum gubernationem pertinent, unde et hominum custodes dicuntur. Supra hunc autem est ordo archangelorum, per quem hominibus ea quae sunt supra rationem nuntiantur, sicut mysteria fidei. Supremus autem huius hierarchiae ordo secundum Gregorium virtutes dicuntur, ex eo quod ea quae sunt supra naturam operantur in argumentum eorum quae nobis supra rationem nuntiantur: unde ad virtutes pertinere dicitur miracula facere. Secundum Dionysium vero supremus ordo huius hierarchiae principatus dicitur, ut principes intelligamus qui singulis gentibus praesunt, angelos qui singulis hominibus, archangelos qui singularibus hominibus ea quae sunt ad communem salutem pertinentia denuntiant.

Et quia inferior potentia in virtute superioris agit, inferior ordo ea quae sunt superioris exercet inquantum agit eius virtute, superiores vero ea quae sunt inferiorum propria excellentius habent; unde omnia in eis sunt

angels of this order are called cherubim, from the fullness of their knowledge. To the third order belongs the consideration in God himself of how creatures share in intelligible exemplars as adapted to effects. And so angels of this order are called thrones, from having God seated within them.

The second way of understanding is to contemplate the exemplars of effects as they exist in universal causes. This is proper to the second hierarchy, which is likewise divided into three orders, corresponding to the three characteristics that pertain to universal causes, especially such as operate under the guidance of the intellect. The first of these characteristics is to plan beforehand what is to be done. Thus among artificers the highest arts are directive, and are called architectonic. From this fact angels belonging to the first order of this hierarchy are known as dominations; for direction and planning are functions of a master (or *dominus*). The second characteristic observed in universal causes is something that initiates action toward the work, as having primacy of execution. For this reason angels belonging to the second order of this hierarchy are called principalities, according to Gregory, or virtues, according to Dionysius, understanding virtues in the sense that to take the initiative in action is virtuosity in a high degree. The third characteristic discerned in universal causes is the removal of obstacles to execution. And so the third order of this hierarchy is that of the powers, whose office is to constrain whatever could impede the execution of the divine command; hence, also, the powers are said to hold demons in check.

The third way of understanding is to contemplate the exemplars of effects in the effects themselves. And this is proper to the third hierarchy, which is placed in immediate charge of us, who obtain knowledge of effects from effects themselves. This hierarchy, too, has three orders. The lowest of these is that of the angels, who are so called because they announce to men details that pertain to their government; hence they are also called guardians of men. Above this order is that of the archangels. The office of this order is to announce to men matters that transcend reason, such as the mysteries of faith. The highest order of this hierarchy is said by Gregory to be that of the virtues, because they perform deeds beyond the power of nature in proof of the mysteries transcending reason that are announced to us. Consequently, the working of miracles is said to pertain to the virtues. According to Dionysius, however, the highest order of this hierarchy is that of the principalities; in his reckoning we are to understand that the princes are they who have charge over individual peoples, while the angels have charge over individual men, and the archangels announce to individual men those affairs that pertain to the salvation of all.

Since a lower power acts in virtue of a higher power, a lower order performs actions proper to a higher order by acting in virtue of that higher power. But the higher orders possess in a more eminent way whatever is proper to the

quodammodo communia, tamen propria nomina sortiuntur ex his quae unicuique secundum se conveniunt. Infimus autem ordo commune sibi nomen retinuit quasi in virtute omnium agens. Et quia superioris est in inferiorem agere, actio vero intelligibilis est instruere vel docere, superiores angeli inquantum inferiores instruunt dicuntur eos purgare, illuminare et perficere. Purgare quidem, inquantum nescientiam removent; illuminare vero, inquantum suo lumine inferiorum intellectus confortant ad aliquid altius capiendum; perficere vero, inquantum eos ad superioris scientiae perfectionem perducunt. Nam haec tria ad assumptionem scientiae pertinent, ut Dionysius dicit.

Nec tamen per hoc removetur quin omnes angeli etiam infimi divinam essentiam videant: licet enim unusquisque beatorum spirituum Deum per essentiam videat, unus tamen alio eum perfectius videt, ut ex superioribus patere potest. Quanto autem aliqua causa perfectius cognoscitur, tanto plures effectus eius cognoscuntur in ea; de effectibus igitur divinis quos superiores angeli cognoscunt in Deo prae aliis, inferiores instruunt, non autem de essentia divina quam omnes immediate vident.

lower orders. Thus all things are in a certain sense common to the various orders. However, they receive their proper names from properties that are characteristic of each order. Nevertheless, the lowest order of all retains the common name of angels for itself, for the reason that it acts, as it were, in virtue of all the rest. Furthermore, since the higher naturally influences the lower, and since intellectual action consists in instructing or teaching, the higher angels, in instructing the lower angels, are said to purify, illuminate, and perfect them. Higher angels purify the lower angels by removing their ignorance. They illuminate them by fortifying the intellects of the lower angels with their own light, thus enabling them to comprehend higher objects. And they perfect lower angels by guiding them to the perfection of higher knowledge. These three operations pertain to the acquisition of knowledge, as Dionysius remarks.

This inequality does not prevent all the angels, even the lowest, from seeing the divine essence. Even though each of the blessed spirits sees God in his essence, some may behold him more perfectly than others. This should be clear from what was said above. However, the more perfectly a cause is known, the more numerous are the effects discerned in it. The divine effects which the higher angels perceive in God more clearly than the other angels constitute the subject matter in which they instruct the lower angels. But higher angels do not instruct lower angels concerning the divine essence, which they all perceive directly.

CHAPTER 127

That lower bodies, but not the human intellect, are disposed by higher bodies

Sicut igitur intellectualium substantiarum una per alteram divinitus gubernatur, inferior scilicet per superiorem, ita et inferiora corpora per superiora divinitus disponuntur. Unde omnes motus inferiorum a motibus corporum caelestium causantur, et ex virtute caelestium corporum haec inferiora formas et species consequuntur, sicut et rationes rerum intelligibiles ad inferiores spiritus per superiores deveniunt.

Cum autem intellectualis substantia in ordine rerum omnibus corporibus praeferatur, non est conveniens secundum praedictum providentiae ordinem ut per aliquam corporalem substantiam intellectualis quaecumque substantia regatur a Deo. Cum igitur anima humana sit intellectualis substantia, impossibile est quod, secundum hoc quod est intelligens et volens, secundum motus corporum caelestium disponatur; neque igitur in intellectum humanum neque in voluntatem corpora caelestia directe impressionem habent.

Just as among intellectual substances, therefore, some are divinely governed by others, that is, the lower by the higher, so too lower bodies are controlled, in God's plan, by higher bodies. Hence every movement of lower bodies is caused by the movements of heavenly bodies. Lower bodies acquire forms and species from the influence thus exercised by heavenly bodies, just as the intelligible exemplars of things descend to lower spirits through higher spirits.

However, since an intellectual substance is superior to all bodies in the hierarchy of beings, the order of providence has suitably disposed matters in such a way that no intellectual substance is ruled by God through a bodily substance. Accordingly, since the human soul is an intellectual substance, it cannot, so far as it is endowed with intelligence and will, be subject to the movements of heavenly bodies. Heavenly bodies cannot directly act upon or influence either the human intellect or the human will.

Item, nullum corpus agit nisi per motum; omne igitur quod ab aliquo corpore patitur, movetur ab eo. Animam autem humanam secundum intellectivam partem, in qua est voluntas, impossibile est motu corporali moveri, cum intellectus non sit actus alicuius organi corporalis; impossibile est igitur quod anima humana secundum intellectum aut voluntatem a corporibus caelestibus aliquid patiatur.

Adhuc, ea quae ex impressione corporum caelestium in istis inferioribus proveniunt naturalia sunt. Si igitur operationes intellectus et voluntatis ex impressione caelestium corporum provenirent, ex naturali instinctu procederent, et sic homo non differret in suis actibus ab aliis animalibus, quae naturali instinctu moventur ad suas actiones; et periret liberum arbitrium et consilium et electio et omnia huiusmodi quae homo prae ceteris animalibus habet.

Again, no body acts except by movement. Hence whatever is acted upon by a body is moved by it. But the human soul, according to its intellectual part, in which is the will, cannot be moved by bodily movement, since the intellect is not the act of any bodily organ. Therefore, it is impossible that the human soul, as far as intellect and will are concerned, suffer any influence emanating from heavenly bodies.

Furthermore, things that come about in lower bodies from the impression of heavenly bodies are natural. Therefore, if the operations of the intellect and will resulted from the impression made by heavenly bodies, they would proceed from natural instinct. And so man would not differ in his activity from other animals, which are moved to their actions by natural instinct. And thus free will and deliberation and choice and all perfections of this sort, which distinguish man from other animals, would perish.

CHAPTER 128

How the human intellect is indirectly subject to heavenly bodies

Sed tamen considerandum est quod intellectus humanus a potentiis sensitivis accipit suae cognitionis originem: unde perturbata phantastica et imaginativa vel memorativa parte animae perturbatur cognitio intellectus, et praedictis potentiis bene se habentibus convenientior fit acceptio intellectus. Similiter etiam immutatio appetitus sensitivi aliquid operatur ad immutationem voluntatis, quae est appetitus rationis, ex ea parte qua bonum apprehensum est obiectum voluntatis; ex eo enim quod diversimode dispositi sumus secundum concupiscentiam, iram et timorem et alias passiones, diversimode nobis aliquid bonum vel malum videtur.

Omnes autem potentiae sensitivae partis, sive sint apprehensivae sive appetitivae, quarundam corporalium partium actus sunt, quibus immutatis necesse est per accidens ipsas quoque potentias immutari. Quia igitur immutatio inferiorum corporum subiacet motui caeli, eidem motui etiam potentiarum sensitivarum operationes licet per accidens subduntur, et sic indirecte motus caelestis aliquid operatur ad actum intellectus et voluntatis humanae, inquantum scilicet per passiones voluntas ad aliquid inclinatur.

Sed quia voluntas passionibus non subditur ut earum impetum ex necessitate sequatur, sed magis in potestate sua habet reprimere passiones secundum iudicium rationis, consequens est ut nec etiam impressionibus corporum caelestium in corpora humana voluntas hu-

Nevertheless, we should not lose sight of the fact that the human intellect is indebted to the sense powers for the origin of its knowledge. This is why intellectual knowledge is thrown into confusion when the soul's faculties of phantasm, imagination, or memory are impaired. On the other hand, when these powers are in good order, intellectual apprehension becomes more efficient. Likewise, a modification in the sensitive appetite tends to bring about a change in the will, which is a rational appetite, as we know from the fact that the object of the will is the good as apprehended. According as we are variously disposed in the matter of concupiscence, anger, fear, and other emotions, a thing will at different times appear to us as good or evil.

Now, all the powers of the sensitive part of our soul, whether they are apprehensive or appetitive, are the acts of certain bodily organs. If these undergo modification, the faculties themselves must, indirectly, undergo some change. Therefore, since change in lower bodies is influenced by the movement of the heavens, the operations of the sensitive faculties are also subject to such movement, although only accidentally. And thus heavenly movement has some indirect influence on the activity of the human intellect and will, so far as the will may be inclined this way or that by the emotions.

Nevertheless, since the will is not subject to the emotions in such a way as necessarily to follow their enticement, but on the contrary has it in its power to repress emotion by the judgment of reason, the human will is not subject to impressions emanating from heavenly bodies. It retains free

mana subdatur, sed liberum iudicium habet eas sequi vel resistere cum videbitur expedire: quod tantum sapientum est, sequi vero corporales passiones et inclinationes est multorum, qui scilicet sapientia et virtute carent.

judgment either to follow or to resist their attractions, as may seem to it expedient. Only the wise act thus; the masses follow the lead of bodily emotions and urgings. For they lack wisdom and virtue.

CHAPTER 129

That God alone, and not a created thing, moves the will of man

Cum autem omne mutabile et multiforme in aliquod primum immobile et unum reducatur sicut in causam, hominis autem intelligentia et voluntas mutabilis et multiformis appareat, necesse est quod in aliquam superiorem causam immobilem et uniformem reducantur. Et quia non reducuntur sicut in causam in corpora caelestia, ut ostensum est, oportet eas reducere in causas altiores.

Aliter autem se habet circa intelligentiam et voluntatem: nam actus intellectus est secundum quod res intellectae sunt in intellectu, actus autem voluntatis attenditur secundum inclinationem voluntatis ad res volitas. Intellectus igitur natus est perfici ab aliquo exteriori quod comparetur ad ipsum sicut ad potentiam: unde homo ad actum intellectus adiuvari potest a quolibet exteriori quod est magis perfectum secundum esse intelligibile, non solum a Deo, sed etiam ab angelo et etiam ab homine magis instructo, aliter tamen et aliter.

Homo enim iuvatur ab homine ad intelligendum per hoc quod unus alteri proponit intelligibile quod non considerabat, non autem ita quod lumen intellectus unius hominis ab altero homine perficiatur, quia utriusque lumen naturale est unius speciei.

Sed quia lumen naturale angeli est secundum naturam sublimius naturali lumine hominis, homo ab angelo iuvari potest ad intelligendum non solum ex parte obiecti quod ei ab angelo proponitur, sed etiam ex parte luminis quod per lumen angeli confortatur. Non tamen lumen naturale hominis ab angelo est, cum natura rationalis animae, quae per creationem esse accipit, non nisi a Deo instituta sit;

Deus igitur ad intelligendum hominem iuvat non solum ex parte obiecti quod homini proponitur a Deo, aut per additionem luminis, sed etiam per hoc quod ipsum lumen naturale hominis quo intellectualis est a Deo est; et per hoc etiam quod, cum ipse sit veritas prima a qua omnis alia veritas certitudinem habet, sicut secundae propositiones a primis in syllogismis demonstrativis, nihil intellectui certum fieri potest nisi virtute

Everything that is changeable and multiform is traced back, as to its cause, to some first principle that is immobile and is one. Since man's intellect and will are clearly changeable and multiform, they must be traced back to some higher cause that is immobile and uniform. The heavenly bodies are not the cause to which they are reduced, as we have shown; therefore they must be traced back to yet higher causes.

In this matter the case of the intellect differs from that of the will. The act of the intellect is brought about by the presence of the things understood in the intellect; but the act of the will is accounted for by the inclination of the will toward the things willed. Thus the intellect is adapted by its nature to be perfected by something external that is related to it as act to potency. Hence man can be aided to elicit an act of the intellect by anything external that is more perfect in intelligible being: not only by God but also by an angel or even by a man who is better informed; but differently in each instance.

A man is helped to understand by a man when one of them proposes to the other an intelligible object not previously contemplated; but not in such a way that the light of the intellect of one man is perfected by the other, because the natural light of both is of the same species.

But the natural light of an angel is by nature of a higher excellence than the natural light of man, and so an angel can aid a man to understand, not only on the part of the object proposed to him by the angel, but also on the part of the light, which is strengthened by the angel's light. However, man's natural light does not come from an angel, for the nature of the rational soul, which receives existence through creation, is produced by God alone.

God helps man to understand, not only on the part of the object proposed by God to man, or by an increase of light, but also by the very fact that man's natural light, which is what makes him intellectual, is from God. Moreover, God himself is the first truth from which all other truth has its certitude, just as secondary propositions in demonstrative sciences derive their certitude from primary propositions. For this reason nothing can become certain for the

divina, sicut nec conclusiones fiunt certae in scientiis nisi secundum virtutem primorum principiorum.

· Sed cum actus voluntatis sit inclinatio quaedam ab interiori ad exterius procedens et comparetur inclinationibus naturalibus, sicut inclinationes naturales rebus naturalibus sunt a causa suae naturae, ita actus voluntatis a solo Deo est, qui solus causa est naturae rationalis voluntatem habentis. Unde patet quod non est contra arbitrii libertatem si Deus voluntatem hominis movet, sicut non est contra naturam quod Deus in rebus naturalibus operatur, sed tam inclinatio naturalis quam voluntaria a Deo est, utraque proveniens secundum conditionem rei cuius est: sic enim Deus res movet secundum quod competit earum naturae.

Patet igitur ex praedictis quod in corpus humanum et virtutes corporeas eius imprimere possunt corpora caelestia, sicut et in alia corpora; non autem in intellectum, sed hoc potest creatura intellectualis. In voluntatem autem solus Deus imprimere potest.

intellect except through God's power, just as conclusions do not achieve certitude in science except in virtue of primary principles.

But with regard to the will, its act is a certain inclination flowing from the interior to the exterior, and has much in common with natural inclinations. Accordingly, as natural inclinations are placed in natural things exclusively by the cause of their nature, the act of the will is from God alone, for he alone is the cause of a rational nature endowed with will. Therefore, if God moves man's will, this is evidently not opposed to freedom of choice, just as God's activity in natural things is not contrary to their nature. Both the natural inclination and the voluntary inclination are from God; each of them issues in action according to the condition of the thing to which it pertains. For thus God moves things in a way that is consonant with their nature.

From all that has been said, it is clear that heavenly bodies can exert an influence on the human body and its bodily powers, as they can on other bodies. But they cannot influence the intellect, although an intellectual creature can. And God alone can act upon the will.

CHAPTER 130

That God is in all things and extends his providence to all

Quia vero causae secundae non agunt nisi per virtutem primae causae, sicut instrumenta agunt per directionem artis, necesse est quod omnia alia agentia per quae Deus ordinem suae gubernationis adimplet, virtute ipsius Dei agant. Agere igitur cuiuslibet ipsorum a Deo causatur, sicut motus mobilis a motione moventis; movens autem et motum oportet esse simul: oportet igitur quod Deus cuilibet agenti assit interius quasi in ipso agens, dum ipsum ad agendum movet.

Adhuc, non solum agere agentium secundorum causatur a Deo sed ipsum eorum esse, sicut in superioribus est ostensum. Non autem sic intelligendum est quod esse rerum causetur a Deo sicut esse domus causatur ab aedificatore, quo remoto adhuc remanet esse domus. Aedificator enim non causat esse domus nisi inquantum movet ad esse domus, quae quidem motio est factio domus; unde directe est causa fieri ipsius domus, quod quidem cessat aedificatore remoto. Deus autem est per se directe causa ipsius esse, quasi esse communicans omnibus rebus, sicut sol communicat lumen aeri et aliis quae ab ipso illuminantur. Et sic, sicut ad conservationem luminis in aere requiritur perseverans illuminatio solis, ita ad hoc quod res conserventur in esse requiritur quod Deus esse incessanter tribuat rebus; et sic omnia non so-

Because second causes do not act except through the power of the first cause, as instruments operate under the direction of art, it is necessary that all the agents through which God carries out the order of his government act only through the power of God himself. The action of any of them is caused by God, just as the movement of a mobile object is caused by the motion of the mover. In such event the mover and the one moved must be simultaneous. Hence God must be inwardly present to any agent as acting therein whenever he moves the agent to act.

Moreover, not only the action of secondary agents, but their very existence, is caused by God, as was shown above. However, we are not to suppose that the existence of things is caused by God in the same way as the existence of a house is caused by its builder. When the builder departs, the house still remains standing. For the builder causes the existence of the house only in the sense that he moves toward the house's existence, and his motion is the building of the house. Thus the builder is directly the cause of the becoming of the house, a process that ceases when he leaves. But God is directly, by himself, the cause of a creature's very being, and communicates existence to all things just as the sun communicates light to the air and to other things illuminated by the sun. The continuous shining of the sun is required for the preservation of light in the air; similarly,

lum inquantum esse incipiunt, sed etiam inquantum in esse conservantur, comparantur ad Deum sicut factum ad faciens. Faciens autem et factum oportet esse simul, sicut movens et motum; oportet igitur Deum adesse omnibus rebus inquantum esse habent. Esse autem est id quod rebus omnibus intimius adest; oportet igitur Deum in omnibus rebus esse.

Item, quicumque exequitur suae providentiae ordinem per aliquas medias causas, necesse est quod effectus illarum mediarum causarum cognoscat et ordinet, alioquin extra ordinem providentiae suae caderent; et tanto perfectior est providentia gubernantis, quanto eius cognitio et ordinatio magis descendit ad singularia, quia si aliquid singularium cognitioni gubernantis subtrahitur, determinatio ipsius singularis eius providentiam diffugiet. Ostensum est autem supra quod necesse est omnia divinae providentiae subdi; et manifestum est quod divina providentia perfectissima est, quia quidquid de Deo dicitur secundum maximum convenit ei: oportet igitur quod ordinatio providentiae ipsius se extendat usque ad minimos effectus.

God must unceasingly confer existence on things if they are to persevere in existence. Thus all things are related to God as an object made is to its maker, and this not only so far as they begin to exist, but so far as they continue to exist. But a maker and the object made must be simultaneous, just as in the case of a mover and the object moved. Hence God is necessarily present to all things to the extent that they have existence. But existence is that which is the most intimately present in all things. Therefore, God must be in all things.

Likewise, whoever carries out the order he has foreseen through the agency of intermediate causes must know and arrange the effects of these intermediate causes. Otherwise, the effects would occur outside the order he has foreseen. The prearranged plan of a governor is more perfect in proportion as his knowledge and design descend to details. For if any detail escapes the governor's awareness, the disposition of that detail will elude his foresight. We showed above that all things are necessarily subject to divine providence; and divine providence must evidently be most perfect, because whatever is predicated of God must befit him in the highest possible degree. Consequently, his providential arrangements must extend to the most minute effects.

CHAPTER 131

That God disposes all things immediately

Secundum hoc igitur patet quod, licet rerum gubernatio fiat a Deo mediantibus causis secundis quantum pertinet ad providentiae executionem, tamen ipsa dispositio seu ordinatio divinae providentiae immediate se extendit ad omnia. Non enim sic prima et universalia ordinat ut ultima et singularia aliis disponenda committat; hoc enim apud homines agitur propter debilitatem cognitionis ipsorum, quae non potest simul vacare pluribus: unde superiores gubernatores disponunt de magnis et minima aliis disponenda committunt. Sed Deus simul multa potest cognoscere, ut supra ostensum est, unde non retrahitur ab ordinatione maximorum per hoc quod dispensat minima.

In the light of the foregoing, it is clear that, although God's government of things is effected through the agency of secondary causes, as far as the carrying out of his providence is concerned, yet the plan itself or ordination of divine providence extends directly to all details. God does not arrange the first and universal matters in such a way as to turn over to others the disposal of the last and most particular things. Men act thus because of the limitations of their knowledge, which cannot at any one time take in many items. This is why higher rulers personally take charge of great concerns, and entrust the management of unimportant affairs to others. But God can take cognizance of a multitude of things simultaneously, as was indicated above. Hence the fact that he attends to the slightest details does not keep him from organizing the weightiest matters.

CHAPTER 132

Arguments that seem to show that God does not have providence over particulars

Posset tamen alicui videri quod singularia non disponantur a Deo. Nullus enim per suam providentiam disponit nisi quae cognoscit. Deo autem singularium cognitio deesse videri potest ex hoc quod singularia non intellectu sed sensu cognoscuntur; in Deo autem, qui omnino incorporeus est, non potest esse sensitiva, sed solum intellectiva cognitio. Potest igitur alicui videri ex hoc, quod singularia divina providentia non ordinentur.

Item, cum singularia sint infinita, infinitorum autem non possit esse cognitio, infinitum enim inquantum huiusmodi ignotum est, videtur quod singularia divinam cognitionem et providentiam effugiant.

Adhuc, singularium multa contingentia sunt; horum autem non potest esse certa scientia: cum igitur scientiam Dei oporteat esse certissimam, videtur quod singularia non cognoscantur nec dispensentur a Deo.

Praeterea, singularia non omnia simul sunt, quia quibusdam succedentibus alia corrumpuntur. Eorum autem quae non sunt non potest esse scientia; si igitur singularium Deus scientiam habeat, sequetur quod quaedam scire incipiat et desinat, ex quo sequitur eum esse mutabilem. Non igitur videtur singularium cognitor et dispositor esse.

Nevertheless, some may think that singulars are not arranged by God. For a person arranges by planning only what he knows. But knowledge of singulars may well seem to be lacking in God, for the reason that singulars are known not by the intellect but by the senses. God, who is wholly non-bodily, can have no sense knowledge, but only intellectual knowledge. Consequently, singulars may seem to lie outside the scope of divine providence.

Moreover, singulars are infinite, and knowledge of infinity is impossible, since the infinite as such is unknown. Therefore, singulars seemingly escape the divine knowledge and providence.

Again, many singulars are contingent. But it is impossible to have certain knowledge of such things. Accordingly, since God's knowledge must be absolutely certain, it seems that singulars are not known or regulated by God.

Besides, singulars do not all exist simultaneously, for some things decay only to have others take their place. But there can be no knowledge of non-existent things. Hence, if God has knowledge of singulars, there must be some things which he begins and ceases to know, and this would lead to the conclusion that he is mutable. Apparently, therefore, he does not know and arrange singulars.

CHAPTER 133

Refutation of the aforesaid arguments

Sed haec facile solvuntur, si quis rei veritatem consideret. Cum enim Deus se ipsum perfecte cognoscat, oportet quod cognoscat omne quod in ipso est quocumque modo. Cum autem ab ipso sit omnis essentia et virtus entis creati, quod autem est ab aliquo virtute in ipso est, necesse est quod se ipsum cognoscens cognoscat essentiam entis creati et quidquid virtute in eo est; et sic cognoscit omnia singularia quae virtute sunt in ipso et in aliis suis causis.

Nec est simile de cognitione intellectus divini et nostri, ut prima ratio procedebat. Nam intellectus noster cognitionem de rebus accipit per species abstractas, quae sunt similitudines formarum et non materiae, nec materialium dispositionum quae sunt individuationis principia: unde intellectus noster singularia cognoscere non potest, sed solum universalia. Intellectus autem divinus cognoscit res per essentiam suam, in qua sicut

But these objections are easily answered if we consider the truth of the matter. God knows himself perfectly, and therefore he must have knowledge of all that exists in himself in any manner whatever. Since every essence and power of created being is from him, and since whatever comes from anyone exists virtually in him, we necessarily conclude that in knowing himself he knows the essence of a created being and whatever is virtually contained in him. And thus he knows all the singulars that are virtually in him and in all their other causes.

The knowledge possessed by the divine intellect is not like our knowledge, as the first objection urged. Our intellect derives knowledge of things through the species it abstracts, and these are the likenesses of forms and not of matter or of material dispositions, which are principles of individuation. Therefore, our intellect cannot know particulars, but only universals. But the divine intellect knows things through its own essence, in which, as in the first

in primo principio virtute continetur non solum forma sed etiam materia; et ideo non solum universalium, sed singularium cognitor est.

Similiter etiam non est inconveniens Deum infinita cognoscere, quamvis intellectus noster infinita cognoscere non possit. Intellectus enim noster non potest simul actu plura considerare, et sic si infinita cognosceret considerando ea, oporteret quod numeraret infinita unum post unum, quod est contra rationem infiniti; sed virtute et in potentia intellectus noster infinita cognoscere potest, utpote omnes species numerorum vel proportionum, inquantum habet sufficiens principium ad omnia cognoscenda. Deus autem simul multa cognoscere potest, ut supra ostensum est; et id per quod omnia cognoscit, scilicet sua essentia, est sufficiens principium omnia cognoscendi, non solum quae sunt sed quae esse possunt. Sicut igitur intellectus noster potentia et virtute cognoscit infinita quorum cognitionis principium habet, ita Deus omnia infinita actu considerat.

Manifestum est etiam quod, licet singularia corruptibilia et temporalia non simul sint, tamen eorum Deus simul cognitionem habet: cognoscit enim ea secundum modum sui esse, quod est aeternum et sine successione. Sicut igitur materialia immaterialiter et multa per unum cognoscit, sic et quae non simul sunt uno intuitu conspicit: et sic non oportet quod eius cognitioni aliquid addatur vel subtrahatur per hoc quod singularia cognoscit.

Ex quo etiam manifestum fit quod de contingentibus certam cognitionem habet, quia etiam antequam fiant intuetur ea prout sunt actu in suo esse, et non solum prout sunt futura et virtute in suis causis, sicut nos aliqua futura cognoscere possumus. Contingentia autem, licet prout sunt in suis causis virtute futura existentia non sint determinata ad unum, ut de eis certa cognitio haberi possit, tamen prout sunt actu in suo esse iam sunt determinata ad unum, et potest de eis certa haberi cognitio: nam Socratem sedere dum sedet, per certitudinem visionis cognoscere possumus. Et similiter Deus per certitudinem cognoscit omnia, quaecumque per totum decursum temporis aguntur, in suo aeterno: nam aeternitas sua praesentialitate totum temporis decursum attingit et ultra transcendit; ut sic consideremus Deum in sua aeternitate fluxum temporis cognoscere, sicut qui in altitudine speculae constitutus totum transitum viatorum simul intuetur.

principle of being, is virtually contained not only form, but matter. And so God knows not only universals but also particulars.

Likewise, God is able to know an infinite number of objects, even though our intellect cannot know the infinite. Our intellect cannot actually contemplate many things at the same time. Hence, if it knew and considered an infinite number of objects, it would have to number them one by one, which is contrary to the very notion of infinity. However, our intellect can know infinity virtually and potentially: for example, it can know all the species of numbers or of proportions, seeing that it possesses an adequate principle for knowing all things. But God can know many things simultaneously, as was indicated above; and that whereby he knows all things (namely, his essence) is an adequate principle for knowing not only all that is, but all that can be. Therefore, as our intellect potentially and virtually knows those infinite objects for which it has a principle of cognition, so God actually contemplates all the infinite objects.

Furthermore, although bodily and temporal particulars do not exist simultaneously, God surely has simultaneous knowledge of them. For he knows them according to his manner of being, which is eternal and without succession. Consequently, as he knows material things in an immaterial way, and many things through one, so in a single glance he beholds objects that do not exist at the same time. And so his knowledge of particulars does not involve the consequence that anything is added to, or subtracted from, his knowledge.

This also makes it clear that he has certain knowledge of contingent things. Even before they come into being, he sees them as they are in act in their own being, and not merely as things yet to come and as virtually present in their causes, in the way we are able to know some future things. Contingent things, regarded as future realities virtually present in their causes, are not sufficiently determinate to admit of certain knowledge about them; but, regarded as actually possessing existence, they are determinate, and hence certain knowledge of them is possible. Thus we can know, through vision's certitude, that Socrates is sitting while he is seated. With like certitude God knows, in his eternity, all that takes place throughout the whole course of time: for his eternity is in present contact with the whole course of time, and even passes beyond time. And thus we may contemplate that God knows the flight of time in his eternity, in the way that a person standing on top of a watchtower embraces in a single glance a whole caravan of passing travelers.

CHAPTER 134

That God alone knows singular future contingents

Manifestum est autem quod hoc modo futura contingentia cognoscere prout sunt actu in suo esse, quod est certitudinem de ipsis habere, solius Dei proprium est, cui proprie et vere competit aeternitas; unde futurorum praenunciatio certa ponitur esse divinitatis signum, secundum illud Ysaiae XL:23 *Futura quaoque nuncietis et dicemus quia dii estis vos.* Sed cognoscere futura in suis causis etiam aliis competere potest; sed haec cognitio non est certa sed coniecturalis magis, nisi circa effectus qui de necessitate ex suis causis sequuntur: et per hunc modum medicus pronunciat infirmitates futuras et nauta tempestates.

Now it is clear that to know future contingents in this way, as actually existing (which is to have certitude about them), is restricted to God alone, to whom alone belongs eternity in the true and proper sense. For this reason, certain prediction of future events is accounted a proof of divinity. This accords with Isaiah 41:23: *Tell us what is to come hereafter, that we may know that you are gods.* Of course, others can know future events in their causes, but such knowledge is not certain, but is rather conjectural, except as regards effects that necessarily flow from their causes. In this way a physician foretells future illnesses, and a sailor predicts storms.

CHAPTER 135

That God is in all things by power, essence, and presence, and disposes all immediately

Sic igitur nihil impedit quin Deus etiam singularium effectuum cognitionem habeat et eos immediate ordinet per se ipsum, licet per causas medias exequatur. Sed et in ipsa executione quodammodo immediate se habet ad omnes effectus, inquantum omnes causae mediae agunt in virtute causae primae, ut quodammodo ipse in omnibus agere videatur; et omnia opera secundarum causarum ei possunt attribui sicut artifici attribuitur opus instrumenti: convenientius enim dicitur quod faber facit cultellum quam martellus. Habet etiam se immediate ad omnes effectus, inquantum ipse est per se causa essendi et omnia ab ipso servantur in esse.

Thus there is no reason why God should not have knowledge of singular effects, or why he should not directly order them by himself, even though he may carry them out through intermediate causes. However, in the very execution he is, in some fashion, in immediate touch with all effects to the extent that all intermediate causes operate in virtue of the first cause, so that in a certain way he himself appears to act in them all. Thus all the achievements of secondary causes can be attributed to him, as the effect produced by a tool is ascribed to the artisan; for it is more fittingly said that an artisan makes the knife than that a hammer does. God is also in immediate contact with all effects inasmuch as he is the essential cause of their existence, and so far as everything is kept in being by him.

Et secundum hos tres immediationis modos dicitur Deus in omnibus esse per essentiam, potentiam et praesentiam. Per essentiam quidem, inquantum esse cuiuslibet est quaedam participatio divini esse, et sic essentia divina cuilibet existenti adest inquantum habet esse, sicut causa proprio effectui; per potentiam vero, inquantum omnia in virtute ipsius agunt; per praesentiam vero, inquantum ipse immediate omnia ordinat et disponit.

Corresponding to these three immediate modes of influence, God is said to be in everything by essence, power, and presence. He is in everything by his essence inasmuch as the existence of each thing is a certain participation in the divine essence, and thus the divine essence is present to every existing thing to the extent that it has existence, as a cause is present to its proper effect. God is in all things by his power, inasmuch as all things act in virtue of him. And God is in all things by his presence, inasmuch as he directly orders and disposes all things.

CHAPTER 136

That doing miracles belongs to God alone

Quia igitur totus ordo causarum secundarum et virtus earum est a Deo, ipse autem non producit suos effectus per necessitatem, sed libera voluntate, ut supra ostensum est, manifestum est quod praeter ordinem causarum secundarum agere potest, sicut quod sanet illos qui secundum operationem naturae sanari non possunt, vel faciat aliqua huiusmodi quae non sunt secundum ordinem naturalium causarum: sunt tamen secundum ordinem divinae providentiae, quia hoc ipsum quod aliquando aliquid a Deo fiat praeter ordinem causarum naturalium, a Deo dispositum est propter aliquem finem.

Cum autem aliqua huiusmodi divinitus fiunt praeter ordinem causarum secundarum, talia facta miracula dicuntur, quia mirum est cum effectus videtur sed causa ignoratur. Cum igitur Deus sit causa simpliciter nobis occulta, cum aliquid ab eo fit praeter ordinem causarum secundarum nobis notarum, simpliciter miracula dicuntur; si autem fiat aliquid ab aliqua alia causa occulta huic vel illi, non est simpliciter miraculum sed quoad illum qui causam ignorat: unde contingit quod aliquid apparet mirum uni, quod non est alii mirum qui causam cognoscit.

Sic autem praeter ordinem causarum secundarum operari solius Dei est, qui est huius ordinis institutor et huic ordini non obligatur. Alia vero omnia huic ordini subduntur; unde miracula facere solius Dei est, secundum illud Psalmi *qui facit mirabilia magna solus.* Cum igitur ab aliqua creatura miracula fieri videntur, vel non sunt vera miracula quia fiunt per aliquas virtutes naturalium rerum, licet nobis occultas, sicut est de miraculis daemonum quae magicis artibus fiunt; vel si sunt vera miracula, impetrantur per aliquem a Deo, ut scilicet talia operetur. Quia ergo huiusmodi miracula solum divinitus fiunt, convenienter in argumentum fidei assumuntur quae soli Deo innititur; quod enim aliquid prolatum ab homine auctoritate divina dicatur, numquam convenientius ostenditur quam per opera quae solus Deus facere potest.

Huiusmodi autem miracula, quamvis praeter ordinem causarum secundarum fiant, non tamen sunt simpliciter dicenda contra naturam, quia hoc ipsum naturalis ordo habet ut inferiora actionibus superiorum subdantur. Unde quae in corporibus inferioribus ex impressione caelestium corporum proveniunt non dicuntur simpliciter esse contra naturam; licet forte

The entire order of secondary causes, as well as their power, comes from God. He himself, however, produces his effects not out of necessity, but by free will, as was shown above. Clearly, then, he can act outside the order of secondary causes, as when he cures those who are incurable from the standpoint of natural causality, or when he does something else of this kind that is not within the order of natural causes but is nevertheless consonant with the order of divine providence. What God occasionally does in this way, outside of the order of natural causes, he arranges for a definite end.

When effects are thus wrought by divine power outside the order of secondary causes, they are called 'miracles,' or wonders: for when we perceive an effect without knowing its cause, we wonder at it. Since God is a cause that is completely hidden from us, when some effect is wrought by him outside the order of secondary causes known to us, it is called simply a miracle. But if an effect is produced by some other cause that is unknown to this or that person, it is not a miracle simply as such, but only with regard to him who is ignorant of the cause. Thus an event may appear miraculous to one person without seeming miraculous to another who is acquainted with its cause.

To act in this way, outside the order of secondary causes, is possible for God alone, who is the founder of this order and is not confined to it. All other beings are subject to this order; and so God alone can work miracles, as the Psalmist says: *who alone does wondrous things* (Ps 72 [71]:18). Therefore, when miracles are apparently worked by some creature, either they are not true miracles, but are effects produced by the power of natural agents, which may be concealed from us, as happens in the case of miracles of demons that are worked by magical arts; or else, if they are true miracles, someone obtains the power to work them by praying to God that he might do such things. Since such miracles are wrought exclusively by divine power, they are rightly appealed to in proof of the faith, which has God alone as its author. For a pronouncement issued by a man with a claim to divine authority is never more fittingly attested than by works which God alone can perform.

Although such miracles occur outside the order of secondary causes, we should not simply say that they are against nature, because the natural order demands precisely that the lower be subject to the activity of the higher. For example, effects brought about in lower bodies in consequence of the influence emanating from the heavenly bodies are not said to be simply against nature, although they

quandoque sit contra naturam particularem huius vel illius rei, sicut patet de motu aquae in fluxu et refluxu maris qui accidit ex actione lunae. Sic igitur et ea quae in creaturis accidunt Deo agente, licet videantur esse contra particularem ordinem causarum secundarum, est tamen secundum ordinem universalem naturae; non igitur miracula sunt contra naturam.

may at times be against the particular nature of this or that thing, as we observe in the movement of water in the ebb and flow of the tide, which is produced by the action of the moon. In the same way, effects produced in creatures by the action of God may seem to be against some particular order of secondary causes; yet they are in accord with the universal order of nature. Therefore, miracles are not contrary to nature.

CHAPTER 137

That some things are said to be by chance and fortuitous

Quamvis autem omnia etiam minima divinitus dispensentur, ut ostensum est, nihil tamen prohibet aliqua accidere a casu et fortuna. Contingit enim aliquid respectu inferioris causae esse fortuitum vel casuale, dum praeter eius intentionem aliquid agitur quod tamen non est fortuitum vel casuale respectu superioris causae, praeter cuius intentionem non agitur; sicut patet de domino qui duos servos ad eundem locum mittit ita quod unus ignoret de alio: horum igitur concursus casualis est quantum ad utrumque, non autem quantum ad dominum.

Sic igitur cum aliqua accidunt praeter intentionem causarum secundarum, fortuita sunt vel casualia habito respectu ad illas causas; et simpliciter casualia dici possunt, quia effectus simpliciter denominantur secundum conditionem proximarum causarum. Si vero habeatur respectus ad Deum, non sunt fortuita sed provisa.

Although all events, even the most trifling, are disposed according to God's plan, as we have shown, there is nothing to prevent some things from happening by chance or accident. An occurrence may be accidental or fortuitous with respect to a lower cause when an effect not intended is brought about, and yet not be accidental or fortuitous with respect to a higher cause, inasmuch as the effect does not take place apart from the latter's intention. For example, a master may send two servants to the same place, but in such a way that neither is aware of the mission of the other. Their meeting is accidental so far as each of them is concerned, but not as regards the master.

So, when certain events occur apart from the intention of secondary causes, they are accidental or fortuitous with respect to those causes; and they may be said to be fortuitous simply speaking, because effects are described simply in terms of their proximate causes. But if God's point of view is considered, they are not fortuitous, but foreseen.

CHAPTER 138

Whether fate is a nature, and what it is

Ex hoc autem patet quae sit ratio fati. Cum enim multi effectus invenirentur casualiter provenire secundum considerationem secundarum causarum, quidam huiusmodi effectus in nullam superiorem causam ordinantem eos reducere voluerunt, quos totaliter negare fatum necesse est. Quidam vero hos effectus qui videntur casuales et fortuiti, in superiorem causam ordinantem eos reducere voluerunt, sed corporalium ordinem non transcendentes, attribuerunt ordinationem horum corporibus primis, scilicet caelestibus: et hi fatum esse dixerunt vim positionis siderum ex qua huiusmodi effectus contingere dicebant. Sed quia ostensum est quod intellectus et voluntas, quae sunt propria prin-

This suggests what we ought to think of fate. Many effects are found to occur haphazardly if they are regarded from the standpoint of secondary causes. Some thinkers are unwilling to refer such effects to a higher cause that ordains them. In consequence, they must utterly reject fate. On the other hand, others have desired to trace back these seemingly accidental and fortuitous effects to a higher cause that plans them. But, failing to rise above the order of bodily entities, they attributed such devising to the highest bodies, namely, the heavenly bodies. And so they contended that fate is a force deriving from the position of the stars, and that this accounts for happenings of this kind. But we showed above that the intellect and will, which are the true

cipia humanorum actuum, corporibus caelestibus non subduntur, non potest dici quod ea quae casualiter vel fortuito in rebus humanis accidere videntur, reducantur in corpora caelestia sicut in causam ordinantem.

Fatum autem non videtur esse nisi de rebus humanis, in quibus est et fortuna; de his enim solent aliqui inquirere futura cognoscere volentes, et de his a divinantibus responderi consuevit, unde et fatum a fando est appellatum. Et ideo sic fatum ponere est alienum a fide.

Sed quia non solum res naturales sed etiam res humanae divinae providentiae subduntur, huiusmodi quae casualiter in rebus humanis accidere videntur in ordinationem divinae providentiae reducere oportet. Et sic necesse est ponere fatum ponentibus divinae providentiae omnia subiacere. Fatum enim sic acceptum se habet ad divinam providentiam sicut proprius eius effectus: est enim explicatio divinae providentiae rebus adhibita, secundum quod Boetius dicit quod fatum est *dispositio*, id est ordinatio, *immobilis rebus mobilibus inhaerens*.

Sed quia cum infidelibus quantum possumus nec nomina debemus habere communia, ne a non intelligentibus erroris occasio sumi possit, cautius est fidelibus ut fati nomen reticeant propter hoc quod fatum communius secundum primam acceptionem sumitur. Unde et Augustinus dicit in V *de Civitate Dei*, quod, si quis secundo modo fatum esse credat, *sententiam teneat et linguam corrigat*.

principles of human acts, are not in any proper sense subject to heavenly bodies. Hence we cannot maintain that events which seemingly occur at random and by chance in human affairs are to be referred to heavenly bodies as to the ordering cause.

There seems to be no place for fate except in human affairs, in which fortune has a part to play. It is only about such events that men are accustomed to inquire in their craving to know the future, and it is also about these that an answer is usually given by fortunetellers. Hence fate is a word formed from the Latin verb *fari*, to foretell. To acknowledge fate thus understood is opposed to faith.

Since, however, not only natural things but also human affairs are under divine providence, those events that seem to happen at random in men's lives must be referred to the ordination of divine providence. Consequently, those who hold that all things are subject to divine providence must admit the existence of fate. Fate taken in this sense is related to divine providence as a real effect of the latter. For it is an unfolding of divine providence as applied to things, and is in agreement with the definition given by Boethius, who says that fate is an *unchangeable disposition*, that is, ordination, *inherent in changeable things*.

Yet, since we ought not to have even words in common with infidels, so far as possible, lest an occasion for going astray be taken by those who do not understand, it is more prudent for the faithful to abstain from the word 'fate,' for the reason that fate is more properly and generally used in the first sense. Therefore, Augustine says in the *City of God* that if anyone believes in the existence of fate in the second sense, *he may keep to his opinion but should correct his language*.

Chapter 139

That not everything is of necessity

Quamvis autem ordo divinae providentiae rebus adhibitus sit certus, ratione cuius Boetius dicit quod fatum est *dispositio immobilis rebus mobilibus inhaerens*, non tamen propter hoc sequitur omnia ex necessitate accidere; nam effectus necessarii vel contingentes dicuntur secundum conditionem proximarum causarum. Manifestum est enim quod si causa prima fuerit necessaria et causa secunda fuerit contingens, effectus sequitur contingens, sicut prima causa in rebus corporalibus generationis in istis inferioribus est motus caelestis corporis; qui cum ex necessitate proveniat, generatio tamen et corruptio in istis inferioribus provenit contingenter, propter hoc quod causae inferiores contingentes sunt et

The order of divine providence as carried out in things is certain. This is why Boethius could say that fate is *an unchangeable disposition inherent in changeable things*. But we may not conclude from this that all things happen of necessity. For effects are said to be necessary or contingent according to the condition of proximate causes. Evidently, if the first cause is necessary and the second cause is contingent, a contingent effect will follow. Thus in the case of lower bodies, the first cause of generation is the movement of a heavenly body; although this movement takes place necessarily, generation and corruption in those lower bodies occur contingently, because the lower causes are contingent and can fail. As we demonstrated above, God carries

deficere possunt. Ostensum est autem quod Deus suae providentiae ordinem per causas inferiores exequitur; erunt igitur aliqui effectus divinae providentiae contingentes secundum conditionem inferiorum causarum.

out the order of his providence through the intermediacy of lower causes. Therefore, some of the effects of divine providence will be contingent, in keeping with the condition of the lower causes.

CHAPTER 140

That even under divine providence, many things are contingent

Nec tamen effectuum contingentia seu causarum certitudinem providentiae perturbare potest. Tria enim sunt quae providentiae certitudinem praestare videntur: scilicet infallibilitas divinae praescientiae, efficacia divinae voluntatis, et sapientia divinae dispositionis quae vias sufficientes ad effectum consequendum adinvenit; quorum nullum congingentiae rerum repugnat. Nam prescientia Dei infallibilis est etiam contingentium futurorum, inquantum Deus intuetur in suo aeterno futura prout sunt actu in suo esse, ut supra expositum est.

Voluntas etiam Dei, cum sit universalis rerum causa, non solum est de hoc quod aliquid fiat, sed ut sic fiat; hoc igitur ad efficaciam divinae voluntatis pertinet ut non solum fiat quod Deus vfieri uult, sed ut hoc modo fiat quo illud fieri vult. Vult autem quaedam fieri necessario et quaedam contingenter, quia utrumque requiritur ad completum esse universi. Ut igitur utroque modo res provenirent, quibusdam adaptauit necessarias causas, quibusdam vero contingentes, ut sic dum quaedam fiunt necessario, quaedam contingentes, divina voluntas efficaciter impleatur.

Manifestum est etiam quod per sapientiam divinae dispositionis providentiae certitudo servatur, contingentia rerum manente. Nam si hoc per prudentiam hominis fieri potest, ut causae quae deficere potest ab effectu sic ferat auxilium ut interdum indeficienter sequatur effectus, sicut patet in medico sanante et in vineae cultore contra sterilitatem vitis adhibendo remedium: multo magis hoc ex sapientia divinae dispositionis contingit, ut quamvis causae contingentes deficere possint quantum est de se ab effectu, tamen aliquibus adminiculis adhibitis indeficienter sequatur effectus, quod eius contingentiam non tollit. Sic igitur manifestum est quod rerum contingentia divinae providentiae certitudinem non excludit.

The contingency of effects or of causes cannot upset the certainty of divine providence. Three things seem to guarantee the certainty of providence: the infallibility of divine foreknowledge, the efficaciousness of the divine will, and the wisdom of the divine management, which discovers adequate ways of procuring an effect. None of these factors is opposed to the contingency of things. God's infallible knowledge embraces even future contingents, inasmuch as God beholds in his eternity future events as actually existing. But we dealt with this question above.

Moreover, God's will, since it is the universal cause of things, decides not only that something will come to pass, but that it will come about in this or that manner. The efficaciousness of the divine will demands not only that what God wishes will happen, but that it will happen in the way he wishes. But he wills that some things should happen necessarily and that other things should happen contingently; both are required for the perfection of the universe. That events may occur in both ways, he applies necessary causes to some things and contingent causes to others. In this manner, with some things happening necessarily and other things happening contingently, the divine will is efficaciously carried out.

Furthermore, it is clear that the certainty of providence is safeguarded by the wisdom of the divine dispensation, without prejudice to the contingency of things. Even the providence exercised by man can enable him so to bolster up a cause which can fail to produce an effect so that, in some cases, the effect will inevitably follow. We find that a physician acts thus in exercising his healing art, as also does the vine-dresser who employs the proper remedy against barrenness in his vines. Much more, then, does the wisdom of the divine economy bring it about that, although contingent causes left to themselves can fail to produce an effect, the effect will inevitably follow when certain supplementary measures are employed; nor does this do away with the contingency of the effect. Evidently, therefore, contingency in things does not exclude the certainty of divine providence.

CHAPTER 141

That the certainty of divine providence does not exclude evil from things

Eodem etiam modo perspici potest quod, divina providentia manente, mala in mundo accidere possunt propter defectum causarum secundarum. Videmus enim in causis ordinatis accidere malum in effectu ex defectu causae secundae, qui tamen defectus a causa prima nullo modo causatur, sicut malum claudicationis causatur a curvitate cruris, non autem a virtute motiua animae; unde quidquid est in claudicatione de motu refertur in virtutem motivam sicut in causam, quod autem est ibi de obliquitate non causatur a virtute motiva, sed a curvitate cruris. Sic igitur quidquid in rebus malum accidit, quantum ad id quod esse vel speciem vel naturam aliquam habet, reducitur in Deum sicut in causam non enim potest esse malum nisi in bono, ut ex supradictis patet; quantum vero ad id quod habet de defectu, reducitur in causam inferiorem defectibilem. Et sic licet Deus sit universalis omnium causa, non tamen est causa malorum inquantum sunt mala, sed quidquid boni eis adiungitur causatur a Deo.

The same process of reasoning enables us to perceive that, without prejudice to divine providence, evil can arise in the world because of defects in secondary causes. Thus in causes that follow one another in order, we see that evil finds its way into an effect owing to some fault in a secondary cause, although this fault is by no means the product of the first cause. For example, the evil of lameness is caused by a curvature in the leg, not by the motive power of the soul. Whatever movement there is in the progress of a lame man is attributed to the motive power as to its cause; but the unevenness of the progress is caused by the curvature of the leg, not by the motive power. Similarly, the evil that arises in things, so far as it has existence or species or a certain nature, is referred to God as to its cause; for there can be no evil unless it resides in something good, as is clear from what we said above. But with regard to the defect that disfigures it, the evil is referred to a lower, defectible cause. Accordingly, although God is the universal cause of all things, he is not the cause of evil as evil. But whatever good is bound up with the evil has God as its cause.

CHAPTER 142

That it does not derogate from God's goodness that he permits evils

Nec tamen hoc bonitati divinae repugnat quod mala esse permittit in rebus ab eo gubernatis. Primo quidem quia providentiae non est naturam gubernatorum perdere, sed salvare. Requirit autem hoc perfectio universi ut sint quaedam in quibus malum non possit accidere, quaedam vero quae defectum mali pati possint secundum suam naturam. Si igitur malum totaliter excluderetur a rebus per providentiam divinam, non regerentur res secundum earum naturam, quod esset maior defectus quam singulares defectus qui tollerentur.

Secundo, quia bonum unius non potest interdum accidere sine malo alterius, sicut videmus quod generatio unius non est sine corruptione alterius, et nutrimentum leonis non est sine occisione alicuius animalis, et patientia iusti non est sine persecutione iniusti. Si igitur malum totaliter excluderetur a rebus, sequeretur quod multa etiam bona tollerentur. Non igitur pertinet ad divinam

God's permission of evil in the things governed by him is not inconsistent with the divine goodness. For, in the first place, the function of providence is not to destroy but to save the nature of the beings governed. The perfection of the universe requires the existence of some beings that are not subject to evil, and of other beings that can suffer the defect of evil in keeping with their nature. If evil were completely eliminated from things, they would not be governed by divine providence in accord with their nature; and this would be a greater defect than the particular defects eradicated.

Second, the good of one cannot be realized without the suffering of evil by another. For instance, we find that the generation of one being does not take place without the corruption of another being, and that the nourishment of a lion is impossible without the destruction of some other animal, and that the patient endurance of the just involves persecution by the unjust. If evil were completely excluded

providentiam ut malum totaliter excludat a rebus, sed ut mala quae proveniunt ad aliquod bonum ordinentur.

from things, much good would be rendered impossible. Consequently, it is the concern of divine providence not that evil be totally excluded from things, but to see to it that the evil which arises is ordered to some good.

Tertio, quia ex ipsis malis particularibus commendabiliora redduntur bona dum eis comparantur, sicut ex obscuritate nigri magis declaratur claritas albi. Et sic per hoc quod mala permittuntur esse in mundo, divina bonitas magis declaratur in bonis, et sapientia in ordinatione malorum ad bona.

Third, good is rendered more estimable when compared with particular evils. For example, the brilliance of white is brought out more clearly when set off by the dinginess of black. And so, by permitting the existence of evil in the world, the divine goodness is more emphatically asserted in the good, just as is the divine wisdom when it forces evil to promote good.

CHAPTER 143

That God specially provides for man by grace

Quia ergo divina providentia rebus singulis secundum earum modum providet, creatura autem rationalis per liberum arbitrium est domina sui actus prae ceteris creaturis, necesse est ut etiam ei singulari modo provideatur quantum ad duo. Primo quidem quantum ad adiumenta operis quae ei dantur a Deo; secundo quantum ad ea quae pro suis operibus ei redduntur.

Creaturis enim irrationalibus haec solum adiumenta dantur divinitus ad agendum quibus naturaliter moventur ad agendum; creaturis vero rationalibus dantur documenta et praecepta vivendi. Non enim praeceptum dari competit nisi ei qui est dominus sui actus, quamvis et creaturis irrationalibus praecepta per quandam similitudinem Deus dare dicatur, secundum illud Psalmi *praeceptum posuit et non praeteribit*: quod quidem praeceptum nihil aliud est quam dispositio divinae providentiae movens res naturales ad proprias actiones.

Similiter etiam actiones creaturarum rationalium imputantur eis ad culpam vel ad laudem pro eo quod habent dominium sui actus, non solum hominibus ab homine praesidente sed etiam a Deo, cum homines non solum regantur ab homine sed etiam a Deo. Cuiuscumque autem regimini aliquis subditur, ab eo sibi imputatur quod laudabiliter vel culpabiliter agit. Et quia pro bene actis debetur praemium, culpae vero debetur poena, ut supra dictum est, creaturae rationales secundum iustitiam divinae providentiae et puniuntur pro malis et praemiantur pro bonis. In creaturis autem irrationalibus non habet locum poena et praemium, sicut nec culpari vel laudari.

Quia vero ultimus finis creaturae rationalis facultatem naturae ipsius excedit, ea vero quae sunt ad finem debent esse fini proportionata secundum rectum providentiae ordinem, consequens est ut creaturae rationali

Accordingly, divine providence governs individual beings in keeping with their nature. Since rational creatures, because of the gift of free will, enjoy dominion over their actions in a way impossible to other creatures, a special providence must be exercised over them in two respects. First, with regard to the aids God gives to rational creatures in their activity; second, with regard to the recompense allotted for their works.

God gives to irrational creatures only those aids by which they are naturally moved to act. But to rational creatures are issued instructions and commands regulating their lives. A precept is not fittingly given except to a being that is master of his actions, although in an analogous sense God is said to also give commands to irrational creatures, about which Psalm 148:6 says: *He set a law which cannot pass away*. But this sort of decree is nothing else than the dispensation of divine providence moving natural things to their proper actions.

The deeds of rational creatures are imputed to them in blame or in praise, because they have dominion over their acts. The actions of men are ascribed to them not only by a man who is placed over them, but also by God. Thus any praiseworthy or blameworthy action that a man performs is imputed to him by the person to whose rule he is subject. Since good actions merit a reward and sin calls for punishment, as was said above, rational creatures are punished for the evil they do and are rewarded for the good they do according to the measure of justice fixed by divine providence. But there is no place for reward or punishment in dealing with irrational creatures, just as there is none for praise or blame.

Since the last end of rational creatures exceeds the capacity of their nature and since whatever conduces to the end must be proportionate to the end according to the right order of providence, rational creatures are given divine aids

etiam adiutoria divinitus conferantur, non solum quae sunt proportionata naturae, sed etiam quae facultatem naturae excedunt. Unde supra naturalem facultatem rationis imponitur divinitus homini lumen gratiae, per quod interius perficitur ad virtutes: et quantum ad cognitionem, dum elevatur mens hominis per lumen huiusmodi ad cognoscendum ea quae rationem excedunt, et quantum ad actionem et affectionem, dum per lumen huiusmodi affectus hominis super omnia creata elevatur ad Deum diligendum et sperandum in ipso, et ad agendum ea quae talis amor requirit.

Huiusmodi autem auxilia supernaturaliter homini data, gratuita vocantur duplici ratione: primo quidem quia gratis divinitus dantur, non enim potest in homine aliquid inveniri cui condigne huiusmodi auxilia debeantur, cum haec facultatem humanae naturae excedant; secundo vero quia speciali quodam modo per huiusmodi dona homo Deo efficitur gratus. Cum enim dilectio Dei sit causa bonitatis in rebus, non a praeexistente bonitate provocata sicut est dilectio nostra, necesse est quod quibus aliquos speciales bonitatis effectus largitur, respectu horum specialis ratio dilectionis divinae consideretur. Unde eos maxime et simpliciter diligere dicitur, quibus tales bonitatis effectus largitur per quos ad ultimum finem perveniant, quod est ipse qui est fons bonitatis.

that are not merely proportionate to nature but that transcend the capacity of nature. God infuses into man, over and above the natural faculty of reason, the light of grace whereby he is internally perfected for the exercise of virtue, both as regards knowledge, inasmuch as man's mind is elevated by this light to the knowledge of truths surpassing reason, and as regards action and affection, inasmuch as man's affective power is raised by this light above all created things to the love of God, to hope in him, and to the performance of acts that such love imposes.

These gifts or aids supernaturally given to man are called 'graces' for two reasons. First, because they are given by God gratis. There is nothing found in man which makes him such aids due to him by right, for they exceed the capacity of nature. Second, because in a very special way man is made *gratus* (or pleasing) to God by such gifts. Since God's love is the cause of goodness in things and is not called forth by any preexisting goodness, as our love is, a special intensity of divine love must be discerned in those whom he showers with such extraordinary effects of his goodness. Therefore, God is said chiefly and simply to love those whom he endows with these effects of his love by which they are enabled to reach their last end, which is he himself, the fountainhead of all goodness.

CHAPTER 144

That God remits sins by freely-given gifts

Et quia peccata contingunt ex hoc quod actiones deficiunt a recto ordine ad finem, ad finem autem homo ordinatur non solum per naturalia auxilia sed per gratuita, necesse est quod peccata hominum non solum naturalibus auxiliis sed etiam gratuitis contrarientur. Contraria autem se invicem expellunt: unde sicut per peccata huiusmodi auxilia gratuita ab homine tolluntur, ita per gratuita dona peccata homini remittuntur; alioquin malitia hominis in peccando plus posset dum removet gratiam, quam divina bonitas ad removendum peccata per gratiae dona.

Item, Deus rebus providet secundum eorum modum. Hic est autem modus mutabilium rerum ut in eis contraria alternari possint, sicut generatio et corruptio in materia corporali, et album et nigrum in corpore colorato; homo autem mutabilis est secundum voluntatem quandiu in hac vita vivit. Sic igitur divinitus gratuita dona homini dantur ut ea possit per peccatum amittere, et sic peccata imputat ut ea per gratuita dona remitti possint.

Sins arise when actions deflect from the right course leading to the end. Since man is conducted to his end not only by natural aids, but by the aids of grace, the sins men commit must be counteracted not by natural aids alone, but also by the helps which grace confers. Contraries exclude each other; therefore, as the aids of grace are taken from man by sin, so sins are forgiven by the gifts of grace. Otherwise man's malice in committing sin would be more powerful in banishing divine grace than the divine goodness is in expelling sin by the gifts of grace.

Furthermore, God's providence over things is in harmony with their mode of being. Changeable things are so constituted that contraries can succeed each other in them; examples are generation and corruption in bodily matter, and white and black in a colored object. Man is changeable in will as long as he lives his earthly life. Hence man receives from God the gifts of grace in such a way that he is able to forfeit them by sin; and the sins man commits are such that they can be remitted by the gifts of grace.

Praeterea, in his quae supra naturam aguntur, possibile et impossibile attenditur secundum potentiam divinam, non secundum potentiam naturalem: quod enim caecus illuminari possit vel mortuus resurgere, non est naturalis potentiae sed divinae. Dona autem gratuita sunt supernaturalia; quod igitur ea aliquis consequi possit, ad divinam potentiam pertinet. Dicere igitur quod aliquis post peccatum gratuita dona consequi non possit, est divinae potentiae derogare. Gratuita autem dona simul cum peccato esse non possunt, cum per gratuita dona homo ordinetur ad finem a quo per peccatum avertitur. Dicere igitur peccata irremissibilia esse, divinae omnipotentiae contrariatur.

Besides, in things done above nature, possible and impossible are regarded from the standpoint of divine power, not from the standpoint of natural power. The fact that a blind man can be made to see or that a dead man can rise is owing not to natural power but to divine power. But the gifts of grace are supernatural. Therefore, a person's capacity to receive them depends on divine power. To say that, once a person has sinned he cannot receive the gifts of grace is derogatory to the power of God. Of course, grace cannot coexist with sin; for by grace man is rightly ordered to his end, from which he is turned away by sin. But the contention that sin is irremissible takes away God's power.

Chapter 145

That sins are not unforgivable

Si quis autem dicat peccata irremissibilia esse, non propter divinam impotentiam, sed quia hoc habet divina iustitia ut qui cadit a gratia ulterius non revertatur ad ipsam: hoc patet esse falsum. Non enim hoc habet ordo iustitiae ut quandiu aliquis est in via, sibi detur quod pertinet ad terminum viae. Immobiliter autem se habere vel in bono vel in malo, hoc pertinet ad terminum viae, immobilitas enim et quies est terminus motus; tota autem praesens vita est status viae, quod demonstrat mutabilitas hominis et quantum ad corpus et quantum ad animam: non igitur hoc habet divina iustitia ut homo post peccatum immobiliter maneat in eo.

Adhuc, ex divinis beneficiis periculum homini non irrogatur, et praecipue ex maximis. Esset autem periculosum homini mutabilem vitam agenti gratiam accipere, si post gratiam peccare posset et iterum redire ad gratiam non posset, praesertim cum peccata quae gratiam praecedunt remittantur per gratiam, quae interdum maiora sunt his quae post gratiam susceptam homo committit. Non est igitur dicendum quod peccata hominis irremissibilia sunt, sive ante susceptam grativam sive post committantur.

The suggestion might be put forward that sins are unforgivable not through any lack of power on God's part, but because divine justice has decided that anyone who falls from grace shall never more be restored to it. But such a position is clearly erroneous. There is no provision in the order of divine justice to the effect that, while a person is on the road, he should have assigned to him what belongs to the end of the journey. But unyielding adherence to good or to evil pertains to the end of life's course; unchangeableness and cessation from activity are the terminus of movement. But the whole of our present life is a time of wayfaring, as is shown by man's changeableness both in body and in soul. Accordingly, divine justice does not determine that after sinning a man must remain immovably in the state of sin.

Moreover, divine benefits do not expose man to danger, particularly in affairs of supreme moment. But it would be dangerous for man, while leading a life subject to change, to accept grace if, after receiving grace, he could sin but could not again be restored to grace. This is so especially in view of the fact that sins preceding grace are remitted by the infusion of grace; and at times such sins are more grievous than those man commits after receiving grace. Therefore, we may not hold that man's sins are unforgivable either before or after they are committed.

CHAPTER 146

That God alone can remit sins

Peccata vero remittere solus Deus potest. Culpa enim contra aliquem commissa ille solus remittere potest contra quem committitur. Peccata autem imputantur homini ad culpam non solum ab homine sed a Deo, ut supra dictum est; sic autem nunc agimus de peccatis prout imputantur homini a Deo: Deus igitur solus peccata remittere potest.

Adhuc, cum per peccata homo avertatur ab ultimo fine, remitti non possunt nisi homo reordinetur in finem; hoc autem fit per gratuita dona quae sunt solum a Deo, cum excedant facultatem naturae solus igitur Deus potest peccata remittere.

Item, peccatum homini imputatur ad culpam inquantum voluntarium est. Voluntatem autem immutare solus Deus potest solus igitur ipse potest remittere peccata.

God alone can forgive sin. For only the one against whom an offense is directed can forgive the offense. Sin is imputed to a man as an offense not only by another man, but also by God, as we said above. However, we are now considering sin as imputed to a man by God. Accordingly, God alone can forgive sin.

Again, since by sin man is deflected from his last end, sins cannot be forgiven unless man is again rightly ordered to his end. This is accomplished through the gifts of grace which come from God alone, since they transcend the power of nature. Therefore, only God can remit sin.

Further, sin is imputed to man as an offense because it is voluntary. But only God can effect a change in the will. Consequently, he alone can truly forgive sins.

CHAPTER 147

Of certain articles of faith that are taken up with the effects of divine government

Hic est igitur secundus Dei effectus gubernatio rerum, et specialiter creaturarum rationalium quibus et gratiam tribuit et peccata remittit. Qui quidem effectus in Symbolo fidei tangitur et quantum ad hoc quod omnia in finem divinae bonitatis ordinantur, per hoc quod Spiritum Sanctum profitemur *Dominum*, nam domini est ad finem suum subditos ordinare; et quantum ad hoc quod omnia movet, per hoc quod dicit *et vivificantem*: sicut enim motus qui est ab anima in corpus est vita corporis, ita motus quo universum movetur a Deo est quasi quaedam vita universi. Et quia tota ratio divinae gubernationis a bonitate divina sumitur, quae Spiritui Sancto appropriatur qui procedit ut amor, convenienter effectus divinae providentiae circa personam Spiritus Sancti ponuntur.

quantum autem ad effectum supernaturalis cognitionis quam per fidem in hominibus Deus facit, dicit *sanctam Ecclesiam catholicam*, nam Ecclesia congregatio fidelium est; quantum vero ad gratiam quam hominibus communicat, dicit *sanctorum communionem*; quantum vero ad remissionem culpae dicit *peccatorum remissionem*.

This, then, is the second of God's effects, namely, the government of things, and especially of rational creatures, to whom God gives grace and whose sins he forgives. This effect is touched on in the Creed. When we profess that the Holy Spirit is *the Lord*, we imply that all things are ordained to the end of divine goodness, since it belongs to a lord to order his subjects to their end. And the words of the Creed which express our belief that the Holy Spirit is *the Life-giver* suggest that God moves all things. For, as the movement flowing from the soul to the body is the life of the body, so the movement whereby the universe is moved by God is, so to speak, a certain life of the universe. Further, since the entire process of divine government is derived from the divine goodness, which is appropriated to the Holy Spirit, who proceeds as love, the effects of divine providence are fittingly thought of in connection with the person of the Holy Spirit.

As regards the effect of supernatural knowledge, which God produces in men through faith, the Creed proclaims *the holy Catholic Church*; for the Church is the congregation of the faithful. Concerning the grace which God communicates to men the Creed states: *the communion of saints*. And with respect to the remission of sin it says: *the forgiveness of sins*.

Chapter 148

That all things were made for the sake of man

Cum autem omnia, sicut ostensum est, in divinam bonitatem ordinentur sicut in finem, eorum autem quae ad hunc finem ordinantur quaedam aliis propinquiora sunt fini, quae plenius divinam bonitatem participant, consequens est ut ea quae sunt inferiora in rebus creatis, minus de bonitate divina participantia, ordinentur etiam quodammodo sicut in fines in entia superiora. In omni enim ordine finium, quae sunt propinquiora ultimo fini sunt etiam fines eorum quae sunt magis remota: sicut potio medicinae est propter purgationem, purgatio autem propter maciem, macies autem propter sanitatem, et sic macies finis quodammodo est purgationis, sicut et purgatio potionis. Et hoc rationabiliter accidit. Sicut enim in ordine causarum agentium virtus primi agentis pervenit ad ultimos effectus per medias causas, ita in ordine finium quae sunt magis remota a fine pertingunt ad ultimum finem mediantibus his quae sunt magis propinqua fini sicut potio non ordinatur ad sanitatem nisi per purgationem. Unde et in ordine universi inferiora consequuntur praecipue ultimum finem inquantum ordinantur ad superiora.

Hoc etiam manifeste apparet ipsum rerum ordinem consideranti. Cum enim ea quae naturaliter fiunt sic nata sunt agi sicut aguntur, videmus autem imperfectiora cedere in usum nobiliorum, utpote quod plantae nutriantur ex terra, animalia ex plantis, haec autem ad usum hominis cedunt: consequens est ut inanimata sint propter animata, et plantae propter animalia, et haec propter hominem. Cum autem ostensum sit quod natura intellectualis sit superior corporali, consequens fit ut tota natura corporalis ad intellectualem ordinetur. Inter naturas autem intellectuales, quae maxime corpori est vicina est anima rationalis, quae est hominis forma: igitur quodammodo propter hominem, inquantum est rationale animal, tota natura corporalis esse videtur. Ex consummatione igitur hominis consummatio totius creaturae corporalis quodammodo dependet.

All things are directed to the divine goodness as to their end, as we have shown. Among things ordained to this end, some are closer to the end than others, and so participate in the divine goodness more abundantly. Consequently, lower creatures, which have a lesser share in the divine goodness, are also in some way ordered to higher beings as to their ends. For in any series of ends, beings that are closer to the ultimate end are also ends with respect to beings that are more remote. For instance, a dose of medicine is administered to procure a purge, the purge is designed to promote slimness, and slimness is desirable for health; and thus slimness is, in a way, the purpose of the purging, as the purging is the purpose of the medicine. And such subordination is reasonable. For just as in a series of efficient causes, the power of the first agent reaches the ultimate effects through intermediate causes, so in a series of ends, whatever is farther removed from the end attains to the ultimate end through the intermediacy of beings that are closer to the end. Thus, in our example, the medicine is only ordered to health through the purging. Similarly, in the order of the universe, lower beings obtain their last end chiefly insofar as they are ordered to higher beings.

The same conclusion is manifest if we turn our attention to the order of things in itself. Things that come into being naturally are born to be treated as they are treated. Now we observe that more imperfect things are used by more noble beings; for example, plants draw their nutriment from the earth, animals feed on plants, and these in turn serve man's use. We conclude, then, that lifeless beings exist for the sake of living beings, plants for the sake of animals, and these for the sake of men. And since, as we have shown, intellectual nature is superior to material nature, it follows that the whole of material nature is subordinate to intellectual nature. But among intellectual natures, that which has the closest ties with the body is the rational soul, which is the form of man. In a certain sense, therefore, we may say that the whole of bodily nature exists for man, inasmuch as he is a rational animal. And so the consummation of the whole of bodily nature depends, in some way, on man's consummation.

CHAPTER 149

Man's ultimate goal

Consummatio autem hominis est in adeptione ultimi finis qui est perfecta beatitudo sive felicitas, quae consistit in divina visione, ut supra ostensum est. Visionem autem divinam consequitur immutabilitas et intellectus et voluntatis: intellectus quidem, quia cum perventum fuerit ad primam causam in qua omnia cognosci possunt, inquisitio intellectus cessat; mobilitas autem voluntatis cessat, quia adepto ultimo fine in quo est plenitudo totius bonitatis, nihil est quod desiderandum restet. Ex hoc autem voluntas mutatur quia desiderat aliquid quod nondum habet. Manifestum est igitur quod ultima consummatio hominis in perfecta quietatione vel immobilitate consistit, et quantum ad intellectum et quantum ad voluntatem.

Man's consummation consists in the attainment of his last end, which is perfect beatitude or happiness, and this consists in the vision of God, as was shown above. The divine vision results in unchangeability in the intellect and in the will. In the intellect, because its inquiry ceases when it comes to the first cause, in which all truth can be known. And the will's moveability ceases because when one has attained the last end, in which is found the fullness of all goodness, nothing remains to be desired. But the reason the will changes is because it desires what it does not yet have. Clearly, therefore, the final consummation of man consists in perfect repose or unchangeableness, both as regards the intellect and as regards the will.

Chapter 150

How man arrives at eternity as to consummation

Ostensum est autem in praemissis quod aeternitatis ratio ex immobilitate consequitur. Sicut enim ex motu causatur tempus in quo prius et posterius invenitur, ita oportet quod remoto motu cesset prius et posterius: et sic ratio aeternitatis relinquitur, quae est *tota simul*. In ultima igitur sua consummatione homo aeternitatem vitae consequitur, non solum quantum ad hoc quod immortaliter secundum animam vivat, quod habet anima rationalis ex sua natura, ut supra ostensum est, sed etiam quantum ad hoc quod ad perfectam immobilitatem perducitur.

We showed in an earlier chapter that the idea of eternity follows from unchangeability. For as motion causes time, in which priority and posteriority are discerned, so the cessation of motion puts a stop to priority and posteriority; and so there is left the idea of eternity, which is *simultaneously whole*. Therefore, in his final consummation man attains eternity of life, not only in the sense that he lives immortally in his soul, which the rational soul has by its nature, as was shown above, but also in the sense that he is brought to perfect unchangeability.

Chapter 151

How the rational soul must be reunited with the body for perfect beatitude

Considerandum est autem quod non potest esse omnimoda immobilitas voluntatis, nisi naturale desiderium totaliter impleatur. Quaecumque autem nata sunt uniri secundum suam naturam, naturaliter sibi uniri appetunt: unumquodque enim appetit id quod est sibi conveniens secundum suam naturam. Cum igitur anima humana naturaliter corpori uniatur, ut supra ostensum est, naturale ei desiderium inest ad corporis unionem; non poterit igitur esse perfecta quietatio voluntatis, nisi iterato anima corpori coniungatur: quod est hominem a morte resurgere.

Item, finalis perfectio requirit perfectionem primam. Prima autem perfectio uniuscuiusque rei est ut sit perfectum in sua natura, finalis vero perfectio consistit in consecutione ultimi finis. Ad hoc igitur quod anima humana omnimode perficiatur in fine, necesse est quod sit perfecta in sua natura: quod non potest esse nisi sit corpori unita. Natura enim animae est quod sit pars hominis ut forma; nulla autem pars perfecta est in sua natura nisi sit in suo toto: requiritur igitur ad ultimam hominis beatitudinem ut anima rursus corpori uniatur.

Adhuc, quod est per accidens et contra naturam non potest esse sempiternum. Necesse est autem hoc quod est animam a corpore separatam esse, per accidens esse et contra naturam, si hoc per se et naturaliter inest ani-

We should note that there cannot be unchangeability of will in every way unless natural desire is completely satisfied. Things that are by nature destined for union naturally desire to be united to each other; for any being seeks what is suited to it by nature. Since, therefore, the human soul is naturally united to the body, as was shown above, it has a natural desire for union with the body. Hence the will cannot be perfectly at rest until the soul is again joined to the body—which is for man to rise from the dead.

Besides, a being's final perfection requires its first perfection. But the first perfection of anything is that it be perfect in its nature, while its final perfection consists in attainment of its last end. In order, therefore, that the human soul may be brought to perfection in every way in its end, it must be perfect in its nature. This is impossible unless the soul is united to the body. For the soul's nature is to be a part of man as his form. But no part is perfect in its nature unless it is in its whole. Therefore, man's final happiness requires the soul to be again united to the body.

Moreover, the incidental and all that is contrary to nature cannot be everlasting. But a state wherein the soul is separated from the body must be incidental and contrary to nature, if it is in the soul naturally and of itself that the

mae ut corpori uniatur; non igitur anima in perpetuum erit a corpore separata. Cum igitur eius substantia sit incorruptibilis, ut supra ostensum est, relinquitur quod sit iterato corpori unienda.

soul be united with the body. Therefore, the soul will not be separated from the body forever. Accordingly, since the soul's substance is incorruptible, as was shown above, we conclude that the soul is to be reunited to the body.

CHAPTER 152

How the separation of soul from body is according to nature and how it is contrary to nature

Videtur autem animam a corpore separari non esse per accidens, sed secundum naturam. Corpus enim hominis ex contrariis compositum est; omne autem huiusmodi naturaliter corruptibile est: corpus igitur humanum naturaliter corruptibile est. Corrupto autem corpore necesse est animam separatam remanere, si anima immortalis est, ut supra ostensum est; videtur igitur animam a corpore separari esse secundum naturam.

Considerandum est igitur quomodo sit secundum naturam, et quomodo contra naturam. Ostensum est enim supra quod anima rationalis praeter modum aliarum formarum excedit totius corporalis materiae facultatem: quod eius operatio intellectualis demonstrat, quam sine corpore habet. Ad hoc igitur quod materia corporalis convenienter ei aptata fuerit, necesse fuit ut aliqua dispositio humano corpori superadderetur per quam fieret conveniens materia talis formae. Et sicut haec forma a solo Deo exit in esse per creationem, ita illa dispositio naturam corpoream excedens a solo Deo corpori humano attributa fuit, quae videlicet ipsum corpus incorruptum conservaret, ut sic perpetuitati animae conveniret. Et haec quidem dispositio in corpore hominis mansit quandiu anima hominis Deo adhaesit.

Aversa autem anima hominis per peccatum a Deo, convenienter et corpus humanum illam supernaturalem dispositionem perdidit per quam immobiliter animae subdebatur: et sic homo necessitatem moriendi incurrit.

Si igitur ad naturam corporis respiciatur, mors naturalis est; si vero ad naturam animae, et ad dispositionem quae propter animam supernaturaliter corpori humano a principio indita fuit, est per accidens et contra naturam, cum naturale sit animae corpori esse unitam.

However, it seems that separation of the soul from the body is not incidental but in accord with nature. For man's body is made up of contrary elements. Now, everything of this sort is naturally corruptible. Therefore, the human body is naturally corruptible. But when the body corrupts the soul must survive as a separate entity if the soul is immortal, as was shown above. Apparently, then, separation of the soul from the body is in accord with nature.

Therefore, we must consider how this separation is in accord with nature and how it is against nature. We showed above that the rational soul exceeds the capacity of all bodily matter in a way impossible to other forms. This is demonstrated by its intellectual activity, which it exercises without the body. To the end that bodily matter might be fittingly adapted to the soul, some disposition had to be added to the body that would make it suitable matter for such a form. And just as this form receives existence from God alone through creation, that disposition, transcending as it does bodily nature, was conferred on the human body by God alone, for the purpose of preserving the body itself in a state of incorruption, so that it might match the soul's perpetual existence. This disposition remained in man's body as long as man's soul cleaved to God.

But when man's soul turned from God by sin, the human body deservedly lost that supernatural disposition whereby it was immoveably subservient to the soul. And hence man incurred the necessity of dying.

Accordingly, if we regard the nature of the body, death is natural. But if we regard the nature of the soul and the disposition with which the human body was supernaturally endowed in the beginning for the sake of the soul, death is incidental and contrary to nature, inasmuch as union with the body is natural for the soul.

CHAPTER 153

That the soul takes up again exactly the same body

Cum autem anima corpori uniatur ut forma, unicuique autem formae propria materia respondeat, necesse est quod corpus cui iterato anima unietur sit eiusdem rationis et speciei cum corpore quod deponit per mortem. Non igitur resumet anima in resurrectione corpus caeleste vel aereum, vel corpus alicuius alterius animalis, ut quidam fabulantur, sed corpus humanum ex carnibus et ossibus compositum, organizatum eisdem organis ex quibus nunc consistit.

Rursus, sicut eidem formae secundum speciem debetur eadem materia secundum speciem, ita eidem formae secundum numerum debetur eadem materia secundum numerum: sicut enim anima bovis non potest esse anima corporis equi, ita anima huius bovis non posset esse anima corporis alterius bovis. Oportet igitur quod, cum eadem numero anima rationalis remaneat, quod corpori eidem numero in resurrectione rursus uniatur.

Since the soul is united to the body as its form, and since each form has the right matter corresponding to it, the body to which the soul will be reunited must be of the same nature and species as was the body laid down by the soul at death. At the resurrection the soul will not resume a celestial or ethereal body, or the body of some animal, as certain people fancifully prattle. No, it will resume a human body made up of flesh and bones, and equipped with the same organs it now possesses.

Furthermore, just as the same specific form ought to have the same specific matter, so the same numerical form ought to have the same numerical matter. For even as the soul of an ox cannot be the soul of a horse's body, neither can the soul of this ox be the soul of any other ox. Therefore, since the rational soul that survives remains numerically the same, at the resurrection it must be reunited to numerically the same body.

CHAPTER 154

That the soul takes up again one and the same body solely by the power of God

Ea vero quae secundum substantiam corrumpuntur, non reiterantur eadem numero secundum operationem naturae, sed solum eadem secundum speciem: non enim eadem numero nubes est ex qua pluvia generatur, et quae iterum ex aqua pluente et rursus evaporante generatur. Cum igitur corpus humanum per mortem substantialiter corrumpatur, non potest operatione naturae idem numero reparari. Cum igitur hoc exigat resurrectionis ratio, ut ostensum est, consequens fit quod resurrectio hominum non fiet per actionem naturae, ut quidam posuerunt, post multa annorum curricula redeuntibus caelestibus corporibus ad eundem situm, rursus eosdem numero homines redire; sed resurgentium reparatio sola virtute divina fiet.

Item, manifestum est quod sensus privati restitui non possunt per operationem naturae, neque aliquid eorum quae solum per generationem accipiuntur, eo quod non sit possibile idem numero pluries generari. Si autem aliquid huiusmodi restituatur alicui, puta oculus erutus aut manus abscissa, hoc erit virtute divina, quae supra naturae ordinem operatur, ut supra ostensum est. Cum igitur per mortem omnes sensus et omnia membra

When substances corrupt, the survival of the species, but not the restoration of the individual, is effected by the action of nature. The cloud from which rain is produced and the cloud which is again formed by evaporation from the fallen rain water are not numerically the same. Accordingly, since the human body substantially dissolves in death, it cannot be restored to numerical identity by the action of nature. But the concept of resurrection requires such identity, as we have just shown. Consequently, the resurrection of man will not be brought about by the action of nature, as some philosophers have held in their theory that, when all bodies return to the position formerly occupied after untold cycles of years, then also men will return to life in the same numerical identity. No, the restoration of all who rise will be effected solely by divine power.

Moreover, it is clear that senses once destroyed, and anything possessed solely as a result of generation, cannot be restored by the activity of nature, for the simple reason that the same numerical being cannot be generated several times. If any such perfection is restored to anyone, for example, an eye that has been torn out or a hand that has been cut off, it will be through divine power which operates beyond the order of nature, as we said above. Therefore, since

depereant, impossibile est hominem mortuum rursus reparari ad vitam nisi operatione divina.

Ex hoc autem quod resurrectionem ponimus divina virtute futuram, de facili videri potest quomodo corpus idem numero reparetur. Cum enim supra ostensum sit quod omnia etiam minima sub divina providentia continentur, manifestum est quod materia huius humani corporis, quamcumque formam post mortem hominis accipiat, non effugit neque virtutem neque cognitionem divinam. Quae quidem materia eadem numero manet, inquantum intelligitur sub dimensionibus existens secundum quas haec materia dici potest et est individuationis principium. Hac igitur materia eadem manente, et ex ea virtute divina corpore reparato humano, nec non et anima rationali, quae cum sit incorruptibilis eadem manet, eidem corpori coniuncta, consequens fit ut homo idem numero reparetur.

Nec potest identitas secundum numerum impediri, ut quidam obiiciunt, per hoc quod non sit humanitas eadem numero. Nam humanitas, quae dicitur forma totius, secundum quosdam nihil est aliud quam forma partis quae est anima: quae quidem dicitur forma corporis secundum quod dat ei vitam, forma autem totius secundum quod dat speciem toti; quod si verum est, manifestum est et humanitatem eandem numero remanere, cum anima rationalis eadem numero maneat.

Sed quia humanitas est quam significat definitio hominis, sicut et essentia cuiuslibet rei est quam significat sua definitio, definitio autem hominis non solum significat formam sed etiam materiam, cum in definitionibus rerum naturalium necesse sit materiam poni: convenientius secundum alios dicitur quod in ratione humanitatis et anima et corpus includatur, aliter tamen quam in definitione hominis. Nam in ratione humanitatis includuntur essentialia principia hominis sola, cum praecisione aliorum; cum enim humanitas dicatur qua homo est homo, manifestum est quod omnia de quibus non est verum dicere quod eis homo sit homo, ab humanitate praeciduntur. Cum vero homo dicatur qui humanitatem habet, per hoc vero quod humanitatem habet non excluditur quin et alia habeat, puta albedinem aut aliquid huiusmodi, hoc nomen homo significat sua essentialia principia, non tamen cum praecisione aliorum, licet alia non includantur actu in eius ratione sed potentia tantum: unde homo significatur per modum totius, humanitas vero per modum partis, nec de homine praedicatur. In Socrate vero aut Platone includitur haec materia et haec forma, ut sicut ratio hominis est ex hoc quod componitur ex corpore et anima, ita, si Socrates definiretur, ratio eius esset quod esset compositus ex his carnibus et his ossibus et hac anima. Cum igitur humanitas non sit aliqua alia forma praeter animam et corpus, sed sit aliquid compositum ex utroque, manifestum est

all the senses and all the members of man corrupt in death, a dead man cannot be brought back to life except by divine action.

The fact that the future resurrection will be effected by divine power, as we hold, enables us to perceive readily how the same numerical body will be revived. Since all things, even the very least, are included under divine providence, as we showed above, the matter composing this human body of ours, whatever form it may take after man's death, evidently does not elude the power or the knowledge of God. Such matter remains numerically the same, in the sense that it exists under quantitative dimensions, by reason of which it can be said to be this particular matter, and is the principle of individuation. When this same matter remains, and the human body is refashioned from it by divine power, and likewise the rational soul which remains the same in its incorruptibility is united to the same body, it follows that identically the same man is restored.

Numerical identity cannot be impeded, as some object, by the consideration that the humanity is not numerically the same as before. In the view of some philosophers, humanity, which is said to be the form of the whole, is nothing else than the form of a part, namely, the soul, and they admit that humanity is the form of the body, in the sense that it confers species on the whole. If this is true, evidently the humanity remains numerically the same, since the rational soul remains numerically the same.

Humanity, however, is that which is signified by the definition of man, as the essence of anything whatever is that which is signified by its definition. But the definition of man signifies not form alone but also matter, since matter must be comprised in the definition of material things. Hence we shall do better to say, with others, that both soul and body are included in the notion of humanity, although otherwise than in the definition of man. The notion of humanity embraces only the essential principles of man, leaving out all other factors. For, since humanity is understood to be that whereby man is man, whatever cannot truly be said to constitute man as man is evidently cut off from the notion of humanity. But when we speak of man, who has humanity, the fact that he has humanity does not exclude the possession of other attributes, for instance, whiteness and the like. The term 'man' signifies man's essential principles, but not to the exclusion of other factors, even though these other factors are not actually, but only potentially, contained in the notion of man. Hence 'man' signifies in the manner of a whole whereas 'humanity' signifies in the manner of a part and is not predicated of man. In Socrates, then, or in Plato, this determinate matter and this particular form are included. Just as the notion of man implies composition of matter and form, so if Socrates were to be defined, the notion of him would imply that he is composed of this flesh and these bones and this soul. Consequently, since humanity is not some third form in addition to soul and body, but

quod eodem corpore reparato et eadem anima manente, eadem numero humanitas erit.

Neque etiam praedicta identitas secundum numerum impeditur ex hoc quod corporeitas non redeat eadem numero, cum corrupto corpore corrumpatur. Nam si per corporeitatem intelligatur forma substantialis per quam aliquid in genere substantiae corporeae ordinatur, cum non sit unius nisi una forma substantialis, talis corporeitas non est aliud quam anima; nam hoc animal per hanc animam non solum est animal, sed animatum corpus et corpus et etiam hoc aliquid in genere substantiae existens: alioquin anima adveniret corpori existenti in actu, et sic esset forma accidentalis. Subiectum enim substantialis formae non est actu hoc aliquid, sed potentia tantum: unde cum accipit formam substantialem non dicitur tantum generari hoc aut illud, sicut dicitur in formis accidentalibus, sed dicitur simpliciter generari, quasi simpliciter esse accipiens; et sic corporeitas accepta eadem numero manet, rationali anima incorruptibili existente.

Si vero corporeitatis nomine forma quaedam intelligatur a qua denominatur corpus quod ponitur in genere quantitatis, sic est quaedam forma accidentalis, cum nihil aliud significet quam trinam dimensionem. Unde licet non eadem numero redeat, identitas subiecti non impeditur ad quam sufficit unitas essentialium principiorum; et eadem ratio est de omnibus aliis accidentibus, quorum diversitas identitatem secundum numerum non tollit. Unde cum unio sit quaedam relatio ac per hoc sit accidens, eius diversitas secundum numerum non tollit identitatem subiecti. Similiter etiam nec diversitas secundum numerum potentiarum animae sensitivae et vegetativae, si tamen corrumpi ponantur: sunt enim in genere accidentis potentiae naturales coniuncti existentes; nec a sensu sumitur sensibile secundum quod est differentia constitutiva animalis, sed ab ipsa substantia animae sensitivae, quae in homine est eadem secundum substantiam cum rationali.

is composed of both, we see clearly that, if the same body is restored and if the same soul remains, the humanity will be numerically the same.

The numerical identity in question is not frustrated on the ground that the corporeity recovered is not numerically the same, for the reason that it corrupts when the body corrupts. If by corporeity is meant the substantial form by which a thing is classified in the genus of bodily substance, such corporeity is nothing else than the soul, seeing that there is but one substantial form for each thing. In virtue of this particular soul, this animal is not only animal, but is animated body, and body, and also this thing existing in the genus of substance. Otherwise the soul would come to a body already existing in act, and so would be an accidental form. The subject of a substantial form is something existing only in potency, not in act. When it receives the substantial form it is not said to be generated merely in this or that respect, as is the case with accidental forms, but is said to be generated simply, as simply receiving existence. And therefore the corporeity that is received remains numerically the same, since the same rational soul continues to exist.

If, however, the word 'corporeity' is taken to mean a form designating a body, which is placed in the genus of quantity, such a form is accidental, since it signifies nothing else than three-dimensional existence. Even though the same numerical form, thus understood, is not recovered, the identity of the subject is not thereby impeded, for unity of the essential principles suffices for this. The same reasoning holds for all the accidents, the diversity among which does not destroy numerical identity. Consequently, since union is a kind of relation, and therefore an accident, its numerical diversity does not prevent the numerical identity of the subject; nor, for that matter, does numerical diversity among the powers of the sensitive and vegetative soul, if they are supposed to have corrupted. For the natural powers existing in the human composite are in the genus of accident; and what we call 'sensible' is derived not from the senses according as sense is the specific difference constituting animal, but from the very substance of the sensitive soul, which in man is essentially identical with the rational soul.

CHAPTER 155

That men rise to incorruptible life

Quamvis autem homines iidem numero resurgant, non tamen eundem modum vivendi habebunt: nunc enim corruptibilem vitam habent, tunc vero incorruptibilem. Si enim natura in generatione hominis perpetuum esse intendit, multo magis Deus in hominis reparatione; quod enim natura perpetuum esse intendat, habet ex hoc quod a Deo movetur. Non autem in reparatione hominis resurgentis intenditur perpetuum esse speciei, quia hoc per continuam generationem poterat optineri; relinquitur igitur quod intendatur perpetuum esse individui: homines igitur resurgentes in perpetuum vivent.

Praeterea, si homines resurgentes moriantur, animae a corporibus separatae non in perpetuum absque corpore remanebunt: hoc enim est contra naturam animae, ut supra dictum est. Oportebit igitur quod iterato resurgant; et hoc idem continget, si post secundam resurrectionem iterum moriantur. Sic igitur in infinitum mors et vita circulariter circa eundem hominem reiterabuntur: quod videtur esse vanum. Convenientius est igitur ut stetur in primo, ut scilicet in prima resurrectione homines immortales resurgant.

Nec tamen mortalitatis ablatio diversitatem vel secundum speciem vel secundum numerum inducet. Mortale enim secundum propriam rationem differentia specifica hominis esse non potest, cum passionem quandam designet; sed ponitur loco differentiae hominis, ut per hoc quod dicitur mortale designetur materia hominis, quod scilicet est ex contrariis compositus, sicut per hoc quod rationale designatur proprie forma eius: res enim naturales non possunt sine materia definiri. Non autem auferetur mortalitas per ablationem propriae materiae: non enim resumet anima corpus caeleste vel aereum, ut supra habitum est, sed corpus humanum ex contrariis compositum. Incorruptibilitas tamen adveniet ex virtute divina, per quam anima supra corpus usque ad hoc dominabitur quod corrumpi non possit; tandiu enim res conservatur in esse, quandiu forma supra materiam dominatur.

Although men will rise as the same individuals, they will not have the same kind of life as before. Now their life is corruptible; then it will be incorruptible. If nature aims at perpetual existence in the generation of man, much more so does God in the restoration of man. Nature's tendency toward never-ending existence comes from an impulse implanted by God. The perpetual existence of the species is not in question in the restoration of risen man, for this could be procured by repeated generation. Therefore, what is intended is the perpetual existence of the individual. Accordingly, risen men will live forever.

Besides, if men once risen were to die, the souls separated from their bodies would not remain forever deprived of the body, for this would be against the nature of the soul, as we said above. Therefore, they would have to rise again; and the same thing would happen if they were to die again after the second resurrection. Thus death and life would revolve around each man in cycles of infinite succession, which seems futile. Surely a halt is better called at the initial stage, so that men might rise to immortal life at the first resurrection.

However, the conquest of mortality will not introduce any diversity either in species or in number. The idea of mortality contains nothing that could make it a specific difference of man, since it signifies only something suffered. It is used to serve as a specific difference of man in the sense that the nature of man is designated by calling him mortal to bring out the fact that he is composed of contrary elements, just as his proper form is designated by the predicate 'rational'; material things cannot be defined without including matter. However, mortality is not overcome by taking away man's proper matter. For the soul will not resume a celestial or ethereal body, as was mentioned above; it will resume a human body made up of contrary elements. Incorruptibility will come as an effect of divine power, whereby the soul will gain dominion over the body to the point that the body cannot corrupt. For a thing continues in being as long as form has dominion over matter.

CHAPTER 156

That after the resurrection the use of food and generation will cease

Quia vero subtracto fine removeri oportet ea quae sunt ad finem, oportet quod remota mortalitate a resurgentibus, ea etiam subtrahantur quae ad statum mortalis vitae ordinantur. Huiusmodi autem sunt cibi et potus, qui ad hoc sunt necessarii ut mortalis vita sustentetur, dum id quod per calorem naturalem resolvitur per cibos restauratur; non igitur post resurrectionem erit usus cibi et potus.

Similiter etiam nec vestimentorum, cum vestimenta ad hoc homini necessaria sint ne corpus ab exterioribus corrumpatur per calorem vel frigus. Similiter etiam necesse est et venereorum usum cessare, cum ad generationem animalium ordinetur; generatio autem mortali vitae deservit, ut quod secundum individuum conservari non potest, conservetur saltem in specie. Cum igitur homines iidem numero in perpetuum conservabuntur, generatio in eis locum non habebit, unde nec venereorum usus.

Rursus, cum semen sit superfluum alimenti, cessante usu ciborum necesse est ut etiam venereorum usus cesset.

Non autem potest convenienter dici quod propter solam delectationem remaneat usus cibi et potus et venereorum. nihil enim inordinatum in illo finali statu erit, quia tunc omnia suo modo perfectam consummationem accipient: inordinatio autem perfectioni opponitur. Et praeterea, cum reparatio hominis per resurrectionem sit immediate a Deo, non poterit in illo statu aliqua inordinatio esse, cum *quae a Deo sunt ordinata sunt*, ut dicitur Ro. XIII. Est autem hoc inordinatum ut usus cibi et potus vel venereorum propter solam delectationem quaeratur, unde et nunc apud homines vitiosum reputatur. Non igitur propter solam delectationem in resurgentibus usus cibi et potus et venereorum esse poterit.

When an end is removed, the means leading to that end must also be removed. Therefore, after mortality is done away with in those who have risen, the means serving the condition of mortal life must cease to have any function. Such are food and drink, which are necessary for the sustenance of mortal life, during which what is dissolved by natural heat has to be restored by food. Consequently, there will be no use of food or drink after the resurrection.

Nor will there be any need of clothing. Man needs clothes so that the body does not suffer harm from heat or cold, which beset him from outside. Likewise, exercise of the reproductive functions, which is designed for the generation of animals, must cease. Generation serves the ends of mortal life, so that what cannot be preserved in the individual may be preserved at least in the species. Since the same individual men will continue in eternal existence, generation will have no place among them; nor, consequently, will the exercise of reproductive power.

Again, since semen is the superfluous part of nourishment, cessation of the use of food necessarily entails cessation of the exercise of the reproductive functions.

On the other hand, we cannot fittingly maintain that the use of food, drink, and the reproductive powers will remain solely for the sake of pleasure. Nothing inordinate will occur in that final state, because then all things, each in its own way, will receive their perfect consummation, but inordinance is opposed to perfection. Also, since the restoration of man through resurrection will be effected directly by God, no inordinance will be able to find its way into that state: *those that exist have been ordained by God* (Rom 13:1). But desire for the use of food and the exercise of the reproductive powers for pleasure alone would be inordinate; indeed, even during our present life people regard such conduct as vicious. Among the risen, consequently, the use of food, drink, and the reproductive functions for mere pleasure can have no place.

Chapter 157

That nevertheless all bodily members will be resurrected

Quamvis autem usus talium rerum resurgentibus desit, non tamen eis deerunt membra ad usus tales ordinata, quia sine his corpus resurgentis integrum non esset. Conveniens est autem ut in reparatione hominis resurgentis, quae erit immediate a Deo cuius perfecta sunt opera, natura integre reparetur. Erunt igitur huiusmodi membra in resurgentibus propter integritatem naturae conservandam, et non propter actus quibus nunc deputantur.

Item, si in illo statu homines pro actibus quos nunc agunt poenam vel praemium consequentur, ut postea manifestabitur, conveniens est ut eadem membra homines habeant quibus peccato vel iustitiae deservierunt in hac vita, ut in quibus peccaverunt vel meruerunt, puniantur vel praemientur.

Although risen men will not occupy themselves with activities of this sort, they will not lack the organs requisite for such functions. Without the organs in question the risen body would not be complete. But it is fitting that nature should be completely restored at the renovation of risen man, for such renovation will be accomplished directly by God, whose works are perfect. Therefore, all the members of the body will have their place in the risen, for the preservation of nature in its entirety rather than for the exercise of their normal functions.

Moreover, as we shall bring out later, men will receive punishment or reward in that future state for the acts they perform now. This being the case, it is no more than right that men should keep the organs with which they served the reign of sin or of justice during the present life, so that they may be punished or rewarded in the members they employed for sin or for merit.

Chapter 158

That they will not rise up with any defect

Similiter autem conveniens est ut omnes naturales defectus a corporibus resurgentium auferantur; per omnes enim huiusmodi defectus integritati naturae derogatur. Si igitur conveniens est ut in resurrectione natura humana integraliter reparetur a Deo, consequens est ut etiam huiusmodi defectus tollantur.

Praeterea, huiusmodi defectus ex defectu virtutis naturalis quae fuit generationis humanae principium provenerunt; in resurrectione autem non erit virtus agens nisi divina, in quam defectus non cadit: non igitur huiusmodi defectus qui fuerunt in hominibus generatis, erunt in hominibus per resurrectionem reparatis.

In like manner, it is fitting that all natural defects should be corrected in the risen body. Any defect of this sort is prejudicial to the integrity of nature. And so, if human nature is to be completely renewed by God at the resurrection, such defects must be taken away.

Besides, these defects arose from a deficiency in the natural power which is the principle of human generation. But in the resurrection there will be no active causality other than the divine, which does not admit of deficiency. Therefore, such defects as are found in men naturally begotten will have no place in men restored by the resurrection.

CHAPTER 159

That only those things that are of the truth of human nature rise up

Quod autem dictum est de integritate resurgentium, referri oportet ad id quod est de veritate humanae naturae. Quod enim de veritate humanae naturae non est, in resurgentibus non resumetur; alioquin oporteret immoderatam esse magnitudinem resurgentium, si quidquid ex cibis in carnem et sanguinem est conversum in resurgentibus resumetur. Veritas autem uniuscuiusque naturae secundum suam speciem et formam attenditur. Partes igitur hominis secundum speciem omnes integraliter in resurgentibus erunt, non solum partes organicae, sed etiam partes consimiles, ut caro, nervus et huiusmodi ex quibus membra organica componuntur. Non autem totum quidquid materialiter fuit sub his partibus resumetur, sed quantum sufficiens erit ad dispositionem partium reintegrandam.

Nec tamen propter hoc homo idem numero aut integer non erit, si totum quidquid materialiter in eo fuit non resurget. Manifestum est enim quod in statu huius vitae a principio usque ad finem homo idem numero manet; id tamen quod materialiter in eo est sub specie partium non idem manet, sed paulatim fluit et refluit, ac si ignis idem conservaretur consumptis et appositis lignis. Et tunc est integer quando species et quantitas speciei debita conservatur.

These remarks about the integrity of risen men should be understood as referring to whatever pertains to the truth of human nature. What is not required for the truth of human nature will not be resumed by risen man. Thus, if all the accretion of matter from the food that has been changed into flesh and blood were to be resumed, the size of risen man would exceed all bounds. The truth of any nature is looked to according to its species and form. Accordingly, all the parts that are consonant with the human species and form will be integrally present in risen man: not only organic parts, but other parts of like nature, such as flesh and sinews, which enter into the composition of the various organs. Of course, not all the matter that was ever contained in those parts during man's natural life will again be taken up, but only so much as will be enough to constitute the species of the parts in integrity.

Even though not all the material elements ever possessed by man will arise, we cannot say on this account that man will not be the same individual, or that he will not be complete. For in this present life it is manifest that a man remains one and the same in number from the beginning all the way to the end. That, however, which is in him materially under the aspect of parts does not remain the same, but undergoes gradual flux and reflux (as if the same fire were preserved by logs being consumed and replaced). And then he is a complete man when the species and the quantity due to the species are preserved.

CHAPTER 160

That God will supply all things to the reformed body, or whatever will be lacking of matter

Sicut autem non totum quod materialiter fuit in corpore hominis ad reparationem corporis resurgentis Deus resumet, ita etiam si quid materialiter defuit Deus supplebit. Si enim hoc officio naturae fieri potest ut puero, qui non habet debitam quantitatem, ex aliena materia per assumptionem cibi et potus tantum addatur quod ei sufficiat ad perfectam quantitatem habendam, nec propter hoc desinit esse idem numero qui fuit: multo magis hoc virtute divina fieri potest ut suppleatur minus habentibus ex extrinseca materia, quod eis in hac vita defuit ad integritatem membrorum naturalium vel debitae quantitatis. Sic igitur licet aliqui in hac vita

For the same reason that God, in restoring the risen body, does not reclaim all the material elements once possessed by man's body, he will supply whatever is wanting to the proper amount of matter. Nature itself has such power. In infancy we do not as yet possess our full quantity; but by assimilating food and drink we receive enough matter from outside sources to round out our perfect quantity; nor on this account does a man cease to be the same individual he was before. Surely, then, divine power can do the same thing much more easily, so that those who do not have sufficient quantity may be supplied from outside matter with whatever was lacking to them in this life as regards

aliquibus membris caruerint, vel perfectam quantitatem nondum attigerint in quantulacumque quantitate defuncti, virtute divina in resurrectione perfectionem debitam consequentur et membrorum et quantitatis.

integrity of natural members or suitable size. Consequently, although some may have lacked certain of their members during this life, or may not have attained to perfect size, the amount of quantity possessed at the moment of death makes no difference; at the resurrection they will receive, through God's power, the due complement of members and quantity.

CHAPTER 161

Solution of possible objections

Ex hoc autem solvi potest quod quidam contra resurrectionem obiiciunt. Dicunt enim possibile esse quod aliquis homo carnibus humanis vescatur, et ulterius sic nutritus filium generet qui simili cibo utatur. Si igitur nutrimentum convertitur in substantiam carnis, videtur quod impossibile sit integraliter utrumque resurgere, cum carnes unius conversae sint in carnem alterius; et quod difficilius videtur, si semen est ex superfluo nutrimenti, ut philosophi tradunt, sequitur quod semen unde natus est filius sit sumptum ex carnibus alterius, et ita impossibile videtur puerum ex tali semine genitum resurgere, si homines quorum carnes et pater et ipse comederant integraliter resurgunt.

Sed hoc communi resurrectioni non repugnat. Dictum est enim supra quod non est necessarium quidquid materialiter fuit in aliquo homine, in ipso resurgente resumi, sed tantum quantum sufficit ad modum debitae quantitatis servandum. Dictumque est etiam quod, si alicui aliquid defuit de materia ad quantitatem perfectam, supplebitur divina virtute.

Considerandum est insuper quod aliquid, materialiter in corpore hominis existens, secundum diversos gradus ad veritatem naturae humanae pertinere invenitur. Nam primo et principaliter quod a parentibus sumitur sub veritate humanae speciei tanquam purissimum perficitur ex virtute formativa; secundario autem, quod ex cibis aggeneratum est necessarium ad debitam quantitatem membrorum, quia semper admixtio extranei debilitat virtutem rei, unde et finaliter necesse est augmentum deficere et corpus senescere et dissolvi, sicut et vinum per admixtionem aquae tandem redditur aquosum. Ulterius autem ex cibis aliquae superfluitates in corpore hominis aggenerantur, quarum quaedam sunt necessariae ad aliquem usum, ut semen ad generationem, et capilli ad tegumentum et ornatum; quaedam vero omnino ad nihil, ut quae expelluntur per sudorem et varias egestiones, vel interius retinentur in gravamen naturae.

This enables us to answer the objections that some raise against the resurrection. For instance, they say that a cannibal may have eaten human flesh, and later, thus nourished, may beget a son, who eats the same kind of food. If what is eaten is changed into the substance of the eater's flesh, it seems impossible for both to rise in their full integrity, for the flesh of one has been changed into the flesh of the other. The difficulty apparently grows if semen is the product of surplus food, as the philosophers teach; for the semen whereby the son is begotten would then be derived from the flesh of another person. And so it seems impossible for a boy begotten from such seed to rise, if the men whose flesh the father and the son himself devoured rise intact.

But this state of affairs is not incompatible with a general resurrection. As was pointed out above, not all the material elements ever present in any man need be resumed when he rises; only so much matter is required as suffices to keep up the amount of quantity he ought to have. We also pointed out that if anyone is lacking in the matter required for perfect quantity, divine power will supply what is needed.

We should note, moreover, that the material elements existing in man's body are found to pertain to true human nature in various degrees. First and foremost, what is received from one's parents is brought to perfection within the truth of the human species, as its purest element, by the parents' formative causality. Second, what is contributed by food is necessary for the proper quantity of the body's members. Since, finally, the introduction of a foreign substance always weakens a thing's energy, growth must eventually cease and the body must become old and decay, just as wine eventually becomes watery if water is mixed in with it. Moreover, certain superfluities are engendered in man's body from food. Some of these are required for special purposes: for instance, semen for reproduction and hair for covering and adornment. But other superfluities serve no useful end, and these are expelled through perspiration and other eliminating processes, or else are retained in the body, with inconvenience to nature.

Hoc igitur in communi resurrectione secundum divinam providentiam attendetur, quod si idem numero materialiter in diversis hominibus fuit, in illo resurget in quo principaliorem gradum optinuit. Si autem in duobus extitit secundum unum et eundem gradum, resurget in eo in quo primo fuit, in alio vero supplebitur ex divina virtute. Et sic patet quod carnes humanae comestae ab aliquo non resurgent in comedente, sed in eo cuius prius fuerunt; resurgent tamen in eo qui ex tali semine generatus est quantum ad id quod in eis fuit de humido nutrimentali, aliud vero resurget in primo, Deo unicuique supplente quod deest.

At the general resurrection all this will be adjusted in accord with divine providence. If the same matter existed in different men, it will rise in that one in whom it fulfilled the higher function. If it existed in two men in exactly the same way, it will rise in him who had it first; in the other, the lack will be made up by divine power. And so we can see that the flesh of a man that was devoured by another will rise not in the cannibal, but in him to whom it belonged originally. But as regards the nutritive fluid present in it, it will rise in the son begotten of semen formed from that flesh. The rest of it will rise in the first man in this series, and God will supply what is wanting to each of the three.

CHAPTER 162

That the resurrection of the dead is expressed in the articles of faith

Ad hanc igitur fidem resurrectionis confitendam, in Symbolo Apostolorum positum est *Carnis resurrectionem*; nec sine ratione additum est *carnis*, quia fuerunt quidam, etiam tempore apostolorum, qui carnis resurrectionem negabant, solam spiritualem resurrectionem confitentes per quam homo a morte peccati resurgit. Unde Apostolus II ad Timotheum II dicit de quibusdam quod dixerunt *resurrectionem iam esse factam et subverterunt multorum fidem*; ad quorum removendum errorem, ut resurrectio futura credatur, dicitur in Symbolo Patrum *Exspecto resurrectionem mortuorum*.

That we may give expression to our faith in the resurrection, we are instructed to say in the Apostles' Creed: *I believe . . . in the resurrection of the body.* The word *body* was inserted not without reason: even in the age of the Apostles there were some who denied the resurrection of the body and admitted no more than a spiritual resurrection, whereby a man rises from the death of sin. Therefore, the Apostle, in 2 Timothy 2:18, has occasion to refer to certain individuals who said that *the resurrection is past already, and have subverted the faith of many.* To abolish this error, so that belief in the future resurrection may be professed, the Creed of the Fathers proclaims: *I look for the resurrection of the dead.*

CHAPTER 163

What sort of activity will belong to the risen

Oportet autem considerare ulterius qualis sit operatio resurgentium. Necesse est enim cuiuslibet viventis esse aliquam operationem cui principaliter intendit, et in hoc dicitur vita eius consistere: sicut qui voluptatibus principaliter vacant, dicuntur vitam voluptuosam agere; qui vero contemplationi, contemplativam; qui vero civitatibus gubernandis, civilem. Ostensum est autem quod resurgentibus neque ciborum neque venereorum aderit usus, ad quem omnia corporalia exercitia ordinari videntur. Subtractis autem corporalibus exercitiis remanent spirituales operationes, in quibus ultimum hominis finem consistere diximus: quem quidem finem adipisci resurgentibus competit a statu corruptionis et mutabilitatis liberatis, ut ostensum est. Non autem in quibuscumque spiritualibus actibus ultimus hominis finis consistit, sed in hoc quod Deus per essentiam videatur, ut supra ostensum est. Deus autem aeternus est: unde oportet quod intellectus Deo coniunctus aeternitati coniungatur. Sicut igitur qui voluptati vacant voluptuosam vitam agere dicuntur, ita qui divina visione potiuntur aeternam optinent vitam, secundum illud Io. XVII *Haec est vita aeterna, ut cognoscant Deum verum.*

We go on to consider what sort of activity risen men will have. Each living being must have some activity that mainly engrosses its attention, and its life is said to consist in this occupation. Thus those who give their time to pleasure more than anything else are said to lead a life of pleasure; those who give their time to contemplation are said to lead a contemplative life; and those who devote their time to civil government are said to lead a political life. We have shown that risen men will have no occasion to use food or the reproductive functions, to which all bodily activity seems to be ordered. But, even if the exercise of bodily functions ceases, there remain spiritual activities, in which we have said that man's ultimate end consists; and achieving this end befits the risen once they are freed from their condition of corruption and changeableness. Of course, man's last end does not consist in spiritual acts of just any sort, but in the vision of God according to his essence, as was shown above. Now, God is eternal; hence the intellect joined to God must joined with eternity. Accordingly, just as those who give their time to pleasure are said to lead a life of pleasure, so those who acquire the vision of God possess eternal life, as is indicated in John 17:3: *This is eternal life, that they know thee the only true God.*

CHAPTER 164

That God will be seen in his essence, and not through a likeness

Videtur autem Deus per essentiam ab intellectu creato, non per aliquam sui similitudinem, qua in intellectu praesente res intellecta possit distare, sicut lapis per suam similitudinem praesens est oculo, per substantiam vero absens; sed, sicut supra ostensum est, ipsa Dei essentia intellectui creato coniungitur quodammodo ut Deus per essentiam videri possit. Sicut igitur in illo ultimo fine videbitur quod prius de Deo credebatur, ita quod sperabatur ut distans tenebitur ut praesens; et hoc comprehensio nominatur, secundum illud Apostoli Phil. III: *Sequor autem, si quo modo comprehendam.*

The created intellect sees God in his essence, and not through any likeness of him. When a likeness of this sort is present in the intellect, the object understood may be at a distance; for example, a stone is present to the eye by its likeness, but is absent in substance. But, as was shown above, God's very essence is in some way united to the created intellect, so that God may be seen through his essence. So, just as in that last end what was formerly believed about God will be seen, so also what was hoped for as distant will be closely embraced as present. This is called comprehension, according to the expression used by the Apostle

Quod non est intelligendum secundum quod comprehensio inclusionem importat, sed secundum quod importat praesentialitatem et tentionem quandam eius quod dicitur comprehendi.

in Philippians 3:12: *I follow after, if I may by any means comprehend*. This is not to be understood in the sense that comprehension implies all-inclusive knowledge, but in the sense that it denotes the presence and a certain possessing of what is said to be comprehended.

CHAPTER 165

That to see God is highest perfection and delight

Rursus considerandum est quod ex apprehensione convenientis delectatio generatur, sicut visus delectatur in pulchris coloribus et gustus in suavibus saporibus. Sed haec quidem delectatio in sensu impediri potest propter organi indispositionem: nam *oculis aegris odiosa est lux, quae puris est amabilis*. Sed quia intellectus non intelligit per organum corporale, ut supra ostensum est, delectationi quae est in consideratione veritatis nulla tristitia contrariatur. Potest tamen per accidens ex consideratione intellectus tristitia sequi inquantum id quod intelligitur apprehenditur ut nocivum, ut sic delectatio quidem assit intellectui de cognitione veritatis, tristitia autem in voluntate sequatur de re quae cognoscitur, non inquantum cognoscitur sed inquantum suo actu nocet. Deus autem hoc ipsum quod est veritas est: non potest igitur intellectus Deum videns in eius visione non delectari.

Itemque, Deus est ipsa bonitas, quae est ratio dilectionis: unde necesse est ipsam diligi ab omnibus apprehendentibus ipsam. Licet enim aliquid quod bonum est possit non diligi, vel etiam odio haberi, hoc non erit inquantum apprehenditur ut bonum, sed inquantum apprehenditur ut nocivum. In visione igitur Dei, qui est ipsa bonitas et veritas, oportet sicut comprehensionem ita delectationem seu delectabilem fruitionem adesse, secundum illud Ys. ult.: *Videbitis, et gaudebit cor vestrum.*

We should further understand that delight is engendered by the apprehension of a suitable good. Thus sight rejoices in beautiful colors, and taste in sweet savors. But this delight of the senses can be prevented if the organ is indisposed; for *the same light that is charming to healthy eyes is annoying to sore eyes.*[3] However, since the intellect does not understand by employing a bodily organ, as we showed above, no sorrow mars the delight that consists in the contemplation of truth. Of course, sadness can indirectly attend the mind's contemplation, when the object of truth is apprehended as harmful. Thus knowledge of truth may cause pleasure in the intellect, while at the same time the object known may engender sorrow in the will, not precisely because the object is known, but because its action is pernicious. But God himself is truth. Therefore, the intellect that sees God cannot but delight in the vision of him.

Besides, God is goodness itself, and goodness is the cause of love. Hence God's goodness must necessarily be loved by all who apprehend it. Although an object that is good may fail to call forth love, or may even be hated, the reason is not that it is apprehended as good, but that it is apprehended as harmful. Consequently, in the vision of God, who is goodness and truth itself, there must be love or delightful enjoyment no less than comprehension. This accords with Isaiah 66:14: *You shall see, and your heart shall rejoice.*

---

3. Augustine, *de Verbis Domini*, serm. XVIII, al. LXXXVIII, n. 4.

CHAPTER 166

That all who see God have a will firmly fixed in good

Ex hoc autem apparet quod anima videns Deum, vel quaecumque alia spiritualis creatura, habet voluntatem confirmatam in ipso, ut ad contrarium de cetero non flectatur. Cum enim obiectum voluntatis sit bonum, impossibile est voluntatem inclinari in aliquid nisi sub aliqua ratione boni. Possibile est autem in quocumque particulari bono aliquid deficere, quod ipsum cognoscenti relinquatur in alio quaerendum: unde non oportet voluntatem videntis quodcumque bonum particulare, in illo solo consistere ut extra eius ordinem non divertat. Sed in Deo, qui est bonum universale et ipsa bonitas, nihil boni deest quod alibi quaeri possit, ut supra ostensum est; quicumque igitur essentiam videt, non potest voluntatem ab eo divertere quin in omnia secundum rationem ipsius tendat.

Est etiam hoc videre per simile in intelligibilibus. Intellectus enim noster potest dubitando hac atque illac divertere, quousque ad primum principium veniatur in quo necesse est intellectum firmari. Quia igitur finis in appetibilibus est sicut principium in intelligibilibus, potest quidem voluntas ad contraria flecti quousque ad fruitionem ultimi finis veniatur, in qua necesse est ipsam firmari. Esset etiam contra rationem perfectae felicitatis, si homo in contrarium tranvsuerti posset: non enim totaliter excluderetur timor de amittendo, et sic non esset totaliter desiderium quietatum. Unde Apoc. III dicitur de beato *foras non egredietur amplius*.

This enables us to understand that the soul which sees God—and the same is true of any other spiritual creature—has its will firmly fixed in him, so that it can never turn to what is opposed to him. For, since the object of the will is the good, the will cannot incline to anything whatever unless it exhibits some aspect of good. Any particular good may be wanting in some perfection which the knower is then free to seek in another. Therefore, the will of him who beholds some particular good need not rest content with its possession, but may search farther afield beyond its orbit. But God, who is the universal good and very goodness itself, is not lacking in any good that may be sought elsewhere, as was shown above. And so whoever sees God's essence cannot turn his will from him, but must rather desire all things under the aspect of him.

Something similar is observed in the process of understanding. Our mind, when in doubt, can turn this way and that until it reaches a first principle; then the intellect must come to a halt. Since the end has the same function in things desired that a principle has in things understood, the will can veer in opposite directions until it comes to the enjoyment of the last end, in which it must rest. It would also be contrary to the notion of perfect happiness if man could turn to what is opposed to it. For then fear of losing happiness would not be wholly excluded, and so desire would not be completely satisfied. Hence the Revelation 3:12 says of the blessed one that *he shall go out no more*.

CHAPTER 167

That bodies will be altogether obedient to souls

Quia vero corpus est propter animam, sicut materia propter formam et organum propter artificem, animae vitam praedictam consecutaure tale corpus in resurrectione adiungetur divinitus quale competat beatitudini animae: quae enim propter finem sunt, disponi oportet secundum exigentiam finis. Animae autem ad summum operationis intellectualis pertingenti non convenit corpus habere per quod aliquatenus impediatur aut retardetur. Corpus autem humanum ratione suae corruptibilitatis impedit animam et retardat, ut neque continue contemplationi insistere valeat, neque ad summum contemplationis pervenire: unde per abstractionem a sensibus corporis homines aptiores ad divina quaedam capienda redduntur. Nam propheticae

The body is for the soul, as matter is for form and a tool for the craftsman. At the resurrection, therefore, when the life we have been speaking of is attained, God will join to the soul a body such as befits the beatitude of the soul; for whatever exists for the sake of an end must be duly disposed in accord with the demands of the end. A soul that has arrived at the peak of intellectual activity cannot appropriately have a body that would in any way impede or slow it down. But the human body, by reason of its corruptibility, does obstruct and slow down the soul, so that the soul can neither devote itself to uninterrupted contemplation nor reach the heights of contemplation. This is why men are able to grasp certain divine truths more readily when they are withdrawn from the bodily senses. For prophetic reve-

revelationes dormientibus vel in aliquo excessu mentis existentibus manifestantur, secundum illud Numeri XII: *Si quis fuerit inter vos propheta Domini, per somnium aut in visione loquar ad eum.* Corpora igitur resurgentium beatorum non erunt corruptibilia et animam retardantia ut nunc, sed magis incorruptibilia et totaliter animae obedientia, ut in nullo ei resistant.

lations are made to men when asleep, or when they are rapt in mental ecstasy, as we read in Numbers 12:6: *If there is a prophet among you, I the Lord make myself known to him in a vision, I speak with him in a dream.* Therefore, the bodies of risen saints will not be corruptible and will not burden down the soul, as they do now. On the contrary, they will be incorruptible and will be wholly obedient to the soul, so as not to resist it in any way whatever.

Chapter 168

Of the gifts of glorified bodies

Ex hoc autem perspici potest qualis sit dispositio corporum beatorum. Anima enim est corporis forma et motor. Inquantum autem est forma, non solum est principium corpori quantum ad esse substantiale, sed etiam quantum ad propria accidentia, quae causantur in subiecto ex unione formae ad materiam. Quanto autem forma fuerit fortior, tanto impressio formae in materia minus potest impediri a quocumque exteriori agente: ut patet in igne, cuius forma, quia est nobilissima inter elementares formas, hoc confert igni ut non de facili transmutetur a sua naturali dispositione patiendo ab aliquo agente.

Quia igitur anima beata in summo nobilitatis et virtutis erit, utpote primo rerum principio coniuncta, conferet corpori sibi divinitus unito, primo quidem esse substantiale nobilissimo modo, totaliter ipsum sub se continendo, unde subtile vel spirituale erit; dabit etiam sibi qualitatem nobilissimam, scilicet gloriam claritatis; et propter virtutem animae a nullo agente a sua dispositione poterit transmutari, quod est ipsum impassibile esse; et quia obediet totaliter animae ut instrumentum motori, agile reddetur. Erunt igitur quatuor conditiones corporum beatorum: subtilitas, claritas, impassibilitas et agilitas.

Unde Apostolus I Cor. XV dicit: corpus quod per mortem *seminatur in corruptione, surget in incorruptione,* quantum ad impassibilitatem; *seminatur in infirmitate, surget in virtute,* quantum ad agilitatem; *seminatur in ignobilitate, surget in gloria,* quantum ad claritatem; *seminatur animale, surget spirituale,* quantum ad subtilitatem.

This doctrine gives us an insight into the disposition of the bodies of the blessed. The soul is both the form and the motive force of the body. In its function as form, the soul is the principle of the body not only as regards the body's substantial being, but also as regards its proper accidents, which arise in the subject from the union of form with matter. The more dominant the form is, the less can any outside cause interfere with the impression made by the form on matter. We see this verified in the case of fire, whose form, which is said to be the noblest of all elementary forms, confers on fire the power of not being easily diverted from its natural disposition by the influence emanating from any cause.

Since the blessed soul, owing to its union with the first principle of all things, will be raised to the pinnacle of nobility and power, it will communicate substantial existence in the most perfect degree to the body that has been joined to it by divine action. And thus, holding the body completely under its sway, the soul will render the body subtle and spiritual. The soul will also bestow on the body a most noble quality, namely, the radiant beauty of clarity. Further, because of the influence emanating from the soul, the body's stability will not be subject to alteration by any cause, which means that the body will be impassible. Lastly, since the body will be wholly submissive to the soul, as a tool is to him who plies it, it will be endowed with agility. Hence the properties of the bodies belonging to the blessed will be these four: subtlety, clarity, impassibility, and agility.

This is the sense of the Apostle's words in 1 Corinthians 15:42–44. In death the body *is sown in corruption, it shall rise in incorruption*; this refers to impassibility. *It is sown in dishonor, it shall rise in glory*; this refers to clarity. *It is sown in weakness, it shall rise in power,* and hence will have agility. *It is sown a natural body, it shall rise a spiritual body*; in other words, it will be endowed with subtlety.

Chapter 169

That man will then be renewed, and all bodily creation

Manifestum est autem quod ea quae sunt ad finem disponuntur secundum exigentiam finis; unde si id propter quod sunt aliqua alia varietur secundum perfectum et imperfectum, ea quae ad ipsum ordinantur diversimode disponi oportet, ut ei deserviant secundum utrumque statum; cibus enim et vestimentum aliter praeparatur puero, et aliter viro. Ostensum est autem supra quod creatura corporalis ordinatur ad rationalem naturam sicut ad finem; oportet igitur quod homine accipiente ultimam perfectionem per resurrectionem, creatura corporalis diversum statum accipiat: et secundum hoc dicitur innovari mundus, homine resurgente, secundum illud Apoc. XXII: *Vidi caelum novum et terram novam*, et Ys. LXV: *Ecce ego creo caelos novos et terram novam.*

It is manifest that all things existing for some definite end are arranged according as the end requires. Therefore, if that for the sake of which other things exist can vary from perfect to imperfect, the things ordered to it must be arranged in various ways so as to serve the end in either state. Food and clothing, for instance, are prepared otherwise for a child than for a grown man. We have already called attention to the fact that material creation is ordered to rational nature as to its end. Consequently, when man is admitted to his final perfection through the resurrection, material creation must take on a new condition. This is why we are told that the world is to undergo renovation when man rises, in accord with Revelation 21:1: *I saw a new heaven and a new earth*, and Isaiah 65:17: *For behold, I create new heavens and a new earth.*

Chapter 170

Which creatures will be renewed, and which will remain

Considerandum tamen est quod diversa genera creaturarum corporalium secundum diversam rationem ad hominem ordinantur. Manifestum est enim quod plantae et animalia deserviunt homini in auxilium infirmitatis ipsius, dum ex eis habet victum et vestitum et vehiculum, et cetera huiusmodi quibus humana infirmitas sustentatur. In statu autem ultimo per resurrectionem tolletur ab homine omnis talis infirmitas: neque enim indigebunt homines ulterius cibis ad vescendum, cum sint incorruptibiles, ut supra ostensum est; neque vestimentis ad operiendum, utpote qui claritate gloriae vestientur; neque animalibus ad vehiculum, quibus agilitas aderit; neque aliquibus remediis ad sanitatem conservandam, utpote qui impassibiles erunt. Huiusmodi igitur corporeas creaturas, scilicet plantas et animalia et alia huiusmodi corpora mixta, conveniens est in statu illius ultimae consummationis non remanere.

Quatuor vero elementa, scilicet ignis, aer, aqua et terra, ordinantur ad hominem non solum quantum ad usum corruptibilis vitae, sed etiam ad constitutionem corporis eius: nam corpus humanum ex elementis constitutum est. Sic igitur essentialem ordinem habent elementa ad corpus humanum; unde homine consummato in corpore et anima, conveniens est ut etiam elementa remaneant, sed in meliorem dispositionem mutata.

It is, however, to be considered that the different kinds of material creatures are subordinated to man in different ways. Plants and animals serve man by aiding him in his weakness, in the sense that they supply him with food, clothing, transportation, and like conveniences which strengthen human feebleness. But in the final state that comes after the resurrection all such defects will be eliminated from man. Men will no longer need food to eat, since they will be incorruptible, as we have pointed out. Nor will men need garments to cover their nakedness, because they will be clothed with the radiance of glory. Nor will they require animals to carry them, as they will be endowed with agility. Nor will they need medicines to keep them in health, since they will be impassible. In that state of final consummation, therefore, it is fitting that no material creatures of this kind, namely, plants, animals, and other like mixed bodies, remain.

But the four elements, fire, air, water, and earth, are ordered to man not only as regards their utility in bodily life, but also as regards the composition of his body. The human body is made up of these elements. And so the elements have an essential ordination to the human body. Hence, when man is glorified in body and soul, the elements have to remain also, although they will be changed to a better condition of existence.

Corpora vero caelestia quantum ad sui substantiam neque in usum corruptibilis vitae ab homine assumuntur, neque corporis humani substantiam intrant; deserviunt tamen homini inquantum ex eorum specie et magnitudine excellentiam sui Creatoris demonstrant: unde frequenter in Scripturis admonetur homo ad considerandum caelestia corpora ut ex eis adducatur in reverentiam divinam, ut patet Ys. XL, ubi dicitur *Levate in excelsum oculos vestros et videte quis creavit haec.* Et quamvis in statu perfectionis illius homo ex creaturis sensibilibus in Dei notitiam non adducatur, cum Deum videat in se ipso, tamen delectabile est et iocundum etiam cognoscenti causam, considerare qualiter eius similitudo resplendeat in effectu: unde et sanctis cedet ad gaudium considerare refulgentiam divinae bonitatis in corporibus, et praecipue caelestibus, quae aliis praeminere videntur. Habent etiam corpora caelestia essentialem quodammodo ordinem ad corpus humanum secundum rationem causae agentis, sicut elementa secundum rationem causae materialis: *homo enim generat hominem et sol*; unde et hac etiam ratione convenit corpora caelestia remanere.

Nec solum ex comparatione ad hominem, sed etiam ex praedictarum corporearum creaturarum naturis idem apparet. Quod enim secundum nihil sui est incorruptibile, non debet remanere in illo incorruptionis statu. Corpora quidem caelestia incorruptibilia sunt secundum totum et partem; elementa vero secundum totum, sed non secundum partem; homines vautem secundum partem, scilicet secundum animam rationalem, sed non secundum totum quia compositum per mortem dissolvitur; animalia vero alia et plantae et omnia corpora mixta neque secundum totum neque secundum partem incorruptibilia sunt. Convenienter igitur in illo ultimo incorruptionis statu remanebunt quidem homines et elementa et corpora caelestia, non autem alia animalia, neque plantae aut corpora mixta.

Rationabiliter etiam idem apparet ex ratione universi. Cum enim homo quaedem pars sit universi corporei, in ultima hominis consummatione necesse est universum corporeum remanere; non enim videtur pars esse perfecta si fuerit sine toto. Universum autem corporeum remanere non potest nisi partes essentiales ipsius remaneant. Sunt autem partes essentiales eius corpora caelestia et elementa, utpote ex quibus tota mundialis machina consistit; cetera vero ad integritatem corporei universi pertinere non videntur, sed magis ad quendam ornatum et decorem ipsius qui competit statui mutabilitatis, secundum quod ex corpore caelesti ut agente, et elementis ut materialibus, generantur animalia et

As for the heavenly bodies, their substance is not utilized for the support of man's corruptible life, and does not enter into the substance of the human frame. However, they serve man in the sense that by their beauty and enormous size they show forth the excellence of their Creator. For this reason man is often exhorted in Sacred Scripture to contemplate the heavenly bodies, so as to be moved by them to sentiments of reverence toward God. This is exemplified in Isaiah 40:26: *Lift up your eyes on high and see who created these.* And although, in the state of consummated perfection, man is not brought to the knowledge of God by a consideration of sensible creatures, since he sees God as he is in himself, still it is pleasing and enjoyable for one who knows the cause to observe how the likeness of the cause shines forth in the effect. Thus a consideration of the divine goodness as mirrored in bodies, and particularly in the heavenly bodies, which appear to have a preeminence over other bodies, gives joy to the saints. Moreover, the heavenly bodies have some sort of essential relationship with the human body under the aspect of efficient causality, just as the elements have under the aspect of material causality: *man generates man, and the sun, too, has some part in this operation.*[4] This, then, is another reason why the heavenly bodies should remain in existence.

The doctrine here advocated follows not only from the relationship which various bodies have with man, but also from an examination of the natures of the material creatures we have been discussing. No object wanting in an intrinsic principle of incorruptibility ought to remain in the state that is characterized by incorruption. The heavenly bodies are incorruptible in whole and in part. The elements are incorruptible as wholes, but not as parts. Man is incorruptible in part (namely, in his rational soul), but not as a whole because the composite is dissolved by death. Animals and plants and all mixed bodies are incorruptible neither in whole nor in part. In the final state of incorruption, therefore, men and the elements and the heavenly bodies will fittingly remain, but not other animals or plants or mixed bodies.

We can argue reasonably to the same conclusion from the nature of the universe. Since man is a part of the material universe, the material universe should remain when man is brought to his final consummation; a part would seem to lack its proper perfection if it were to exist without the whole. On the other hand, the material universe cannot remain in existence without its essential parts. But the essential parts of the universe are the heavenly bodies and the elements, for the entire world machine is made up of them. Other bodies do not, apparently, pertain to the integrity of the material universe, but contribute rather to its adornment and beauty. They befit its changeable state in the sense that, with a heavenly body acting as efficient cause, and

---

4. Aristotle, *Physics* II, 2.

plantae et corpora mineralia. In statu autem ultimae consummationis alius ornatus elementis attribuetur qui deceat incorruptionis statum. Remanebunt igitur in illo statu homines et elementa et corpora caelestia, non autem animalia et plantae et corpora mineralia.

CHAPTER 171

That heavenly bodies will cease moving

Sed cum corpora caelestia continue moveri videantur, potest alicui videri quod si eorum substantia remaneat, quod tunc etiam in illo consummationis statu moveantur. Et quidem si ea ratione motus corporibus caelestibus adesset qua ratione adest elementis, rationabilis esset sermo. Motus enim elementis gravibus vel levibus adest propter eorum perfectionem consequendam: tendunt enim suo motu naturali in proprium locum, ubi melius est eis esse; unde in illo ultimo consummationis statu unumquodque elementum et quaelibet pars eius in suo proprio loco erit.

Sed hoc de motu corporum caelestium dici non potest, cum corpus caeleste nullo loco optento quiescat, sed sicut naturaliter movetur ad quodcumque ubi, ita et naturaliter discedit ab eo. Sic ergo non deperit aliquid corporibus caelestibus, si motus eis auferatur, ex quo motus eis non inest ut ipsa perficiantur. Ridiculum autem est dicere quod, sicut corpus leve per suam naturam movetur sursum, ita corpus caeleste per suam naturam circulariter moveatur sicut per activum principium. Manifestum est enim quod natura semper intendit ad unum; unde illud quod ex sui ratione unitati repugnat, non potest esse ultimus finis naturae. Motus autem unitati repugnat, inquantum id quod movetur alio et alio modo se habet dum movetur. Natura igitur non producit motum propter se ipsum, sed causat motum intendens terminum motus, sicut natura levis intendit locum sursum in ascensu, et sic de aliis.

Cum igitur motus circularis caelestis corporis non sit ad aliquod ubi determinatum, non potest dici quod motus circularis caelestis corporis principium activum sit natura, sicut est principium motus gravium et levium. Unde manente eadem natura corporum caelestium, nihil prohibet ipsa quiescere, licet ignem impossibile sit quiescere extra proprium ubi existentem, dummodo remaneat eadem natura ipsius. Dicitur tamen motus caelestis corporis naturalis, non propter principium ac-

Since the heavenly bodies are in constant motion, so far as we can judge, it may seem that if their substance remains, they will keep on moving also in the state of consummation. And, indeed, if motion were possessed by heavenly bodies for the same reason as that for which it is possessed by elements, such an assertion would be logical. Motion is found in heavy or light elements to promote the perfection they are to attain: by their natural motion they tend to the place that suits them, where they are in a better condition. Hence in the ultimate state of consummation each element and each part thereof will be in its own proper place.

But this cannot be maintained of the motion of heavenly bodies, for a heavenly body does not come to rest in any place it may occupy; as it travels naturally to any particular place, it no less naturally departs thence. Therefore, heavenly bodies suffer no loss if they are deprived of motion, because motion is not found in them for their own perfection. Also, it would be ridiculous to contend that a heavenly body is moved in circles by its nature as an active principle, in the way that a light body is impelled upward by its nature. For, as is evident, nature tends invariably in the direction of unity; and therefore that which by its very concept opposes unity cannot be the ultimate goal of nature. But motion is opposed to unity, in the sense that what moves varies in its mode of being by the very fact that it is in motion. Therefore, nature does not produce motion just for the sake of motion, but in causing motion has in view the terminus to be reached by motion. For instance, a body that is naturally light seeks an elevated place in its ascent; and so of other bodies.

Consequently, since the circular motion of a heavenly body does not tend to a definite position, we cannot say that the active principle of a heavenly body's circular motion is nature, in the sense that nature is the principle of the motion of heavy and light bodies. Accordingly, there is no reason why heavenly bodies should not come to rest without any change in their nature, even though fire, if its nature is to remain constant, cannot cease from its restlessness as long as it exists outside its proper sphere. Nevertheless, we

tivum motus, sed propter ipsum mobile quod habet aptitudinem ut sic moveatur. Relinquitur quod motus caelestis corporis sit ab aliquo intellectu.

Sed cum intellectus non moveat nisi ex intentione finis, considerare oportet quis sit finis motus caelestium corporum. Non autem potest dici quod ipse motus sit finis: motus enim cum sit via ad perfectionem, non habet rationem finis, sed magis eius quod est ad finem. Similiter etiam non potest dici quod renovatio situum sit finis motus caelestis corporis, ut scilicet propter hoc caeleste corpus moveatur ut omne ubi ad quod est in potentia adipiscatur in actu, quia hoc infinitum est; infinitum autem repugnat rationi finis.

Oportet igitur hinc considerare finem motus caeli. Manifestum est enim quod omne corpus motum ab intellectu est instrumentum ipsius; finis autem motus instrumenti est forma a principali agente concepta, quae per motum instrumenti in actum educitur. Forma autem divini intellectus quam per motum caeli complet, est perfectio rerum per viam generationis et corruptionis; generationis autem et corruptionis ultimus finis est nobilissima forma quae est anima humana, cuius ultimus finis est vita aeterna, ut supra ostensum est: est igitur ultimus finis motus caeli multiplicatio hominum perducendorum ad vitam aeternam.

Haec autem multitudo non potest esse infinita, nam intentio cuiuslibet intellectus stat in aliquo finito; completo igitur numero hominum ad vitam aeternam perducendorum, et eis in vita aeterna constitutis, motus caeli cessabit, sicut motus cuiuslibet instrumenti cessat postquam fuerit opus perfectum. Cessante autem motu caeli, cessabit per consequens omnis motus in inferioribus corporibus, nisi solus motus qui erit ab anima in hominibus. Et sic totum universum corporeum habebit aliam dispositionem et formam, secundum illud Apostoli I Cor. VII: *Praeterit figura huius mundi.*

say that the motion of a heavenly body is natural; but it is natural not by reason of an active principle of motion in it, but by reason of the mobile body itself that has an aptitude for such motion. We conclude, therefore, that motion is communicated to a heavenly body by some intellect.

However, since an intellect does not impart movement except in view of some end, we must inquire what is the end of the motion of heavenly bodies. The motion itself cannot be said to be this end. For motion is the way leading to perfection, and so does not have the notion of end, but rather pertains to that which is tending toward an end. Likewise, we cannot maintain that a succession of locations is the term of the movement of a heavenly body, as though a heavenly body moved for the purpose of actually occupying every position for which it has a potency; this would entail endless wandering, and what is endless contradicts the notion of end.

We ought to think of the end of the heaven's motion somewhat as follows. Any body set in motion by an intellect is evidently an instrument of the latter. But the end of an instrument's motion is a form conceived by the principal agent, a form that is reduced to act by the motion of the instrument. The form conceived by the divine intellect, to be realized by the motion of the heavens, is the perfection of things as achieved by way of generation and corruption. But the ultimate end of generation and corruption is the noblest of all forms, the human soul; and the soul's ultimate end is eternal life, as we said above. Accordingly, the ultimate end of the movement of the heavens is the multiplication of men, who are to be brought into being for eternal life.

Such a multitude cannot be infinite; the intention to be realized by any intellect comes to rest in something definite. Consequently, once the number of men who are to be brought into being for eternal life is filled out, and they are actually established in the possession of eternal life, the movement of the heavens will cease, just as the motion of any instrument ceases after a project has been carried through to completion. And when the movement of the heavens ceases, all movement in lower bodies will cease by way of consequence, excepting only the movement that will be in men as flowing from their souls. And thus the entire material universe will have a different arrangement and form, in accordance with the truth proclaimed in 1 Corinthians 7:31: *The form of this world is passing away.*

CHAPTER 172

Of the reward of man according to his works, or of his misery

Considerandum est autem quod, si est determinata via perveniendi ad aliquem finem, illum finem consequi non possunt qui per contrariam viam incedunt, aut a recta via deficiunt: non enim sanatur aeger, si contrariis utatur quae medicus prohibet, nisi forte per accidens. Est autem determinata via perveniendi ad felicitatem per virtutem. Non enim consequitur aliquid finem suum, nisi quod sibi proprium est bene operando: neque enim planta fructum faceret, si naturalis operationis modus non servaretur in ipsa; neque cursor perveniret ad bravium aut miles ad palmam, nisi uterque secundum proprium officium recte operaretur. Recte autem operari hominem propriam operationem est operari ipsum secundum virtutem, nam virtus uniuscuiusque rei est quae bonum facit habentem et opus eius bonum reddit. Cum igitur ultimus finis hominis sit vita aeterna de qua dictum est, non omnes ad eam perveniunt, sed soli qui secundum virtutem operantur.

Praeterea, ostensum est supra sub divina providentia contineri non solum naturalia, sed etiam res humanas, non in universali tantum sed etiam in singulari. Ad eum autem qui singularium hominum curam habet, pertinet praemia virtuti reddere et poenas peccato, quia poena est medicina culpae et ordinativa ipsius, ut supra habitum est; virtutis autem praemium felicitas est, quod ex bonitate divina homini datur: pertinet ergo ad Deum his qui contra virtutem agunt, non felicitatem sed contrarium in poenam reddere, scilicet extremam miseriam.

This leads to our next point. If there is a definite way of reaching a fixed end, they who travel along a road leading in the opposite direction or who turn aside from the right road cannot reach the goal. A sick man is not cured by using the wrong medicines, forbidden by the doctor, except, perhaps, quite by accident. Now, there is a definite way of arriving at happiness: namely, through the practice of virtue. Nothing will reach its end unless it performs well the operations proper to it. A plant will not bear fruit if its natural manner of operation is not preserved. A runner will not win a trophy or a soldier an award, unless each of works rightly in accord with his proper function. To say that a man rightly carries out his proper work is to say that he acts in accord with virtue; for the virtue of any being is that which makes its possessor good and also makes his work good. Accordingly, since the ultimate end of man is eternal life, of which we spoke previously, not all attain it, but only those who act in accord with virtue.

Besides, we showed above that, not just natural things but also human affairs are contained under divine providence, and this not only in general but in particular. But it belongs to one who has care of individual men to bestow awards for virtue and the punishments for sin, for punishment has a medicinal value with regard to sin and restores right order when violated by sin, as we stated above. Now, the reward of virtue is happiness, which is granted to man by God's goodness. Therefore, it belongs to God not to grant happiness to those who act against virtue, but to assign as punishment the opposite of happiness, namely, extreme misery.

CHAPTER 173

That man's reward or misery comes after this life

Considerare autem oportet quod contrariorum contraria sunt effectus. Operationi autem secundum virtutem contraria est operatio secundum malitiam; oportet igitur quod miseria, ad quam per operationem malitiae pervenitur, contraria sit felicitati quam meretur operatio virtutis. Contraria autem sunt unius generis: cum igitur felicitas ultima, ad quam pervenitur per operationem virtutis, non sit aliquod bonum huius vitae, sed post hanc vitam, ut ex supradictis patet, consequens erit quod etiam ultima miseria ad quam malitia perducit, sit aliquod malum post hanc vitam.

In this matter we should note that contrary causes beget contrary effects. Thus action that proceeds from malice is contrary to action that proceeds from virtue. Accordingly, the wretchedness at which evil action arrives is the opposite of the happiness that virtuous action merits. Now, contraries belong to the same genus. Therefore, since ultimate happiness, which is reached by virtuous action, is a good that belongs not to this life but to the next life, as is clear from what was said above, consequently ultimate misery also, to which vice leads, must be an evil after this life.

Praeterea, omnia bona vel mala huius vitae inveniuntur ad aliud ordinari: bona enim exteriora et etiam bona corporalia organice deserviunt ad virtutem, quae est directa via perveniendi ad beatitudinem apud eos qui praedictis rebus bene utuntur; sicut et apud eos qui eis male utuntur, sunt instrumenta malitiae per quam ad miseriam pervenitur. Et similiter mala his opposita, ut puta infirmitas, paupertas et huiusmodi, quibusdam sunt ad profectum virtutis, quibusdam ad malitiae augmentum, secundum quod eis homines diversimode utuntur. Quod autem ordinatur ad aliud non est ultimum praemium vel poena: non igitur ultima felicitas neque ultima miseria in bonis vel malis huius vitae consistit.

Besides, all goods and ills of this life are found to be ordered to something else. For external goods and even bodily goods are organically subservient to virtue, which is the direct path to beatitude for those who use such goods well. And for those who use these goods ill, they are instruments of vice, which leads to misery. Similarly, the ills opposed to such goods, such as sickness, poverty, and the like, are an occasion of progress in virtue for some but aggravate the viciousness of others, according as men use them in different ways. But what is ordered to something else cannot be the ultimate reward or punishment. Therefore, neither ultimate happiness nor ultimate misery consists in the goods or ills of this life.

Chapter 174

In what consists the misery of man, as regards the punishment of the damned

Quia igitur miseria ad quam ducit malitia contrariatur felicitati ad quam ducit virtus, oportet ea quae ad miseriam pertinent sumere per oppositum eorum quae de felicitate sunt dicta. Dictum est autem superius quod ultima hominis felicitas, quantum ad intellectum quidem consistit in plena Dei visione, quantum ad affectum vero in hoc quod voluntas hominis in prima bonitate sit immobiliter firmata. Erit igitur extrema miseria hominis in hoc quod intellectus totaliter divino lumine privetur, et affectus a Dei bonitate obstinate avertatur: et haec est praecipua miseria damnatorum, quae vocatur poena damni.

Considerandum tamen est quod, sicut ex supradictis patet, malum non potest totaliter excludere bonum, cum omne malum in aliquo bono fundetur. Miseria igitur, quamvis felicitati quae ab omni malo erit immunis opponatur, oportet tamen quod in bono naturae fundetur. Bonum autem intellectualis naturae in hoc consistit quod intellectus respiciat verum et voluntas tendat in bonum. Omne autem verum et omne bonum derivatur a primo vero et bono, quod Deus est. Unde oportet quod intellectus hominis in illa extrema miseria constituti, aliquam Dei cognitionem habeat et aliquam Dei dilectionem, secundum scilicet quod est principium naturalium perfectionum, quae est dilectio naturalis: non autem secundum quod in se ipso est, neque secundum quod est principium virtutum et gratiarum, seu quorumcumque bonorum quibus intellectualis natura ab ipso perficitur, quae est dilectio virtutis et gloriae.

Nec tamen homines in tali miseria constituti libero arbitrio carent, quamvis habeant voluntatem immobiliter firmatam in malo, sicut nec beati quamvis habeant voluntatem firmatam in bono. Libertas enim arbitrii proprie ad electionem se extendit, electio autem est eorum quae sunt ad finem; ultimus autem finis naturaliter appetitur ab unoquoque, unde omnes homines ex hoc quod intellectuales sunt, appetunt naturaliter felicitatem tanquam ultimum finem, et adeo immobiliter quod nullus potest velle fieri miser. Nec hoc libertati repugnat arbitrii, quae non se extendit nisi ad ea quae sunt ad finem.

Since the wretchedness to which vice leads is opposed to the happiness to which virtue leads, whatever pertains to wretchedness must be understood as being the opposite of all we have said about happiness. We pointed out above that, as regards his intellect, man's ultimate happiness consists in the full vision of God; while as regards man's affection, happiness consists in the immovable repose of his will in the first Good. Therefore, man's extreme misery will consist in the fact that his intellect is completely shut off from the divine light, and that his affections are stubbornly turned away from God's goodness. And this is the chief misery of the damned. It is known as the punishment of loss.

However, as is clear from what we have said already, evil cannot wholly exclude good, since every evil is founded on some good. Consequently, although misery is opposed to that happiness which will be free from all evil, nonetheless it must be rooted in a good of nature. The good of an intellectual nature consists in the fact that the intellect looks to the truth and the will tends to the good. But every truth and every good is derived from the first and supreme good, which is God. Therefore, the intellect of a man situated in the extreme misery of hell must have some knowledge of God and some love of God, namely, according as he is the principle of natural perfections. This is natural love. But the soul in hell cannot know and love God as he is in himself, nor so far as he is the principle of virtue or of grace or of any other goods by which intellectual nature is brought to perfection by him; for this is the love that belongs to virtue and glory.

Nevertheless, men buried in the misery of hell are not deprived of free choice, even though their will is immovably attached to evil. In the same way the blessed retain the power of free choice, even though their will is fixed on the Good. For freedom of choice, properly speaking, has to do with choice, and choice is concerned with the means leading to an end. Now, the last end is naturally desired by every being. Hence all men, by the very fact that they are intellectual, naturally desire happiness as their last end, and they do so with such immovable fixity of purpose that no one can wish to be miserable. But this is not incompatible with free will, which extends only to means leading to the end.

Quod autem in hoc particulari hic ultimum suam felicitatem, ille autem in illo ponat, non convenit huic aut illi inquantum est homo, cum in tali aestimatione et appetitu homines differant, sed unicuique hoc competit secundum quod est aliqualis. Dico autem aliqualis secundum aliquam passionem aut habitum: unde si transmutetur, aliud ei optimum videbitur. Et hoc maxime patet in his qui ex passione appetunt aliquid ut optimum, cessante autem passione, ut irae vel concupiscentiae, non similiter iudicant illud bonum ut prius. Habitus autem permanentiores sunt, unde firmius perseverant in his quae ex habitu prosequuntur; tamen quandiu habitus mutari potest, et aestimatio et appetitus hominis de ultimo fine mutatur.

Hoc autem contingit tantum hominibus in hac vita, in qua sunt in statu mutabilitatis: anima enim post hanc vitam intransmutabilis est secundum alterationem, quia huiusmodi transmutatio non competit ei nisi per accidens secundum aliquam transmutationem factam circa corpus. Resumpto vero corpore, non sequetur ipsa mutationes corporis, sed potius e converso: nunc enim anima infunditur corpori seminato, et ideo convenienter transmutationes corporis sequitur; tunc vero corpus unietur animae praeexistenti, unde totaliter sequetur eius conditiones. Anima igitur quemcumque finem sibi ultimum praestituisse invenitur in statu mortis, in eo fine perpetuo permanebit appetens illud ut optimum, sive sit bonum sive malum, secundum illud Eccl. XI quod lignum si praecisum fuerit *ubicumque ceciderit, ibi erit.*

Sic igitur post hanc vitam qui in morte boni inveniuntur, habebunt perpetuo voluntatem firmatam in bono; qui autem mali tunc invenientur, erunt perpetuo obstinati in malo.

The fact that one man places his happiness in this particular good while another places it in that good does not pertain to this or that man insofar as he is a man, since in such opinions and desires men differ. Rather, this variety is explained by each man's condition. By this I mean an emotion or habit; and so if it were to change, some other good would appeal to the man as most desirable. And this appears most clearly in men who are led by emotion to crave some good as the best: when the emotion, whether of anger or lust, dies away, they no longer judge that good as they did before. Habits are more permanent, and so men persevere more steadily in seeking things pursued by habit. Yet, so long as habit is capable of change, man's desire and his judgment as to what constitutes the last end are subject to change.

This possibility is open to men only during the present life, while they are in the state of changeability. After this life the soul is not subject to change as regards alteration, because such a change can affect it only indirectly, in consequence of some change undergone by the body. However, when the body is resumed, the soul will not be governed by changes occurring in the body, but rather the other way around. For at present the soul is infused into a body that has been generated of seed, and therefore is fittingly affected by changes experienced in the body. But then the body will be united to a preexisting soul, and so will be completely governed by the latter's conditions. Accordingly, whatever end the soul is found to have set for itself at the time of death, it will remain in that end forever, desiring it as the best, whether it is good or evil. This is the meaning of Ecclesiastes 11:3: *In the place where the tree falls, there it will lie.*

After this life, therefore, those who are found good at death will have their wills forever fixed in good. But those who are found evil will be forever obstinate in evil.

Chapter 175

That mortal sins are not forgiven after this life, but rather venial sins

Ex hoc autem considerari potest quod peccata mortalia post hanc vitam non dimittuntur, venialia vero dimitti possunt. Nam peccata mortalia sunt per aversionem a fine ultimo, circa quem homo immobiliter firmatur post mortem, ut dictum est; peccata vero venialia non respiciunt ultimum finem, sed viam ad finem ultimum. Sed si voluntas malorum post mortem obstinate firmatur in malo, semper appetent ut optimum quod prius appetierant; non ergo dolebunt se peccasse, nullus enim dolet se prosecutum esse quod aestimat esse optimum.

This enables us to perceive that mortal sins are not forgiven in the next world, while venial sins can be forgiven. Mortal sins are committed by turning away from our last end, about which man is irrevocably settled after death, as we have just said. Venial sins, however, do not regard our last end, but rather the road leading to that end. If the will of evil men is obstinately confirmed in evil after death, they forever continue to desire as the best what they previously desired. Therefore, they are not sorry they have sinned; for no one is sorry he has pursued what he judges to be the best.

Sed sciendum est quod damnati ad ultimam mise-riam ea quae appetierant ut optima habere post mortem non poterunt: non enim ibi dabitur luxuriosis facul-tas luxuriandi, aut iratis vel invidis facultas offendendi et impediendi alios, et idem est de singulis vitiis. Co-gnoscent autem eos qui secundum virtutem vixerunt se obtinere quod appetiverunt ut optimum. Dolent er-go quia peccata commiserunt, non propter hoc quod peccata eis displiceant, quia etiam tunc mallent peccata illa committere, si facultas daretur, quam Deum habere; sed propter hoc quod illud quod elegerunt habere non possunt, et id quod respuerunt possent habere. Sic igitur et voluntas eorum perpetuo manet obstinata in malo, et tamen gravissime dolebunt de culpa commissa et de gloria amissa: et hic dolor vocatur remorsus conscien-tiae, qui methaphorice in Scripturis vermis nominatur, secundum illud Ys. ult. *Vermis eorum non morietur.*

But we should understand that those who are con-demned to final misery cannot have after death what they craved as the best. Libertines in hell will have no opportu-nity to gratify their cravings; the wrathful and the envious will have no victims to offend or obstruct; and so of all the vices in turn. But the condemned will be aware that men who have lived a virtuous life in conformity with the pre-cepts of virtue obtain what they desired as best. Therefore, the wicked regret the sins they have committed, not because sin displeases them, for even in hell they would rather com-mit those same sins, if they had the chance, than possess God; but because they cannot have what they have chosen, and can have only what they have detested. Hence their will must remain forever obstinate in evil, and at the same time they will grieve most agonizingly for the sins they have committed and the glory they have lost. This anguish is called remorse of conscience, and in Scripture is referred to metaphorically as a worm, as we read in Isaiah 66:24: *Their worm shall not die.*

CHAPTER 176

That the bodies of the damned will be passible and yet complete, and without glorious qualities

Sicut autem in sanctis beatitudo animae quodammo-do ad corpora derivatur, ut supra dictum est, ita etiam et miseria animae derivabitur ad corpora damnatorum: hoc tamen observato quod, sicut miseria bonum naturae non excludit ab anima, ita etiam nec a corpore. Erunt igitur corpora damnatorum integra in sui natura, non tamen illas conditiones habebunt quae pertinent ad glo-riam beatorum: non enim erunt subtilia et impassibilia, sed magis in sua grossitie et passibilitate remanebunt, vel etiam haec augebuntur in eis; non erunt agilia, sed vix ab anima portabilia; non erunt clara sed obscura, ut ob-scuritas animae in corporibus demonstretur, secundum illud Ys. XIII *Facies combustae vultus eorum.*

Even as we said above, in speaking of the saints, that the beatitude of the soul will in some manner flow over to the body, so too the suffering of souls will flow over to the bodies of the damned. Yet we must observe that mis-ery does not exclude the good of nature from the body, any more than it does from the soul. Therefore, the bodies of the damned will be complete in their kind, although they will not have those qualities that go with the glory of the blessed. That is, they will not be subtle and impassible; rather, they will remain in their grossness and capacity for suffering, or these defects will even be heightened in them. Nor will they be agile, but scarcely maneuverable by the soul. Lastly, they will not be radiant but will be dark, so that the darkness of the soul may be displayed in the body, as is intimated in Isaiah 13:8: *Their countenances shall be as faces burnt.*

CHAPTER 177

That the bodies of the damned, although passible, will nevertheless be incorruptible

Sciendum tamen est quod, licet damnatorum corpora passibilia sint futura, non tamen corrumpentur, quamvis hoc esse videatur contra rationem eorum quae nunc experimur, nam passio magis facta abicit a substantia. Erit tamen tunc duplex ratio quare passio in perpetuum continuata passibilia corpora non corrumpet.

Prima quidem quia cessante motu caeli, ut supra dictum est, necesse est omnem mutationem naturae cessare; non igitur aliquid alterari poterit alteratione naturae, sed solum alteratione animae. Dico autem alterationem naturae, sicut cum aliquid ex calido fit frigidum, vel qualitercumque variatur secundum naturale esse qualitatum; Alterationem autem animae dico, sicut cum aliquid recipit qualitatem non secundum esse naturale qualitatis sed secundum esse spirituale ipsius: sicut pupilla non recipit formam coloris ut sit colorata, sed ut colorem sentiat. Sic igitur et corpora damnatorum patientur, vel ab igne vel a quocumque alio corporeo, non ut alterentur ad speciem vel qualitatem ignis, sed ut sentiant excellentias qualitatum eius: et hoc erit afflictivum, inquantum huiusmodi excellentiae contrariantur harmoniae in qua consistit et delectatur sensus; non tamen erit corruptivum, quia spiritualis receptio formarum naturam corporis non transmutat, nisi forte per accidens.

Secunda ratio erit ex parte animae, ad cuius perpetuitatem corpus trahetur divina virtute: unde anima damnati, inquantum est forma et natura talis corporis, dabit ei esse perpetuum; non tamen dabit ei ut pati non possit, propter suam imperfectionem. Sic igitur semper patientur illa corpora, non tamen corrumpentur.

Nevertheless, it should be known that although the bodies of the damned will be capable of suffering, they will yet not be subject to corruption, even though this may seem to disagree with present experience, according to which heightened suffering tends to deteriorate substance. In spite of this, there are two reasons why suffering that lasts forever will not corrupt the bodies undergoing it.

First, when the movement of the heavens ceases, as we said above, all transformation of nature must come to a stop. Nothing will be capable of alteration by alteration of its nature, but only by alteration of the soul. In speaking of an alteration of nature, I mean, for instance, a change from hot to cold in a thing, or any other such variation in the natural being of qualities. And by alteration of the soul I mean when a thing receives a quality not according to the quality's natural mode of being, but according to its spiritual mode of being; for example, the pupil of the eye does not receive the form of a color such that it is colored itself, but such that it perceives color. In this way the bodies of the damned will suffer from fire or from some other material agent, not that they may be transformed into the likeness or quality of fire, but that they may experience the distinguishing characteristics of its qualities. And this experience will be painful, because such distinguishing characteristics are opposed to the harmony in which the pleasure of sense consists. Yet the action of hellfire will not cause corruption, because spiritual reception of forms does not modify bodily nature, except perhaps indirectly.

The second reason is on the side of the soul, in whose perpetual duration the body will be forced, by divine power, to share. The condemned person's soul, insofar as it is the form and nature of such a body, will confer never-ending existence on the latter. But because of its imperfection, the soul will not bestow on the body immunity from suffering. Consequently, the bodies of the damned will suffer forever, but will not undergo dissolution.

CHAPTER 178

That before the resurrection the souls of some obtain happiness while others live in misery

Sic igitur secundum praedicta patet quod tam felicitas quam miseria principaliter consistit in anima, secundario autem et per quandam derivationem in corpore. Non igitur felicitas vel miseria animae dependet ex felicitate vel miseria corporis, sed magis e converso. Cum igitur post mortem animae remaneant ante resumptionem corporum, quaedam quidem cum merito beatitudinis, quaedam cum merito miseriae, manifestum est quod etiam ante resurrectionem animae quorundam praedicta felicitate potiuntur, secundum illud Apostoli II Cor. V: *Scimus quoniam si terrestris domus nostra huius habitationis dissolvatur, domum habemus a Deo non manufactam, conservatam in caelis*; et infra *Audemus et bonam voluntatem habemus peregrinari a corpore et praesentes esse Domino.* Quorundam vero animae in miseria vivent, secundum illud Luc. XVI: *Mortuus est dives et sepultus est in inferno.*

In keeping with what has been said, it is clear that both happiness and misery are found chiefly in the soul, and in the body secondarily and by a certain derivation. Hence the happiness or misery of the soul will not depend on the well-being or suffering of the body, but rather the other way around. However, souls remain in existence after death before the resumption of the body, some deserving beatitude, others deserving misery. Therefore, we can see that even before the resurrection the souls of some men obtain happiness, as the Apostle indicates in 2 Corinthians 5:1: *For we know that if the earthly tent we live in is destroyed, we have a building from God, a house not made with hands, eternal in the heavens.* A little below, in verse 8, he adds: *We are of good courage, and we would rather be away from the body and at home with the Lord.* But the souls of some will live in misery, in accord with Luke 16:22: *The rich man also died, and was buried in hell.*

CHAPTER 179

That the punishment of the damned is in the wicked by things both spiritual and bodily

Considerandum tamen est quod sanctarum animarum felicitas in solis bonis spiritualibus erit, poena vero animarum damnatarum ante resurrectionem non solum erit in malis spiritualibus, ut aliqui putaverunt, sed etiam poenas corporeas sustinebunt. Cuius diversitatis ratio est quia animae sanctorum, dum in hoc mundo fuerunt corporibus unitae, suum ordinem servaverunt, se rebus corporalibus non subiiciendo sed soli Deo, in cuius fruitione tota eorum felicitas consistit, non autem in aliquibus corporalibus bonis; malorum vero animae, naturae ordine non servato, se per affectum rebus corporalibus subdiderunt, divina et spiritualia contemnentes: unde consequens est ut puniantur non solum ex privatione spiritualium bonorum, sed etiam per hoc quod rebus corporalibus subdantur. Et ideo si qua in Scripturis sacris inveniantur quae sanctis animabus corporalium bonorum retributionem repromittant, mystice sunt exponenda, secundum quod in praedictis Scripturis spiritualia sub corporalium similitudinibus designari solent. Quae vero animabus damnatorum praenuntiant poenas corporeas, utpote quod ab igne inferni cruciabuntur, sunt secundum litteram intelligenda.

We should realize that the happiness enjoyed by the souls of the saints will consist exclusively in spiritual goods. On the other hand, the punishment inflicted on the souls of the damned, even before the resurrection, will not consist solely in spiritual evils, as some have thought; lost souls will also undergo bodily punishment. The reason for this difference is as follows. When the souls of the saints were united to their bodies here in this world, they observed right order, not subjecting themselves to material things but serving God alone. And so their whole happiness consists in the enjoyment of him, not in any material goods. But the souls of the wicked, in violation of the order of nature, set their affections on material things, scorning divine and spiritual goods. In consequence, they are punished not only by being deprived of spiritual goods, but by being subjected to the tyranny of material things. Accordingly, if Sacred Scripture is found to promise a reward of material goods to the souls of the saints, such passages are to be interpreted in a mystical sense; for spiritual things are often described in Scripture in terms of their likeness to material things. But texts that portend the bodily punishments of the souls of the damned, specifying that they will be tormented by the fires of hell, are to be understood literally.

Chapter 180

Whether the soul can suffer from bodily fire

Ne autem alicui absurdum videatur animam a corpore separatam ab igne corporeo pati, considerandum est non esse contra naturam spiritualia substantiae corpori alligari. Hoc enim et per naturam fit, sicut patet in unione animae ad corpus; et per magicas artes, per quas aliquis spiritus imaginibus aut anulis aut aliquibus huiusmodi alligatur. Hoc igitur ex divina virtute fieri potest ut aliquae spirituales substantiae, quamvis secundum suam naturam sint supra omnia corporalia elevatae, aliquibus corporibus alligentur, utputa igni infernali; non ita quod ipsum vivificent, sed quod eo quodammodo astringantur: et hoc ipsum consideratum a spirituali substantia, quod scilicet rei tam infimae quodammodo subditur, est ei afflictivum.

Inquantum igitur huiusmodi consideratio est spiritualis substantiae afflictiva, verificatur quod dicitur quod *anima, eo ipso quod se aspicit cremari, crematur*; et iterum quod ignis ille spiritualis sit, nam immediatum affligens est ignis apprehensus ut alligans. Inquantum vero ignis cui alligatur corporeus est, sic verificatur quod dicitur a Gregorio, quod *anima non solum videndo sed etiam experiendo ignem patitur*.

Et quia ignis ille non ex sua natura, sed ex virtute divina habet quod substantiam spiritualem alligare possit, convenienter dicitur a quibusdam, quod ignis ille agit in animam ut instrumentum divinae iustitiae vindicantis: non quidem ita quod agat in spiritualem substantiam sicut agit in corpora calefaciendo, desiccando, dissolvendo, sed alligando, ut dictum est. Et quia proximum afflictivum spiritualis substantiae est apprehensio ignis alligantis in poenam, manifeste perpendi potest quod afflictio non cessat, etiam si ad horam dispensative contingat substantiam spiritualem igne non ligari; sicut alicui qui esset ad perpetua vincula damnatus, ex hoc continuam afflictionem sentiret, etiam si ad horam a vinculis solveretur.

The assertion that a soul separated from its body can be tortured by bodily fire should not seem nonsensical when we reflect that it is not contrary to the nature of a spiritual substance to be confined to a body. This happens in the ordinary course of nature, as we see in the union of the soul with the body. The same effect is sometimes produced by magical arts, by which a spirit is imprisoned in images or amulets or other such objects. The power of God can undoubtedly bring it about that spiritual substances, which are raised above the material world by their nature, may nevertheless be tied down to certain bodies, such as hellfire; not in the sense that they animate the body in question, but that they are in some way fettered to it. And this very fact (namely, that it is subjected in a way to the dominion of a lowly creature), considered by a spiritual substance, is grievous to it.

Inasmuch as this awareness is distressing to the spiritual substance, the contention that the soul *burns by the very fact that it perceives itself to be in fire*, is substantiated. Thus understood, the fire is plainly spiritual, for what directly causes the distress is the fire apprehended as imprisoning. But inasmuch as the fire in which the spirit is imprisoned is bodily fire, the further statement made by Gregory is borne out, namely, that *the soul is in agony not only because it sees, but also because it experiences, the fire.*[5]

Furthermore, since this fire has the power of imprisoning the spiritual substance not of its own nature, but by the might of God, the view is fittingly expressed by some that the fire acts on the soul as an instrument of God's vindictive justice. This does not mean that the fire acts on the spiritual substance as it acts on bodies, by heating, parching, and consuming; its action is restrictive, as we said. And since that which directly afflicts the spiritual substance is the awareness that the fire incarcerates it for its punishment, we can reasonably suppose that the suffering does not cease even if, by God's dispensation, the spiritual substance should happen for a time to be released from the fire. In the same way a criminal who has been sentenced to perpetual irons feels no diminution of his continual affliction even though the chains should be struck off for an hour.

5. Gregory, *Dialogues*, IV.

CHAPTER 181

That after this life there are certain punishments of purgatory that are not eternal

Licet autem aliquae animae statim cum a corporibus absolvuntur, beatitudinem aeternam consequantur, ut dictum est, aliquae tamen ab hac consecutione retardantur ad tempus. Contingit enim quandoque aliquos pro peccatis commissis, de quibus tamen finaliter poenitent, poenitentiam non implesse in hac vita. Et quia ordo divinae iustitiae habet ut pro culpis poenae reddantur, oportet dicere quod post hanc vitam animae poenam exsolvant quam in hoc mundo non solverunt; non autem ita quod ad ultimam miseriam damnatorum deveniant, cum per poenitentiam ad statum caritatis sint reductae, per quam Deo sicut ultimo fini adhaeserunt: per quod vitam aeternam meruerunt. Unde relinquitur post hanc vitam esse quasdam purgatorias poenas, quibus poenitentiae non impletae implentur.

Although some souls attain to eternal beatitude as soon as they are released from their bodies, others are held back from this attainment for a time. For it sometimes happens that during their lives people have not done full penance for the sins they have committed, but of which they repented in the end. Since the order of divine justice demands that punishment be undergone for sins, we must hold that souls pay after this life the penalty they have not paid while on earth. This does not mean that they are banished to the ultimate misery of the damned, since by their repentance they have been brought back to the state of charity, whereby they cleave to God as their last end, so that they have merited eternal life. Hence we conclude that there are certain purgatorial punishments after this life, by which the debt of penalty not previously paid is discharged.

CHAPTER 182

That some punishments of purgatory are for venial sins

Simul etiam contingit aliquos ex hac vita decedere sine peccato mortali, sed tamen cum peccato veniali per quod ab ultimo fine non avertuntur, licet circa ea quae sunt ad finem indebite inhaerendo peccaverint. Quae quidem peccata in quibusdam perfectis viris ex fervore caritatis purgantur; in aliis autem oportet per aliquam poenam huiusmodi peccata purgari, quia ad vitam aeternam consequendam non perducitur nisi qui ab omni peccato et defectu fuerit immunis. Oportet igitur ponere purgatorias poenas aliquas post hanc vitam.

Habent autem huiusmodi poenae quod sint purgatoriae ex conditione eorum qui eas patiuntur, in quibus est caritas per quam voluntatem suam divinae voluntati conformant; ex cuius caritatis virtute poenae quas patiuntur eis ad purgationem prosunt; unde in his qui sine caritate sunt, sicut in damnatis, poenae non purgant, sed semper infectio peccati remanet, et ideo poena semper durat.

It also happens that some men depart this life free from mortal sin but nevertheless with venial sin. The commission of such sins does not, indeed, turn them from their last end, but they have sinned by cleaving unduly to the means leading to the end. In the case of some perfect men such sins are purged by their charity's fervor. But in others these sins must be purged by punishment of some sort, because no one is admitted to the possession of eternal life unless he is free from all sin and imperfection. Therefore, we must acknowledge the existence of purgatorial punishment after this life.

Such punishments derive their cleansing power from the condition of those who suffer them. For the souls in purgatory have charity, by which their wills are conformed to the divine will; it is owing to this charity that the punishments they suffer avail them for cleansing. This is why punishment has no cleansing force in those who lack charity, such as the damned. The defilement of their sin remains forever, and so their punishment endures forever.

CHAPTER 183

Whether suffering eternal punishment is opposed to
divine justice, since the guilt was momentary

Non est autem contra rationem divinae iustitiae si aliquis poenam perpetuam patiatur, quia nec secundum leges humanas hoc exigitur ut poena commensuretur culpae in tempore. Nam pro peccato adulterii vel homicidii, quod in tempore brevi committitur, lex humana infert quandoque perpetuum exilium, aut etiam mortem, per quae aliquis in perpetuum a societate civitatis excluditur; et quod exilium non in perpetuum durat, hoc per accidens contingit, quia vita hominis non est perpetua sed intentio iudicis ad hoc esse videtur ut eum sicut potest perpetuo puniat. Unde etiam non est iniustum, si pro momentaneo peccato et temporali Deus poenam aeternam infert.

Simul etiam considerandum est quod peccatori poena aeterna infertur qui de peccato non poenitet, et sic in ipso usque ad mortem perdurat; et quia in suo aeterno peccat, rationabiliter a Deo in aeternum punitur.

Habet etiam et quodlibet peccatum contra Deum commissum quandam infinitatem ex parte Dei contra quem committitur. Manifestum est enim quod quanto maior est contra quem peccatur, tanto peccatum est gravius: sicut qui dat alapam militi, gravius reputatur quam si daret rustico, et adhuc multo gravius si principi vel regi. Et sic cum Deus sit infinite magnus, offensa contra ipsum commissa est quodammodo infinita, unde et aliqualiter ei poena infinita debetur. Non autem potest esse poena infinita intensive, quia nihil creatum sic infinitum esse potest; unde relinquitur quod peccato mortali debetur poena infinita duratione.

Item, in eo qui corrigi potest, poena temporalis infertur ad eius correctionem vel purgationem. Si igitur aliquis a peccato corrigi non potest, sed voluntas eius obstinate firmata est in peccato, sicut supra de damnatis dictum est, eius poena terminari non debet.

The suffering of eternal punishment is not opposed to the character of divine justice. Even in the laws men make, punishment need not correspond to the offense in point of time. For the crime of adultery or murder, either of which may be committed in a brief span of time, human law may prescribe lifelong exile or even death, by both of which the criminal is banned forever from the society of the state. Exile, it is true, does not last forever, but this is purely accidental, owing to the fact that man's life is not everlasting; but the intention of the judge, it seems, is to sentence the criminal to perpetual punishment, so far as he can. In the same way it is not unjust for God to inflict eternal punishment for a sin committed in a moment of time.

We should also take into consideration the fact that eternal punishment is inflicted on a sinner who does not repent of his sin, and so he continues in his sin up to his death. And since he sins in his own eternity, he is reasonably punished by God eternally.

Furthermore, any sin committed against God has a certain infinity on the side of the God against whom it is committed. For, clearly, the greater the person who is offended, the more grievous is the offense. He who strikes a soldier is held more gravely accountable than if he struck a peasant; and his offense is much more serious if he strikes a prince or a king. Accordingly, since God is infinitely great, an offense committed against him is in a certain respect infinite; and so a punishment that is in a certain respect infinite is due to it. Such a punishment cannot be infinite in intensity, for nothing created can be infinite in this way. Consequently, a punishment of infinite duration is due for mortal sin.

Moreover, while a person is still capable of correction, temporal punishment is imposed for his emendation or cleansing. But if a sinner is incorrigible, so that his will is obstinately fixed in sin, as we said above is the case with the damned, his punishment should never end.

CHAPTER 184

That the aforesaid things belong also to other spiritual substances

Quia vero homo in natura intellectuali cum angelis convenit, in quibus etiam potest esse peccatum sicut et in hominibus, ut supra dictum est, quaecumque dicta sunt de gloria vel poena animarum, intelligenda etiam sunt de gloria bonorum et poena malorum angelorum. Hoc tamen solum inter homines et angelos differt, quod confirmationem voluntatis in bono et obstinationem in malo animae quidem humanae habent cum a corpore separantur, sicut supra dictum est, angeli vero quando primo cum voluntate deliberata sibi finem praestituerunt vel Deum vel aliquid creatum, et ex tunc beati vel miseri facti sunt. In animabus enim humanis mutabilitas esse potest non solum ex libertate voluntatis, sed etiam ex mutabilitate corporis, in angelis vero ex sola libertate arbitrii; et ideo angeli ex prima electione immutabilitatem consequuntur, animae vero non nisi cum fuerint a corporibus exutae.

Ad ostendendum igitur remunerationem bonorum, in Symbolo fidei dicitur *vitam aeternam*: quae quidem non est intelligenda aeterna solum propter durationem, sed magis propter aeternitatis fruitionem. Sed quia circa hoc etiam multa alia credenda occurrunt quae dicta sunt de poenis damnatorum et de finali statu mundi, ut omnia haec comprehenderentur, in Symbolo Patrum positum est *vitam futuri saeculi*; futurum enim saeculum omnia huiusmodi comprehendit.

In his intellectual nature man resembles the angels, who are capable of sin, as is man. We spoke of this above. Hence all that has been set forth about the punishment or glory of souls should be understood also of the glory of good angels and the punishment of bad angels. Men and angels exhibit only one point of difference in this regard: the wills of human souls receive confirmation in good or obstinacy in evil when they are separated from their bodies, as was said above; whereas angels were immediately made blessed or eternally wretched as soon as, with a deliberate will, they fixed either upon God or some created good as their end. The variability found in human souls can be accounted for not only by freedom of will, but also by changeableness of body; but in the angels such variability comes from the freedom of will alone. And so angels achieve unchangeability at the very first choice they make; but souls are not rendered immutable until they leave their bodies.

To express the reward of the good, we say in the Creed: *I believe . . . in life eternal.* This life is to be understood as eternal not only because of its duration, but even more on account of the enjoyment of eternity. But because in this connection there are proposed for our belief many other truths that concern the punishments of the damned and the final state of the world, the Creed of the Fathers sums up all these things where it says: *the life of the world to come.* For the world to come encompasses all such things.

CHAPTER 185

On faith in the humanity of Christ

Quia, sicut in principio dictum est, christiana fides circa duo praecipue versatur, scilicet circa divinitatem Trinitatis et circa humanitatem Christi, praemissis his quae ad divinitatem pertinent et effectus eius, considerandum restat de his quae pertinent ad humanitatem Christi.

Et quia, ut dicit Apostolus I Tim. I *Christus Iesus venit in hunc mundum peccatores salvos facere*, praemittendum videtur quomodo humanum genus in peccatum inciderit, ut sic evidentius acognoscatur quomodo per Christi humanitatem homines a peccatis liberantur.

As was remarked in the beginning of this work, the Christian faith revolves about two main doctrines: the divinity of the Trinity and the humanity of Christ. Having reviewed the truths that pertain to the divinity and its effects, we now turn to a consideration of matters pertaining to the humanity of Christ.

Since, however, as the Apostle remarks in 1 Timothy 1:15, *Christ Jesus came into the world to save sinners*, it seems best to inquire first how the human race fell into sin, so that we may understand more clearly how men are freed from their sins through Christ's humanity.

CHAPTER 186

On man's perfection in the first state

Sicut autem supra dictum est, homo in sui conditione taliter institutus fuit a Deo ut corpus omnino esset animae subiectum; rursumque inter partes animae inferiores vires rationi absque repugnantia subiicerentur, et ipsa ratio hominis esset Deo subiecta. Ex hoc autem quod corpus erat animae totaliter subiectum, contingebat quod nulla passio in corpore posset accidere quae dominio animae super corpus repugnaret, unde nec mors nec infirmitas in homine locum habebat. Ex subiectione vero inferiorum virium ad rationem erat in homine omnimoda mentis tranquillitas, quia ratio humana nullis inordinatis passionibus turbabatur. Ex hoc vero quod voluntas hominis erat Deo subiecta, homo referebat omnia in Deum sicut in ultimum finem, in quo eius iustitia et innocentia consistebat.

Horum autem trium ultimum erat causa aliorum: non enim hoc erat ex natura corporis, si eius componentia considerentur, quod in eo dissolutio sive quaecumque passio vitae repugnans locum non haberet, cum esset ex contrariis elementis compositum. Similiter etiam non erat ex natura animae quod vires sensibiles absque repugnantia rationi subiicerentur, cum vires sensibiles naturaliter moveantur in ea quae sunt delectabilia secundum sensum, quae multotiens rectae rationi repugnant.

We saw above that man was originally constituted by God in such a condition that his body was completely subject to his soul. Further, among the faculties of the soul, the lower powers were subject to reason without any rebelliousness, and man's reason itself was subject to God. In consequence of the perfect subjection of the body to the soul, no emotion could arise in the body that would in any way conflict with the soul's dominion over the body. Therefore, neither death nor illness had any place in man. And from the subjection of the lower powers to reason there resulted in man complete peace of mind, for the human reason was troubled by no inordinate emotions. Finally, owing to the submission of man's will to God, man referred all things to God as to his last end, and in this his justice and innocence consisted.

Of these three subordinations, the last was the cause of the other two. For man's freedom from dissolution, or from any suffering that would be a threat to his life, did not come from the nature of his body, as we see if we regard its component parts; for the body was made up of contrary elements. Similarly, the fact that man's sense faculties were subservient to reason without any rebelliousness did not come from the nature of the soul, since the sense powers naturally tend toward things that cause pleasure in the senses, which things are often at odds with right reason.

Erat igitur hoc ex virtute superioris, scilicet Dei, qui sicut animam rationalem corpori coniunxit, omnem proportionem corporis et corporearum virtutum cuiusmodi sunt sensibiles transcendentem, ita dedit animae rationali virtutem ut supra conditionem corporis ipsum continere posset et vires sensibiles, secundum quod rationali animae competebat. Ut igitur ratio inferiora sub se firmiter contineret, oportebat quod ipsa firmiter sub Deo contineretur, a quo virtutem praedictam habebat supra conditionem naturae.

Fuit igitur homo sic institutus ut nisi eius ratio subduceretur a Deo, neque corpus eius subduci poterat a vita animae, neque vires sensibiles a rectitudine rationis: unde quodammodo immortalis et impassibilis erat, quia scilicet nec mori nec pati poterat si non peccaret. Peccare tamen poterat, voluntate eius nondum confirmata per adeptionem ultimi finis; et sub hoc eventu poterat et mori et pati.

Et in hoc differt impassibilitas et immortalitas quam primus homo habuit, ab ea quam post resurrectionem sancti habebunt, qui numquam poterunt nec pati nec mori, voluntate eorum omnino confirmata in Deo, sicut supra dictum est. Differebat etiam quantum ad aliud, quia post resurrectionem homines neque cibis neque venereis utentur, primus autem homo sic conditus fuit ut necesse haberet vitam cibis sustentare, et ei incumberet generationi operam dare ut genus humanum multiplicaretur ex uno. Unde duo praecepta accepit in sui conditione. Ad primum pertinet quod ei dictum est *de omni ligno quod est in paradiso comede*; ad secundum quod ei dictum est *crescite et multiplicamini, et replete terram*.

This harmony came from the power of something higher, namely God. Just as God united to the body the rational soul that so immeasurably surpasses the body and the bodily faculties, such as the sense powers, so he gave to the rational soul power to control the body and the sensible powers in a manner that exceeded the body's natural condition, in a way befitting a rational soul. In order, therefore, that reason might firmly hold the lower faculties under its sway, reason itself had to be firmly kept under the dominion of God, from whom it received this power surpassing the condition of nature.

Therefore, man was so constituted that, unless his reason was subservient to God, his body could not be made subject to the life of the soul, nor his sense powers be brought under the rule of reason. Hence in that state life was in a certain way immortal and impassible: that is, man could neither die nor suffer, so long as he did not sin. Nevertheless, since his will was not yet confirmed in good by the attainment of the last end, he retained the power to sin; should this happen, man could suffer and die.

It is precisely in this respect that the impassibility and immortality possessed by the first man differ from the impassibility and immortality to be enjoyed after the resurrection by the saints, who will never be subject to suffering and death, since their wills will be wholly fixed upon God, as we said above. There was also another difference: after the resurrection men will have no use for food or the reproductive functions; but the first man was so constituted that he had to sustain his life with food, and he had a mandate to perform the work of generation; for the human race was to be multiplied from this one parent. Hence he received two commands, in keeping with his condition. The first is that mentioned in Genesis 2:16: *You may eat of every tree of the garden.* The other is reported in Genesis 1:28: *Be fruitful and multiply, and fill the earth.*

CHAPTER 187

That that perfect state may be called original justice

Hic autem hominis tam ordinatus status originalis iustitia nominatur, per quam et ipse homo suo superiori subditus erat, et ei omnia inferiora subiiciebantur, secundum quod de eo dictum est *Praesit piscibus maris et volatilibus caeli*; et inter partes etiam eius inferior absque repugnantia superiori subdebatur. Qui quidem status primo homini fuit concessus non ut cuidam personae singulari, sed ut primo humanae naturae principio, ita quod per ipsum simul cum natura traduceretur in posteros.

This wonderfully ordered state of man is called original justice. By it man himself was submissive to what was higher than him, and to him all lower creatures were subjected, as is indicated in Genesis 1:26: *Let him have dominion over the fishes of the sea and the fowls of the air.* And among man's component parts, the lower were subservient to the higher without any conflict. This state was granted to man, not as to a private individual, but as to the first principle of human nature, so that through him it was to be handed down to his descendants together with human nature.

Et quia unicuique debetur locus secundum convenientiam suae conditionis, homo sic ordinate institutus positus est in loco temperatissimo et delicioso, ut non solum interiorum molestiarum sed etiam exteriorum omnis ei vexatio tolleretur.

Moreover, since every one ought to have a habitation befitting his condition, man thus harmoniously constituted was placed in a most temperate and delightful region, so that all inconvenience, not only of internal annoyance, but also of external surroundings, might be far removed from him.

CHAPTER 188

On the tree of the knowledge of good and evil, and the commandment for the first man

Quia vero praedictus status hominis ex hoc dependebat quod voluntas humana Deo subiiceretur, ut homo a principio assuefieret ad Dei voluntatem sequendam, proposuit Deus homini quaedam praecepta, ut scilicet omnibus aliis lignis paradisi vesceretur, prohibens sub mortis comminatione ne de ligno scientiae boni et mali vesceretur; cuius quidem ligni esus non ideo prohibitus est quia secundum se malus esset, sed ut homo saltem in hoc modico aliquid observaret ea sola ratione quia esset a Deo praeceptum: unde praedicti ligni esus factus est malus, quia prohibitus. Dicebatur autem lignum illud *scientiae boni et mali*, non quia haberet virtutem scientiae causativam, sed propter eventum sequentem, quia scilicet homo per eius esum experimento didicit quid intersit inter obedientiae bonum et inobedientiae malum.

Now, this state enjoyed by man depended on the submission of the human will to God. In order therefore that man might become accustomed from the very beginning to following God's will, God laid certain precepts on him: man could eat of all the other trees in Paradise, but he was forbidden under pain of death to eat of the tree of knowledge of good and evil. Eating of the fruit of this tree was prohibited, not because it was evil in itself, but that at least in this slight matter man might have some precept to observe for the sole reason that it was so commanded by God. Hence eating of the fruit of this tree was evil because it was forbidden. The tree was called the tree *of knowledge of good and evil*, not because it had the power to cause knowledge, but because of would happen afterward, namely, because by eating of it man learned by experience the difference between the good of obedience and the evil of disobedience.

CHAPTER 189

On the seduction of Eve by the devil

Diabolus igitur qui iam peccaverat, videns hominem taliter institutum ut ad perfectam felicitatem pervenire posset a qua ipse deciderat, et quod nihilominus posset peccare, eum conatus est a rectitudine iustitiae abducere, aggrediens hominem ex parte debiliori, tentans feminam in qua minus vigebat sapientiae bonum. Et ut ad transgressionem praecepti facilius inclinaret, exclusit mendaciter metum mortis; et illa promisit quae homo naturaliter appetit, scilicet vitationem ignorantiae, dicens *aperientur oculi vestri*; et excellentiam dignitatis, dicens *eritis sicut dii*; et perfectionem scientiae, cum dicit *scientes bonum et malum*. Homo enim ex parte intellectus naturaliter fugit ignorantiam et scientiam appetit; ex parte vero voluntatis, quae naturaliter libera est, appetit celsitudinem, ut nulli, vel quanto paucioribus potest, subdatur.

The devil, who had already fallen into sin, saw that man was so equipped that he could arrive at everlasting happiness, from which the devil himself had been cast out. Yet, as he knew, man could still sin. So he sought to lead man astray from the straight path of justice, by attacking him on his weaker side: that is, he tempted the woman, in whom the good of wisdom was less vigorous. The more easily to induce her to break the command, he lyingly drove from her mind the fear of death, and promised her things that man naturally desires, namely, the overcoming of ignorance, saying: *your eyes shall be opened*; and the excellence of dignity: *you shall be as gods*; and the perfection of knowledge: *knowing good and evil* (Gen 3:5). On the part of his intellect man naturally shuns ignorance and desires knowledge; and on the part of his will, which is naturally free, he desires high station, so that he may be subject to no one, or at any rate to as few as possible.

CHAPTER 190

What was the woman's motivation

Mulier igitur repromissam celsitudinem simul et perfectionem scientiae concupivit. Accessit etiam ad hoc pulchritudo et suavitas fructus alliciens ad edendum, et sic metu mortis contempto, Dei praeceptum transgressa est de vetito ligno edendo.

Et sic eius peccatum multiplex invenitur: primo quidem superbiae, qua excellentiam inordinate appetiit; secundo curiositatis, qua scientiam ultra terminos sibi praefixos concupivit; tertio gulae, qua suavitate cibi permota est ad edendum; quarto falsam aestimationem de Deo, dum credidit verbis diaboli contra Deum loquentis; quinto inobedientiam, praeceptum Dei transgrediendo.

The woman craved both the promised exaltation and the perfection of knowledge. Added to this were the beauty and sweetness of the fruit, which attracted her to eat of it. And so, scorning the fear of death, she violated God's command by eating of the forbidden tree.

And thus she is found to have committed several sins. First, there was a sin of pride, whereby she inordinately desired excellence. Her second sin was one of curiosity, whereby she coveted knowledge beyond the limits fixed for her. The third sin was that of gluttony, whereby the sweetness of the fruit enticed her to eat. A fourth sin was a false estimation of God, when she believed the words of the devil who spoke against God. Fifth, there was a sin of disobedience, by transgressing God's command.

CHAPTER 191

How sin came to the man

Ex persuasione autem mulieris peccatum usque ad virum devenit; qui tamen, ut Apostolus dicit, *non est seductus* ut mulier, in hoc scilicet quod crederet verbis diaboli contra Deum loquentis: non enim in eius mente cadere poterat Deum mendaciter aliquid comminatum esse, neque inutiliter a re utili prohibuisse. Allectus tamen fuit promissione diaboli, excellentiam et scientiam indebite appetendo; ex quo voluntas eius a rectitudine iustitiae discessisset, uxori suae morem gerere volens, in transgressione divini praecepti eam secutus est edendo de fructu ligni vetiti.

The sin came to the man through the woman's persuasion. He, however, as the Apostle says in 1 Timothy 2:14, *was not seduced*, as the woman was. That is, he did not believe the words the devil spoke against God. The thought could not cross his mind that God would utter a lying threat or that he would uselessly forbit a useful thing. Nevertheless, he was enticed by the devil's promise by unduly desiring excellence and knowledge. As a result, his will fell away from the uprightness of justice and, wanting to go along with his wife, he followed her in transgressing the divine command by eating of the fruit of the forbidden tree.

CHAPTER 192

On the lower powers' rebellion against reason

Quia igitur status praedicti tam ordinata integritas tota causabatur ex subiectione humanae voluntatis ad Deum, ut dictum est, consequens fuit ut subducta humana voluntate a subiectione divina, deperiret illa perfecta subiectio inferiorum virium ad rationem et corporis ad animam: unde consecutum est ut homo sentiret in inferiori appetitu sensibili concupiscentiae et irae et ceterarum passionum inordinatos motus, non secundum ordinem rationis sed magis ei repugnantes, et eam plerumque obnubilantes et quasi pertrahentes. Et haec est pugna carnis ad spiritum de qua Scriptura loquitur. Nam quia appetitus sensitivus, sicut et ceterae sensitivae vires, per instrumentum corporeum operatur, ratio autem absque aliquo organo corporali, convenienter quod ad appetitum sensitivum pertinet carni imputatur; quod vero ad rationem spiritui, secundum quod spirituales substantiae dici solent quae sunt a corporibus separatae.

Because the harmonious integrity of the original state depended entirely on the submission of man's will to God, as was said, consequently as soon as the human will was withdrawn from subjection to God, the perfect subjection of the lower powers to reason and of the body to the soul likewise perished. As a result, man experienced in his lower, sensitive appetite the inordinate stirrings of concupiscence, anger, and all the other emotions. These movements no longer followed the order set by reason but rather resisted reason, frequently overclouding the mind and, so to speak, dragging it about. This is that rebellion of the flesh against the spirit which Scripture mentions. For, since the sensitive appetite, like all the other sense powers, operates through a bodily instrument, whereas reason functions without any bodily organ, what pertains to the sensitive appetite is fittingly ascribed to the flesh, while what pertains to reason is attributed to the spirit, in accord with the fact that substances that are without bodies are commonly called spiritual substances.

CHAPTER 193

On suffering and the necessity of dying

Consecutum est etiam ut in corpore sentirentur corruptionis defectus, ac per hoc homo incurrere necessitatem moriendi, quasi anima iam non valente corpus in perpetuum continere, vitam ei praebendo: unde homo factus est passibilis et mortalis, non solum quasi potens pati et mori ut antea, sed quasi necessitatem habens ad patiendum et moriendum.

A further consequence was that the defect of corruption was experienced in the body, and so man incurred the necessity of dying, the soul being no longer able to sustain the body forever by conferring life on it. Thus man became subject to suffering and death, not only in the sense that he was capable of suffering and dying as before, but in the sense that he was now under the necessity of suffering and dying.

CHAPTER 194

On other defects that followed in intellect and will

Consecuti sunt etiam in homine per consequens multi alii defectus. Abundantibus enim in appetitu inferiori inordinatis motibus passionum, simul etiam et in ratione deficiente lumine sapientiae, quo divinitus illustrabatur dum voluntas erat Deo subiecta, per consequens affectum suum rebus sensibilibus subdidit, in quibus aberrans a Deo multipliciter peccavit; et ulterius immundis spiritibus se subdidit, per quos credidit in huiusmodi rebus acquirendis sibi auxilium praestari, et sic in humano genere idolatria et diversa peccatorum genera processerunt. Et quo magis homo in his corruptus fuit, eo amplius a cognitione et desiderio bonorum spiritualium et divinorum recessit.

Many other defects also began to appear in man as a consequence. Inordinate stirrings of the lower appetite abounded, while at the same time the light of wisdom, which supernaturally illuminated man as long as his will was submissive to God, grew dim in his intellect. As a result, man subjected his affections to sensible things. Immersed in these, he wandered far from God and fell into repeated sins. Furthermore, he subjected himself to unclean spirits who he thought would help him to acquire such things. Through this process, idolatry and various kinds of sins arose in the human race. The more man was corrupted by these things, the farther he withdrew from the knowledge and desire of spiritual and divine goods.

CHAPTER 195

How these defects are handed down to posterity

Et quia praedictum originalis iustitiae bonum sic humano generi in primo parente divinitus attributum fuit, ut tamen per ipsum derivaretur in posteros, remota autem causa removetur effectus, consequens fuit ut primo homine praedicto bono per proprium peccatum privato, omnes posteri privarentur; et sic de cetero, post scilicet primi parentis peccatum, omnes absque originali iustitia et cum defectibus consequentibus sunt exorti.

Nec hoc est contra ordinem iustitiae, quasi Deo puniente in filiis quod primus parens deliquit, quia ista poena non est nisi subtractio eorum quae supernaturaliter primo homini divinitus sunt concessa per ipsum in alios derivanda: unde aliis non debebantur, nisi quatenus per primum parentem in eos erant transitura. Sicut si rex det feudum militi transiturum per ipsum ad heredes, si miles contra regem peccat ut feudum mereatur amittere, non potest postmodum ad eius posteros devenire: unde iuste privantur posteri per culpam parentis.

The good of original justice was conferred by God on the human race in its first parent, yet in such a way that it was to be transmitted to his posterity through him. But when a cause is removed, the effect is removed as well. Therefore, when the first man stripped himself of this good by his sin, all his descendants were likewise deprived of it. And so thenceforward, that is, ever since the sin of the first parent, all men come into the world bereft of original justice and burdened with the defects that attend its loss.

Nor is this in any way against the order of justice, as though God were punishing the sons for the crime of their first father. For the punishment in question is no more than the withdrawing of goods that were supernaturally granted by God to the first man for transmission, through him, to others. These goods were not owed to others, except insofar as these goods were to be passed on to them through their first parent. In the same way a king may give a soldier an estate, which will be handed on by him to his heirs. If the soldier then commits a crime against the king, and so deserves to forfeit the estate, it cannot afterwards pass to his heirs. In this case the sons are justly dispossessed in consequence of their father's crime.

CHAPTER 196

Whether the privation of original justice has the nature of sin in posterity

Sed remanet quaestio magis urgens: utrum defectus originalis iustitiae in his qui ex primo parente prodierunt, rationem culpae possit habere. Hoc enim ad rationem culpae pertinere videtur, sicut supra dictum est, ut malum quod culpabile dicitur sit in potestate eius cui reputatur in culpam. Nullus enim culpatur de eo quod non est in ipso facere vel non facere. Non est autem in potestate eius qui nascitur, ut cum originali iustitia nascatur vel sine ea; unde videtur quod talis defectus rationem culpae habere non possit.

Sed haec quaestio de facili solvitur, si distinguatur inter personam et naturam. Sicut enim in una persona multa sunt membra, ita in una humana natura multae sunt personae, ut participatione speciei humanae multi homines intelligantur quasi unus homo, ut Porfirius dicit. Est autem hoc advertendum in peccato unius hominis, quod diversis membris diversa peccata exercentur; nec requiritur ad rationem culpae quod singula peccata sint voluntaria voluntate membrorum quibus exercentur, sed voluntate eius quod est in homine principale, scilicet intellectivae partis: non enim potest manus non percutere aut pes non ambulare, voluntate iubente.

Per hunc igitur modum defectus originalis iustitiae est peccatum naturae, inquantum derivatur ex inordinata voluntate primi principii in natura humana, scilicet primi parentis, et sic est voluntarium habito respectu ad naturam, voluntate scilicet primi principii naturae; et sic transit in omnes qui ab ipso naturam humanam accipiunt, quasi in quaedam membra ipsius: et propter hoc dicitur originale peccatum, quia per originem a primo parente in posteros derivatur. Unde cum alia peccata, scilicet actualia, immediate respiciant personam peccantem, hoc peccatum directe respicit naturam; nam primus parens suo peccato infecit naturam, et natura infecta inficit personas filiorum qui ipsam a primo parente suscipiunt.

But there remains a more pressing question: whether the lack of original justice can have the character of sin in those who descend from the first parent. The notion of sin seems to require, as we said above, that a culpable evil be in the power of him to whom it is imputed as fault. No one is blamed for that which is beyond his power to do or not to do. But it is not in the power of a person who is born to be born with or without original justice. Hence it seems that such a lack cannot have the character of sin.

But this question is easily solved if we distinguish between person and nature. As there are many members in one person, so there are many persons in one human nature. Thus, by sharing in the same species, many men may be thought of as one man, as Porphyry remarks. Now we should note that in the sin of one man different sins are committed by different members. Nor does the notion of sin require that each sin be voluntary by the will of the members whereby they are committed, but that they be voluntary by the will of that which is principal in man, that is, his intellectual part. For the hand cannot but strike, and the foot cannot help walking, when the will so commands.

In this manner, then, the lack of original justice is a sin of nature in the sense that it has its origin in the inordinate will of the first principle in human nature: namely, of the first parent. And so it is voluntary with respect to nature, that is, by the will of the first principle of nature. And so it is transmitted to all who receive human nature from him, as though to his members. This is why it is called original sin, for it is transferred from the first parent to his descendants by their origin from him. So while other sins, that is, actual sins, have immediately to do with the person sinning, this sin has to do with the nature. For the first parent infected nature by his sin, and nature thus contaminated thereupon infects the persons of the children who receive their nature from the first parent.

CHAPTER 197

That not all sins are transmitted to posterity

Nec tamen oportet quod omnia alia peccata, vel primi parentis vel etiam ceterorum, traducantur in posteros, quia primum peccatum primi parentis sustulit donum totum quod supernaturaliter erat collatum in humana natura personae primi parentis, et sic dicitur corrupisse vel infecisse naturam: unde peccata consequentia non inveniunt aliquid huiusmodi quod possint subtrahere a tota natura, sed auferunt ab homine aut diminuunt aliquod bonum personale, nec corrumpunt naturam nisi inquantum pertinet ad hanc vel illam personam. Homo autem non generat sibi similem in persona, sed in natura: et ideo non traducitur a parente in posteros peccatum quod vitiat personam, sed primum peccatum quod vitiavit naturam.

It does not follow, however, that all other sins, either of the first parent or of other parents, are handed down to posterity. For only the first sin of the first parent removed in its entirety the gift that had been supernaturally granted to human nature in the first father's person. This is the reason why sin is said to have corrupted or infected nature. Subsequent sins do not encounter anything of this sort that they can uproot from the whole of human nature. Such sins do take away from a man or diminish some personal good; but they do not corrupt the nature except insofar as it pertains to this or that person. Since a man begets his like not in person but only in nature, the sin that defiles the person is not handed down from a parent to his descendants, but only the first sin that defiled the nature.

CHAPTER 198

That Adam's merit did not avail his posterity for reparation

Quamvis autem peccatum primi parentis totam naturam humanam infecerit, non tamen potuit per eius poenitentiam vel quodcumque eius meritum tota natura reparari. Manifestum est enim quod poenitentia Adae, vel quodcumque aliud eius meritum, fuit actus singularis personae; actus autem alicuius individui non potest in totam naturam speciei. Causae enim quae possunt in totam speciem sunt causae aequivocae, et non univocae: sol enim est causa generationis in tota specie humana, sed hic homo non potest esse causa generationis in tota specie humana, sed est causa generationis huius hominis. Meritum ergo singulare Adae, vel cuiuscumque puri hominis, sufficiens esse non potuit ad totam naturam reintegrandam. Quod autem per actum singularem primi hominis tota natura vitiata est, per accidens est consecutum, inquantum eo privato innocentiae statu per ipsum in alios derivari non potuit.

Et quamvis per poenitentiam redierit ad gratiam, non tamen redire potuit ad pristinam innocentiam, cui divinitus praedictum originalis iustitiae donum concessum erat. Simul etiam manifestum est quod praedictus originalis iustitiae status fuit quoddam speciale donum gratiae; gratia autem meritis non acquiritur, sed gratis a Deo datur: sicut igitur primus homo a principio originalem iustitiam non ex merito habuit, sed ex dono divino, ita etiam, et multo minus, post peccatum eam mereri potuit poenitendo, vel quodcumque aliud opus agendo.

Although the sin of the first parent infected the whole of human nature, neither his repentance nor any merit of his was able to restore nature in its entirety. Adam's repentance (or any other merit of his) was clearly the act of an individual person. But no act of any individual can affect the entire nature of the species. Causes that can affect a whole species are equivocal causes, not univocal: the sun is a cause of generation in the whole human species, but a particular man cannot be the cause of generation for the whole human species, but is a cause of the generation of a particular man. Hence the individual merit of Adam, or of any other mere man, could not suffice to re-establish the whole of nature. The fact that all nature was corrupted by a single act of the first man followed only indirectly, inasmuch as once the state of innocence had been removed in him, it could not be conveyed through him to others.

Even though Adam were to recover grace through penance, he could not return to that pristine innocence to which God had granted the gift of original justice. At the same time, it is clear that the state of original justice was a special gift of grace. Grace, however, is not acquired by merits, but is freely given by God. As, therefore, the first man had original justice not by merit but by a divine gift, much less could he merit it by repentence after his sin, nor by doing any other work.

Chapter 199

On the reparation of human nature through Christ

Oportebat autem quod humana natura praedicto modo infecta, ex divina providentia repararetur. Non enim poterat ad perfectam beatitudinem pervenire, nisi tali infectione remota: quia beatitudo cum sit perfectum bonum, nullum defectum compatitur, et maxime defectum peccati, quod aliquo modo virtuti opponitur quae est via in ipsam, ut dictum est. Et sic cum homo propter beatitudinem factus sit, quia ipsa est ultimus eius finis, sequeretur quod opus Dei in tam nobili creatura frustraretur, quod reputat inconveniens Psalmista cum dicit: *Numquid enim vane constituisti filios hominum?* Sic igitur oportebat humanam naturam reparari.

Praeterea, bonitas divina excedit potentiam creaturae ad bonum. Patet autem ex supradictis quod talis est hominis conditio quod, quandiu in hac mortali vita vivit, sicut nec confirmatur in bono immobiliter, ita nec immobiliter obstinatur in malo. Pertinet igitur hoc ad conditionem humanae naturae ut ab infectione peccati possit purgari. Non fuit igitur conveniens quod divina bonitas hanc potentiam totaliter dimitteret vacuam, quod fuisset si ei reparationis remedium non procurasset.

Nevertheless, human nature, infected in the aforesaid way, ought to be repaired by divine providence. It could not be admitted to perfect beatitude unless it were freed of its defilement. Beatitude, being a perfect good, tolerates no defect, especially the defect of sin; for sin is, in its own way, opposed to virtue, which is the path leading to beatitude, as was said. And so, since man was made for beatitude, for it is his ultimate end, one might conclude that God's work in creating so noble a being was doomed to frustration. But this the Psalmist holds to be inadmissible, for he says in Psalm 89 [88]:48: *For what vanity thou hast created all the sons of men?* Accordingly, it was fitting that human nature should be restored.

Furthermore, divine goodness exceeds the creature's capacity for good. As long as man leads a mortal life in this world, we know that his condition is such that he is neither immovably confirmed in good nor immovably obstinate in evil. Hence the very condition of human nature implies that it is capable of being cleansed from the contamination of sin. Surely the divine goodness would hardly allow this capacity to remain forever unrealized; but this would have been so had God not provided a remedy devised for man's restoration.

Chapter 200

That only through God incarnate ought nature to be repaired

Ostensum est autem quod neque per Adam neque per aliquem alium purum hominem poterat reparari: tum quia nullus homo singularis praeeminebat toti naturae, tum quia nullus purus homo potest esse gratiae causa. Eadem etiam ratione nec per angelum potuit reparari, quia neque angelus potest esse gratiae causa, neque etiam praeminet homini quantum ad ultimam beatitudinem perfectam ad quam oportebat hominem revocari, quia in ea sunt pares. Relinquitur igitur quod per solum Deum talis reparatio fieri poterat.

Sed si Deus hominem sola sua voluntate et virtute reparasset, non servaretur divinae iustitiae ordo, secun-

It was shown that the reparation of human nature could not be effected either by Adam or by any other mere man. For no individual man ever occupied a position of preeminence over the whole of nature; nor can any mere man be the cause of grace. The same reasoning shows that not even an angel could be the author of man's restoration. An angel cannot be the cause of grace, just as he cannot be man's recompense with regard to the ultimate perfection of beatitude, to which man was to be recalled. In this matter of beatitude angels and men are on a footing of equality. Nothing remains, therefore, but that such restoration could be effected by God alone.

But if God had restored man solely by his will and power, the order of divine justice would not have been ob-

dum quam exigitur satisfactio pro peccato. In Deo autem satisfactio non cadit, sicut nec meritum, hoc enim est sub alio existentis. Sic igitur neque Deo competebat satisfacere pro peccato totius naturae humanae, neque purus homo poterat, ut ostensum est. Conveniens igitur fuit Deum hominem fieri, ut sic unus et idem esset qui et reparare et satisfacere posset. Et hanc causam divinae Incarnationis assignat Apostolus I Tim. I *Christus Iesus venit in hunc mundum peccatores salvos facere.*

served, according to which satisfaction is demanded for sin. But to God there cannot belong satisfaction, just as neither can there belong merit, for this pertains to one who is subject to another. Thus it did not belong to God to satisfy for the sin of the whole of human nature; and a mere man was unable to do so, as we have just shown. Hence it was fitting that God become man, so that in this way it would be one and the same person who would be able both to repair and to offer satisfaction. This is the reason for the divine Incarnation assigned by the Apostle in 1 Timothy 1:15: *Christ Jesus came into this world to save sinners.*

CHAPTER 201

Other reasons for the Incarnation of the Son of God

Sunt tamen et aliae rationes Incarnationis divinae. Quia enim homo a spiritualibus recesserat et totum se rebus corporalibus dederat, ex quibus in Deum per se ipsum redire non poterat, divina Sapientia, quae hominem fecerat, per naturam corpoream assumptam hominem in corporalibus iacentem visitavit, ut per corporis sui mysteria eum ad spiritualia revocaret.

Fuit etiam necessarium humano generi ut Deus homo fieret ad demonstrandam humanae naturae dignitatem, ut sic homo neque se daemonibus subderet neque corporalibus rebus.

Simul etiam per hoc quod Deus homo fieri voluit manifeste ostendit immensitatem sui amoris ad homines, ut ex hoc iam homines Deo subderentur, non propter metum mortis quem primus homo contempsit, sed per caritatis affectum.

Datur etiam per hoc homini quoddam exemplum illius beatae unionis qua intellectus creatus increato Spiritui intelligendo unietur. Non enim restat incredibile quin intellectus creatus Deo uniri possit eius essentiam videndo, ex quo Deus homini unitus est naturam eius assumendo.

Perficitur etiam per hoc quodammodo totius operis divini universitas, dum homo, qui est ultimo creatus, circulo quodam in suum redit principium, ipsi rerum principio per opus Incarnationis unitus.

There are also other reasons for the divine Incarnation. Man had withdrawn from spiritual things and had delivered himself up wholly to material things, from which he was unable by his own efforts to make his way back to God. Therefore, divine Wisdom, who had made man, took to himself a bodily nature and visited man immersed in things of the body, so that by the mysteries of his bodily life he might recall man to spiritual life.

Furthermore, the human race had need that God should become man to show forth the dignity of human nature, so that man might not be subjugated either by devils or by things of the body.

At the same time, by willing to become man, God clearly displayed the immensity of his love for men, so that henceforth men might serve God, no longer out of fear of death, which the first man had scorned, but out of the love of charity.

Moreover, the Incarnation holds up to man an exemplar of that blessed union whereby the created intellect is joined, in an act of understanding, to the uncreated Spirit. It is no longer unbelievable that a creature's intellect should be capable of union with God by beholding the divine essence, since the time when God became united to man by taking a human nature to himself.

Lastly, the Incarnation puts the finishing touch to the whole vast work envisaged by God. For man, who was the last to be created, returns by a sort of circulatory movement to his first beginning, being united by the work of the Incarnation to the very principle of all things.

CHAPTER 202

On the error of Photinus about the Incarnation of the Son of God

Hoc autem divinae Incarnationis mysterium Fotinus, quantum in se fuit, evacuavit. Nam Ebionem et Cerinthum et Paulum Samosatenum sequens, Dominum Iesum Christum purum hominem fuisse asseruit, nec ante Mariam Virginem extitisse, sed quod per beatae vitae meritum et patientiam mortis gloriam divinitatis promeruit, ut sic Deus diceretur non per naturam, sed per adoptionis gratiam. Sic igitur non esset facta unio Dei et hominis, sed homo esset per gratiam deificatus: quod non singulare est Christo sed commune omnibus sanctis, quamvis in hac gratia aliqui excellentiores aliis habeantur.

Hic autem error auctoritatibus divinae Scripturae contradicit. Dicitur enim Io. I *in principio erat Verbum*, et postea subdit *Verbum caro factum est.* Verbum ergo quod *erat in principio apud Deum* carnem assumpsit, non autem homo qui ante non fuerat per gratiam adoptionis deificatus. Item, Dominus dicit Io. VI *Descendi de caelo non ut faciam voluntatem meam, sed voluntatem eius qui misit me*; secundum autem Fotini errorem non conveniret Christo descendisse sed solum ascendisse, cum tamen Apostolus dicat Eph. IV *Quod autem ascendit, quid est nisi quia primo descendit in inferiores partes terrae?* Ex quo manifeste datur intelligi quod in Christo non haberet locum Ascensio, nisi descensio praecessisset.

So far as he could, Photinus made void this mystery of the divine Incarnation. Following Ebion, Cerinthus, and Paul of Samosata, he asserted that our Lord Jesus Christ was no more than a man and that he did not exist before the Virgin Mary, but earned the glory of divinity by the merit of a blessed life and by patiently enduring death; and thus he was called God, not on account of his nature, but by the grace of adoption. In this event no union of God with man would have been effected, but a man would be deified by grace. Elevation of this sort is not peculiar to Christ, but is common to all the saints, although some may be considered more highly endowed with such grace than others.

This error contradicts the authority of Sacred Scripture. In John 1:1 we read: *In the beginning was the Word.* Shortly after the Evangelist adds: *and the Word was made flesh.* Hence the Word that *in the beginning was with God* assumed flesh—not that a man who did not exist beforehand was deified by the grace of adoption. Likewise, in John 6:38 the Lord says: *I came down from heaven, not to do my own will, but the will of him that sent me.* According to the error of Photinus, Christ could not have come down from heaven, but could only have gone up to heaven. Against him is the Apostle, who says in Ephesians 4:9: *In saying, "He ascended," what does it mean but that he had also descended into the lower parts of the earth?* This enables us to understand clearly that the Ascension would have no place in Christ unless his descent from heaven had preceded.

CHAPTER 203

Nestorius' error about the Incarnation and his refutation

Hoc igitur volens declinare Nestorius, partim quidem a Fotini errore discessit, quia posuit Christum Filium Dei dici non solum per adoptionis gratiam, sed per naturam divinam in qua Patri extitit coaeternus; partim vero cum Fotino concordat, dicens Filium Dei non sic esse unitum homini ut una persona fieret Dei et hominis, sed per solam inhabitationem: et sic homo ille sicut secundum Fotinum per solam gratiam Deus dicitur, sic et secundum Nestorium Dei Filius dicitur, non quia ipse vere sit Deus, sed propter Filii Dei inhabitationem in ipso quae est per gratiam.

Hic etiam error auctoritati sacrae Scripturae repugnat. Hanc enim unionem Dei et hominis Apostolus

Nestorius wished to avoid this contradiction. In part he disagreed with the error of Photinus; for Nestorius held that Christ was the Son of God not only by the grace of adoption, but by the divine nature in which he existed coeternal with the Father. In part, however, he sided with Photinus, saying that the Son of God was united to man not in such a way that there came to be one person of both God and man, but merely by dwelling in him. And so that man who, according to Photinus, is called God through grace alone, is called the son of God by Nestorius, not because he is truly God, but because the Son of God dwells in him through the inhabitation effected by grace.

This error is likewise opposed to the authority of Sacred Scripture. For the union of God with man is called by the

exinanitionem nominat, dicens Phil. II de Filio Dei: *Qui cum in forma Dei esset, non rapinam arbitratus est esse se aequalem Deo, sed semet ipsum exinanivit formam servi accipiens*; non est autem exinanitio Dei quod creaturam rationalem inhabitat per gratiam, alioquin et Pater et Spiritus Sanctus exinanirentur quia et ipsi creaturam rationalem per gratiam inhabitant, dicente Domino de se et de Patre, Io. XIV *ad eum veniemus, et mansionem apud eum faciemus*, et Apostolus de Spiritu sancto I Cor. III: *Spiritus Dei habitat in vobis*.

Item, non conveniret homini illi voces divinitatis emittere, si personaliter Deus non esset; praesumptuosissime ergo dixisset *Ego et Pater unum sumus*, vel *antequam Abraham fieret ego sum*: ego enim personam loquentis demonstrat, homo autem erat qui loquebatur; est igitur eadem persona Dei et hominis.

Ad hos igitur errores excludendos, in Symbolo tam Apostolorum quam Patrum, facta mentione de persona Filii, subditur *qui conceptus est et natus, passus, mortuus et resurrexit*. Non enim ea quae sunt hominis de Filio Dei praedicarentur, nisi eadem esset persona Filii Dei et hominis, quia quae uni personae conveniunt non ex hoc ipso de altera praedicantur: sicut quae conveniunt Paulo non ex hoc ipso praedicantur de Petro.

Apostle an *emptying*; in Philippians 2:6–7 he says of the Son of God: *Who, though he was in the form of God, did not count equality with God a thing to be grasped, but emptied himself, taking the form of a servant*. But there is no emptying of God when he dwells in a rational creature by grace. Otherwise the Father and the Holy Spirit would be emptied out also, since they too dwell in the rational creature by grace. Thus in John 14:23 our Lord says of himself and the Father: *We will come to him and make our home with him*. And in 1 Corinthians 3:16 the Apostle says of the Holy Spirit: *God's Spirit dwells in you*.

Moreover, the man in question could hardly use words signifying divinity unless he were personally God. He would have been guilty of supreme presumption in saying, as he does in John 10:30: *I and the Father are one*, and also in 8:58: *Before Abraham was, I am*. For the pronoun *I* indicates the person of the speaker; but he who uttered these words was a man. Hence the person of God and this man are one and the same.

To preclude such errors, both the Apostles' Creed and the Creed of the Nicene Fathers, after mentioning the person of the Son, add that *He was conceived of the Holy Spirit, was born, suffered, died, and rose*. For what pertains to the man would not be predicated of the Son of God unless the person of the Son of God and of the man were the same. What is proper to one person is, by that very fact, not said of another person; for example, what is proper to Paul is, for that precise reason, not predicated of Peter.

CHAPTER 204

Arius' error about the Incarnation and his refutation

Ut ergo unitatem Dei et hominis confiterentur quidam haeretici in partem contrariam diverterunt, dicentes Dei et hominis esse unam non solum personam, sed etiam naturam. Cuius quidem erroris primum principium fuit ab Arrio, qui ut ea quae in Scripturis dicuntur de Christo quibus ostenditur minor Patre, non nisi ad ipsum Dei Filium possent referri secundum assumentem naturam, posuit in Christo aliam animam non esse quam Dei Verbum, quod dixit corpori Christi fuisse pro anima: et sic cum dicit *Pater maior me est*, vel cum orasse legitur aut tristatus, ad ipsam naturam Filii Dei sit referendum. Hoc autem posito, sequitur quod unio Filii Dei ad hominem facta sit non solum in persona sed etiam in natura; manifestum est enim quod ex anima et corpore constituitur unitas naturae humanae.

Et huius quidem positionis falsitas quantum ad id quod Filium minorem Patre asserit esse, supra declarata

Therefore, in order to proclaim the unity of God and man in Christ, some heretics went to the opposite extreme and taught that not only was there one person, but also a single nature, in God and man. This error took its first origin from Arius. To ensure that those scriptural passages where Christ is represented as being inferior to the Father must refer to the Son of God himself, regarded in his assuming nature, Arius taught that in Christ there is no other soul than the Word of God who, he maintained, took the place of the soul in Christ's body. Thus when Christ says, in John 14:28, *The Father is greater than I*, or when he is read to pray or be sad, such matters are to be referred to the very nature of the Son of God. If this were so, the union of God's Son with man would be effected not only in the person, but also in the nature. For, as we know, the unity of human nature arises from the union of soul and body.

The falsity of this position, so far as regards the assertion that the Son is less than the Father, was brought out above,

est cum ostendimus Filium Patri aequalem. Quantum vero ad hoc quod dicit Verbum Dei Christo fuisse pro anima, huius erroris ex praemissis falsitas ostendi potest. Ostensum est enim supra animam corpori uniri ut formam; Deum autem impossibile est formam corporis esse, sicut supra ostensum est. Et ne forte Arrius diceret hoc de summo Deo Patre intelligendum, idem et de angelis ostendi potest, quod secundum suam naturam corpori non possunt uniri per modum formae, cum sint secundum suam naturam a corporibus separati. Multo igitur minus Filius Dei per quem facti sunt angeli, ut etiam Arrius confitetur, corporis forma esse non potest.

Praeterea, Filius Dei etiam si sit creatura, ut Arrius mentitur, tamen secundum ipsum beatitudine praecedit omnes spiritus creatos. Est autem tanta angelorum beatitudo quod tristitiam habere non possunt; non enim esset vera et plena felicitas, si aliquid eorum votis deficeret, est enim de ratione beatitudinis ut sit finale et perfectum bonum totaliter appetitum quietans. Multo igitur minus Dei Filius tristari potest aut timere secundum suam naturam. Legitur autem tristatus, cum dicitur *cepit Iesus pavere et taedere, et mestus esse*; et ipse etiam suam tristitiam profitetur dicens, *Tristis est anima mea usque ad mortem*. Manifestum est autem tristitiam corporis non esse, sed alicuius apprehensivae substantiae; oportet igitur praeter Verbum et corpus in Christo aliam fuisse substantiam quae tristitiam pati posset, et hanc dicimus animam.

Rursus, si Christus propterea assumpsit quae nostra sunt ut nos a peccatis mundaret, magis autem necessarium erat nobis mundari secundum animam, a qua origo peccati processerat et quae est subiectum peccati: non igitur corpus assumpsit sine anima, sed principalius animam, et corpus cum anima.

when we showed that the Son is equal to the Father. And with respect to the theory that the Word of God took the place of the soul in Christ, the absurdity of this error can be shown by reverting to a point previously set forth. For, as we demonstrated above, the soul is united to the body as the latter's form. But God cannot be the form of a body, as we also demonstrated above. Arius could not counter by maintaining that this is to be understood of God the Father on high, since the same can be proved even of the angels: namely, that they cannot, of their very nature, be united to a body in the manner of a form, seeing that by nature they are separated from bodies. Much less, then, can the Son of God be the form of a body, by whom the angels were made, as even Arius admits.

Besides, even if the Son of God were a creature, as Arius falsely teaches, he nevertheless excels all created spirits in beatitude, according to Arius himself. But the beatitude of the angels is so great that they can suffer no sadness. Their happiness would not be true and complete if anything were wanting to their desires, since the very notion of beatitude requires that it be the ultimate and perfect good wholly satisfying all desire. Much less can the Son of God be subject to sadness or fear in his own nature. Yet we read that he was sad: *Jesus began to be greatly distressed and troubled, and to be sorrowful* (Mark 14:33; Matt 26:37). And he himself gave witness of his sorrow, saying, *My soul is sorrowful even unto death* (Mark 14:34). Sadness, assuredly, pertains not to the body, but to some substance capable of apprehension. Therefore, besides the Word and the body, there must have been in Christ another substance that could suffer sadness; and this we call the soul.

Moreover, if Christ assumed what is ours for the purpose of cleansing us of sin, and if our greater need was to be cleansed in soul, from which sin arises and which is the subject of sin, we must conclude that he did not assume a body without a soul, but most principally the soul, and the body with the soul.

CHAPTER 205

Apollinaris' error about the Incarnation and his refutation

Ex quo etiam excluditur error Apollinaris, qui primo quidem Arrium secutus in Christo aliam animam esse non posuit quam ipsum Dei Verbum. Sed quia non sequebatur in hoc Arrium quod Filium Dei diceret creaturam, multa autem dicuntur de Christo quae nec corpori attribui possunt nec Creatori convenire, ut tristitia, timor et huiusmodi, coactus tandem fuit ponere quidem aliquam animam in Christo quae corpus sensificaret et harum passionum posset esse subiectum; quae tamen ratione et intellectu careret, ipsum autem Verbum homini Christo pro intellectu et ratione fuisse.

Hoc autem multipliciter falsum esse ostenditur. Primo quidem quia hoc est contra naturae rationem ut anima non rationalis cum formam corporis habeat; nihil autem monstruosum et innaturale in Christi Incarnatione fuisse putandum est. Secundo quia hoc fuisset contra Incarnationis finem qui est reparatio humanae naturae, quae quidem principalius incipit reparari quantum ad intellectivam partem, quae particeps peccati esse potest: unde praecipue conveniens fuit ut intellectivam hominis partem assumeret. Legitur etiam Christus ammiratus fuisse; ammirari autem non est nisi animae rationalis, Deo vero omnino convenire non potest. Sic igitur, sicut tristitia cogit in Christo ponere partem animae sensitivam, sic ammiratio cogit ponere in ipso partem animae intellectivam.

These considerations also refute the error of Apollinaris, who at first followed Arius in refusing to admit any soul in Christ other than the Word of God. But since he did not follow Arius in teaching that the Son of God was a creature, and many things are narrated of Christ which cannot be ascribed to the body, and which are inadmissible in the Creator, such as sadness, fear, and the like, he was eventually driven to acknowledge the existence in Christ of some soul which gave sense life to the body and could be the subject of such emotions. Yet this soul was without reason and intellect, and the Word himself took the place of intellect and reason in the man Christ.

This theory is shown to be false on many grounds. In the first place, the very concept of nature is incompatible with the opinion that a non-rational soul is the form of man, whose body nevertheless must have some form. But nothing monstrous or unnatural can be thought of in connection with Christ's Incarnation. Second, this hypothesis would be inconsistent with the purpose of the Incarnation, which is the reparation of human nature. Above all, human nature needs to be restored in the intellectual sphere, for that which can have part in sin is precisely the rational soul. Hence it chiefly befitted God's Son to assume man's intellectual nature. Besides, Christ is said to have marveled. But wonder cannot be experienced without a rational soul, and of course is wholly inadmissible in God. Therefore, as the sorrow Christ experienced forces us to admit that he had a sensitive soul, so the wonder he expressed compels us to acknowledge the existence of a rational soul in him.

CHAPTER 206

Eutyches' error of placing union in the nature

Hos autem quantum ad aliquid secutus est Eutices: posuit enim unam naturam fuisse Dei et hominis post Incarnationem, non tamen posuit quod Christo deesset vel anima vel intellectus, vel aliquid eorum quae ad integritatem spectant naturae.

Sed et huius opinionis falsitas manifeste apparet. Divina enim natura in se perfecta est et incommutabilis. Natura autem quae in se perfecta est, cum altera non potest in unam naturam convenire, nisi vel ipsa convertatur in alteram sicut cibus in cibatum, vel alterum convertatur in ipsum sicut in ignem ligna, vel utrumque transmutetur in tertium sicut elementa in corpus mix-

In a certain respect, Eutyches embraced the error of these men. He taught that there was one nature common to both God and man after the Incarnation. However, he did not hold that Christ was lacking in soul or in intellect or in anything pertaining to the integrity of nature.

But the falsity of this theory is plainly apparent. The divine nature is perfect in itself, and is incapable of change. But a nature that is perfect in itself cannot combine with another nature to form a single nature unless it is changed into that other nature (as food is changed into the eater), or unless the other nature is changed into it (as wood is changed into fire), or unless both natures are transformed

tum. Haec autem omnia removet divina immutabilitas: non enim immutabile est neque quod in alterum convertitur, neque in quod alterum converti potest. Cum igitur natura divina in se sit perfecta, nullo modo potest esse quod simul cum alia natura in unam naturam conveniat.

Rursus, si quis rerum ordinem consideret, additio maioris perfectionis variat naturae speciem. Alterius enim speciei est quod est et vivit quam quod est tantum; quod autem est et vivit et sentit, ut animal, est alterius speciei quam quod est et vivit tantum, ut planta; itemque quod est, vivit, sentit et intelligit, ut homo, est alterius speciei quam quod est, vivit et sentit tantum, ut animal brutum.

Si igitur illa una natura quae ponitur esse Christi, supra haec omnia habuit quod divinum est, consequens est quod illa natura fuerit alterius speciei a natura humana, sicut natura humana a natura bruti animalis; neque igitur Christus fuit homo eiusdem speciei. Quod falsum esse ostenditur ex hoc quod ab hominibus secundum carnem progenitus fuit, sicut Matthaeus ostendit in principio Euangelii sui dicens *liber generationis Iesu Christi, filii David, filii Abraham.*

into a third nature (as elements are when they combine to form a mixed body). The divine immutability excludes all these alternatives. For neither that which is changed into another thing, nor that into which another thing can be changed, is immutable. Since, therefore, the divine nature is perfect in itself, it can in no way combine with some other nature to form one nature.

Moreover, as we see if we reflect on the order of things, the addition of a greater perfection causes variation in the species of a nature. Thus a thing that not only exists but lives differs in species from a thing that merely exists. And that which exists and lives and senses, for instance, an animal, differs in species from the plant, which merely exists and lives. Likewise a being that exists, lives, senses, and understands, namely, a man, differs in species from that which merely exists, lives, and feels, such as a brute animal.

Accordingly, if the single nature which the Eutychean theory ascribes to Christ has the perfection of divinity in addition to all these other perfections, that nature necessarily differs in species from human nature, in the way that human nature differs specifically from the nature of a brute animal. On this supposition, consequently, Christ would not be a man of the same species as other men, a conclusion shown to be false by Christ's descent from men according to the flesh. This is brought out by Matthew in the beginning of his Gospel, saying, *The book of the generation of Jesus Christ, the son of David, the son of Abraham.*

CHAPTER 207

Against the error of the Manichaeans, who said that Christ did not have a true body but a phantastical one

Sicut autem Photinus evacuavit Incarnationis mysterium divinam naturam Christo auferendo, ita Manichaeus auferendo humanam. Quia enim ponebat totam creaturam corpoream a diabolo fuisse creatam, nec erat conveniens ut boni Dei Filius assumeret diaboli creaturam, posuit Christum non habuisse veram carnem sed phantasticam tantum; et omnia quae in Euangelio de Christo narrantur ad humanam naturam pertinentia, in phantasia et non in veritate facta fuisse asserebat.

Haec autem positio manifeste sacrae Scripturae contradicit, quae Christum asserit de Virgine natum, circumcisum, esurisse, comedisse et alia pertulisse quae pertinent ad humanae carnis naturam; falsa igitur esset Euangeliorum scriptura haec narrans de Christo.

Rursus, ipse Christus de se dicit *In hoc natus sum et ad hoc veni in mundum, ut testimonium perhibeam*

Just as Photinus emptied the mystery of the Incarnation by denying Christ's divine nature, so the Manichaean did the same by denying Christ's human nature. He held that the whole of material creation was the work of the devil and that the Son of the good God could not becomingly take to himself a creature of the devil. Therefore, he taught that Christ did not have real flesh but only phantom flesh. Consequently, he asserted that everything narrated in the Gospel as pertaining to the human nature of Christ was done in appearance only and not in very truth.

This theory plainly contradicts Sacred Scripture, which relates that Christ was born of the Virgin, that he was circumcised, that he was hungry, that he ate, and that he had other experiences common to the nature of human flesh. Hence in recording such things of Christ, what is written in the Gospels would be false.

Besides, Christ says of himself: *For this I was born, and for this I have come into the world, to bear witness to the*

veritati; non fuisset autem veritatis testis, sed magis falsitatis, si in se demonstrasset quod non erat: praesertim cum praedixerit se passurum quae sine vera carne pati non potuisset, scilicet quod traderetur in manus hominum, quod conspueretur, flagellaretur et crucifigeretur. Dicere ergo Christum veram carnem non habuisse, nec huiusmodi in veritate sed solum in phantasia eum fuisse perpessum, est Christo imponere falsitatem.

Adhuc, veram opinionem a cordibus hominum removere est hominis fallacis; Christus autem hanc opinionem a cordibus discipulorum removit. Cum enim post resurrectionem discipulis appareret qui eum spiritum vel phantasma esse existimabant, ad huiusmodi suspicionem de cordibus eorum tollendam dixit *Palpate et videte, quia spiritus carnem et ossa non habet sicut me videtis habere*; et in alio loco, cum supra mare ambularet, aestimantibus discipulis eum esse phantasma et ob hoc eis in timore constitutis, Dominus dixit *Ego sum, nolite timere*. Si igitur haec opinio vera est, necesse est dicere Christum fuisse fallacem; Christus autem Veritas est, ut ipse de se dicit. Est igitur hec opinio falsa.

truth (John 18:37). If he had displayed in himself what really did not exist, he would have been a witness not of truth but rather of error; especially since he foretold that he would suffer that which he could not suffer without a body: namely, that he would be betrayed into the hands of men, that he would be spat upon, scourged, and crucified. Accordingly, to say that Christ did not have true flesh and that he suffered such indignities not in truth but only in appearance is to accuse him of lying.

Furthermore, to banish true conviction from men's minds is the act of a liar. Christ did expel the Manichaean view from the minds of his disciples. After his resurrection he appeared to the disciples, who thought that he was a spirit or a specter. To banish suspicion of this kind from their hearts, he said to them: *Handle me, and see; for a spirit has not flesh and bones as you see that I have.* (Luke 24:39). On another occasion, when he was walking on the sea, and his disciples were terrified because they thought that he was an phantom, our Lord said: *It is I; have no fear* (Matt 14:27). If, therefore, this opinion were true, it is necessary to say that Christ was deceitful. But Christ is the Truth, as he testified of himself. Therefore, the Manichaean theory is false.

CHAPTER 208

That Christ had a true body, not one from heaven, against Valentinus

Valentinus autem etsi verum corpus Christum habuisse confiteretur, dicebat tamen eum non assumpsisse carnem de Virgine, sed attulisse corpus de caelo formatum quod transivit per Virginem, nihil ex ea accipiens, sicut aqua per canalem.

Hoc etiam veritati Scripturae contradicit. Dicit enim Apostolus ad Romanos de Christo *qui factus est ei ex semine David secundum carnem*, et ad Galatas dicit quod *Misit Deus Filium suum factum ex muliere*; Matthaeus etiam dicit quod *Iacob genuit Ioseph virum Mariae, de qua natus est Iesus qui vocatur Christus*, et postmodum eam eius matrem nominat subdens *Cum esset desponsata mater eius Maria Ioseph*. Haec autem vera non essent, si Christus de Virgine carnem non assumpsisset; falsum est igitur quod corpus caeleste attulerit.

Sed quod Apostolus ad Corinthios dicit *secundus homo de caelo caelestis*, intelligendum est quod de caelo descendit secundum divinitatem, non autem secundum substantiam corporis.

Adhuc, nulla ratio esset quare corpus de caelo afferens Dei Filius uterum Virginis introisset, si ex eo nihil

Valentinus admitted that Christ had a real body. However, he insisted that our Lord did not take flesh from the Blessed Virgin, but rather brought down with him a body formed of celestial matter. This body passed through the Virgin without receiving anything from her, like water through a canal.

This view also contradicts the truth of Scripture. In Romans 1:3 the Apostle says that God's Son *was descended from David according to the flesh*. And in Galatians 4:4 St. Paul writes: *God sent forth his Son, born of woman*. Matthew likewise relates: *And Jacob begot Joseph, the husband of Mary, of whom was born Jesus, who is called Christ* (Matt 1:16). A little later Matthew refers to her as Christ's mother, *when his mother Mary had been betrothed to Joseph*. None of this would be true if Christ had not received his flesh from the Virgin. Accordingly, the doctrine that Christ brought with him a celestial body is false.

But what the Apostle states in 1 Corinthians 15:47, namely, that *the second man* was *from heaven, heavenly*, should be understood in the sense that he came down from heaven in his divinity, not according to the substance of his body.

Moreover, there would be no reason why the Son of God, bringing his body from heaven, should have entered

assumeret; sed magis videretur esse fictio quaedam, dum ex utero matris egrediens demonstraret se ab ea accepisse carnem quam non acceperat. Cum igitur omnis falsitas a Christo sit aliena, simpliciter confitendum est quod Christus sic processit ex utero Virginis quod ex ea carnem accepit.

the Virgin's womb, if he were to receive nothing from her. Such a procedure would seem to be a kind of deceit if, by coming forth from his Mother's womb, he were to intimate that he had received from her a body which in fact he had not received. Since, therefore, all falsehood is foreign to Christ, we must acknowledge without reservation that he came forth from the Virgin's womb in such a way that he really took his flesh from her.

CHAPTER 209

The teaching of the faith about the Incarnation

Ex praemissis igitur colligere possumus quod in Christo, secundum catholicae fidei veritatem, fuit verum corpus nostrae naturae, vera anima rationalis, et simul cum hoc perfecta deitas. Hae autem tres substantiae in unam personam convenerunt, non autem in unam naturam.

Ad huius autem veritatis expositionem aliqui per quasdam vias erroneas processerunt. Considerantes enim quidam quod omne quod advenit alicui post esse completum accidentaliter ei adiungitur, ut homini vestis, posuerunt quod humanitas accidentali unione fuerit in persona Filii divinitati coniuncta, ita scilicet quod natura assumpta se haberet ad personam Filii Dei sicut vestis ad hominem; ad cuius confirmationem inducebant quod Apostolus dicit ad Philippenses de Christo, quod *habitu est inventus ut homo*. Rursus, considerabant quod ex unione animae et corporis efficitur individuum quoddam rationalis naturae, quod nominatur persona; si igitur anima in Christo fuisset corpori unita, videre non poterant quin sequeretur quod ex tali unione constitueretur persona. Sequeretur igitur in Christo duas esse personas, scilicet personam assumentem et personam assumptam; in homine enim induto non sunt duae personae, quia indumentum rationem personae non habet: si autem vestis esset persona, sequeretur in homine vestito duas esse personas. Ad hoc igitur excludendum, posuerunt animam Christi corpori unitam numquam fuisse, sed quod persona Filii Dei animam et corpus separatim assumpsit.

Sed dum haec opinio unum inconveniens vitare nititur, incidit in maius: sequitur enim ex necessitate quod Christus non fuerit verus homo. Veritas enim humanae naturae requirit animae et corporis unionem, nam homo est quod ex utroque componitur. Sequeretur etiam quod caro Christi non fuerit vera caro, nec aliquod membrum eius habuerit veritatem: remota enim anima, non est oculus aut manus aut caro et os nisi aequivoce, sicut

We can gather together the various points established in the foregoing chapters and say that, according to the true teaching of Catholic faith, Christ had a real body of the same nature as ours, a true rational soul, and, together with these, perfect deity. These three substances are united in one person, but do not combine to form one nature.

In undertaking to explain this truth, some theologians have taken the wrong path. Persuaded that everything accruing to a being subsequent to its complete existence is joined to it accidentally, as a garment is joined to a man, they taught that humanity was joined to divinity in the person of the Son by an accidental union, in such a way that the assumed nature would be related to the person of God's Son as clothing is related to a man. To bolster up this view, they brought forward what the Apostle says of Christ in Philippians 2:7, that he was *in habit found as a man*. Likewise, they reflected that from the union of soul and body an individual possessed of rational nature is formed, and that such an individual is called a person. If, therefore, the soul was united to the body in Christ, they were unable to see how they could escape the conclusion that a person would be constituted by such a union. In this event there would be two persons in Christ, the person who assumes and the person who is assumed. For there are not two persons in a man who is clothed, because clothing does not possess what is required for the notion of a person; but if the clothes were a person, there would be two persons in a clothed man. To avoid this conclusion, therefore, some proposed that Christ's soul was never united to his body, but that the person of God's Son assumed soul and body separately.

This view, while trying to escape one absurdity, falls into a greater, for it entails the necessary consequence that Christ would not be true man. For true human nature requires the union of soul and body; 'man' is what is made up of both. A further consequence is that Christ's flesh would not be true flesh, and that none of his members would be a true member. For if the soul is taken away, there is no eye or hand or flesh and bone, except in an equivocal sense, as

pictus aut lapideus. Sequeretur etiam quod Christus vere mortuus non fuerit: mors enim est privatio vitae; manifestum est autem quod divinitatis vita per mortem privari non potuit, corpus autem vivum esse non potuit si ei anima coniuncta non fuit. Sequeretur etiam ulterius quod Christi corpus sentire non potuit, non enim sentit corpus nisi per animam sibi coniunctam.

Adhuc, haec opinio in errorem Nestorii relabitur, quem tamen declinare intendit. In hoc enim erravit Nestorius quod potuit Verbum Dei homini Christo fuisse unitum secundum inhabitationem gratiae, ita quod Verbum Dei fuerit in illo homine sicut in templo suo; nihil autem refert dicere, quantum ad propositum pertinet, quod Verbum est in homine sicut in templo, et quod natura humana Verbo adveniat ut vestimentum vestito: nisi quod in tantum haec opinio est deterior, quia Christum verum hominem confiteri non potest. Est igitur haec opinio non immerito condemnata.

Adhuc, homo vestitus non potest dici esse persona vestis aut indumenti, neque aliquo modo dici potest quod sit in specie indumenti. Si igitur Filius Dei humanam naturam ut vestimentum assumpsit, nullo modo dici poterit persona humanae naturae; nec etiam dici poterit quod Filius Dei sit eiusdem speciei cum aliis hominibus, de quo tamen Apostolus dicit quod *est in similitudine hominum factus.* Unde patet hanc opinionem esse totaliter evitandam.

when these parts of the body are depicted in paint or fashioned in stone. Further, it would follow that Christ did not really die. For death is the privation of life. But obviously the divinity could not be deprived of life by death, and the body could not be alive if a soul were not united to it. A final consequence would be that Christ's body could not experience sensation; for the body has no sensation except through the soul united to it.

Furthermore, this theory falls back into the heresy of Nestorius, which it set out to overthrow. The error of Nestorius consisted in holding that the Word of God was united to Christ the man by the indwelling of grace, so that the Word of God would reside in that man as in his temple. It makes no difference, with regard to the doctrine at hand, whether we say that the Word is in the man as in a temple, or whether we say that human nature is joined to the Word as a garment to the person wearing it, except that the second opinion is the worse, inasmuch as it cannot admit that Christ was true man. Accordingly, this view is condemned, and deservedly so.

Moreover, the man who is clothed cannot be the person of the clothes or garment, nor can he in any way be said to be in the species of clothing. If, therefore, the Son of God took human nature to himself as a garment, he cannot in any sense be called the person of the human nature, nor could the Son of God be said to belong to the same species as the rest of men. Yet the Apostle says of him that he was *made in the likeness of men* (Phil 2:7). Clearly, therefore, this theory is to be utterly rejected.

CHAPTER 210

That in him there are not two supposita

Alii vero praedicta inconvenientia vitare volentes, posuerunt quidem in Christo animam corpori fuisse unitam, et ex tali unione quendam hominem constitutum fuisse quem dicunt a Filio Dei in unitatem personae assumptum; ratione cuius assumptionis illum hominem dicunt esse Filium Dei, et Filium Dei dicunt esse illum hominem. Et quia assumptionem praedictam ad unitatem personae dicunt esse terminatam, confitentur quidem in Christo unam personam Dei et hominis; sed quia hic homo, quem ex anima et corpore constitutum dicunt, est quoddam suppositum vel hypostasis humanae naturae, ponunt in Christo duo supposita et duas hypostases: unum humanae naturae creatum et temporale, aliud divinae naturae increatum et aeternum.

Haec autem positio, licet ab errore Nestorii verbotenus recedere videatur, tamen si quis eam interius perscrutetur, in idem cum Nestorio labitur.

Other theologians, wishing to avoid these absurdities, proposed that in Christ the soul was indeed united to the body, and that this union constituted a certain man who, they maintained, was assumed by the Son of God in unity of person. By reason of this assumption they said that the man in question was the Son of God and that the Son of God was that man. Further, since this assumption had unity of person as its terminus, they admitted that in Christ there was one person of God and man. But since this man who, they maintain, is composed of soul and body, is a certain suppositum or hypostasis of human nature, they place two supposita and two hypostases in Christ: one of human nature, created and temporal; the other of divine nature, uncreated and eternal.

Verbally, this view appears to recede from the error of Nestorius. But if we examine it a little more closely, we find that it slips into the heresy identified with Nestorius.

Manifestum est enim quod persona nihil aliud est quam substantia individua rationalis naturae; humana autem natura natura rationalis est: unde ex hoc ipso quod ponitur in Christo aliqua hypostasis vel suppositum humanae naturae temporale et creatum, ponitur etiam aliqua persona in Christo temporalis et creata: hoc enim est quod nomine suppositi vel hypostasis significatur, scilicet individua substantia. Ponentes igitur in Christo duo supposita vel duas hypostases, si quod dicunt intelligunt, necesse habent ponere duas personas.

Item, quaecumque supposito differunt, ita se habent quod ea quae sunt propria unius, alteri convenire non possunt. Si igitur non est idem suppositum Filius Dei et filius hominis, sequetur quod ea quae sunt filii hominis non possunt attribui Filio Dei, nec e converso; non ergo poterit dici Deus crucifixus aut natus ex Virgine quod est Nestorianae impietatis.

Si quis autem ad haec dicere velit, quod ea quae sunt hominis illius Filio Dei attribuuntur, et e converso, propter unitatem personae, quamvis sint diversa supposita: hoc omnino stare non potest. Manifestum est enim quod suppositum aeternum Filii Dei non est aliud quam ipsa eius persona; quaecumque igitur dicuntur de Filio Dei ratione suae personae, dicentur de ipso ratione sui suppositi. Sed ea quae sunt hominis non dicuntur de eo ratione suppositi, quia ponitur Filius Dei a filio hominis supposito differre: neque igitur ratione personae de Filio Dei dici poterunt quae sunt propria filii hominis, ut nasci de Virgine, mori et similia.

Adhuc, si de supposito aliquo temporali Dei nomen praedicetur, hoc erit recens et novum; sed omne quod recenter et de novo dicitur Deus, non est Deus nisi quia est factum Deus: quod autem est factum Deus non est naturaliter Deus, sed per adoptionem. Sequetur ergo quod ille homo non fuerit vere et naturaliter Deus, sed solum per adoptionem: quod etiam ad errorem Nestorii pertinet.

For a person, clearly, is nothing else than an individual substance possessed of rational nature. But human nature is rational. Therefore, by the very fact that a hypostasis or suppositum of human nature, temporal and created, is admitted in Christ, a person that is temporal and created is also admitted in him. This is precisely what the name of suppositum or hypostasis signifies: namely, an individual substance. Accordingly, if these people understand what they are saying, they must place two persons in Christ when they place two supposita or two hypostases in him.

Another consideration is the following. Things that differ as supposita exist in such a way that what is proper to one cannot belong to another. Therefore, if the Son of God is not the same suppositum as the Son of man, it follows that what belongs to the Son of man cannot be attributed to the Son of God, and vice versa. Hence we could not say that God was crucified or born of the Virgin: which is characteristic of the Nestorian impiety.

If anyone should undertake to protest, in reply to this, that what pertains to the man in question is ascribed to the Son of God, and conversely, because of the unity of person, even though the supposita may be different, his answer simply cannot stand. Evidently the eternal suppositum of the Son of God is nothing else than his very person. Hence whatever is said of the Son of God by reason of his person would also be said of him by reason of his suppositum. But what pertains to the man is not said of him by reason of his suppositum, for the Son of God is represented as differing from the son of man in suppositum. Therefore, what is proper to the Son of man, such as to be born of the Virgin, to die, and the like, cannot be said of the Son of God by reason of the person.

Furthermore, if the name of God is predicated of a temporal suppositum, this will be something recent and new. But any being that is recently and newly called God is not God unless it has been made God. What is made God, however, is God not by nature, but only by adoption. Consequently, the man in question would be God not in fact and by nature, but merely by adoption: which, again, pertains to the error of Nestorius.

CHAPTER 211

That in Christ there is only one suppositum and only one person

Sic igitur oportet dicere quod in Christo non solum sit una persona Dei et hominis, sed etiam unum suppositum et una hypostases; natura autem non una sed duae.

Ad cuius evidentiam considerare oportet quod haec nomina 'persona,' 'hypostasis' et 'suppositum' integrum quoddam designant. Non enim potest dici quod manus aut caro aut quaecumque alia partium sit persona vel hypostasis aut suppositum, sed hoc totum quod est hic homo. Ea vero nomina quae sunt communia individuis substantiarum et accidentium, ut 'individuum' et 'singulare,' possunt et toti et partibus aptari; nam partes aliquid cum accidentibus habent commune, scilicet quod non per se existunt sed aliis insunt, licet secundum modum diversum. Potest igitur dici quod manus Socratis et Platonis est quoddam individuum vel quoddam singulare, licet non sit hypostasis vel suppositum vel persona.

Est etiam considerandum ulterius quod aliquorum coniunctio, per se considerata, quandoque quidem facit aliquod integrum, quae in alio propter alterius additionem non constituit aliquod integrum, sicut in lapide commixtio quatuor elementorum facit aliquod integrum: unde id quod est ex elementis constitutum in lapide potest dici suppositum vel hypostasis, quod est hic lapis, non autem persona quia non est hypostasis rationalis naturae. Compositio autem elementorum in animali non constituit aliquod integrum, sed constituit partem, scilicet corpus, quia necesse est aliquid aliud advenire ad completionem animalis, scilicet animam; unde compositio elementorum in animali non constituit suppositum vel hypostasim, sed hoc animal totum est hypostasis vel suppositum. Nec tamen propter hoc minus est efficax in animali elementorum compositio quam in lapide, sed multo amplius, quia est ordinata ad rem nobiliorem.

Sic igitur in aliis hominibus unio animae et corporis constituit hypostasim et suppositum, quia nihil aliud advenit praeter haec duo. In Domino autem Iesu Christo praeter animam et corpus advenit tertia substantia divinitatis; unde non est seorsum suppositum vel hypostasis, sicut nec persona, id quod est ex corpore et anima constitutum, sed suppositum, hypostasis vel persona est id quod constat ex tribus substantiis, corpore scilicet, anima et deitate: et sic in Christo sicut est una tantum persona, ita una hypostasis et unum suppositum.

Accordingly, we must say that in Christ there is not only one person of God and man, but also that there is but one suppositum and one hypostasis. There is not, however, only one nature, but two natures.

To see that this is so, we have to consider that the names 'person,' 'hypostasis,' and 'suppositum' signify a certain whole. We cannot say that a hand or flesh or any of the other parts is a person or a hypostasis or a suppositum; but this whole, which is this man, is such. But names that are common to individuals in the line of substance and accident, such as 'individual' and 'singular,' can be applied both to a whole and to its parts. Parts have something in common with accidents in the sense that they do not exist by themselves, but inhere in other things, although in a different way. We can say, therefore, that the hand of Socrates or Plato is a certain individual or singular thing, even though it is not a hypostasis or a suppositum or a person.

Furthermore, we should note that a combination of various ingredients, considered just in itself, sometimes constitutes an integral whole, which same combination does not constitute an integral whole in another being because of the addition of some other component. Thus in a stone the combination of the four elements constitutes an integral whole; and so the object composed of the elements can, in the stone, be called a suppositum or hypostasis, which is this stone. It cannot, of course, be called a person, because it is not a hypostasis endowed with rational nature. But the combination of elements in an animal constitutes not an integral whole, but only a part, namely, the body. Something else must be added to make up the complete animal, and this is the soul. Hence the combination of elements in an animal does not constitute a suppositum or hypostasis; rather, this whole animal is the hypostasis or suppositum. Nevertheless, the combination of the elements is not, on this account, any less effectual in an animal than in a stone, but is rather more so, because it is ordained to the formation of a nobler being.

In all other men, therefore, the union of soul and body constitutes a hypostasis and suppositum, because in their case the hypostasis or suppositum is nothing else but these two components. But in our Lord Jesus Christ, besides soul and body, a third substance enters in, namely, divinity. In him, therefore, the composite of body and soul is not a separate suppositum or hypostasis, nor is it a person. The suppositum, hypostasis, or person is that which is made up of three substances: namely, the body, the soul, and the divinity. And thus in Christ, just as there is but one person, so there is but one suppositum and one hypostasis.

Alia autem ratione advenit anima corpori, et divinitas utrique. Nam anima advenit corpori ut forma eius existens, unde ex his duobus constituitur una natura, quae dicitur humana natura. Divinitas autem non advenit animae et corpori per modum formae nec per modum partis, hoc enim est contra rationem divinae perfectionis; unde ex divinitate et anima et corpore non constituitur una natura, sed ipsa divina natura in se ipsa integra et pura existens, sibi quodam incomprehensibili et ineffabili modo uniuit humanam naturam ex anima et corpore constitutam: quod ex infinita virtute eius processit. Videmus enim quod quanto aliquod agens est maioris virtutis, tanto magis sibi applicat aliquod instrumentum ad aliquod opus perficiendum; sicut igitur divina virtus propter sui infinitatem est infinita et incomprehensibilis, ita modus quo sibi univit humanam naturam Christi, quasi organum quoddam ad humanae salutis effectum, est nobis ineffabilis et excellens omnem aliam unionem Dei ad creaturam.

Et quia, sicut iam diximus, persona, hypostasis et suppositum designant aliquod integrum, si divina natura in Christo est ut pars et non ut aliquod integrum, sicut anima in compositione hominis, una persona Christi non se teneret tantum ex parte divinae naturae, sed esset quoddam constitutum ex tribus, sicut et in homine persona, hypostasis et suppositum est quod ex anima et corpore constituitur. Sed quia divina natura est aliquod integrum quod sibi assumpsit per quandam ineffabilem unionem humanam naturam, persona se tenet ex parte divinae naturae, et similiter hypostasis et suppositum; anima vero et corpus trahuntur ad personalitatem divinae personae, ut sic persona Filii Dei sit etiam persona filii hominis et hypostasis et suppositum.

Potest autem huiusmodi exemplum aliquale in creaturis inveniri. Subiectum enim et accidens non sic uniuntur ut ex eis aliquod tertium constituatur, unde subiectum in tali unione non se habet ut pars, sed est integrum quoddam quod est persona, hypostasis et suppositum; accidens autem trahitur ad personalitatem subiecti, ut sit eadem persona hominis et albi, et similiter eadem hypostasis et idem suppositum. Sic igitur secundum similitudinem quandam persona, hypostasis et suppositum Filii Dei est persona, hypostasis et suppositum humanae naturae in Christo; unde quidam propter huiusmodi similitudinem, dicere praesumpserunt quod humana natura in Christo degenerat in accidens, et quod accidentaliter Dei Filio uniretur, veritatem a similitudine non discernentes.

Patet igitur ex praemissis quod in Christo non est alia persona nisi aeterna, quae est persona Filii Dei, nec alia hypostasis aut suppositum; unde cum dicitur 'hic homo', demonstrato Christo, importatur suppositum aeternum.

But the way his soul is joined to his body differs from the way his divinity is united to both. His soul is joined the body as being its form, so that one nature, which is called human nature, is composed of these two. But divinity does not come to the soul and body as a form or as a part; this is against the very concept of divine perfection. Therefore, the divinity and the soul and the body do not constitute one nature; but the divine nature, complete in itself and existing in its purity, united to itself the human nature composed of soul and body in a way that is incomprehensible and indescribable. This called for an exercise of God's infinite power. For we see that the stronger an agent is, the more closely he connects to himself an instrument to carry out an undertaking. Therefore, as the divine power is infinite and incomprehensible because of its infinity, so too the way God united Christ's human nature to himself (as a sort of organ for accomplishing man's salvation) is beyond human expression and surpasses every other union of God with creation.

We pointed out above that person, hypostasis, and suppositum signify an integral whole. Hence if the divine nature in Christ had the function of a part, like the soul in the composition of a man, and were not something whole, then the one person of Christ would not be accounted for by the divine nature alone, but would be a certain composite of three elements, just as in man the person, hypostasis, and suppositum is what is constituted of soul and body. However, since the divine nature is an integral whole that took human nature to itself by an ineffable union, the person is accounted for by the divine nature, as also is the hypostasis and suppositum. Yet the soul and body are drawn to the personhood of the divine person, such that the person of the Son of God is also the person and the hypostasis and suppositum of the Son of man.

Some sort of example of this can be found in creatures. Thus subject and accident are not united in such a way that some third thing is formed from them. In a union of this kind, the subject does not have the function of a part, but is an integral whole, which is a person, hypostasis, and suppositum. But the accident is drawn to the personhood of the subject, so that the person of the man and of the color of whiteness is one and the same, and the hypostasis or suppositum is likewise the same. In a somewhat similar fashion the person, hypostasis, and suppositum of the Son of God is the person, hypostasis, and suppositum of the human nature in Christ. Influenced by comparisons of this sort, some theologians went so far as to say that the human nature in Christ deteriorates into an accident and is accidentally united to the Son of God; they were unable to discriminate between literal truth and likeness.

Therefore, the foregoing exposition makes it clear that there is no other person in Christ but the eternal person, who is the person of the Son of God. Nor is there any other hypostasis or suppositum. Hence when we say, 'this man,'

Nec tamen propter hoc aequivoce dicitur hoc nomen homo de Christo et aliis hominibus. Aequivocatio enim non attenditur secundum diversitatem suppositionis, sed secundum diversitatem significationis; nomen autem hominis attributum Petro et Christo idem significat, scilicet naturam humanam, sed non idem supponit, quia hic supponit suppositum aeternum Filii Dei, ibi autem suppositum creatum.

Quia vero de unoquoque supposito alicuius naturae possunt dici ea quae competunt illi naturae cuius est suppositum, idem autem suppositum est in Christo humanae et divinae naturae, manifestum est quod de hoc supposito utriusque naturae, sive supponatur per nomen significans humanam naturam sive per nomen significans divinam naturam aut personam, possunt dici indifferenter et quae sunt divinae et quae sunt humanae naturae ut puta si dicamus quod Filius Dei est aeternus et quod Filius Dei est natus de Virgine, et similiter dicere possumus quod hic homo est Deus et creavit stellas, et quod est natus, mortuus et sepultus.

Quod autem praedicatur de aliquo supposito, praedicatur de eo secundum aliquam formam vel naturam, sicut Socrates est albus secundum albedinem et est rationalis secundum animam. Dictum est autem supra quod in Christo sunt duae naturae et unum suppositum. Si ergo ad suppositum referatur, indifferenter sunt praedicanda de Christo humana et divina; est tamen discernendum secundum quid utrumque dicatur, quia divina dicuntur de ipso secundum divinam naturam, humana vero secundum humanam.

pointing to Christ, we mean the eternal suppositum. Nevertheless, the name 'man' is not for that reason predicated equivocally of Christ and of other men. Equivocation does not follow diversity of supposition, but follows diversity of signification. The name of man, as attributed to Peter and to Christ, signifies the same thing, namely, human nature. But it does not have the same supposition; for in the one case it takes the eternal suppositum of the Son of God as what underlies, while in the other case it takes a created suppositum as what underlies.

Since, however, we can predicate of a suppositum of some nature all that is proper to that nature of which it is the suppositum, and since in Christ the suppositum of the human nature is the same as the suppositum of the divine nature, it is evident that everything belonging to the divine nature and everything belonging to the human nature can be predicated indifferently of this suppositum, which is the suppositum of both natures. This is true both when the name we use signifies the divine nature or person, and when it signifies the human nature. We can say, for example, that the Son of God is eternal, and that the Son of God was born of the Virgin. Likewise we can say that this man is God, that he created the stars, and that he was born, died, and was buried.

What is predicated of a suppositum, is predicated of it according to some form or matter. Thus Socrates is white according to the whiteness of his skin and is rational according to his soul. But, as we pointed out in the beginning of this chapter, in Christ there are two natures and one suppositum. Therefore, if reference is made to the suppositum, human and divine things are to be predicated indifferently of Christ. Yet we must discern in what respect each thing is predicated; that is, divine attributes are predicated of Christ according to his divine nature, and human attributes are predicated of him according to his human nature.

CHAPTER 212

On the things that are spoken of as one or many in Christ

Quia igitur in Christo est una persona et duae naturae, ex horum consequentia considerandum est quid in Christo unum dici debeat, et quid multa.

Quaecumque enim secundum naturae diversitatem multiplicantur, necesse est quod in Christo plura esse confiteamur. Inter quae primo considerandum est quod, cum per generationem sive nativitatem natura recipiatur, necesse est quod sicut in Christo sunt duae naturae, ita etiam esse duas generationes sive nativitates: una aeterna, secundum quam accepit naturam divinam

Since there are in Christ one person and two natures, we have to examine the relationship between them to determine what is to be spoken of as one and what is to be spoken of as multiple in him.

Whatever is multiplied in accord with the diversity of Christ's natures must be acknowledged to be plural in him. In this connection we must consider, first of all, that nature is received by generation or birth. Consequently, as there are two natures in Christ, there must also be two generations or births: one that is eternal, whereby he received divine nature from his Father, and one that occurred in time,

a Patre; alia temporalis, secundum quam accepit humanam naturam a matre. Similiter etiam quaecumque communiter Deo et homini attribuuntur ad naturam pertinentia, necesse est plura dicere in Christo. Attribuitur autem Deo intellectus et voluntas et horum perfectiones, puta scientia seu sapientia, et caritas sive iustitia, quae etiam homini attribuuntur ad humanam naturam pertinentia; nam voluntas et intellectus sunt partes animae, horum autem perfectiones sunt sapientia et iustitia et huiusmodi. Necesse est ergo in Christo ponere duos intellectus, humanum et divinum, et similiter duas voluntates, duplicem etiam scientiam et iustitiam sive caritatem, creatam scilicet et increatam.

Ea vero quae ad suppositum sive hypostasim pertinent, unum tantum in Christo confiteri oportet. Unde si esse accipiatur secundum quod unum esse est unius suppositi, videtur dicendum quod in Christo sit unum tantum esse. Manifestum est enim quod partes divisae singulae proprium esse habent, secundum autem quod in toto considerantur, non habent singule suum esse, sed omnes sunt per esse totius. Sic igitur si consideremus ipsum Christum ut quoddam integrum suppositum duarum naturarum, erit eius unum tantum esse, sicut et est unum suppositum.

Quia vero operationes suppositorum sunt, visum fuit aliquibus quod sicut in Christo non est nisi unum suppositum, ita non est nisi una operatio. Sed non recte consideraverunt: nam in unoquoque individuo inveniuntur plures operationes si sunt plura operationum principia, sicut in ipso homine alia est operatio intelligendi et alia sentiendi propter differentiam sensus et intellectus; sed et in igne alia est operatio calefactionis et alia ascensionis propter differentiam caloris et levitatis. Natura autem comparatur ad operationem ut operationis principium; non igitur est una operatio in Christo propter unum suppositum, sed duae propter duas naturas, sicut e converso in Sancta Trinitate est una operatio trium personarum propter unam naturam.

Participat tamen operatio humanitatis in Christo aliquid de virtute operationis divinae. Omnium enim eorum quae conveniunt in unum suppositum, ei quod principalius est instrumentaliter cetera deserviunt, sicut ceterae partes hominis sunt instrumenta intellectus. Sic igitur in Domino Iesu Christo humanitas quasi quoddam organum divinitatis censetur. Manifestum est autem quod instrumentum agit in virtute principalis agentis; unde in actione instrumenti non solum invenitur virtus instrumenti, sed etiam virtus principalis agentis, sicut per actionem securis fit arca inquantum dirigitur ab artifice. Ita igitur et operatio ipsius humanae naturae in Christo quandam vim ex deitate habebat supra virtutem humanam: quod enim tangeret leprosum, humanitatis actio fuit, sed quod tactus ille

whereby he received human nature from his Mother. Likewise, whatever is attributed both to God and man as pertaining to nature must be predicated of Christ in the plural. To God are ascribed intellect and will and their perfections, such as knowledge or wisdom, and charity, and justice; these are also attributed to man as pertaining to human nature; for will and intellect are faculties of the soul, and their perfections are wisdom, justice, and the like. Therefore, we must acknowledge two intellects in Christ, one human and one divine, and likewise two wills, as well as a double knowledge and charity, namely, the created and the uncreated.

But whatever belongs to the suppositum or hypostasis must be declared to be one in Christ. Hence if existence is taken in the sense that one suppositum has one existence, it seems that we must say that there is only one existence in Christ. Of course, as is evident, when a whole is divided, each separate part has its own proper existence; but according as parts are considered in a whole, they do not have their own existence, for they all exist with the existence of the whole. Therefore, if we look upon Christ as an integral suppositum having two natures, his existence will be but one, just as there is but one suppositum.

Since actions belong to supposita, some have thought that, as there is but one suppositum in Christ, so there is only one activity in him. But they did not rightly weigh the matter. For many activities are discerned in any individual if there are many principles of activity in him. Thus in man the activity of understanding differs from the activity of sense perception, because of the difference between sense and intellect. Likewise, in fire the activity of heating differs from the activity of soaring upward, because of the difference between heat and lightness. Now, nature is related to activity as its principle. Therefore, it is not true that Christ has only activity because of the one suppositum. Rather, there are two activities in him, because of the two natures, just as, conversely, there is in the Holy Trinity but one activity of the three persons because of the one nature.

Nevertheless, the activity of Christ's humanity participates in a certain way in the power of his divine activity. For of all the factors that come together in a suppositum, that which is the most eminent is served by the rest in an instrumental capacity, just as all the lesser faculties of man are instruments of his intellect. Thus in Christ the human nature is held to be, as it were, the organ of his divine nature. But it is clear that an instrument acts in virtue of the principal agent. This is why, in the action of an instrument, we are able to discern not only the power of the instrument but also the power of the principal agent. A chest is made by the action of an axe, but only so far as the axe is directed by the carpenter. In like manner, the activity of the human nature in Christ received a certain efficacy from the divine nature, over and above its human power. When Christ touched a

curaret a lepra, ex virtute divinitatis processit. Et per hunc modum omnes eius actiones et passiones humanae virtute divinitatis salutares fuerunt: et ideo Dionysius vocat humanam Christi operationem 'theandricam,' id est deivirilem, quia scilicet sic procedebat ex humanitate quod tamen in ea vigeret divinitatis virtus.

Vertitur etiam a quibusdam in dubium de filiatione, utrum sit una tantum in Christo propter unitatem suppositi, vel duae propter dualitatem nativitatis. Videtur autem quod sint duae, quia multiplicata causa multiplicatur effectus; est autem causa filiationis nativitas: cum igitur sint duae nativitates Christi, consequens videtur quod etiam sint duae filiationes.

Nec obstat quod filiatio est relatio personalis, id est personam constituens: hoc enim verum est de filiatione divina, filiatio vero humana non constituit personam, sed accidit personae constitutae. Similiter etiam non obstat quod unus homo una filiatione refertur ad patrem et matrem, quia eadem nativitate nascitur ab utroque parente. Ubi autem est eadem causa relationis, et relatio est una realiter, quamvis multiplicentur respectus. Sicut enim nihil prohibet aliquid habere respectum ad alterum absque hoc quod realiter insit ei relatio, sicut scibile refertur ad scientiam relatione in eo non existente: ita nihil prohibet una tantum realis relatio plures respectus habere. Nam sicut relatio ex causa sua habet quod sit res quaedam, ita etiam quod sit una vel multiplex; et sic cum Christus non eadem nativitate nascatur ex Patre et matre, duae filiationes reales in eo esse videntur propter duas nativitates.

Sed est aliud quod obviat propter quod non possunt esse plures filiationes reales in Christo. Non enim omne quod nascitur ex aliquo filius dici potest, sed solum completum suppositum; manus enim alicuius hominis non dicitur filia, nec pes filius, sed totum singulare quod est Petrus vel Iohannes: proprie igitur subiectum filiationis est ipsum suppositum. Ostensum est autem supra quod in Christo non est aliud suppositum quam increatum, cui non potest ex tempore aliqua realis relatio advenire; sed, sicut supra diximus, omnis relatio Dei ad creaturam est secundum rationem tantum. Oportet igitur quod filiatio qua suppositum aeternum Filii refertur ad Virginem matrem, non sit realis relatio sed respectus rationis tantum.

Nec propter hoc impeditur quin Christus sit vere et realiter filius Virginis matris quasia realiter ab ea natus, sicut etiam Deus vere et realiter est dominus creaturae

leper, the action belonged to his human nature; but the fact that the touch cured the man of his leprosy flowed from the power of the divine nature. In this way all the human actions and sufferings of Christ were efficacious for our salvation in virtue of his divinity. This is why Dionysius calls the human activity of Christ 'theandric,' that is, divine-human, because actions of this sort proceeded from his human nature in such a way that the power of the divinity was operative in them.

A doubt is raised by some theologians concerning sonship: whether there is only one filiation in Christ because of the oneness of the suppositum, or two filiations because of the duality of his birth. It may seem that there are two filiations, for when a cause is multiplied the effect is multiplied, and the cause of sonship is being born. Since, therefore, there are two births of Christ, the consequence may seem to follow that there are also two filiations.

This view is not undermined by the fact that filiation is a personal relation, that is, that it constitutes a person. In the case of Christ, this is true of the divine filiation; the human filiation does not constitute a person, but comes to a person already constituted as such. In the same way there is no reason why one man should not be related to his father and mother by a single filiation; he is born of both parents by the same birth. Wherever the cause of a relation is the same, the relation is in reality but one, even though it may have many respects. There is nothing to prevent a thing from having a reference to another thing, even though no relation is really in it; for example, the knowable is referred to knowledge, although no relation exists in it. So, too, there is no reason why a single real relation should not have a number of respects. Just as a relation depends on its cause for its existence as a certain thing, so it also depends on its cause for the fact that it is one or multiple. Therefore, since Christ does not proceed from his Father and his Mother by the same nativity, there may seem to be in him two real filiations because of the two nativities.

But there is a different reason why several real filiations cannot be attributed to Christ. Not everything that is generated by another can be called a son: only a complete suppositum can be called a son. Not a man's hand or foot, but the whole individual, Peter or John, is called son. Hence the proper subject of filiation is the suppositum itself. But we have shown that the only suppositum in Christ is the uncreated suppositum, which cannot receive any real relation beginning in time; as we intimated above, every relation of God to creatures is purely one of reason. Consequently, the filiation whereby the eternal suppositum of the Son is related to his Virgin Mother cannot be a real relation, but must be one of reason alone.

However, this does not prevent Christ from being really and truly the Son of his Virgin Mother, because he was truly born of her. In the same way God is really and truly the

quasi realem habens potentiam cohercendi creaturam, et tamen dominii relatio solum secundum rationem Deo attribuitur. Si autem in Christo essent plura supposita, ut quidam posuerunt, nihil prohiberet ponere in Christo duas filiationes, quia filiationi temporali subiiceretur suppositum creatum.

Lord of his creatures, because he possesses real power to coerce them; yet the relation of dominion is attributed to God only by reason. Of course, if there were several supposita in Christ, as some have held, there would be nothing to keep us from admitting two filiations in Christ, for in that case the created suppositum would be subject to temporal sonship.

Chapter 213

That Christ had to be perfect in grace and in the wisdom of truth

Quia vero, sicut iam dictum est, humanitas Christi ad eius divinitatem comparatur quasi quoddam organum eius, organorum autem dispositio et qualitas pensatur praecipue quidem ex fine, et etiam ex decentia instrumento utentis, secundum hos modos conveniens est ut consideremus qualitatem humanae naturae a Verbo Dei assumptae. Finis autem assumptionis humanae naturae a Verbo Dei est salus et reparatio humanae naturae; talem igitur oportuit esse Christum secundum humanam naturam ut convenienter esse posset auctor humanae salutis. Salus autem humana consistit in fruitione divina per quam homo beatus efficitur: et ideo oportuit Christum secundum humanam naturam fuisse perfecte Deo fruentem, principium enim in unoquoque genere oportet esse perfectum. Fruitio autem divina secundum duo existit, scilicet secundum voluntatem et secundum intellectum: secundum voluntatem quidem Deo perfecte per amorem inhaerentem, secundum intellectum autem perfecte Deum cognoscentem.

Perfecta autem inhaesio voluntatis ad Deum per amorem est per gratiam, per quam homo iustificatur secundum illud Ro. III *iustificati gratis per gratiam eius*: ex hoc enim homo iustus est quod Deo per amorem inhaeret. Perfecta autem cognitio Dei est per lumen sapientiae, quae est cognitio divinae veritatis. Oportuit igitur Verbum Dei incarnatum perfectum in gratia et in sapientia veritatis existere; unde et Io. I dicitur *Verbum caro factum est et habitavit in nobis: et vidimus gloriam eius, gloriam quasi unigeniti a Patre, plenum gratiae et veritatis.*

As was mentioned in the preceding chapter, the humanity of Christ is related to his divinity as a sort of organ belonging to it. Now, the disposition and quality of organs are gauged chiefly by the purpose, though also by the dignity, of the person using them. Consequently, we are to esteem the quality of the human nature assumed by the Word of God in accord with these norms. The purpose the Word of God had in assuming human nature was the salvation and reparation of human nature. Therefore, Christ had to be of such excellence in his human nature that he could fittingly be the author of man's salvation. But the salvation of man consists in the enjoyment of God, whereby man is beatified; and so Christ must have had in his human nature a perfect enjoyment of God. For the principle in any genus must be perfect. But enjoyment of God has a twofold aspect: namely, according to will and according to intellect. The will must adhere unreservedly to God by love, while the intellect must know God perfectly.

Perfect attachment of the will to God through love is brought about by grace, whereby man is justified, according to Romans 3:24: *They are justified by his grace as a gift*. For man is made just by union with God through love. Perfect knowledge of God is effected by the light of wisdom, which is the knowledge of divine truth. Therefore, the incarnate Word of God had to be perfect in grace and in the wisdom of truth. Hence we read in John 1:14: *The Word became flesh and dwelt among us, full of grace and truth; we have beheld his glory, glory as of the only Son from the Father.*

CHAPTER 214

On the fullness of Christ's grace

Primo autem videndum est de plenitudine gratiae ipsius. Circa quod considerandum est quod nomen gratiae a duobus assumi potest: uno modo ex eo quod est gratum esse, dicimus enim aliquem alicuius gratiam habere quia est ei gratus; Alio modo ex eo quod est gratis dari, dicitur enim aliquis alicui gratiam facere qui ei aliquod beneficium gratis confert.

Nec istae duae acceptiones gratiae penitus separatae sunt. Ex eo enim aliquid alteri gratis datur, quod is cui datur gratus est danti vel simpliciter vel secundum quid. Simpliciter quidem, quando ad hoc recipiens gratus est danti ut eum sibi coniungat secundum aliquem modum: hos enim quos gratos habemus, nobis pro posse attrahimus secundum quantitatem et modum quo nobis grati existunt.

Secundum quid autem, quando ad hoc recipiens gratus est danti ut aliquid ab eo recipiat, non autem ad hoc ut assumatur ab ipso. Unde patet quod omnis qui habet gratiam aliquid habet quod gratis datur; non autem omnis qui habet aliquid gratis datum, gratus danti existit. Et ideo duplex gratia distingui solet: una scilicet quae solum gratis est data, alia quae etiam gratum facit.

Gratis autem dari dicitur quod nequaquam est debitum. Dupliciter autem aliquid debitum existit: uno quidem modo secundum naturam, alio modo secundum operationem. Secundum naturam quidem debitum est rei quod ordo naturalis illius rei exposcit, sicut debitum est homini quod habeat rationem aut manus et pedes; secundum operationem autem, sicut merces operanti debetur. Illa ergo dona sunt hominibus divinitus gratis data quae et ordinem naturae excedunt, et meritis non acquiruntur; quamvis et ea quae pro meritis divinitus dantur interdum gratiae rationem non amittant: tum quia principium merendi fuit a gratia, tum etiam quia superabundantius dantur quam merita humana requirant, sicut dicitur Ro. VI *gratia Dei vita aeterna*.

Huiusmodi autem donorum quaedam quidem et naturae humanae facultatem excedunt, et meritis non redduntur, nec tamen ex hoc ipso quod homo ea habet redditur Deo gratus, sicut donum prophetiae, miraculorum operationis, scientiae et doctrinae, vel si qua talia divinitus conferuntur. Per haec enim et huiusmodi homo non coniungitur Deo, nisi forte per similitudinem quandam, prout aliquid de eius bonitate participat, per

First we shall deal with the question of the fullness of grace in Christ. In this matter we should observe that the term grace can be taken from two roots. In one way, it can be taken from the word *gratum*, or gratifying: we say that someone is in the good graces of another because he is gratifying to him. In another way, it can be taken from giving something 'gratis': a person is said to grant a grace to another when he confers gratis a benefit on that other.

These two meanings of grace are not wholly unconnected. A thing is given gratis to another because he to whom it is given is gratifying to the giver, either simply or in some respect. The recipient is simply gratifying to the giver when he is gratifying to such an extent that the giver associates him with himself in some way. For those whom we hold in our good graces we draw to ourselves as far as we can, according to the quantity and degree in which they are dear to us.

But the recipient is gratifying to the giver only in some respect when he is gratifying to the extent that he receives something from him, although not to the extent that he is taken into association by the donor. Clearly, therefore, everyone who is in another's good graces has something given to him gratis; but not everyone who has something given to him gratis is gratifying to the donor. Hence we ordinarily distinguish between two kinds of grace: one, namely, which is only given gratis, and the other which also makes one gratifying.

A thing is said to be given gratis if it is in no way due. A thing may be due in two ways: either according to nature or according to operation. According to nature, whatever the natural order of a thing requires is due to it; thus the possession of reason and hands and feet is due to man. According to operation, a thing is due in the way that a recompense is due to a worker. Therefore, those gifts are given gratis by God to men which exceed the order of nature and are not acquired by merits; although even gifts that are conferred by God because of merits sometimes retain the name and character of grace, because the principle of meriting comes from grace, and also because rewards are given over and above what human merits require, as we learn from Romans 6:23: *the grace of God, life everlasting.*

Among such gifts, some exceed the capacity of human nature and are not given for merits. However, the fact that a man has these gifts does not prove that he is thereby rendered pleasing to God. Examples are the gifts of prophecy, of working miracles, of knowledge, of teaching, or any other such gifts divinely conferred. By these and like gifts man is not united to God, except, perhaps, by a certain similarity, so far as he shares to some extent in his goodness,

quem modum omnia Deo similantur. Quaedam vero hominem Deo gratum reddunt et eum ipsi coniungunt, et huiusmodi dona non solum gratiae dicuntur ex eo quod gratis dantur, sed etiam ex eo quod hominem faciunt Deo gratum.

Coniunctio autem hominis ad Deum est duplex. Una quidem per affectum: et haec est per caritatem, quae quodammodo facit per affectum hominem unum cum Deo, secundum illud I Cor. VI *Qui adhaeret Deo unus spiritus est.* Per hanc etiam Deus hominem inhabitat, secundum illud Io. XIV *Si quis diligit me, sermonem meum servabit, et Pater meus diliget eum, et ad eum veniemus et mansionem apud eum faciemus.* Facit etiam hominem esse in Deo, secundum illud I Io. IV *Qui manet in caritate, in Deo manet et Deus in eo.* Ille igitur per acceptum donum gratuitum efficitur Deo gratus, qui usque ad hoc perducitur quod per caritatis amorem unus spiritus cum Deo fiat, quod ipse in Deo sit et Deus in eo: unde Apostolus dicit I Cor. XIII quod sine caritate cetera dona homini non prosunt, quia eum gratum Deo facere non possunt nisi caritas assit.

Haec autem gratia est omnium sanctorum communis; unde hanc gratiam homo Christus discipulis orando impetrans, dicit Io. XVII *ut sint unum* in nobis, scilicet per connexionem amoris, *sicut et nos unum sumus.*

Alia vero coniunctio est hominis ad Deum non solum per affectum aut inhabitationem, sed per unitatem hypostasis sive personae, ut scilicet una et eadem hypostasis vel persona sit Deus et homo. Et haec quidem coniunctio ad Deum est propria Iesu Christi, de qua coniunctione plura iam dicta sunt. Haec igitur est hominis Christi gratia singularis, quod est Deo unitus in unitate personae: hoc enim et gratis datum est, quia et naturae facultatem excedit et hoc donum merita nulla praecedunt; sed et gratissimum Deo facit, ita quod de ipso singulariter dicatur *Hic est Filius meus dilectus in quo mihi complacui,* Matth. III et XVII.

Hoc tamen interesse videtur inter utramque gratiam, quod gratia quidem per quam homo Deo unitur per affectum aliquid habituale existit in anima: quia cum per actum amoris sit ista coniunctio, actus autem perfecti procedant ab habitu, consequens est ut ad istum perfectissimum actum quo anima Deo coniungitur per amorem, aliqua habitualis gratia animae infundatur. Esse autem personale vel ypostaticum non est per aliquem habitum, sed per ipsas naturas quarum sunt hypostases vel personae. Unio igitur humanae naturae ad Deum in unitate personae non fit per aliquam habitualem gratiam, sed per ipsam naturarum coniunctionem in persona una.

Inquantum autem creatura aliqua magis ad Deum accedit, intantum de bonitate eius magis participat, et abundantioribus donis ex eius influentia repletur, sicut et ignis calorem magis participant quae ei magis appropin-

in the way that everything is assimilated to God. Yet some gifts do render man pleasing to God, and join man to him. Such gifts are called graces, not only because they are given gratis, but also because they make man pleasing to God.

The union of man with God is twofold. One way is by affection, and this is brought about by charity, which in a certain sense makes man one with God in affection, as is said in 1 Corinthians 6:17: *He who is united to the Lord becomes one spirit with him.* Through this virtue God dwells in man, according to John 14:23: *If a man loves me, he will keep my word, and my Father will love him, and we will come to him and make our home with him.* It also causes man to be in God, according to 1 John 4:16: *He who abides in love abides in God, and God abides in him.* By receiving this gratuitous gift, therefore, man is made pleasing to God, and he is brought so far that by the love of charity he becomes one spirit with God: he is in God and God is in him. Hence the Apostle teaches, in 1 Corinthians 13:1–3, that without charity the other gifts do not profit men: they cannot make men pleasing to God unless charity is present.

This grace is common to all the saints. And so the man Christ, when asking for this grace for his disciples in prayer, begs *that they may be one* in us, namely, by the bond of love, *even as we are one* (John 17:22).

There is another conjunction of man with God that is brought about not only by affection or inhabitation, but also by the unity of hypostasis or person, so that one and the same hypostasis or person is both God and man. And this conjunction of man with God is proper to Jesus Christ. We have already spoken at length of this union. Therefore, this is a singular grace of the man Christ, that he is united to God in unity of person, for it was given gratis, both since it exceeds the capacity of nature and since no merits preceded this gift. But it also makes him supremely pleasing to God, so that the Father says of him in a unique sense: *This is my beloved Son, with whom I am well pleased* (Matt 3:17; 17:5).

Yet there seems to be this difference between the two graces. On the one hand, the grace whereby man is united to God by affection exists in the soul as something habitual. For that union is accomplished through an act of love, and perfect acts issue from habit; consequently, some habitual grace is infused into the soul to produce that eminently perfect habit whereby the soul is united to God by love. On the other hand, personal or hypostatic being is constituted, not by any habit, but by the very natures to which the hypostases or persons pertain. Therefore, the union of human nature with God in unity of person is brought about, not by some habitual grace, but by the conjunction of the natures themselves in one person.

Now, the closer any creature draws to God, the more it shares in his goodness, and the more abundantly it is filled with gifts infused by him. Thus he who comes closer to a fire shares to a greater extent in its heat. But there can be

quant. Nullus autem modus esse aut excogitari potest, quo aliqua creatura propinquius Deo adhaereat quam quod ei in unitate personae coniungatur. Ex ipsa igitur unione naturae humanae ad Deum in unitate personae, consequens est ut anima Christi donis gratiarum etiam habitualibus prae ceteris fuerit plena; ut sic habitualis gratia in Christo non sit dispositio ad unionem, sed magis unionis effectus, quod ex ipso modo loquendi quo Euangelista utitur in verbis praemissis manifeste apparet, cum dicit *Vidimus eum quasi unigenitum a Patre, plenum gratiae et veritatis.* Est autem unigenitus a Patre homo Christus, inquantum Verbum caro factum est; ex hoc igitur quod Verbum caro factum est, hoc effectum est ut esset plenus gratiae et veritatis.

In his autem quae aliqua perfectione vel bonitate replentur, illud magis plenum esse invenitur ex quo etiam in alia redundat, sicut plenius lucet quod alia illuminare potest. Quia igitur homo Christus summam plenitudinem gratiae optinuit quasi unigenitus a Patre, consequens fuit ut etiam ab ipso in alios gratia redundaret, ita quod Filius Dei factus homo homines faceret deos et filios Dei, secundum illud Apostoli Gal. IV *Misit Deus Filium suum factum ex muliere, ut adoptionem filiorum reciperemus.*

Ex hoc autem quod a Christo ad alios gratia et veritas derivatur, convenit ei ut sit caput Ecclesiae. Nam a capite ad alia membra, quae sunt ei conformia in natura, quodammodo sensus et motus derivatur; sic a Christo gratia et veritas ad alios homines derivatur, unde dicitur Eph. I *et ipsum dedit caput super omnem Ecclesiam, quae est corpus eius.* Dici etiam potest caput non solum hominum, sed etiam angelorum quantum ad excellentiam et influentiam, licet non quantum ad conformitatem naturae secundum eandem speciem: unde ante praedicta verba Apostolus praemittit quod Deus *constituit illum,* scilicet Christam, *ad dexteram suam in caelestibus supra omnem principatum et potestatem et virtutem et dominationem.*

Sic igitur secundum praemissa triplex gratia consuevit assignari in Christo. Primo quidem gratia unionis, secundum quod humana natura nullis meritis praecedentibus hoc donum accepit ut uniretur Dei Filio in persona; secundo gratia singularis, qua anima Christi prae ceteris fuit gratia et veritate repleta; tertio gratia capitis, secundum quod ab ipso in alios gratia redundat. Quae tria Euangelista congruo ordine prosequitur: nam quantum ad gratiam unionis dicit *Verbum caro factum*

no way, nor can any be conceived, by which a creature more closely adheres to God than by being united to him in unity of person. Therefore, in consequence of the very union of his human nature with God in unity of person, Christ's soul was filled with habitual gifts of graces beyond all other souls. And so habitual grace in Christ is not a disposition for union, but is rather an effect of union. This appears clearly in the very way of speaking used by the Evangelist when he says, in words previously quoted: *We saw him as it were the only begotten of the Father, full of grace and truth* (John 1:14). The man Christ is, indeed, the only-begotten of the Father, inasmuch as the Word was made flesh. The very fact that the Word was made flesh brought it about that he was full of grace and truth.

But among things that are filled with any goodness or perfection, the one from which goodness or perfection also flows out upon other things is found to be more full than the others; for example, what can shed light on other objects, shines more brilliantly than they. Therefore, since the man Christ possessed supreme fullness of grace, as being the only-begotten of the Father, the result was that grace overflowed from him to others, so that the Son of God, made man, might make men gods and sons of God, according to the Apostle's words in Galatians 4:4–5: *God sent forth his Son, born of woman, born under the law, to redeem those who were under the law, so that we might receive adoption as sons.*

Because of the fact that grace and truth come to others from Christ, it befits him to be the head of the Church. Sensation and movement are, in a way, conveyed from the head to the other members that are conformed to the head in nature. In like manner, grace and truth are conveyed from Christ to other men. Hence we are told in Ephesians 1:22–23 that God *has made him the head over all the church, which is his body.* Christ is not the head of men alone; he can also be called the head of the angels with respect to his excellence and influence, although not with respect to conformity of nature in the same species. This is why, before the words just quoted, the Apostle says that God *made him,* namely Christ, *sit on his right hand in the heavenly places, above all principality and power and virtue and dominion.*

In accord with this doctrine, a threefold grace is usually pointed out in Christ. The first is the grace of union, whereby the human nature, with no merits preceding, received the gift of being united in person to the Son of God. The second is the singular grace whereby the soul of Christ was filled with grace and truth beyond all other souls. The third is the grace of being head, in virtue of which grace flows from him to others. The Evangelist presents these three kinds of grace in due order (John 1:14, 16). Regard-

est; quantum ad gratiam singularem dicit *vidimus eum quasi unigenitum a Patre, plenum gratiae et veritatis*; quantum ad gratiam capitis subdit *et de plenitudine eius nos omnes accepimus.*

ing the grace of union he says: *the Word was made flesh.* Regarding Christ's singular grace he says: *We saw him as it were the only begotten of the Father, full of grace and truth.* Regarding the grace of head he adds: *and of his fullness we all have received.*

CHAPTER 215

On the infinity of Christ's grace

Est autem proprium Christi quod eius gratia sit infinita, quia secundum testimonium Iohannis Baptistae, *non ad mensuram dat Deus spiritum* homini Christo, ut dicitur Io. III; aliis autem datur spiritus ad mensuram, secundum illud Eph. IV *Unicuique data est gratia secundum mensuram donationis Christi.* Et quidem si hoc referatur ad gratiam unionis, nullam dubitationem habet quod dicitur. Nam aliis quidem sanctis datum est deos aut filios Dei esse per participationem ex influentia alicuius doni, quod quia creatum est, necesse est ipsum sicut et ceteras creaturas esse finitum. Sed Christo secundum humanam naturam datum est ut sit Deus Filius Dei non per participationem, sed per naturam. Naturalis autem divinitas est infinita: ex ipsa igitur unione accepit donum infinitum, unde gratia unionis absque omni dubitatione est infinita.

Sed de gratia habituali dubium esse potest an fuerit infinita. Cum enim huiusmodi gratia sit etiam donum creatum, confiteri oportet quod habeat essentiam finitam; potest tamen infinita dici triplici ratione.

Primo quidem ex parte recipientis. Manifestum est enim uniuscuiusque naturae creatae capacitatem esse finitam, quia etsi infinitum bonum recipere possit cognoscendo, amando et fruendo, non tamen ipsum recipit infinite. Est igitur cuiuslibet creaturae secundum suam speciem et naturam determinata capacitatis mensura, quae tamen divinae potestati non praeiudicat quin posset aliam creaturam maioris capacitatis facere; sed iam non esset eiusdem naturae secundum speciem, sicut si ternario addatur unitas, iam erit alia species numeri. Quando igitur alicui non tantum datur de bonitate divina quanta est capacitas naturalis speciei suae, videtur ei secundum aliquam mensuram donatum. Quando vero tota naturalis capacitas impletur, non videtur ei secundum mensuram donatum, quia etsi sit mensura ex parte recipientis, non est mensura ex parte dantis qui totum paratus est dare: sicut si aliquis vas ad fluvium deferens, absque mensura invenit aquam sibi praeparatam, quamvis ipse cum mensura accipiat propter vasis determinatam quantitatem. Sic igitur gratia Christi habitualis finita quidem est secundum essentiam, sed infinite et

The possession of infinite grace is proper to Christ. According to the testimony of John the Baptist, *It is not by measure that God gives the Spirit* to the man Christ (John 3:34). But to others the Spirit is given in measure, as we read in Ephesians 4:7: *Grace was given to each of us according to the measure of Christ's gift.* If this refers to the grace of union, no doubt can arise about what is here stated. To other saints is given the grace of being gods or sons of God by participation, through the infusion of some gift. Such a gift, being created, must itself be finite, just as all other creatures are. But to Christ, in his human nature, is given the grace to be the Son of God not by participation, but by nature. But natural divinity is infinite. Through that union, therefore, he received an infinite gift. Hence beyond all doubt the grace of union is infinite.

Concerning habitual grace, however, a doubt can be raised as to whether it is infinite. Since such grace is a created gift, we have to acknowledge that it has a finite essence. Yet it can be said to be infinite for three reasons.

First, on the part of the recipient. The capacity of any created nature is evidently finite. Even though it is able to receive an infinite good by knowing, loving, and enjoying it, the creature does not receive that good infinitely. Therefore, each creature has a definite measure of capacity in keeping with its species and nature. This does not prevent the divine power from being able to make another creature with a greater capacity; but such a creature would no longer be of the same nature with regard to species. Thus if one is added to three, a different species of number will result. Consequently, when the divine goodness that is bestowed on anyone does not completely exhaust the natural capacity of his nature, we judge that what is given to him has been apportioned according to some measure. But when the whole of his natural capacity is filled up, we conclude that what he receives is not parceled out to him according to measure. For although there is a measure on the part of the recipient, there is no measure on the part of the giver, who is ready to give all; if a person, for instance, takes a pitcher down to the river, he finds water at hand without measure, although he himself receives with measure because of the limited size

non secundum mensuram dari dicitur, quia tantum datur quantum natura creata potest esse capax.

Secundo vero ex parte ipsius doni recepti. Considerandum enim quod nihil prohibet aliquid esse secundum essentiam finitum, quod tamen secundum rationem alicuius formae specialis infinitum existit. Infinitum enim secundum essentiam est quod habet totam essendi plenitudinem, quod quidem soli Deo convenit qui est ipsum esse. Si autem ponatur esse aliqua forma specialis non in subiecto existens, puta albedo vel calor, non quidem haberet essentiam infinitam, quia essentia eius esset limitata ad genus vel speciem, sed tamen totam plenitudinem illius speciei possideret; unde secundum rationem speciei absque termino vel mensura esset, habens quidquid ad illam speciem pertinere potest. Si autem in aliquo subiecto recipiatur albedo vel calor, non habet semper totum quidquid pertinet ad rationem huius formae de necessitate et semper, sed solum quando sic perfecte habetur sicut perfecte haberi potest, ita scilicet quod modus habendi adaequet rei habitae potestatem. Sic igitur gratia Christi habitualis finita quidem fuit secundum essentiam: sed tamen dicitur absque termino et mensura fuisse, quia quidquid ad rationem gratiae poterat pertinere totum Christus accepit; Alii autem non totum accipiunt, sed unus sic, alius autem sic: *divisiones enim gratiarum sunt*, ut dicitur I Cor. XII.

Tertio autem ex parte causae. In causa enim quodammodo habetur effectus; cuicumque ergo adest causa infinitae virtutis ad influendum, habet quod influitur absque mensura et quodammodo infinite: puta si quis haberet fontem qui aquam in infinitum posset effluere, aquam absque mensura et infinite diceretur habere. Sic igitur anima Christi infinitam et absque mensura gratiam habet ex hoc ipso quod habet Verbum sibi unitum, quod est totius emanationis creaturarum indeficiens et infinitum principium.

Ex hoc autem quod gratia singularis animae Christi est modis praedictis infinita, evidenter colligitur quod gratia ipsius secundum quod est Ecclesiae caput, est etiam infinita. Ex hoc enim quod habet, effundit; unde quia absque mensura spiritus dona accepit, habet virtutem absque mensura ipsa effundendi, quod ad gratiam capitis pertinet: ut scilicet sua gratia non solum sufficiat ad salutem hominum aliquorum, sed homianum totius mundi, secundum illud I Io. II *Ipse est propitiatio pro peccatis nostris, et non solum pro nostris, sed etiam pro totius mundi.* Addi autem potest et plurium mundorum, si essent.

of the vessel. In this way Christ's habitual grace is finite in its essence, but may be said to be given infinitely and not according to measure, because as much is given as created nature is able to receive.

Second, grace may be said to be infinite on the part of the gift itself that is received. We must take into consideration that nothing prevents a thing from being finite in its essence while yet being infinite according to the nature of some form. Infinite according to essence is that which possesses the whole fullness of being; this, of course, is proper to God alone, who is being itself. But if we suppose that there is some particular form not existing in a subject, such as whiteness or heat, it would not, indeed, have an infinite essence, for its essence would be confined to a genus or species; but it would possess the entire fullness of that species. With respect to the species in question, it would be without limit or measure, because it would have whatever could pertain to that species. But if whiteness or heat is received into some subject, the latter does not always possess everything that necessarily and invariably pertains to the nature of that form, but does so only when the form is possessed as perfectly as it can be possessed, that is, when the manner of possessing is equal to the thing's capacity for being possessed. In this way, then, Christ's habitual grace was finite in its essence; but it is said to have been without limit and measure because Christ received all that could pertain to the nature of grace. Other men do not receive the whole: one man receives grace in this measure, another in that. *There are diversities of graces*, as we learn from 1 Corinthians 12:4.

In the third place, grace may be called infinite on the part of its cause. For an effect is in some way contained in its cause. Therefore, if a cause with infinite power to influence is at hand, it is able to influence without measure and, in a certain sense, infinitely; for example, if a person had a fountain capable of pouring forth water infinitely, he could be said to possess water without measure and infinitely. In this way Christ's soul has grace that is infinite and without measure, owing to the fact that it possesses, as united to itself, the Word who is the inexhaustible and infinite principle of every emanation of creatures.

From the fact that the singular grace of Christ's soul is infinite in the ways described, we readily infer that the grace which is his as head of the Church is likewise infinite. For he pours forth from what he has. And since he has received the gifts of the Spirit without measure, he has the power of pouring forth without measure all that pertains to the grace of the head, so that his grace is sufficient for the salvation not of some men only, but of the whole world, in keeping with 1 John 2:2: *He is the expiation for our sins, and not for ours only but also for the sins of the whole world*; and, we may add, of many worlds, if such existed.

Chapter 216

On the fullness of Christ's wisdom

Oportet autem consequenter dicere de plenitudine sapientiae Christi. Ubi primo considerandum occurrit quod, cum in Christo sint duae naturae, divina scilicet et humana, quidquid ad utramque naturam pertinet necesse est quod geminetur in Christo, ut supra dictum est. Sapientia autem et divinae naturae convenit et humanae. Dicitur enim de Deo Iob IX *sapiens corde est, et fortis robore*; sed et homines interdum Scriptura sapientes appellat sive secundum sapientiam mundanam, secundum illud Ier. IX *Non glorietur sapiens in sapientia sua*, sive secundum sapientiam divinam, secundum illud Matth. XXIII *Ecce ego mitto ad vos sapientes et scribas*. Oportet igitur confiteri duas esse in Christo sapientias secundum duas naturas, sapientiam scilicet increatam quae ei competit secundum quod est Deus, et sapientiam creatam quae ei competit secundum quod est homo.

Et secundum quidem quod Deus est et Verbum Dei, est genita Sapientia Patris, secundum illud I Cor. I *Christum Dei virtutem et Dei sapientiam*; nihil enim aliud est verbum interius uniuscuiusque intelligentis nisi conceptio sapientiae eius. Et quia Verbum Dei supra diximus esse perfectum et unicum, necesse est quod Dei Verbum sit perfecta conceptio sapientiae Dei Patris, ut scilicet quidquid in sapientia Dei Patris continetur per modum ingeniti, totum in Verbo contineatur per modum geniti vel concepti. Et inde est quod dicitur Col. II quod *in ipso*, scilicet Christo, *sunt omnes thesauri sapientiae et scientiae Dei absconditi*.

Hominis autem est duplex cognitio. Una quidem deiformis, secundum quod Deum per essentiam videt et alia videt in Deo, sicut et ipse Deus intelligendo se ipsum intelligit omnia, per quam visionem et ipse Deus beatus est, et omnis creatura rationalis perfecte Deo fruens. Quia igitur Christum diximus esse humanae salutis auctorem, necesse est dicere quod talis cognitio sic animae Christi conveniat ut decet auctorem. Principium autem et immobile esse oportet, et virtute praestantissimum; conveniens igitur fuit ut illa Dei visio in qua beatitudo hominum et salus aeterna consistit, excellentius prae ceteris Christo conveniat et tamquam immobili principio. Haec autem differentia invenitur mobilium ad immobilia, quod mobilia propriam perfectionem non a principio habent inquantum mobilia sunt, sed eam per successionem temporis assequuntur; immobilia vero, inquantum huiusmodi, semper optinent suas perfectiones ex quo esse incipiunt. Conveniens igitur fuit Christum humanae salutis auctorem ab ipso suae Incarnationis principio plenam Dei visionem possedisse, non autem

We treat next of the fullness of wisdom in Christ. In this matter, the first point that comes up for consideration is the truth that, since Christ has two natures, the divine and the human, whatever pertains to both natures must be twofold in Christ, as was stated above. But wisdom belongs to both the divine nature and the human nature. The assertion of Job 9:4: *He is wise in heart and mighty in strength*, is spoken of God. At times Scripture also calls men wise, whether with reference to worldly wisdom, as in Jeremiah 9:23: *Let not the wise man glory in his wisdom*, or with reference to divine wisdom, as in Matthew 23:34: *Behold, I send to you prophets and wise men and scribes*. Hence we must acknowledge two wisdoms in Christ, conformably with his two natures: uncreated wisdom, which pertains to him as God, and created wisdom, which pertains to him as man.

Inasmuch as Christ is God and the Word of God, he is the begotten Wisdom of the Father, in accord with 1 Corinthians 1:24: *Christ the power of God and the wisdom of God*. For the interior word of any intellectual being is nothing else than the conception of its wisdom. And since, as we said above, the Word of God is perfect and singular, he must be the perfect conception of the wisdom of God the Father. Consequently, whatever is contained in the wisdom of God the Father as unbegotten, is contained wholly in the Word as begotten and conceived. And so we are told, in Colossians 2:3, that *in him*, namely, in Christ, *are hid all the treasures of wisdom and knowledge*.

Indeed, even as man, Christ has a twofold knowledge. The one is godlike, whereby he sees God in his essence, and other things in God, just as God himself, by knowing himself, knows all other things. Through this vision God himself is happy, as is every rational creature admitted to the perfect fruition of God. Therefore, since we hold that Christ is the author of man's salvation, we must also hold that such knowledge as befits the author of salvation pertains to the soul of Christ. But a principle must be immovable and must also be preeminent in power. Hence that vision of God in which men's beatitude and eternal salvation consist ought to be found to be more excellent in Christ than in others, and ought to be found in him as in an immovable principle. The difference between what is movable and what is immovable comes to this: movable things, so far as they are movable, do not possess their proper perfection from the beginning, but acquire it in the course of time; but immovable things, as such, always possess their perfections from the first moment of their existence. Accordingly, it was fitting for Christ, the author of man's salvation, to have pos-

per temporis successionem pervenisse ad ipsam, ut alii sancti perveniunt.

Conveniens etiam fuit ut prae ceteris creaturis illa anima divina visione beatificaretur quae Deo propinquius coniungebatur; in qua quidem visione gradus attenditur secundum quod aliqui clarius aliis Deum vident qui est omnium rerum causa. Quanto autem aliqua causa plenius cognoscitur, tanto in ipsa plures eius effectuum perspici possunt; non enim magis cognoscitur causa nisi virtus eius plenius cognoscatur, cuius virtutis cognitio sine cognitione effectuum esse non potest: nam quantitas virtutis secundum effectus mensurari solet. Et inde est quod eorum qui Dei essentiam vident, aliqui plures effectus vel rationes divinorum operum in ipso Deo inspiciunt quam alii qui minus clare vident: et secundum hoc inferiores angeli a superioribus instruuntur, ut supra iam diximus.

Anima igitur Christi summam perfectionem divinae visionis optinens inter creaturas ceteras, omnia divina opera et rationes ipsorum, quaecumque sunt, erunt vel fuerunt, in ipso Deo plene intuetur, ut non solum homines sed etiam supremos angelorum illuminet; et ideo Apostolus dicit Col. II quod *in ipso sunt omnes thesauri sapientiae et scientiae Dei absconditi*, et Hebr. IV quod *omnia nuda et aperta sunt oculis eius.*

Non tamen anima Christi ad comprehensionem divinitatis pertingere potest. Nam, ut supra dictum est, illud cognoscendo comprehenditur quod tantum cognoscitur quantum cognoscibile est. Unumquodque autem cognoscibile est inquantum est ens et verum; esse autem divinum est infinitum, similiter et veritas eius: infinite igitur Deus cognoscibilis est. Nulla autem creatura infinite cognoscere potest, etsi infinitum sit quod cognoscit; nulla igitur creatura Deum videndo comprehendere potest. Est autem anima Christi creatura, et quidquid in Christo ad humanam tantum naturam pertinet creatum est, alioquin non esset in Christo alia natura humanitatis a natura divinitatis, quae sola increata est. Hypostasis autem Dei Verbi sive persona increata est, quae est una in duabus naturis: ratione cuius Christum non dicimus creaturam, loquendo simpliciter, quia hoc nomine importatur hypostasis; dicimus tamen animam Christi vel corpus Christi esse creaturam. Anima igitur Christi Deum non comprehendit, sed Christus Deum comprehendit sua sapientia increata, secundum quem modum Dominus dicit Matth. XI *Nemo novit Filium nisi Pater, neque Patrem quis novit nisi Filius*, de comprehensionis notitia loquens.

Est autem considerandum quod eiusdem rationis est comprehendere essentiam alicuius rei et virtutem ipsius: unumquodque enim potest agere inquantum est actu.

sessed the full vision of God from the very beginning of his Incarnation, and not to have attained to it in the course of time, as other saints do.

It was also appropriate that that soul which was united to God more closely than all others should be beatified by the vision of God beyond the rest of creatures. Gradation is possible in this vision, according as some see God, the cause of all things, more clearly than others. The more comprehensively a cause is known, the more numerous are the effects that can be discerned in it. For a more perfect knowledge of a cause entails a fuller knowledge of its power, and there can be no knowledge of this power without a knowledge of its effects, since the magnitude of a power is ordinarily gauged from its effects. This is why, among those who behold the essence of God some perceive more effects in God himself or more exemplars of the divine works than do others who see less clearly. It is because of this fact that lower angels are instructed by higher angels, as we have previously observed.

Accordingly, the soul of Christ, possessing the highest perfection of the divine vision among all creatures, clearly beholds in God himself all the divine works and the exemplars of all things that are, will be, or have been; and so he enlightens not only men, but also the highest of the angels. Hence the Apostle says, in Colossians 2:3, that in Christ *are hid all the treasures of wisdom and knowledge* of God; and in Hebrews 4:13 he points out that *all things are naked and open to his eyes.*

Nonetheless, the soul of Christ cannot attain to a comprehension of the divinity. For, as we said above, a thing is comprehended by knowledge when it is known to the full extent that it is knowable. Any object is knowable to the degree that it is a being and is true; but the divine being is infinite, as likewise is its truth. Therefore, God is infinitely knowable. But no creature can know infinitely, even if what it knows is infinite. Hence no creature can comprehend God by seeing him. But Christ's soul is a creature, and whatever in Christ pertains exclusively to his human nature is created. Otherwise there would not be in Christ a human nature that is other than the divine nature, which alone is uncreated. However, the hypostasis or person of the Word of God, which is one in two natures, is uncreated. For this reason we do not call Christ a creature, speaking absolutely, because the hypostasis is connoted by the name 'Christ.' But we do say that the soul of Christ or the body of Christ is a creature. Therefore, Christ's soul does not comprehend God, but Christ comprehends God by his uncreated wisdom. Our Lord had this uncreated wisdom in mind when, speaking of his knowledge of comprehension, he said in Matthew 11:27: *No one knows the Son except the Father, and no one knows the Father except the Son.*

In this connection we may note that comprehension of a thing's essence and comprehension of its power are of the same nature; a thing is able to act so far as it is a being in

Si igitur anima Christi essentiam divinitatis comprehendere non valet, ut ostensum est, impossibile est ut divinam virtutem comprehendat; comprehenderet autem eius virtutem si cognosceret quidquid Deus facere potest, et quibus rationibus effectus producere possit: non igitur anima Christi cognoscit quidquid Deus facere potest, vel quibus rationibus possit operari.

Sed quia Christus, etiam secundum quod homo, omni creaturae a Deo Patre praepositus est, conveniens est ut omnium quae a Deo qualitercumque facta sunt, in ipsius divinae essentiae visione plenam cognitionem percipiat: et secundum hoc anima Christi omnisciens dicitur, quia plenam notitiam habet omnium quae sunt, erunt vel fuerunt. Aliarum vero creaturarum Deum videntium quaedam plenius et quaedam minus plene praedictorum effectuum in ipsa Dei visione cognitionem percipiunt.

Praeter hanc autem rerum cognitionem qua res ab intellectu creato cognoscuntur in ipsius divinae essentiae visione, sunt alii modi cognitionis quibus a creaturis habetur rerum cognitio. Nam angeli praeter cognitionem matutinam qua res in Verbo cognoscunt, habent cognitionem vespertinam qua cognoscunt res in propriis naturis. Huiusmodi autem cognitio aliter competit hominibus secundum suam naturam, atque aliter angelis. Nam homines secundum naturae ordinem intelligibilem rerum veritatem a sensibus colligunt, ut Dionysius dicit, ita scilicet quod species intelligibiles in eorum intellectibus actione intellectus agentis a phantasmatibus abstrahuntur; angeli vero per influxum divini luminis rerum scientiam acquirunt, ut scilicet sicut a Deo res in esse prodeunt, ita etiam in intellectu angelico a Deo rerum rationes sive similitudines imprimuntur. In utrisque autem, tam hominibus quam angelis, supra rerum cognitionem quae competit eis secundum naturam, invenitur quaedam supernaturalis cognitio mysteriorum divinorum, de quibus et angeli illuminantur ab angelis, et homines etiam de his prophetica revelatione instruuntur.

Et quia nulla perfectio creaturis exhibita, animae Christi, quae est creaturarum excellentissima, deneganda est, convenienter praeter cognitionem qua Dei essentiam videt et omnia in ipsa, triplex alia cognitio est ei attribuenda. Una quidem experimentalis, sicut et aliis hominibus, inquantum aliqua per sensus cognovit ut competit humanae naturae. Alia vero divinitus infusa, ad cognoscendaum omnia illa ad quae naturalis hominis cognitio se extendere potest. Conveniens enim fuit ut humana natura a Dei Verbo assumpta in nullo a perfectione deficeret, utpote per quam esset tota natura humana restauranda. Est autem imperfectum omne quod in potentia existit antequam reducatur in actum; intellectus autem humanus est in potentia ad

act. Therefore, if Christ's soul is incapable of comprehending the essence of the divinity, as we have shown is the case, it cannot comprehend the divine power. But it would comprehend the divine power if it knew all that God is able to accomplish and all the examplars by which he can produce his effects. But this is impossible. Therefore, Christ's soul does not know all that God can do, nor all the exemplars by which he can work.

However, since Christ, even as man, is placed by God the Father over every creature, it is fitting that in his vision of the divine essence he should perceive with full knowledge all things that in any way have been wrought by God. In this sense the soul of Christ is said to be omniscient, for it has complete knowledge of all things that are, will be, or have been. Among the other creatures that see God, some enjoy a more perfect knowledge, others a less perfect, of these effects in their vision of God.

In addition to this knowledge of things, whereby things are known by the created intellect in the vision of the divine essence itself, there are other ways of knowing by which creatures possess a knowledge of things. The angels, besides morning knowledge, whereby they know things in the Word, also have evening knowledge, whereby they know things in their proper natures. This kind of knowledge pertains to men in one way, in keeping with their nature, and to angels in another way. For men, consistent with the order of nature, derive the intelligible truth of things from their senses, as Dionysius observes, in such a way that the intelligible species in their intellects are abstracted from phantasms by the agent intellect. But angels acquire knowledge of things through an influx of divine light so that, in the same way that things themselves come forth into being from God, representations or likenesses of things are imprinted on the angelic intellect by God. In men and angels alike, however, over and above the knowledge of things they have by nature, there is found a certain supernatural knowledge of divine mysteries, about which angels are enlightened by angels, and men, for their part, are instructed by prophetic revelation.

Accordingly, since no perfection vouchsafed to creatures may be withheld from Christ's soul, which is the most excellent of creatures, a threefold knowledge is fittingly to be attributed to him, in addition to the knowledge whereby he beholds the essence of God and all things in that essence. One kind of knowledge is experiential, as in other men, so far as Christ knew some things through the senses in keeping with his human nature. A second knowledge is divinely infused, granted to Christ so that he might know all truths to which man's natural knowledge extends or can extend. The human nature assumed by the Word of God ought not to have been lacking in any perfection whatever, since through it the whole of human nature was to be restored. But everything that exists in potency is imperfect

intelligibilia quae naturaliter homo intelligere potest: omnium igitur horum scientiam anima Christi divinitus accepit per species influxas, quibus tota potentia intellectus humani fuit reducta ad actum. Sed quia Christus secundum humanam naturam non solum fuit reparator naturae sed etiam gratiae propagator, affuit ei et tertia cognitio qua plenissime cognovit quidquid ad mysteria gratiae potest pertinere, quae naturalem hominis cognitionem excedunt, sed cognoscuntur ab hominibus per donum sapientiae vel per spiritum prophetiae. Nam ad huiusmodi etiam cognoscenda est in potentia intellectus humanus, licet altiori agente reducatur in actum; nam ad naturalia cognoscenda reducitur in actum per lumen intellectus agentis, horum autem cognitionem consequitur per lumen divinum.

Patet igitur ex praedictis quod anima Christi summum cognitionis gradum inter creaturas optinuit quantum ad Dei visionem, qua Dei essentia videtur et alia in ipsa; similiter etiam quantum ad cognitionem mysteriorum gratiae, necnon quantum ad cognitionem naturalium scibilium: unde in nullo horum trium Christus proficere potuit. Sed manifestum est quod res sensibiles per temporis successionem magis ac magis sensibus corporis experiendo cognovit, et ideo solum quantum ad cognitionem experimentalem Christus proficere potuit, secundum illud Luc. II *Puer proficiebat sapientia et aetate*; quamvis possit et hoc aliter intelligi, ut profectus sapientiae Christi dicatur non quo ipse sit sapientior, sed quo sapientia proficiebat in aliis, quia scilicet per eius sapientiam magis ac magis instruebantur. Quod dispensative factum est, ut se aliis hominibus conformem ostenderet, ne si in puerili aetate perfectam sapientiam demonstrasset, Incarnationis mysterium phantasticum videretur.

before it is reduced to act. Thus the human intellect is in potency to the intelligibles which man can know naturally. Hence the soul of Christ received knowledge of all such objects through divinely infused species, by which the entire potency of his human intellect was reduced to act. Furthermore, since Christ in his human nature was not only the restorer of our nature, but was also the fountainhead of grace, he was endowed with a third knowledge whereby he knew most perfectly all that can pertain to the mysteries of grace, which transcend man's natural knowledge, although they are known by men through the gift of wisdom or through the spirit of prophecy. The human intellect is in potency with regard to the acquisition of such knowledge, even though an agency belonging to a higher sphere is required to reduce it to act. When there is question of knowing natural things, the mind is reduced to act by the light of the agent intellect; but it acquires knowledge of these mysteries through divine light.

From all that has been said, it is clear that the soul of Christ reached the highest degree of knowledge among all creatures as regards the vision of God, whereby the essence of God is seen, and other things in it; likewise as regards knowledge of the mysteries, and also as regards knowledge of things naturally knowable. Consequently, Christ could not advance in any of these three kinds of knowledge. But obviously he knew sensible things more and more with the passing of time by experiencing them through the bodily senses. Therefore, Christ could advance only with respect to experimental knowledge. That he actually did so we learn from Luke 2:52: *The boy advanced in wisdom and years.* However, this can be understood also in another way, so that Christ's increase of wisdom would mean not that he himself became wiser, but that wisdom increased in others, in the sense that they were more and more instructed by his wisdom. This was done for a good reason: that he might show that he was like other men. If he had made a display of his perfect wisdom at a tender age, the mystery of the Incarnation might well have seemed phantastical.

CHAPTER 217

Concerning the matter of Christ's body

Secundum praemissa igitur evidenter apparet qualis debuit esse corporis Christi formatio. Poterat siquidem Deus corpus Christi ex limo terrae formare vel ex quacumque materia, sicut formavit corpus primi parentis; sed hoc humanae restaurationi propter quam Filius Dei, ut diximus, carnem assumpsit, congruum non fuisset. Non enim sufficienter natura humani generis ex primo parente derivata, quae sananda erat, in pristinum honorem restituta esset, si aliunde corpus assumeret diaboli victor et mortis triumphator, sub quibus humanum genus captivum tenebatur propter peccatum primi parentis. Dei autem perfecta sunt opera, et ad perfectum perducit quod reparare intendit, ut etiam plus adiiciat quam fuerat subtractum, secundum illud Apostoli Ro. V: quod *gratia Dei per Christum amplius abundavit quam delictum Adae.* Convenientius igitur fuit ut Dei Filius corpus assumeret de natura ab Adam propagata.

Adhuc, Incarnationis mysterium hominibus per fidem proficuum redditur: nisi enim homines crederent Dei Filium esse eum qui homo videbatur, non sequerentur eum homines ut salutis auctorem, quod Iudaeis accidit, qui ex Incarnationis mysterio propter incredulitatem damnationem potius quam salutem sunt consecuti. Ut ergo hoc ineffabile mysterium facilius crederetur, Filius Dei sic omnia dispensavit ut se verum hominem esse ostenderet, quod non ita videretur si aliunde materiam sui corporis acciperet quam ex natura humana. Conveniens igitur fuit ut corpus a primo parente propagatum assumeret.

Item, Filius Dei homo factus humano generi salutem adhibuit, non solum conferendo gratiae remedium, sed etiam praebendo exemplum quod repudiari non potest. Alterius enim hominis et doctrina et vita in dubium venire potest propter imperfectum humanae cognitionis et virtutis; sed sicut quod Filius Dei docet indubitanter creditur verum, ita quod operatur indubitanter creditur bonum. Oportuit autem ut in eo exemplum acciperemus et gloriae quam speramus, et virtutis qua ipsam meremur; utrumque autem exemplum minus efficax esset, si aliunde materiam corporis assumpsisset quam unde alii homines assumunt. Si cui enim persuaderetur quod toleraret passiones sicut Christus sustinuit, quod speraret se resurrecturum sicut Christus resurrexit, posset ex-

The foregoing exposition clearly indicates the way the formation of Christ's body ought to have taken place. God could, indeed, have fashioned Christ's body from the dust of the earth or from any other matter, in the way he fashioned the body of our first parent. But this would not have been in keeping with the restoration of man, which is the reason why the Son of God assumed flesh, as we have pointed out. The nature of the human race, which was derived from the first parent and which was to be healed, would not have been so well restored to its pristine honor if the victor over the devil and the conqueror of death, under which the human race was held captive because of the sin of the first father, had taken his body from some other source. The works of God are perfect, and what he means to restore he brings to perfection. He even adds more than had been taken away: *Through Christ the grace of God has abounded more than the offense of Adam*, as the Apostle teaches in Romans 5:15, 20. Hence it was fitting that the Son of God should assume a body from the nature propagated by Adam.

Moreover, the mystery of the Incarnation becomes profitable to men by faith. Unless men believed that he who appeared in the guise of a man was the Son of God, they would not follow him as the author of salvation. This was the case with the Jews, who drew upon themselves damnation rather than salvation from the mystery of the Incarnation, because of their unbelief. In order, therefore, that this ineffable mystery might more readily be believed, the Son of God disposed all things in such a way as to show that he was a true man. This would not have seemed to be so if he had taken his bodily nature from some other source than from human nature. Fittingly, therefore, he assumed a body stemming from the first parent.

Furthermore, the Son of God, made man, brought salvation to the human race, not only by conferring the remedy of grace, but also by giving an example that cannot be ignored. Doubts may be raised about the teaching and the life of any other man because of a defect in his human knowledge and his mastery of truth. But what the Son of God teaches is believed without hesitation to be true and what he does is accepted without misgiving as good. We ought to accept him as an example of the glory we hope for and of the virtue whereby we may merit it. In both instances the example would have been less effective if he had taken his bodily nature from another source than that from which the rest of men receive theirs. Otherwise, if we tried to persuade a man that he should endure sufferings as Christ en-

cusationem praetendere ex diversa corporis conditione. Ut igitur exemplum Christi efficacius redderetur, conveniens fuit ut non aliunde corporis materiam assumeret quam de natura quae a primo parente propagatur.

dured them, and that he should hope to rise as Christ rose, he could allege as an excuse the different condition of his body. Therefore, to give greater effectiveness to his example, it was fitting that Christ assumed his bodily nature from no other source than from the nature that is propagated from the first parent.

Chapter 218

On the formation of Christ's body, which was not from male seed

Non tamen fuit conveniens ut eodem modo formaretur corpus Christi de humana natura, sicut formantur aliorum hominum corpora. Cum enim ad hoc Filius Dei naturam humanam assumeret ut ipsam a peccato mundaret, oportebat ut tali modo assumeret quod nullum contagium peccati incurreret. Homines autem peccatum originale incurrunt ex hoc quod generantur per virtutem activam quae est in virili semine, quod est secundum seminalem rationem in Adam peccante praeextitisse. Sicut enim primus homo originalem iustitiam transfudisset in posteros simul cum transfusione naturae, ita etiam originalem culpam transfudit transfundendo naturam, quod est per virtutem activam virilis seminis; oportuit igitur absque virili semine corpus Christi formari.

Item, virtus activa virilis seminis naturaliter agit, et ideo homo qui ex virili semine generatur non subito perducitur ad perfectum, sed determinatis processibus: omnia enim naturalia per determinata media ad determinatos fines procedunt. Oportebat autem corpus Christi in ipsa assumptione perfectum esse et anima rationali informatum, quia corpus est assumptibile a Dei Verbo inquantum est animae rationali unitum, licet non esset perfectum secundum debitam quantitatem; non ergo corpus Christi formari debuit per virilis seminis virtutem.

Nevertheless, the body of Christ could not becomingly have been fashioned in human nature in the same way as the bodies of other men are formed. Since he assumed this nature for the purpose of cleansing it from sin, he ought to have assumed it in such a way that he would incur no contagion of sin. Men incur original sin by the fact that they are begotten through the active human power residing in the male seed; which is according to the seminal principle preexisting in Adam the sinner. Just as the first man would have transmitted original justice to his posterity along with the transmission of nature, so he transmitted original sin by transmitting nature; and this is brought about by the active power of the male seed. Hence the body of Christ ought to have been formed without male seed.

Moreover, the active power of the male seed operates naturally, and so man, who is begotten of male seed, is brought to perfection, not at once, but by definite processes. For all natural things advance to fixed ends through fixed intermediary stages. But Christ's body ought to have been perfect and informed by a rational soul at its very assumption; for a body is capable of being assumed by the Word of God so far as it is united to a rational soul, even though it was not at first perfect with regard to its full measure of quantity. Accordingly, the body of Christ ought not to have been formed through the power of the male seed.

CHAPTER 219

On the cause of the formation of Christ's body

Cum autem corporis humani formatio naturaliter sit ex virili semine, quocumque alio modo corpus Christi formatum fuerit, supra naturam fuit talis formatio. Solus autem Deus institutor naturae est qui supernaturaliter in rebus naturalibus operatur, ut supra dictum est; unde relinquitur quod solus Deus illud corpus miraculose formavit ex materia humanae naturae. Sed cum omnis Dei operatio in creatura sit tribus personis communis, tamen per quandam convenientiam formatio corporis Christi attribuitur Spiritui Sancto. Est enim Spiritus Sanctus amor Patris et Filii, quo se invicem et nos diligunt; Deus autem, ut Apostolus ad Ephesios dicit, *propter nimiam caritatem suam qua dilexit nos*, Filium suum incarnari constituit: convenienter igitur carnis eius formatio Spiritui Sancto attribuitur.

Item, Spiritus Sanctus omnium gratiarum est actor, cum sit primum donum in quo omnia dona gratis donantur; hoc autem fuit superabundantis gratiae ut humana natura in unitatem divinae personae assumeretur, ut ex supradictis apparet: Ad demonstrandam igitur huiusmodi gratiam formatio corporis Christi Spiritui Sancto attribuitur.

Convenit etiam hoc secundum similitudinem humani verbi et spiritus. Verbum enim humanum in corde existens sinvlitudinem gerit aeterni Verbi secundum quod existit in Patre. Sicut autem humanum verbum vocem assumit ut sensibiliter hominibus innotescat, ita et Verbum Dei carnem assumpsit ut visibiliter hominibus appareret; vox autem humana per hominis spiritum formatur: unde et caro Verbi Dei per Spiritum Verbi Dei debuit formari.

Since the formation of the human body is naturally effected by the male seed, any other way of fashioning the body of Christ was above nature. God alone is the author of nature, and he works supernaturally in natural things, as was remarked above. Hence we conclude that God alone miraculously formed that body from matter supplied by human nature. However, although every action of God in creation is common to the three divine persons, the formation of Christ's body is, by a certain appropriation, attributed to the Holy Spirit. For the Holy Spirit is the love of the Father and the Son, who love each other and us in him. Since God decreed that his Son should become incarnate *because of his great love with which he loved us*, as the Apostle says in Ephesians 2:4, the formation of Christ's flesh is fittingly ascribed to the Holy Spirit.

Besides, the Holy Spirit is the author of all grace, since he is the first in whom all gifts are given gratis. But the taking up of human nature into the unity of a divine person was a communication of superabundant grace, as is clear from what was said above. Accordingly, to emphasize the greatness of this grace, the formation of Christ's body is attributed to the Holy Spirit.

Another reason for the appropriateness of this teaching is the relationship between the human word and spirit. The human word, as existing in the heart, bears a resemblance to the eternal Word as existing in the Father. And as the human word takes voice that it may become sensibly perceptible to men, so the Word of God took flesh that it might appear visibly to men. But the human voice is formed by man's breath or spirit. In the same way the flesh of the Word of God ought to have been formed by the Spirit of the Word.

CHAPTER 220

Explanation of the article in the Creed about the conception and birth of Christ

Ad excludendum igitur errorem Ebionis et Cerinthi, qui corpus Christi ex virili semine formatum dixerunt, dicitur in Symbolo Apostolorum *qui conceptus est de Spiritu Sancto*; loco cuius in Symbolo Patrum dicitur *et incarnatus est de Spiritu Sancto*, ut non corpus phantasticum secundum Manichaeos, sed veram carnem assumpsisse credatur. Additum est autem in Symbolo Patrum *propter nos homines*, ad excludendum Origenis errorem, qui posuit virtute passionis Christi etiam daemones liberandos. Additum est etiam in eodem *propter*

To exclude the error of Ebion and Cerinthus, who taught that Christ's body was formed from male seed, the Apostles' Creed states: *who was conceived by the Holy Spirit*. In place of this, the Creed of the Nicene Fathers has: *he was made flesh by the Holy Spirit*, so that we may believe that he assumed true flesh and not a phantastical body, as the Manichaeans claimed. And the Creed of the Fathers adds: *on account of us men*, to exclude the error of Origen, who alleged that by the power of Christ's Passion even the devils were to be set free. In the same Creed the phrase, *for our*

nostram salutem, ut mysterium Incarnationis Christi sufficiens ad humanam salutem ostendatur, contra haeresim Nazaraeorum, qui fidem Christi sine operibus legis ad salutem humanam sufficere non putabant. Additum est etiam *descendit de caelis*, ad excludendum errorem Fotini, qui Christum purum hominem asserebat dicens eum ex Maria sumpsisse initium, ut magis per bonae vitae meritum in terris habens principium ad caelum ascenderet, quam caelestem habens originem assumendo carnem descendisset ad terram. Additur etiam *Et homo factus est*, ad excludendum errorem Nestorii, secundum cuius positionem Filius Dei, de quo Symbolum loquitur, magis inhabitator hominis quam homo esse diceretur.

salvation, is appended to show that the mystery of Christ's Incarnation suffices for men's salvation, against the heresy of the Nazarenes, who thought that faith was not enough for human salvation apart from the works of the Law. The words, *he came down from heaven*, were added to exclude the error of Photinus, who asserted that Christ was no more than a man and that he took his origin from Mary. In this heresy the false teaching that Christ had an earthly beginning and later ascended to heaven by the merit of a good life, replaces the truth that he had a heavenly origin and descended to earth by assuming flesh. Lastly, the words, *and he was made man*, were added to exclude the error of Nestorius, according to whose contention the Son of God, of whom the Creed speaks, would be said rather to dwell in man than to be man.

CHAPTER 221

That it was fitting for Christ to be born of a virgin

Cum autem ostensum sit quod de materia humanae naturae conveniebat Filium Dei carnem assumere, materiam autem in humana generatione ministrat femina, conveniens fuit ut Christus de femina carnem assumeret, secundum illud Apostoli ad Galatas IV: *Misit Deus Filium suum factum ex muliere*. Femina autem indiget viri commixtione ad hoc quod materia quam ipsa ministrat formetur in corpus humanum; formatio autem corporis Christi fieri non debuit per virtutem virilis seminis, ut supra iam dictum est: unde absque commixtione virilis seminis illa femina concepit ex qua Filius Dei carnem assumpsit.

Tanto autem aliquis magis spiritualibus donis repletur, quanto magis a carnalibus separatur: nam per spiritualia homo sursum trahitur, per carnalia vero deorsum. Cum autem formatio corporis Christi fieri debuerit per Spiritum Sanctum, oportuit illam feminam de qua Christus carnem assumpsit maxime spiritualibus donis repleri, ut per Spiritum Sanctum non solum anima fecundaretur virtutibus, sed etiam venter prole divina. Unde oportuit non solum mentem eius esse a peccato immunem, sed etiam corpus eius ab omni corruptela carnalis concupiscentiae elongari; unde non solum ad concipiendum Christum virilem commixtionem non est experta, sed nec ante nec postea.

Hoc etiam conveniebat ei qui nascebatur ex ipsa. Ad hoc enim Filius Dei veniebat in mundum carne assumpta ut nos ad resurrectionis statum promoveret, in quo *neque nubent neque nubentur, sed erunt homines sicut angeli in caelo*: unde et continentiae et integritatis

Since, as we have shown, the Son of God was to take flesh from matter supplied by human nature, and since in human generation the woman provides matter, Christ appropriately took flesh from a woman. This is taught by the Apostle in Galatians 4:4: *God sent forth his Son, born of woman*. A woman needs the cooperation of a man in order that the matter she supplies may be fashioned into a human body. But the formation of Christ's body ought not to have been effected through the power of the male seed, as we said above. Hence that woman from whom the Son of God assumed flesh conceived without the admixture of male seed.

Now the more anyone is detached from the things of the flesh, the more such a person is filled with spiritual gifts. For man is raised up by spiritual things, whereas he is dragged down by carnal things. Accordingly, since the formation of Christ's body was to be accomplished by the Holy Spirit, it was necessary that the woman from whom Christ took his body should wholly filled with spiritual gifts, so that not only her soul would be endowed with virtues by the Holy Spirit, but also her womb would be made fruitful with divine offspring. Therefore, her soul had to be free from sin, and her body had to be far removed from every taint of carnal concupiscence. And so, not only did she have no experience of commingling with a man at the conceiving of Christ, but neither did she have it before or after.

This was also due to him who was born of her. The Son of God assumed flesh and came into the world for the purpose of raising us to the state of resurrection, in which men *neither marry nor are given in marriage, but are like angels of God in heaven* (Matt 22:30). This is why he established the

doctrinam introduxit, ut in fidelium vita aliqualiter resplendeat gloriae futurae imago; conveniens ergo fuit ut et in suo ortu integritatem commendaret nascendo ex Virgine. Et ideo in Symbolo Apostolorum dicitur *natus ex Maria Virgine*. In Symbolo autem Patrum *incarnatus ex Maria Virgine* dicitur, per quod Valentini error excluditur, ceterorumque qui corpus Christi dixerunt aut esse phantasticum, aut esse alterius naturae, et non esse ex corpore Virginis sumptum atque formatum.

doctrine of continence and of virginal integrity: so that an image of the glory that is to come might, in some degree, shine forth in the lives of the faithful. Consequently, he did well to extol purity of life at his very birth by being born of a virgin; and so the Apostles' Creed says that he was *born of the Virgin Mary*. In the Creed of the Fathers he is said to have been *made flesh of the Virgin Mary*. This excludes the error of Valentinus and others, who taught that the body of Christ was either phantastical or was of another nature and was not taken and formed from the body of the Virgin.

CHAPTER 222

That the Blessed Virgin is the mother of Christ

Ex hoc etiam excluditur error Nestorii, qui beatam Mariam matrem Dei confiteri nolebat. In utroque enim Symbolo dicitur quod Filius Dei est natus vel incarnatus ex Virgine; femina autem ex qua aliquis homo nascitur, mater illius dicitur ex eo quod materiam ministrat humano conceptui: unde beata Virgo Maria, quae materiam ministravit conceptioni Filii Dei, vera mater Filii Dei dicenda est. Non enim refert ad rationem matris, quacumque virtute materia ministrata ab ipsa formetur: non minus igitur mater est quae materiam ministravit Spiritu Sancto formandam, quam quae materiam ministrat formandam virtute virilis seminis.

Si quis autem dicere velit beatam Virginem Dei matrem non debere dici, quia non est ex ea assumpta divinitas, sed caro sola, sicut dicebat Nestorius, manifeste vocem suam ignorat. Non enim ex hoc aliqua dicitur alicuius mater, quia totum quod in ipso est ex ea sumatur. Homo enim constat ex anima et corpore, magisque est homo id quod est secundum animam quam secundum corpus; Anima autem nullius hominis a matre sumitur, sed vel a Deo immediate creatur, ut veritas habet, vel si esset ex traduce, ut quidam posuerunt, non sumeretur a matre sed magis a patre, quia in generatione ceterorum animalium, secundum philosophorum doctrinam, masculus dat animam, femina vero corpus.

Sicut igitur cuiuslibet hominis mater aliqua femina dicitur ex hoc quod ab ea corpus eius assumitur, ita Dei mater beata Virgo Maria dici debet, si corpus ex ea assumptum est corpus Dei. Oportet autem dicere quod sit corpus Dei, si assumitur in unitatem personae Filii Dei, qui, est verus Deus; confitentibus igitur humanam naturam esse assumptam a Filio Dei in unitatem per-

The error of Nestorius, who refused to acknowledge that Blessed Mary is the Mother of God, is likewise excluded. Both Creeds assert that the Son of God was born or was made flesh of the Virgin Mary. The woman of whom any person is born is called his mother, for the reason that she supplies the matter for human conception. Hence the Blessed Virgin Mary, who provided the matter for the conception of the Son of God, should be called the true mother of the Son of God. As far as the definition of motherhood is concerned, the power whereby the matter furnished by a woman is formed does not enter into the question. She who supplied matter to be formed by the Holy Spirit is no less a mother than a woman who supplies matter that is to be formed by the power of male seed.

If anyone insists on maintaining that the Blessed Virgin ought not to be called the Mother of God because flesh alone and not divinity was derived from her, as Nestorius contended, he clearly is not aware of what he is saying. A woman is not called a mother for the reason that everything that is in her child is derived from her. Man is made up of body and soul; and a man is what he is more in virtue of his soul than in virtue of his body. But no man's soul is derived from his mother. The soul is either created by God directly, as truth has it, or, if it were produced by traduction, as some have fancied, it would be derived from the father rather than from the mother. For in the generation of other animals, according to the teaching of philosophers, the male gives the soul, the female gives the body.

Consequently, just as any woman is a mother from the fact that her child's body is derived from her, so the Blessed Virgin Mary ought to be called the Mother of God if the body of God is derived from her. But we have to hold that it is the body of God if it is taken up into the unity of the person of God's Son, who is true God. Therefore, all who admit that human nature was assumed by the Son of God

sonae, necesse est dicere quod beata Virgo Maria sit mater Dei. Sed quia Nestorius negabat unam personam esse Dei et hominis Iesu Christi, ideo et ex consequenti negabat Virginem Mariam esse matrem Dei.

into the unity of his person must admit that the Blessed Virgin Mary is the Mother of God. But because Nestorius denied that the person of God and of the man Jesus Christ was one, consequently he denied that the Virgin Mary was the Mother of God.

CHAPTER 223

That the Holy Spirit is not the father of Christ

Licet autem Filius Dei dicatur de Spiritu Sancto et ex Maria Virgine incarnatus, et de Spiritu Sancto conceptus, non tamen dicendum est quod Spiritus Sanctus sit pater hominis Christi, licet beata Virgo Maria mater eius dicatur.

Primo quidem, quia in beata Maria Virgine invenitur totum quod pertinet ad matris rationem: materiam enim ministravit Christi conceptui Spiritu Sancto formandam, ut requirit ratio 'matris.' Sed ex parte Spiritus Sancti non invenitur totum quod ad rationem patris exigitur. Est enim de ratione patris ut ex sua natura filium sibi connaturalem producat; unde si fuerit aliquod agens quod faciat aliquid non ex sua substantia, nec producat ipsum in similitudinem suae naturae, pater eius dici non poterit: non enim dicimus quod homo sit pater eorum quae facit per artem, nisi forte secundum methaphoram. Spiritus autem Sanctus est quidem Christo connaturalis secundum naturam divinam, secundum quam pater Christi non est, sed magis ab ipso procedens; secundum autem naturam humanam non est Christo connaturalis, est enim alia natura humana et divina in Christo, ut supra dictum est; neque in naturam humanam est versum aliquid de natura divina, ut supra dictum est. Relinquitur ergo quod Spiritus Sanctus pater hominis Christi dici non possit.

Item, in unoquoque filio id quod principalius in ipso est, a patre est; quod autem secundarium, a matre: in aliis enim animalibus anima est a patre, corpus vero a matre. In homine autem etsi anima rationalis a patre non sit, sed a Deo creata, virtus tamen paterni seminis dispositive operatur ad formam. Id autem quod principalius est in Christo est persona Verbi, quae nullo modo est a Spiritu Sancto. Relinquitur ergo quod Spiritus Sanctus pater Christi dici non possit.

Although the Son of God is said to have been made flesh and to have been conceived by the Holy Spirit and of the Virgin Mary, we are not to conclude that the Holy Spirit is the father of the man Christ, even though the Blessed Virgin is called his Mother.

The first reason for this is that everything pertaining to the idea of mother is verified in the Blessed Virgin Mary. She furnished the matter to be formed by the Holy Spirit for the conception of Christ, as the idea of 'mother' requires. But not all the elements required for the idea of fatherhood are found on the part of the Holy Spirit. The idea of fatherhood requires that the father produce from his nature a son who is of like nature with himself. Therefore, if some agent would make a thing that is not derived from its own substance, and would not produce such a thing unto the likeness of its own nature, that agent could not be called the thing's father. We do not say that a man is the father of things he makes by artistry, unless perhaps in a metaphorical sense. The Holy Spirit is, indeed, connatural with Christ as regards the divine nature; in this respect, however, he is not the father of Christ, but rather proceeds from him. With respect to the human nature, the Holy Spirit is not connatural with Christ. For the human nature in Christ is other than the divine nature, as we said above. Nor is anything of the divine nature changed into human nature, as we also said above. Consequently, the Holy Spirit cannot be called the father of the man Christ.

Moreover, that which is principal in any son comes from his father, and what is secondary comes from his mother. Thus in other animals the soul is from the father, and the body from the mother. In man, of course, the rational soul does not come from the father, but is created by God; yet the power of the paternal seed operates dispositively toward the form. But that which is principal in Christ is the person of the Word, who is in no way derived from the Holy Spirit. We conclude, therefore, that the Holy Spirit cannot be called the father of Christ.

CHAPTER 224

On the sanctification of the mother of Christ[6]

Quia igitur, ut ex praedictis apparet, beata Virgo Maria mater Filii Dei facta est, de Spiritu Sancto concipiens, decuit ut excellentissima puritate mundaretur, per quam congrueret tanto mysterio; et ideo credendum est eam ab omni labe actualis peccati fuisse immunem, non tantum mortalis sed etiam venialis, quod nulli sanctorum convenire potest post Christum, cum apostolus Iohannes dicat I Io. I *Si dixerimus quia peccatum non habemus, nos ipsos seducimus, et veritas in nobis non est.* Sed de beata Virgine matre Dei intelligi potest quod in Cant. IV dicitur *Tota pulchra es, amica mea, et macula non est in te.*

Nec solum a peccato actuali immunis fuit, sed etiam a peccato originali speciali privilegio mundata. Oportuit siquidem ut cum peccato originali conciperetur, utpote quae ex utriusque sexus commixtione concepta fuit: hoc enim privilegium sibi soli servabatur ut virgo conciperet Filium Dei. Commixtio autem sexus, quae sine libidine esse non potest post peccatum primi parentis, transmittit peccatum originale in prolem. Simul etiam quia si cum peccato originali concepta non fuisset, non indigeret per Christum redimi, et sic Christus non esset universalis hominum redemptor: quod derogat dignitati Christi. Est ergo tenendum quod cum peccato originali concepta fuit, sed ab eo quodam speciali modo, ut dictum est, purgata fuit.

Quidam enim a peccato originali purgantur post nativitatem ex utero, sicut qui in baptismo sanctificantur; quidam autem quodam privilegio gratiae etiam in maternis uteris sanctificati leguntur, sicut de Ieremia dicitur Ier. I *Priusquam te formarem in utero, novi te,* et de Iohanne Baptista angelus dicit *Spiritu Sancto replebitur adhuc ex utero matris suae.*

Quod autem praestitum est Christi praecursori et prophetae, non debet credi denegatum esse matri ipsius: et ideo creditur in utero sanctificata, ante scilicet quam ex utero nasceretur.

Non autem talis sanctificatio praecessit infusionem animae, sic enim numquam fuisset originali peccato subiecta, et redemptione non indiguisset non enim subiectum peccati esse potest nisi natura rationalis.

As appears from the foregoing exposition, the Blessed Virgin Mary became the mother of God's Son by conceiving of the Holy Spirit. Therefore, it was fitting that she should be adorned with the highest degree of purity, that she might be made conformable to such a Son. And so we are to believe that she was free from every stain of actual sin—not only of mortal sin but of venial sin. Such freedom from sin can pertain to none of the saints after Christ, as we know from 1 John 1:8: *If we say that we have no sin, we deceive ourselves, and the truth is not in us.* But what is said in the Canticle of Canticles 4:7, *You are all fair, my love; there is no flaw in you,* can well be understood of the Blessed Virgin, Mother of God.

Mary was not only free from actual sin, but she was also, by a special privilege, cleansed from original sin. She had, indeed, to be conceived with original sin, inasmuch as her conception resulted from the commingling of both sexes: for this privilege was reserved exclusively to her who as a virgin conceived the Son of God. But the commingling of the sexes which, after the sin of our first parent, cannot take place without lust, transmits original sin to the offspring. Likewise, if Mary had been conceived without original sin, she would not have had to be redeemed by Christ, and so Christ would not be the universal redeemer of men, which detracts from his dignity. Accordingly, we must hold that she was conceived with original sin, but was cleansed from it in some special way.

Some men are cleansed from original sin after their birth from the womb, as is the case with those who are sanctified in baptism. Others are reported to have been sanctified in the wombs of their mothers, in virtue of an extraordinary privilege of grace. Thus we are told with regard to Jeremiah: *Before I formed you in the womb I knew you; and before you came forth out of the womb I sanctified you* (Jer 1:5). And in Luke 1:15 the angel says of John the Baptist: *He will be filled with the Holy Spirit even from his mother's womb.*

We cannot suppose that the favor granted to the precursor of Christ and to the prophet was denied to Christ's own mother. Therefore, we believe that she was sanctified in her mother's womb, that is, before she was born.

Yet such sanctification did not precede the infusion of her soul. In that case she would never have been subject to original sin, and so would have had no need of redemption. For only a rational creature can be the subject of sin. Fur-

---

6. Pius IX, Ineffabilis Deus, Dec. 8, 1854: We declare, pronounce, and define that the doctrine which holds that the most Blessed Virgin Mary, in the first instance of her conception, by a singular grace and privilege granted by Almighty God, in view of the merits of Jesus Christ, the Savior of the human race, was preserved free from all stain of original sin, is a doctrine revealed by God and therefore to be believed firmly and constantly by all the faithful.

Similiter etiam sanctificationis gratia per prius in anima radicatur, nec ad corpus potest pervenire nisi per animam: unde post infusionem animae credendum est eam sanctificatam fuisse.

Eius autem sanctificatio amplior fuit quam aliorum in utero sanctificatorum. Alii namque sanctificati in utero sunt quidem a peccato originali mundati, non tamen eis est praestitum ut post non peccarent, saltem venialiter; sed beata Virgo Maria tanta abundantia gratiae sanctificata fuit, ut deinceps ab omni peccato conservaretur immunis, non solum mortali sed etiam veniali. Et quia veniale peccatum interdum ex surreptione contingit, ex hoc scilicet quod aliquis inordinatus concupiscentiae motus insurgit, aut alterius passionis, praeveniens rationem, ratione cuius primi motus dicuntur esse peccata, consequens est, quia beata Virgo Maria numquam venialiter peccauit, quod inordinatos passionum motus non senserit. Contingunt autem huiusmodi motus inordinati ex hoc quod appetitus sensitivus, qui est harum passionum subiectum, non sic subiicitur rationi quin interdum ad aliquid praeter ordinationem rationis moveatur, et quandoque etiam contra rationem, in quo consistit motus peccati. Sic igitur fuit in beata Virgine appetitus sensitivus rationi subiectus per virtutem gratiae ipsam sanctificantis, quod numquam contra rationem moveretur; poterat tamen habere aliquos motus subitos non preordinatos ratione.

In Domino autem Iesu Christo aliquid amplius fuit. Sic enim inferior appetitus in eo rationi subiiciebatur ut ad nihil moveretur nisi secundum ordinem rationis, secundum scilicet quod ratio ordinabat vel permittebat appetitum inferiorem moveri proprio motu. Hoc autem videtur ad integritatem primi status pertinuisse ut inferiores vires totaliter rationi subderentur: quae quidem subiectio per peccatum primi parentis est sublata, non solum in ipso sed etiam in aliis qui ab eo contrahunt originale peccatum, in quibus etiam postquam a culpa originali mundantur per gratiae sacramentum, remanet rebellio vel inobedientia inferiorum virium ad rationem, quae dicitur fomes peccati; qui in Christo nullatenus fuit secundum praedicta.

Sed quia in beata Virgine Maria non erant inferiores vires totaliter rationi subiectae, ut scilicet nullum motum haberent a ratione non praeordinatum, et tamen sic cohibebantur per virtutem gratiae ut nullo modo contra rationem moverentur: propter hoc solet dici quod in beata Virgine post sanctificationem remansit quidem fomes peccati secundum substantiam, sed ligatus.

thermore, the grace of sanctification is rooted primarily in the soul, and cannot extend to the body except through the soul. Hence we must believe that Mary was sanctified after the infusion of her soul.

But her sanctification was more ample than that of others who were sanctified in the wombs of their mothers. Others thus sanctified in the womb were, it is true, cleansed from original sin; but the grace of being unable to sin later on, even venially, was not granted to them. The Blessed Virgin Mary, however, was sanctified with such a wealth of grace that thenceforth she was preserved free from all sin, and not only from mortal sin, but also from venial sin. Moreover, venial sin sometimes creeps up on us unawares, owing to the fact that an inordinate motion of concupiscence or of some other emotion arises prior to the advertence of the mind, yet in such a way that the first motions are called sins. Hence we conclude that the Blessed Virgin Mary never committed a venial sin, for she did not experience such inordinate motions of emotion. Inordinate motions of this kind arise because the sensitive appetite, which is the subject of these emotions, is not so obedient to reason as not sometimes to move toward an object outside the order of reason, or even, occasionally, against reason; and this is what engenders the sinful impulse. In the Blessed Virgin, accordingly, the sensitive appetite was rendered so subject to reason by the power of the grace which sanctified it that it was never aroused against reason, but was always in conformity with the order of reason. Nevertheless, she could experience some spontaneous movements not ordered by reason.

In our Lord Jesus Christ there was something more. In him the lower appetite was so perfectly subject to reason that it did not move in the direction of any object except in accord with the order of reason, that is, so far as reason regulated the lower appetite or permitted it to go into action of its own accord. So far as we can judge, a characteristic pertaining to the integrity of the original state was the complete subjection of the lower powers to reason. This subjection was destroyed by the sin of our first parent not only in himself, but in all the others who contract original sin from him. In all of these the rebellion or disobedience of the lower powers to reason, which is called concupiscence, or the *fomes peccati*, remains even after they have been cleansed from sin by the sacrament of grace. But such was by no means the case with Christ, according to the explanation given above.

In the Blessed Virgin Mary, however, the lower powers were not so completely subject to reason as never to experience any movement not preordained by reason. Yet they were so restrained by the power of grace that they were at no time aroused contrary to reason. Because of this we usually say that after the Blessed Virgin was sanctified concupiscence remained in her according to its substance, but that it was shackled.

CHAPTER 225

On the perpetual virginity of the mother of Christ

Si autem per primam sanctificationem sic fuit contra omnem motum peccati munita, multo magis in ea excrevit gratia, et fomes peccati est debilitatus vel etiam totaliter sublatus, Spiritu Sancto in ipsam secundum verbum angeli superveniente ad corpus Christi ex ea formandum. Unde postquam facta est sacrarium Spiritus Sancti, habitaculum Filii Dei, nephas est credere non solum aliquem motum peccati in ea fuisse, sed nec etiam carnalis concupiscentiae delectationem eam fuisse expertam. Et ideo abhominandus est error Elvidii, qui etsi asserat Christum ex Virgine conceptum et natum, dixit tamen eam postmodum ex Ioseph alios filios genuisse.

Nec hoc eius errori suffragatur quod Matthae. I dicitur, quod *non cognovit eam* Ioseph, scilicet Mariam, *donec peperit filium suum primogenitum*, quasi postquam peperit eam cognoverit; quia in hoc loco *donec* non significat tempus finitum, sed indeterminatum. Est enim consuetudo sacrae Scripturae ut usque tunc specialiter aliquid asserat factum vel non factum, quousque in dubium poterat venire; sicut dicitur in Psalmo *Sede a dextris meis, donec ponam inimicos tuos scabellum pedum tuorum*: dubium enim esse poterat an Christus sederet ad dexteram Dei, quandiu non videntur inimici ei esse subiecti, quod postquam innotuerit nullus remanebit dubitandi locus. Similiter dubium esse poterat an ante partum Filii Dei Ioseph Mariam cognoverit; unde hoc evangelista removere curavit, quasi indubitabile relinquens quod post partum non fuerit cognita.

Nec etiam ei suffragatur quod Christus dicitur primogenitus eius, quasi post ipsum alios habuerit filios; solet enim in Scriptura primogenitus dici ante quem nullus genitus, etiam si post ipsum nullus sequatur, sicut patet de primogenitis qui secundum legem sanctificabantur Domino et sacerdotibus offerebantur.

Nec etiam ei suffragatur quod in Euangelio aliqui dicuntur fratres Christi fuisse, quasi mater eius alios habuerit filios. Solet enim Scriptura 'fratres' dicere omnes qui sunt cognationis eiusdem, sicut Abraham Loth fratrem suum nominavit, cum tamen esset nepos eius. Et secundum hoc nepotes Mariae, et alii eius consanguinei, fratres Christi dicuntur, et etiam consanguinei Ioseph qui pater Christi putabatur.

Et ideo in Symbolo dicitur *qui natus est de Virgine Maria*. Quae quidem virgo dicitur absolute, quia et ante

If Mary was thus strengthened against every movement of sin by her first sanctification, much more did grace grow in her and much more was concupiscence weakened or even completely uprooted in her when the Holy Spirit came upon her, according to the angel's word, to form of her the body of Christ. After she had been made the shrine of the Holy Spirit and the tabernacle of the Son of God, it would be wicked to believe that there was ever any inclination to sin in her, or that she ever experienced any pleasure of carnal concupiscence. And so we must view with revulsion the error of Helvidius who, while admitting that Christ was conceived and born of the Virgin, asserted that she later bore other sons to Joseph.

Certainly this error finds no support in Matthew's statement that Joseph *knew her not*, namely, Mary, *until she brought forth her first-born Son* (Matt 1:25); as though he knew her after she gave birth to Christ. The word *until* in this text does not signify definite time but indicates indeterminate time. Sacred Scripture frequently asserts with emphasis that something was done or not done up to a certain time, as long as the issue could remain in doubt. Thus we read in Psalm 110 [109]:1: *Sit at my right hand until I make your enemies your footstool.* There could be some doubt whether Christ would sit at the right hand of God as long as his enemies did not seem to be subject to him; but once we know that they are, no room for doubt could remain. Similarly there could be some doubt as to whether Joseph knew Mary before the birth of God's Son. The Evangelist took pains to remove this doubt, thus giving us to understand beyond all question that she was not known after giving birth.

Nor does the fact that Christ is called Mary's first-born give any support to the error, as though she bore other sons after him. For in scriptural usage the son before whom no other is born is called the first-born, even though no other should follow him. This is clear from the case of the first-born sons who, according to the law, were consecrated to the Lord and offered to the priests.

Again, the error of Helvidius receives no support from the Gospel narrative that certain individuals are called the brethren of Christ, as though his mother had other sons. Scripture is accustomed to apply the name 'brethren' to all who belong to the same relationship. For example, Abraham called Lot his brother, although Lot was his nephew. In the same way Mary's nephews and other relatives are called Christ's brethren, as also are the relatives of Joseph, who was reputed to be the father of Christ.

Accordingly, the Creed states: *who was born of the Virgin Mary.* And, indeed, she is called a virgin without any

partum, et in partu, et post partum virgo permansit. Et quidem quod ante partum et post partum eius virginitati derogatum non fuerit, satis iam dictum est. Sed nec in partu est eius virginitas violata; corpus enim Christi, quod ad discipulos *ianuis clausis* intravit, potuit eadem potestate de utero clauso matris exire. Non enim decebat ut integritatem nascendo tolleret, qui ad hoc nascebatur ut corrupta in integrum reformaret.

qualification, for she remained a virgin before the birth, at the birth, and after the birth of Christ. That there was no impairment of her virginity before and after Christ's birth is clear from what has been said. More than that: her virginity was not violated even in the act of giving birth. Christ's body, which appeared to the disciples *when the doors were closed* (John 20:26), could by the same power come forth from the closed womb of his mother. It was not seemly that he, who was born for the purpose of restoring what was corrupt to its pristine integrity, should destroy integrity in being born.

CHAPTER 226

On the defects assumed by Christ

Sicut autem conveniens fuit ut Filius Dei humanam naturam assumens propter hominum salutem, in natura assumpta salutis humanae finem ostenderet per gratiae et sapientiae perfectionem, ita etiam conveniens fuit quod in humana natura assumpta a Dei Verbo conditiones aliquae existerent quae congruerent decentissimo liberationis modo generis humani. Fuit autem convenientissimus modus ut homo, qui per iniustitiam perierat, per iustitiam repararetur. Exigit autem hoc iustitiae ordo ut qui poenae alicuius peccando factus est debitor, per solutionem poenae illius liberetur. Quia vero quae per amicos facimus aut patimur, aliqualiter nos ipsi facere aut pati videmur, eo quod amor est unitiua virtus ex duobus se amantibus quodammodo faciens unum, non discordat a iustitiae ordine, si aliquis liberetur amico eius satisfaciente pro ipso.

Per peccatum autem primi parentis perditio in totum humanum genus devenerat, nec alicuius hominis poena sufficere poterat ut totum humanam genus liberaret. Non enim erat condigna satisfactio et aequivalens, ut uno homine puro satisfaciente omnes homines absolverentur; similiter etiam nec sufficiebat secundum iustitiam ut angelus ex amore humani generis pro ipso satisfaceret: angelus enim non habet infinitam dignitatem, ut eius satisfactio pro infinitis et infinitorum peccatis sufficere posset. Solus autem Deus est infinitae dignitatis, qui carne assumpta pro homine sufficienter satisfacere poterat, ut supra iam diximus. Talem igitur oportuit ut humanam naturam assumeret in qua pati posset pro homine ea quae homo peccando meruit ut pateretur, ad satisfaciendum pro homine.

Non autem omnis poena quam homo peccando incurrit, est ad satisfaciendum idonea. Provenit enim peccatum hominis ex hoc quod a Deo avertitur, conversus ad commutabilia bona; punitur autem homo pro peccato in utrisque: nam et privatur gratia et ceteris donis quibus Deo coniungitur, et meretur etiam pati molestiam et defectum in his propter quae a Deo aversus est. Ordo igitur satisfactionis requirit ut per poenas quas peccator in bonis commutabilibus patitur, revocetur ad Deum.

Huic autem revocationi contrariae sunt illae poenae quibus homo separatur a Deo; nullus igitur per hoc Deo satisfacit quod privatur gratia, vel quod ignorat Deum,

In assuming human nature for the salvation of man, the Son of God appropriately showed in the nature he assumed, by the perfection of its grace and wisdom, what was to be the goal of human salvation. No less appropriately was the human nature assumed by the Word of God characterized by certain conditions befitting the most suitable way of liberating the human race. The most suitable way was that man, who had perished through his injustice, should be restored by justice. But the order of justice requires that the one who has become liable to some punishment by sinning should be freed by paying the penalty. Since, however, what we do or suffer through our friends, we ourselves are considered in some fashion to do or to suffer, inasmuch as love is a force that in a way makes two lovers one, the order of justice is not violated if a person is set free by the satisfaction his friend offers for him.

By the sin of the first parent ruin had come upon the entire human race. No punishment undergone by any man could suffice to liberate the whole human race. No worthy satisfaction was available; no satisfaction offered by any mere man was great enough in value to free all men. Similarly, justice would not be fully met if even an angel, out of love for the human race, were to offer satisfaction for it. An angel does not possess infinite dignity, and hence any satisfaction he offered would not be capable of sufficing for indefinitely many people and their sins. God alone is of infinite dignity, and so he alone, in the flesh assumed by him, could adequately satisfy for man, as has already been noted. Therefore, it was right for him to assume a human nature so constituted that he could suffer for man in it what man himself deserved to suffer on account of his sin, and thus offer satisfaction on man's behalf.

However, not every punishment incurred for sin is suitable for making satisfaction. Man's sin comes from the fact that in turning to transient goods he turns away from God. And man is punished for sin on both counts. He is deprived of grace and the other gifts by which union with God is effected, and besides this he deserves to suffer chastisement and loss with respect to the object for whose sake he turned away from God. Therefore, the order of satisfaction requires that the sinner should be led back to God by punishments suffered in relation to transient goods.

However, the punishments by which man is separated from God stand in the way of such recall. No one offers satisfaction to God by being deprived of grace, or by being

187

vel quod habet inordinatam animam, quamvis haec sint poena peccati, sed per hoc quod in se ipso dolorem aliquem sentit et in exterioribus rebus damnum.

Non igitur Christus illos defectus assumere debuit quibus homo separatur a Deo, licet sint poena peccati, sicut privatio gratiae, ignorantia et huiusmodi. Per hoc enim minus idoneus ad satisfaciendum redderetur; quinimmo ad hoc quod esset actor humanae salutis, requirebatur ut plenitudinem gratiae et sapientiae possideret, sicut iam dictum est.

Sed quia homo propter peccatum in hoc punitus erat ut necessitatem moriendi haberet, et ut secundum corpus et animam esset passibilis, huiusmodi defectus Christus suscipere voluit, ut mortem pro hominibus patiendo genus humanum redimeret.

Est tamen attendendum quod huiusmodi defectus, etsi sint Christo et nobis communes. Alia tamen ratione inveniuntur in ipso et in nobis. Huiusmodi enim defectus, ut dictum est, poena sunt primi peccati; quia igitur nos per vitiatam originem culpam originalem contrahimus, per consequens hos defectus dicimur contractos habere. Christus autem nullam ex sua origine maculam peccati contraxit; hos autem defectus sua voluntate accepit, unde non debet dici quod habuit hos defectus contractos, sed magis assumptos: illud enim contrahitur quod cum alio ex necessitate trahitur. Christus autem potuit assumere humanam naturam sine huiusmodi defectibus, sicut et sine culpa assumpsit: et hoc rationis ordo poscere videbatur ut qui fuit immunis a culpa, esset immunis a poena. Et sic patet quod nulla necessitate neque vitiatae originis, neque iustitiae, huiusmodi defectus fuerunt in eo: unde relinquitur quod non contracti sed voluntarie assumpti fuerunt.

Quia vero corpus nostrum praedictis defectibus subiacet in poenam peccati, nam ante peccatum ab his eramus immunes, convenienter Christus, inquantum huiusmodi defectus in sua carne assumpsit, dicitur similitudinem peccati gessisse secundum illud Apostoli Ro. VIII *Deus misit Filium suum in similitudinem carnis peccati*; unde et ipsa Christi passibilitas vel passio ab Apostolo peccatum nominatur, cum subditur *et de peccato damnavit peccatum in carne*, et Ro. V: *Quod mortuus est peccato, mortuus est semel*. Et quod est mirabilius, hac etiam ratione dicit Apostolus Gal. III quod est *factus pro nobis maledictum*. Hac etiam ratione dicitur simplam nostram vetustatem assumpsisse, scilicet poenae, ut duplam nostram consumeret, scilicet culpae et poenae.

Est autem considerandum ulterius quod defectus poenales in corpore duplices inveniuntur: quidam communes omnibus, ut esuries, sitis, lassitudo post laborem, dolor, mors et huiusmodi; quidam vero non sunt omnibus communes, sed quorundam hominum proprii,

ignorant of God, or by the fact that his soul is in a state of disorder, even though such afflictions are punishment for sin; man can satisfy only by enduring some pain in himself and by undergoing loss in external goods.

Accordingly, Christ ought not to have assumed those defects which separate man from God, such as privation of grace, ignorance, and the like, although they are punishment for sin. Defects of this kind would but render him less apt for offering satisfaction. Indeed, to be the author of man's salvation, he had to possess fullness of grace and wisdom, as we pointed out above.

Yet, since man by sinning was placed under the necessity of dying and of being subjected to suffering in body and soul, Christ wished to assume the same kind of defects, so that by undergoing death for men he might redeem the human race.

Defects of this kind, we should note, are common to Christ and to us. Nevertheless they are found in Christ otherwise than in us. For, as we have remarked, such defects are the punishment of the first sin. Since we contract original sin through our vitiated origin, we are in consequence said to have contracted these defects. But Christ did not contract any stain in virtue of his origin. He accepted these defects by his own free will. Hence we should not say that he contracted these defects, but rather that he assumed them; for that is contracted (*contrahitur*) which is necessarily drawn along with (*cum trahitur*) some other thing. Christ could have assumed human nature without such defects, just as he actually did assume it without the defilement of sin; and indeed the order of reason would seem to demand that he who was free from sin should also be free from punishment. Thus it is clear that defects of this sort were not in him by any necessity either of vitiated origin or of justice. Therefore, in him they were not contracted but were voluntarily assumed.

Yet, since our bodies are subject to the aforesaid defects in punishment for sin—for prior to sin we were immune from them—Christ, so far as he assumed such defects in his flesh, is rightly deemed to have borne the likeness of sin, as the Apostle says in Romans 8:3: *God, sending his own Son in the likeness of sinful flesh*. Hence Christ's very passibility or suffering is called sin by the Apostle, when he adds that God *condemned sin in the flesh*, and observes in Romans 6:10: *In that he died to sin, he died once*. For the same reason the Apostle uses an even more astonishing expression in Galatians 3:13, saying that Christ was *made a curse for us*. This is also why Christ is said to have assumed our single oldness, namely, of punishment, in order to relieve us of our double burden, namely, sin and punishment.

We should call to mind, further, that the penal defects afflicting our bodies are of two kinds. Some are common to all men, such as hunger, thirst, weariness after labor, pain, death, and the like. Others, however, are not common to all, but are peculiar to certain individuals, such as blind-

sicut caecitas, lepra, febris, membrorum mutilatio et huiusmodi. Horum autem defectuum haec est differentia, quod defectus communes in nobis ab alio traducuntur, scilicet ex primo parente qui eos pro peccato incurrit; defectus autem proprii ex particularibus causis in singulis hominibus innascuntur. Christus autem ex se ipso nullam causam defectus habebat, nec ex anima quae erat gratia et sapientia plena et Verbo Dei unita, nec ex corpore quod erat optime omnipotenti virtute Spiritus Sancti compactum, sed sua voluntate quasi dispensative ad nostram salutem procurandam aliquos defectus suscepit.

Illos igitur suscipere debuit qui ab alio derivantur ad alios, scilicet communes, non proprios, qui in singuli ex causis propriis innascuntur. Simul etiam quia principaliter venerat ad restaurandum humanam naturam, illos defectus suscipere debuit qui in tota natura inveniebantur.

Patet igitur secundum praedicta quod, sicut Damascenus dicit, Christus assumpsit defectus nostros indetractabiles, id est quibus detrahi non potest. Si enim defectum scientiae vel gratiae suscepisset, aut etiam lepram auel caecitatem auel aliquid huiusmodi, hoc ad derogationem dignitatis Christi pertinere videretur, et esset hominibus detrahendi occasio, quae nulla datur ex defectibus totius naturae.

ness, leprosy, fever, mutilation of the members, and similar ills. The difference between these defects is this: common defects are passed on to us from another, namely, our first parent, who incurred them through sin; but personal defects are produced in individual men by particular causes. But Christ had no cause of defect in himself, either in his soul, which was full of grace and wisdom and was united to the Word of God, or in his body, which was excellently organized and disposed, having been fashioned by the omnipotent power of the Holy Spirit. On the contrary, he took upon himself certain defects by the free decision of his own will, with a view to procuring our salvation.

Accordingly, Christ fittingly took on himself those defects that are handed down from one man to others, namely, the common defects, but not the special defects that arise in individuals from particular causes. Again, since he came chiefly to restore human nature, he fittingly assumed those defects that are found universally in nature.

The doctrine thus set forth also makes it clear that, as Damascene points out, Christ assumed our irreprehensible defects, that is, those which are not open to slander. If Christ had taken to himself a deficiency in knowledge or in grace, or even such ills as leprosy or blindness, this would seem to detract from his dignity, and might provide men with an occasion for defaming him. But no such occasion is given by defects attaching to the whole of nature.

CHAPTER 227

Why Christ willed to die

Manifestum est ergo secundum praedicta quod Christus aliquos defectus nostros suscepit, non ex necessitate, sed propter aliquem finem, scilicet propter nostram salutem. Omnis autem potentia et habitus sive habilitas ordinatur ad actum sicut ad finem: unde passibilitas ad satisfaciendum vel merendum non sufficit sine passione in actu. Non enim aliquis dicitur bonus vel malus ex eo quod potest talia agere, sed ex eo quod agit, nec laus et vituperium potentiae debetur, sed actui; unde et Christus non solum passibilitatem nostram suscepit ut nos salvaret, sed etiam ut pro peccatis nostris satisfaceret voluit pati. Passus est autem pro nobis ea quae ut nos pateremur ex peccato primi parentis meruimus, quorum praecipuum est mors, ad quam omnes aliae passiones humanae ordinantur sicut ad ultimum: *Stipendia enim peccati mors est*, ut Apostolus dicit Ro. V.

Unde et Christus pro peccatis nostris voluit mortem pati ut, dum poenam nobis debitam ipse sine culpa

Evidently, therefore, as we see from this discussion, Christ took some of our defects on himself not out of necessity, but for a definite purpose, namely, for our salvation. But every potency and every habit or capacity are ordained toward act as their end. Hence capacity to suffer is not enough for satisfaction or merit apart from actual suffering. A person is called good or evil not because he is able to perform good or evil actions, but because he performs them; praise and blame are duly rendered not for power to act but for acting. To save us, consequently, Christ was not content merely to make our passibility his portion, but he willed actually to suffer that he might satisfy for our sins. He endured for us those sufferings which we deserved to suffer in consequence of the sin of our first parent. Of these the chief is death, to which all other human sufferings are ordered as to their final term. *For the wages of sin is death*, as the Apostle says in Romans 6:23.

Accordingly, Christ willed to submit to death for our sins so that, in taking on himself without any fault of his

susciperet, nos a reatu mortis liberaret, sicut aliquis a debito poenae liberatur, alio pro eo poenam sustinente.

Mori etiam voluit ut non solum mors eius esset nobis satisfactionis remedium, sed etiam salutis sacramentum, ut ad similitudinem mortis eius nos carnali vitae moriamur in spiritualem vitam translati, secundum illud I Pe. III *Christus semel pro peccatis nostris mortuus est, iustus pro iniustis, ut nos offerret Deo, mortificatos quidem carne, vivificatos autem spiritu.*

Mori etiam voluit ut nobis mors eius esset perfectae virtutis exemplum. Quantum ad caritatem quidem, quia *maiorem caritatem nemo habet quam ut animam suam ponat quis pro amicis suis*, ut dicitur Io. XV; tanto enim quisque magis amare ostenditur, quanto plura et graviora pro amico pati non refugit: omnium autem humanorum malorum gravius est mors, per quam tollitur vita humana, unde nullum maius signum dilectionis esse potest quam quod homo pro amico se morti exponat.

Quantum ad fortitudinem vero, quae propter adversa a iustitia non recedit, quia maxime ad fortitudinem pertinere videtur ut etiam nec timore mortis aliquis a virtute recedat, unde dicit Apostolus Hebr. II de Christi passione loquens *Ut per mortem destrueret eum qui habebat mortis imperium, et liberaret eos qui per totam vitam timore mortis obnoxii erant servituti.* Dum enim pro veritate mori non recusavit, exclusit timorem moriendi, propter quem homines servituti peccati plerumque subduntur.

Quantum ad patientiam vero, quae in adversis tristitiam hominem absorbere non sinit, quia quanto sunt maiora adversa, tanto magis in his relucet patientiae virtus unde in maximo malorum quod est mors, perfectae patientiae datur exemplum, si absque mentis turbatione sustineatur, quod de Christo propheta praedixit dicens Ys. LIII *tamquam agnus coram tondente se obmutescet, et non aperiet os suum.*

Quantum ad obedientiam vero, quia tanto laudabilior est obedientia quanto in difficilioribus quis obedit; omnium autem difficillimum est mors: unde ad perfectam obedientiam Christi commendandam dicit Apostolus Phil. II quod *factus est obediens Patri usque ad mortem.*

own the punishment due to us, he might free us from the death to which we had been sentenced, in the way that anyone would be freed from a debt of penalty if another person undertook to pay the penalty for him.

Another reason why he wished to die was that his death might be for us not only a remedy of satisfaction but also a sacrament of salvation, so that we, transferred to a spiritual life, might die to our carnal life, in the likeness of his death. This is in accord with 1 Peter 3:18: *For Christ also died for sins once for all, the righteous for the unrighteous, that he might bring us to God, being put to death in the flesh but made alive in the spirit.*

Christ also wished to die that his death might be an example of perfect virtue for us. He gave an example of charity, for *greater love has no man than this, that a man lay down his life for his friends* (John 15:13). The more numerous and grievous are the sufferings a person does not refuse to bear for his friend, the more strikingly his love is shown forth. But of all human ills the most grievous is death, by which human life is snuffed out. Hence no greater proof of love is possible than that a man should expose himself to death for a friend.

By his death Christ also gave an example of fortitude, which does not abandon justice in the face of adversity; refusal to give up the practice of virtue even under fear of death seems to pertain most emphatically to fortitude. Thus the Apostle says in Hebrews 2:14–15, with reference to Christ's Passion: *That through death he might destroy him who has the power of death, that is, the devil, and deliver all those who through fear of death were subject to lifelong bondage.* In not refusing to die for truth, Christ overcame the fear of dying, which is the reason men for the most part are subject to the slavery of sin.

Further, he gave an example of patience, a virtue that prevents sorrow from overwhelming man in time of adversity; the greater the trials, the more splendidly does the virtue of patience shine forth in them. Therefore, an example of perfect patience is afforded in the greatest of evils, which is death, if it is borne without mental turbulence. Such tranquility the prophet foretold of Christ: *He shall be like a lamb that before its shearers is dumb, and shall not open his mouth* (Isa 53:7).

Lastly, our Lord gave an example of obedience, for the more difficult are the precepts one obeys, the more praiseworthy is the obedience. But the most difficult of all the objects of obedience is death. Hence, to commend the perfect obedience of Christ, the Apostle says, in Philippians 2:8, that *he was obedient to the Father even unto death.*

CHAPTER 228

On the death of the cross

Ex eisdem etiam causis apparet quare mortem crucis voluit pati. Primo quidem quia hoc convenit quantum ad remedium satisfactionis convenienter enim homo punitur per ea in quibus peccavit; *in quo enim peccat quis, per hoc et torquetur*, ut dicitur Sap. XI. Peccatum autem hominis primum fuit per hoc quod pomum arboris ligni scientiae boni et mali contra praeceptum decerpsit; loco cuius Christus se ligno affigi permisit, ut *exsolveret quae non rapuit*, sicut de eo Psalmus dicit.

Convenit etiam quantum ad sacramentum. Voluit enim Christus ostendere sua morte, ut sic moreremur vitae carnali quod spiritus noster in superna elevaretur; unde et ipse dicebat Io. XII *Ego si exaltatus fuero a terra, omnia traham ad me ipsum.*

Convenit etiam quantum ad exemplum perfectae virtutis. Homines enim quandoque non minus refugiunt vituperabile genus mortis quam mortis acerbitatem; unde ad perfectionem virtutis pertinere videtur ut propter bonum virtutis aliquis vetiam vituperabilem mortem non refugiat pati. Unde Apostolus ad commendandam perfectam obedientiam Christi, cum dixisset de eo quod *factus est obediens usque ad mortem*, subdidit *mortem autem crucis*: quae quidem mors turpissima videbatur, secundum illud Sap. II *Morte turpissima condemnemus eum.*

The same reasons reveal why Christ willed to suffer the death of the cross. In the first place, such a death was suitable as a salutary means of satisfaction. Man is fittingly punished in the things wherein he has sinned, as is said in Wisdom 11:16: *One is punished by the very things by which he sins.* But the first sin of man was the fact that he ate the fruit of the tree of knowledge of good and evil, contrary to God's command. In his stead Christ permitted himself to be fastened to a tree, so that *he might pay for what he did not carry off*, as Psalm 68 [67]:5 says of him.

Death on the cross was also appropriate as a sacrament. Christ wished to make clear by his death that we ought so to die in our carnal life that our spirit might be raised to higher things. Hence he himself says, in John 12:32: *I, when I am lifted up from the earth, will draw all men to myself.*

This kind of death was likewise fitting as an example of perfect virtue. Sometimes men shrink no less from a disgraceful kind of death than from the painfulness of death. Accordingly, the perfection of virtue seems to require that a person should not refuse to suffer even a disgraceful death for the good of virtue. Therefore, to commend the perfect obedience of Christ, the Apostle, after saying of him that he was *obedient unto death*, added: *even to the death of the cross* (Phil 2:8). This sort of death was looked on as the most ignominious of all, in the words of Wisdom 2:20: *Let us condemn him to a shameful death.*

CHAPTER 229

On the death of Christ

Cum autem in Christo convenerint in unam personam tres substantiae, scilicet corpus, anima et divinitas Verbi, quarum duae, scilicet anima et corpus, unitae sunt in unam naturam, in morte quidem Christi separata est unio corporis et animae: Aliter enim corpus vere mortuum non fuisset, mors enim corporis nihil est aliud quam separatio animae ab ipso.

Neutrum tamen separatum est a Dei Verbo quantum ad unionem personae. Ex unione autem animae et corporis resultat humanitas: unde separata anima a corpore Christi per mortem, in triduo mortis homo dici non potuit. Dictum est autem supra quod propter unionem in persona humanae naturae ad Dei Verbum, quidquid dicitur de homine Christo potest convenienter de Dei Filio praedicari; unde cum in morte manserit

In Christ three substances, the body, the soul, and the divinity of the Word, are joined together in one person. Two of these, the soul and the body, are united to form one nature. Accordingly, at the death of Christ the union between body and soul was dissolved. Otherwise the body would not have been truly dead, since death of the body is nothing else than the separation of the soul from it.

But neither soul nor body was separated from the Word of God, as far as union with the person is concerned. Human nature results from the union of soul and body; hence Christ could not be said to be a man during the three days of his death, when his soul remained separated from his body by death. However, as was shown above, on account of the union of the human nature with the Word of God in one person, whatever is said of the man Christ can rightly

unio personalis Filii Dei tam ad animam quam ad corpus Christi, quidquid de utroque eorum dicitur, poterat de Dei Filio praedicari. Unde et in Symbolo dicitur de Filio Dei quod *sepultus est*, propter hoc quod corpus sibi unitum iacuit in sepulcro, et quod *descendit ad inferos*, anima descendente.

Est etiam considerandum quod masculinum genus designat personam, neutrum vero naturam: unde in Trinitate dicimus quod Filius est alius a Patre, non aliud. Secundum hoc ergo in triduo mortis Christus fuit totus in sepulcro, totus in inferno, totus in caelo, propter personam quae unita erat et carni in sepulcro iacenti, et animae infernum exspolianti, et subsistebat in natura divina in caelo regnante; sed non potest dici quod totum fuerit in sepulcro aut in inferno, quia non tota humana natura, sed pars in sepulcro aut in inferno fuit.

be predicated also of the Son of God. Consequently, since the personal union of the Son of God both with the soul and with the body of Christ remained in death, whatever is said of either of them could be predicated of the Son of God. Hence the Creed asserts that the Son of God *was buried*, for the reason that the body united to him lay in the tomb, and likewise that *he descended into hell*, because his soul descended.

We should also recall that the masculine gender designates a person, and that the neuter gender designates nature. Thus in speaking of the Trinity we say that the Son is another person (*alius*) than the Father, but not that he is another thing (*aliud*). Accordingly, during the three days of his death Christ was whole in the sepulcher, whole in hell, and whole in heaven, because of his person which remained united to his flesh reposing in the tomb and to his soul which was emptying hell, and which continued to subsist in the divine nature reigning in heaven. But we cannot say that the whole of Christ was in the sepulcher or in hell, because only a part of the human nature and not the whole of it was in the sepulcher or in hell.

Chapter 230

That the death of Christ was voluntary

Fuit igitur mors Christi nostrae morti conformis quantum ad id quod est de ratione mortis, quod est animam a corpore separari; sed quantum ad aliquid mors Christi a nostra morte differens fuit. Nos enim morimur quasi morti subiecti ex necessitate vel naturae, vel alicuius violentiae nobis illatae; Christus autem mortuus est non necessitate, sed potestate et propria voluntate: unde ipse dicebat Io. X *Potestatem habeo ponendi animam meam, et iterum sumendi eam.*

Huius autem differentiae ratio est, quia naturalia voluntati nostrae non subiacent; coniunctio autem animae ad corpus est naturalis, unde voluntati nostrae non subiacet quod anima corpori unita remaneat vel a corpore separetur, sed oportet hoc ex virtute alicuius agentis provenire. Quidquid autem in Christo secundum humanam naturam erat naturale, totum eius voluntati subiacebat propter divinitatis virtutem cui subiacet tota natura. Erat igitur in potestate Christi, ut quandiu vellet anima eius corpori unita remaneret, et statim cum vellet separaretur ab ipso.

Huius autem divinae virtutis indicium centurio cruci Christi assistens sensit, dum eum vidit clamantem expirare, per quod manifeste ostendebatur quod non sicut ceteri homines ex defectu naturae moriebatur: non

Christ's death was like our death as regards the essence of death, which consists in the separation of the soul from the body. But in another respect the death of Christ was different from ours. We die because we are subject to death by a necessary law of nature, or in consequence of some violence done to us. But Christ did not die because of any necessity. He gave up his life by his power and his own will, as he himself attested: *I have power to lay my life down, and I have power to take it again* (John 10:18).

The reason for this difference is that natural things are not subject to our will. But the joining of the soul to the body is natural. Hence the fact that the soul remains united to the body or that it is separated from the body is not subject to our will, but must be brought about by the power of some agent. But whatever was natural in Christ as regards his human nature was completely subject to his will because of the power of his divinity, to which all nature is subject. Therefore, Christ had it in his power that so long as he willed, his soul would remain united to his body, and that the instant he willed, the soul would depart from the body.

The centurion standing near the cross of Christ felt the presence of this divine power when he saw him expire with a loud cry. By this Christ clearly showed that he was not dying like other men, from the breaking down of nature.

enim possunt homines cum clamore spiritum emittere, cum in illo mortis articulo vix etiam possint palpitando linguam movere; unde quod Christus clamans expiravit, in eo divinam manifestavit virtutem, et propter hoc centurio dixit *Vere Filius Dei erat iste.*

Non tamen dicendum est quod Iudaei non occiderunt Christum, vel quod Christus ipse se ipsum occiderit. Ille enim dicitur aliquem occidere qui ei causam mortis inducit, non tamen mors sequitur nisi causa mortis naturam vincat quae vitam conservat. Erat autem in potestate Christi ut natura causae corrumpenti cederet vel resisteret quantum ipse vellet: ideo et ipse voluntarie Christus mortuus fuit, et tamen Iudaei eum occiderunt.

For men cannot send forth their last breath with a loud cry; in the moment of death they can scarcely move their tongue in a quavering whisper. Hence the fact that Christ died uttering a loud cry gave evidence of the divine power in him. It was for this reason that the centurion said: *Truly, this was the Son of God* (Matt 27:54).

Yet we may not say that the Jews did not kill Christ, or that Christ took his own life. For the one who brings the cause of death to bear on a person is said to kill him. But death does not ensue unless the cause of death prevails over nature, which conserves life. Christ had it in his power either to submit his nature to the destructive cause or to resist that influence, just as he willed. Thus Christ died voluntarily, and yet the Jews killed him.

CHAPTER 231

On the Passion of Christ as regards the body

Non solum autem Christus mortem pati voluit, sed et alia quae ex peccato primi parentis in posteros pervenerunt, ut dum poenam peccati integraliter susciperet, nos perfecte a peccato satisfaciendo liberaret. Horum autem quaedam praecedunt mortem, quaedam mortem subsequuntur. Praecedunt quidem mortem corporis passiones tam naturales, ut fames, sitis, lassitudo et cetera huiusmodi, quam etiam violentae, ut vulneratio, flagellatio et similia: quae omnia Christus pati voluit tamquam provenientia ex peccato; si enim homo non peccasset, nec famis aut sitis aut lassitudinis vel frigoris afflictionem sensisset, nec ab exterioribus pertulisset violentam passionem.

Has tamen passiones alia ratione Christus pertulit quam alii homines patiantur. In aliis enim hominibus non est aliquid quod his passionibus repugnare possit; in Christo autem erat unde his passionibus resisteretur, non solum virtus divina increata, sed etiam animae beatitudo, cuius tanta vis est, ut Augustinus dicit, ut eius beatitudo suo modo redundet ad corpus: unde post resurrectionem ex hoc ipso quod anima glorificata erit per Dei visionem apertam et plenam fruitionem, corpus gloriosae animae unitum gloriosum reddetur, impassibile et immortale. Cum igitur anima Christi perfecta visione Dei frueretur, quantum est ex virtute huius visionis, consequens erat ut corpus impassibile et immortale redderetur per redundantiam gloriae ab anima in corpus; sed dispensative factum est ut anima Dei visione fruente simul corpus pateretur, nulla redundantia gloriae ab anima in corpus facta. Suberat enim, ut dictum est, quod

Christ wished to suffer not only death, but also the other ills that flow from the sin of the first parent to his posterity, so that, bearing in its entirety the penalty of sin, he might perfectly free us from sin by offering satisfaction. Of these ills, some precede death, others follow death. Prior to the death of the body come natural sufferings, such as hunger, thirst, and weariness, and also sufferings inflicted by violence, such as wounding, scourging, and the like. Christ wished to endure all these sufferings, since they stem from sin. If man had not sinned, he would not have experienced the affliction of hunger or of thirst or of fatigue or of cold, and he would not have had to undergo the suffering caused by external violence.

Christ bore these sufferings for a different reason from that on account of which other men endure them. In other men there is nothing that can resist these sufferings. But in Christ there was that from which these emotions would be resisted: not only the uncreated power of his divinity, but also the beatitude of his soul, which is so powerful that, as Augustine says, its happiness in its own way flows over into the body. Thus, after the resurrection, by the very fact that the soul will be glorified by the vision of God in unrestricted and full fruition, the body united to the glorified soul will be rendered glorious, impassible, and immortal. Therefore, since the soul of Christ enjoyed the vision of God in the highest degree of perfection, his body should in consequence, so far as the power of this vision is concerned, have been rendered impassible and immortal by an overflowing of glory from the soul to the body. But it was done dispositively[7] that Christ's body would suffer at the

---

7. i.e., by the divine economy.

erat naturale Christo secundum humanam naturam eius voluntati: unde poterat naturalem redundantiam a superioribus partibus in inferiores pro suo libito impedire, ut sineret unamquamque partem pati aut agere quod sibi proprium esset absque alterius partis impedimento, quod in aliis hominibus esse non potest.

Inde etiam est quod in passione Christus maximum corporis dolorem sustinuit, quia corporalis dolor in nullo mitigabatur per superius gaudium rationis, sicut nec e converso dolor corporis rationis gaudium impediebat.

Hinc etiam apparet quod solus Christus simul viator et comprehensor fuit. Sic enim divina visione fruebatur, quod ad comprehensorem pertinet, ut tamen corpus passionibus subiectum remaneret, quod pertinet ad viatorem. Et quia proprium est viatoris ut per bona quae ex caritate agit mereatur vel sibi vel aliis, inde est quod Christus, quamvis comprehensor esset, meruit tamen per ea quae fecit et passus est, et sibi et nobis.

Sibi quidem non gloriam animae, quam a principio suae conceptionis habuerat, sed gloriam corporis, ad quam patiendo pervenit. Nobis etiam suae singulae passiones et operationes fuerunt proficuae ad salutem, non solum per modum exempli, sed etiam per modum meriti, inquantum propter abundantiam caritatis et gratiae nobis potuit gratiam promereri, ut sic de plenitudine capitis membra acciperent.

Erat siquidem quaelibet passio eius, quantumcumque minima, sufficiens ad redimendum humanum genus, si consideretur dignitas patientis. Quanto enim aliqua passio in personam digniorem infertur, tanto videtur maior iniuria: puta si quis percutiat principem quam si percutiat quendam de populo. Cum igitur Christus sit dignitatis infinitae, quaelibet passio eius habet infinitam aestimationem, ut sic sufficeret ad infinitorum peccatorum abolitionem. Non tamen per quamlibet fuit consummata humani generis redemptio, sed per mortem, quam propter rationes supra positas ad hoc pati voluit ut genus humanum redimeret a peccatis; in emptione enim qualibet non solum requiritur quantitas valoris, sed deputatio pretii ad emendum.

very time his soul was enjoying the vision of God, with no overflow of glory from the soul to the body. For, as we have said, all that was natural in Christ's human nature was subject to his will. Hence at his good pleasure he could prevent natural flowing-over from his higher to his lower parts, and so could allow any part to suffer or do whatever would be proper to it without interference from any other part. This, of course, is impossible in other men.

This also accounts for the fact that during his Passion Christ suffered the most excruciating pain of body. For his bodily pain was in no way lessened by the higher joy of his rational soul, just as, conversely, pain of body did not obstruct the joy of his rational soul.

This reveals, too, that Christ alone was both a viator and a comprehensor. He enjoyed the vision of God, which characterizes the comprehensor, but in such a way that his body remained subject to sufferings, which characterizes the wayfarer. And since a wayfarer has power to merit, either for himself or for others, by the good works he performs from charity, Christ too, although he was a comprehensor, merited both for himself and for others by his works and sufferings.

For himself Christ merited, not indeed glory of soul, which he had from the first instant of his conception, but glory of body, which he won by suffering. For us, too, each of his sufferings and actions was profitable unto salvation, not only by way of example, but also by way of merit; owing to the abundance of his charity and grace, he could merit grace for us, so that thus the members might receive of the fullness of the head.

Any suffering of his, however slight, was enough to redeem the human race, if the dignity of the sufferer is considered. For the more exalted the person on whom suffering is inflicted, the greater is the injury judged to be; for instance, a greater outrage is committed if one strikes a prince than if one strikes a common man of the people. Consequently, since Christ is a person of infinite dignity, any suffering of his has an infinite value, and so suffices for the abolition of infinitely many sins. Yet the redemption of the human race was accomplished not by this or that slight suffering, but by Christ's death, which, for reasons listed above, he chose to endure to redeem the human race from its sins. For in any purchasing transaction there is required, not only an amount of value, but also the stipulation of the price of the purchase.

CHAPTER 232

On the passibility of Christ's soul

Quia vero anima est forma corporis, consequens est ut patiente corpore, etiam anima quodammodo patiatur; unde pro statu illo quo Christus corpus passibile habuit, etiam anima eius passibilis fuit.

Est autem considerandum quod duplex est animae passio: una quidem ex parte corporis, alia vero ex parte obiecti; quod in una aliqua potentiarum considerari potest, sic enim se habet anima ad corpus sicut pars animae ad partem corporis. Potentia autem visiva patitur quidem ab obiecto, sicut cum ab excellenti fulgido visus obtunditur; ex parte vero organi, sicut cum laesa pupilla hebetatur visus.

Si igitur consideretur passio animae Christi ex parte corporis, sic tota anima patiebatur corpore patiente. Est enim anima forma corporis secundum suam essentiam, in essentia vero animae omnes potentiae radicantur: unde relinquitur quod corpore patiente quaelibet potentia animae quodammodo pateretur.

Si vero consideretur animae passio ex parte obiecti, non omnis potentia animae patiebatur, secundum quod passio proprie sumpta nocumentum importat: non enim ex parte obiecti cuiuslibet potentiae poterat aliquid esse nocivum. Iam enim supra dictum est quod anima Christi perfecta Dei visione fruebatur. Superior igitur ratio animae Christi, quae rebus aeternis contemplandis et consulendis inhaeret, nihil habebat adversum aut repugnans ex quo aliqua nocumenti passio in ea locum haberet.

Potentiae vero sensitivae, quarum obiecta sunt res corporeae, habere poterant aliquod nocumentum ex corporis lesione: unde sensibilis dolor in Christo fuit corpore patiente. Et quia laesio corporis sicut a sensu sentitur noxia, ita etiam interior imaginatio eam ut nocivam apprehendit, unde sequitur interior tristitia etiam cum dolor in corpore non sentitur: et hanc etiam passionem tristitiae dicimus in Christo fuisse. Non solum autem imaginatio, sed etiam inferior ratio nociva corporis apprehendit; et ideo etiam ex apprehensione inferioris rationis, quae circa temporalia versatur, poterat passio tristitie locum in Christo habere, inquantum scilicet mortem et aliam corporis laesionem inferior ratio apprehendebat ut noxiam et appetitui naturali contrariam.

Contingit autem ex amore qui facit duos homines quasi unum, ut aliquis tristitiam patiatur non solum ex his quae per imaginationem vel per inferiorem rationem apprehendit ut sibi nociva, sed etiam ex his quae appre-

Since the soul is the form of the body, any suffering undergone by the body must in some way affect the soul. Therefore, in that state in which the body of Christ was passible, his soul was passible also.

We may note that the suffering of the soul is of two kinds. One kind of suffering arises from the body, the other from the object that causes suffering, and this can be observed in any one of the faculties. For the soul is related to the body in the same way that a part of the soul is related to a part of the body. Thus suffering may be caused in the faculty of sight by some object, as when vision is dimmed by an excessively bright light; suffering can also arise from the organ itself, as when vision is dulled because of an injured pupil.

Accordingly, if the suffering of Christ's soul is regarded as arising from the body, the whole soul suffered when the body suffered. For the soul in its essence is the form of the body, and the faculties, too, are all rooted in the essence of the soul. Consequently, if the body suffers, every power of the soul suffers in some way.

But if the suffering of the soul is considered as arising from an object, not every power of Christ's soul suffered, understanding suffering in the proper sense as connoting harm. For nothing that arose from the object of any of these powers could be harmful, since, as we saw above, the soul of Christ enjoyed the perfect vision of God. Thus the higher reason of Christ's soul, which is immersed in the contemplation and meditation of eternal things, embraced nothing adverse or repugnant that could cause it to suffer any harm.

But the sense faculties, whose objects are material things, could receive some injury from the suffering of the body; and so Christ experienced sensible pain when his body suffered. Furthermore, just as laceration of the body is felt by the senses to be injurious, so the inner imagination apprehends it as harmful; hence interior distress follows even when pain is not felt in the body. We assert that suffering of such distress was experienced by the soul of Christ. More than this: not the imagination alone, but also the lower reason apprehends objects harmful to the body; and so, as a result of such apprehension by the lower reason, which is concerned with temporal affairs, the suffering of sorrow could have place in Christ, so far as the lower reason apprehended death and other maltreatment of the body as injurious and as contrary to natural appetite.

Moreover, in consequence of love, which makes two persons like one, a man may be afflicted with sadness not only on account of objects he apprehends through his imagination or his lower reason as harmful to himself, but also

hendit ut noxia aliis quos amat. Unde ex hoc tristitiam Christus patiebatur quod aliis, quos ex caritate amabat, periculum imminere cognoscebat culpae vel poenae, unde non solum sibi, sed etiam aliis doluit.

Et quamvis dilectio proximi ad superiorem rationem quodammodo pertineat, inquantum proximus ex caritate diligitur propter Deum, superior tamen ratio in Christo de proximorum defectibus tristitiam habere non potuit, sicut in nobis habere potest. Quia enim superior ratio Christi plena Dei visione fruebatur, hoc modo apprehendebat quidquid ad aliorum defectus pertinet secundum quod in divina sapientia continetur, secundum quam decenter ordinatum existit et quod aliquis peccare permittitur, et quod pro peccato punitur. Et ideo nec anima Christi, nec aliquis beatus Deum videns, de defectibus proximorum tristitiam pati potest. Secus autem est in viatoribus, qui ad rationem sapientiae videndam non attingunt; hi enim etiam secundum rationem superiorem de defectibus aliorum tristantur, dum ad honorem Dei et exaltationem fidei pertinere existimant quod aliqui salventur, qui tamen damnantur.

Sic igitur de eisdem de quibus Christus dolebat secundum sensum, imaginationem et rationem inferiorem, secundum superiorem gaudebat, inquantum ea ad ordinem divinae sapientiae referebat. Et quia referre aliquid ad alterum est proprium opus rationis, ideo solet dici quod mortem ratio Christi refugiebat quidem si consideretur ut natura, quia scilicet naturaliter est mors odibilis: volebat tamen eam pati, si consideretur ut ratio.

Sicut autem in Christo fuit tristitia, ita etiam et aliae passiones quae ex tristitia oriuntur, ut puta timor, ira et huiusmodi. Ex his enim quae tristitiam praesentia ingerunt, timor in nobis causatur dum futura aestimantur; et dum aliquo laedente contristati sumus, contra eum irascimur. Hae tamen passiones aliter fuerunt in Christo quam in nobis. In nobis enim plerumque iudicium rationis praeveniunt, et interdum modum rationis excedunt; in Christo autem numquam praeveniebant iudicium rationis, nec modum a ratione taxatum excedebant, sed tantum movebatur inferior appetitus, qui est passioni subiectus, quantum ratio ordinabat eum debere moveri. Poterat igitur contingere quod secundum inferiorem partem anima Christi refugiebat aliquid quod secundum superiorem optabat. Non tamen erat contrarietas appetituum in ipso, vel rebellio carnis ad spiritum, quae in nobis contingit ex hoc quod appetitus inferior iudicium et modum rationis transcendit; sed in Christo movebatur secundum iudicium rationis, inquantum permittebat unicuique inferiorum virium moveri proprio motu, secundum quod Christum decebat.

on account of objects he apprehends as harmful to others whom he loves. Thus Christ suffered sadness from his awareness of the perils of sin or of punishment threatening other men whom he loved with the love of charity. And so he grieved for others as well as for himself.

However, although the love of our fellow men pertains in a certain way to the higher reason, inasmuch as our neighbor is loved out of charity for God's sake, the higher reason in Christ could not experience sorrow on account of the defects of his fellow men, as it can in us. For, since Christ's higher reason enjoyed the full vision of God, it apprehended all that pertains to the defects of others as contained in the divine wisdom, in the light of which the fact that a person is permitted to sin and is punished for his sin is seen to be in accord with becoming order. And so neither the soul of Christ nor of any of the blessed who behold God can be afflicted with sadness by the defects of their neighbors. But the case is otherwise with wayfarers who do not rise high enough to perceive the plan of wisdom. Such persons are saddened by the defects of others even in their higher reason, when they think that it pertains to the honor of God and the exaltation of the faith that some should be saved who nevertheless are damned.

Thus, with regard to the very things for which he was suffering in sense, imagination, and lower reason, Christ was rejoicing in his higher reason, so far as he referred them to the order of divine wisdom. And since the referring of one thing to another is the proper task of reason, we generally say that Christ's reason, if it is considered as nature, shrank from death, meaning that death is naturally abhorrent, but that if it is considered as reason, it was willing to suffer death.

Just as Christ was afflicted with sadness, so he experienced other emotions that stem from sadness, such as fear, wrath, and the like. Fear is caused in us by those things whose presence engenders sorrow, when they are thought of as future evils; and when we are grieved by someone who is hurting us, we become angry at him. Such emotions existed otherwise in Christ than in us. In us they frequently anticipate the judgment of reason, and sometimes pass the bounds of reason. In Christ they never anticipated the judgment of reason, and never exceeded the moderation imposed by reason; his lower appetite, which was subject to emotion, was moved just so far as reason decreed that it should be moved. Therefore, Christ's soul could desire something in its higher part that it shrank from in its lower part, and yet there was no conflict of appetites in him or rebellion of the flesh against the spirit, such as occurs in us owing to the fact that the lower appetite exceeds the judgment and measure of reason. In Christ this appetite was moved in accord with the judgment of reason, to the extent that he permitted each of his lower powers to be moved by its own impulse, according as it was fitting.

His igitur consideratis manifestum est quod superior ratio Christi tota quidem fruebatur et gaudebat per comparationem ad suum obiectum, non enim ex hac parte aliquid ei occurrere poterat quod esset tristitiae causa; sed etiam tota patiebatur ex parte subiecti, ut supra dictum est. Nec illa fruitio minuebat passionem, nec passio impediebat fruitionem, cum non fieret redundantia ex una potentia in aliam, sed quaelibet potentiarum permitteretur agere quod sibi proprium erat, sicut iam supra dictum est.

In the light of all this we see clearly that the whole higher reason of Christ was happy and full of joy in respect to its proper object. On the part of this object, nothing that might engender sorrow could arise in him; but also the whole was suffering on the part of the subject, as was said above. Yet that enjoyment did not lessen the suffering, nor did the suffering prevent the enjoyment, since no overflowing from one power to another took place; each of the powers was allowed to exercise the function proper to it, as we mentioned above.

CHAPTER 233

On the prayer of Christ

Quia vero oratio est desiderii expositiva, ex diversitate appetituum ratio sumi potest orationis quam Christus imminente passione proposuit dicens Matth. XXVI *Pater, si fieri potest, transeat a me calix iste: verumtamen non sicut ego volo, sed sicut tu vis.* In hoc enim quod ait *transeat a me calix iste*, motum inferioris appetitus et naturalis designat, quo naturaliter unusquisque refugit mortem et appetit vitam; in hoc autem quod dicit *verumptamen non sicut ego volo, sed sicut tu vis*, exprimit motum superioris rationis omnia considerantis prout sub ordinatione divinae sapientiae contineantur. Ad quod etiam pertinet quod dicit *si fieri potest*, hoc solum fieri posse demonstrans quod secundum ordinem divinae voluntatis procedit.

Et quamvis calix passionis non transiverit ab eo quin ipsum biberit, non tamen dici debet quod eius oratio exaudita non fuerit; nam secundum Apostolum Hebr. V, in omnibus *exauditus est pro sua reverentia*. Cum enim oratio, ut dictum est, sit desiderii expositiva, illud simpliciter oramus quod simpliciter volumus: unde et desiderium iustorum orationis vim optinet apud Deum, secundum illud Psalmi *Desiderium pauperum exaudivit Dominus.* Illud autem simpliciter volumus quod secundum rationem superiorem appetimus, ad quam solam pertinet consentire in opus. Et ideo simpliciter oravit Christus ut Patris voluntas fieret, non autem quod calix ab eo transiret, quia nec hoc simpliciter voluit sed secundum inferiorem paratem, ut dictum est.

Since prayer manifests desire, the nature of the prayer Christ offered when his Passion was upon him may be gathered from the different desires he expressed. In Matthew 26:39 he begs: *My Father, if it be possible, let this chalice pass from me. Nevertheless, not as I will, but as thou wilt.* In saying, *let this chalice pass from Me*, he indicates the movement of his lower appetite and natural desire, whereby all naturally shrink from death and desire life. And in saying, *nevertheless not as I will, but as Thou wilt*, he gives expression to the movement of his higher reason, which looks on all things as comprised under the ordinations of divine wisdom. The same is the bearing of the added words, *if this cannot pass unless I drink it, thy will be done* (Matt 26:42), whereby he showed that only those events can occur which take place according to the order of the divine will.

Although the chalice of the Passion did not pass from him, but he had to drink it, we may not say that his prayer went unheard. For, as the Apostle assures us in Hebrews 5:7, in all things Christ *was heard for his reverence*. Since prayer, as we have remarked, is expressive of desire, we pray unconditionally for what we wish unconditionally; and so the very desires of the just have the force of prayer with God, according to Psalm 10 [9]:17: *The Lord hath heard the desire of the poor.* But we wish unconditionally only what we desire with our higher reason, which alone has the power of assenting to an undertaking. Christ prayed absolutely that the Father's will might be done, for this was what he wished absolutely. But he did not thus pray that the chalice might pass from him, because he wished this, not absolutely, but according to his lower reason, as we have stated.

CHAPTER 234

On the burial of Christ

Consequuntur autem hominem ex peccato post mortem alii defectus, et ex parte corporis, et ex parte animae. Ex parte corporis quidem, quod corpus redditur terrae ex qua sumptum est; hic autem defectus in nobis quidem secundum duo attenditur, scilicet secundum positionem et secundum resolutionem. Secundum positionem quidem, inquantum corpus mortuum sub terra ponitur sepultum; secundum resolutionem vero, inquantum corpus in elementa resolvitur ex quibus est compactum.

Horum autem defectuum primum quidem Christus pati voluit, ut scilicet corpus eius sub terra poneretur; Alium autem defectum passus non fuit, ut scilicet corpus eius in terram resolveretur: unde de ipso Psalmus dicit *Non dabis sanctum tuum videre corruptionem*, id est corporis putrefactionem. Huius autem ratio est quia corpus Christi materiam sumpsit de natura humana, sed formatio eius non fuit virtute humana sed virtute Spiritus Sancti. Et ideo propter substantiam materiae subterraneum locum, qui corporibus mortuis deputari consuevit, voluit pati locus enim corporibus debetur secundum naturam praedominantis elementi; sed dissolutionem corporis per Spiritum Sanctum fabricati pati non voluit, quia quantum ad hoc ab aliis hominibus differebat.

In consequence of sin, other defects, both on the part of the body and on the part of the soul, overtake man after death. With regard to defects on the part of the body, the body returns to the earth from which it was taken. This defect on the part of the body has two phases in the case of ourselves: it is laid away and it corrupts. It is laid away, inasmuch as the dead body is placed beneath the earth in burial; and it corrupts, inasmuch as the body is resolved into the elements of which it was composed.

Christ wished to be subject to the first of these defects, namely, the placing of his body beneath the earth. But he did not submit to the other defect, the dissolving of his body into dust. Thus Psalm 15 [14]:10 says of him, *Nor will you give your holy one to see corruption*, that is, decay of the body. The reason for this is plain: although Christ's body received matter from human nature, its formation was accomplished not by any human power but by the power of the Holy Spirit. Accordingly, the substance of his matter being what it was, he wished to be subject to the place beneath the earth usually given over to dead bodies; for that place which is in keeping with the matter of the predominant element in bodies is rightly assigned to them. But he did not wish the body that had been formed by the Holy Spirit to undergo dissolution, since in this respect he was different from other men.

CHAPTER 235

On Christ's descent into hell

Ex parte vero animae sequitur in hominibus ex peccato post mortem ut ad infernum descendant, non solum quantum ad locum sed etiam quantum ad poenam. Sicut autem corpus Christi fuit quidem sub terra secundum locum, non autem secundum concomitantem resolutionis defectum, ita et anima Christi descendit quidem ad inferos secundum locum, non autem ut ibi poenam subiret, sed magis ut alios a poena absolveret qui propter peccatum primi parentis illuc detinebantur, pro quo plene iam satisfecerat mortem patiendo: unde post mortem nihil ei patiendum restabat, sed absque omni poenae passione localiter ad infernum descendit, ut se vivorum et mortuorum liberatorem ostenderet. Et hinc etiam dicitur quod solus *inter mortuos fuit liber*, quia nec anima eius in inferno subiacuit poenae, nec corpus eius in sepulcro corruptioni.

On the part of the soul, death among men is followed, in consequence of sin, by descent into hell not only as a place, but as a state of punishment. However, just as Christ's body was buried beneath the earth regarded as a place but not with respect to the common defect of dissolution, so his soul went down to hell as a place, not to undergo punishment there, but rather to release from punishment others who were detained there because of the sin of the first parent for which he had already made full satisfaction by suffering death. Hence nothing remained to be suffered after death, and so without undergoing any punishment he descended locally into hell that he might manifest himself as the Savior of the living and the dead. For this reason Psalm 87 [86]:6 says he alone *among the dead was free*, since his soul was not subject to punishment in hell and his body was not subject to corruption in the grave.

Quamvis autem Christus descendens ad inferos, eos liberaverit qui pro peccato primi parentis ibi tenebantur, illos tamen reliquit qui pro peccatis propriis ibidem poenis erant addicti; et ideo dicitur momordisse infernum, non absorbuisse, quia scilicet partem liberavit, et partem dimisit.

Hos igitur Christi defectus Symbolum fidei tangit, cum dicit *Passus sub Pontio Pilato, crucifixus, mortuus et sepultus, descendit ad inferos.*

When Christ descended into hell he freed those who were detained there for the sin of our first parent, but left behind those who were being punished for their own sins. And so he is said to have bitten into hell[8] but not to have swallowed it, for he freed a part and left a part.

The Creed of our faith touches on the various defects of Christ when it states: *He suffered under Pontius Pilate, was crucified, died and was buried; he descended into hell.*

---

8. See Hosea 13:14: "O death, I will be thy death; O hell, I will be thy bite."

Chapter 236

On the resurrection of Christ and the time of his resurrection

Quia ergo per Christum humanum genus liberatum est a malis quae ex peccato primi parentis derivata erant, oportuit quod sicut ipse mala nostra sustinuit ut ab eis nos liberaret, ita etiam reparationis humanae per ipsum factae in eo primitiae apparerent; ut utroque modo Christus proponeretur nobis in signum salutis, dum ex eius passione consideramus quid pro peccato incurrimus et quid nobis patiendum est ut a peccato liberemur, et per eius exaltationem consideramus quid nobis per ipsum sperandum proponitur.

Superata igitur morte quae ex peccato primi parentis provenerat, primus ad immortalem vitam resurrexit: ut sicut in Adam peccante primo mortalis vita apparuit, ita in Christo pro peccato satisfaciente primo immortalis vita appareret. Redierant quidem ad vitam alii ante Christum, vel ab eo vel a prophetis suscitati, tamen iterum morituri; sed *Christus resurgens ex mortuis iam non moritur*, unde quia primus necessitatem moriendi evasit, dicitur *princeps mortuorum* et *primitiae dormientium*, quia scilicet primus a somno mortis surrexit, iugo mortis excusso.

Eius autem resurrectio non tardari debuit, nec statim post mortem esse. Si enim statim post mortem redisset ad vitam, mortis veritas comprobata non fuisset; si vero diu resurrectio tardaretur, signum superatae mortis in eo non appareret, nec hominibus daretur spes ut per ipsum liberarentur a morte. Unde resurrectionem usque ad tertium diem distulit, quia hoc tempus et satis sufficiens videbatur ad mortis veritatem comprobandam, nec erat nimis prolixum ad spem liberationis tollendam. Nam si amplius dilata fuisset, iam fidelium spes debilitationem pateretur, unde et quasi deficiente iam spe quidam dicebant tertia die, Lucae ult. *Nos sperabamus quod ipse redempturus esset Israel.*

Non tamen per tres integros dies Christus mortuus remansit. Dicitur tamen tribus diebus et tribus noctibus in corde terrae fuisse illo modo locutionis quo pars pro toto poni solet. Cum enim ex die et nocte unus naturalis dies constituatur, quacumque parte diei vel

Since the human race was freed by Christ from the evils flowing from the sin of our first parent, it was fitting that, as he bore our ills to free us from them, the first fruits of man's restoration effected by him should make their appearance in him. This was done that Christ might be held up to us as a sign of salvation in two ways. First, we learn from his Passion what we brought down on ourselves by sin and what suffering had to be undergone for us to free us from sin. Second, we see in his exaltation what is proposed to us to hope for through him.

In triumph over death, which resulted from our first parent's sin, Christ was the first of all men to rise to immortal life. Thus, as life first became mortal through Adam's sin, immortal life made its first appearance in Christ through the atonement for sin he offered. Others, it is true, raised up either by Christ or by the prophets, had returned to life before him; yet they had to die a second time. But *Christ, being raised from the dead, will never die again* (Rom 6:9). As he was the first to escape the necessity of dying, he is called *the first-born of the dead* (Rev 1:5) and *the first fruits of those who have fallen asleep* (1 Cor 15:20). He was the first to rise from the sleep of death, having thrown off the yoke of death.

Christ's resurrection was not to be long delayed, nor, on the other hand, was it to take place immediately after death. If he had returned to life immediately after death, the truth of his death would not have been well established; and if the resurrection had been long delayed, the sign of vanquished death would not have appeared in him, and men would not have been given the hope that they would be rescued from death by him. Therefore, he put off the resurrection until the third day, for this interval was judged sufficient to establish the truth of his death, and was not too long to wither away the hope of liberation. If it had been delayed for a longer time, the hope of the faithful might have begun to suffer doubt. Indeed, on the third day, as though hope were already running out, some were saying: *We had hoped that he was the one to redeem Israel* (Luke 24:21).

However, Christ did not remain dead for three full days. He is said to have been in the heart of the earth for three days and three nights, according to that figure of speech whereby a part is often taken for the whole. For, since one natural day is made up of a day and a night, whichever part

noctis computata Christus fuit in morte, tota illa die dicitur in morte fuisse.

Secundum autem Scripturae consuetudinem nox cum sequenti die computatur, eo quod Hebraei tempora secundum cursum lunae observant, quae de sero incipit apparere. Fuit autem Christus in sepulcro ultima parte sextae feriae, quae si cum nocte praecedenti computetur, erit dies artificialis et nox quasi dies unus naturalis; nocte vero sequente sextam feriam cum integra die sabbati fuit in sepulcro, et sic sunt duo dies. Iacuit etiam mortuus in sepulcro in sequenti nocte, quae praecedit diem dominicum, in qua resurrexit vel media nocte secundum Gregorium, vel diluculo secundum alios: unde si computetur vel tota nox, vel pars eius cum sequenti die dominico, erit dies tertius naturalis.

Nec vacat a mysterio quod tertia die resurgere voluit, ut per hoc manifestetur quod virtute totius Trinitatis resurrexit, unde et quandoque dicitur Pater eum resuscitasse, quandoque autem quod ipse propria virtute surrexit: quod non est contrarium, cum eadem sit virtus divina Patris et Filii et Spiritus Sancti; et ut etiam ostenderetur quod reparatio vitae non fuit facta in prima die saeculi, id est sub lege naturali, nec secunda die, id est sub lege mosayca, sed tertia die, id est tempore gratiae.

Habet etiam rationem quod Christus una die integra et duabus noctibus integris iacuit in sepulcro: quia Christus una vetustate quam suscepit, scilicet poenae, duas nostras vetustates consumpsit, scilicet culpae et poenae, quae per duas noctes significantur.

of day or night Christ is reckoned to have been in death, he is said to have been in death for all of it.

Moreover, in the usual practice of Scripture, night is figured in with the following day, because the Hebrews reckon time by the course of the moon, which begins to shine in the evening. Christ was in the sepulcher during the latter part of the sixth day, and if this is counted along with the preceding night, it will be as one natural day. He reposed in the tomb during the night following the sixth day, together with the whole of the Sabbath day, and so we have two days. He lay dead also during the next night, which preceded the Lord's Day, on which he rose, and this occurred either at midnight, according to Gregory, or at dawn, as others think. Therefore, if either the whole night, or a part of it together with the Lord's Day following, is taken into our calculation, we shall have the third natural day.

The fact that Christ wished to rise on the third day is not without mysterious significance; for so he was able to show that he rose by the power of the whole Trinity. Sometimes the Father is said to have raised him up, and sometimes Christ himself is said to have risen by his own power. These two statements do not contradict each other, for the divine power of the Father is identical with that of the Son and of the Holy Spirit. Another purpose was to show that the restoration of life was accomplished, not on the first day of the world, that is, under the natural law, nor on the second day, that is, under the Mosaic law, but on the third day, that is, in the era of grace.

The fact that Christ lay in the sepulcher for one whole day and two whole nights also has its meaning: for by the one ancient debt that Christ took upon himself, namely, that of punishment, he blotted out our two ancient debts, namely, sin and punishment, which are represented by the two nights.

CHAPTER 237

On the quality of the risen Christ

Non solum autem Christus recuparavit humano generi quod Adam peccando amiserat, sed etiam hoc ad quod Adam merendo pervenire potuisset. Multo enim maior fuit Christi efficacia ad merendum quam hominis ante peccatum. Incurrit siquidem Adam peccando necessitatem moriendi, amissa facultate qua mori non poterat si non peccaret; Christus autem non solum necessitatem moriendi exclusit, sed etiam necessitatem non moriendi acquisivit: unde corpus Christi post resurrectionem factum est impassibile et immortale, non

Christ recovered for the human race not merely what Adam had lost through sin, but all that Adam could have attained through merit. For Christ's power to merit was far greater than that of man prior to sin. By sin Adam incurred the necessity of dying, because he lost the power which would have enabled him to avoid death if he had not sinned. Christ not only did away with the necessity of dying, but even gained the power of not being able to die. Therefore, his body after the resurrection was rendered impassible and immortal—not like that of the first man, which

quidem sicut primi hominis potens non mori, sed omnino non potens mori, quod in futurum de nobis ipsis expectamus.

Et quia anima Christi ante mortem passibilis erat secundum corporis passionem, consequens etiam est ut corpore impassibili facto, et anima impassibilis redderetur.

Et quia iam impletum erat humanae redemptionis mysterium, propter quod dispensative continebatur fruitionis gloria in superiori animae parte ne fieret redundantia ad inferiores partes et ad ipsum corpus, sed permitteretur unumquodque agere aut pati quod sibi proprium erat: consequens fuit ut iam per redundantiam gloriae a superiori animae parte totaliter corpus glorificaretur, et inferiores animae vires; et inde est quod cum ante passionem Christus esset et comprehensor propter fruitionem animae, et viator propter corporis passibilitatem, iam post resurrectionem viator ultra non fuerit, sed solum comprehensor.

had the power not to die, but rather, altogether unable to die. And this is what we await in the future life for ourselves.

And because Christ's soul before his death was capable of suffering in company with the suffering of his body, as a consequence when his body became incapable of suffering, his soul was also rendered incapable of suffering.

And because now accomplished was the mystery of man's redemption, on account of which the glory of fruition had, in God's dispensation, been restricted to the superior part of his soul so that no overflowing to the lower parts and to the body itself would occur, but each faculty would be allowed to do or suffer what was proper to it, now as a consequence [of the redemption having been accomplished] the body and the lower powers were wholly glorified by an overflow of glory from the higher part of the soul. Accordingly, Christ, who before the Passion had been a comprehensor because of the fruition enjoyed by his soul and a wayfarer because of the passibility of his body, was now, after the resurrection, no longer a wayfarer, but exclusively a comprehensor.

Chapter 238

How Christ's resurrection is proved by fitting arguments

Et quia, ut dictum est, Christus resurrectionem anticipavit ut eius resurrectio argumentum nobis spei existeret, ut nos etiam resurgere speraremus, oportuit ad spem resurrectionis fundandam, ut eius resurrectio, nec non et resurgentis qualitas, congruentibus indiciis manifestaretur. Non autem omnibus indifferenter suam resurrectionem manifestavit, sicut humanitatem et passionem, sed solis *testibus praeordinatis a Deo*, scilicet discipulis quos elegerat ad procurandam humanam salutem. Nam status resurrectionis, ut dicturn est, pertinet ad gloriam comprehensoris, cuius cognitio non debetur omnibus, sed his tantum qui se dignos reddiderunt. Manifestavit autem eis Christus et veritatem resurrectionis, et gloriam resurgentis.

Veritatem quidem resurrectionis manifestauit ostendendo quod idem ipse qui mortuus fuerat resurrexit, et quantum ad naturam et quantum ad suppositum. Quantum ad naturam quidem, quia se verum corpus humanum habere demonstravit, dum ipsum palpandum et videndum discipulis praebuit, quibus dixit Luc. ult. *Palpate et videte, quia spiritus carnem et ossa non habet, sicut me videtis habere.* Manifestavit etiam exercendo actus qui naturae humanae conveniunt, cum discipulis suis manducans et bibens, et cum eis multotiens loquens

As we stated above, Christ anticipated the general resurrection in order that his resurrection might bolster up our hope of our own resurrection. To foster our hope of resurrection, Christ's resurrection and the qualities of his risen nature had to be made known by suitable proofs. He manifested his resurrection, not to all alike, in the way that he manifested his human nature and his Passion, but only *to witnesses preordained by God* (Acts 10:41), namely, the disciples whom he had selected to bring about man's salvation. For the state of resurrection, as was mentioned above, belongs to the glory of the comprehensor, and knowledge of this is not due to all, but only to such as make themselves worthy. To the witnesses he had chosen Christ revealed both the truth of his resurrection and the glory of his risen nature.

He made known the truth of his resurrection by showing that he, the very one who had died, rose again both in his nature and in his suppositum. As regards nature, he showed that he had a true human body when he offered himself to be touched and seen by the disciples, to whom he said: *Handle me, and see; for a spirit has not flesh and bones as you see that I have* (Luke 24:39). He gave further evidence of the same by performing actions that belong to human nature, eating and drinking with his disciples, and often conversing with them and walking about. These are

et ambulans, qui sunt actus hominis viventis; quamvis illa comestio necessitatis non fuerit, non enim incorruptibilia resurgentium corpora ulterius cibo indigebunt, cum in eis nulla fiat deperditio quam oporteat per cibum restaurari. Unde et cibus a Christo assumptus non cessit in corporis eius nutrimentum, sed fuit resolutum in praeiacentem materiam. Verumtamen ex hoc ipso quod comedit et bibit, se verum hominem demonstravit.

Quantum vero ad suppositum, ostendit se esse eundem qui mortuus fuerat, per hoc quod indicia suae mortis eis in suo corpore demonstravit, scilicet vulnerum cicatrices; unde dicit Thomae, Io. XX *Infer digitum tuum huc et mitte manum tuam in latus meum* et cognosce loca clauorum; et Luc. ult. dixit discipulis *Videte manus meas et pedes meos, quia ego ipse sum.* Quamvis hoc etiam dispensationis fuerit quod cicatrices vulnerum in suo corpore reservavit, ut per eas resurrectionis veritas probaretur: corpori enim incorruptibili resurgenti debetur omnis integritas. Licet dici possit quod etiam in martyribus quaedam indicia praecedentium vulnerum apparebunt cum quodam decore in testimonium virtutis. Ostendit etiam se esse eundem secundum suppositum et ex modo loquendi, et ex aliis consuetis operibus ex quibus homines recognoscuntur: unde et discipuli recognoverunt eum *in fractione panis*, Luc. ult., et ipse etiam in Galilaea appariturum se eis denunciavit, ubi cum eis erat solitus conversari.

Gloriam vero resurgentis manifestavit dum *ianuis clausis* ad eos intravit, Io. XX, dum *ab oculis eorum evanuit*, Luc. ult. Hoc enim pertinet ad gloriam corporis resurgentis, ut in potestate habeat apparere oculo non glorioso quando vult, vel non apparere quando voluerit. Quia tamen resurrectionis fides difficultatem habebat, propterea per plura indicia veritatem resurrectionis quam gloriam resurgentis corporis demonstravit. Nam si inusitatam conditionem glorificati corporis totaliter demonstrasset, fidei resurrectionis praeiudicium attulisset, quia immensitas gloriae opinionem exclusisset eiusdem naturae. Hec etiam omnia non solum visibilibus signis, sed etiam intelligibilibus documentis manifestavit, dum *aperuit eorum sensum ut Scripturas intelligerent*, et per Scripturas prophetarum se resurrecturum ostendit.

the actions of a living man. Of course such eating was not dictated by necessity. The incorruptible bodies of the risen will have no further need of food, for there occurs in them no loss that has to be restored by nourishment. Hence the food consumed by Christ did not become nourishment for his body but was dissolved into preexisting matter. Yet he proved that he was a true man by the very fact that he ate and drank.

As regards his suppositum, Christ showed that he was the same person who had died by displaying to his disciples the marks of his death on his body, namely, the scars of his wounds. In John 20:27 he says to Thomas: *Put your finger here, and see my hands; and put out your hand, and place it in my side.* And in Luke 24:39 he says: *See my hands and feet, that it is I myself.* It was by divine dispensation that he kept the scars of his wounds in his body, so that the truth of the resurrection might be demonstrated by them; for complete integrity is the proper condition of the incorruptible risen body, although we may say that in the case of the martyrs some indications of the wounds they bore will appear with a certain splendor, in testimony of their virtue. Christ further showed that he was the same suppositum by his manner of speech and by other familiar actions whereby men are recognized. Thus the disciples knew him *in the breaking of the bread* (Luke 24:35). Also, he openly showed himself to them in Galilee, where he was accustomed to converse with them.

Christ manifested the glory of his risen nature when he came among them, *the doors being shut* (John 20:26), and when *he vanished out of their sight* (Luke 24:31). For the glory of risen man gives him the power to be seen in glorious vision when he wishes, or not to be seen when he so wishes. Christ demonstrated the truth of his resurrection and the glory of his risen body by so many proofs because faith in the resurrection is difficult. If he had displayed the extraordinary condition of his glorified body in its full splendor, he would have engendered prejudice against faith in the resurrection: the very immensity of its glory would have excluded belief that it was the same nature. Further, he manifested the truth not only by visible signs, but also by proofs appealing to the intellect, as when *he opened their minds to understand the Scriptures* (Luke 24:45), and showed that according to the writings of the prophets he was to rise again.

Chapter 239

On the power of the Lord's resurrection

Sicut autem Christus sua morte mortem nostram destruxit, ita sua resurrectione vitam nostram reparavit. Est autem hominis duplex mors et duplex vita: una quidem mors est corporis per separationem ab anima, alia vero mors est animae per separationem a Deo. Christus aigitur, in quo secunda mors locum non habuit, per primam mortem quam subiit, scilicet corporalem, utramque in nobis mortem destruxit, scilicet corporalem et spiritualem.

Similiter autem per oppositum intelligitur duplex vita: una quidem corporis ab anima, quae dicitur vita naturae, alia animae a Deo, quae dicitur vita iustitiae vel vita gratiae: et haec est per fidem, per quam Deus habitat in nobis, secundum illud Abac. II *Iustus autem meus ex fide vivit.* Et secundum hoc etiam est duplex resurrectio: una corporalis, qua anima iterato coniungitur corpori; alia spiritualis, qua anima iterato coniungitur Deo. Et haec quidem secunda resurrectio in Christo locum non habuit, quia numquam eius anima fuit per peccatum separata a Deo. Per resurrectionem igitur suam corporalem utriusque resurrectionis, scilicet corporalis et spiritualis, nobis est causa.

Considerandum tamen est quod, sicut dicit Augustinus *Super Iohannem*, Verbum Dei resuscitat animas, sed Verbum caro factum resuscitat corpora: animam enim vivificare solius Dei est. Quia tamen caro assumpta a Verbo Dei est divinitatis eius instrumentum, instrumentum autem agit in virtute causae principalis, utraque resurrectio nostra, et spiritualis et corporalis, in corporalem Christi resurrectionem refertur ut in causam. Omnia enim quae in Christi carne facta sunt nobis salutaria fuerunt virtute divinitatis unitae, unde et Apostolus resurrectionem Christi causam nostrae spiritualis resurrectionis ostendens, dicit Ro. IV quod *traditus est propter peccata nostra, et resurrexit propter iustificationem nostram.* Quod autem resurrectio Christi nostrae corporalis resurrectionis sit causa, ostendit I Cor. XV *Si Christus resurrexit, quomodo quidam dicunt quod mortui non resurgent?*

Pulchre autem Apostolus peccatorum remissionem morti Christi attribuit, iustificationem vero nostram resurrectioni, ut designetur conformitas et similitudo effectus ad causam. Nam sicut peccatum deponitur cum remittitur, ita Christus moriendo deposuit passibilem vitam in qua erat similitudo peccati. Cum autem aliquis iustificatur, novam vitam adipiscitur ita Christus resurgendo novitatem gloriae consecutus est. Sic igitur mors Christi causa est remissionis peccati nostri et effectiva

As Christ destroyed our death by his death, so he restored our life by his resurrection. Man has a twofold death and a twofold life. The first death is the death of the body, brought about by separation from the soul; the second death is brought about by separation from God. Christ, in whom the second death had no place, destroyed both of these deaths in us, that is, the bodily and the spiritual, by the first death he underwent, namely, that of the body.

Similarly, opposed to this twofold death, we are to understand that there is a twofold life. One is a life of the body, imparted by the soul, and this is called the life of nature. The other comes from God, and is called the life of justice or the life of grace. This life is given to us through faith, by which God dwells in us, according to Habakkuk 2:4: *The just shall live by his faith.* Accordingly, resurrection is also twofold: one is a bodily resurrection, in which the soul is united to the body for the second time; the other is a spiritual resurrection, in which the soul is again united to God. This second resurrection had no place in Christ, because his soul was never separated from God by sin. By his bodily resurrection, therefore, Christ is the cause of both the bodily and the spiritual resurrection in us.

However, as Augustine says in his *Commentary on St. John*, we are to understand that the Word of God raises up souls, but that the Word made flesh raises up bodies: for to give life to the soul belongs to God alone. Yet, since the flesh is the instrument of his divinity, and since an instrument operates in virtue of the principal cause, our double resurrection, bodily and spiritual, is referred to Christ's bodily resurrection as cause. For everything done in Christ's flesh was salutary for us by reason of the divinity united to that flesh. Hence the Apostle, indicating the resurrection of Christ as the cause of our spiritual resurrection, says, in Romans 4:25, that Christ *was put to death for our trespasses and raised for our justification.* And in 1 Corinthians 15:12 he shows that Christ's resurrection is the cause of our bodily resurrection: *Now if Christ is preached as raised from the dead, how can some of you say that there is no resurrection of the dead?*

Most aptly does the Apostle attribute remission of sins to Christ's death and our justification to his resurrection, thus tracing out conformity and likeness of effect to cause. As sin is discarded when it is remitted, so Christ by dying laid aside his passible life, in which the likeness of sin was discernible. But when a person is justified, he receives new life; in like manner Christ, by rising, obtained newness of glory. Therefore, Christ's death is the cause of the remission of our sin: the efficient cause instrumentally, the

instrumentaliter et exemplaris sacramentaliter et meritoria; resurrectio autem Christi fuit causa resurrectionis nostrae effectiva quidem instrumentaliter et exemplaris sacramentaliter, non autem meritoria: tum quia Christus iam non erat viator, ut sibi mereri competeret, tum quia claritas resurrectionis fuit praemium passionis, ut per Apostolum patet, Phil. II.

Sic igitur manifestum est quod Christus potest dici *primogenitus resurgentium ex mortuis*, non solum ordine temporis, quia primus resurrexit secundum praedicta, sed etiam ordine causae, quia eius resurrectio est causa resurrectionis aliorum, et in ordine dignitatis, quia prae cunctis gloriosior resurrexit.

Hanc igitur fidem de resurrectione Christi Symbolum fidei continet dicens *tertia die resurrexit a mortuis*.

exemplary cause sacramentally, and the meritorious cause. In like manner Christ's resurrection was the cause of our resurrection: the efficient cause instrumentally and the exemplary cause sacramentally. But it was not a meritorious cause, for Christ was no longer a wayfarer, and so was not in a position to merit; and also because the glory of the resurrection was the reward of his Passion, as the Apostle declares in Philippians 2:9–11.

Thus we see clearly that Christ can be called *the first-born of those who rise from the dead* (Col 1:18). This is true not only in the order of time, inasmuch as Christ was the first to rise, as was said above, but also in the order of causality, because his resurrection is the cause of the resurrection of other men, and in the order of dignity, because he rose more gloriously than all others.

This belief in Christ's resurrection is expressed in the words of the Creed: *on the third day he arose again from the dead.*

CHAPTER 240

On the twofold reward of the humiliation, namely, resurrection and ascension

Quia vero secundum Apostolum exaltatio Christi praemium fuit humiliationis ipsius, conveniens fuit ut duplici eius humiliationi duplex exaltatio responderet.

Humiliaverat namque se primo secundum mortis passionem in carne passibili quam assumpserat; secundo quantum ad locum, corpore posito in sepulcro et anima ad inferos descendente. Primae igitur humiliationi respondet gloria resurrectionis, in qua a morte ad vitam rediit immortalem; secunde autem humiliationi respondet exaltatio ascensionis, unde Apostolus dicit Eph. IV *Qui descendit, ipse est et qui ascendit super omnes caelos.*

Sicut autem de Filio Dei dicitur quod est conceptus, natus, passus, mortuus et sepultus, et resurrexit, non tamen secundum divinam naturam, sed secundum humanam: ita et de Filio Dei dicitur quod ascendit in caelum, non quidem secundum divinam naturam, sed secundum humanam. Nam secundum divinam naturam numquam a caelo discessit, semper ubique existens: unde ipse dicit Io. III *Nemo ascendit in caelum nisi qui de caelo descendit, Filius hominis qui est in caelo*; per quod datur intelligi quod sic descendisse de caelo dicitur naturam assumendo terrenam, quod tamen in caelo semper permansit. Ex quo etiam considerandum est quod solus Christus propria virtute caelos ascendit. Locus enim ille debebatur ei qui de caelo descenderat ratione suae origi-

According to the Apostle, the exaltation of Christ was the reward of his humiliation. Therefore, a twofold exaltation had to correspond to his twofold humiliation.

Christ had humbled himself first by suffering death in the passible flesh he had assumed; second, he had undergone humiliation with reference to place, when his body was laid in the sepulcher and his soul descended into hell. The exaltation of the resurrection, in which he returned from death to immortal life, corresponds to the first humiliation. And the exaltation of the ascension corresponds to the second humiliation. Hence the Apostle says, in Ephesians 4:10: *He who descended is he who also ascended far above all the heavens.*

However, as it is narrated of the Son of God that he was born, suffered and was buried, and rose again, not according to his divine nature but according to his human nature, so also, we are told, he ascended into heaven, not according to his divine nature but according to his human nature. According to his divine nature he had never left heaven, existing always everywhere. He indicates this himself when he says: *No one has ascended into heaven but he who descended from heaven, the Son of man who is in heaven* (John 3:13). By this we are given to understand that he came down from heaven by assuming an earthly nature, yet in such a way that he continued to remain in heaven. The same consideration leads us to conclude that Christ alone has gone up to heaven by his own power. By reason of his origin, that

nis; alii vero per se ipsos ascendere non possunt, sed per Christi virtutem, eius membra effecti.

Et sicut ascendere in caelum convenit Filio Dei secundum humanam naturam, ita additur alterum quod convenit ei secundum divinam naturam, scilicet quod sedeat ad dexteram Patris. Non enim est ibi cogitanda dextera vel sessio corporalis, sed quia dextera est potior pars animalis, datur per hoc intelligi quod Filius considet Patri non aliquo minoratus ab ipso secundum divinam naturam, sed omnino in eius aequalitate existens. Potest tamen et hoc ipsum attribui Filio Dei secundum humanam naturam, ut secundum divinam naturam intelligamus Filium in ipso Patre esse secundum essentiae unitatem, cum quo habet unam sedem regni, id est potestatem eandem. Sed quia solent regibus aliqui assidere, quibus scilicet aliquid de regia potestate communicant, ille autem potissimus in regno esse videtur quem rex ad dexteram suam ponit, merito Filius Dei etiam secundum humanam naturam dicitur ad dexteram Patris sedere, quasi super omnem creaturam in dignitate caelestis regni exaltatus.

Utroque igitur modo sedere ad dexteram est proprium Christi: unde Apostolus Hebr. II dicit *Ad quem autem dixit aliquando angelorum: Sede a dextris meis?*

Hanc igitur Christi ascensionem confitemur in Symbolo, dicentes *Ascendit in caelum, sedet ad dexteram Dei Patris.*

abode belonged by right to him who had come down from heaven. Other men cannot ascend of themselves, but are taken up by the power of Christ, whose members they have been made.

As ascent into heaven befits the Son of God according to his human nature, so something else is added that becomes him according to his divine nature, namely, that he should sit at the right hand of his Father. In this connection we are not to think of a literal right hand or a bodily sitting. Since the right side of an animal is the stronger, this expression gives us to understand that the Son is seated with the Father as being in no way inferior to him according to the divine nature, but on a par with him in all things. Yet this same prerogative may be ascribed to the Son of God in his human nature, thus enabling us to perceive that in his divine nature the Son is in the Father himself according to unity of essence, and that together with the Father he possesses a single kingly throne, that is, an identical power. Since other persons ordinarily sit near kings, namely, ministers to whom kings assign a share in governing power, and since the one whom the king places at his right hand is judged to be the most powerful man in the kingdom, the Son of God is rightly said to sit at the Father's right hand even according to his human nature, as being exalted in rank above every creature of the heavenly kingdom.

In both senses, therefore, Christ properly sits at the right hand of God. And so the Apostle asks, in Hebrew 1:13: *To what angel has he ever said, "Sit at my right hand"?*

We profess our faith in this ascension of Christ when we say in the Creed: *He ascended into heaven and sits at the right hand of God the Father.*

Chapter 241

That Christ will judge according to his human nature

Ex his igitur quae dicta sunt manifeste colligitur quod per Christi passionem et mortem, resurrectionis atque ascensionis gloriam, a peccato et morte liberati sumus, et iustitiam et immortalitatis gloriam, hanc in re, illam in spe, adepti. Haec autem quae praediximus, scilicet passio, mors, resurrectio et ascensio, sunt in Christo completa secundum humanam naturam; consequenter igitur dici oportet quod, secundum ea quae in humana natura Christus vel passus est vel fecit, nos a malis tam spiritualibus quam corporalibus liberando, ad spiritualia et aeterna bona promovit.

Est autem conveniens ut qui aliquibus aliqua bona acquirit, eadem ipsis dispenset. Dispensatio autem bonorum in multos requirit iudicium, ut unusquisque secundum suum gradum accipiat; convenienter igi-

We clearly gather from all this, that by the Passion and death of Christ and by the glory of his resurrection and ascension, we are freed from sin and death, and have received justice and the glory of immortality, the former in actual fact, the latter in hope. All these events we have mentioned (the Passion, the death, the resurrection, and also the ascension) were accomplished in Christ according to his human nature. Therefore, we must conclude that Christ has rescued us from spiritual and bodily evils, and has put us in the way of spiritual and eternal goods, by what he suffered or did in his human nature.

It is fitting that the one who acquires goods for people should also distribute them. But the distribution of goods among many requires judgment, so that each may receive what corresponds to his degree. Therefore, Christ, in the

tur Christus secundum humanam naturam, secundum quam mysteria humanae salutis implevit, iudex constituitur a Deo super homines quos salvavit: unde dicitur Io. V: *Potestatem dedit ei,* scilicet Pater Filio, *iudicium facere, quia Filius hominis est.*

Quamvis et hoc habeat aliam rationem. Est enim conveniens ut iudicem videant iudicandi; Deum autem, apud quem iudicii auctoritas residet, in sua natura videre est praemium quod per iudicium redditur: oportuit igitur quod Deus iudex, non in natura propria, sed in natura assumpta ab hominibus videretur qui iudicandi sunt, tam bonis quam malis. Mali enim si Deum in natura deitatis viderent, iam praemium reportarent quo se reddiderunt indignos.

Est etiam et hoc conveniens exaltationis praemium humiliationi Christi respondens, qui usque ad hoc humiliari voluit ut sub homine iudice iudicaretur iniuste: unde ad hanc humilitatem exprimendam signanter in Symbolo eum sub Pontio Pilato passum fatemur. Hoc igitur ei exaltationis praemium debebatur, ut ipse secundum humanam naturam iudex a Deo omnium hominum mortuorum et vivorum constitueretur, secundum illud Iob XXXVI: *Causa tua quasi impii iudicata est: iudicium causamque recipies.*

Et quia potestas iudiciaria ad Christi exaltationem pertinet sicut et resurrectionis gloria, Christus in iudicio apparebit, non in humilitate quae pertinebat ad meritum, sed in forma gloriosa ad praemium pertinente: unde dicitur in Euangelio quod *videbunt Filium hominis venientem in nube cum potestate magna et maiestate.* Visio autem claritatis ipsius electis quidem, qui eum dilexerunt, erit ad gaudium, quibus promittitur Ys. XXIII *regem in decore suo videbunt*; impiis autem erit ad confusionem et luctum, quia iudicantis gloria et potestas damnationem timentibus tristitiam et metum inducit: unde dicitur Ysa. XXVI *Videant et confundantur zelantes populi, et ignis hostes tuos devoret.*

Et quamvis in forma gloriosa se ostendat, apparebunt tamen in eo indicia passionis non cum defectu sed cum decore et gloria, ut ex his visis et electi accipiant gaudium, qui per passionem Christi se liberatos recognoscunt, et peccatores tristitiam, qui tantum beneficium contempserunt: unde dicitur Apoc. I *Videbunt in quem confixerunt, et plangent se super eum omnes tribus terrae.*

human nature in which he has accomplished the mysteries of man's salvation, is fittingly appointed by God to be judge over the men he has saved. We are told that this is so, in John 5:27: *He hath given him,* that is, the Father has given the Son, *authority to execute judgment, because he is the Son of man.*

There is also another reason. Those who are to be judged ought to see the judge. But the sight of God, in whom the judicial authority resides, in his own proper nature, is the reward that is meted out in the judgment. Hence the men to be judged, the good as well as the wicked, ought to see God as judge, not in his proper nature, but in his assumed nature. If the wicked saw God in his divine nature, they would be receiving the very reward of which they had made themselves unworthy.

Furthermore, the office of judge is a suitable recompense by way of exaltation, corresponding to the humiliation of Christ, who was willing to be humiliated to the point of being unjustly judged by a human judge. To give expression to our belief in this humiliation, we say explicitly in the Creed, that he suffered under Pontius Pilate. Therefore, this exalted reward of being appointed by God to judge all men, the living and the dead, in his human nature, was due to Christ, according to Job 36:17: *Your cause hath been judged as that of the wicked. Cause and judgment you shall recover.*

Moreover, since this judicial power pertains to Christ's exaltation, as does the glory of his resurrection, Christ will appear at the judgment not in humility, which belonged to the time of merit, but in the glorious form that is indicative of his reward. We are assured in the Gospel that *they will see the Son of man coming in a cloud with power and great glory* (Luke 21:27). And the sight of his glory will be a joy to the elect who have loved him; to these is made the promise, in Isaiah 33:17, that *they shall see the King in his beauty.* But to the wicked this sight will mean confusion and lamentation, for the glory and power of the judge will bring grief and dread to those who fear damnation. We read of this in Isaiah 26:11: *Let them see thy zeal for thy people, and be ashamed, and let the fire for thy adversaries consume them.*

Although Christ will show himself in his glorious form, the marks of the Passion will appear in him not with disfigurement, but with beauty and splendor, so that at the sight of them the elect, who will perceive that they have been saved through the sufferings of Christ, will be filled with joy; but sinners, who have scorned so great a benefit, will be filled with dismay. Thus we read in Revelation 1:7: *Every eye shall see him, and they also that pierced him. And all the tribes of the earth shall bewail themselves because of him.*

CHAPTER 242

That the Father who knows the hour of judgment will give all judgment to the Son

Sed quia *Pater omne iudicium dedit Filio*, ut dicitur Io. V, nunc autem humana vita iusto Dei iudicio dispensatur, ipse enim *est qui iudicat omnem carnem*, ut Abraham dixit Gen. XVIII, non est dubitandum etiam hoc iudicium quo in hoc mundo reguntur homines, ad Christi potestatem iudiciariam pertinere: unde et ad ipsum introducuntur in Psalmo verba Patris dicentis *Sede a dextris meis, donec ponam inimicos tuos scabellum pedum tuorum*. Assidet enim dextris Dei Christus secundum humanam naturam, inquantum ab eo recipit iudiciariam potestatem: quam quidem etiam nunc exercet, etiam antequam manifeste appareant omnes inimici pedibus eius subiecti, unde et ipse statim post resurrectionem dixit Matth. ult. *Data est mihi omnis potestas in caelo et in terra.*

Est autem et aliud Dei iudicium, quo unicuique in exitu mortis suae retribuit quantum ad animam secundum quod meruit: iusti enim dissoluti manent cum Christo, ut Paulus desiderat, peccatores autem mortui in inferno sepeliuntur. Non est autem putandum hanc discretionem absque Dei iudicio fieri, aut hoc iudicium ad Christi potestatem iudiciariam non pertinere, praesertim cum ipse discipulis suis dicat Io. XIV *Si abiero et praeparavero vobis locum, iterum veniam et tollam vos ad me ipsum, ut ubi sum ego, et vos sitis*. Quod quidem 'tolli' nihil est aliud quam dissolvi ut cum Christo esse possimus, quia *quandiu sumus in corpore peregrinamur a Domino*, II Cor. V.

Sed quia retributio hominis non solum consistit in bonis animae, sed etiam in bonis corporis iterato per resurrectionem ab anima resumendi, omnisque retributio requirit iudicium, oportet et aliud iudicium esse, quo retribuatur hominibus secundum ea quae gesserunt non solum in anima, verum etiam in corpore. Et hoc etiam iudicium Christo debetur, ut sicut ipse pro nobis mortuus resurrexit in gloria et caelos ascendit, ita etiam ipse sua virtute resurgere faciat corpora humilitatis nostrae configurata corpori claritatis suae, et secum ea in caelum transferat, quo ipse praecessit *ascendens et pandens iter ante* nos, ut fuerat per Michaeam praedictum. Resurrectio autem omnium hominum simul fiet, et in fine saeculi huius, ut supra iam diximus: unde hoc iudicium commune et finale iudicium erit, ad quod faciendum Christus creditur secundo venturus cum gloria.

Sed quia in Psalmo dicitur *Iudicia Dei abyssus multa*, et Apostolus dicit Ro. XI quod *incomprehensibilia*

Since *the Father has given all judgment to the Son*, as is said in John 5:22, and since human life even at present is regulated by the just judgment of God—for *it is he who judges all flesh*, as Abraham declared in Genesis 18:25—we cannot doubt that this judgment, by which men are governed in the world, pertains likewise to the judicial power of Christ. To him are directed the words of the Father reported in Psalm 110 [109]:1: *Sit at my right hand until I make your enemies your footstool*. He sits at the right hand of God according to his human nature inasmuch as he receives his judicial power from the Father. And this power he exercises even now before all his enemies are clearly seen to lie prostrate at his feet. He himself bore witness to this fact shortly after his resurrection, in Matthew 28:18: *All authority in heaven and on earth has been given to me.*

There is another judgment of God whereby, at the moment of death, everyone receives the recompense he has deserved, as regards his soul. The just who have been dissolved in death remain with Christ, as Paul desired for himself (Phil 1:23); but sinners who have died are buried in hell. We may not suppose that this division takes place without God's judgment, or that this judgment does not pertain to the judicial power of Christ, especially as he himself tells his disciples in John 14:3: *If I go and prepare a place for you, I will come again and will take you to myself, so that where I am, there you may be also*. 'To be taken' in this way means nothing else than to be dissolved in death, so that we may be with Christ; for *while we are at home in the body we are away from the Lord*, as is said in 2 Corinthians 5:6.

However, since man's recompense is not confined to goods of the soul, but embraces goods of the body which is to be again resumed by the soul at the resurrection, and since every recompense requires judgment, there has to be another judgment by which men are rewarded for what they have done in the body as well as for what they have done in the soul. This judgment, too, belongs rightfully to Christ, in order that, as he rose and ascended into heaven in glory after dying for us, he may also by his own power cause the bodies of our lowliness to rise again in the likeness of his glorified body, and may transport them up to heaven where he has preceded us, *ascending and opening the way before us*, as had been foretold by Micah 2:13. This resurrection of all men will take place simultaneously at the end of the world, as we have already indicated. Therefore, this judgment will be a general and final judgment, and we believe that Christ will come a second time, in glory, to preside at it.

In Psalm 36 [35]:6 we read: *Your judgments are the great deep*; and in Romans 11:33 the Apostle exclaims: *How in-*

sunt iudicia eius, in singulis praemissorum iudiciorum est aliquid profundum et incomprehensibile humanae cognitioni. In primo enim Dei iudicio quo praesens vita hominum dispensatur, tempus quidem iudicii manifestum est omnibus sed retributionum ratio latet, praesertim quia et bonis plerumque mala in hoc mundo eveniunt, et malis bona. In aliis autem duobus Dei iudiciis retributionum quidem ratio in evidenti erit sed tempus manet occultum, quia et mortis suae tempus homo ignorat, secundum illud Eccl. X *Nescit homo finem suum*, et finem huius saeculi homo prescire non potest. Non enim praescimus futura, nisi quorum comprehendimus causas; causa autem finis mundi est Dei voluntas, quae est nobis ignota: unde nec finis mundi ab aliqua creatura potest praesciri, sed a solo Deo secundum illud Matth. XXIV *De die illa et hora nemo scit, neque angeli caelorum, nisi solus Pater.*

Sed quia in Marco legitur *neque Filius*, sumpserunt hinc aliqui errandi materiam, dicentes Filium Patre minorem quia ea ignorat quae Pater novit. Posset autem hoc evitari, ut diceretur quod Filius haec ignorat secundum humanam naturam assumptam, non autem secundum divinam, secundum quam unam sapientiam habet cum Patre vel, ut expressius dicatur, est ipsa sapientia in corde Patris concepta. Sed et hoc inconveniens videtur ut Filius, etiam secundum naturam assumptam, diem ignoret iudicii, cum eius anima, Euangelista testante, plena sit omni gratia et veritate, ut supra dictum est. Neque etiam videtur habere rationem ut, cum Christus potestatem iudicandi accepit *quia Filius hominis est*, tempus sui iudicii secundum humanam naturam ignoret: non enim omne iudicium Pater ei dedisset, si determinandi temporis sui adventus esset ei subtractum iudicium.

Est ergo hoc intelligendum secundum usitatum modum loquendi in Scripturis, prout dicitur tunc Deus aliquid scire quando illius rei notitiam praebet, sicut dixit ad Abraham Gen. XXII *Nunc cognovi quod timeas Dominum*, non quod tunc nosse inciperet qui omnia ab aeterno cognoscit, sed quia eius devotionem per illud factum ostenderat. Sic igitur et Filius dicitur diem iudicii ignorare, quia eius notitiam discipulis non dedit, sed eis respondit Act. I *Non est vestrum nosse tempora vel momenta quae Pater posuit in sua potestate*. Pater autem isto modo non ignorat, quia saltem Filio huius rei notitiam dedit per generationem aeternam. Quidam autem

comprehensible are his judgments! Each of the judgments mentioned contains something profound and incomprehensible to human knowledge. In the first of God's judgments, by which the present life of mankind is regulated, the time of the judgment is, indeed, manifest to men, but the reason for the recompenses is concealed, especially as evils for the most part are the lot of the good in this world, while good things come to the wicked. In the other two judgments of God the reason for the requitals will be clearly known, but the time remains hidden, because man does not know the hour of his death, as is noted in Ecclesiastes 9:12: *Man does not know his end*; and no one can know the end of this world. For we do not foreknow future events, except those whose causes we understand. But the cause of the end of the world is the will of God, which is unknown to us. Therefore, the end of the world can be foreseen by no creature, but only by God, according to Matthew 24:36: *Of that day and hour no one knows, not even the angels of heaven, but the Father only.*

In this connection, some have found an occasion for going astray in the added words, *nor the Son*, which are read in Mark 13:32. They contend that the Son is inferior to the Father, on the score that he is ignorant of matters which the Father knows. The difficulty could be avoided by replying that the Son is ignorant of this event in his assumed human nature, but not in his divine nature, in which he has one and the same wisdom as the Father or, to speak with greater propriety, he is wisdom itself intellectually conceived. But the Son could hardly be unaware of the divine judgment even in his assumed nature, since his soul, as the Evangelist attests, is full of God's grace and truth, as was pointed out above. Nor does it seem reasonable that Christ, who has received the power to judge *because he is the Son of man* (John 5:27), should be ignorant in his human nature of the time appointed for him to judge. The Father would not really have given all judgment to him if the judgment of determining the time of his coming were withheld from him.

Accordingly, this text is to be interpreted in the light of the usual style of speech found in the Scriptures, in which God is said to know a thing when he imparts knowledge of that thing, as when he said to Abraham, in Genesis 22:12: *Now I know that you fear God*. The meaning is not that he who knows all things from eternity began to know at that moment, but that he made known Abraham's devotedness by that declaration. In a similar way the Son is said to be ignorant of the day of judgment because he did not impart that knowledge to the disciples, but replied to them, Acts 1:7: *It is not for you to know times or seasons which the Father has fixed by his own authority*. But the Father is not

brevius se expediunt, dicentes hoc esse intelligendum de filio adoptivo.

Ideo autem voluit Dominus tempus futuri iudicii esse occultum, ut homines sollicite vigilarent, ne forte tempore iudicii imparati inveniantur, propter quod etiam voluit tempus mortis uniuscuiusque esse ignotum. Talis enim unusquisque in iudicio comparebit, qualis hinc per mortem exierit: unde Dominus dixit Matth. XXIV *Vigilate, quia nescitis qua hora Dominus vester venturus sit.*

ignorant in this way, since in any case he gave knowledge of the matter to the Son through the eternal generation. Some authors extricate themselves from the difficulty in fewer words, saying that Mark's expression is to be understood of an adopted son.

However that may be, the Lord wished the time of the future judgment to remain hidden so that men might watch with care lest they be found unprepared at the hour of judgment. For the same reason he also wished the hour of each one's death to be unknown. For each man will appear at the judgment in the state in which he departs from this world by death. Therefore, the Lord admonishes us in Matthew 24:42: *Watch, therefore, for you do not know in what hour your Lord is coming.*

CHAPTER 243

Whether all will be judged or not

Sic igitur secundum praedicta patet quod Christus habet iudiciariam potestatem super vivos et mortuos. Exercet enim iudicium et in eos qui in praesenti saeculo vivunt, et in eos qui ex hoc saeculo transeunt moriendo. In finali autem iudicio iudicabit simul et *vivos et mortuos*: sive per *vivos* intelligantur iusti qui per gratiam vivunt, per *mortuos* autem peccatores qui a gratia exciderunt; sive per *vivos* intelligantur qui in adventu Domini vivi reperientur, per *mortuos* autem qui antea decesserunt.

Hoc autem non est sic intelligendum, quod aliqui sic vivi iudicentur quod numquam senserint corporis mortem, sicut aliqui posuerunt. Manifeste enim Apostolus dicit I Cor. XV *Omnes quidem resurgemus*, et alia littera habet *Omnes quidem dormiemus*, id est moriemur; et si in aliquibus libris habeatur *non omnes quidem dormiemus*, ut Ieronymus dicit in Epistola ad Minervium de resurrectione carnis, praedictae sententiae firmitatem non tollit. Nam paulo ante praemiserat Apostolus *Sicut in Adam omnes moriuntur, ita et in Christo omnes vivificabuntur*; et sic illud quod dicitur *non omnes dormiemus* non potest referri ad mortem corporis, quae in omnes transivit per peccatum primi parentis, ut dicitur Ro. V; sed exponendum esset de dormitione peccati, de qua dicitur Eph. V: *Surge qui dormis, surge a mortuis et illuminabit tibi Christus.*

Distinguuntur ergo qui in adventu Domini reperientur, ab his qui antea decesserunt, non quia ipsi numquam moriantur, sed quia in ipso raptu quo rapientur *in*

According to the doctrine thus set forth, Christ clearly has judicial power over the living and the dead. He exercises judgment both over those who are living in the world at present and over those who pass from this world by death. At the Last Judgment, however, he will judge *the living and the dead* at once. In this expression *the living* may be taken to mean the just who live by grace, and *the dead* may be taken to mean sinners who have fallen from grace. Or else by *the living* may be meant those who will be found still alive at the Lord's coming, and by *the dead* those who have died in previous ages.

We are not to understand by this that certain of the living will be judged without ever having undergone death of the body, as some have argued. For the Apostle says clearly, in 1 Corinthians 15:51, *We shall all indeed rise again.* Another reading has *we shall indeed sleep*, that is, we shall die; or, according to some books, *we shall not indeed all sleep*, as Jerome notes in his letter to Minervius on the resurrection of the body. But this variant does not destroy the force of the doctrine under discussion. For a little previously the Apostle had written: *As in Adam all die, so also in Christ all shall be made alive* (1 Cor 15:22). Hence the text which reads, *we shall not all sleep*, cannot refer to death of the body, which has come down to all through the sin of our first parent, as is stated in Romans 5:12, but must be interpreted as referring to the sleep of sin, concerning which we are exhorted in Ephesians 5:14: *Awake, O sleeper, and arise from the dead, and Christ shall give you light.*

Accordingly, those who are found alive at the Lord's coming will be marked off from those who have died before not because they will never die, but because in the very act

nubibus obviam Christo in aera morientur et statim resurgent, ut Augustinus dicit.

Considerandum tamen est quod ad iudicium tria concurrere videntur: primo quidem quod aliquis iudici praesentetur, secundo quod eius merita discutiantur, tertio quod sententiam accipiat.

Quantum igitur ad primum, omnes boni et mali a primo homine usque ad ultimum iudicio Christi subdentur, quia, ut dicitur II Cor. V, *omnes nos oportet astare ante tribunal Christi*; a quorum generalitate non excluduntur etiam parvuli qui vel sine baptismo vel cum baptismo decesserunt, ut Glosa dicit ibidem.

Quantum vero ad secundum, scilicet ad discussionem meritorum, non omnes iudicabuntur, nec boni nec mali. Ibi enim necessaria est iudicii discussio ubi bona malis permisceantur; ubi vero est bonum absque commixtione mali, vel malum absque commixtione boni, ibi discussio locum non habet. Bonorum igitur quidam sunt qui totaliter bona temporalia contemnunt, soli Deo vacantes et his quae sunt Dei. Quia ergo peccatum committitur per hoc quod spreto incommutabili bono bonis commutabilibus adhaeretur, nulla videtur in his esse notabilis commixtio boni et mali, non quod absque peccato vivant, cum ex eorum persona dicatur I Io. I *Si dixerimus quia peccatum non habemus, nos ipsos seducimus*, sed quia in eis levia quaedam peccata inveniuntur quae fervore caritatis quodammodo consumuntur, ut nihil esse videantur: unde hi in iudicio non iudicabuntur per meritorum discussionem.

Qui vero terrenam vitam agentes, rebus saecularibus intendentes eis utuntur non quidem contra Deum, sed eis plus debito inhaerentes, habent aliquid mali bono fidei et caritatis permixtum secundum aliquam notabilem quantitatem, ut non de facili apparere possit quid in eis praevaleat: unde tales iudicabuntur etiam quantum ad discussionem meritorum.

Similiter etiam ex parte malorum, notandum est quod principium accedendi ad Deum est fides, secundum illud Hebr. XI *Accedentem ad Deum oportet credere*. Qui ergo fidem non habet, nihil boni in eo invenitur cuius ad mala permixtio faciat eius dubiam damnationem, et ideo condemnabitur absque meritorum discussione. Qui vero fidem habet sed caritatem non habet, nec opera bona, habet quidem aliquid unde Deo coniungitur; unde necessaria est meritorum discussio, ut evidenter appareat quid in ipso praeponderet, utrum bonum vel malum: unde talis cum discussione meritorum damnabitur, sicut rex terrenus civem peccantem cum audientia damnat, hostem vero absque omni audientia punit.

by which they are taken up *in the clouds to meet Christ in the air* (1 Thess 4:16), they will die and immediately rise again, as Augustine teaches.

In discussing this matter, we must take cognizance of the three phases which seem to constitute a judicial process. First, someone is haled into court; second, his cause is examined; and third, he receives sentence.

As to the first phase, all men, good and evil, from the first man down to the very last, will be subject to Christ's judgment, for, as we are told in 2 Corinthians 5:10, *we must all appear before the judgment seat of Christ*. Not even those who have died in infancy, whether they were baptized or not, are exempt from this universal law, as the Gloss on this text explains.

With regard to the second phase, namely, the examination of the case, not all, either of the good or of the wicked, will be judged. A judicial investigation is not necessary unless good and evil actions are intermingled. When good is present without admixture of evil, or evil without admixture of good, discussion is out of place. Among the good there are some who have wholeheartedly despised temporal possessions, and have dedicated themselves to God alone and to the things that are of God. Accordingly, since sin is committed by cleaving to changeable goods in contempt of the changeless Good, such souls exhibit no mingling of good and evil. This is not to imply that they live without sin, for in their person is asserted what we read in 1 John 1:8: *If we say that we have no sin, we deceive ourselves*. Although certain lesser sins are found in them, these are, so to speak, consumed by the fire of charity, and so seem to be nothing. At the judgment, therefore, such souls will not be judged by an investigation of their deeds.

On the other hand, those who lead an earthly life and in their preoccupation with things of this world use them, not indeed against God, but with excessive attachment to them, have a notable amount of evil mixed up with the good of faith and charity, so that the element predominating in them cannot easily be perceived. Such souls will undergo judgment by an examination of their merits.

Similarly, with reference to the wicked, we should recall that the principle of approach to God is faith, according to Hebrews 11:6: *Whoever would draw near to God must believe*. Therefore, in him who lacks faith there is found nothing of good which, mixed with evil, might render his damnation doubtful. And so such a one will be condemned without any inquiry into merits. Again, he who has faith but has no charity and, consequently, no good works, possesses, indeed, some point of contact with God. Hence an examination of his case is necessary, so that the element predominating in him, whether good or evil, may clearly emerge. Such a person will be damned with an investigation of his case. In the same way an earthly king condemns a criminal citizen after hearing him, but punishes an enemy without any hearing.

Quantum vero ad tertium, scilicet sententiae prolationem, omnes iudicabuntur, quia omnes ex Christi sententia vel gloriam vel poenam reportabunt: unde dicitur II Cor. V: *Ut referat unusquisque propria corporis quae gessit, sive bona sive mala.*

Lastly, with regard to the third phase of a judgment, that is, the pronouncement of the sentence, all will be judged, for all will receive glory or punishment in accord with the sentence. The reason is given in 2 Corinthians 5:10: *So that each one may receive good or evil, according to what he has done in the body.*

CHAPTER 244

Of the manner and place of the judgment

Non est autem aestimandum quod discussio iudicii sit necessaria ut iudex informetur, sicut contingit in humanis iudiciis, cum *omnia sint nuda et aperta oculis eius*, ut dicitur Hebr. IV; sed ad hoc est necessaria praedicta discussio, ut unicuique innotescat et de se ipso et de aliis quomodo sunt digni poena vel gloria, ut sic boni in omnibus de Dei iustitia gaudeant, et mali contra se ipsos irascantur.

Nec est aestimandum quod huiusmodi discussio meritorum verbotenus fiat. Immensum enim tempus requireretur ad enarrandum singulorum cogitata, dicta et facta, bona vel mala: unde Lactantius deceptus fuit ut poneret diem iudicii mille annis duraturum, quamvis nec hoc tempus sufficere videatur, cum ad unius hominis iudicium modo praedicto complendum plures dies requirerentur. Fiet ergo virtute divina ut statim unicuique occurrant omnia bona vel mala quae fecit, pro quibus est praemiandus vel puniendus, et non solum unicuique de se ipso, sed etiam unicuique de aliis. Ubi ergo intantum bona excedunt quod mala nullius videntur esse momenti, aut e converso, nulla videbitur esse concertatio bonorum ad mala secundum aestimationem humanam, et propter hoc sine discussione praemiari vel puniri dicuntur.

In illo autem iudicio licet omnes Christo assistant, different tamen boni a malis non solum quantum ad causam meritorum, sed etiam loco segregabuntur ab eis. Nam mali, qui terrena diligentes a Christo recesserunt, remanebunt in terra; boni vero, qui Christo adhaeserunt, obviam Christo occurrent in aera sublevati ut Christo conformentur, non solum configurati gloriae claritatis eius, sed etiam loco ei consociati, secundum illud Matth. XXIV, *Ubicumque fuerit corpus, congregabuntur et aquilae*, per quas sancti significantur. Signanter autem loco *corporis* in hebraeo *ioathon* dicitur, secundum Ieronymum, quod cadaver significat, ad commemorandum Christi passionem per quam et Christus potestatem iu-

We are not to suppose that judicial examination will be required so that the judge may receive information, as is the case in human courts; for *all things are naked and open to his eyes*, as we are told in Hebrews 4:13. The examination is necessary for the purpose of making known to each person, concerning himself and others, the reasons why each is worthy of punishment or of glory, so that the good may joyfully acknowledge God's justice in all things and the wicked may be roused to anger against themselves.

Nor should we imagine that this examination is to be conducted by oral discussion. Endless time would be required to recount the thoughts, words, and deeds, good or evil, of each person. Therefore, Lactantius was deceived when he suggested that the day of judgment would last a thousand years. Even this time would scarcely be enough, as several days would be required to complete the judicial process for a single man in the manner proposed. Accordingly, the divine power will bring it about that in an instant everyone will be apprised of all the good or evil he has ever done, for which he is to be rewarded or punished. And all this will be made known to each person not only about himself, but also about the rest. Hence, wherever the good is so much in excess that the evil seems to be of no consequence (or vice versa), there will seem to be no conflict between the good and the evil in human estimation. This is what we meant when we said that such persons will be rewarded or punished without examination.

Although all men will appear before Christ at that judgment, the good will not only be set apart from the wicked by reason of the meritorious cause, but will be separated from them in locality. The wicked, who have withdrawn from Christ in their love of earthly things, will remain on earth; but the good, who have clung to Christ, will be raised up into the air when they go to meet Christ, that they may be made like Christ not only by being conformed to the splendor of his glory, but by being associated with him in the place he occupies. This is indicated in Matthew 24:28: *Wherever the body is, there the eagles* (by which the saints are signified) *will be gathered together.* According to Jerome, instead of *body* the Hebrew has the

diciariam promeruit, et homines conformari passioni eius ad societatem gloriae ipsius assumuntur, secundum illud Apostoli *Si compatimur, et conregnabimus*, II Tim. II.

Et inde est quod circa locum dominicae passionis creditur Christus ad iudicium descensurus, secundum illud Ioel III *Congregabo omnes gentes, et disceptabo cum eis in valle Iosaphat*, quae subiacet monti Oliveti, unde Christus ascendit.

Inde etiam est quod veniente Domino ad iudicium, signum crucis et alia passionis indicia demonstrabuntur, secundum illud Matth. XXIV, *Apparebit signum Filii hominis in caelo*, ut impii videntes in quem confixerunt, doleant et crucientur, et hi qui redempti sunt gaudeant de gloria redemptoris. Et sicut Christus a dextris Dei sedere dicitur secundum humanam naturam inquantum est ad bona potissima Patris sublimatus, ita iusti in iudicio a dextris eius dicuntur consistere, quasi honorabilissimum apud eum locum habentes.

significant word *joatham*, which means 'corpse,' to commemorate Christ's Passion, whereby Christ merited the power to judge. And men who have been conformed to his Passion are admitted into the company of his glory, as we are told by the Apostle in 2 Timothy 2:12: *If we suffer, we shall also reign with him.*

And therefore it is believed that Christ will come down to hold judgment around the place of the Lord's Passion, according to the text of Joel 3:2: *I will gather all the nations and bring them down to the valley of Josaphat, and I will enter into judgment with them there.* This valley lies at the foot of Mount Olivet, from which Christ ascended into heaven.

For the same reason, when Christ comes for the judgment the sign of the cross and other signs of the Passion will be displayed, as is said in Matthew 24:30: *Then will appear the sign of the Son of man in heaven*, so that the wicked, looking upon him whom they have pierced, will be distressed and tormented, and those who have been redeemed will exult in the glory of their Redeemer. And as Christ is said to sit at God's right hand according to his human nature, inasmuch as he has been lifted up to share in the most excellent goods of the Father, so at the judgment the just are said to stand at Christ's right, as being entitled to the most honorable place near him.

CHAPTER 245

That the saints will judge

Non solum autem Christus in illo iudicio iudicabit, sed etiam alii. Quorum quidam iudicabunt sola comparatione, scilicet boni minus bonos, aut mali magis malos, secundum illud Matth. XII: *Ninivitae surgent in iudicio, et condemnabunt generationem istam.* Quidam vero iudicabunt per sententiae approbationem, et sic omnes iusti iudicabunt, secundum illud Sap. III: *Iudicabunt sancti nationes.* Quidam vero iudicabunt quasi iudiciariam potestatem accipientes a Christo, secundum illud Psalmi: *Gladii ancipites in manibus eorum.*

Hanc autem ultimam iudiciariam potestatem Dominus apostolis repromisit Matth. XIX dicens: *Vos qui secuti estis me, in regeneratione cum sederit Filius hominis in sede maiestatis suae, sedebitis et vos super sedes duodecim iudicantes duodecim tribus Israel.*

Non est autem aestimandum quod soli Iudaei qui ad duodecim tribus Israel pertinent per apostolos iudicentur, sed per duodecim tribus Israel omnes fideles

Christ will not be the only one to judge on that day; others will be associated with him. Of these, some will judge only in the sense of serving as a basis for comparison. In this way the good will judge the less good, or the wicked will judge the more wicked, according to Matthew 12:41: *The men of Nineveh will arise at the judgment with this generation and condemn it.* And some will judge by giving their approval to the sentence; in this way all the just shall judge, according to Wisdom 3:8: *The just shall judge nations.* But some will judge with a certain judicial power delegated to them by Christ, having *two-edged swords in their hands*, as is indicated in Psalm 149:6.

This last kind of judicial power the Lord promised to the apostles, in Matthew 19:28, when he said: *In the new world, when the Son of man shall sit on his glorious throne, you who have followed me will also sit on twelve thrones, judging the twelve tribes of Israel.*

We are not to conclude from this that only the Jews who belong to the twelve tribes of Israel will be judged by the apostles, for by the twelve tribes of Israel are understood

intelliguntur qui in fidem Patriarcharum sunt assumpti; nam infideles non iudicantur, sed iam iudicati sunt.

Similiter etiam non soli duodecim Apostoli qui tunc erant cum Christo iudicabunt, nam neque Iudas iudicabit; neque Paulus, qui plus aliis laboravit, carebit iudiciaria dignitate, praesertim cum ipse dicat *Nescitis quoniam angelos iudicabimus?* Sed ad illos proprie haec dignitas pertinet qui omnibus relictis Christum sunt secuti; hoc enim premiserat Petrus quaerens *Ecce nos reliquimus omnia et secuti sumus te quid ergo erit nobis?* unde Iob XXXVI dicitur *Iudicium pauperibus tribuet.* Et hoc rationabiliter: ut enim dictum est, iudicii discussio erit de actibus hominum qui rebus terrenis bene vel male sunt usi; requiritur autem ad rectitudinem iudicii ut animus iudicis sit liber ab his de quibus habet iudicare: et ideo per hoc quod aliqui animum suum a rebus terrenis totaliter abstrahunt, dignitatem iudiciariam merentur.

Facit etiam ad meritum huius dignitatis praeceptorum divinorum annuntiatio: unde Matth. XXV Christus *cum angelis* ad iudicandum dicitur esse venturus, per quos *praedicatores* intelliguntur, ut Augustinus in libro *De poenitentia* dicit; decet enim ut illi discutiant actus hominum circa observantiam divinorum praeceptorum qui praecepta vitae annuntiaverunt.

Iudicabunt autem praedicti inquantum cooperabuntur ad hoc quod unicuique appareat causa salvationis et damnationis, tam sui quam aliorum, eo modo quo superiores angeli inferiores vel etiam homines illuminare dicuntur.

Hanc igitur potestatem iudiciariam confitemur in Christo, in Symbolo Apostolorum dicentes *inde venturus est iudicare vivos et mortuos.*

all the faithful who have been admitted to the faith of the patriarchs. As for infidels, they will not be judged, but have already been judged.

Similarly, the twelve apostles who walked with Christ during his earthly life are not the only ones who will judge. Judas assuredly will not judge, nor shall Paul, who labored more than the rest, lack judicial power, especially as he himself says: *Do you not know that we are to judge angels?* (1 Cor 6:3). This dignity pertains properly to those who have left all to follow Christ, for such was the promise made to Peter in answer to his question in Matthew 19:27: *Lo, we have left everything and followed you. What then shall we have?* The same thought occurs in Job 36:6: *He gives judgment to the poor.* And this is reasonable, because, as we said, the investigation will deal with the actions of men who have used earthly things well or ill. Correctness of judgment requires that the mind of the judge should be unswayed by those matters about which he has to judge; and so the fact that some have their minds completely detached from earthly things gives them a title to judicial authority.

The announcing of the divine commandments also contributes to the meriting of this dignity. In Matthew 25:31 we read that Christ will come to judge *accompanied by angels,* that is, *by preachers,* as Augustine suggests in a work on penance. For they who have made known the precepts of life ought to have a part in examining the actions of men regarding the observance of the divine precepts.

The persons mentioned will judge by cooperating in the task of revealing to each individual the cause of the salvation or damnation both of himself and of others, in the way that higher angels are said to illuminate the lower angels and also men.

We profess that this judicial power belongs to Christ when we say, in the Apostles' Creed, *from thence he shall come to judge the living and the dead.*

Chapter 246

On the distinction of the articles of faith

His igitur consideratis quae pertinent ad christianae fidei veritatem, sciendum est quod omnia praemissa ad certos articulos reducuntur: secundum quosdam quidem ad duodecim, secundum alios autem ad quatuordecim.

Cum enim fides sit de his quae sunt incomprehensibilia rationi, ubi aliquid novum occurrit rationi incomprehensibile, ibi oportet esse novum articulum. Est igitur unus articulus pertinens ad divinitatis unitatem: quamvis enim Deum esse unum ratione probetur, tamen eum sic praeesse immediate omnibus ut sin-

Having reviewed the doctrines pertaining to the truth of the Christian faith, we should know that all the teachings thus set forth are reduced to certain articles: twelve in number, as some think, or fourteen, according to others.

Faith has to do with truths incomprehensible to reason. Hence, whenever a new truth incomprehensible to reason is proposed, a new article is required. One article pertains to the divine unity. For, even though we prove by reason that God is one, the fact that he governs all things directly or that he wishes to be worshiped in some particular way, is a

gulariter sit colendus, fidei subiacet. De tribus autem personis ponuntur tres articuli. De tribus autem effectibus Dei, scilicet creationis quae pertinet ad naturam, iustificationis quae pertinet ad gratiam, remunerationis quae pertinet ad gloriam, ponuntur tres alii: et sic de divinitate in universo ponuntur septem articuli.

Circa humanitatem vero Christi ponuntur septem alii, ut primus sit de Incarnatione et conceptione, secundus de nativitate quae habet specialem difficultatem propter exitum a clauso Virginis utero, tertius de passione, morte et sepultura, quartus de descensu ad inferos, quintus de resurrectione, sextus de ascensione, septimus de adventu ad iudicium: et sic in universo sunt quatuordecim articuli.

Alii vero satis rationabiliter fidem trium personarum sub uno articulo comprehendunt, eo quod non potest credi Pater quin credatur et Filius et amor nectens utrumque, qui est Spiritus Sanctus; sed distinguunt articulum resurrectionis ab articulo remunerationis: et sic duo articuli sunt de Deo, unus de unitate, alius de Trinitate; quatuor de effectibus, unus de creatione, alius de iustificatione, tertius de communi resurrectione, quartus de remuneratione. Similiter circa fidem humanitatis Christi, conceptionem et nativitatem sub uno articulo comprehendunt, sicut passionem et mortem. Fiunt igitur in universo secundum istam computationem duodecim articuli.

Et haec de fide sufficiant.

matter relating to faith. Three articles are reserved for the three divine persons. Three other articles are formulated about the effects produced by God: creation, which pertains to nature; justification, which pertains to grace; and reward, which pertains to glory. Thus seven articles altogether are devoted to the divinity.

Concerning the humanity of Christ, seven more are proposed. The first is on the Incarnation and conception of Christ. The second deals with the nativity, which involves a special difficulty because of our Lord's coming forth from the closed womb of the Virgin. The third article is on the death, Passion, and burial; the fourth on the descent into hell; the fifth on the resurrection; the sixth on the ascension; and the seventh treats of Christ's coming for the judgment. And so there are fourteen articles in all.

Other authorities, reasonably enough, include faith in the three persons under one article, on the ground that we cannot believe in the Father without believing in the Son and also in the Holy Spirit, the bond of love uniting the first two persons. However, they distinguish the article on the resurrection from the article on eternal reward. Accordingly, there are two articles about God, one on the unity, the other on the Trinity. Four articles deal with God's effects: one with creation, the second with justification, the third with the general resurrection, and the fourth with reward. Similarly, as regards belief in the humanity of Christ, these authors comprise the conception and the nativity under one article, and they also include the Passion and death under one article. According to this way of reckoning, therefore, we have twelve articles in all.

And this should be enough on faith.

Book II

On Hope

Chapter 1

In which it is shown that the virtue of hope is necessary for the perfection of Christian life

Quia secundum principis apostolorum sententiam admonemur ut non solum rationem reddamus de fide, sed etiam *de ea quae in nobis est spe*, post praemissa, in quibus fidei Christianae sententiam breviter prosecuti sumus, restat ut de iis quae ad spem pertinent, compendiosam tibi expositionem faciamus.

Est autem considerandum, quod in aliqua cognitione desiderium hominis requiescere potest, cum homo naturaliter scire desideret veritatem, qua cognita eius desiderium quietatur. Sed in cognitione fidei desiderium hominis non quiescit: fides enim imperfecta est cognitio, ea enim creduntur quae non videntur, unde apostolus eam vocat *argumentum non apparentium*, ad Hebr. XI, 1.

Habita igitur fide, adhuc remanet animae motus ad aliud, scilicet ad videndum perfecte veritatem quam credit et assequendum ea per quae ad veritatem huiusmodi poterit introduci. Sed quia inter cetera fidei documenta unum esse diximus ut credatur Deus providentiam de rebus humanis habere, insurgit ex hoc in animo credentis motus spei, ut scilicet bona quae naturaliter desiderat, ut edoctus ex fide, per eius auxilium consequatur. Unde post fidem ad perfectionem Christianae vitae spes necessaria est, sicut supra iam diximus.

The Prince of the Apostles has left us an admonition urging us to render an account not only of our faith, but also *of the hope that is in us* (1 Pet 3:15). In the first part of the present work we have briefly set forth the teaching of Christian faith. We now turn to the task of undertaking, in compendious fashion, an exposition of the truths pertaining to hope.

We should recall that in one kind of knowledge, man's desire can come to rest. We naturally desire to know truth, and when we do know it, our craving in this direction is satisfied. But in the knowledge of faith man's desire never comes to rest. For faith is imperfect knowledge: the truths we accept on faith are not seen. This is why the Apostle calls faith *the evidence of things that appear not* (Heb 11:1).

Accordingly, even when we have faith, there still remains in the soul an impulse toward something else: namely, the perfect vision of the truth assented to by faith, and the attainment of whatever can lead to such truth. Now, we have said that among faith's other teachings, there is one by which we believe in God's providence over human affairs. From this, stirrings of hope arise in the believer's soul that by God's help he may gain possession of the goods he naturally desires, once he learns of them through faith. Therefore, as we mentioned at the very beginning, next after faith, the virtue of hope is necessary for the perfection of Christian living.

CHAPTER 2

That prayer is recommended to men to obtain what they hope from God, and on the diversity of prayers to God and man

Quia vero secundum divinae providentiae ordinem unicuique attribuitur modus perveniendi ad finem secundum convenientiam suae naturae, est etiam hominibus concessus congruus modus obtinendi quae sperat a Deo secundum humanae conditionis tenorem. Habet enim hoc humana conditio ut aliquis interponat deprecationem ad obtinendum ab aliquo, praesertim superiori, quod per eum se sperat adipisci: et ideo indicta est hominibus oratio per quam homines a Deo obtineant quod ab ipso consequi sperant.

Aliter tamen necessaria est oratio ad obtinendum aliquid ab homine, aliter a Deo. Interponitur enim ad hominem primum quidem, ut desiderium orantis et necessitas exprimatur, secundo ut deprecati animus ad concedendum flectatur: sed haec in oratione quae ad Deum funditur, locum non habent. Non enim in orando intendimus necessitates nostras aut desideria Deo manifestare, qui omnium est cognitor, unde et Psal. XXVII, 10 dicit ei: *Domine, ante te omne desiderium meum*, et in Evangelio dicitur Matth. VI, 32: *Scit pater vester quia his omnibus indigetis*. Nec etiam divina voluntas verbis humanis flectitur ad volendum quod prius noluerat, quia, ut dicitur Num. XXIII, 19: *non est Deus quasi homo ut mentiatur, nec ut filius hominis, ut mutetur*. Nec poenitudine flectitur, ut dicitur I Reg. XV, 29.

Sed oratio ad obtinendum a Deo est homini necessaria propter seipsum qui orat, ut scilicet ipsemet suos defectus consideret, et animum suum flectat ad ferventer et pie desiderandum quod orando sperat obtinere: per hoc enim ad recipiendum idoneus redditur. Est autem et alia differentia consideranda orationis quae ad Deum et hominem fit. Nam ad orationem quae fit ad hominem, praeexigitur familiaritas, per quam sibi deprecandi aditus pateat; sed ipsa oratio quae ad Deum emittitur, familiares nos Deo facit, dum mens nostra elevatur ad ipsum, et quodam spirituali affectu Deo colloquitur, in spiritu et veritate ipsum adorans, et sic familiaris effectus orando aditum sibi parat ut iterum fiducialius oret. Unde dicitur in Psal. XVI, 6: *ego clamavi*, scilicet fiducialiter orando, *quoniam exaudisti me Deus*, quasi per primam orationem in familiaritatem receptus, secundo fiducialius clamet.

Et propter hoc in oratione divina assiduitas vel petitionum frequentia non est importuna, sed reputatur

In the order of divine providence, each being has assigned to it a way of reaching its end in keeping with its nature. To men, too, is appointed a suitable way, that befits the conditions of human nature, of obtaining what they hope for from God. Human nature inclines us to have recourse to petition for the purpose of obtaining from another, especially from a person of higher rank, what we hope to receive from him. And so prayer is recommended to men that by it they may obtain from God what they hope to secure from him.

But the reason why prayer is necessary for obtaining something from a man is not the same as the reason for obtaining a favor from God. Prayer is addressed to man first to lay bare the desire and the need of the petitioner, and second, to incline the mind of him to whom the prayer is addressed to grant the petition. These purposes have no place in the prayer that is sent up to God. When we pray we do not intend to manifest our needs or desires to God, for he knows all things. The Psalmist says to God: *Lord, all my longing is known to thee* (Psalm 38 [37]:10); and in the Gospel we are told: *Your heavenly Father knows that you need them all* (Matt 6:32). Again, the will of God is not influenced by human words to will what he had previously not willed. For, as we read in Numbers 23:19, *God is not man, that he should lie, or a son of man, that he should be changed*; nor is God *moved to repentance* (1 Sam 15:29).

Prayer, then, for obtaining something from God is necessary for man on account of the very one who prays, that he may reflect on his shortcomings and may turn his mind to desiring fervently and piously what he hopes to gain by his petition. In this way he is rendered fit to receive the favor. Yet a further difference between the prayer offered to God and that addressed to man is to be marked. Prayer addressed to a man presupposes a certain intimacy that may afford the petitioner an opportunity to present his request. But when we pray to God, the very prayer we send forth makes us intimate with him, inasmuch as our soul is raised up to God and converses with him in spiritual affection, and adores him in spirit and truth. The familiar affection thus experienced in prayer begets an inducement in the petitioner to pray again with yet greater confidence. And so we read in Psalm 17 [16]:6: *I have cried to you*, that is, in trusting prayer, *for you, O God, have heard me*; as though, after being admitted to intimacy in the first prayer, the Psalmist cries out with all the greater confidence in the second.

For this reason, in prayer to God, perseverance or repetition of our supplication is not unseemly, but is regarded

Deo accepta. *Oportet enim semper orare et non deficere, ut dicitur Luc. XVIII, 1. Unde et dominus ad petendum invitat, dicens Matth. VII, 7, petite, et dabitur vobis . . . pulsate, et aperietur vobis.* In oratione vero quae ad hominem fit, petitionum assiduitas redditur importuna.

as acceptable to God. Indeed, we *ought always to pray and not lose heart*, as we learn from Luke 18:1. Our Lord, too, invites us to pray, for he said: *Ask, and it will be given you . . . knock, and it will be opened to you* (Matt 7:7). But in prayer addressed to man, persistence in begging becomes irritating.

CHAPTER 3

That Christ fittingly gave us a form of prayer for hope's consummation

Quia igitur ad salutem nostram post fidem etiam spes requiritur, opportunum fuit ut salvator noster sicut auctor et consummator nobis factus est fidei reservando caelestia sacramenta; ita etiam nos in spem vivam induceret, nobis formam orandi tradens, per quam maxime spes nostra in Deum erigitur, dum ab ipso Deo edocemur quid ab ipso petendum sit. Non enim ad petendum induceret nisi proponeret exaudire, nullusque ab alio petit nisi de quo sperat, et ea ipse petit quae sperat. Sic igitur dum nos docet a Deo aliqua petere, in Deo nos sperare admonet, et quid ab ipso sperare debeamus ostendit per ea quae petenda esse demonstrat.

Sic igitur prosequentes ea quae in oratione dominica continentur, demonstrabimus quidquid ad spem Christianorum pertinere potest: scilicet in quo spem ponere debeamus, et propter quam causam, et quae ab eo sperare debeamus. Spes quidem nostra debet esse in Deo, quem etiam orare debemus, secundum illud Psal. LXI, v. 9: *sperate in eo*, scilicet Deo, *omnis congregatio populi; effundite coram illo*, scilicet orando, *corda vestra.*

Since, in addition to faith, hope is also necessary for our salvation, our Savior, who inaugurated and perfected our faith by instituting the heavenly sacraments, thought it well to carry us on to a living hope by giving us a form of prayer that mightily raises up our hope to God. Thus we are taught by God himself what we ought to request from him. He would not urge us to pray unless he were determined to hear us; no one asks another for a favor unless he has hope in him, and he asks only what he hopes for. Therefore, in teaching us to ask God for benefits, Christ exhorts us to hope in God, and he shows us what we ought to hope for from him by making known to us what to request.

Accordingly, we shall go through the petitions contained in the Lord's Prayer, and shall point out all that may relate to the hope of Christians. We shall indicate the person in whom we ought to place our hope, and why, and what we should expect from him. Our hope ought to be anchored in God to whom we are to pray, as we are told in Psalm 62 [61]:8: *Trust in him*, namely, in God, *at all times, O people; pour out your heart before him*, that is, by praying.

CHAPTER 4

Why we ought to pray to God himself for what we hope

Causa autem quare in eo sperandum est, haec praecipua est, quia pertinemus ad ipsum sicut effectus ad causam. Nihil autem in vanum operatur, sed propter aliquem finem certum. Pertinet igitur ad unumquodque agens sic effectum producere ut ei non desint per quae possit pervenire ad finem: et inde est quod in his quae naturalibus agentibus fiunt, natura deficere in necessariis non invenitur, sed attribuit unicuique generato quae sunt ad consistentiam sui esse, et ad perficiendum operationem qua pertingat ad finem, nisi forte hoc impediatur per defectum agentis, qui sit insufficiens ad haec exhibenda.

The chief reason why we must hope in God is that we belong to him as effect belongs to cause. God does nothing in vain, but always acts for a definite purpose. Every active cause has the power of producing its effect in such a way that the effect will not be wanting in whatever can advance it toward its end. This is why, in effects produced by natural causes, nature is not found to be deficient in anything that is necessary, but confers on every effect whatever goes into its composition and is required to carry through the action whereby it may reach its end. Of course, some impediment may arise from a defect in the cause, which then may be unable to furnish all this.

Agens autem per intellectum non solum in ipsa effectus productione ea confert suo effectui quae sunt necessaria ad finem intentum, sed etiam opere iam perfecto disponit de usu ipsius, qui est operis finis, sicut faber non solum cultellum fabricat, sed etiam disponit de incisione ipsius. Homo autem a Deo est productus ut artificiatum ab artifice, unde dicitur Isai. LXIV, 8: *Et nunc, domine, fictor noster es tu, nos vero lutum*: et ideo sicut vas fictile, si sensum haberet, sperare de figulo posset ut bene disponeretur, ita etiam homo debet habere spem de Deo, ut recte gubernetur ab eo, unde dicitur Ier. XVIII, 6: *sicut lutum in manu figuli, sic vos, domus Israel, in manu mea.*

Haec autem fiducia quam homo habet de Deo, debet esse certissima. Dictum enim est quod agens a recta sui operis dispositione non recedit nisi propter aliquem eius defectum. In Deo autem nullus defectus cadere potest neque ignorantia, quia *omnia nuda et aperta sunt oculis eius*, ut dicitur Hebr. IV, 13, neque impotentia, quia: *non est abbreviata manus eius ut salvare non possit*, ut dicitur Isai. LIX, 1, neque iterum defectus bonae voluntatis, quia *bonus est dominus sperantibus in eum, animae quaerenti illum*, ut dicitur Thren. III, 25. Et ideo spes qua aliquis de Deo confidit, sperantem *non confundit*, ut dicitur Rom. V, 5.

Est autem considerandum ulterius, quod etsi respectu omnium creaturarum providentia dispositionis invigilet, speciali tamen ratione curam habet de rationabilibus, quae scilicet dignitate imaginis ipsius sunt insignitae, et ad eum cognoscendum et amandum possunt pertingere, et suorum actuum dominium habent, ut boni et mali discretionem habentes: unde competit eis fiduciam habere de Deo, non solum ut conserventur in esse secundum conditionem suae naturae, quod competit ceteris creaturis, sed etiam ut recedendo a malo et operando bonum, aliquid promereantur ab ipso. Unde in Psal. XXXV, v. 7, dicitur: *homines et iumenta salvabis*, inquantum scilicet hominibus simul cum irrationabilibus creaturis confert ea quae pertinent ad subsidium vitae; sed postea subdit: *filii autem hominum in tegmine alarum tuarum sperabunt*, quasi speciali quadam cura protecti ab ipso.

Ulterius autem considerare oportet, quod perfectione quacumque accedente, superadditur facultas aliquid faciendi vel adipiscendi, sicut aer illuminatus a sole facultatem habet ut possit esse medium visionis, et aqua calefacta ab igne facultatem habet decoquendi, et hoc sperare posset si sensum haberet. Homini autem supra animae naturam additur perfectio gratiae, per quam efficitur *divinae consors naturae*, ut dicitur II Pet. I, 4: unde et secundum hoc dicimur regenerari in filios Dei, secundum illud Ioan. I, 12: *dedit eis potestatem filios Dei fieri*. Filii autem effecti convenienter possunt heredita-

A cause that operates intellectually not only confers on the effect, in the act of producing it, all that is required for the result intended, but also, when the product is finished, controls its use, which is the end of the object. Thus a smith, in addition to forging a knife, orders its cutting efficiency. Man is made by God somewhat as an article is made by an artificer. Something of this sort is said in Isaiah 64:8: *And now, Lord, you are our Father and we are clay, and you are our Maker*. Accordingly, just as an earthen vessel, if it were endowed with sense, might hope to be put to good use by the potter, so man ought to cherish the hope of being rightly provided for by God. Thus we are told in Jeremiah 18:6: *Behold, like the clay in the potter's hand, so are you in my hand, O house of Israel.*

The confidence which man has in God ought to be most certain. As we just intimated, a cause does not refrain from rightly controlling its product unless it labors under some defect. But no defect or ignorance can occur in God, because *all things are naked and open to his eyes*, as is said in Hebrews 4:13. Nor does he lack power, for *the hand of the Lord is not shortened that it cannot save*, as we read in Isaiah 59:1. Nor is he wanting in good will, for *the Lord is good to those who hope in him, to the soul that seeks him*, as we are reminded in Lamentations 3:25. Therefore, the hope with which a person trusts in God *does not confound* him that hopes, as is said in Romans 5:5.

We should also bear in mind that, while providence watches solicitously over all creatures, God exercises special care over rational beings. For the latter are exalted to the dignity of God's image, and can rise to the knowledge and love of him, and have dominion over their actions, since they are able to discriminate between good and evil. Hence they should have confidence in God not only that they may be preserved in existence in keeping with the condition of their nature—for this pertains also to other creatures—but that, by avoiding evil and doing good, they may merit some reward from him. We are taught a salutary lesson in Psalm 36 [35]:6: *Man and beast thou savest, O Lord*, that is, God bestows on men and irrational creatures alike whatever pertains to the sustaining of life. And then the Psalmist adds, in the next verse: *The children of men take refuge in the shadow of thy wings*, indicating that they will be protected by God with special care.

We should observe, further, that when any perfection is conferred, an ability to do or acquire something is also added. For example, when the air is illuminated by the sun, it has the capacity to serve as a medium for sight, and when water is heated by fire it can be used to cook, and it could hope for this if it had a mind. To man is given, over and above the nature of his soul, the perfection of grace, by which he is made *a partaker in the divine nature*, as we are taught in 2 Peter 1:4. As a result of this, we are said to be regenerated and to become sons of God, according to John 1:12: *He gave power to become children of God*. Thus

tem sperare, secundum illum Rom. VIII, v. 17: *si filii et heredes*. Et ideo secundum hanc spiritualem regenerationem competit homini quandam altiorem spem de Deo habere, hereditatis scilicet aeternae consequendae, secundum illud I Pet. I, 3: *regeneravit nos in spem vivam per resurrectionem Christi ex mortuis, in hereditatem incorruptibilem et incontaminatam et immarcescibilem, conservatam in caelis.*

Et quia per spiritum adoptionis quem accepimus, clamamus *abba, pater*, ut dicitur Rom. VIII, 15, ideo dominus ut ex hac spe nobis esse orandum ostenderet, suam orationem a patris invocatione inchoavit dicens, *pater*. Similiter etiam ex hoc quod dicitur, *pater*, praeparatur hominis affectus ad pure orandum, et ad obtinendum quod sperat. Debent etiam filii imitatores parentum existere, unde qui patrem Deum confitetur, debet conari ut Dei imitator existat, vitando scilicet illa quae Deo dissimilem reddunt, et his insistendo quae nos Deo assimilant: unde dicitur Ier. III, 19: *patrem vocabis me, et post me ingredi non cessabis*. Si ergo ut Gregorius Nyssenus dicit *ad res mundanas intuitum dirigis, aut humanam gloriam ambis, aut sordes passibilis appetitus: quomodo qui corrupta vivis vita, patrem vocas incorruptibilitatis genitorem?*

raised to be sons, men may reasonably hope for an inheritance, as we learn from Romans 8:17: *if sons, then heirs*. In keeping with this spiritual regeneration, man should have a yet higher hope in God, namely, the hope of receiving an eternal inheritance, according to 1 Peter 1:3–4: *We have been born anew to a living hope through the resurrection of Jesus Christ from the dead, and to an inheritance which is imperishable, undefiled, and unfading, kept in heaven for you.*

Through this spirit of adoption that we receive, we cry: *Abba, Father*, as is said in Romans 8:15. Hence our Lord began his prayer by calling upon the Father, saying, *Father*, to teach us that our prayer must be based on this hope. By uttering the name, *Father*, man's affection is prepared to pray with a pure disposition, and also to obtain what he hopes for. Moreover, sons ought to be imitators of their parents. Therefore, he who professes that God is his Father ought to try to be an imitator of God, by avoiding things that make him unlike God and by earnestly praying for those perfections that make him like to God. Hence we are commanded in Jeremiah 3:19: *You shall call me Father and shall not cease to walk after me*. If, then, as Gregory of Nyssa reminds us, *you turn your gaze to worldly affairs, or seek human honor or the filth of passionate craving: how can you, who lead such a corrupt life, call the source of incorruption your Father?*[9]

CHAPTER 5

That God, from whom we beg the object of our hope in prayer, ought to be called "Our Father" and not "My Father"

Inter alia vero praecipue qui se Dei filium recognoscit, debet in caritate dominum imitari, secundum illud Ephes. V, 1: *estote imitatores Dei, sicut filii carissimi et ambulate in dilectione*. Dei autem dilectio non privata est, sed communis ad omnes: *diligit enim omnia quae sunt*, ut dicitur Sap. XI, 25; et specialiter homines, secundum illud Deut. XXXIII, 3: *Dilexit populos*. Et ideo, ut Cyprianus dicit, *publica est nobis et communis oratio; et quando oramus, non pro uno tantum, sed pro populo toto oramus, quia totus populus unum sumus*. Pro se igitur orare, ut Chrysostomus dicit, *necessitas cogit, pro altero autem caritas fraternitatis hortatur*. Et ideo non dicimus, *pater meus*, sed *pater noster*.

Simul etiam considerandum est, quod si spes nostra principaliter divino auxilio innitatur, ad invicem tamen iuvamur ut facilius obtineamus quod petimus, unde dicitur II Cor. I, 10–11: *eripiet nos adiuvantibus et*

He who looks on himself as a son of God, ought, among other things, to imitate our Lord especially in his love, as we are urged to do in Ephesians 5:1–2: *Be, therefore, followers of God as most dear children, and walk in love*. God's love is not restricted to any individual, but embraces all in common; for God *loves all things that are*, as is said in Wisdom 11:25. Most of all he loves men, according to Deuteronomy 33:3: *He loved the people*. Consequently, in Cyprian's words, *our prayer is public and is offered for all; and when we pray, we do not pray for one person alone, but for the whole people, because we are all together one people*.[10] Or, as Chrysostom says, *Necessity forces us to pray for ourselves, but fraternal charity impels us to pray for others*.[11] This is why we say *Our Father*, and not simply *My Father*.

At the same time we should remember that, although our hope rests chiefly on God's help, we can aid one another to obtain more easily what we ask for. St. Paul says, in 2 Corinthians 1:10–11: *God will deliver us, and with you*

---

9. Gregory of Nyssa, *De Oratione Dominica*, II.
10. *Liber de oratione dominica*, VIII
11. Pseudo-Chrysostom, *In Evangelium Matthaei*, hom. XIV.

vobis in oratione pro nobis; unde et Iac. V, 16, dicitur: *orate pro invicem ut salvemini*. Ut enim dicit Ambrosius, *multi minimi, dum congregantur et unanimes fiunt, fiunt magni, et multorum preces impossibile est ut non impetrent*, secundum illud Matth. XVIII, 19: *si duo ex vobis consenserint super terram de omni re quamcumque petierint, fiet illis a patre meo qui in caelis est*. Et ideo non singulariter orationem porrigimus, sed quasi ex unanimi consensu dicimus, *pater noster*.

Considerandum est etiam, quod spes nostra est ad Deum per Christum, secundum illud Rom. V, 1: *iustificati ex fide pacem habeamus ad Deum per dominum nostrum Iesum Christum, per quem habemus accessum per fidem in gratiam istam, in qua stamus, et gloriamur in spe gloriae filiorum Dei*. Per ipsum enim qui est unigenitus Dei filius naturalis, efficimur filii adoptivi, quia, ut dicitur Gal. IV, 4, *misit Deus filium suum . . . ut adoptionem filiorum reciperemus*. Tali igitur tenore Deum patrem profiteri debemus, ut privilegio unigeniti non derogetur, unde Augustinus dicit: *noli tibi aliquid specialiter vindicare. Solius Christi specialiter est pater, nobis omnibus in communi pater est, quia illum solum genuit, nos creavit*. Et ideo dicitur, *pater noster*.

helping in prayer for us. And in James 5:16 we are exhorted: *Pray one for another, that you may be saved*. For, as Ambrose reminds us, *Many insignificant people, when they are gathered together and are of one mind, become powerful, and the prayers of many cannot but be heard*.[12] This agrees with Matthew 18:19: *If two of you agree on earth about anything they ask, it will be done for them by my Father in heaven*. Therefore, we do not pour forth our prayers as individuals, but with unanimous accord we cry out, *Our Father*.

Let us also reflect that our hope reaches up to God through Christ, according to Romans 5:1–2: *Since we are justified by faith, we have peace with God through our Lord Jesus Christ. Through him we have obtained access to this grace in which we stand, and we rejoice in our hope of sharing the glory of God*. Through him who is the only-begotten Son of God by nature, we are made adopted sons: *God sent forth his Son . . . so that we might receive adoption as sons*, as is said in Galatians 4:4–5. Hence, in acknowledging that God is our Father, we should do so in such a way that the prerogative of the Only-begotten is not disparaged. In this connection Augustine admonishes us: *Do not make any exclusive claims for yourself. In a special sense, God is the Father of Christ alone, and is the Father of all the rest of us in common. For the Father begot him alone, but created us*.[13] This, then, is why we say: *Our Father*.

Chapter 6

God's power to grant our petitions is shown by saying, "Who art in heaven"

Solet autem contingere spei defectus propter impotentiam eius a quo auxilium esset sperandum. Non enim sufficit ad spei fiduciam quod ille cui spes innititur, voluntatem habeat adiuvandi, nisi adsit potestas. Satis autem voluntatis divinae promptitudinem ad iuvandum exprimimus patrem eum profitendo. Sed ne de excellentia potestatis eius dubitetur, subditur: *qui es in caelis*. Non enim esse in caelis dicitur sicut a caelis contentus, sed sicut caelos sua virtute comprehendens, secundum illud Eccli. XXIV, 8: *gyrum caeli circuivi sola*: quinimmo super totam caelorum magnitudinem virtus eius elevata est, secundum illud Psal. VIII, 2: *elevata est magnificentia tua super caelos, Deus*. Et ideo ad spei fiduciam confirmandam, virtutem eius profitemur, quae caelos sustinet et transcendit.

Per hoc etiam impedimentum quoddam orationis excluditur. Sunt enim aliqui qui res humanas fatali necessitati siderum subdunt, contra illud quod dicitur

It often happens that hope is lost because of the powerlessness of the one from whom help was expected. To have confidence in hope, the mere willingness of a peson to help is not sufficient, unless that person also has the power to help. We sufficiently express our conviction that the divine will is ready to help us when we proclaim that God is our Father. But to exclude all doubt as to the perfection of his power, we add: *who art in heaven*. The Father is not said to be in heaven as though he were contained by heaven; on the contrary, he encompasses heaven in his power, as is said in Sirach 24:8: *Alone I have made the circuit of the vault of heaven*. Indeed, God's power is raised above the whole immensity of heaven, according to Psalm 8:2: *Your magnificence is elevated above the heavens*. And so, to strengthen the confidence of our hope, we hail the power of God which sustains and transcends the heavens.

This same phrase removes a certain obstacle that may stand in the way of our prayer. Some people act as though human affairs were subjected to a deterministic fatalism

---

12. Ambrosiaster, *In epistolam ad Romanos*, XV.
13. Really Ambrose, *de Sacramentis*, V. 19.

Ier. X, 2: *a signis caeli nolite metuere quae gentes timent.* Secundum autem hunc errorem tollitur orationis fructus: nam si necessitati siderum vita nostra subiicitur, non potest circa hoc aliquid immutari. Frustra igitur orando peteremus vel aliqua bona consequi, vel liberari a malis. Ut igitur nec hoc orantium fiduciae obsit, dicimus: *qui es in caelis,* idest tamquam motor et moderator eorum. Et sic per virtutem caelestium corporum auxilium quod a Deo speramus, impediri non potest.

Sed etiam ad hoc quod oratio sit efficax apud Deum, oportet ut ea petat homo quae dignum est expectare a Deo. Dicitur enim quibusdam, Iac. IV, 3: *petitis et non accipitis, eo quod male petatis.* Illa enim male petuntur quae terrena sapientia suggerit, non caelestis. Et ideo Chrysostomus dicit: cum dicimus, *qui es in caelis,* non Deum ibi concludimus, sed a terra abducitur orantis animus, et excelsis regionibus affigitur.

Est autem et aliud orationis sive fiduciae impedimentum, quod orans habet de Deo, scilicet si putet aliquis humanam vitam a divina providentia esse remotam, secundum quod ex persona impiorum dicitur Iob XXII, 14: *nubes latibulum eius, nec nostra considerat, et circa cardines caeli perambulat*; et Ezech. VIII, 12: *non videt dominus nos; dereliquit dominus terram.*

Contrarium autem apostolus Paulus Atheniensibus praedicans ostendit, dicens: *non longe est ab unoquoque nostrum, in ipso enim vivimus, movemur et sumus,* quia scilicet per ipsum nostrum esse conservatur, vita gubernatur, motus dirigitur, secundum illud Sap. XIV, 3: *tua autem, pater, providentia ab initio cuncta gubernat,* tantum quod nec eius providentiae minima animalia subtrahuntur, secundum illud Matth. X, 29–30: *nonne duo passeres asse veneunt et unus ex illis non cadet super terram sine patre vestro? Vestri autem et capilli capitis omnes numerati sunt.*

Intantum tamen excellentiori modo sub cura divina homines ponuntur, ut horum comparatione dicat apostolus: *non est cura Deo de bobus,* non quod omnino eorum curam non habeat, sed quia nec sic eorum curam habet ut hominum, quos punit aut remunerat pro bonis aut malis, et eos ad aeternitatem praeordinat: unde et post praemissa verba dominus subdit: *vestri autem capilli capitis omnes numerati sunt,* tanquam totum quod est hominis, sit in resurrectione reparandum.

imposed by the stars, contrary to what is commanded in Jeremiah 10:2: *Be not dismayed at the signs of the heavens because the nations are dismayed at them.* If this error had its way, it would rob us of the fruit of prayer. For if our lives were subjected to a necessity decreed by the stars, nothing in our course could be changed. In vain we should plead in our prayer for the granting of some good or for deliverance from evil. To prevent this error from undermining confidence in prayer, we say, *who art in heaven,* thus acknowledging that God moves and regulates the heavens. Accordingly, the assistance we hope to obtain from God cannot be obstructed by the power of heavenly bodies.

In order that prayer may be efficacious at the court of God, man must ask for those benefits which he may worthily expect from God. Of old some petitioners were rebuked: *You ask and do not receive, because you ask wrongly* (Jas 4:3). Something is asked wrongly when suggested by earthly wisdom rather than by heavenly wisdom. And so Chrysostom assures us that the words, *who art in heaven,* do not imply that God is confined to that locality, but rather indicate that the mind of him who prays is raised up from the earth and comes to rest in that celestial region.[14]

There is another obstacle to prayer or confidence in God that would deter one from praying. This is the notion that human life is far removed from divine providence. The thought is given expression, in the person of the wicked, in Job 22:14: *Thick clouds enwrap him, so that he does not see, and he walks on the vault of heaven.* Also in Ezekiel 8:12: *The Lord does not see us, the Lord has forsaken the land.*

But the Apostle Paul taught the contrary in his sermon to the Athenians, when he said that God *is not far from each one of us, for in him we live and move and have our being* (Acts 17:27–28). That is, our being is preserved, our life is governed and our activity is directed by him. This is confirmed by Wisdom 14:3: *Your providence, Father, governs all things from the beginning.* Not even the most insignificant of living things are withdrawn from God's providence, as we are told in Matthew 10:29–30: *Are not two sparrows sold for a penny? And not one of them will fall to the ground without your Father's will. But even the hairs of your head are all numbered.*

Men are placed under the divine care in a yet more excellent way, so that in comparison with them the Apostle could ask: *Is it for oxen that God is concerned?* (1 Cor 9:9). The meaning is not that God has no concern at all for such animals, but that he does not take care of them in the same way he does of men, whom he punishes or rewards in accordance with their good or evil actions, and whom he foreordains to eternal life. This is why, in the words quoted from Matthew, our Lord says: *Even the hairs of your head are all numbered,* thus indicating that everything belonging to man is to be recovered at the resurrection.

---

14. *In Matthaeum,* hom. XIX, 4.

Et ex hoc omnis diffidentia a nobis debet excludi, unde et ibidem subdit: *nolite ergo timere. Multis passeribus pluris estis vos.* Et propter hoc, ut supra dictum est, in Psal. XXXV, 8, dicitur: *filii hominum in tegmine alarum tuarum sperabunt.*

Et quamvis propter specialem curam omnibus hominibus Deus dicatur propinquus esse, specialissime tamen dicitur esse propinquus bonis qui ei fide et dilectione appropinquare nituntur, secundum illud Iac. IV, 8: *appropinquate Deo et appropinquabit vobis*; unde in Psal. CXLIV, v. 18, dicitur: *prope est dominus omnibus invocantibus eum, omnibus invocantibus eum in veritate.* Nec solum eis appropinquat, sed etiam eos per gratiam inhabitat, secundum illud Ier. XIV, 9: *tu in nobis es domine.*

Et ideo ad sanctorum spem augendam dicitur: *qui es in caelis,* idest *in sanctis,* ut Augustinus exponit. Tantum enim, ut ipse dicit, spiritualiter interesse videtur inter iustos et peccatores, quantum corporaliter inter caelum et terram. Huius rei significandae gratia orantes ad orientem convertimur, unde caelum surgit. Ex quo etiam spes sanctis augetur et orandi fiducia non solum ex propinquitate divina, sed etiam ex dignitate quam sunt consecuti a Deo, qui eos per Christum caelos fecit, secundum illud Isai. LI, 16: *ut plantes caelos, et fundes terram.* Qui enim eos caelos fecit, bona eis caelestia non negabit.

Consequently, all diffidence should be banished from our lives. For as our Lord adds in the same context: *Fear not, therefore; you are of more value than many sparrows* (Matt 10:31). This clarifies the passage we called attention to above: *The children of men take refuge in the shadow of thy wings* (Ps 36 [35]:7).

Although God is said to be near to all men by reason of his special care over them, he is exceptionally close to the good who strive to draw near to him in faith and love, as we are assured in James 4:8: *Draw near to God, and he will draw near to you.* Confirmation of this is found in Psalm 145 [144]:18: *The Lord is near to all who call upon him: to all who call upon him in truth.* Indeed, he not only draws near to them: he even dwells in them through grace, as is intimated in Jeremiah 14:9: *You, O Lord, are in the midst of us.*

Therefore, to increase the hope of the saints, we are bidden to say: *who art in heaven,* that is, *in the saints,* as Augustine explains.[15] For, as the same doctor adds, the spiritual distance between the just and sinners seems to be as great as the spatial distance between heaven and earth. To symbolize this idea, we turn toward the east when we pray, because it is in that direction that heaven rises. The hope of the saints and their confidence in prayer are increased by the divine nearness, and also by the dignity they have received from God, who through Christ has caused them to be heavens, as is indicated in Isaiah 51:16: *That you might plant the heavens and found the earth.* He who has made them heavens will not withhold heavenly goods from them.

CHAPTER 7

Of the objects and reason of hope

His praemissis, ex quibus homines spem de Deo concipiunt, oportet considerare quae sunt ea quae a Deo sperare debemus. Ubi considerandum est, quod spes desiderium praesupponit: unde ad hoc quod aliquid sit sperandum, primo requiritur quod sit desideratum. Quae enim non desiderantur, sperari non dicuntur, sed timeri vel etiam despici. Secundo oportet quod id quod speratur, possibile esse aestimetur ad consequendum, et hoc spes supra desiderium addit: potest enim homo desiderare etiam ea quae non aestimat se posse adipisci, sed horum spes esse non potest. Tertio requiritur quod id quod sperandum est, sit aliquid arduum, nam ea quae parva sunt, magis despicimus quam speremus, vel si ea desideramus, quasi in promptu ea habentes,

Having treated of the truths that lead men to hope in God, we must go on to inquire what are the blessings we ought to hope to receive from him. In this connection we should observe that hope presupposes desire. Before a thing can be hoped for, it must first be desired. Things that are not desired are not said to be objects of hope; rather, they are feared or even despised. Second, we must judge that what is hoped for is possible to obtain; hope includes this factor over and above desire. True, a man can desire things he does not believe he is able to attain; but he cannot cherish hope with regard to such objects. Third, hope necessarily implies the idea that the good hoped for is hard to get: trifles are the object of contempt rather than of hope. Or, if we desire certain things and have them, as it were, to hand, we

---

15. *de Sermone Domini in monte,* II, 5.

non videmur ea sperare quasi futura, sed habere quasi praesentia.

Ulterius autem considerandum est, quod arduorum quae quis se sperat adepturum, quaedam aliquis se sperat adipisci per alium, quaedam vero per se ipsum. Inter quae hoc differre videtur, quod ad ea obtinenda quae per se homo consequi sperat, conatum propriae virtutis adhibet: ad ea vero obtinenda quae se ab alio consequi sperat, interponit petitionem: et si quidem ab homine illud se adipisci sperat, vocatur simplex petitio; si autem sperat illud obtinere a Deo, vocatur oratio, quae, ut Damascenus dicit, *est petitio decentium a Deo.*

Non autem ad virtutem spei pertinet spes quam habet aliquis de seipso, nec etiam quam habet de alio homine, sed solum spes quam habet de Deo, unde dicitur Ierem. XVII, 5: *maledictus homo qui confidit in homine, et ponit carnem brachium suum*, et post subditur: *benedictus homo qui confidit in domino, et erit dominus fiducia eius.* Sic igitur ea quae dominus in sua oratione petenda esse docuit, ostenduntur homini esse consideranda possibilia, et tamen ardua, ut ad ea non humana virtute, sed divino auxilio perveniatur.

are not deemed to hope for them as future goods, but to possess them as present to us.

We should further note that among the difficult things a person hopes to obtain, there are some he hopes to get through the good offices of another, and some that he hopes to acquire through his own efforts. The difference between these two classes of goods seems to come to this: to obtain the things he hopes to acquire by himself, a man employs the resources of his own power; to obtain what he hopes to receive from another, he has recourse to petition. If he hopes to receive such a benefit from a man, his request is called simple petition; if he hopes to obtain a favor from God, it is called prayer, which, as Damascene says, *is a petition addressed to God for suitable goods.*[16]

However, the hope a man places in his own powers or in another man does not pertain to the virtue of hope; that virtue is limited to the hope he has in God. Hence we are told in Jeremiah 17:5: *Cursed is the man who trusts in man, and makes flesh his arm*; and a little farther on: *Blessed be the man who trusts in the Lord, and the Lord shall be his confidence.* This shows us that the goods our Lord teaches us to ask for in his prayer are to be regarded as possible, yet not easy to get; access to them is afforded by God's help and not by human power.

CHAPTER 8

The first petition: we are taught to desire that the knowledge of God begun in us would be perfected

Oportet igitur considerare desiderii ordinem ex caritate prodeuntem, ut secundum hoc etiam sperandorum et petendorum a Deo ordo accipi possit. Habet autem hoc ordo caritatis ut Deus super omnia diligatur, et ideo primum desiderium nostrum movet caritas ad ea quae sunt Dei. Sed cum desiderium sit boni futuri, Deo autem, secundum quod in se consideratur, nihil in futurum adveniat, sed aeternaliter eodem modo se habeat, desiderium nostrum non potest ferri ad ea quae Dei sunt prout in seipsis considerantur, ut scilicet Deus aliqua bona obtineat quae non habet. Sic autem ad ipsa fertur nostra dilectio, ut ea tanquam existentia amemus. Potest tamen hoc desiderari de Deo ut in opinione et reverentia omnium magnificetur, qui in seipso semper magnus existit.

Hoc autem non est tanquam impossibile reputandum. Cum enim ad hoc factus sit homo, ut magnitudinem divinam cognoscat, si ad eam percipiendam

In this connection we must heed the order of desire as regulated by charity, so that a corresponding order of goods to be hoped and asked for from God may be established. The order of charity requires us to love God above all things. And so charity moves our first desire in the direction of the things that are of God. But desire has to do with future good, and nothing in the future can accrue to God, considered as he is in himself, since he is eternally the same. Therefore, our desire cannot bear on things that belong to God as they are considered in themselves: we may not entertain the idea that God can acquire some goods he does not already possess. Rather, our love regards these goods in such a way that we love them as existing. However, we can desire, with respect to God, that he who exists forever great in himself, may be magnified in the thoughts and reverence of all men.

This is not to be dismissed as impossible. For, since man was made for the very purpose of knowing God's greatness, he would seem to have been created in vain if he were un-

16. *de Fide orthodoxa*, III, 24.

pervenire non possit, videretur in vanum constitutus esse, contra id quod in Psal. LXXXVIII, 48, dicitur: *numquid enim vane constituisti omnes filios hominum?* Esset quoque inane naturae desiderium, quo omnes naturaliter desiderant aliquid cognoscere de divinis, unde nullus est qui Dei cognitione totaliter privetur, secundum illud Iob XXXVI, 25: *omnes homines vident eum.* Est tamen hoc arduum, ut omnem facultatem humanam excedat, secundum illud Iob XXXVI, 26: *ecce Deus magnus, vincens scientiam nostram.*

Unde cognitio divinae magnitudinis et bonitatis hominibus provenire non potest nisi per gratiam revelationis divinae, secundum illud Matth. XI, 27: *nemo novit filium nisi pater, neque patrem quis novit nisi filius, et cui voluerit filius revelare.* Unde Augustinus super Ioannem dicit: *Deum nullus cognoscit, si non se indicat ipse qui novit.*

Indicat se quippe Deus aliqualiter hominibus naturali quadam cognitione cognoscendum per hoc quod hominibus lumen rationis infundit, et creaturas visibiles condidit, in quibus bonitatis et sapientiae ipsius aliqualiter relucent vestigia, secundum illud Rom. I, 19: *quod notum est Dei,* idest quod cognoscibile est de Deo per naturalem rationem, *manifestum est illis,* scilicet gentilibus hominibus: *Deus enim illis revelavit,* scilicet per lumen rationis, et per creaturas quas condidit, unde subdit: *invisibilia enim ipsius a creatura mundi per ea quae facta sunt, intellecta conspiciuntur, sempiterna quoque eius virtus et divinitas.*

Ista tamen cognitio imperfecta est, quia nec ipsa creatura perfecte ab homine conspici potest, et etiam creatura deficit a perfecta Dei repraesentatione, quia virtus huius causae in infinitum excedit effectum, unde dicitur Iob XI, 7: *forsitan vestigia Dei comprehendes, et usque ad perfectum omnipotentem reperies?* Et Iob XXVI, 25, postquam dixit: *omnes homines vident eum:* subdit: *unusquisque intuetur procul.*

Ex huius autem cognitionis imperfectione consecutum est ut homines a veritate discedentes diversimode circa cognitionem Dei errarent, intantum quod sicut apostolus dicit Roman. I, 21–22 *quidam evanuerunt in cogitationibus suis, et obscuratum est insipiens cor eorum: dicentes enim se esse sapientes, stulti facti sunt, et mutaverunt gloriam incorruptibilis Dei in similitudinem corruptibilis hominis, et volucrum et quadrupedum et serpentium.* Et ideo ut ab hoc errore homines Deus revocaret, expressius notitiam suam hominibus dedit in veteri lege, per quam homines ad cultum unius Dei revocantur, secundum illud Deuter. VI, 4: *audi Israel, dominus Deus tuus unus est.* Sed haec de Deo cognitio erat figurarum obscuritatibus implicita, et infra

able to attain to the perception of this attribute, contrary to what is said in Psalm 89 [88]:47: *For what vanity thou hast created all the sons of men?* If this were the case, the desire of nature, whereby all men naturally desire to know something of the divine perfections, would be fruitless. Indeed, no man is completely deprived of knowledge of God, as we are taught in Job 36:25: *All men see him.* Yet such knowledge of God is hard to obtain; indeed, it is beyond all human power, according to Job 36:26: *Behold, God is great, exceeding our knowledge.*

Accordingly, knowledge of God's greatness and goodness cannot come to men except through the grace of divine revelation, as we are told in Matthew 11:27: *No one knows the Son except the Father, and no one knows the Father except the Son and any one to whom the Son chooses to reveal him.* Hence Augustine says, in his commentary on John, that *no one knows God unless he who knows manifests himself.*[17]

To some extent God makes himself known to men through a certain natural knowledge, by imbuing them with the light of reason and by giving existence to visible creatures, in which are reflected some glimmerings of his goodness and wisdom, as we read in Romans 1:19: *That which is known of God,* that is, what is knowable about God by natural reason, *is plain to them,* namely, is disclosed to pagan peoples. *Because God has shown it to them* through the light of reason and through the creatures he has put in the world. The Apostle adds: *Ever since the creation of the world his invisible nature, namely, his eternal power and deity, has been clearly perceived in the things that have been made.*

But this knowledge is imperfect, because not even creatures can be perfectly comprehended by man, and also because creatures are unable to represent God perfectly, since the excellence of the cause infinitely surpasses its effect. Therefore, in Job 11:7 the question is put: *Can you comprehend the deep things of God? Can you find out the limit of the Almighty?* And in Job 36:25, after affirming, *All men see him,* the speaker adds, *Everyone gazes from afar.*

As a result of the imperfection of this knowledge, it happened that men, wandering from the truth, erred in various ways concerning the knowledge of God, to such an extent that, as the Apostle says in Romans 1:21–22, *Some became vain in their thoughts, and their foolish heart was darkened; for, professing themselves to be wise, they became fools, and they changed the glory of the incorruptible God into the likeness of the image of a corruptible man and of birds and of four-footed beasts and of creeping things.* To recall men from this error, God gave them a clearer knowledge of himself in the Old Law, through which men were brought back to the worship of the one God. Thus the truth is announced in Deuteronomy 6:4: *Hear, O Israel: The Lord our God is one Lord.* But this information about God was wrapped up

---

17. *In Joannis Evangelium,* LVIII, 3.

unius Iudaicae gentis terminos clausa, secundum illud Psal. LXXV, 1: *notus in Iudaea Deus, in Israel magnum nomen eius.*

Ut ergo toti humano generi vera Dei cognitio proveniret, verbum suae virtutis unigenitum Deus pater misit in mundum, ut per eum totus mundus ad veram cognitionem divini nominis perveniret, et hoc quidem ipse dominus facere inchoavit in suis discipulis, secundum illud Ioan. XVII, 6: *manifestavi nomen tuum hominibus quos dedisti mihi de mundo.* Nec in hoc terminabatur eius intentio ut illi soli deitatis haberent notitiam, sed ut per eos divulgaretur in mundum universum, unde postea subdit: *ut mundus credat quia tu me misisti.* Quod quidem per apostolos et successores eorum continue agit, dum ad Dei notitiam per eos homines adducuntur, quousque per totum mundum nomen Dei sanctum et celebre habeatur, sicut praedictum est Mal. I, v. 11: *ab ortu solis usque ad occasum magnum est nomen meum in gentibus, et in omni loco sacrificatur et offertur nomini meo oblatio munda.*

Ut igitur id quod inchoatum est, ad consummationem perveniat, petimus dicentes: *sanctificetur nomen tuum.* Quod, ut Augustinus dicit, *non sic petitur quasi non sit sanctum Dei nomen, sed ut sanctum habeatur ab omnibus, idest, ita innotescat Deus, ut non aestimetur aliquid sanctius.* Inter alia vero indicia quibus sanctitas Dei manifestatur hominibus, evidentissimum signum est sanctitas hominum, qui ex divina inhabitatione sanctificantur. Ut enim Gregorius Nyssenus dicit, *quis est tam bestialis, qui videns in credentibus vitam puram, non glorificet nomen invocatum in tali vita?* Secundum illud quod apostolus dicit I Cor. XIV, 24: *si omnes prophetent, intret autem quis infidelis vel idiota, convincitur ab omnibus;* et postea subdit: *et ita cadens in faciem, adorabit Deum, pronuntians, quod vere Deus in vobis sit.*

Et ideo, sicut Chrysostomus dicit, in hoc quod dicit, *sanctificetur nomen tuum,* rogare etiam iubet orantem per nostram glorificari vitam, ac si dicat: ita fac nos vivere, ut per nos te universi glorificent. Sic autem per nos Deus sanctificatur in mentibus aliorum, inquantum nos sanctificamur per ipsum: unde dicendo, *sanctificetur nomen tuum,* optamus, sicut dicit Cyprianus, ut *nomen eius sanctificetur in nobis.* Quia enim Christus dicit, *sancti estote, quia ego sanctus sum,* id petimus ut qui in Baptismo sanctificati sumus, in eo quod esse

in the obscurities of figurative language, and was confined within the limits of one nation, the Jewish people, as is indicated in Psalm 75 [74]:2: *In Judea God is known; his name is great in Israel.*

In order that true knowledge of God might spread throughout the whole human race, God the Father sent the only-begotten Word of his majesty into the world, that through him the entire world might come to a true knowledge of the divine name. Our Lord himself began this work among his disciples, as he tells us in John 17:6: *I have manifested your name to the men whom you gave me out of the world.* But his intention in imparting knowledge of the Deity was not limited to the disciples; he wished this knowledge to be promulgated through them to the whole world. This is why he adds the prayer: *that the world may believe that you have sent me* (John 17:21). He carries on his task without intermission through the apostles and their successors; by their ministry men are brought to the knowledge of God, to the end that the name of God may be held in benediction and honor throughout the entire world, as was foretold in Malachi 1:11: *From the rising of the sun to its setting my name is great among the nations, and in every place incense is offered to my name, and a pure offering.*

When we say in our prayer, *hallowed be Your name,* we ask that the work thus begun may be brought to completion. *In making this petition,* says St. Augustine, *we do not mean to imply that the name of God is not holy, but we ask that it may be regarded by all men as holy; that is, that God may become so well known that men will not judge anything to be holier.*[18] Among the various indications that make the holiness of God known to men, the most convincing sign is the holiness of men, who are sanctified by the divine indwelling. Gregory of Nyssa asks: *Who is so bereft of the finer sensibilities as not, on beholding the spotless life of believers, to glorify the name that is invoked by those who lead such a life?*[19] The Apostle speaks in like vein, in 1 Corinthians 14:24–25. After saying: *If all prophesy, and an unbeliever or outsider enters, he is convicted by all,* he adds: *and so, falling on his face, he will worship God and declare that God is really among you.*

Therefore, as Chrysostom points out, in teaching us the words, *hallowed be Your name,* our Lord also bids us, when we pray, to ask that God may be glorified by our lives, and the sense of the prayer is this: *grant us so to live, that all men may glorify You through us.*[20] God is sanctified or hallowed in the minds of other men through us to the extent that we are sanctified by him. Hence when we say: *hallowed be Your name,* we pray, as Cyprian remarks, that *God's name may be hallowed in us.*[21] Following the lead of Christ, who says, *Be holy, because I am holy,* we beg that we, who have been

---

18. *De sermone Domini in monte,* II, 5.
19. *De oratione dominica,* III.
20. *In Matthaeum,* hom. XIX, 4.
21. *Liber de oratione dominica,* XII.19.

coepimus perseveremus. Quotidie etiam deprecamur ut sanctificemur, ut qui quotidie delinquimus, delicta nostra sanctificatione assidua purgemus.

Ideo autem haec petitio primo ponitur, quia, sicut Chrysostomus dicit, digna est Deum deprecantis oratio nihil ante patris gloriam petere, sed omnia laudi eius postponere.

sanctified in baptism, may persevere in the state in which we began. Furthermore, we pray daily to be sanctified in order that we, who daily fall, may wash away our sins by a constant process of purification.

This petition is put first because, as Chrysostom observes, he who would offer a worthy prayer to God should ask for nothing before the Father's glory, but should make everything come after the praise of him.

CHAPTER 9

The second petition: prayer for participation in God's glory

Post desiderium autem et petitionem divinae gloriae, consequens est ut homo appetat et requirat particeps gloriae divinae fieri. Et ideo secunda petitio ponitur: *adveniat regnum tuum.* Circa quam, sicut et in praemissa petitione, oportet primo considerare, quod regnum Dei convenienter desideretur. Secundo vero quod ad id adipiscendum homo possit pervenire. Tertio vero quod ad illud pertingere non possit propria virtute, sed solo auxilio divinae gratiae. Et sic quarto considerandum est, quomodo regnum Dei advenire petamus.

Est igitur circa primum considerandum quod unicuique rei naturaliter appetibile est proprium bonum, unde et bonum convenienter definiunt esse quod omnia appetunt. Proprium autem bonum uniuscuiusque rei est id quo res illa perficitur: dicimus enim unamquamque rem bonam, ex eo quod propriam perfectionem attingit. Intantum vero bonitate caret, inquantum propria perfectione caret, unde consequens est ut unaquaeque res suam perfectionem appetat, unde et homo naturaliter appetit perfici. Et cum multi sint gradus perfectionis humanae, illud praecipue et principaliter in eius appetitum naturaliter cadit, quod ad ultimam eius perfectionem spectat. Hoc autem bonum hoc indicio cognoscitur, quod naturale desiderium hominis in eo quiescit. Cum enim naturale desiderium hominis non tendat nisi in bonum proprium, quod in aliqua perfectione consistit, consequens est quod quamdiu aliquid desiderandum restat, nondum pervenit homo ad ultimam perfectionem suam.

Dupliciter autem adhuc restat aliquid desiderandum. Uno modo, quando id quod desideratur, propter aliquid aliud quaeritur, unde oportet quod eo obtento adhuc desiderium non quiescat, sed feratur in aliud. Alio modo, quando non sufficit ad obtinendum id quod homo desiderat, sicut modicus cibus non sufficit ad sustentationem naturae, unde naturalem appetitum non satiat.

After desiring and praying for the glory of God, man is led to desire and ask that he may be given a share in divine glory. And so the second petition is worded: *your kingdom come.* In discussing this petition, we shall follow the same procedure as we observed in treating of the preceding petition. We shall consider, first, that we do right to desire the kingdom of God; second, that man can attain to the possession of this kingdom; third, that he can attain to it not by his own powers, but only with the help of divine grace. And then, in the fourth place, we must inquire into the sense in which we pray that the kingdom of God may come.

As to the first point, we should note that to every being its own good is naturally desirable. Hence good is fittingly defined as that which all desire. The proper good of any being is that whereby it is brought to perfection: we say that a thing is good inasmuch as it reaches its proper perfection. On the other hand, a thing lacks goodness so far as it is lacking in its proper perfection. Consequently, each thing seeks its own perfection, and so man, too, naturally desires to be perfected. And, since there are many degrees of human perfection, that good chiefly and primarily comes under man's desire which looks to his ultimate perfection. This good is recognized by the sure sign that man's natural desire comes to rest in it. For, since man's natural desire always inclines toward his own good which consists in some perfection, the consequence is that as long as something remains to be desired, man has not yet reached his final perfection.

Something can thus remain to be desired in two ways. First, when the thing desired is sought for the sake of something else; when it is obtained, desire cannot cease, but must be borne along toward that other object. Second, when a thing does not suffice to provide what man desires; for instance, a meager portion of food is not enough to sustain nature, and so does not satisfy natural appetite.

Illud ergo bonum quod homo primo et principaliter desiderat, tale debet esse ut non quaeratur propter aliud, et sufficiat homini. Hoc autem bonum communiter felicitas nominatur, inquantum est bonum hominis principale: per hoc enim aliquos felices esse dicimus, quod eis credimus bene esse. Vocatur etiam beatitudo, inquantum excellentiam designat. Potest et pax vocari, inquantum quietat, nam quies appetitus pax interior esse videtur, unde in Psal. CXLVII, 3, dicitur: *qui posuit fines tuos pacem.*

Sic igitur apparet quod in corporalibus bonis, hominis felicitas vel beatitudo esse non potest. Primo quidem, quia non sunt propter se quaesita, sed naturaliter propter aliud desiderantur: conveniunt enim homini ratione sui corporis. Corpus autem hominis ordinatur ad animam sicut ad finem, tum quia corpus est instrumentum animae moventis, omne autem instrumentum est propter artem quae utitur eo, tum etiam quia corpus comparatur ad animam sicut materia ad formam. Forma autem est finis materiae, sicut et actus potentiae. Ex quo consequens est ut neque in divitiis neque in honoribus neque in sanitate aut pulchritudine, neque in rebus aliquibus huiusmodi ultima hominis felicitas consistat.

Secundo, quia impossibile est ut corporalia bona sufficiant homini; quod multipliciter apparet. Uno quidem modo, quia cum in homine sit duplex vis appetitiva, scilicet intellectiva et sensitiva, et per consequens desiderium duplex, desiderium intellectivi appetitus principaliter in bona intelligibilia tendit, ad quae bona corporalia non attingunt. Alio modo quia bona corporalia tanquam infima in rerum ordine, non collectam sed dispersam recipiunt bonitatem, ita scilicet ut hoc habeat hanc bonitatis rationem, puta delectationem, illud aliam, puta corporis salubritatem, et sic de aliis. Unde in nullo eorum appetitus humanus, qui naturaliter in bonum universale tendit, sufficientiam potest invenire. Sed neque in multis eorum, quantumcumque multiplicentur, quia deficiunt ab infinitate universalis boni: unde dicitur Eccle. V, 9: quod *avarus non implebitur pecunia.* Tertio quia cum homo apprehendat per intellectum bonum universale, quod neque loco neque tempore circumscribitur, consequens est quod appetitus humanus bonum desideret secundum convenientiam ad apprehensionem intellectus, quod tempore non circumscribatur: unde naturale est homini ut perpetuam stabilitatem desideret, quae quidem non potest inveniri in corporalibus rebus, quae sunt corruptioni et multiplici subiectae variationi. Unde conveniens est quod in corporalibus bonis appetitus humanus non inveniat sufficientiam quam requirit. Sic igitur in eis non potest esse ultima felicitas hominis.

Consequently, that good which man primarily and principally desires must be of such a nature that it is not sought for the sake of something else and that it satisfies man. This good is commonly called 'happiness,' inasmuch as it is man's foremost good: we say that certain people are happy because we believe that everything goes well with them. It is also known as 'beatitude,' a word that stresses its excellence. It can also be called 'peace,' so far as it brings quiet; for cessation of appetite appears to imply interior peace. This is indicated in the words of Psalm 147:14: *He makes peace in your borders.*

We see clearly that man's happiness or beatitude cannot consist in material goods. The first reason for this is that such goods are not sought for their own sake, but are naturally desired because of something else. They are suitable for man by reason of his body. But man's body is subordinated to his soul as to its end. For the body is the instrument of the soul that moves it, and every instrument exists for the good of the art that employs it. Furthermore, the body is related to the soul as matter is related to form. But form is the end of matter, just as act is the end of potency. Consequently, man's final happiness does not consist in riches or in honors or in health and beauty or in any goods of this kind.

The second reason why happiness is not to be found in material goods is that such goods cannot satisfy man. This is clear on many scores. In the first place, man has a twofold appetitive power, one intellectual, the other sensitive. Consequently, he has a twofold desire. But the desire of the intellectual appetite veers chiefly toward intelligible goods, which exceed the competency of material goods. Second, material goods, as being the lowest in the order of nature, do not contain all goodness but possess only a portion of goodness, so that one object has this particular aspect of goodness, for example, the power to give pleasure, while another object has a different advantage, for instance, the power to cause bodily well-being, and so on of the rest. In none of them can the human appetite, which naturally tends toward universal good, find complete satisfaction. Nor can full satisfaction be found even in a large number of such goods, no matter how much they may be multiplied, for they fall short of the infinity of universal good. Thus we are assured in Ecclesiastes 5:10 that *he who loves money will not be satisfied with money.* Third, since man by his intellect apprehends the universal good that is not circumscribed by space or time, the human appetite, consistently with the apprehension of the intellect, desires a good that is not circumscribed by time. Hence man naturally desires perpetual stability. But this cannot be found in material things, which are subject to corruption and to many kinds of change. Therefore, the human appetite cannot find the sufficiency it needs in material goods. Accordingly, man's ultimate happiness cannot consist in such goods.

Sed quia vires sensitivae corporeas operationes habent, utpote per organa corporea operantes, quae circa corporalia operantur, consequens est quod neque in operationibus sensitivae partis ultima hominis felicitas consistat, puta in quibuscumque delectationibus carnis. Habet etiam intellectus humanus aliquam circa corporalia operationem, dum et corpora cognoscit homo per speculativum intellectum, et res corporales dispensat per practicum. Et sic consequens fit quod nec in propria ipsa operatione intellectus speculativi vel practici quae corporalibus rebus intendit, ultima hominis felicitas, et perfectio possit poni.

Similiter etiam nec in operatione intellectus humani qua in se ipsam anima reflectitur, duplici ratione. Primo quidem quia anima secundum se considerata non est beata, alioquin non oporteret eam operari propter beatitudinem acquirendam. Non igitur beatitudinem acquirit ex hoc solo quod sibi intendit. Secundo, quia felicitas est ultima perfectio hominis, ut supra dictum est. Cum autem perfectio animae in propria operatione eius consistat, consequens est ut ultima perfectio eius attendatur secundum optimam eius operationem, quae quidem est secundum optimum obiectum, nam operationes secundum obiecta specificantur. Non autem anima est optimum in quod sua operatio tendere potest. Intelligit enim aliquid esse melius se, unde impossibile est quod ultima beatitudo hominis consistat in operatione qua sibi intendit vel quibuscumque aliis superioribus substantiis, dummodo eis sit aliquid melius, in quod humanae animae operatio tendere possit. Tendit autem operatio hominis in quodcumque bonum, quia universale bonum est quod homo desiderat, cum per intellectum universale bonum apprehendat: unde ad quemcumque gradum se porrigit bonum, aliqualiter extenditur operatio intellectus humani, et per consequens voluntatis. Bonum autem summe invenitur in Deo, qui per essentiam suam bonus est, et omnis bonitatis principium: unde consequens est ut ultima hominis perfectio et finale bonum ipsius sit in hoc quod Deo inhaeret, secundum illud Psal. LXXII, 28: *mihi adhaerere Deo bonum est.*

Hoc etiam manifeste apparet, si quis ad ceterarum rerum participationem inspiciat. Omnes enim singulares homines huius praedicationis recipiunt veritatem, per hoc quod ipsam essentiam speciei participant. Nullus autem eorum ex hoc dicitur homo quod similitudinem participet alterius hominis, sed ex eo solo quod participat essentiam speciei, ad quam tamen participandam unus inducit alium per viam generationis, pater scilicet filium. Beatitudo autem, sive felicitas, nihil est aliud quam bonum perfectum. Oportet igitur per solam participationem divinae beatitudinis, quae est bonitas hominis, omnes beatitudinis participes esse beatos, quamvis unus per alium ad tendendum ad

Moreover, since the sense faculties have bodily activities (inasmuch as they operate through bodily organs which exercise their functions on corporeal objects), man's ultimate happiness cannot consist in the activities of his sensitive nature: for example, in certain pleasures of the flesh. The human intellect, too, has some activity with reference to corporeal things, for man knows bodies by his speculative intellect and manages corporeal things by his practical intellect. And so man's ultimate happiness and perfection cannot be placed in the proper activity of the speculative intellect or of the practical intellect that deals with material things.

Likewise, such happiness is not found in that activity of the human intellect whereby the soul reflects on itself. There are two reasons for this. In the first place the soul, considered in its own nature, is not beatified. Otherwise it would not have to labor for the attainment of beatitude. Therefore, it does not acquire beatitude from the mere contemplation of itself. In the second place, happiness is the ultimate perfection of man, as was stated above. Since the perfection of the soul consists in its proper activity, its ultimate perfection is to be looked for on the plane of its best activity, and this is determined by its best object, for activities are specified according to their objects. But the soul is not the best object to which its activity can tend. For it is aware that something exists that is better than itself. Hence man's ultimate beatitude cannot consist in the activity whereby he makes himself or any of the other higher substances the object of his intellection, as long as there is something better to which the action of the human soul can turn. Man's activity may extend to any good whatever, for the universal good is what man desires, since he apprehends universal good with his intellect. Therefore, whatever may be the degree to which goodness extends, the action of the human intellect, and hence also of the will, reaches out toward it in some way. But good is found supremely in God, who is good by his very essence, and is the source of every good. Consequently, man's ultimate perfection and final good consist in union with God, according to Psalm 72 [71]:28: *It is good for me to adhere to my God.*

This truth is clearly perceived if we examine the way other things participate in being. Individual men all truly receive the predication 'man,' because they share in the very essence of the species. None of them is said to be a man on the ground that he shares in the likeness of some other man, but only because he shares in the essence of the species. This is so even though one man brings another to such participation by way of generation, as a father does with regard to his son. Now beatitude or happiness is nothing else than perfect good. Therefore, all who share in beatitude can be happy only by participation in the divine beatitude, which is man's essential goodness, even though one man may be helped by another in his progress toward beatitude. This is

beatitudinem adiuvetur. Unde Augustinus dicit in libro *de Vera religione* quod neque nos videndo angelos beati sumus, sed videndo veritatem, qua ipsos diligimus, et his congratulamur.

Contingit autem humanam mentem ferri in Deum dupliciter: uno modo per se, alio modo per aliud. Per se quidem, puta cum in seipso videtur, et per seipsum amatur. Per aliud autem, cum ex creaturis ipsius, animus elevatur in Deum, secundum illud Rom. I, 20: *Invisibilia Dei per ea quae facta sunt, intellecta conspiciuntur.*

Non est autem possibile ut perfecta beatitudo consistat in hoc quod aliquis per aliud in Deum tendit. Primo quidem, quia cum beatitudo significet omnium humanorum actuum finem, non potest vera beatitudo et perfecta consistere in eo quod habet rationem non quidem termini, sed magis mutationis in finem. Quod autem Deus per aliud agnoscatur et ametur, quodam humanae mentis motu agitur, inquantum per unum in aliud devenitur. Non est ergo in hoc vera et perfecta beatitudo.

Secundo, quia si in hoc quod mens humana Deo inhaereat, eius beatitudo consistat, consequens est ut perfecta beatitudo perfectam inhaesionem ad Deum requirat. Non autem est possibile ut per aliquam creaturam mens humana Deo perfecte inhaereat neque per cognitionem neque per amorem. Quaelibet enim forma creata in infinitum deficiens est a repraesentatione divinae essentiae. Sicut ergo non est possibile ut per formam inferioris ordinis cognoscantur ea quae sunt superioris ordinis, puta per corpus spiritualis substantia, vel per elementum corpus caeleste; ita multo minus possibile est ut per aliquam formam creatam Dei essentia cognoscatur. Sed sicut per considerationem inferiorum corporum superiorum naturas negative percipimus, puta quod non sunt gravia neque levia, et per corporum considerationem negative de angelis concipimus quod sunt immateriales vel incorporei, ita etiam per creaturas de Deo non cognoscimus quid est, sed potius quid non est. Similiter etiam quaecumque creaturae bonitas quoddam minimum est respectu bonitatis divinae, quae est bonitas infinita: unde bonitates in rebus provenientes a Deo, quae sunt Dei beneficia, non sublevant mentem usque ad perfectum Dei amorem. Non est igitur possibile quod vera et perfecta beatitudo consistat in hoc quod mens Deo per aliud inhaereat.

Tertio, quia secundum rectum ordinem minus nota, per ea quae sunt magis nota, cognoscuntur; et similiter ea quae sunt minus bona per ea quae sunt magis bona amantur. Quia igitur Deus, qui est prima veritas et summa bonitas, secundum se summe cognoscibilis et

why Augustine says in his book, *de Vera religione*, that we are beatified not by beholding the angels, but by seeing the Truth in which we love the angels and are happy along with them. [22]

Man's spirit is carried up to God in two ways: by God himself, and by some other thing. It is borne up to God by God himself when God is seen in himself and is loved for himself. It is raised up by something else when the soul is elevated to God by his creatures, according to Romans 1:20: *The invisible things of God . . . are clearly seen, being understood by the things that are made.*

Perfect beatitude cannot consist in a person's movement toward God through the agency of something else. For, first, since beatitude denotes the ultimate term of all human actions, true and perfect happiness cannot be found in that which is of the nature of change in the direction of the end rather than of a final term. Knowledge and love of God through the medium of something other than God is brought about by a certain movement of the human mind, as it advances through one stage to another. True and perfect beatitude, therefore, is not discovered in this process.

Second, if man's beatitude consists in the adhering of the human mind to God, perfect beatitude must require a perfect adhering to God. But the human mind cannot adhere perfectly to God through the medium of any creature, whether by way of knowledge or by way of love. All created forms fall infinitely short of representing the divine essence. Objects pertaining to a higher order of being cannot be known through a form belonging to a lower order. For example, a spiritual substance cannot be known through a body, and a heavenly body cannot be known through one of the elements. Much less can the essence of God be known through any created form. Yet, just as we gain a negative insight into higher bodies from a study of lower bodies, thus learning, for instance, that they are neither heavy nor light, and just as we conceive a negative idea about angels from a consideration of bodies, judging that they are immaterial or incorporeal, so by examining creatures we come to know not what God is, but rather what he is not. Likewise, any goodness possessed by a creature is a definite minimum in comparison with the divine goodness, which is infinite goodness. Hence the various degrees of goodness emanating from God and discerned in things, which are benefits bestowed by God, fail to raise the mind to a perfect love of God. Therefore, true and perfect beatitude cannot consist in the adherence of the mind to God through some alien medium.

Third, according to right order, things that are less familiar become known through things that are more familiar. Likewise, things that are less good are loved because of their connection with things that possess greater goodness. Consequently, as God is the first truth and supreme

---

22. LV, 110.

amabilis est, hoc naturalis ordo habet ut omnia cognoscantur et amentur per ipsum. Si igitur oportet alicuius mentem in Dei cognitionem et amorem per creaturas perduci, hoc ex eius imperfectione contingit. Nondum ergo consecutus est perfectam beatitudinem, quae omnem imperfectionem excludit.

Relinquitur ergo quod perfecta beatitudo sit in hoc quod mens Deo per se inhaereat cognoscendo et amando. Et quia regis est subditos disponere et gubernare, illud in homine regere dicitur secundum quod cetera disponuntur, unde apostolus monet Rom. VI, 12: *non regnet peccatum in vestro mortali corpore.* Quia igitur ad perfectam beatitudinem requiritur ut ipse Deus per se cognoscatur et ametur, ut per eum animus feratur ad alta, vere et perfecte in bonis Deus regnat, unde dicitur Isai. XLIX, 10: *miserator eorum reget eos, et ad fontes aquarum potabit eos,* scilicet per ipsum in quibuscumque potissimis bonis reficientur.

Est enim considerandum, quod cum intellectus per aliquam speciem seu formam intelligat omne quod novit, sicut etiam visus exterior per formam lapidis lapidem videt, non est possibile quod intellectus Deum in sua essentia videat per aliquam creatam speciem seu formam quasi divinam essentiam repraesentantem. Videmus enim quod per speciem inferioris ordinis rerum non potest repraesentari res superioris ordinis quantum ad suam essentiam: unde fit quod per nullam speciem corporalem potest intelligi spiritualis substantia quantum ad suam essentiam. Cum igitur Deus supergrediatur totum creaturae ordinem, multo magis quam spiritualis substantia excedat ordinem corporalium rerum, impossibile est quod per aliquam speciem corporalem Deus secundum suam essentiam videatur.

Hoc etiam manifeste apparet, si quis consideret quid sit rem aliquam per suam essentiam videre. Non enim essentiam hominis videt qui aliquid eorum quae essentialiter homini conveniunt apprehendit, sicut nec cognoscit essentiam hominis qui cognoscit animal absque rationali. Quidquid autem de Deo dicitur, essentialiter convenit ei. Non est autem possibile quod una creata species repraesentet Deum quantum ad omnia quae de Deo dicuntur. Nam in intellectu creato alia est species per quam apprehendit vitam et sapientiam et iustitiam, et omnia alia huiusmodi, quae sunt Dei essentia. Non est igitur possibile quod intellectus creatus informetur aliqua una specie sic repraesentante divinam essentiam, quod Deus in ea per suam essentiam possit videri. Si autem per multas, deficiet unitas, quae idem est quod Dei essentia. Non est igitur possibile quod intellectus creatus elevari possit ad videndum Deum in seipso

goodness, and is eminently knowable and lovable in himself, the order of nature would require that all things should be known and loved through him. Therefore, if the mind of any person has to be brought to the knowledge and love of God through creatures, this results from his imperfection. Accordingly, such a one has not yet achieved perfect beatitude, which excludes all imperfection.

We conclude, therefore, that perfect beatitude consists in the direct union of the spirit with God in knowledge and love. In the same way that a king has the office of directing and governing his subjects, that tendency is said to predominate in man which is the norm for regulating everything else in him. This is the reason for the Apostle's warning in Romans 6:12: *Let not sin therefore reign in your mortal body.* Accordingly, since the notion of perfect beatitude requires that God be known and loved in himself, so that the soul embraces other objects only through him, God reigns truly and perfectly in the good. Hence we are told in Isaiah 49:10: *He who has mercy on them will lead them, and by springs of water will give them drink.* In other words, they shall be refreshed by him with all the most excellent goods, of whatever kind they may be.

We should recall, further, that the intellect understands all it knows by means of a certain likeness or form; in a similar way the external organ of sight perceives a stone by means of a form of the stone. Consequently, the intellect cannot behold God as he is in his essence by means of a created likeness or form that would represent the divine essence. For we are aware that an object belonging to a higher order of being cannot be represented, so far as its essence is concerned, by a likeness pertaining to a lower order. Thus a spiritual substance cannot, if there is question of its essence, be understood by means of any bodily likeness. And so, as God transcends the whole order of creation much more than a spiritual substance excels the order of material things, he cannot be seen in his essence through the medium of a corporeal likeness.

The same truth is quite evident if we but reflect on what the vision of a thing in its essence implies. He who apprehends some property pertaining essentially to man does not perceive the essence of man, just as a person who knows what an animal is, but does not know what rationality is, fails to understand the essence of man. Any perfection predicated of God belongs to him essentially. But no single created likeness can represent God with respect to all the perfections predicated of him. For in the created intellect the likeness whereby man apprehends the life of God differs from the likeness whereby he apprehends God's wisdom, and so on with regard to justice and all the other perfections that are identical with God's essence. Therefore, the created intellect cannot be informed by a single likeness representing the divine essence in such a way that the essence of God can be seen therein. And if such likenesses are multiplied, they will be lacking in unity, which is iden-

per suam essentiam aliqua una specie creata, vel etiam pluribus. Relinquitur ergo quod oportet, ad hoc quod Deus per suam essentiam videatur ab intellectu creato, quod ipsa divina essentia per seipsam, non per aliam speciem videatur,

et hoc per quandam unionem intellectus creati ad Deum. Unde Dionysius dicit, I capite *de Divinis nomin.*, quod quando beatissimum consequemur finem, Dei apparitione, adimpleti erimus per quandam superintellectualem cognitionem ad Deum. Est autem hoc singulare divinae essentiae ut ei possit intellectus uniri absque omni similitudine, quia et ipsa divina essentia est eius esse, quod nulli alii formae competit.

Unde oportet quod omnis forma sit in intellectu: et ideo si aliqua forma, quae per se existens non potest esse informativa intellectus, puta substantia angeli, cognosci debeat ab intellectu alterius, oportet quod hoc fiat per aliquam eius similitudinem intellectum informantem, quod non requiritur in divina essentia, quae est suum esse.

Sic igitur per ipsam Dei visionem mens beata fit in intelligendo unum cum Deo. Oportet igitur intelligens et intellectum esse quodammodo unum. Et ideo Deo regnante in sanctis, et ipsi etiam cum Deo conregnabunt, et ideo ex eorum persona dicitur Apoc. V, 10: *fecisti nos Deo nostro regnum et sacerdotes, et regnabimus super terram.* Dicitur enim hoc regnum quo Deus regnat in sanctis et sancti cum Deo, regnum caelorum, secundum illud Matth. III, 2: *poenitentiam agite, appropinquavit enim regnum caelorum*: eo modo loquendi quo esse in caelo Deo attribuitur, non quia corporalibus caelis contineatur, sed ut per hoc designetur Dei eminentia super omnem creaturam, sicut caeli eminent super omnem aliam creaturam corpoream, secundum illud Psal. CXII, 4: *excelsus super omnes gentes dominus, et super caelos gloria eius.*

Sic igitur et beatitudo sanctorum regnum caelorum dicitur, non quia eorum remuneratio sit in corporalibus caelis, sed in contemplatione supercaelestis naturae, unde et de angelis dicitur Matth. XVIII, 10: *angeli eorum in caelis semper vident faciem patris mei qui in caelis est.* Unde et Augustinus, in libro *de Sermone domini in monte* dicit, exponens illud quod dicitur Matth. V, 12: *merces vestra copiosa est in caelis: non hic caelos dici puto superiores partes huius visibilis mundi: non enim merces nostra in rebus volubilibus collocanda est; sed in caelis*

tical with God's essence. Consequently, the created intellect cannot be raised so high by a single created likeness, or even by many of them, as to see God as he is in himself, in his own essence. In order, therefore, that God may be seen in his essence by a created intellect, the divine essence must be perceived directly in itself, and not through the medium of some likeness.

Such vision requires a certain union of the created intellect with God. Dionysius observes, in the first chapter of his book, *de Divinis nominibus*, that when we arrive at our most blessed end and God appears, we shall be filled with a superintellectual knowledge of God.[23] The divine essence, however, has this exclusive characteristic, that our intellect can be united to it without the medium of any likeness. The reason is that the divine essence itself is its own existence or esse, which is true of no other form.

Knowledge always requires the presence of some form in the intellect; and so, if any form that exists by itself (for example, the substance of an angel) cannot inform an intellect, and yet is to be known by the intellect of another, such knowledge has to be brought about by some likeness of the thing informing the intellect. But this is not necessary in the case of the divine essence, which is its own existence.

Accordingly, the soul that is beatified by the vision of God is made one with him in understanding. The knower and the known must somehow be one. And so, when God reigns in the saints, they too reign along with God. In their person are uttered the words of Revelation 5:10: *You have made us to our God a kingdom and priests, and we shall reign on the earth.* This kingdom, in which God reigns in the saints and the saints reign with God, is called the kingdom of heaven, according to Matthew 3:2: *Repent, for the kingdom of heaven is at hand.* This is the same manner of speaking as that whereby presence in heaven is ascribed to God, not in the sense that he is housed in the material heavens, but to show forth the eminence of God over every creature, in the way that heaven towers high above every other material creature, as is indicated in Psalm 113 [112]:4: *The Lord is high above all nations, and his glory above the heavens.*

The beatitude of the saints is called the kingdom of heaven, therefore, not because their reward is situated in the material heavens, but because it consists in the contemplation of super-celestial nature. This is also the reason for the statement about the angels in Matthew 18:10: *Their angels always behold the face of my Father who is in heaven.* Hence Augustine, in his explanation of the passage in Matthew 5:12, *Your reward is great in heaven*, says in his book, *de Sermone Domini in monte* I, 5: *I do not think that heaven here means the loftier regions of this visible world. For our re-*

---

23. De Div. Nom. I, 4.

dictum puto in spiritualibus firmamentis, ubi habitat sempiterna iustitia.

Dicitur etiam et hoc finale bonum, quod in Deo consistit vita aeterna, eo modo loquendi quo actio animae vivificantis dicitur vita: unde tot modi vitae distinguuntur, quot sunt genera animae actionum, inter quas suprema est operatio intellectus, et secundum philosophum *actio intellectus est vita.* Et quia actus ex obiecto speciem accipit, inde est quod visio divinitatis vita aeterna nominatur, secundum illud Ioannis XVII, 3: *haec est vita aeterna ut cognoscant te solum Deum verum.*

Hoc etiam finale bonum comprehensio nominatur, secundum illud Philip. III, 12: *sequor autem, si quo modo comprehendam.* Quod quidem non dicitur eo modo loquendi quo comprehensio inclusionem importat: quod enim ab alio includitur, totum et totaliter ab eo continetur. Non est autem possibile quod intellectus creatus Dei essentiam totaliter videat, ita scilicet quod attingat ad completum et perfectum modum visionis divinae, ut scilicet Deum videat quantum visibilis est: est enim Deus visibilis secundum suae veritatis claritatem, quae infinita est, unde infinite visibilis est, quod convenire intellectui creato non potest, cuius est finita virtus in intelligendo. Solus igitur Deus per infinitam virtutem sui intellectus se infinite intelligens, totaliter se intelligendo comprehendit seipsum.

Repromittitur autem sanctis comprehensio prout comprehensionis nomen importat quamdam tentionem. Cum enim aliquis insequitur aliquem, dicitur comprehendere eum, quando potuerit eum manu tenere. Sic igitur *quandiu sumus in corpore,* ut dicitur II Cor. V, 6, *peregrinamur a domino; per fidem enim ambulamus et non per speciem,* et ita in eum tendimus ut in aliquid distans. Sed quando per speciem videbimus, praesentialiter eum in nobismetipsis tenebimus, unde Cant. III, 4, sponsa quaerens quem diligit anima sua, tandem vero eum inveniens dicit: *tenui eum, nec dimittam.*

Habet autem praedictum finale bonum perpetuum et plenum gaudium, unde dominus dicit Ioan. XVI, 24: *petite et accipietis, ut gaudium vestrum plenum sit.* Non potest autem esse plenum gaudium de aliqua creatura, sed de solo Deo, in quo est tota plenitudo bonitatis, unde et dominus dicit servo fideli: *intra in gaudium domini tui,* ut scilicet de domino tuo gaudeas, secundum illud Iob XXII, 26: *super omnipotentem deliciis afflues.* Et quia Deus praecipue de seipso gaudet, dicitur servus fidelis intrare in gaudium domini sui, scilicet inquantum intrat ad gaudium quo dominus eius gaudet, secundum quod

ward . . . is not to be in evanescent things. I think that the expression, 'in heaven,' refers rather to the spiritual firmament, where eternal justice dwells.

This ultimate good, which consists in God, is also called eternal life. The word is used in the sense in which the action of the animating soul is called life. Hence we distinguish as many kinds of life as there are kinds of action performed by the soul, among which the action of the intellect is supreme; and, according to the Philosopher, *the action of the intellect is life.*[24] Furthermore, since an act receives species from its object, the vision of the divinity is called eternal life, as we read in John 17:3: *This is eternal life, that they know thee the only true God.*

The ultimate good is also known as comprehension, a word suggested by Philippians 3:12: *I follow after, if I may by any means comprehend.* The term is not, of course, used in the sense according to which comprehension implies enclosing; for what is enclosed by another is completely contained by it as a whole. The created intellect cannot completely see God's essence, that is, in such a way as to attain to the ultimate and perfect degree of the divine vision, and so to see God to the extent that he is capable of being seen. For God is knowable in a way that is proportionate to the clarity of his truth, and this is infinite. Hence he is infinitely knowable. But infinite knowledge is impossible for a created intellect, whose power of understanding is finite. God alone, therefore, who knows himself infinitely well with the infinite power of his intellect, comprehends himself by completely understanding himself.

Nevertheless, comprehension is promised to the saints, in the sense of the word 'comprehension' that implies a certain grasp. Thus when one man pursues another, he is said to comprehend the latter when he can grasp him with his hand. Accordingly, *while we are in the body,* as the matter is put in 2 Corinthians 5:6–7, *we are away from the Lord, for we walk by faith, not by sight.* And so we press on toward him as toward some distant goal. But when we see him by direct vision we shall hold him present within ourselves. Thus in the Song of Songs 3:4, the spouse seeks him whom her soul loves; and when at last she finds him she says: *I held him, and I will not let him go.*

The ultimate good we have been speaking of contains perpetual and full joy, as our Lord says in John 16:24: *Ask, and you will receive, that your joy may be full.* Full joy, however, can be gained from no creature, but only from God, in whom the entire plenitude of goodness resides. And so our Lord says to the faithful servant in Matthew 25:21: *Enter into the joy of your master,* that you may have the joy of your Lord, as is indicated in Job 22:26: *You will delight yourself in the Almighty.* Since God rejoices most of all in himself, the faithful servant is said to enter into the joy of his Lord inasmuch as he enters into the joy wherein his Lord rejoices, as

---

24. *Metaphysics*, XII, 7, 1072 b 27.

alibi dominus discipulis, Luc. XXII, 29, promittit dicens: *ego dispono vobis, sicut disposuit mihi pater meus regnum, ut edatis et bibatis super mensam meam in regno meo:* non quod in illo finali bono corporalibus cibis sancti utantur, incorruptibiles iam effecti, sed per mensam significatur refectio gaudii quod habet Deus de seipso, et sancti de eo.

Oportet ergo plenitudinem gaudii attendi non solum secundum rem de qua gaudetur, sed secundum dispositionem gaudentis, ut scilicet rem de qua gaudet, praesentem habeat, et totus affectus gaudentis per amorem feratur in gaudii causam. Iam autem ostensum est, quod per visionem divinae essentiae mens creata praesentialiter tenet Deum: ipsa etiam visio totaliter affectum accendit ad divinum amorem. Si enim unumquodque est *amabile inquantum est pulchrum et bonum,* secundum Dionysium *de Divinis nominibus* cap. IV, impossibile est quod Deus, qui est ipsa essentia pulchritudinis et bonitatis, absque amore videatur. Et ideo ex perfecta eius visione sequitur perfectus amor: unde et Gregorius dicit *super Ezech.: amoris ignis qui hic ardere inchoat, cum ipsum quem amat viderit, in amore ipsius amplius ignescit.* Tanto autem maius est gaudium de aliquo praesentialiter habito, quanto magis amatur, unde sequitur quod illud gaudium sit plenum non tantum ex parte rei de qua gaudetur, sed etiam ex parte gaudentis. Et hoc gaudium est humanae beatitudinis consummativum, unde et Augustinus dicit X *Confessionum,* quod beatitudo est *gaudium de veritate.*

Est autem ulterius considerandum, quod quia Deus est ipsa essentia bonitatis, per consequens ipse bonum est omnis boni, unde eo viso omne bonum videtur, secundum quod dominus dicit Moysi, Exod. XXXIII, 19: *ego ostendam tibi omne bonum.* Per consequens igitur eo habito omne bonum habetur, secundum illud Sapient. VII, 11: *venerunt mihi omnia bona pariter cum illa.* Sic igitur in illo finali bono, videndo Deum, habebimus omnium bonorum plenam sufficientiam, unde et fideli servo repromittit dominus Matth. XXIV, 47: quod *super omnia bona sua constituet eum.*

Quia vero malum bono opponitur, necesse est ut ad praesentiam omnis boni malum universaliter excludatur. Non est enim participatio iustitiae cum iniquitate, nec societas lucis ad tenebras, ut dicitur II Corinth. VI, 14. Sic igitur in illo finali bono non solum aderit perfecta sufficientia habentibus omne bonum, sed etiam aderit plena quies et securitas per immunitatem omnis mali, secundum illud Prov. I, 33: *qui me audiet absque terrore requiescet, et abundantia perfruetur, terrore malorum sublato.*

our Lord said on another occasion when he made a promise to his disciples: *As my Father appointed a kingdom for me, so do I appoint for you that you may eat and drink at my table in my kingdom* (Luke 22:29–30). Not that the saints, once they have been made incorruptible, have any use for bodily foods in that final state of good; no, by *table* is meant rather the replenishment of joy that God has in himself and that the saints have from him.

This fullness of joy must be understood not only of the object of the rejoicing, but also with reference to the disposition of him who rejoices. In other words, the object of the rejoicing must be present, and the entire affection of the joyful person must be centered on the cause of the joy. As we have shown, in the vision of the divine essence the created spirit possesses God as present; and the vision itself sets the affections completely on fire with divine love. If any object is *lovable so far as it is beautiful and good,* as Dionysius remarks in *de Divinis nominibus* IV, 10, surely God, who is the very essence of beauty and goodness, cannot be gazed at without love. Therefore, perfect vision is followed by perfect love. Gregory observes in one of his homilies on Ezekiel:[25] *The fire of love which begins to burn here on earth flares up more fiercely with love of God when he who is loved is seen.* Moreover, joy over an object embraced as present is keener the more that object is loved; consequently that joy is full not only because of the object that gives joy, but also on the part of him who rejoices. This joy is what crowns human beatitude. Hence Augustine writes in his *Confessions* X, 23 that happiness is *joy in truth.*

Another point to consider is this: as God is the very essence of goodness, he is the good of every good. Therefore, all good is beheld when he is beheld, as the Lord intimated when he said to Moses: *I will show you all good* (Exod 33:19). Consequently, if God is possessed all good is possessed, as is suggested in Wisdom 7:11: *All good things came to me along with her.*[26] In that final state of good, when we see God, we shall have a full abundance of all goods; and so our Lord promises the faithful servant in Matthew 24:47 that *he shall place him over all his goods.*

Since evil is opposed to good, the presence of all good requires the utter banishment of evil. Justice has no participation with injustice, and light has no fellowship with darkness, as we are told in 2 Corinthians 6:14. In that final state of good, therefore, those who possess all good will not only have a perfect sufficiency, but they will enjoy complete serenity and security as a result of their freedom from all evil, according to Proverbs 1:33: *He who listens to me will dwell secure and will be at ease, without dread of evil.*

25. *In Ezechielem homiliae,* II, 2.
26. I.e., with Wisdom.

Ex hoc autem ulterius sequitur quod sit ibi futura omnimoda pax. Non enim impeditur pax hominis nisi vel per interiorem desideriorum inquietudinem, dum desiderat habere quae nondum habet, vel per aliquorum malorum molestiam, quae vel patitur vel pati timet. Ibi autem nihil timetur: cessabit enim inquietudo desiderii propter plenitudinem omnis boni; cessabit etiam omnis molestia exterior per absentiam omnis mali; unde relinquitur quod ibi sit perfecta pacis tranquillitas. Hinc est quod dicitur Isai. XXXII, 18: *sedebit populus meus in pulchritudine pacis*, per quod pacis perfectio designatur: et ad ostendendum causam pacis subditur, *et in tabernaculis fiduciae*, quae scilicet erit subtracto timore malorum, *in requie opulenta*, quae pertinet ad affluentiam omnis boni.

Huius autem finalis boni perfectio in perpetuum durabit. Non enim poterit deficere per defectum bonorum quibus homo fruetur, quia sunt aeterna et incorruptibilia, unde dicitur Isai. XXXIII, v. 20: *oculi tui videbunt Ierusalem, civitatem opulentam, tabernaculum quod nequaquam transferri poterit*. Et postmodum subditur causa: *quia solummodo ibi erit magnificus dominus Deus noster*. Tota enim illius status perfectio erit in fruitione divinae aeternitatis.

Consimiliter etiam non poterit ille status deficere per corruptionem ibidem existentium, quia vel sunt naturaliter incorruptibiles, sicut angeli, vel in incorruptionem transferentur, sicut homines: *oportet enim corruptibile hoc induere incorruptionem*, ut dicitur I Corinth. XV, 53. Unde et Apoc. III, 12, dicitur: *qui vicerit, faciam illum columnam in templo Dei mei, et foras non egredietur amplius*.

Nec etiam poterit ille status deficere per hoc quod voluntas hominis fastidiendo se avertat, quia quanto Deus, qui est bonitatis essentia, magis videtur, tanto necesse est ut magis ametur, unde et magis eius fruitio desiderabitur, secundum illud Eccli. XXIV, 29: *qui edunt me, adhuc esurient; et qui bibunt me, adhuc sitient*. Propter quod et de angelis Deum videntibus dicitur I, 12: *in quem desiderant angeli prospicere*.

Similiter etiam non deficiet ille status per hostis alicuius impugnationem, quia cessabit ibi omnis mali molestia, secundum illud Isai. XXXV, 9: *non erit ibi leo*, idest diabolus impugnans, *et mala bestia*, idest malus homo, *non ascendet per eam, nec invenietur ibi*; unde et dominus dicit Ioan. X, de ovibus suis, quod *non peribunt in aeternum, et quod non rapiet eas quisquam de manu sua*.

Sed nec finiri poterit ille status per hoc quod a Deo aliqui inde excludantur. Non enim aliquis ab illo statu repelletur propter culpam, quae omnino non erit, ubi deerit omne malum, unde dicitur Isai. LX, 21: *populus tuus omnes iusti*, neque etiam propter promotionem ad melius bonum, sicut in hoc mundo Deus interdum

A further consequence is that absolute peace will reign in heaven. Man's peace is blocked either by the inner restlessness of desire, when he covets what he does not yet possess, or by the irksomeness of certain evils which he suffers or fears he may suffer. But in heaven there is nothing to fear. All restlessness of craving will come to an end, because of the full possession of all good. And every external cause of disturbance will cease, because all evil will be absent. Hence the perfect tranquillity of peace will be enjoyed there. This is alluded to in Isaiah 32:18: *My people shall sit in the beauty of peace*, by which the perfection of peace is meant. To show forth the cause of peace the Prophet adds: *And in the tabernacles of confidence*, for confidence will reign when the fear of evils is abolished; *and in wealthy rest*, which refers to the overflowing abundance of all good.

The perfection of this final good will endure forever. It cannot fail through any lack of the goods which man enjoys, for these are eternal and incorruptible. We are assured of this in Isaiah 33:20: *Your eyes will see Jerusalem, a quiet habitation, an immovable tent*. The cause of this stability is given in the next verse: *Because only there our Lord is magnificent*. The entire perfection of that state will consist in the enjoyment of divine eternity.

Similarly, that state cannot fail through the corruption of the beings existing there. These are either naturally incorruptible, as is the case with the angels, or they will be transferred to a condition of incorruption, as is the case with men. *For this corruptible must put on incorruption*, as we are informed in 1 Corinthians 15:53. The same is indicated in Revelation 3:12: *He who conquers, I will make him a pillar in the temple of my God*.

Nor can that state fail by reason of the turning away of man's will in disgust. The more clearly God, the essence of goodness, is seen, the more he must be loved; and so enjoyment of him will be desired ever more keenly, according to Sirach 24:29: *Those who eat me will hunger for more, and those who drink me will thirst for more*. For this reason the words of 1 Peter 1:12, *on whom the angels desire to look*, were spoken of the angels who see God.

That state will not be overthrown by the attack of an enemy, for no disturbing interference of any evil will be found there, as we read in Isaiah 35:9: *No lion shall be there*, that is, no assaulting devil, *nor shall any ravenous beast*, that is, any evil man, *come up on it, nor be found there*. Hence our Lord says of his sheep in John 10:28: *I give them eternal life, and they shall never perish, and no one shall snatch them out of my hand*.

Furthermore, that state cannot come to an end as a result of the banishment of some of its inhabitants by God. No one will be expelled from that state on account of sin, which will be simply non-existent in a place where every evil will be absent; hence we are told in Isaiah 60:21: *Your people shall all be righteous*. Again, none will be exiled for

etiam iustis spirituales consolationes subtrahit, et alia sua beneficia, ut avidius quaerant, et suum defectum recognoscant, quia status ille non est emendationis aut profectus, sed perfectionis finalis: et ideo dominus dicit Ioan. VI, 37: *eum qui venit ad me, non eiiciam foras.* Habebit igitur status ille omnium praedictorum bonorum perpetuitatem, secundum illud Psal. V, 12: *in aeternum exultabunt, et habitabis in eis.* Est igitur praedictum regnum beatitudo perfecta, utpote immutabilem omnis boni sufficientiam habens. Et quia beatitudo naturaliter desideratur ab hominibus, consequens est quod regnum Dei ab omnibus desideretur.

the purpose of urging them on to greater good, as happens at times in this world, when God withdraws spiritual consolations even from the just and takes away some of his other benefits so that men may seek them with greater eagerness and may acknowledge their own powerlessness. For that state is not one of correction or progress, but is a life of final perfection. This is why our Lord says in John 6:37: *Him who comes to me I will not cast out.* Therefore, that state will consist in the everlasting enjoyment of all the goods mentioned, as is said in Psalm 5:12: *They shall rejoice forever, and you shall dwell in them.* Consequently, the kingdom we have been discussing is perfect happiness, for it contains all good in changeless abundance. And, since happiness is naturally desired by men, the kingdom of God, too, is desired by all.

CHAPTER 10

That is it possible to reach the kingdom

Oportet autem ulterius ostendere, quod homo ad illud regnum pervenire possit: alioquin frustra speraret et pateretur. Primo autem apparet hoc esse possibile ex promissione divina, dicit enim dominus, Luc. XII, 32: *nolite timere pusillus grex, quia complacuit patri vestro dare vobis regnum.* Est autem divinum beneplacitum efficax ad implendum omne quod disponit, secundum illud Isai. XLVI, 10: *consilium meum stabit, et omnis voluntas mea fiet. Voluntati enim eius quis resistit?* Ut dicitur ad Roman. IX, 19. Secundo ostenditur hoc esse possibile ex evidenti exemplo.

We must go on to show that man can reach that kingdom. Otherwise, it would be hoped for and prayed for in vain. In the first place, the divine promise makes this possibility clear. Our Lord says, in Luke 12:32: *Fear not, little flock, for it is your Father's good pleasure to give you the kingdom.* God's good pleasure is efficacious in carrying out all that he plans, according to Isaiah 46:10: *My counsel shall stand, and I will accomplish all my purpose.* For, as we read in Romans 9:19: *Who can resist his will?* Second, an evident example shows that attainment of the kingdom is possible.

On the Principles
of Nature

Chapter 1

Act and potency

Nota quod quoddam potest esse licet non sit, quoddam vero est. Illud quod potest esse dicitur esse potentia, illud quod iam est dicitur esse actu. Sed duplex est esse, scilicet esse essentiale rei sive substantiale, ut hominem esse, et hoc est esse simpliciter; est autem aliud esse accidentale, ut hominem esse album, et hoc est esse aliquid.

Ad utrumque esse est aliquid in potentia: aliquid enim est in potentia ut sit homo, ut sperma et sanguis menstruus, aliquid est in potentia ut sit album, ut homo. Tam illud quod est in potentia ad esse substantiale quam illud quod est in potentia ad esse accidentale potest dici materia, sicut sperma hominis et homo albedinis; sed in hoc differt quia materia quae est in potentia ad esse substantiale dicitur materia ex qua, quae autem est in potentia ad esse accidentale dicitur materia in qua.

Item proprie loquendo quod est in potentia ad esse accidentale dicitur subiectum, quod vero est in potentia ad esse substantiale dicitur proprie materia. Quod autem illud quod est in potentia ad esse accidentale dicatur subiectum, signum est quia dicuntur esse accidentia in subiecto, non autem quod forma substantialis sit in subiecto. Et secundum hoc differt materia a subiecto, quia subiectum est quod non habet esse ex eo quod advenit, sed per se habet esse completum, sicut homo non habet esse ab albedine; sed materia habet esse ex eo quod ei advenit, quia de se habet esse incompletum. Unde, simpliciter loquendo forma dat esse materiae, sed subiectum accidenti, licet aliquando unum sumatur pro altero, scilicet materia pro subiecto et e converso.

Sicut autem omne quod est in potentia potest dici materia, ita omne a quo aliquid habet esse, quodcumque esse sit, sive substantiale sive accidentale, potest dici forma: sicut homo cum sit potentia albus fit actu albus per albedinem, et sperma cum sit potentia homo fit actu homo per animam. Et quia forma facit esse in actu, ideo forma dicitur esse actus; quod autem facit actu esse substantiale est forma substantialis, et quod facit actu esse accidentale dicitur forma accidentalis.

Note that some things can be, although they are not, and some things now are. Those which can be and are not are said to be in potency, but those which already exist are said to be in act. But existence is twofold: one is the essential or substantial existence of a thing (for example, man exists). And this is existence simply speaking. The other is accidental existence, (for example, man is white): and this is existence in a certain respect.

Moreover, for each existence there is something in potency. Something is in potency to be man, as sperm or the menstrual blood, and something is in potency to be white, as man. Both that which is in potency to substantial existence and that which is in potency to accidental existence can be called matter: for example sperm is the matter of man and man is the matter of whiteness. But these differ, because that which is in potency to substantial existence is called the matter from which, but that which is in potency to accidental existence is called the matter in which.

Again, properly speaking, that which is in potency to substantial existence is called 'prime matter,' but that which is in potency to accidental existence is called 'the subject.' Thus we say that accidents are in a subject; but we do not say that the substantial form is in a subject. In this way matter differs from subject because the subject is that which does not have existence by reason of something which comes to it; rather, it has complete existence of itself, just as man does not have existence through whiteness. But matter has existence by reason of what comes to it because, of itself, it has incomplete existence. Hence, simply speaking, the form gives existence to matter. The accident, however, does not give existence to the subject; rather, the subject gives existence to the accident, although sometimes the one is used for the other (namely, matter for subject, and conversely).

But, just as everything which is in potency can be called matter, so also everything from which something has existence (whether that existence be substantial or accidental) can be called form; for example, man, since he is white in potency, becomes actually white through whiteness, and sperm, since it is man in potency, becomes actually man through the soul. Also, because form causes existence in act, we say that the form is the act. However, that which causes substantial existence in act is called substantial form, and that which causes accidental existence in act is called accidental form.

Et quia generatio est motus ad formam, duplici formae respondet duplex generatio: formae substantiali respondet generatio simpliciter, formae vero accidentali generatio secundum quid. Quando enim introducitur forma substantialis, dicitur aliquid fieri simpliciter; quando autem introducitur forma accidentalis, non dicitur aliquid fieri simpliciter sed fieri hoc: sicut quando homo fit albus, non dicimus simpliciter hominem fieri vel generari, sed fieri vel generari album. Et huic duplici generationi respondet duplex corruptio, scilicet simpliciter et secundum quid; generatio vero et corruptio simpliciter non sunt nisi in genere substantiae, sed generatio et corruptio secundum quid sunt in aliis generibus.

Et quia generatio est quaedam mutatio de non esse vel ente ad esse vel ens, e converso autem corruptio debet esse de esse ad non esse, non ex quolibet non esse fit generatio, sed ex non ente quod est ens in potentia: sicut idolum ex cupro, quod idolum est in potentia, non in actu.

Ad hoc ergo quod sit generatio tria requiruntur: scilicet ens potentia quod est materia, et non esse actu quod est privatio, et id per quod fit actu, scilicet forma. Sicut quando ex cupro fit idolum, cuprum quod est potentia ad formam idoli est materia, hoc autem quod est infiguratum sive indispositum dicitur privatio; figura autem a qua dicitur idolum est forma, non autem substantialis quia cuprum ante adventum formae seu figurae habet esse in actu, et eius esse non dependet ab illa figura, sed est forma accidentalis: omnes enim formae artificiales sunt accidentales, ars enim non operatur nisi supra id quod iam constitutum est in esse perfecto a natura.

Because generation is a motion to form, there is a twofold generation corresponding to this twofold form. Generation simply speaking corresponds to the substantial form, and generation in a certain respect corresponds to the accidental form. When a substantial form is introduced, we say that something comes into being simply speaking: for example, we say that man comes into being or man is generated. But when an accidental form is introduced, we do not say that something comes into being simply speaking, but that it comes into being as this. For example, when man comes into being as white, we do not say simply that man comes into being or is generated, but that he comes into being or is generated as white. There is a twofold corruption opposed to this twofold generation: simply speaking, and in a certain respect. Generation and corruption simply speaking are only in the genus of substance, but generation and corruption in a certain respect are in all the other genera.

Also, because generation is a change from nonexistence to existence, contrarily, corruption should be from existence to nonexistence. However, generation does not take place from just any non-being, but from the nonbeing which is being in potency. For example, a statue comes to be from bronze, which is a statue in potency and not in act.

In order that there be generation three things are required: being in potency, which is matter; non-existence in act, which is privation; and that through which something comes to be in act, which is form. For example, when a statue is made from bronze, the bronze which is in potency to the form of the statue is the matter; the shapeless or undisposed something is the privation; and the shape because of which it is called a statue is the form. But it is not a substantial form because the bronze, before it receives the shape, has existence in act, and its existence does not depend upon that shape. Rather, it is an accidental form, because all artificial forms are accidental. Art operates only on that which is already constituted in existence by nature.

CHAPTER 2

The three principles of nature

Sunt igitur tria principia naturae, scilicet materia, forma et privatio, quorum alterum, scilicet forma, est id ad quod est generatio, alia duo sunt ex parte eius ex quo est generatio. Unde materia et privatio sunt idem subiecto, sed differunt ratione; illud idem quod est aes est infiguratum ante adventum formae, sed ex alia ratione dicitur aes, et ex alia infiguratum. Unde privatio dicitur esse principium non per se sed per accidens, quia scilicet concidit cum materia; sicut dicimus quod hoc est per accidens medicus aedificat: non enim ex eo quod medicus, sed ex eo quod aedificator, quod concidit medico in uno subiecto.

Sed duplex est accidens, scilicet necessarium quod non separatur a re, ut risibile hominis, et non necessarium quod separatur, ut album ab homine. Unde licet privatio sit principium per accidens, non sequitur quod non sit necessarium ad generationem, quia materia a privatione non denudatur; in quantum enim est sub una forma, habet privationem alterius et e converso, sicut in igne est privatio aeris et in aere privatio ignis.

Et sciendum quod, cum generatio sit ex non esse, non dicimus quod negatio sit principium, sed privatio; quia negatio non determinat sibi subiectum: 'non videt' enim potest dici etiam de non entibus, ut 'chimaera non videt', et iterum de entibus quae non nata sunt habere visum, sicut de lapidibus. Sed privatio non dicitur nisi de determinato subiecto, in quo scilicet natus est fieri habitus, sicut caecitas non dicitur nisi de his quae sunt nata videre.

Et quia generatio non fit ex non ente simpliciter, sed ex non ente quod est in aliquo subiecto, et non in quolibet sed in determinato—non enim ex quolibet non igne fit ignis sed ex tali non igne circa quod nata sit fieri forma ignis—ideo dicitur quod privatio est principium. Sed in hoc differt ab aliis, quia alia sunt principia et in esse et in fieri: ad hoc enim quod fiat idolum oportet quod sit aes, et quod ultima sit figura idoli.

Et iterum quando iam idolum est oportet haec duo esse; sed privatio est principium in fieri et non in esse, quia dum fit idolum oportet quod non sit idolum: si enim esset non fieret, quia quod fit non est, nisi in successivis. Sed ex quo iam idolum est, non est ibi privatio

Therefore, there are three principles of nature: matter, form, and privation. One of these, form, is that by reason of which generation takes place; the other two are found on the part of that from which there is generation. Hence matter and privation are the same in subject but they differ in definition, because bronze and what is shapeless are the same before the advent of the form; but for one reason it is called bronze and for another reason it is called shapeless. Wherefore, privation is not said to be a principle essentially, but rather a principle accidentally, because it is coincident with matter. For example we say that it is accidental that the doctor builds, because he does not do this insofar as he is a doctor but insofar as he is a builder, which is coincident with being a doctor in the same subject.

But there are two kinds of accidents: the necessary, which is not separated from the thing (for example, risible in man); and the non-necessary, which can be separated (for example, white from man). Thus, although privation is an accidental principle, still it does not follow that it is not necessary for generation, because matter is never entirely without privation. For insofar as it is under one form it has the privation of another, and conversely, just as there is the privation of fire in air and the privation of air in fire.

Also, we should note that, although generation is from non-existence, we do not say that negation is the principle but that privation is the principle, because negation does not determine a subject. Non-seeing can be said even of non-beings: for example, we say that the chimaera does not see, and we say the same of beings which are not apt to have sight, such as stones. But privation is said only of a determined subject: namely, that in which the habit is apt to come to be; for example, blindness is said only of those things which are apt to see.

Also, because generation does not come to be from non-being simply speaking, but from the non-being which is in some subject, and not in just any subject, but in a determined subject—because fire does not come to be from just any non-fire, but from such non-fire as is apt to receive the form of fire—therefore, we say that privation is the principle, and not negation. Privation differs from the other principles because the others are principles both in existence and in becoming. In order for a statue to come to be, there must be bronze; further, there must be the shape of the statue.

Again, when the statue already exists, it is necessary that these two exist. But privation is a principle in becoming, and not in existing, because until the statue comes to be it must not be a statue. For, if it were, it would not come to be, because whatever comes to be is not, except in successive

243

idoli, quia affirmatio et negatio non sunt simul, similiter nec privatio et habitus. Item privatio est principium per accidens, ut supra expositum est, alia duo sunt principia per se.

Ex dictis igitur patet quod materia differt a forma et a privatione secundum rationem. Materia enim est id in quo intelligitur forma et privatio, sicut in cupro intelligitur figura et infiguratum; quandoque quidem materia nominatur cum privatione, quandoque sine privatione: sicut aes cum sit materia idoli non importat privationem, quia ex hoc quod dico 'aes' non intelligitur indispositum seu infiguratum; sed farina cum sit materia respectu panis, importat in se privationem formae panis, quia ex hoc quod dico farinam significatur indispositio sive inordinatio opposita formae panis. Et quia in generatione materia sive subiectum permanet, privatio vero non, neque compositum ex materia et privatione, ideo materia quae non importat privationem est permanens, quae autem importat est transiens.

Sed sciendum quod quaedam materia habet compositionem formae, sicut aes cum sit materia respectu idoli, ipsum tamen aes est compositum ex materia et forma, et ideo aes non dicitur materia prima quia habet materiam. Ipsa autem materia quae intelligitur sine qualibet forma et privatione, sed subiecta formae et privationi, dicitur materia prima, propter hoc quod ante ipsam non est alia materia: et hoc etiam dicitur *yle*. Et quia omnis definitio et omnis cognitio est per formam, ideo materia prima per se non potest cognosci vel definiri, sed per comparationem, ut dicatur quod illud est materia prima quod hoc modo se habet ad omnes formas et privationes sicut aes ad idolum et infiguratum: et haec dicitur simpliciter prima. Potest etiam aliquid dici materia prima respectu alicuius generis, sicut aqua est materia liquabilium, non tamen est prima simpliciter quia est composita ex materia et forma, unde habet materiam priorem.

Et sciendum quod materia prima, et etiam forma, non generatur neque corrumpitur, quia omnis generatio est ad aliquid ex aliquo; id autem ex quo est generatio est materia, id ad quod est forma: si igitur materia vel forma generaretur, materiae esset materia et formae forma in infinitum. Unde generatio non est nisi compositi proprie loquendo.

Sciendum est etiam quod materia prima dicitur una numero in omnibus. Sed unum numero dicitur duobus modis, scilicet quod habet unam formam determinatam in numero, sicut Socrates: et hoc modo materia prima

things: for example, in time and motion. But from the fact that the statue already exists, the privation of statue is not there, because affirmation and negation are not found together, and neither are privation and habit. Likewise, privation is an accidental principle, as was explained above, but the other two are essential principles.

Therefore, from what was said, it is plain that matter differs from form and privation by definition. Matter is that in which the form and privation are understood, just as in bronze the shape and the shapeless is understood. Still, matter sometimes designates privation and sometimes does not designate privation. For example, when bronze becomes the matter of the statue, it does not imply a privation, because when I speak of 'bronze' in this way I do not mean what is undisposed or shapeless. Flour, on the other hand, since it is the matter with respect to bread, implies in itself the privation of the form of bread, because when I say 'flour' the lack of disposition or the inordination opposed to the form of bread is signified. Also, because in generation the matter or the subject remains, but the privation does not (nor does the composite of matter and privation); therefore, that matter which does not imply privation is permanent, but that which implies privation is transient.

We should notice, too, that some matter has a composition of form: bronze, for example. For, although it is the matter with respect to the statue, the bronze itself is composed of matter and form. Therefore, bronze is not called prime matter, even though it has matter. However, that matter which is understood without any form and privation, but rather is subject to form and privation, is called 'prime matter' by reason of the fact that there is no other matter before it. This is also called *hyle*. Also, because all knowledge and every definition comes by way of the form, prime matter cannot be defined or known in itself but only through the composite. Consequently, it might be said that that is prime matter which is related to all forms and privations as bronze is to the statue and the shapeless; and this is called first simply speaking. A thing can also be called prime matter with respect to some genus, as water with respect to aqueous solutions; this, however, is not first simply speaking because it is composed of matter and form. Hence it has a prior matter.

Note, also, that prime matter, and likewise form, is neither generated nor corrupted, because every generation goes from something to something. But that from which generation takes place is matter, and that in which generation terminates is form. Therefore, if matter and form were generated, there would be a matter of matter and a form of form, and so on forever. Hence, properly speaking, there is only generation of the composite.

Again, notice that prime matter is said to be numerically one in all things. But to be numerically one can be said in two ways, such as that which has a determined numerically one form, like Socrates. Prime matter is not said to be nu-

non dicitur unum numero, cum in se non habeat aliquam formam. Dicitur etiam aliquid unum numero quia est sine dispositionibus quae faciunt differre secundum numerum: et hoc modo dicitur materia prima unum numero, quia intelligitur sine omnibus dispositionibus a quibus est differentia in numero.

Et sciendum quod, licet materia non habeat in sua natura aliquam formam vel privationem, sicut in ratione aeris neque est figuratum neque infiguratum, tamen nunquam denudatur a forma et privatione: quandoque enim est sub una forma, quandoque sub alia. Sed per se nunquam potest esse, quia, cum in ratione sua non habeat aliquam formam, non habet esse in actu, cum esse in actu non sit nisi a forma, sed est solum in potentia; et ideo quicquid est actu non potest dici materia prima.

merically one in this way, since it does not have in itself a form. Also, something is said to be numerically one because it is without the dispositions which would cause it to differ numerically. Prime matter is said to be numerically one in this way because it is understood without all the dispositions which would cause it to differ numerically.

Notice, likewise, that, although prime matter does not have in its definition any form or privation (for example, neither shaped nor shapeless is in the definition of bronze), nevertheless, matter is never completely without form and privation, because it is sometimes under one form and sometimes under another. Moreover, it can never exist by itself: for, since it does not have any form in its definition, it cannot exist in act, since existence in act is only from the form. Rather, it exists only in potency. Therefore, whatever exists in act cannot be called prime matter.

CHAPTER 3

The four causes

Ex dictis igitur patet tria esse naturae principia, scilicet materia, forma et privatio; sed haec non sunt sufficientia ad generationem. Quod enim est in potentia non potest se reducere ad actum, sicut cuprum quod est potentia idolum non facit se idolum, sed indiget operante qui formam idoli extrahat de potentia in actum. Forma etiam non extraheret se de potentia in actum: et loquor de forma generati, quam diximus esse terminum generationis; forma enim non est nisi in facto esse, quod autem operatur est in fieri, idest dum res fit. Oportet ergo praeter materiam et formam esse aliquod principium quod agat, et hoc dicitur esse efficiens, vel movens, vel agens, vel unde est principium motus.

Et quia, ut dicit Aristoteles in II *Metaphysicae*, omne quod agit non agit nisi intendendo aliquid, oportet esse aliud quartum, id scilicet quod intenditur ab operante: et hoc dicitur finis. Et sciendum quod omne agens, tam naturale quam voluntarium, intendit finem; non tamen sequitur quod omne agens cognoscat finem, vel deliberet de fine. Cognoscere enim finem est necessarium in his quorum actiones non sunt determinatae, sed se habent ad opposita, sicut se habent agentia voluntaria; et ideo oportet quod cognoscant finem per quem suas actiones determinent. Sed in agentibus naturalibus sunt actiones determinatae, unde non est necessarium eligere ea quae sunt ad finem.

Et ponit exemplum Avicenna de citharaedo, quem non oportet de qualibet percussione chordarum deliberare, cum percussiones sint determinatae apud ipsum: alioquin esset inter percussiones mora, quod esset absonum. Magis autem videtur de operante voluntarie quod deliberet quam de agente naturali: et ita patet per locum a maiori quod possibile est agens naturale sine deliberatione intendere finem. Et hoc intendere nihil aliud erat quam habere naturalem inclinationem ad aliquid.

Ex dictis ergo patet quod sunt quatuor causae, scilicet materialis, efficiens, formalis et finalis. Licet autem principium et causa dicantur convertibiliter, ut dicitur in V *Metaphysicae*, tamen Aristoteles in libro *Physicorum* ponit quatuor causas et tria principia. Causas autem accipit tam pro extrinsecis quam pro intrinsecis: materia et forma dicuntur intrinsecae rei eo quod sunt partes constituentes rem, efficiens et finalis dicuntur extrin-

From this it is plain, therefore, that there are three principles of nature: matter, form and privation. But these are not sufficient for generation. What is in potency cannot reduce itself to act: for example, the bronze which is in potency to being a statue cannot cause itself to be a statue. Rather, it needs an agent so that the form of the statue can pass from potency to act. Neither can the form draw itself from potency to act. I mean the form of the thing generated which we say is the term of generation, because the form exists only in that which has been made to be. However, what is made is in the state of becoming as long as the thing is coming to be. Therefore, it is necessary that besides the matter and form there be some principle which acts. This is called the efficient, moving, or agent cause, or that from which the principle of motion is.

Also, because, as Aristotle says in the second book of the *Metaphysics*, everything which acts, acts only by intending something, there must be some fourth thing: namely, that which is intended by the agent; and this is called the end. Again, we should notice that, although every agent, both natural and voluntary, intends an end, still it does not follow that every agent knows the end or deliberates about the end. To know the end is necessary in those whose actions are not determined, but which may act for opposed ends (as, for example, voluntary agents). Therefore, it is necessary that these know the end by which they determine their actions. But in natural agents the actions are determined; hence, it is not necessary to choose those things which are for the end.

Avicenna gives the following example. A harpist does not have to deliberate about the notes in any particular chord, since these are already determined for him; otherwise, there would be a delay between the notes, which would cause discord. However, it seems more reasonable to attribute deliberation to a voluntary agent than to a natural agent: and thus it is clear, by reasoning from the greater thing to the lesser, that a natural agent can intend the end without deliberation. Therefore, it is possible for the natural agent to intend the end without deliberation; and to intend this is nothing else than to have a natural inclination to something.

From the above it is plain that there are four causes: material, efficient, formal and final. But, although principle and cause are used convertibly, as is said in the fifth book of the *Metaphysics*, still, in the *Physics*, Aristotle gives four causes and three principles, because he takes as causes both what is extrinsic and what is intrinsic. Matter and form are said to be intrinsic to the thing because they are parts constituting the thing; the efficient and final causes are said to

secae quia sunt extra rem; sed principia accipit solum causas intrinsecas. Privatio autem non nominatur inter causas, quia est principium per accidens, ut dictum est. Et cum dicimus quatuor causas, intelligimus de causis per se, ad quas tamen causae per accidens reducuntur, quia omne quod est per accidens reducitur ad id quod est per se.

Sed licet principia ponat Aristoteles pro causis intrinsecis in I *Physicorum*, tamen, ut dicitur in XI *Metaphysicae*, principium dicitur proprie de causis extrinsecis, elementum de causis quae sunt partes rei, id est de causis intrinsecis, causa dicitur de utrisque; tamen aliquando unum ponitur pro altero: omnis enim causa potest dici principium et omne principium causa. Sed tamen causa videtur addere supra principium communiter dictum, quia id quod est primum, sive consequatur esse posterius sive non, potest dici principium, sicut faber dicitur principium cultelli ut ex eius operatione est esse cultelli; sed quando aliquid movetur de nigredine ad albedinem, dicitur quod nigrum est principium illius motus, et universaliter omne id a quo incipit esse motus dicitur principium: tamen nigredo non est id ex quo consequatur esse albedo. Sed causa solum dicitur de illo primo ex quo consequitur esse posterioris: unde dicitur quod causa est ex cuius esse sequitur aliud; et ideo illud primum a quo incipit esse motus non potest dici causa per se, etsi dicatur principium. Et propter hoc privatio ponitur inter principia et non inter causas, quia privatio est id a quo incipit generatio; sed potest etiam dici causa per accidens, in quantum concidit materiae, ut supra expositum est.

Elementum vero non dicitur proprie nisi de causis ex quibus est compositio rei, quae proprie sunt materiales; et iterum non de qualibet causa materiali, sed de illa ex qua est prima compositio, sicut nec membra elementa sunt hominis, quia membra etiam sunt composita ex aliis: sed dicimus quod terra et aqua sunt elementa, quia haec non componuntur ex aliis corporibus, sed ex ipsis est prima compositio corporum naturalium. Unde Aristoteles in V *Metaphysicae* dicit quod *elementum est id ex quo componitur res primo, et est in ea, et non dividitur secundum formam.*

Expositio primae particulae, *ex quo componitur res primo*, patet per ea quae diximus. Secunda particula, scilicet *et est in ea*, ponitur ad differentiam illius materiae quae ex toto corrumpitur per generationem, sicut panis est materia sanguinis, sed non generatur sanguis nisi corrumpatur panis, unde panis non remanet in sanguine: unde non potest dici panis elementum sanguinis;

be extrinsic because they are outside the thing. But he takes as principles only the intrinsic causes. Privation, however, is not listed among the causes because it is an accidental principle, as was said. When we say that there are four causes we mean the essential causes, to which all the accidental causes are reduced, because everything which is accidental is reduced to that which is essential.

And, although Aristotle calls intrinsic causes 'principles' in the first book of the *Physics*, still, principle is applied properly to extrinsic causes, as is said in the eleventh book of the *Metaphysics*. 'Element' is used for those causes which are parts of the thing (namely, for the intrinsic causes). 'Cause' is applied to both. Nevertheless, one is sometimes used for the other: every cause can be called a principle and every principle a cause. However, cause seems to add something to principle as commonly used, because that which is primary, whether the existence of a posterior follows from it or not, can be called a principle: for example, the smith is called the principle of the knife because the existence of the knife comes from his operation. But when something is moved from whiteness to blackness, whiteness is said to be the principle of that motion; and universally, everything from which motion begins is called a principle. However, whiteness is not that from which the existence of blackness follows. But cause is said primarily only of that from which the existence of the posterior follows. Hence we say that a cause is that from whose existence another follows. Therefore, that primarily from which motion begins cannot really be called a cause, even though it may be called a principle. Because of this, privation is placed among the principles and not among the causes, because privation is that from which generation begins. But it can also be called an accidental cause insofar as it is coincident with matter, as was said above.

Element, on the other hand, is applied properly only to the causes of which the thing is composed, which are properly the materials. Moreover, it is not said of just any material cause, but of that one of which a thing is primarily composed; for example, we do not say that the members of the body are the elements of man, because the members also are composed of other things. Rather, we say that earth and water are the elements, because these are not composed of other bodies, but natural bodies are primarily composed of them. Hence Aristotle says, in the fifth book of the *Metaphysics*, that *an element is that of which a thing is primarily composed, which is in that thing, and which is not divided by a form.*

The explanation of the first part of the definition, *that of which a thing is primarily composed*, is plain from the preceding. The second part, *which is in that thing*, differentiates it from that matter which is entirely corrupted by generation; for example, bread is the matter of blood, but blood is generated only by the corruption of bread. Thus bread does not remain in blood; and therefore bread cannot be called

sed elementa oportet aliquo modo manere cum non corrumpantur, ut dicitur in libro *de Generatione*. Tertia particula, scilicet *et non dividitur secundum formam*, ponitur ad differentiam eorum scilicet quae habent partes diversas in forma, id est in specie, sicut manus cuius partes sunt caro et ossa quae differunt secundum speciem; sed elementum non dividitur in partes diversas secundum speciem, sicut aqua cuius quaelibet pars est aqua. Non enim oportet ad esse elementi ut non dividatur secundum quantitatem, sed sufficit si non dividatur secundum speciem; et si etiam non dividatur, dicitur elementum, sicut litterae dicuntur elementa dictionum. Patet igitur quod principium quodammodo in plus habet se quam causa, et causa in plus quam elementum: et hoc est quod dicit Commentator in V *Metaphysicae*.

an element of blood. But the elements must remain in some way, since they are not entirely corrupted, as is said in the book *On Generation*. The third part, *and which is not divided by a form*, differentiates an element from those things which have parts diverse in form (that is, in species), as the hand whose parts are flesh and bone, which differ according to species. An element is not divided into parts diverse according to species: rather, it is like water whose every part is water. For an element to exist, it need not be undivided by quantity; rather, it is sufficient that it be undivided by form. Even if it is in no way divided, it is called an element, just as letters are the elements of words. This it is plain from what was said that 'principle,' in some way, applies to more than does 'cause,' and 'cause' to more than does 'element.' This is what the Commentator says in the fifth book of the *Metaphysics*.

CHAPTER 4

Coincidence of causes

Viso igitur quod quatuor sunt causarum genera, sciendum est quod non est impossibile quod idem habeat plures causas, ut idolum cuius causa est cuprum et artifex, sed artifex ut efficiens, cuprum ut materia. Non autem est impossibile ut idem sit causa contrariorum, sicut gubernator est causa salutis navis et submersionis, sed huius per absentiam, illius quidem per praesentiam.

Sciendum est etiam quod possibile est ut aliquid idem sit causa et causatum respectu eiusdem, sed diversimode: ut deambulatio est causa sanitatis ut efficiens, sed sanitas est causa deambulationis ut finis, deambulatio enim est aliquando propter sanitatem; et etiam corpus est materia animae, anima vero est forma corporis. Efficiens enim dicitur causa respectu finis, cum finis non sit in actu nisi per operationem agentis; sed finis dicitur causa efficientis, cum non operetur nisi per intentionem finis. Unde efficiens est causa illius quod est finis—ut sit sanitas—non tamen facit finem esse finem; et ita non est causa causalitatis finis, id est non facit finem esse finalem: sicut medicus facit sanitatem esse in actu, non tamen facit quod sanitas sit finis.

Finis autem non est causa illius quod est efficiens, sed est causa ut efficiens sit efficiens; sanitas enim non facit medicum esse medicum—et dico sanitatem quae fit operante medico—sed facit ut medicus sit efficiens. Unde finis est causa causalitatis efficientis, quia facit efficiens esse efficiens; similiter facit materiam esse materiam et formam esse formam, cum materia non suscipiat formam nisi per finem, et forma non perficiat materiam nisi per finem. Unde dicitur quod finis est causa causarum, quia est causa causalitatis in omnibus causis.

Materia enim dicitur causa formae in quantum forma non est nisi in materia; et similiter forma est causa materiae in quantum materia non habet esse in actu nisi per formam: materia enim et forma dicuntur relative ad invicem, ut dicitur in II *Physicorum*; dicuntur enim ad compositum sicut partes ad totum et simplex ad compositum.

Sed quia omnis causa in quantum est causa naturaliter prior est causato, sciendum quod prius dicitur

Now that we have seen that there are four genera of causes, we must understand that it is not impossible that the same thing have many causes. For example, the statue whose causes are both the bronze and the artist: the artist is the efficient cause while the bronze is the material cause. Nor is it impossible that the same thing be the cause of contraries; for example, the captain is the cause of the safety of the ship and of its sinking. He is the cause of the latter by his absence and of the former by his presence.

Also, notice that it is possible that the same thing be a cause and the thing caused with respect to the same thing, but in diverse ways. For example, walking is sometimes the cause of health, as the efficient cause, but health is the cause of the walking, as the end: walking is sometimes on account of health. Also, the body is the matter of the soul, but the soul is the form of the body. The efficient cause is called a cause with respect to the end, since the end is actual only by the operation of the agent. But the end is called the cause of the efficient cause, since the efficient cause does not operate except by the intention of the end. Hence the efficient cause is the cause of that which is the end—for example, walking in order to be healthy. However, the efficient cause does not cause the end to be the end. Therefore, it is not the cause of the causality of the end; that is, it does not cause the end to be the final cause. For example, the doctor causes health to actually exist, but he does not cause health to be the end.

Also, the end is not the cause of that which is the efficient cause, but it is the cause of the efficient cause being an efficient cause. For example, health does not cause the doctor to be a doctor—I am speaking of the health which comes about by the doctor's activity—but it causes the doctor to be an efficient cause. Therefore, the end is the cause of the causality of the efficient cause, because it causes the efficient cause to be an efficient cause. Likewise, the end causes the matter to be the matter and the form to be the form, since matter receives the form only for the sake of the end and the form perfects the matter only through the end. Therefore, we say that the end is the cause of causes, because it is the cause of the causality in all causes.

Also, we say that matter is the cause of the form, insofar as the form exists only in matter. Likewise, the form is the cause of the matter, insofar as matter has existence in act only through the form, because matter and form are spoken of in relation to each other, as is said in the second book of the *Physics*. They are also spoken of in relation to the composite, as the part to the whole and as the simple to the composed.

But, because every cause, as cause, is naturally prior to that which it causes, notice that we say a thing is prior in

duobus modis, ut dicit Aristoteles in XVI *de Animalibus*: per quorum diversitatem potest aliquid dici prius et posterius respectu eiusdem et causa et causatum. Dicitur enim aliquid prius altero generatione et tempore, et iterum in substantia et complemento. Cum ergo naturae operatio procedat ab imperfecto ad perfectum et ab incompleto ad completum, imperfectum est prius perfecto secundum generationem et tempus, sed perfectum est prius in complemento: sicut potest dici quod vir est ante puerum in substantia et complemento, sed puer est ante virum generatione et tempore.

Sed licet in rebus generabilibus imperfectum sit prius perfecto et potentia prior actu, considerando in aliquo eodem quod prius est imperfectum quam perfectum et in potentia quam in actu, simpliciter tamen loquendo oportet actum et perfectum prius esse, quia quod reducit potentiam ad actum actu est, et quod perficit imperfectum perfectum est. Materia quidem est prior forma generatione et tempore, prius enim est cui advenit quam quod advenit; forma vero est prior materia perfectione, quia materia non habet esse completum nisi per formam. Similiter efficiens prior est fine generatione et tempore, cum ab efficiente fiat motus ad finem; sed finis est prior efficiente in quantum est efficiens in substantia et complemento, cum actio efficientis non compleatur nisi per finem. Igitur istae duae causae, scilicet materia et efficiens, sunt prius per viam generationis, sed forma et finis sunt prius per viam perfectionis.

Et notandum quod duplex est necessitas, scilicet necessitas absoluta et necessitas conditionalis. Necessitas quidem absoluta est quae procedit a causis prioribus in via generationis, quae sunt materia et efficiens, sicut necessitas mortis quae provenit ex materia et ex dispositione contrariorum componentium: et haec dicitur absoluta, quia non habet impedimentum; haec etiam dicitur necessitas materiae. Necessitas autem conditionalis procedit a causis posterioribus in generatione, scilicet a forma et fine, sicut dicimus quod necessarium est esse conceptionem si debeat generari homo; et ista est conditionalis, quia hanc mulierem concipere non est necessarium simpliciter, sed sub conditione: si debeat generari homo. Et haec dicitur necessitas finis.

Et est sciendum quod tres causae possunt incidere in unum, scilicet forma, finis et efficiens, sicut patet in generatione ignis: ignis enim generat ignem, ergo ignis est causa efficiens in quantum generat; et iterum ignis est forma in quantum facit esse actu quod prius erat

two ways, as Aristotle says in the *History of Animals* XVI. Because of this diversity, we can call something prior and posterior with respect to the same thing, both the cause and the thing caused. We say that one thing is prior to another from the point of view of generation and time, and likewise from the point of view of substance and completeness. Since the operation of nature proceeds from the imperfect to the perfect and from the incomplete to the complete, the imperfect is prior to the perfect (namely, from the point of view of generation and time), but the perfect prior to the imperfect from the point of view of substance. For example, we can say that the man is before the boy according to substance and completeness, but the boy is before the man according to generation and time.

But, although in generable things the imperfect is prior to the perfect and potency to act, when we consider that in one and the same thing the imperfect is prior to the perfect and potency to act, still, simply speaking, the act and the perfect must be prior, because it is what is in act that reduces potency to act and it is the perfect that perfects the imperfect. Matter is prior to form from the point of view of generation and time because that to which something comes is prior to that which comes to it. But form is prior to matter from the point of view of substance and completeness, because matter has completed existence only through the form. Likewise, the efficient cause is prior to the end from the point of view of generation and time, since the motion to the end comes from the efficient cause. But the end is prior to the efficient cause, insofar as it is the efficient cause from the point of view of substance and completeness, since the action of the efficient cause is completed only through the end. Therefore, these two causes, the material and the efficient, are prior by way of generation, but the form and the end are prior by way of perfection.

It must be noted that there are two kinds of necessity: absolute and conditional. Absolute necessity is that which proceeds from the causes prior by way of generation: the material and the efficient causes. An example of this is the necessity of death which comes from the matter: namely, the disposition of the composing contraries. This is called 'absolute' because it does not have an impediment. It is also called the necessity of matter. Conditional necessity, on the other hand, proceeds from causes posterior in generation: namely, the form and the end. For example, we say that conception is necessary if a man is to be generated. This is called 'conditional' because it is not necessary simply that this woman conceive, but only conditionally, namely, if a man is to be generated. This is called the necessity of the end.

Notice, also, that three causes can coincide in one thing—namely, the form, the end and the efficient cause—as is plain in the generation of fire. Fire generates fire; therefore, fire is the efficient cause insofar as it generates. Fire is also the formal cause insofar as it causes to exist actually

potentia; et iterum est finis in quantum est intentum ab agente et in quantum terminantur ad ipsum operationes ipsius agentis.

Sed duplex est finis, scilicet finis generationis et finis rei generatae, sicut patet in generatione cultelli: forma enim cultelli est finis generationis, sed incidere quod est operatio cultelli, est finis ipsius generati, scilicet cultelli. Finis autem generationis concidit ex duabus dictis causis aliquando, scilicet quando fit generatio a simili in specie, sicut homo generat hominem et oliva olivam: quod non potest intelligi de fine rei generatae.

Sciendum autem quod finis incidit cum forma in idem numero, quia illud idem in numero quod est forma generati est finis generationis. Sed cum efficiente non incidit in idem numero, sed in idem specie; impossibile est enim ut faciens et factum sint idem numero, sed possunt esse idem specie: ut quando homo generat hominem, homo generans et generatus sunt diversa in numero sed idem in specie.

Materia autem non concidit cum aliis, quia materia ex eo quod est ens in potentia, habet rationem imperfecti; sed aliae causae cum sint actu, habent rationem perfecti: perfectum autem et imperfectum non concidunt in idem.

that which before was in potency. Again, it is the end insofar as the operations of the agent are terminated in it and insofar as it is intended by the agent.

But the end is twofold: the end of generation and the end of the thing generated, as is plain in the generation of a knife. The form of the knife is the end of generation; but cutting, which is the operation of the knife, is the end of the thing generated, namely, of the knife. Moreover, the end of generation sometimes is coincident with the two aforementioned causes: namely, when generation takes place from what is similar in species, as when man generates man and the olive, an olive. But this cannot be understood of the end of the thing generated.

Notice that the end coincides with the form in something which is numerically the same, because that which is the form of the thing generated and that which is the end of generation are the same numerically. But it does not coincide with the efficient cause in a thing numerically the same, but in a thing specifically the same, because it is impossible that the maker and the thing made be numerically the same, but they can be specifically the same. Thus, when man generates man, the man generating and the one generated are numerically diverse, but they are specifically the same.

However, matter does not coincide with the others. This is because matter, by the fact that it is being in potency, has the nature of something imperfect; but the other causes, since they are in act, have the nature of something perfect. However, the perfect and the imperfect do not coincide in the same thing.

CHAPTER 5

Causes and predication

Viso igitur quod sint quatuor causae, scilicet efficiens, materialis, formalis et finalis, sciendum est quod quaelibet istarum causarum dividitur multis modis. Dicitur enim aliquid causa per prius et aliquid per posterius: sicut dicimus quod ars et medicus sunt causa sanitatis, sed ars est causa per prius et medicus per posterius; et similiter in causa formali et in aliis causis. Et nota quod semper debemus reducere quaestionem ad primam causam; ut si quaeratur *Quare est iste sanus?* dicendum est *Quia medicus sanavit*; et iterum *Quare medicus sanavit? Propter artem sanandi quam habet.*

Sciendum est quod idem est dictu causa propinqua quod causa posterior, et causa remota quod causa prior; unde istae duae divisiones causarum, alia per prius alia per posterius, et causarum alia remota alia propinqua, idem significant. Hoc autem observandum est quod semper illud quod universalius est causa remota dicitur, quod autem specialius causa propinqua: sicut dicimus quod forma hominis propinqua est sua definitio, scilicet animal rationale mortale, sed animal est magis remota, et iterum substantia remotior est. Omnia enim superiora sunt formae inferiorum. Et similiter materia idoli propinqua est cuprum, sed remota est metallum, et iterum remotius corpus.

Item causarum alia est per se, alia per accidens. Causa per se dicitur causa alicuius rei in quantum huiusmodi, sicut aedificator est causa domus et lignum materia scamni. Causa per accidens est illa quae accidit causae per se, sicut cum dicimus 'Grammaticus aedificat'; grammaticus enim dicitur causa aedificationis per accidens, non enim in quantum grammaticus sed in quantum accidit aedificatori. Et similiter est in aliis causis.

Item causarum quaedam est simplex et quaedam composita. Simplex causa dicitur quando solum dicitur causa illud quod per se est causa, vel etiam solum illud quod est per accidens: sicut si dicamus aedificatorem esse causam domus, et similiter si dicamus medicum esse causam domus. Composita autem dicitur quando utrumque dicitur causa, ut si dicamus *aedificator medicus est causa domus*. Potest etiam dici causa simplex, secundum quod exponit Avicenna, illud quod sine adiunctione alterius est causa, sicut cuprum idoli, sine adiunctione enim alterius materiae ex cupro fit idolum; et sicut dicitur quod medicus facit sanitatem, vel quod ignis calefacit. Composita autem causa est quando

Therefore, now that we have seen that there are four causes—the efficient, formal, material and final—we must note that any of these causes can be spoken of in many ways. We call one thing a prior cause and another a posterior cause. For example, we say that art and the doctor are the cause of health, but art is a prior cause and the doctor is a posterior cause. And it is similar in the formal cause and in the other causes. Notice, also that we must always bring the question back to the first cause. For example, if it be asked: *Why is this man healthy?* we would answer: *Because the doctor has healed him.* Likewise, if it be asked: *Why did the doctor heal him?* we would say: *Because of the art of healing which the doctor has.*

Notice, also, that the proximate cause is the same as the posterior cause and that the remote cause is the same as the prior cause. Hence these two divisions of causes into prior and posterior, remote and proximate signify the same thing. Moreover, it must be observed that that which is more universal is always called the remote cause, but that which is more particular is called the proximate cause. For example, we say that the proximate form of man is his definition, namely, rational animal; but animal is more remote and substance is still more remote. All superiors are forms of the inferiors. Again, the proximate matter of the statue is bronze, but the remote matter is metal, and the still more remote is body.

Further, there is one cause which is an essential cause, another which is accidental. An essential cause is said of one which is the cause of something as such: for example, the builder is the cause of the house and the wood is the matter of the bench. An accidental cause is said of one which happens to an essential cause. For example, we say that 'the grammarian builds'; the grammarian is called the cause of the building accidentally, not insofar as he is a grammarian, but insofar as it happens to the builder that he is a grammarian; and it is similar in other causes.

Likewise, some causes are simple, others are composed. A cause is simple when that alone is said to be the cause which is the essential cause, or that alone which is the accidental cause; as if we were to say that the builder is the cause of the house and likewise if we were to say that the doctor is the cause of the house. A cause is composed when both are said to be the cause, as if we were to say that *the medical builder is the cause of the house.* According to the explanation of Avicenna, that can be called a simple cause also which is a cause without the addition of another. For example, bronze is the cause of the statue without the addition of another matter, because the statue is made of bronze; and we say that the doctor causes health or that fire heats.

oportet plura advenire ad hoc quod sit causa, sicut unus homo non est causa motus navis, sed multi; et sicut unus lapis non est materia domus, sed multi.

Item causarum quaedam est actu, quaedam potentia. Causa in actu est quae actu causat rem, sicut aedificator cum aedificat, vel cuprum cum ex eo est idolum; causa autem in potentia est quae, licet non causet rem in actu, tamen potest causare, ut aedificator dum non aedificat. Et sciendum quod loquendo de causis in actu, necessarium est causam et causatum simul esse, ita quod si unum sit, et alterum: si enim est aedificator in actu, oportet quod aedificet, et si sit aedificatio in actu, oportet quod sit aedificator in actu. Sed hoc non est necessarium in causis quae sunt solum in potentia.

Sciendum est autem quod causa universalis comparatur causato universali, causa vero singularis comparatur causato singulari: sicut dicimus quod aedificator est causa domus, et hic aedificator huius domus.

But a cause is composed when many things must come together in order that there be a cause. For example, not one man, but many, are the cause of the motion of a ship; and not one stone, but many, are the cause of a house.

Again, some causes are in act, others are in potency. A cause in act is one which causes a thing in act, as the builder while he is building or the bronze when a statue is made of it. A cause in potency is one which, although it does not cause a thing in act, can cause it nevertheless, such as a builder when he is not building. Note that in speaking of causes in act, the cause and the thing caused must exist at the same time, so that if one exists the other does also. If there is a builder in act, he must be building and, if there is building in act, it is necessary that there be a builder in act. But this is not necessary in causes which are only in potency.

Moreover, it should be noted that the universal cause is compared to the universal thing that is caused and the singular cause is compared to the singular thing that is caused. For example, we say that a builder is the cause of a house and that this builder is the cause of this house.

CHAPTER 6

Analogy

Sciendum est etiam quod loquendo de principiis intrinsecis, scilicet materia et forma, secundum convenientiam principiatorum et differentiam est convenientia et differentia principiorum. Quaedam enim sunt idem numero, sicut Socrates et 'hic homo' demonstrato Socrate; quaedam sunt diversa numero et sunt idem in specie, ut Socrates et Plato, qui licet conveniant in specie humana, tamen differunt numero. Quaedam autem differunt specie sed sunt idem genere, sicut homo et asinus conveniunt in genere animalis; quaedam autem sunt diversa in genere sed sunt idem solum secundum analogiam, sicut substantia et quantitas, quae non conveniunt in aliquo genere sed conveniunt solum secundum analogiam: conveniunt enim in eo solum quod est ens, ens autem non est genus, quia non praedicatur univoce sed analogice.

Ad huius intelligentiam sciendum est quod tripliciter aliquid praedicatur de pluribus: univoce, aequivoce et analogice. Univoce praedicatur quod praedicatur secundum idem nomen et secundum rationem eamdem, id est definitionem, sicut animal praedicatur de homine et de asino: utrumque enim dicitur animal, et utrumque est substantia animata sensibilis, quod est definitio animalis. Aequivoce praedicatur quod praedicatur de aliquibus secundum idem nomen et secundum diversam rationem, sicut canis dicitur de latrabili et de caelesti, quae conveniunt solum in nomine et non in definitione sive significatione; id enim quod significatur per nomen est definitio, sicut dicitur in IV Metaphysicae. Analogice dicitur praedicari quod praedicatur de pluribus quorum rationes diversae sunt, sed attribuuntur uni alicui eidem, sicut sanum dicitur de corpore animalis et de urina et de potione, sed non ex toto idem significat in omnibus: dicitur enim de urina ut de signo sanitatis, de corpore ut de subiecto, de potione ut de causa. Sed tamen omnes istae rationes attribuuntur uni fini, scilicet sanitati.

Aliquando enim ea quae conveniunt secundum analogiam, id est in proportione vel comparatione vel convenientia, attribuuntur uni fini, sicut patet in praedicto exemplo; aliquando uni agenti, sicut medicus dicitur et de eo qui operatur per artem et de eo qui operatur sine arte, ut vetula, et etiam de instrumentis, sed per attributionem ad unum agens quod est medicina; aliquando autem per attributionem ad unum subiectum, sicut ens dicitur de substantia, de qualitate et quantitate et aliis praedicamentis: non enim ex toto est eadem ratio qua substantia est ens et quantitas et alia, sed omnia dicuntur ex eo quod attribuuntur substantiae, quod est

Also, notice that, when we speak of intrinsic principles (namely, matter and form), according to the agreement and difference of things that are from principles and according to the agreement and difference of principles, we find that some are numerically the same, as are Socrates and this man in the Socrates now pointed out. Others are numerically diverse and specifically the same, as Socrates and Plato who, although they differ numerically, have the same human species. Others differ specifically but are generically the same, as man and ass have the same genus of animal. Others are generically diverse and are only analogically the same, as substance and quantity which have no common genus and are only analogically the same, because they are the same only insofar as they are beings. Being, however, is not a genus because it is not predicated univocally, but only analogically.

In order to understand this last we must notice something is predicated of many things in three ways: univocally, equivocally, and analogically. Something is predicated univocally according to the same name and the same nature (that is, definition), as 'animal' is predicated of man and of ass because each is called animal and each is a sensible, animated substance, which is the definition of animal. That is predicated equivocally which is predicated of some things according to the same name but according to a different nature, as 'dog' is said of the thing that barks and of the star in the heavens, which two agree in the name but not in the definition or in signification, because that which is signified by the name is the definition, as is said in the fourth book of the *Metaphysics*. That is said to be predicated analogically which is predicated of many whose natures are diverse but which are attributed to one same thing, as 'health' is said of the animal body, or of urine and of food. But it does not signify entirely the same thing in all three. It is said of urine as a sign of health, of body as of a subject and of food as of a cause. But all these natures are attributed to one end: namely, to health.

Sometimes those things which agree according to analogy—that is, in proportion, comparison, or agreement—are attributed to one end, as was plain in the preceding example of health. Sometimes they are attributed to one agent, as 'medical' is said of one who acts with art, of one who acts without art (like a midwife), and even of the instruments; but it is said of all by attribution to one agent, which is medicine. Sometimes it is said by attribution to one subject, as 'being' is said of substance, quantity, quality, and the other predicaments, because it is not entirely for the same reason that substance is being, and quantity and the others. Rather, all are called being insofar as they are

subiectum aliorum. Et ideo ens dicitur per prius de substantia et per posterius de aliis; et ideo ens non est genus substantiae et quantitatis, quia nullum genus praedicatur per prius et posterius de suis speciebus, sed praedicatur analogice. Et hoc est quod diximus, quod substantia et quantitas differunt genere sed sunt idem analogia.

Eorum igitur quae sunt idem numero, forma et materia sunt idem numero, ut Tullii et Ciceronis; eorum autem quae sunt idem in specie, diversa numero, etiam materia et forma non est eadem numero sed specie, sicut Socratis et Platonis. Et similiter eorum quae sunt idem genere, et principia sunt idem genere, ut anima et corpus asini et equi differunt specie, sed sunt idem genere. Et similiter eorum quae conveniunt secundum analogiam tantum, principia sunt eadem secundum analogiam tantum sive proportionem. Materia enim et forma et privatio, sive potentia et actus, sunt principia substantiae et aliorum generum; tamen materia substantiae et quantitatis, et similiter forma et privatio, differunt genere, sed conveniunt solum secundum proportionem in hoc quod, sicut se habet materia substantiae ad substantiam in ratione materiae, ita se habet materia quantitatis ad quantitatem. Sicut tamen substantia est causa ceterorum, ita principia substantiae sunt principia omnium aliorum.

attributed to substance, which is the subject of the others. Hence 'being' is said primarily of substance and secondarily of the others. Therefore, being is not a genus of substance and quantity because no genus is predicated of its species according to prior and posterior. Rather, being is predicated analogically. This is what we mean when we say that substance and quantity differ generically but are the same analogically.

Therefore, the form and matter of those things which are numerically the same are themselves likewise numerically the same, as are the form and matter of Tullius and Cicero. The matter and form of those things which are specifically the same and numerically diverse are not the same numerically, but specifically, as the matter and form of Socrates and Plato. Likewise, the matter and form of those things which are generically the same, as the soul and body of an ass and a horse differ specifically but are the same generically. Likewise, the principles of those things which agree only analogically or proportionally are the same only analogically or proportionally, because matter, form and privation or potency and act are the principles of substance and of the other genera. However, the matter, form and privation of substance and of quantity differ generically, but they agree according to proportion only, insofar as the matter of substance is to substance, in the nature of matter, as the matter of quantity is to quantity. Still, just as substance is the cause of the others, so the principles of substance are the principles of all the others.

ON BEING AND ESSENCE

PROLOGUE

Quia parvus error in principio magnus est in fine secundum Philosophum in I *Caeli et mundi,* ens autem et essentia sunt quae primo intellectu concipiuntur, ut dicit Avicenna in principio suae *Metaphysicae,* ideo ne ex eorum ignorantia errare contingat, ad horum difficultatem aperiendam dicendum est quid nomine essentiae et entis significetur et quomodo in diversis inveniatur, et quomodo se habeat ad intentiones logicas, scilicet genus, speciem et differentiam.

Quia vero ex compositis simplicium cognitionem accipere debemus et ex posterioribus in priora devenire, ut a facilioribus incipientes convenientior fiat disciplina, ideo ex significatione entis ad significationem essentiae procedendum est.

A small error at the outset can lead to great errors in the final conclusions, as the Philosopher says in *de Caelo et mundo* 1.5,[1] and thus, since being and essence are the things first conceived of by the intellect, as Avicenna says at the beginning of his *Metaphysics* 1.6, in order to avoid errors arising from ignorance about these two things, we should make plain the difficulties surrounding them by explaining what the terms being and essence each signify and by showing how each may be found in various things and how each is related to the logical intentions of genus, species, and difference.

Since we ought to acquire knowledge of simple things from composite ones and come to know what is prior from what is posterior, we advance in learning more readily when we begin with what is easier, and thus we should first consider the signification of being and then proceed from there to the signification of essence.

CHAPTER 1

On the meaning of the terms 'being' and 'essence'

Sciendum est igitur quod, sicut in V *Metaphysicae* Philosophus dicit, ens per se dupliciter dicitur: uno modo quod dividitur per decem genera, alio modo quod significat propositionum veritatem. Horum autem differentia est quia secundo modo potest dici ens omne illud de quo affirmativa propositio formari potest, etiam si illud in re nihil ponat; per quem modum privationes et negationes entia dicuntur: dicimus enim quod affirmatio est opposita negationi, et quod caecitas est in oculo. Sed primo modo non potest dici ens nisi quod aliquid in re ponit; unde primo modo caecitas et huiusmodi non sunt entia.

Nomen igitur essentiae non sumitur ab ente secundo modo dicto: aliqua enim hoc modo dicuntur entia quae essentiam non habent, ut patet in privationibus; sed sumitur essentia ab ente primo modo dicto. Unde Commentator in eodem loco dicit quod ens primo modo dictum est *quod significat essentiam rei.* Et quia, ut dictum est, ens hoc modo dictum dividitur per decem genera, oportet ut essentia significet aliquid commune omnibus naturis per quas diversa entia in diversis generibus et speciebus collocantur, sicut humanitas est essentia hominis, et sic de aliis.

As the Philosopher says in *Metaphysics* 5.7,[2] 'being' has two senses. In one sense, being signifies that which is divided into the ten categories; in another sense, that which signifies the truth of propositions. The difference between these is that in the second sense, anything can be called a being about which an affirmative proposition can be formed, even if the thing posits nothing in reality. In this way, privations and negations are called beings, as when we say that affirmation is opposed to negation, or that blindness is in the eye. But in the first sense, nothing can be called a being unless it posits something in reality, and thus in this first sense blindness and similar things are not beings.

The term 'essence' is not taken from being in the second sense, for in this sense some things are called beings that have no essence, as is clear with privations. Rather, the term 'essence' is taken from being in the first sense. Thus, in *Metaphysics* 5, com. 14, the Commentator explains the passage from Aristotle mentioned above by saying that being, in the first sense, is *what signifies the essence of a thing.* And since, as was said above, being in this sense is divided into the ten categories, essence signifies something common to all natures through which the various beings are placed in the various genera and species, as humanity is the essence of man, and so on.

---

1. Aristotle, *de Caelo et mundo,* 271b8–13.
2. Aristotle, *Metaphysics,* 1017a22–35.

Et quia illud per quod res constituitur in proprio genere vel specie est hoc quod significatur per diffinitionem indicantem quid est res, inde est quod nomen essentiae a philosophis in nomen quiditatis mutatur; et hoc est etiam quod Philosophus frequenter nominat *quod quid erat esse*, id est hoc per quod aliquid habet esse quid. Dicitur etiam forma, secundum quod per formam significatur certitudo uniuscuiusque rei, ut dicit Avicenna in II *Metaphysicae* suae. Hoc etiam alio nomine natura dicitur, accipiendo naturam secundum primum modum illorum quattuor quos Boethius in libro *de Duabus naturis* assignat: secundum scilicet quod natura dicitur omne illud quod *intellectu quoquo modo capi potest*, non enim res est intelligibilis nisi per diffinitionem et essentiam suam; et sic etiam Philosophus dicit in V *Metaphysicae* quod omnis substantia est natura. Tamen nomen naturae hoc modo sumptae videtur significare essentiam rei secundum quod habet ordinem ad propriam operationem rei, cum nulla res propria operatione destituatur; quiditatis vero nomen sumitur ex hoc quod per diffinitionem significatur. Sed essentia dicitur secundum quod per eam et in ea ens habet esse.

Sed quia ens absolute et primo dicitur de substantiis, et per posterius et quasi secundum quid de accidentibus, inde est quod essentia proprie et vere est in substantiis, sed in accidentibus est quodammodo et secundum quid. Substantiarum vero quaedam sunt simplices et quaedam compositae, et in utrisque est essentia; sed in simplicibus veriori et nobiliori modo, secundum quod etiam esse nobilius habent: sunt enim causa eorum quae composita sunt, ad minus substantia prima simplex quae Deus est. Sed quia illarum substantiarum essentiae sunt nobis magis occultae, ideo ab essentiis substantiarum compositarum incipiendum est, ut a facilioribus convenientior fiat disciplina.

Since that through which a thing is constituted in its proper genus or species is what is signified by the definition indicating what the thing is, philosophers introduced the term 'quiddity' to mean the same as the term essence; and this is the same thing that the Philosopher frequently terms *what it is to be a thing*; that is, that through which something has being as a particular kind of thing. Essence is also called 'form,' for the certitude of every thing is signified through its form, as Avicenna says in his *Metaphysics* 1.6. The same thing is also called 'nature,' taking nature in the first of the four senses that Boethius distinguishes in his book *de Persona et duabus naturis* 1,[3] in the sense, in other words, that nature is what we call everything that *can in any way be captured by the intellect,* for a thing is not intelligible except through its definition and essence. And so the Philosopher says in *Metaphysics* 5.4[4] that every substance is a nature. But the term 'nature' used in this way seems to signify the essence of a thing as it is ordered to the proper operation of the thing, for no thing is without its proper operation. The term 'quiddity,' surely, is taken from the fact that this is what is signified by the definition. But the same thing is called 'essence' because the being has existence through it and in it.

But because being is absolutely and primarily said of substances, and only secondarily and in a certain sense said of accidents, essence too is properly and truly in substances and is in accidents only in a certain way and in a certain sense. Now some substances are simple and some are composite, and essence is in both, though in the simple substances in a truer and more noble way, as these have existence in a nobler way: indeed, the simple substances are the cause of the composite ones, or at least this is true with respect to the first simple substance, which is God. But because the essences of these substances are more hidden from us, we ought to begin with the essences of composite substances, for we advance in learning more readily when we begin with what is easier.

3. PL 64, 1341B.
4. Aristotle, *Metaphysics*, 1014b36.

CHAPTER 2

On the essences of composite substances

In substantiis igitur compositis forma et materia nota est, ut in homine anima et corpus. Non autem potest dici quod alterum eorum tantum essentia esse dicatur. Quod enim materia sola rei non sit essentia, planum est, quia res per essentiam suam et cognoscibilis est, et in specie ordinatur vel genere; sed materia neque cognitionis principium est, neque secundum eam aliquid ad genus vel speciem determinatur, sed secundum id quod aliquid actu est. Neque etiam forma tantum essentia substantiae compositae dici potest, quamvis hoc quidam asserere conentur. Ex his enim quae dicta sunt patet quod essentia est illud quod per diffinitionem rei significatur; diffinitio autem substantiarum naturalium non tantum formam continet sed etiam materiam, aliter enim diffinitiones naturales et mathematicae non differrent. Nec potest dici quod materia in diffinitione substantiae naturalis ponatur sicut additum essentiae eius vel ens extra essentiam eius, quia hic modus diffinitionum proprius est accidentibus, quae perfectam essentiam non habent; unde oportet quod in diffinitione sua subiectum recipiant, quod est extra genus eorum. Patet ergo quod essentia comprehendit et materiam et formam.

Non autem potest dici quod essentia significet relationem quae est inter materiam et formam, vel aliquid superadditum ipsis, quia hoc de necessitate esset accidens et extraneum a re, nec per eam res cognosceretur: quae omnia essentiae conveniunt. Per formam enim, quae est actus materiae, materia efficitur ens actu et hoc aliquid; unde illud quod superadvenit non dat esse actu simpliciter materiae, sed esse actu tale, sicut etiam accidentia faciunt, ut albedo facit actu album. Unde et quando talis forma acquiritur, non dicitur generari simpliciter sed secundum quid.

Relinquitur ergo quod nomen essentiae in substantiis compositis significat id quod ex materia et forma compositum est. Et huic consonat verbum Boethii in commento *Praedicamentorum*, ubi dicit quod *usia* significat compositum; *usia* enim apud Graecos idem est quod *essentia* apud nos, ut ipsemet dicit in libro *de Duabus naturis*. Avicenna etiam dicit quod quiditas substantiarum compositarum est ipsa compositio formae et materiae. Commentator etiam dicit super VII *Metaphysicae*: *Natura quam habent species in rebus generabilibus*

In composite substances we find form and matter, as in man there are soul and body. We cannot say, however, that either of these alone is the essence of the thing. That matter alone is not the essence of the thing is clear, for it is through its essence that a thing is knowable and is placed in a species or genus. But matter is not a principle of cognition; nor is anything determined to a genus or species according to its matter but rather according to what it is in act. Nor is form alone the essence of a composite thing, however much certain people may try to assert this. From what has been said, it is clear that the essence is that which is signified by the definition of the thing. The definition of a natural substance, however, contains not only form but also matter; otherwise, the definitions of natural things and mathematical ones would not differ. Nor can it be said that matter is placed in the definition of a natural substance as something added to the essence or as some being beyond the essence of the thing, for that type of definition is more proper to accidents, which do not have a perfect essence and which include in their definitions a subject beyond their own genus. Therefore, the essence of a composite substance clearly comprises both matter and form.

Nor can it be said that essence signifies the relation between the matter and the form or something superadded to these, for then the essence would of necessity be an accident and extraneous to the thing, and the thing would not be known through its essence, all of which are proper to an essence. Through the form, surely, which is the act of the matter, the matter is made a being in act and a certain kind of thing. Thus, something that supervenes does not give to the matter existence in act simply, but rather existence in act in a certain way, just as accidents do, as when whiteness makes something actually white. Hence, when such a form is acquired, we do not say that the thing is generated simply but only in a certain way.

It remains, therefore, that the term 'essence,' used with respect to composite substances, signifies that which is composed of matter and form. This conclusion is consistent with what Boethius says in his commentary on the *Categories*, namely, that *ousia* signifies what is composite; *ousia*, of course, is for the Greeks what *essence* is for us, as Boethius himself says in his book *de Persona et duabus naturis*.[5] Avicenna even says (*Metaphysics* 5.5) that the quiddity of a composite substance is the very composition of the form and the matter. And commenting on Book 7 of Aris-

---

5. Although quoted by various thirteenth century authors, this statement does not appear in the text of *de Persona et duabus naturis* as we have it.

est aliquod medium, id est compositum ex materia et forma.

Huic etiam ratio concordat, quia esse substantiae compositae non est tantum formae neque tantum materiae, sed ipsius compositi; essentia autem est secundum quam res esse dicitur: unde oportet ut essentia qua res denominatur ens non tantum sit forma, neque tantum materia, sed utrumque, quamvis huiusmodi esse suo modo sola forma sit causa. Sic enim in aliis videmus quae ex pluribus principiis constituuntur, quod res non denominatur ex altero illorum principiorum tantum, sed ab eo quod utrumque complectitur: ut patet in saporibus, quia ex actione calidi digerentis humidum causatur dulcedo, et quamvis hoc modo calor sit causa dulcedinis, non tamen denominatur corpus dulce calore sed sapore qui calidum et humidum complectitur.

Sed quia individuationis principium materia est, ex hoc forte videtur sequi quod essentia, quae materiam in se complectitur simul et formam, sit tantum particularis et non universalis: ex quo sequeretur quod universalia diffinitionem non haberent, si essentia est id quod per diffinitionem significatur. Et ideo sciendum est quod materia non quolibet modo accepta est individuationis principium, sed solum materia signata; et dico materiam signatam quae sub determinatis dimensionibus consideratur. Haec autem materia in diffinitione quae est hominis in quantum est homo non ponitur, sed poneretur in diffinitione Socratis si Socrates diffinitionem haberet. In diffinitione autem hominis ponitur materia non signata: non enim in diffinitione hominis ponitur hoc os et haec caro, sed os et caro absolute quae sunt materia hominis non signata.

Sic ergo patet quod essentia hominis et essentia Socratis non differt nisi secundum signatum et non signatum; unde Commentator dicit super VII *Metaphysicae: Socrates nihil aliud est quam animalitas et rationalitas, quae sunt quiditas eius.* Sic etiam essentia generis et speciei secundum signatum et non signatum differunt, quamvis alius modus designationis sit utrobique: quia designatio individui respectu speciei est per materiam determinatam dimensionibus, designatio autem speciei respectu generis est per differentiam constitutivam quae ex forma rei sumitur. Haec autem determinatio vel designatio quae est in specie respectu generis, non est per aliquid in essentia speciei exsistens quod nullo modo in essentia generis sit; immo quicquid est in specie est etiam in genere ut non determinatum. Si enim animal non esset totum quod est homo sed pars

totle's *Metaphysics,* the Commentator says: *The nature that species in generable things have is something in the middle; that is, it is composed of matter and form (Metaphysics 7, com. 27).*

Moreover, reason supports this view, for the existence of a composite substance is neither form alone nor matter alone but is rather composed of these. The essence is that according to which the thing is said to exist; hence, it is right that the essence by which a thing is denominated a being is neither form alone not matter alone but both, although existence of this kind is caused by the form and not by the matter. Similarly, we see that in other things that are constituted from many principles, the thing is not denominated from just one or the other of the principles but rather from that which embraces both. Thus, with respect to flavors, sweetness is caused by the action of a warm animal body digesting what is wet, and although in this way warmth is the cause of the sweetness, nevertheless a body is not called sweet by reason of the warmth, but rather by reason of the flavor, which embraces both the warmth and the wetness.

But because matter is the principle of individuation, it would perhaps seem to follow that essence, which embraces in itself simultaneously both form and matter, is merely particular and not universal. From this it would follow that universals have no definitions, assuming that essence is what is signified by the definition. Thus, we must point out that the principle of individuation is not matter understood in just any way, but only signate matter is the principle of individuation. I call 'signate matter' matter considered under determinate dimensions. Such matter is not included in the definition of man as man, but it would be included in the definition of Socrates, if Socrates had a definition. In the definition of man, however, is included nonsignate matter: in the definition of man we do not include 'this bone' and 'this flesh' but only bone and flesh absolutely, which are the non-signate matter of man.

Hence, the essence of man and the essence of Socrates do not differ except as the signate differs from the non-signate, and so the Commentator says, in *Metaphysics 7,* com. 20: *Socrates is nothing other than animality and rationality, which are his quiddity.* Similarly, the essence of a genus and the essence of a species differ as signate from non-signate, although in the case of genus and species a different mode of designation is used with respect to each. For the designation of the individual with respect to the species is through matter determined by dimensions, while the designation of the species with respect to the genus is through the constitutive difference, which is taken from the form of the thing. This determination or designation, however, which is made in the species with respect to the genus, is not through something that exists in the essence of the species but in no way exists in the essence of the genus.

eius, non praedicaretur de eo, cum nulla pars integralis de suo toto praedicetur.

Hoc autem quomodo contingat videri poterit, si inspiciatur qualiter differt corpus secundum quod ponitur pars animalis, et secundum quod ponitur genus; non enim potest esse eo modo genus quo est pars integralis. Hoc igitur nomen quod est corpus multipliciter accipi potest. Corpus enim secundum quod est in genere substantiae dicitur ex eo quod habet talem naturam ut in eo possint designari tres dimensiones; ipsae enim tres dimensiones designatae sunt corpus quod est in genere quantitatis. Contingit autem in rebus ut quod habet unam perfectionem, ad ulteriorem etiam perfectionem pertingat; sicut patet in homine, qui et naturam sensitivam habet, et ulterius intellectivam. Similiter etiam et super hanc perfectionem quae est habere talem formam ut in ea possint tres dimensiones designari, potest alia perfectio adiungi, ut vita vel aliquid huiusmodi. Potest ergo hoc nomen corpus significare rem quandam quae habet talem formam ex qua sequitur in ipsa designabilitas trium dimensionum, cum praecisione: ut scilicet ex illa forma nulla ulterior perfectio sequatur, sed si quid aliud superadditur, sit praeter significationem corporis sic dicti. Et hoc modo corpus erit integralis et materialis pars animalis: quia sic anima erit praeter id quod significatum est nomine corporis, et erit superveniens ipsi corpori, ita quod ex ipsis duobus, scilicet anima et corpore, sicut ex partibus constituetur animal.

Potest etiam hoc nomen corpus hoc modo accipi ut significet rem quandam quae habet talem formam ex qua tres dimensiones in ea possunt designari, quaecumque forma sit illa, sive ex ea possit provenire aliqua ulterior perfectio, sive non; et hoc modo corpus erit genus animalis, quia in animali nihil erit accipere quod non implicite in corpore contineatur. Non enim anima est alia forma ab illa per quam in re illa poterant designari tres dimensiones; et ideo cum dicebatur quod *corpus est quod habet talem formam ex qua possunt designari tres dimensiones in eo*, intelligebatur quaecumque forma esset: sive anima, sive lapideitas, sive quaecumque alia. Et sic forma animalis implicite in forma corporis continetur, prout corpus est genus eius.

Et talis est etiam habitudo animalis ad hominem. Si enim animal nominaret tantum rem quandam quae habet talem perfectionem ut possit sentire et moveri per principium in ipso existens, cum praecisione alterius perfectionis, tunc quaecumque alia perfectio ulterior superveniret haberet se ad animal per modum compartis, et non sicut implicite contenta in ratione animalis: et sic animal non esset genus. Sed est genus secundum quod significat rem quandam ex cuius forma potest provenire

On the contrary, whatever is in the species is also in the genus as undetermined. If animal were not all that man is but rather only a part of him, then animal would not be predicated of man, for no integral part may be predicated of its whole.

We can see how this happens by considering how body taken as a part of animal differs from body taken as the genus of animal, for body cannot be a genus in the way it is an integral part. The term 'body' can thus be accepted in several ways. Body is said to be in the genus of substance in that it has a nature such that three dimensions can be designated in it. These three designated dimensions are the body that is in the genus of quantity. Now, it sometimes happens that what has one perfection may attain to a further perfection as well, as is clear in man, who has a sensitive nature and, further, an intellective one. Similarly, above this perfection of having a form such that three dimensions can be designated in it, there can be joined another perfection, as life or some similar thing. This term 'body' therefore can signify a certain thing that has a form such that from the form there follows in the thing designatability in three dimensions exclusively: namely, such that from this form no further perfection follows, but if some other thing is superadded, it is beyond the signification of body thus understood. And understood in this way, body will be an integral and material part of animal, because in this way soul will be beyond what is signified by the term 'body,' and it will supervene on body such that from these two (namely, soul and body), animal is constituted as from parts.

This term 'body' can also be understood as signifying a certain thing that has a form such that three dimensions can be designated in it, whatever form this may be, such that either from the form some further perfection can arise or not. Understood in this way, body will be the genus of animal, for there will be understood in animal nothing that is not implicitly contained in body. Now, the soul is not a form other than that through which there can be designated in the thing three dimensions, and therefore, when we say that *body is what has a form from which three dimensions can be designated in the body*, we understand that there is some kind of form of this type, whether soul, or rockness, or any other form. And thus the form of animal is implicitly contained in the form of body, when body is its genus.

Such too is the relation of animal to man. For if 'animal' named just a certain thing that has a perfection such that it can sense and move by a principle existing in itself, excluding any other perfection, then whatever further perfection may supervene would be related to animal as another part thereof, and not as implicitly contained in the notion of animal, and in this way animal would not be a genus. But animal is a genus when it signifies a certain thing from the form of which sensation and motion can arise, whatever

sensus et motus, quaecumque sit illa forma: sive sit anima sensibilis tantum, sive sensibilis et rationalis simul.

Sic ergo genus significat indeterminate totum id quod est in specie, non enim significat tantum materiam. Similiter etiam et differentia significat totum, et non significat tantum formam; et etiam diffinitio significat totum, et etiam species. Sed tamen diversimode: quia genus significat totum ut quaedam denominatio determinans id quod est materiale in re sine determinatione propriae formae, unde genus sumitur ex materia—quamvis non sit materia—ut patet quia corpus dicitur ex hoc quod habet talem perfectionem ut possint in eo designari tres dimensiones, quae quidem perfectio est materialiter se habens ad ulteriorem perfectionem. Differentia vero e converso est sicut quaedam denominatio a forma determinate sumpta, praeter hoc quod de primo intellectu eius sit materia determinata; ut patet cum dicitur animatum, scilicet illud quod habet animam, non enim determinatur quid sit, utrum corpus vel aliquid aliud; unde dicit Avicenna quod genus non intelligitur in differentia sicut pars essentiae eius, sed solum sicut ens extra essentiam, sicut etiam subiectum est de intellectu passionum. Et ideo etiam genus non praedicatur de differentia per se loquendo, ut dicit Philosophus in III *Metaphysicae* et in IV *Topicorum*, nisi forte sicut subiectum praedicatur de passione. Sed diffinitio vel species comprehendit utrumque, scilicet determinatam materiam quam designat nomen generis, et determinatam formam quam designat nomen differentiae.

Ex hoc patet ratio quare genus, species et differentia se habent proportionaliter ad materiam et formam et compositum in natura, quamvis non sint idem quod illa: quia neque genus est materia, sed a materia sumptum ut significans totum; neque differentia forma, sed a forma sumpta ut significans totum. Unde dicimus hominem esse animal rationale, et non ex animali et rationali sicut dicimus eum esse ex anima et corpore: ex anima enim et corpore dicitur esse homo sicut ex duabus rebus quaedam res tertia constituta quae neutra illarum est, homo enim neque est anima neque corpus. Sed si homo aliquo modo ex animali et rationali esse dicatur, non erit sicut res tertia ex duabus rebus, sed sicut intellectus tertius ex duobus intellectibus. Intellectus enim animalis est sine determinatione specialis formae, exprimens naturam rei ab eo quod est materiale respectu ultimae perfectionis; intellectus autem huius differentiae rationalis consistit in determinatione formae specialis: ex quibus duobus intellectibus constituitur intellectus speciei vel diffinitionis. Et ideo sicut res constituta ex aliquibus non recipit praedicationem earum rerum ex quibus constituitur, ita nec

this form may be, whether a sensible soul only or a soul both sensible and rational.

Therefore, the genus signifies indeterminately the whole of what is in the species and not the matter only. Similarly, the difference also signifies the whole and not the form only. So, too, the definition signifies the whole, as does the species. But although these all signify the same thing, they do so in different ways. For the genus signifies the whole as a certain denomination determining that which is material in the thing without a determination of its proper form, whence the genus is taken from the matter, although it is not the matter. This is clear from the fact that we call something a body in that the thing has a perfection such that in it three dimensions can be designated, and this perfection is related materially to some further perfection. Conversely, the difference is like a certain denomination taken from the determined form, beyond the first conception by which the matter is determined. So, when we speak of something animated (that is, something that has a soul), this does not determine what the thing is, whether it is a body or something else. Hence, Avicenna says (*Metaphysics* 5.6) that the genus is not understood in the difference as a part of its essence but only as a being beyond its essence, even as a subject is with respect to the concept of a passion. And thus the genus is not predicated of the difference in itself, as the Philosopher says in *Metaphysics* 3.8[6] and in *Topics* 4.2,[7] unless perhaps as a subject is predicated of a passion. But the definition or the species comprehends both: namely, the determined matter that the term 'genus' designates and the determined form that the term 'difference' designates.

From this is it clear why the genus, the difference, and the species are related proportionally to the matter, the form, and the composite in nature, although they are not the same as these things. For the genus is not the matter, although it is taken from the matter as signifying the whole; nor is the difference the form, although it is taken from the form as signifying the whole. We thus say that man is a rational animal, but not that he is composed of animal and rational in the sense that we say that man is composed of soul and body: man is said to be composed of soul and body as from two things from which a third thing is constituted different from each of the two, for man is neither body nor soul. But if man is said in some sense to be composed of animal and rational, it will not be as a third thing composed from these two things, but as a third concept composed from these two concepts. The concept of animal is without determination of a special form and expresses the nature of the thing from that which is material with respect to its ultimate perfection; the concept of the difference, rational, consists in the determination of a special form. From these two concepts are constituted the concept of the species or

---

6. Aristotle, *Metaphysics*, 998b24.
7. Aristotle, *Topics*, 122b22–26.

intellectus recipit praedicationem eorum intellectuum ex quibus constituitur: non enim dicimus quod diffinitio sit genus aut differentia.

Quamvis autem genus significet totam essentiam speciei, non tamen oportet ut diversarum specierum quarum est idem genus, sit una essentia, quia unitas generis ex ipsa indeterminatione vel indifferentia procedit. Non autem ita quod illud quod significatur per genus sit una natura numero in diversis speciebus, cui superveniat res alia quae sit differentia determinans ipsum, sicut forma determinat materiam quae est una numero; sed quia genus significat aliquam formam— non tamen determinate hanc vel illam—quam determinate differentia exprimit, quae non est alia quam illa quae indeterminate significabatur per genus. Et ideo dicit Commentator in XI *Metaphysicae* quod materia prima dicitur una per remotionem omnium formarum, sed genus dicitur unum per communitatem formae significatae. Unde patet quod per additionem differentiae remota illa indeterminatione quae erat causa unitatis generis, remanent species per essentiam diversae.

Et quia, ut dictum est, natura speciei est indeterminata respectu individui sicut natura generis respectu speciei: inde est quod, sicut id quod est genus prout praedicabatur de specie implicabat in sua significatione, quamvis indistincte, totum quod determinate est in specie, ita etiam et id quod est species secundum quod praedicatur de individuo oportet quod significet totum id quod est essentialiter in individuo, licet indistincte. Et hoc modo essentia speciei significatur nomine hominis, unde homo de Socrate praedicatur. Si autem significetur natura speciei cum praecisione materiae designatae quae est principium individuationis, sic se habebit per modum partis; et hoc modo significatur nomine humanitatis; humanitas enim significat id unde homo est homo. Materia autem designata non est id unde homo est homo, et ita nullo modo continetur inter illa ex quibus homo habet quod sit homo. Cum ergo humanitas in suo intellectu includat tantum ea ex quibus homo habet quod est homo, patet quod a significatione excluditur vel praeciditur materia designata; et quia pars non praedicatur de toto, inde est quod humanitas nec de homine nec de Socrate praedicatur. Unde dicit Avicenna quod quiditas compositi non est ipsum compositum cuius est quiditas, quamvis etiam ipsa quiditas sit composita; sicut humanitas, licet sit composita, non est homo: immo oportet quod sit recepta in aliquo quod est materia designata.

the definition. Thus, just as a thing constituted from other things does not have predicated of it these other things, so too a concept does not have predicated of it the concepts of which it is constituted: clearly, we do not say that the definition is either the genus or the difference.

Although the genus may signify the whole essence of the species, nevertheless the various species of which it is the genus do not have the same essence, for the unity of the genus proceeds from its very indetermination or undifferentiation. Nor is it the case that what is signified through the genus in the various species is numerically one nature such that to it there supervenes some other thing, which is the difference that determines it, as a form determines matter that is numerically one. Rather, the genus signifies some form (though not determinately this one or that one), which the difference expresses determinately, the very one that is signified indeterminately through the genus. And thus the Commentator says in *Metaphysics* 12,[8] com. 14, that prime matter is called 'one' by the removal of all forms, but the genus is called 'one' through the commonality of forms signified. Hence, once the the indetermination (which was the cause of the unity of the genus) is removed through the addition of the difference, the various species remain diverse by essence.

Furthermore, since, as was said above, the nature of the species is indeterminate with respect to the individual just as the nature of the genus is with respect to the species, and since, further, the genus, as predicated of the species, includes in its signification (although indistinctly) everything that is in the species determinately, so too does the species, as predicated of the individual, signify everything that is in the individual essentially, although it signifies this indistinctly. In this way, the essence of the species is signified by the term 'man,' and so man is predicated of Socrates. If, however, the nature of the species is signified in such a way as to exclude designate matter, which is the principle of individuation, then the species is related to the individual as a part; and this is how the term 'humanity' signifies, for humanity signifies that by which a man is a man. Designate matter, however, is not that by which a man is a man, and it is in no way contained among those things that make a man a man. Since, therefore, the concept of humanity includes only those things by which a man is a man, designate matter is excluded or omitted, and since a part is not predicated of its whole, humanity is predicated neither of man nor of Socrates. Thus, Avicenna says (*Metaphysics* 5.5) that the quiddity of a composite thing is not the composite thing of which it is the quiddity, even though the quiddity itself is composite, just as humanity, while composite, is not man. On the contrary, it must be received in something that is designate matter.

---

8. Aquinas knew this book as Book XI.

Sed quia, ut dictum est, designatio speciei respectu generis est per formam, designatio autem individui respectu speciei est per materiam, ideo oportet ut nomen significans id unde natura generis sumitur, cum praecisione formae determinatae perficientis speciem, significet partem materialem totius, sicut corpus est pars materialis hominis; nomen autem significans id unde sumitur natura speciei, cum praecisione materiae designatae, significat partem formalem. Et ideo humanitas significatur ut forma quaedam, et dicitur quod est forma totius; non quidem quasi superaddita partibus essentialibus, scilicet formae et materiae, sicut forma domus superadditur partibus integralibus eius: sed magis est forma quae est totum, scilicet formam complectens et materiam, tamen cum praecisione eorum per quae nata est materia designari.

Sic igitur patet quod essentiam hominis significat hoc nomen homo et hoc nomen humanitas, sed diversimode, ut dictum est: quia hoc nomen homo significat eam ut totum, in quantum scilicet non praecidit designationem materiae sed implicite continet eam et indistincte, sicut dictum est quod genus continet differentiam; et ideo praedicatur hoc nomen homo de individuis. Sed hoc nomen humanitas significat eam ut partem, quia non continet in significatione sua nisi id quod est hominis in quantum est homo, et praecidit omnem designationem; unde de individuis hominis non praedicatur. Et propter hoc nomen essentiae quandoque invenitur praedicatum de re, dicimus enim Socratem esse essentiam quandam; et quandoque negatur, sicut dicimus quod essentia Socratis non est Socrates.

But since, as was said above, the designation of the species with respect to the genus is through form, and the designation of the individual with respect to the species is through matter, the term signifying that from which the nature of the genus is taken, when it excludes the determinate form that completes the species, signifies the material part of the whole: for example, as body is the material part of man. However, the term signifying that from which the nature of the species is taken, when it excludes designate matter, signifies the formal part. Thus, humanity is signified as a certain form, and it is said that it is the form of the whole: not, certainly, as a form superadded to the essential parts (the form and the matter) as the form of a house is superadded to its integral parts. Rather, humanity is the form that is the whole, embracing both form and matter, although excluding those things through which matter can be designated.

Therefore, the term 'man' and the term 'humanity' both signify the essence of man, though in diverse ways, as was said above. The term 'man' signifies the essence as a whole: in other words, insofar as the essence does not exclude designation of matter but implicitly and indistinctly contains it, in the way in which we said that the genus contains the difference. Hence, the term 'man' is predicated of individuals. But the term 'humanity' signifies the essence of man as a part because it contains in its signification only what belongs to man insofar as he is man, and excludes all designation. Thus, it is not predicated of individual men. And for this reason the term 'essence' is sometimes found predicated of the thing, as when we say that Socrates is a certain essence; and sometimes the term 'essence' is denied of the thing, as when we say that the essence of Socrates is not Socrates.

CHAPTER 3

How essence is related to genus, species, and difference

Viso igitur quid significetur nomine essentiae in substantiis compositis, videndum est quomodo se habeat ad rationem generis speciei et differentiae. Quia autem id cui convenit ratio generis vel speciei vel differentiae praedicatur de hoc singulari signato, impossibile est quod ratio universalis, scilicet generis vel speciei, conveniat essentiae secundum quod per modum partis significatur, ut nomine humanitatis vel animalitatis; et ideo dicit Avicenna quod rationalitas non est differentia sed differentiae principium; et eadem ratione humanitas non est species, nec animalitas genus. Similiter etiam non potest dici quod ratio generis vel speciei conveniat essentiae secundum quod est quaedam res exsistens extra singularia, ut Platonici ponebant, quia sic genus et species non praedicarentur de hoc individuo; non enim potest dici quod Socrates sit hoc quod ab eo separatum est, nec iterum illud separatum proficeret in cognitionem huius singularis. Et ideo relinquitur quod ratio generis vel speciei conveniat essentiae secundum quod significatur per modum totius, ut nomine hominis vel animalis, prout implicite et indistincte continet totum hoc quod in individuo est.

Natura autem vel essentia sic accepta potest dupliciter considerari. Uno modo, secundum rationem propriam, et haec est absoluta consideratio ipsius: et hoc modo nihil est verum de ea nisi quod convenit sibi secundum quod huiusmodi; unde quicquid aliorum attribuatur sibi, falsa est attributio. Verbi gratia homini in eo quod est homo convenit rationale et animal et alia quae in diffinitione eius cadunt; album vero aut nigrum, vel quicquid huiusmodi quod non est de ratione humanitatis, non convenit homini in eo quod homo. Unde si quaeratur utrum ista natura sic considerata possit dici una vel plures, neutrum concedendum est, quia utrumque est extra intellectum humanitatis, et utrumque potest sibi accidere. Si enim pluralitas esset de intellectu eius, nunquam posset esse una, cum tamen una sit secundum quod est in Socrate. Similiter si unitas esset de ratione eius, tunc esset una et eadem Socratis et Platonis nec posset in pluribus plurificari. Alio modo consideratur secundum esse quod habet in hoc vel in illo: et sic de ipsa aliquid praedicatur per accidens ratione eius in quo est, sicut dicitur quod homo est albus quia Socrates est albus, quamvis hoc non conveniat homini in eo quod homo.

Having seen what the term 'essence' signifies in composite substances, we ought next to see how essence is related to the logical intentions of genus, species, and difference. Since that to which the intentions of genus or species or difference is appropriate is predicated of this signate singular, it is impossible that a universal intention, like that of the species or genus, should be appropriate to the essence if the genus or species is signified as a part, as in the term 'humanity' or 'animality.' Thus, Avicenna says (*Metaphysics* 5.6) that rationality is not the difference but the principle of the difference. For the same reason, humanity is not a species, and animality is not a genus. Similarly, we cannot say that the intention of species or genus is appropriate to the essence as to a certain thing existing beyond singulars, as the Platonists used to suppose, for then the species and the genus would not be predicated of an individual: we surely cannot say that Socrates is something that is separated from him, nor would that separate thing advance our knowledge of this singular thing. And so it remains that the intention of genus or species is appropriate to the essence as the essence is signified as a whole, as the term 'man' or 'animal' implicitly and indistinctly contains the whole of what is in the individual.

The nature, however, or the essence thus understood can be considered in two ways. First, we can consider it according to its proper notion, and this is to consider it absolutely. In this way, nothing is true of the essence except what pertains to it absolutely: thus everything else that may be attributed to it will be attributed falsely. For example, to man, in that by which he is man, pertains animal and rational and the other things that fall in his definition; white or black or whatever else of this kind that is not in the notion of humanity does not pertain to man in that by which he is a man. Hence, if it is asked whether this nature, considered in this way, can be said to be one or many, we should concede neither alternative, for both are beyond the concept of humanity, and either may befall the conception of man. If plurality were in the concept of this nature, it could never be one, but nevertheless it is one as it exists in Socrates. Similarly, if unity were in the notion of this nature, then it would be one and the same in Socrates and Plato, and it could not be made many in many individuals. Second, we can also consider the existence the essence has in this thing or in that: in this way something can be predicated of the essence accidentally by reason of what the essence is in, as when we say that man is white because Socrates is white, although this does not pertain to man in that by which he is man.

Haec autem natura duplex habet esse: unum in singularibus et aliud in anima, et secundum utrumque consequuntur dictam naturam accidentia; in singularibus etiam habet multiplex esse secundum singularium diversitatem. Et tamen ipsi naturae secundum suam primam considerationem, scilicet absolutam, nullum istorum esse debetur. Falsum enim est dicere quod essentia hominis in quantum huiusmodi habeat esse in hoc singulari, quia si esse in hoc singulari conveniret homini in quantum est homo, nunquam esset extra hoc singulare; similiter etiam si conveniret homini in quantum est homo non esse in hoc singulari, nunquam esset in eo: sed verum est dicere quod homo, non in quantum est homo, habet quod sit in hoc singulari vel in illo aut in anima. Ergo patet quod natura hominis absolute considerata abstrahit a quolibet esse, ita tamen quod non fiat praecisio alicuius eorum. Et haec natura sic considerata est quae praedicatur de individuis omnibus.

Non tamen potest dici quod ratio universalis conveniat naturae sic acceptae, quia de ratione universalis est unitas et communitas; naturae autem humanae neutrum horum convenit secundum absolutam suam considerationem. Si enim communitas esset de intellectu hominis, tunc in quocumque inveniretur humanitas inveniretur communitas; et hoc falsum est, quia in Socrate non invenitur communitas aliqua, sed quicquid est in eo est individuatum. Similiter etiam non potest dici quod ratio generis vel speciei accidat naturae humanae secundum esse quod habet in individuis, quia non invenitur in individuis natura humana secundum unitatem ut sit unum quid omnibus conveniens, quod ratio universalis exigit. Relinquitur ergo quod ratio speciei accidat naturae humanae secundum illud esse quod habet in intellectu.

Ipsa enim natura humana in intellectu habet esse abstractum ab omnibus individuantibus; et ideo habet rationem uniformem ad omnia individua quae sunt extra animam, prout aequaliter est similitudo omnium et ducens in omnium cognitionem in quantum sunt homines. Et ex hoc quod talem relationem habet ad omnia individua, intellectus adinvenit rationem speciei et attribuit sibi; unde dicit Commentator in principio *de Anima* quod *intellectus est qui agit in rebus universalitatem*; hoc etiam Avicenna dicit in sua *Metaphysica*. Et quamvis haec natura intellecta habeat rationem universalis secundum quod comparatur ad res extra animam, quia est una similitudo omnium, tamen secundum quod habet esse in hoc intellectu vel in illo est quaedam species intellecta particularis. Et ideo patet defectus Commentatoris in III *de Anima*, qui voluit ex universalitate formae intellectae unitatem intellectus in omnibus hominibus concludere; quia non est universalitas illius formae secundum hoc esse quod habet in intellectu,

The nature considered in this way, however, has a double existence. On the one hand, it exists in singulars, and, on the other hand, it exists in the soul, and from each of these the nature acquires certain accidents. In singulars, furthermore, the essence has a multiple existence according to the multiplicity of singulars. Nevertheless, if we consider the essence in the first, or absolute, sense, none of these pertain to the essence. For it is false to say that the essence of man, considered absolutely, has existence in this singular, because if existence in this singular pertained to man insofar as he is man, man would never exist outside this singular. Similarly, if it pertained to man insofar as he is man not to exist in this singular, then the essence would never exist in the singular. But it is true to say that man, but not insofar as he is man, has whatever may be in this singular or in that one, or else in the soul. Therefore, the nature of man considered absolutely abstracts from every existence, though it does not exclude the existence of anything either. And the nature thus considered is the one predicated of each individual.

Nevertheless, the nature understood in this way is not a universal notion, because unity and commonality belong to the notion of a universal, but to human nature, considered absolutely, neither of these belong. For if commonality were in the concept of man, then in whatever humanity were found, there would be found commonality, and this is false, because no commonality is found in Socrates, but rather whatever is in him is individuated. Similarly, the notion of genus or species does not pertain to human nature because of the existence that that nature has in individuals, for human nature is not found in individuals with a unity that it will be one thing in all the individuals, which the notion of a universal demands. It remains, therefore, that the notion of species pertains to human nature according to the existence human nature has in the intellect.

Human nature in the intellect has existence abstracted from everything that individuates, and thus it is related uniformly to all individuals that exist outside the soul, as it is equally a likeness of all of them, and it leads to knowledge of all of them insofar as they are men. Since the nature in the intellect has this relation to each individual, the intellect invents the notion of species and attributes it to the nature. Hence, the Commentator, in *de Anima* 1, com. 8, says that *the intellect is what makes universality in things*; and Avicenna says the same in his *Metaphysics* 5.2. Although this nature understood in the intellect has the notion of a universal in relation to things outside the soul (because it is one likeness of them all), as the nature has existence in this intellect or in that one, it is a certain particular understood species. The Commentator, therefore, is in error in *de Anima* 3, com. 5, when he wants to infer the unity of intellect in all men from the universality of the understood form, because the universality of the form does not arise from the existence the form has in the intellect but rather

sed secundum quod refertur ad res ut similitudo rerum; sicut etiam si esset una statua corporalis repraesentans multos homines, constat quod illa imago vel species statuae haberet esse singulare et proprium secundum quod esset in hac materia, sed haberet rationem communitatis secundum quod esset commune repraesentativum plurium.

Et quia naturae humanae secundum suam absolutam considerationem convenit quod praedicetur de Socrate, et ratio speciei non convenit sibi secundum suam absolutam considerationem sed est de accidentibus quae consequuntur eam secundum esse quod habet in intellectu, ideo nomen speciei non praedicatur de Socrate ut dicatur Socrates est species: quod de necessitate accideret si ratio speciei conveniret homini secundum esse quod habet in Socrate, vel secundum suam considerationem absolutam, scilicet in quantum est homo; quicquid enim convenit homini in quantum est homo praedicatur de Socrate.

Et tamen praedicari convenit generi per se, cum in eius diffinitione ponatur. Praedicatio enim est quiddam quod completur per actionem intellectus componentis et dividentis, habens fundamentum in re ipsa unitatem eorum quorum unum de altero dicitur. Unde ratio praedicabilitatis potest claudi in ratione huius intentionis quae est genus, quae similiter per actum intellectus completur. Nihilominus tamen id cui intellectus intentionem praedicabilitatis attribuit, componens illud cum altero, non est ipsa intentio generis, sed potius illud cui intellectus intentionem generis attribuit, sicut quod significatur hoc nomine animal.

Sic ergo patet qualiter essentia vel natura se habet ad rationem speciei, quia ratio speciei non est de his quae conveniunt ei secundum absolutam suam considerationem, neque est de accidentibus quae consequuntur ipsam secundum esse quod habet extra animam, ut albedo et nigredo; sed est de accidentibus quae consequuntur eam secundum esse quod habet in intellectu. Et per hunc modum convenit etiam sibi ratio generis vel differentiae.

from its relation to things as a likeness of them. It is as if there were a corporeal statue representing many men; that image or species of statue would have a singular and proper existence insofar as it exists in this matter, but it would have the character of commonality insofar as it was a common representative of many men.

Since human nature, considered absolutely, is properly predicated of Socrates, and since the notion of species does not pertain to human nature considered absolutely but only accidentally because of the existence the nature has in the intellect, the term 'species' is not predicated of Socrates, for we do not say that Socrates is a species. We would have to say that Socrates is a species if the notion of species pertained to man arising from the existence that the nature has in Socrates or from the nature considered absolutely, that is, insofar as man is man. For whatever pertains to man insofar as he is man is predicated of Socrates.

But 'to be predicated' pertains to a genus in itself, because being predicated is placed in its definition. Now, predication is completed by the action of the intellect in compounding and dividing, and it has as its basis the unity in the real thing itself of those things one of which is said of another. Hence, the notion of predicability can be placed under the notion of this intention which is the genus, which is itself completed by an act of the intellect. Still, that to which the intellect attributes the intention of predicability by compounding it with another is not itself this intention of genus; it is rather that to which the intellect attributes the intention of genus, as, for instance, to what is signified by the term 'animal.'

We have thus made clear how the essence or nature is related to the notion of species, for the notion of species is not among those that pertain to the essence considered absolutely; nor is it among the accidents that follow from the existence that the essence has outside the soul, as whiteness or blackness. Rather, the notion of species is among the accidents that follow from the existence the essence has in the intellect. And in this way as well do the notions of genus or difference pertain to essences.

Chapter 4

How essences exist in separated substances

Nunc restat videre per quem modum sit essentia in substantiis separatis, scilicet in anima, intelligentia et causa prima. Quamvis autem simplicitatem causae primae omnes concedant, tamen compositionem formae et materiae quidam nituntur inducere in intelligentias et in animam; cuius positionis auctor videtur fuisse Avicebron, auctor libri *Fontis vitae*. Hoc autem dictis philosophorum communiter repugnat, qui eas substantias separatas a materia nominant et absque omni materia esse probant. Cuius demonstratio potissima est ex virtute intelligendi quae in eis est. Videmus enim formas non esse intelligibiles in actu nisi secundum quod separantur a materia et a condicionibus eius, nec efficiuntur intelligibiles in actu nisi per virtutem substantiae intelligentis, secundum quod recipiuntur in ea et secundum quod aguntur per eam. Unde oportet quod in qualibet substantia intelligente sit omnino immunitas a materia, ita quod neque habeat materiam partem sui, neque etiam sit sicut forma impressa in materia ut est de formis materialibus.

Nec potest aliquis dicere quod intelligibilitatem non impediat materia quaelibet, sed materia corporalis tantum. Si enim hoc esset ratione materiae corporalis tantum, cum materia non dicatur corporalis nisi secundum quod stat sub forma corporali, tunc oporteret quod hoc haberet materia, scilicet impedire intelligibilitatem, a forma corporali; et hoc non potest esse, quia ipsa etiam forma corporalis actu intelligibilis est sicut et aliae formae, secundum quod a materia abstrahitur. Unde in anima vel in intelligentia nullo modo est compositio ex materia et forma, ut hoc modo accipiatur essentia in eis sicut in substantiis corporalibus. Sed est ibi compositio formae et esse; unde in commento IX propositionis libri *de Causis* dicitur quod intelligentia est habens formam et esse: et accipitur ibi forma pro ipsa quiditate vel natura simplici.

Et quomodo hoc sit planum est videre. Quaecumque enim ita se habent ad invicem quod unum est causa esse alterius, illud quod habet rationem causae potest habere esse sine altero, sed non convertitur. Talis autem invenitur habitudo materiae et formae quod forma dat esse materiae, et ideo impossibile est esse materiam sine aliqua forma; tamen non est impossibile esse aliquam formam sine materia, forma enim in eo quod est forma non habet dependentiam ad materiam. Sed si inveniantur aliquae formae quae non possunt esse nisi in materia, hoc accidit eis secundum quod sunt distantes a primo principio quod est actus primus et purus. Unde illae

We should now see how essences exist in separated substances, that is, in the soul, in the intelligences, and in the first cause. Now, although everyone concedes the simplicity of the first cause, some people have tried to introduce into the intelligences and the soul a composition of form and matter, a position that seems to have begun with Avicebron, the author of the book called *Fons vitae*. But this view is repugnant to the common teaching of the philosophers, for they call these things substances separated from matter, and they prove them to be wholly without matter. The most cogent demonstration of this proceeds from the excellence of understanding found in these substances. For we see that forms are not actually intelligible except as they are separated from matter and its conditions, and forms are not made actually intelligible except by virtue of an intelligent substance in which they are received and through which they are brought about. Hence, in any intelligent substance there is a complete absence of matter in such a way that the substance has neither a material part itself, nor even is the substance like a form impressed in matter, as is the case with material forms.

Nor can someone say that only corporeal matter, and not some other kind of matter, impedes intelligibility. For, if it were only corporeal mater that impedes intelligibility, then, since matter is called corporeal only insofar as it exists under a corporeal form, it would follow that matter impedes intelligibility by the corporeal form; and this is impossible, for the corporeal form is actually intelligible just like any other form, insofar as it is abstracted from matter. Hence, in no way is there a composition of matter and form in either the soul or the intelligences, such that an essence is received in these as in corporeal substances. Nevertheless, in separate substances there is a composition of form and existence, and so in the *Liber de causis* 9, it is said that the intelligences have form and existence: and in this place form is taken in the sense of a simple quiddity or nature.

It is easy to see how this is the case. Whenever two things are related to each other such that one is the cause of the other, the one that is the cause can have existence without the other, but not conversely. Now, we find that matter and form are related in such a way that form gives existence to matter, and therefore it is impossible that matter exist without a form; but it is not impossible that a form exist without matter, for a form, insofar as it is a form, is not dependent on matter. If we should find some forms that cannot exist except in matter, this happens because such forms are distant from the first principle, which is primary and pure act. Hence, those forms that are nearest the first prin-

formae quae sunt propinquissimae primo principio sunt formae per se sine materia subsistentes, non enim forma secundum totum genus suum materia indiget, ut dictum est; et huiusmodi formae sunt intelligentiae, et ideo non oportet ut essentiae vel quiditates harum substantiarum sint aliud quam ipsa forma.

In hoc ergo differt essentia substantiae compositae et substantiae simplicis, quod essentia substantiae compositae non est tantum forma sed complectitur formam et materiam, essentia autem substantiae simplicis est forma tantum. Et ex hoc causantur aliae duae differentiae. Una est quod essentia substantiae compositae potest significari ut totum vel ut pars, quod accidit propter materiae designationem, ut dictum est. Et ideo non quolibet modo praedicatur essentia rei compositae de ipsa re composita: non enim potest dici quod homo sit quiditas sua. Sed essentia rei simplicis quae est sua forma non potest significari nisi ut totum, cum nihil sit ibi praeter formam quasi formam recipiens; et ideo quocumque modo sumatur essentia substantiae simplicis, de ea praedicatur. Unde Avicenna dicit quod *quiditas simplicis est ipsummet simplex*, quia non est aliquid aliud recipiens ipsam. Secunda differentia est quia essentiae rerum compositarum ex eo quod recipiuntur in materia designata multiplicantur secundum divisionem eius, unde contingit quod aliqua sint idem specie et diversa numero. Sed cum essentia simplicis non sit recepta in materia, non potest ibi esse talis multiplicatio; et ideo oportet ut non inveniantur in illis substantiis plura individua eiusdem speciei, sed quot sunt ibi individua tot sunt ibi species, ut Avicenna expresse dicit.

Huiusmodi ergo substantiae, quamvis sint formae tantum sine materia, non tamen in eis est omnimoda simplicitas nec sunt actus purus, sed habent permixtionem potentiae; et hoc sic patet. Quicquid enim non est de intellectu essentiae vel quiditatis, hoc est adveniens extra et faciens compositionem cum essentia, quia nulla essentia sine his quae sunt partes essentiae intelligi potest. Omnis autem essentia vel quiditas potest intelligi sine hoc quod aliquid intelligatur de esse suo: possum enim intelligere quid est homo vel phoenix et tamen ignorare an esse habeat in rerum natura; ergo patet quod esse est aliud ab essentia vel quiditate. Nisi forte sit aliqua res cuius quiditas sit ipsum suum esse, et haec res non potest esse nisi una et prima: quia impossibile est ut fiat plurificatio alicuius nisi per additionem alicuius differentiae, sicut multiplicatur natura generis in species; vel per hoc quod forma recipitur in diversis materiis, sicut multiplicatur natura speciei in diversis individuis; vel per hoc quod unum est absolutum et aliud in aliquo receptum, sicut si esset quidam calor separatus esset alius a calore non separato ex ipsa sua separatione. Si

ciple are subsisting forms essentially without matter, for not the whole genus of forms requires matter, as said above, and the intelligences are forms of this type. Thus, the essences or quiddities of these substances are not other than the forms themselves.

Therefore, the essence of a composite substance and that of a simple substance differ in that the essence of a composite substance is not form alone but embraces both form and matter, while the essence of a simple substance is form alone. And from this two other differences arise. One is that the essence of a composite substance can be signified as a whole or as a part, which happens because of the designation of the matter, as said above. Hence, the essence of a composite thing is not in every way predicated of the composite thing itself, for we cannot say that a man is his own quiddity. But the essence of a simple thing, which is its form, cannot be signified except as a whole, as in this case there is nothing beyond the form to receive the quiddity. And so, however we take the essence of a simple thing, the essence is predicated of it. Hence, Avicenna says (*Metaphysics* 5.5) that *the quiddity of a simple thing is the simple thing itself*, because there is no other thing to receive the form. The second difference is that the essences of composite things, because they are received in designate matter, are multiplied according to the division of matter, and so it happens that some such things are the same in species but different in number. But since the essence of a simple thing is not received in matter, there can be no such multiplication in this case, and so among such substances we do not find many individuals of the same species, but rather there are as many species as there are individuals, as Avicenna expressly says in *Metaphysics* 5.2.

Although substances of this kind are form alone and are without matter, they are nevertheless not in every way simple, and they are not pure act. Rather, they have an admixture of potency, and this can be seen as follows. Whatever is not in the concept of the essence or the quiddity comes from outside the essence and makes a composition with the essence, because no essence can be understood without the things that are its parts. But every essence or quiddity can be understood without understanding anything about its existence: I can understand what a man is or what a phoenix is, and nevertheless not know whether either has existence in reality. Therefore, it is clear that existence is something other than the essence or quiddity, unless perhaps there is something whose quiddity is its very own existence, and, if so, this thing must be one and primary. For there can be no plurification of something except by the addition of some difference, as the nature of a genus is multiplied in its species; or as the nature of the species is multiplied in diverse individuals since the form is received in diverse matters; or again as when one thing is absolute and another is received in something else, as if there were a certain separate heat

autem ponatur aliqua res quae sit esse tantum ita ut ipsum esse sit subsistens, hoc esse non recipiet additionem differentiae, quia iam non esset esse tantum sed esse et praeter hoc forma aliqua; et multo minus reciperet additionem materiae, quia iam esset esse non subsistens sed materiale. Unde relinquitur quod talis res quae sit suum esse non potest esse nisi una; unde oportet quod in qualibet alia re praeter eam aliud sit esse suum et aliud quiditas vel natura seu forma sua; unde oportet quod in intelligentiis sit esse praeter formam, et ideo dictum est quod intelligentia est forma et esse.

Omne autem quod convenit alicui vel est causatum ex principiis naturae suae, sicut risibile in homine; vel advenit ab aliquo principio extrinseco, sicut lumen in aere ex influentia solis. Non autem potest esse quod ipsum esse sit causatum ab ipsa forma vel quiditate rei, dico sicut a causa efficiente, quia sic aliqua res esset sui ipsius causa et aliqua res se ipsam in esse produceret: quod est impossibile. Ergo oportet quod omnis talis res cuius esse est aliud quam natura sua habeat esse ab alio. Et quia omne quod est per aliud reducitur ad id quod est per se sicut ad causam primam, oportet quod sit aliqua res quae sit causa essendi omnibus rebus eo quod ipsa est esse tantum; alias iretur in infinitum in causis, cum omnis res quae non est esse tantum habeat causam sui esse, ut dictum est. Patet ergo quod intelligentia est forma et esse, et quod esse habet a primo ente quod est esse tantum, et hoc est causa prima quae Deus est.

Omne autem quod recipit aliquid ab alio est in potentia respectu illius, et hoc quod receptum est in eo est actus eius; ergo oportet quod ipsa quiditas vel forma quae est intelligentia sit in potentia respectu esse quod a Deo recipit, et illud esse receptum est per modum actus. Et ita invenitur potentia et actus in intelligentiis, non tamen forma et materia nisi aequivoce. Unde etiam pati, recipere, subiectum esse et omnia huiusmodi quae videntur rebus ratione materiae convenire, aequivoce conveniunt substantiis intellectualibus et substantiis corporalibus, ut in III *de Anima* Commentator dicit. Et quia, ut dictum est, intelligentiae quiditas est ipsamet intelligentia, ideo quiditas vel essentia eius est ipsum quod est ipsa, et esse suum receptum a Deo est id quo subsistit in rerum natura; et propter hoc a quibusdam dicuntur huiusmodi substantiae componi ex quo est et quod est, vel ex quod est et esse, ut Boethius dicit.

that was other than unseparated heat by reason of its separation. But if we posit a thing that is existence only, such that it is subsisting existence itself, this existence will not receive the addition of a difference. For, if there were added a difference, it would be not only existence, but existence and also some form beyond this. Much less would such a thing receive the addition of matter, for then the thing would be not subsisting existence but material. Hence, it remains that a thing that is its own existence cannot be other than one, and so in every other thing, the thing's existence is one thing, and its essence or quiddity or nature or form is another. In the intelligences, therefore, there is existence beyond the form, and so we say that an intelligence is form and existence.

Everything that pertains to a thing, however, either is caused by the principles of its own nature, as risibility in man, or else comes from some extrinsic principle, as light in the air from the influence of the sun. Now, it cannot be that existence itself is caused by the very form or quiddity of the thing (I mean as by an efficient cause), because then the thing would be its own efficient cause, and the thing would produce itself in existence, which is impossible. Therefore, everything the existence of which is other than its own nature has existence from another. And since everything that is through another is reduced to that which is through itself as to a first cause, there is something that is the cause of existence in all things in that this thing is existence only. Otherwise, we would have to go to infinity in causes, for everything that is not existence alone has a cause of its existence, as was said above. It is clear, therefore, that the intelligences are form and existence and have existence from the first being, which is existence alone, and this is the first cause, which is God.

Everything that receives something from another is in potency with respect to what it receives, and that which is received in the thing is its act. Therefore, a quiddity or form that is an intelligence is in potency with respect to the existence that it receives from God, and this received existence is received as its act. And thus there are found in the intelligences both potency and act, but not matter and form, unless in some equivocal sense. Hence it is also clear that 'to suffer,' 'to receive,' 'to be a subject' and everything of this type that seem to pertain to things by reason of their matter are said of intellectual substances and corporeal substances equivocally, as the Commentator says in *de Anima* 3, com. 14. Furthermore, since, as was said above, the quiddity of an intelligence is the intelligence itself, its quiddity or essence is itself the very thing that exists, and its existence received from God is that by which it subsists in reality; and because of this some people say that substances of this kind are composed of what is and that by which it is, or of what is and existence, as Boethius says in *de Hebdomadibus*.[9]

9. PL 64, 1311 B–C.

Et quia in intelligentiis ponitur potentia et actus, non erit difficile invenire multitudinem intelligentiarum, quod esset impossibile si nulla potentia in eis esset. Unde Commentator dicit in III *de Anima* quod si natura intellectus possibilis esset ignota, non possemus invenire multitudinem in substantiis separatis. Est ergo distinctio earum ad invicem secundum gradum potentiae et actus, ita quod intelligentia superior quae magis propinqua est primo habet plus de actu et minus de potentia, et sic de aliis.

Et hoc completur in anima humana, quae tenet ultimum gradum in substantiis intellectualibus. Unde intellectus possibilis eius se habet ad formas intelligibiles sicut materia prima, quae tenet ultimum gradum in esse sensibili, ad formas sensibiles, ut Commentator in III *de Anima* dicit; et ideo Philosophus comparat eam tabulae in qua nihil est scriptum. Et propter hoc quod inter alias substantias intellectuales plus habet de potentia, ideo efficitur in tantum propinqua rebus materialibus ut res materialis trahatur ad participandum esse suum: ita scilicet quod ex anima et corpore resultat unum esse in uno composito, quamvis illud esse prout est animae non sit dependens a corpore. Et ideo post istam formam quae est anima inveniuntur aliae formae plus de potentia habentes et magis propinquae materiae, in tantum quod esse earum sine materia non est; in quibus esse invenitur ordo et gradus usque ad primas formas elementorum, quae sunt propinquissimae materiae: unde nec aliquam operationem habent nisi secundum exigentiam qualitatum activarum et passivarum et aliarum quibus materia ad formam disponitur.

Moreover, since we posit in the intelligences potency and act, it will not be difficult to find a multitude of intelligences, which would be impossible if there were in them no potency. Hence, the Commentator says in *de Anima* 3, com. 5 that if the nature of the possible intellect were unknown, we would not be able to find a multitude of separate substances. There is thus a distinction among separate substances according to their grade of potency and act such that the superior intelligences, which are nearer the first cause, have more act and less potency, and so on.

This scale comes to an end with the human soul, which holds the lowest place among intellectual substances. The soul's possible intellect is related to intelligible forms just as prime matter (which holds the lowest place in sensible existence) is related to sensible forms, as the Commentator says in *de Anima* 3, com. 5. The Philosopher thus compares the soul to a tablet on which nothing has been written, in *de Anima* 3.4.[10] Since the soul has the most potency among the intellectual substances, it is so close to material things that a material thing is brought to participate in its existence: that is, from the soul and the body there results one existence in one composite thing, although this existence, as the existence of the soul, is not dependent on the body. Beyond this form that is the soul, there are other forms having more potency and being closer to matter, and so much so that they have no existence without matter. Among these forms there is an order and gradation down to the primary forms of the elements, which are closest to matter; and so these have no operation except as required by the active and passive qualities and other such qualities by which matter is disposed by form.

---

10. Aristotle, *de Anima*, 430a1.

CHAPTER 5

How essence is found in various kinds of things

His igitur visis, patet quomodo essentia in diversis invenitur. Invenitur enim triplex modus habendi essentiam in substantiis. Aliquid enim est sicut Deus cuius essentia est ipsummet suum esse; et ideo inveniuntur aliqui philosophi dicentes quod Deus non habet quidditatem vel essentiam, quia essentia sua non est aliud quam esse eius. Et ex hoc sequitur quod ipse non sit in genere; quia omne quod est in genere oportet quod habeat quidditatem praeter esse suum, cum quiditas vel natura generis aut speciei non distinguatur secundum rationem naturae in illis quorum est genus vel species, sed esse est diversum in diversis.

Nec oportet, si dicimus quod Deus est esse tantum, ut in illorum errorem incidamus qui Deum dixerunt esse illud esse universale quo quaelibet res formaliter est. Hoc enim esse quod Deus est huius condicionis est ut nulla sibi additio fieri possit, unde per ipsam suam puritatem est esse distinctum ab omni esse; propter quod in commento IX propositionis libri *de Causis* dicitur quod individuatio primae causae, quae est esse tantum, est per puram bonitatem eius. Esse autem commune sicut in intellectu suo non includit aliquam additionem, ita non includit in intellectu suo praecisionem additionis; quia, si hoc esset, nihil posset intelligi esse in quo super esse aliquid adderetur.

Similiter etiam quamvis sit esse tantum, non oportet quod deficiant ei reliquae perfectiones et nobilitates. Immo habet omnes perfectiones quae sunt in omnibus generibus, propter quod perfectum simpliciter dicitur, ut Philosophus et Commentator in V *Metaphysicae* dicunt; sed habet eas modo excellentiori omnibus rebus, quia in eo unum sunt, sed in aliis diversitatem habent. Et hoc est quia omnes illae perfectiones conveniunt sibi secundum esse suum simplex; sicut si aliquis per unam qualitatem posset efficere operationes omnium qualitatum, in illa una qualitate omnes qualitates haberet, ita Deus in ipso esse suo omnes perfectiones habet.

Secundo modo invenitur essentia in substantiis creatis intellectualibus, in quibus est aliud esse quam essentia earum, quamvis essentia sit sine materia. Unde esse earum non est absolutum sed receptum, et ideo limitatum et finitum ad capacitatem naturae recipientis; sed natura vel quiditas earum est absoluta, non recepta in aliqua materia. Et ideo dicitur in libro *de Causis* quod intelligentiae sunt infinitae inferius et finitae superius; sunt

Having treated these matters, we can see clearly how essence is found in various kinds of things. There are thus three ways in which substances may have an essence. First, surely, is the way God has his essence, which is his very existence itself, and so we find certain philosophers saying that God does not have a quiddity or essence because his essence is not other than his existence. From this it follows that he is not in any genus, for everything that is in a genus has a quiddity beyond its existence, since the quiddity or nature of the genus or species is not in the order of nature distinguished in the things of which it is the genus or species, but the existence is diverse in diverse things.

Even though we say that God is existence alone, we should not fall into the error of those who said that God is that universal existence by which everything formally exists. The existence which is God is of such a kind that no addition can be made to it, whence through its purity it is distinct from every other existence; for this reason a comment on the *Liber de causis* 9 says that the individuation of the first cause, which is being alone, is through its pure goodness. But common existence, just as it does not include in its concept any addition, does not exclude any addition in its concept; for, if such existence did in its concept exclude any addition, nothing could be understood to exist in which there was added something beyond existence.

Similarly, although God is existence alone, the remaining perfections and nobilities are not lacking in him. On the contrary, he has all the perfections that exist in every genus, and for this reason he is called perfect without qualification, as the Philosopher, in *Metaphysics* 5.16,[11] and the Commentator, in *Metaphysics* 5, com. 21, each say. But God has these perfections in a more excellent way than all other things have them, because in him they are one, while in other things they are diverse. And this is because all these perfections pertain to God according to his simple existence, just as, if someone through one quality could effect the operations of all qualities, such a person would have in that one quality all the qualities, so too does God in his very existence have all the perfections.

In a second way, essence is found in created intellectual substances in which existence is other than essence, although in these substances the essence is without matter. Hence, their existence is not absolute but received, and so finite and limited by the capacity of the receiving nature; but their nature or quiddity is absolute and is not received in any matter. Thus, it says in the *Liber de causis* 16 that intelligences are infinite with respect to what is inferior to

---

11. Aristotle, *Metaphysics*, 1021b30–33.

enim finitae quantum ad esse suum quod a superiori recipiunt, non tamen finiuntur inferius quia earum formae non limitantur ad capacitatem alicuius materiae recipientis eas.

Et ideo in talibus substantiis non invenitur multitudo individuorum in una specie, ut dictum est, nisi in anima humana propter corpus cui unitur. Et licet individuatio eius ex corpore occasionaliter dependeat quantum ad sui inchoationem, quia non acquiritur sibi esse individuatum nisi in corpore cuius est actus: non tamen oportet ut subtracto corpore individuatio pereat, quia cum habeat esse absolutum ex quo acquisitum est sibi esse individuatum ex hoc quod facta est forma huius corporis, illud esse semper remanet individuatum. Et ideo dicit Avicenna quod individuatio animarum vel multiplicatio pendet ex corpore quantum ad sui principium, sed non quantum ad sui finem.

Et quia in istis substantiis quiditas non est idem quod esse, ideo sunt ordinabiles in praedicamento; et propter hoc invenitur in eis genus et species et differentia, quamvis earum differentiae propriae nobis occultae sint. In rebus enim sensibilibus etiam ipsae differentiae essentiales ignotae sunt; unde significantur per differentias accidentales quae ex essentialibus oriuntur, sicut causa significatur per suum effectum: sicut bipes ponitur differentia hominis. Accidentia autem propria substantiarum immaterialium nobis ignota sunt, unde differentiae earum nec per se nec per accidentales differentias a nobis significari possunt.

Hoc tamen sciendum est quod non eodem modo sumitur genus et differentia in illis substantiis et in substantiis sensibilibus, quia in substantiis sensibilibus genus sumitur ab eo quod est materiale in re, differentia vero ab eo quod est formale in ipsa; unde dicit Avicenna in principio libri sui *de Anima* quod forma in rebus compositis ex materia et forma *est differentia simplex eius quod constituitur ex illa*: non autem ita quod ipsa forma sit differentia, sed quia est principium differentiae, ut idem dicit in sua *Metaphysica*. Et dicitur talis differentia esse differentia simplex quia sumitur ab eo quod est pars quiditatis rei, scilicet a forma. Cum autem substantiae immateriales sint simplices quiditates, non potest in eis differentia sumi ab eo quod est pars quiditatis sed a tota quiditate; et ideo in principio *de Anima* dicit Avicenna quod *differentiam simplicem non habent nisi species quarum essentiae sunt compositae ex materia et forma.*

Similiter etiam in eis ex tota essentia sumitur genus, modo tamen differenti. Una enim substantia separata

them and finite with respect to what is superior to them: they are finite with respect to their existence, which they receive from something superior, although they are not rendered finite with respect to what is inferior to them because their forms are not limited to the capacity of some matter receiving them.

And thus among such substances we do not find a multitude of individuals in one species, as was said above, except in the case of the human soul, and there we do find a multitude of individuals in one species because of the body to which the soul is united. Now, the individuation of the soul depends on the body for the occasion of its inception, for the soul does not acquire for itself individual existence unless in the body of which it is the act. But nevertheless, if we remove the body, the individuation does not perish; rather, its existence remains individuated because, since the soul was made the form of a particular body, it acquired individuated existence and so has absolute existence. And thus Avicenna says (*de Anima* 5.3) that the individuation of souls and their multiplication depend on the body for their beginning but not for their end.

Since in these substances the quiddity is not the same as existence, these substances can be ordered in the categories, and for this reason we find genera, species, and differences among these things, although their proper differences are hidden from us. Even in sensible things, essential differences are unknown to us, and so they are signified through accidental differences that arise from the essential ones, just as a cause is signified through its effect. We take bipedality, for example, as the difference of man. The proper accidents of immaterial substances, however, are also unknown to us, and thus we can signify their differences neither essentially nor through their accidental differences.

We should note, though, that the genus and difference in immaterial substances are not taken in the same way as in sensible substances, for in sensible substances the genus is taken from that which is material in the thing, while the difference is taken from that which is formal in the thing. Hence, Avicenna says in his book *de Anima* 1.1 that, in things composed of form and matter, the form *is its simple difference because the thing is constituted from it*; not, however, because the form is the difference but rather because it is the principle of the difference, as Avicenna himself says in his *Metaphysics* 5.6. Further, this difference is called a simple difference because it is taken from that which is a part of the quiddity of the thing: namely, from the form. But since immaterial substances are simple quiddities, in such substances the difference cannot be taken from that which is a part of the quiddity but only from the whole quiddity, and so in *de Anima* 1.1, Avicenna says that substances *have no simple difference except for those species of which the essences are composed of matter and form.*

Similarly, in immaterial things the genus is taken from the whole essence, though not in the same way as the differ-

convenit cum alia in immaterialitate, et differunt ab invicem in gradu perfectionis secundum recessum a potentialitate et accessum ad actum purum. Et ideo ab eo quod consequitur illas in quantum sunt immateriales sumitur in eis genus, sicut est intellectualitas vel aliquid huiusmodi; ab eo autem quod consequitur in eis gradum perfectionis sumitur in eis differentia, nobis tamen ignota. Nec oportet has differentias esse accidentales quia sunt secundum maiorem et minorem perfectionem, quae non diversificant speciem; gradus enim perfectionis in recipiendo eandem formam non diversificat speciem, sicut albius et minus album in participando eiusdem rationis albedinem: sed diversus gradus perfectionis in ipsis formis vel naturis participatis speciem diversificat, sicut natura procedit per gradus de plantis ad animalia per quaedam quae sunt media inter animalia et plantas, secundum Philosophum in VII *de Animalibus*. Nec iterum est necessarium ut divisio intellectualium substantiarum sit semper per duas differentias veras, quia hoc impossibile est in omnibus rebus accidere, ut Philosophus dicit in XI *de Animalibus*.

Tertio modo invenitur essentia in substantiis compositis ex materia et forma, in quibus et esse est receptum et finitum propter hoc quod ab alio esse habent, et iterum natura vel quiditas earum est recepta in materia signata.

Et ideo sunt finitae et superius et inferius; et in eis iam propter divisionem signatae materiae possibilis est multiplicatio individuorum in una specie. Et in his qualiter se habet essentia ad intentiones logicas dictum est supra.

ence is. Separated substance are alike with respect to their immateriality, but they differ one from another with respect to their grade of perfection according to how far each recedes from potentiality and approaches pure act. And so, in such substances, the genus is taken from that which arises in these substances insofar as they are immaterial, as intellectuality and such things; the difference, however, is taken from that which arises in these substances from their grade of perfection, although these differences are unknown to us. Nor are these differences accidental because they arise from greater and lesser perfection, which do not diversify the species. For, while the grade of perfection in receiving the same form does not diversify the species (as whiter and less white in participating in whiteness of the same type), nevertheless, a different grade of perfection in these participated forms or natures does diversify the species, just as nature proceeds by grades from plants to animals through those things that are median between plants and animals, as the Philosopher says in *de Historia animalium* 8.1.[12] Nor is it necessary that the division of intellectual substances always be made through two true differences, for it is impossible that this happen in all cases, as the Philosopher says in *de Partibus animalium* 1.2.[13]

In a third way, essence is found in substances composed of matter and form, in which existence is both received and limited because such substances have existence from another, and again because the nature or quiddity of such substances is received in signate matter.

And thus such substances are finite both with respect to what is superior to them and with respect to what is inferior to them, and among such substances, because of the division of signate matter, there can be a multiplication of individuals in one species. Finally, we explained above the ways in which essence in such substances is related to the logical intentions.

---

12. Aristotle, *de Historia animalium*, 588b4–12.
13. Aristotle, *de Partibus animalium*, 642b5–7.

Chapter 6

How there are essences in accidents

Nunc restat videre quomodo sit essentia in accidentibus; qualiter enim sit in omnibus substantiis dictum est. Et quia, ut dictum est, essentia est id quod per diffinitionem significatur, oportet ut eo modo habeant essentiam quo habent diffinitionem. Diffinitionem autem habent incompletam, quia non possunt diffiniri nisi ponatur subiectum in eorum diffinitione; et hoc ideo est quia non habent esse per se absolutum a subiecto, sed sicut ex forma et materia relinquitur esse substantiale quando componuntur, ita ex accidente et subiecto relinquitur esse accidentale quando accidens subiecto advenit. Et ideo etiam nec forma substantialis completam essentiam habet nec materia, quia etiam in diffinitione formae substantialis oportet quod ponatur illud cuius est forma, et ita diffinitio eius est per additionem alicuius quod est extra genus eius sicut et diffinitio formae accidentalis; unde et in diffinitione animae ponitur corpus a naturali qui considerat animam solum in quantum est forma physici corporis.

Sed tamen inter formas substantiales et accidentales tantum interest quia, sicut forma substantialis non habet per se esse absolutum sine eo cui advenit, ita nec illud cui advenit, scilicet materia; et ideo ex coniunctione utriusque relinquitur illud esse in quo res per se subsistit, et ex eis efficitur unum per se: propter quod ex coniunctione eorum relinquitur essentia quaedam. Unde forma, quamvis in se considerata non habeat completam rationem essentiae, tamen est pars essentiae completae. Sed illud cui advenit accidens est ens in se completum subsistens in suo esse, quod quidem esse naturaliter praecedit accidens quod supervenit.

Et ideo accidens superveniens ex coniunctione sui cum eo cui advenit non causat illud esse in quo res subsistit, per quod res est ens per se; sed causat quoddam esse secundum sine quo res subsistens intelligi potest esse, sicut primum potest intelligi sine secundo. Unde ex accidente et subiecto non efficitur unum per se sed unum per accidens. Et ideo ex eorum coniunctione non resultat essentia quaedam sicut ex coniunctione formae ad materiam; propter quod accidens neque rationem completae essentiae habet neque pars completae essen-

Having already said how essences are found in all types of substances, we should now see in what way there are essences in accidents. Now, as was said above, the essence is that which is signified by the definition, and so accidents will have essences in the same way in which they have definitions. But accidents have incomplete definitions, because they cannot be defined unless we put a subject in their definitions, and this is because they do not have absolute existence in themselves apart from a subject. Rather, just as from the form and the matter substantial existence results when these are compounded, so too from the accident and the subject does accidental existence result when the accident comes to the subject. Thus, neither the substantial form nor the matter has a complete essence, for even in the definition of the substantial form we place something of which it is the form, and so its definition involves the addition of something that is beyond its genus, just as with the definition of an accidental form. Hence, the natural philosopher places the body in the definition of the soul because he considers the soul only insofar as it is the form of the physical body.

But as between substantial and accidental forms, there is this difference. For, just as the substantial form has no absolute existence in itself without that to which the form comes, so neither does that to which the form comes (namely, matter) have such existence. Rather, from the conjunction of both there results that existence in which the thing subsists in itself, and from these two there is made one thing in itself, and for this reason, from the conjunction of these, there results a certain essence. Hence, although considered in itself the form does not have the complete character of an essence, nevertheless it is part of a complete essence. But that to which an accident comes is in itself a complete being subsisting in its own existence, and this existence naturally precedes the accident that supervenes.

Therefore, the supervening accident, from its conjunction with the thing to which it comes, does not cause that existence in which the thing subsists, the existence through which the thing is a being in itself; it causes, rather, a certain secondary existence without which the subsisting being can be understood to exist, as what is first can be understood without what is second. Hence, from the accident and the subject there is made something that is one accidentally, not essentially; and so from the conjunction of these two there does not result an essence as there does from the conjunc-

tiae est, sed sicut est ens secundum quid, ita et essentiam secundum quid habet.

Sed quia illud quod dicitur maxime et verissime in quolibet genere est causa eorum quae sunt post in illo genere, sicut ignis qui est in fine caliditatis est causa caloris in rebus calidis, ut in II *Metaphysicae* dicitur: ideo substantia quae est primum in genere entis, verissime et maxime essentiam habens, oportet quod sit causa accidentium quae secundario et quasi secundum quid rationem entis participant. Quod tamen diversimode contingit. Quia enim partes substantiae sunt materia et forma, ideo quaedam accidentia principaliter consequuntur formam et quaedam materiam. Forma autem invenitur aliqua cuius esse non dependet ad materiam, ut anima intellectualis; materia vero non habet esse nisi per formam. Unde in accidentibus quae consequuntur formam est aliquid quod non habet communicationem cum materia, sicut est intelligere, quod non est per organum corporale, sicut probat Philosophus in III *de Anima*; aliqua vero ex consequentibus formam sunt quae habent communicationem cum materia, sicut sentire. Sed nullum accidens consequitur materiam sine communicatione formae.

In his tamen accidentibus quae materiam consequuntur invenitur quaedam diversitas. Quaedam enim accidentia consequuntur materiam secundum ordinem quem habet ad formam specialem, sicut masculinum et femininum in animalibus, quorum diversitas ad materiam reducitur, ut dicitur in X *Metaphysicae*; unde remota forma animalis dicta accidentia non remanent nisi aequivoce. Quaedam vero consequuntur materiam secundum ordinem quem habet ad formam generalem; et ideo remota forma speciali adhuc in ea remanent, sicut nigredo cutis est in aethiope ex mixtione elementorum et non ex ratione animae, et ideo post mortem in eo manet.

Et quia unaquaeque res individuatur ex materia et collocatur in genere vel specie per suam formam, ideo accidentia quae consequuntur materiam sunt accidentia individui, secundum quae individua etiam eiusdem speciei ad invicem differunt; accidentia vero quae consequuntur formam sunt propriae passiones vel generis vel speciei, unde inveniuntur in omnibus participantibus naturam generis vel speciei, sicut risibile consequitur in

tion of form and matter. And so an accident has neither the character of a complete essence, nor is it a part of a complete essence; rather, just as an accident is a being only in a certain sense, so too does it have an essence only in a certain sense.

But since that which is greatest and truest in a genus is the cause of the lesser things in the genus (as fire, which is the hottest of all things, is the cause of heat in other hot things, as the Philosopher says in *Metaphysics* 2.1[14]), thus substance, which is first in the genus of beings and which has essence in the truest and greatest way, is the cause of accidents, which participate in the notion of being only secondarily and in a certain sense. But this happens in a variety of ways. Since the parts of substance are matter and form, certain accidents are principally a consequence of form, and certain accidents are principally a consequence of matter. Now, while we find some forms (like the intellectual soul) whose existence does not depend on matter, matter does not have existence except through form. Hence, among those accidents that are a consequence of form, there are some that have no communication with matter, such as understanding, which does not take place through a corporeal organ, as the Philosopher proves in *de Anima* 3.1.[15] Other accidents that are a consequence of form do have communication with matter, and among these is sensation. But no accident that is a consequence of matter is without some communication with form.

Among the accidents that are consequences of matter there is found a certain diversity. Some accidents follow from the order the matter has to a special form, as the masculine and the feminine in animals, the difference between which is reduced to the matter, as the Philosopher says in *Metaphysics* 10.9.[16] Hence, the form of the animal having been removed, these accidents do not remain except in some equivocal sense. Other accidents follow from the order the matter has to a general form, and so with these accidents, if the special form is removed, the accidents still remain in the thing, as the blackness of the skin of an Ethiopian comes from the mixture of the elements and not from the notion of the soul, and hence the blackness remains in the man after death.

Since everything is individuated by matter and is placed in its genus or species through its form, the accidents that follow from the matter are accidents of the individual, and by these accidents individuals of the same species differ one from another. But the accidents that follow from the form are properly passions of the genus or species, and so they are found in all things participating in the nature of the genus or species, as risibility in man follows from the form,

---

14. Aristotle, *Metaphysics*, 993b24–27.
15. Aristotle, *de Anima*, 429a18–b5.
16. Aristotle, *Metaphysics*, 1058b21–23.

homine formam, quia risus contingit ex aliqua apprehensione animae hominis.

Sciendum etiam est quod accidentia aliquando ex principiis essentialibus causantur secundum actum perfectum, sicut calor in igne qui semper est calidus; aliquando vero secundum aptitudinem tantum, sed complementum accidit ex agente exteriori, sicut diaphaneitas in aere quae completur per corpus lucidum exterius; et in talibus aptitudo est accidens inseparabile, sed complementum quod advenit ex aliquo principio quod est extra essentiam rei, vel quod non intrat constitutionem rei, est separabile, sicut moveri et huiusmodi.

Sciendum est etiam quod in accidentibus modo alio sumitur genus, differentia et species quam in substantiis. Quia enim in substantiis ex forma substantiali et materia efficitur per se unum, una quadam natura ex earum coniunctione resultante quae proprie in praedicamento substantiae collocatur, ideo in substantiis nomina concreta quae compositum significant proprie in genere esse dicuntur, sicut species vel genera, ut homo vel animal. Non autem forma vel materia est hoc modo in praedicamento nisi per reductionem, sicut principia in genere esse dicuntur. Sed ex accidente et subiecto non fit unum per se; unde non resultat ex eorum coniunctione aliqua natura cui intentio generis vel speciei possit attribui.

Unde nomina accidentalia concretive dicta non ponuntur in praedicamento sicut species vel genera, ut album vel musicum, nisi per reductionem, sed solum secundum quod in abstracto significantur, ut albedo et musica. Et quia accidentia non componuntur ex materia et forma, ideo non potest in eis sumi genus a materia et differentia a forma sicut in substantiis compositis; sed oportet ut genus primum sumatur ex ipso modo essendi, secundum quod ens diversimode secundum prius et posterius de decem generibus praedicamentorum, sicut dicitur quantitas ex eo quod est mensura substantiae et qualitas secundum quod est dispositio substantiae, et sic de aliis, secundum Philosophum IX *Metaphysicae*.

Differentiae vero in eis sumuntur ex diversitate principiorum, ex quibus causantur. Et quia propriae passiones ex propriis principiis subiecti causantur, ideo subiectum ponitur in diffinitione eorum loco differentiae si in abstracto diffiniuntur, secundum quod sunt proprie in genere, sicut dicitur quod simitas est curvitas nasi. Sed e converso esset si eorum diffinitio sumeretur secundum quod concretive dicuntur; sic enim subiectum in eorum diffinitione poneretur sicut genus,

for laughter comes from a certain kind of understanding in the soul of man.

We should also note that some accidents are caused by the essential principles of a thing to be in perfect act, as heat in fire, which is always actually hot, while other accidents are the result of a mere aptitude in the substance, and in such cases the complete accident arises from an exterior agent, as transparency in air, which is completed through an exterior luminescent body. In such things, the aptitude is an inseparable accident, but the complete accident, which comes from some principle that is beyond the essence of the thing, or that does not enter into the constitution of the thing, is separable, as the ability to be moved, and so on.

We should further note that in accidents, the genus, difference, and species are taken in a way different from that in substances. For in substances, from the substantial form and the matter there is made something one in itself, a certain single nature resulting from the conjunction of these two, and this nature is properly placed in the category of substance. Hence, in substances, the concrete terms (such as the species or genera) that signify the composite are properly said to be in the genus, as, for example, man or animal. But in this way neither the form nor the matter is in a category except by means of reduction, as when we say that principles are in a genus. For from the accident and the subject there does not result something that is one in itself, and thus from the conjunction of these two there does not result a nature to which the intention of genus or species may be attributed.

Therefore, when accidental terms are used concretely like species or genera, such as white or musical, they cannot be placed in a category, except by means of reduction; rather, they can be placed in a category only when they are signified in the abstract, as, for example, whiteness and music. And because accidents are not composed of matter and form, in accidents the genus cannot be taken from the matter nor the difference from the form, as is the case with composite substances; rather, the first genus is taken from their very mode of existing, as being is said in different ways according to what is prior and what is posterior in the ten categories, and thus we call the measure of a substance quantity, the disposition of a substance quality, and so on for the others, as the Philosopher says in *Metaphysics* 9.1.[17]

The differences in accidents are taken from the diversity of principles by which they are caused. Since passions are properly caused by the proper principles of the subject, the subject is placed in the definition of the passion in place of the difference if the passion is being defined in the abstract and properly in its genus, as when we say that snubnosedness is the upward curvature of the nose. But it would be the converse if the definition of the passion were taken according to its concrete sense; in this way, the subject is placed

17. Aristotle, *Metaphysics*, 1045b27–32.

quia tunc diffinirentur per modum substantiarum compositarum in quibus ratio generis sumitur a materia, sicut dicimus quod simum est nasus curvus. Similiter etiam est si unum accidens alterius accidentis principium sit, sicut principium relationis est actio et passio et quantitas; et ideo secundum haec dividit Philosophus relationem in V *Metaphysicae*. Sed quia propria principia accidentium non semper sunt manifesta, ideo quandoque sumimus differentias accidentium ex eorum effectibus, sicut congregativum et disgregativum dicuntur differentiae coloris quae causantur ex abundantia vel paucitate lucis, ex quo diversae species coloris causantur.

Sic ergo patet quomodo essentia est in substantiis et accidentibus, et quomodo in substantiis compositis et simplicibus, et qualiter in his omnibus intentiones universales logicae inveniuntur; excepto primo quod est in fine simplicitatis, cui non convenit ratio generis aut speciei et per consequens nec diffinitio propter suam simplicitatem: in quo sit finis et consummatio huius sermonis. Amen.

in the definition as a genus, for then the passion is defined in the mode of composite substances in which the notion of the genus is taken from the matter, as when we say that a snub nose is an upwardly curving nose. The case is similar even when one accident is the principle of another, as the principle of relation is action and passion and quantity, and thus by reference to these the Philosopher divides relation in *Metaphysics* 5.15.[18] But because the proper principles of accidents are not always manifest, we sometimes take the differences of accidents from their effects, as we do with the concentrative and the diffusive, which are called the differences of color and which are caused by the abundance or the paucity of light, which cause the different species of color.

We have thus made clear how essence is found in substances and in accidents, and how in composite substances and in simple ones, and in what way the universal intentions of logic are found in all of these, except for the first being, which is the height of simplicity and to which, because of its simplicity, the notions of genus, species, and thus definition do not apply. In him let there be an end and consummation of this discourse. Amen.

---

18. Aristotle, *Metaphysics*, 1020b26–32.

ON SEPARATE SUBSTANCES

To Brother Raynald of Piperno

PROLOGUE

Quia sacris angelorum solemniis interesse non possumus, non debet nobis devotionis tempus transire in vacuum, sed quod psallendi officio subtrahitur scribendi studio compensetur. Intendentes igitur sanctorum angelorum excellentiam utcumque depromere, incipiendum videtur ab his quae de angelis antiquitus humana coniectura aestimavit; ut si quid invenerimus fidei consonum accipiamus, quae vero doctrinae repugnant catholicae refutemus.

Since we cannot be present at the holy ceremonies in honor of the angels, we should not let this time of devotion go by fruitlessly; rather, such time as we do not spend in singing their praises, we should spend in writing about them. And because our aim is to present as best we can the excellence of the holy angels, we ought to begin with man's earliest conjectures about the angels. In this way, we shall be in a position to accept whatever we find that agrees with faith, and refute whatever is opposed to Catholic teaching.

CHAPTER 1

On the opinions of the early philosophers and of Plato

Primi quidem igitur philosophantium de rerum naturis sola corpora esse aestimaverunt, ponentes prima rerum principia aliqua corporalia elementa, aut unum aut plura. Et si unum, aut aquam ut Thales Milesius, aut aerem ut Diogenes, aut ignem ut Hippasus, aut vaporem ut Heraclitus. Et si plura, aut finita sicut Empedocles quatuor elementa et cum his duo moventia amicitiam et litem; aut infinita, sicut Democritus et Anaxagoras, quorum uterque posuit infinitas partes minimas esse omnium rerum principia, nisi quod Democritus eas posuit genere similes, differre autem eas solum figura et ordine et positione,

The first of those who philosophized on the natures of things believed that only bodies existed and held that the first principles of things were certain corporeal elements, either one or several.[1] And if they held the first principle to be one, either they thought it was water, as Thales of Miletus did, or air as Diogenes, or fire [as Hippasus, or vapor] as Heraclitus.[2] If they thought the principles to be several, they thought them to be either finite in number, as did Empedocles, who posited four elements and along with them two moving principles, namely, love and strife;[3] or infinite in number, as in the case of Democritus and Anaxagoras, both of whom posited an infinite number of minimal parts as the principles of all things, except that Democritus held that these parts were similar in kind, differing only in figure, order, and position.[4]

Anaxagoras autem diversarum rerum quae sunt similium partium infinitas partes minimas prima rerum

Anaxagoras, on the other hand, thought that in the case of diverse things which have similar parts, the first prin-

---

1. Aristotle, *Metaphysics*, 1, 3–4 (983b 6–985b 22); 11, 5 (1002a 8); *Physics*, IV, 6 (213a 29); St. Augustine, *De Civitate Dei*, VIII, 2 (PL 41, 225). For St. Thomas' use of these texts: ST, I, 44, 2 (BW, I, 428–429); *De Spiritualibus Creaturis*, a. 10 ad 8, ed. L. Keeler, 131–133 (OSC, 121–122); *Q. D. De Potentia* III, 5; A. C. Pegis, A Note on St. Thomas' Summa Theologica, 1, 44, 1–2 in *Mediaeval Studies*, VIII, 1946, 159–168.

2. Palaeographically, there is little justification for this particular reading which we have adopted, since all 12 mss. seem to be representative of a tradition which attributes "vapor" to Heraclitus. Manuscripts "A" and "B," i.e., CAMBRIDGE, *Corpus Christi*, Libr. ms. 35 and TOLEDO, *Bibl. del Cabildo*, 19–15 do omit *Hippasus* but still attribute both fire and "vapor" to Heraclitus. Manuscript "D," i.e., VENICE, S. Marco 31, IV suppresses the phrase "ut Hippasus aut vaporem ut" and substitutes for it "ac" leaving, at the same time, a space between "ac" and "Heraclitus." The scribe of "D" evidently deleted the troublesome phrase and left a space for a future correction. Since no sources of Greek philosophy credit Heraclitus with "vapor," the phrase "ut Hippasus aut vaporem" seems to be an interpolation which, most interestingly, is not found in the 1488 Soncinas nor in the 1490 and 1498 Pizzamanus printed editions. Hence, we have made an emendation by suppressing the obvious interpolation and the text reads: "Et si unum, aut aquam ut Thales Milesius, aut aërem ut Diogenes, aut ignem ut Heraclitus." For the relative value of incunabula in the establishment of a critical text, cf. above, Introduction, 13, 14 and F. Lescoe, *Sancti: Thomae Aquinatis Tractatus de substantiis separatis*, Introduction: Literary Problems.

3. Aristotle, *Physics*, 1, 5 (188b 34).

4. Aristotle, *Metaphysics* I, 4 (985b 3–20); Lucretius, *De Rerum Natura*, I, 421 ff. (Stoic and Epicurean Philosophers, ed. W. Oates, 76 ff.); cf. K. Freeman, *Ancilla to the Pre-Socratic Philosophers*, 91–120; *The Pre-Socratic Philosophers*, 289–326.

principia aestimavit. Et quia omnibus inditum fuit in animo ut illud deum aestimarent quod esset primum rerum principium, prout quisque eorum alicui corporum auctoritatem attribuebat primi principii, eidem etiam divinitatis nomen et dignitatem attribuendam censebat.

Quae quidem ideo dicta sunt quia his omnibus et eorum sequacibus nullas substantias incorporeas esse videbatur quas angelos nominamus. Sed Epicurei ex Democriti doctrinis originem sumentes deos quosdam ponebant, corporeos quidem utpote humana figura figuratos, quos dicebant esse penitus otiosos nihil curantes ut sic perpetuis voluptatibus fruentes possent esse beati; unde haec opinio in tantum invaluit ut usque ad Iudaeos Dei cultores perveniret quorum Sadducaei dicebant non esse angelum neque spiritum.

Huic autem opinioni triplici via antiqui philosophi restiterunt. Primo namque Anaxagoras, etsi cum ceteris philosophis Naturalibus materialia principia corporalia poneret, posuit tamen primus inter philosophos quoddam incorporale principium, scilicet intellectum. Cum enim secundum suam positionem omnia corporalia in omnibus mixta essent, non videbatur quod ab invicem corpora distingui potuissent nisi fuisset aliquod distinctionis principium quod ipsum secundum se penitus esset immixtum et nihil cum natura corporali habens commune.

Sed eius opinio, etsi in veritate alios praecesserit qui solum corporalem naturam ponebant, invenitur tamen a veritate deficere in duobus. Primo quidem quia, ut ex eius positione apparet, non posuit nisi unum intellectum separatum qui hunc mundum effecerat commixta distinguendo; cum autem Deo attribuamus mundi institutionem, secundum hoc etiam de substantiis incorporalibus quas angelos dicimus, quae sunt infra Deum et supra naturas corporeas, ex eius opinione nihil habere poterimus. Secundo quia etiam circa intellectum quem unum ponebat immixtum, in hoc videtur deficere quod eius virtutem et dignitatem non sufficienter expressit. Non enim aestimavit intellectum quem posuit separatum ut universale essendi principium sed solum ut principium distinctivum; non enim ponebat quod corpora invicem commixta esse haberent ab intellectu separato, sed solum quod ab eo distinctionem sortirentur.

Unde Plato sufficientiori via processit ad opinionem primorum Naturalium evacuandam. Cum enim apud antiquos Naturales poneretur ab hominibus cer-

ciples are the infinite minimal parts. Moreover, since all of these philosophers had the natural conviction that they should consider as god that which was the first principle of things, just as each of them had attributed to a certain corporeal element the rank of a first principle, so he likewise felt that the name and honor of divinity should be given to this element.

These things were said for this reason, that for all of these men and their followers, it was the case that no incorporeal substances, which we call angels, existed. The Epicureans, however, who traced their origin to the teachings of Democritus, posited certain corporeal gods, resembling human beings in appearance,[5] whom they held completely free and without any cares, so that by enjoying ceaseless pleasures, they would be blessed. This teaching had such a far-reaching effect that it influenced even Jewish worshipers of God, a sect of whom, the Sadducees, held that neither angels nor spirits existed.[6]

The early philosophers, however, opposed this opinion in three ways. For although at first Anaxagoras posited certain material or corporeal principles with the other natural philosophers, nevertheless, he was the first among the philosophers to assert a certain incorporeal principle, namely, an intellect.[7] Since indeed, according to his view, all corporeal things were mixed in all things, it did not seem possible that corporeal bodies could have been distinguished from one another unless there existed some principle of distinction which was itself completely unmixed and had nothing in common with corporeal nature.

But, although Anaxagoras' opinion was much closer to the truth than that of the philosophers who posited only a corporeal nature, yet it falls short of the truth in two respects. First, because it is apparent from his position that he posited only one separate intellect which had produced this world by distinguishing what was mixed. But since we attribute the establishment of the world to God, from this point of view, we can gather nothing from his opinion as to the incorporeal substances which we call angels, which are below God and above corporeal natures. Second, because concerning the intellect, which he said to be one and unmixed, he seems to have failed in this respect, since he did not sufficiently express its power and eminence. Instead of defining this intellect, which he considered to be separate, as the universal principle of being, he makes it to be only a distinguishing principle, for he did not hold that the bodies that were mixed with one another received being from the separate intellect; they received from it only distinctions.

Plato therefore proceeded by a more adequate way to refute the opinion of these early naturalists.[8] For since the early naturalists had held that man could not know the def-

---

5. St. Thomas, *De Spiritualibus Creaturis*, a. 5, ed. L. Keeler, 65 (OSC, 67) calls them "anthropomorphitae"; cf. St. Augustine, *Epist.* 148, IV (PL 33, 628).

6. Acts 23:8; cf. St. Thomas, ST, I, 50, 1 (BW, 1, 480).

7. Aristotle, *Metaphysics*, 1, 3 (984a 15–22); 1, 8 (989a 30–989b 21); *Physics*, VIII, I (250b 24); Plato, *Phaedo*, 97A.

8. Aristotle, *Metaphysics*, 1, 6–7 (987a 30–988b 16); 1, 9 (992b 7); III, 5 (1009a 38–1009b 33).

tam rerum veritatem sciri non posse, tum propter rerum corporalium continuum fluxum tum propter deceptionem sensuum quibus corpora cognoscuntur, posuit naturas quasdam a materia fluxibilium rerum separatas, in quibus esset veritas fixa et sic eis inhaerendo anima nostra veritatem cognosceret; unde secundum hoc quod intellectus veritatem cognoscens aliqua seorsum apprehendit praeter materiam sensibilium rerum, sic aestimavit esse aliqua a sensibilibus separata.

Intellectus autem noster duplici abstractione utitur circa intelligentiam veritatis. Una quidem secundum quod apprehendit numeros mathematicos et magnitudines et figuras mathematicas sine materiae sensibilis intellectu; non enim intelligendo binarium aut ternarium aut lineam et superficiem aut triangulum et quadratum, simul in nostra apprehensione aliquid cadit quod pertineat ad calidum vel frigidum aut aliquid huiusmodi quod sensu percipi possit. Alia vero abstractione utitur intellectus noster intelligendo aliquid universale absque consideratione alicuius particularis, puta cum intelligimus hominem nihil intelligentes de Socrate vel Platone aut alio quocumque; et idem apparet in aliis. Unde Plato duo genera rerum a sensibilibus abstracta ponebat, scilicet mathematica et universalia quae species sive ideas nominabat. Inter quae tamen haec differentia videbatur quod in mathematicis apprehendere possumus plura unius speciei, puta duas lineas aequales vel duos triangulos aequilateros et aequales: quod in speciebus omnino esse non potest, sed homo in universali acceptus secundum speciem est unus tantum. Sic igitur mathematica ponebat media inter species seu ideas et sensibilia; quae quidem cum sensibilibus conveniunt in hoc quod plura sub eadem specie continentur, cum speciebus autem in hoc quod sunt a materia sensibili separata.

In ipsis etiam speciebus ordinem quemdam ponebat, quia secundum quod aliquid erat simplicius in intellectu secundum hoc prius erat in ordine rerum. Id autem quod primo est in intellectu est unum et bonum, nihil enim intelligit qui non intelligit unum; unum autem et bonum se consequuntur: unde ipsam primam ideam unius, quod nominabat secundum se unum et secundum se bonum, primum rerum principium esse ponebat et hunc summum deum esse dicebat. Sub hoc autem uno diversos ordines participantium et participatorum

inite truth of things, both because of the continuous passing of corporeal things and because of the deception of the senses by which bodies are known, Plato posited certain natures, separate from the matter of flowing things, in which truth remained abiding.[9] By adhering to these natures, our soul knew the truth.[10] Hence, as the intellect in knowing truth apprehends certain things beyond the matter of sensible things, Plato thus believed that there existed certain realities separate from sensible things.[11]

Now, our intellect uses a twofold abstraction in arriving at the understanding of truth: one, according as it grasps mathematical numbers, magnitudes, and figures without the understanding of sensible matter. For in understanding the number two or three, or a line, a surface, a triangle, or a square, there is not included together with it in our apprehension anything pertaining to what is hot or cold (or the like) which is perceptible by sense. The intellect, however, uses another abstraction when it understands something universal without the consideration of something particular, as when we understand man without including in our understanding anything about Socrates, Plato, or any other individual. The same appears in other cases.[12] Plato accordingly posited two classes of beings abstracted from sensible things: namely, mathematicals and universals, to which he gave the name of forms or ideas.[13] There appeared, however, to be this difference between them: namely, that in the case of mathematicals, we can grasp several members of one species (for example, two equal lines or two identical equilateral triangles), whereas with forms, this is absolutely impossible (man, for example, taken universally is only one in form).[14] And so, Plato posited mathematicals between forms or ideas and sensible things, since mathematicals agree with sensible things in that many are contained in the same species, and they agree with the forms in that they are separate from sensible matter.[15]

Further, he posited a certain order among forms themselves, on the ground that according as something was simpler in the intellect, so far was it prior within the order of things. Now that which is first in the intellect is the one and the good; for he understands nothing who does not understand one thing, and the one and the good follow upon each other. Hence Plato held that the first idea of the one, which he called the one-in-itself and the good-in-itself, was the first principle of things, and this idea he said was the highest good.[16] Under this one, he established among the

---

9. Plato, *Phaedo*, 96A, 1001; *Theaetetus*, 156A; cf. Aristotle, *Metaphysics*, I, 9 (991b 3).

10. Cf. St. Augustine, *Liber LXXXIII Quaestionum*, q. 46 (PL 40,30); Avicenna, *Metaphysics*, VII,2 (fol. 96ra).

11. Cf. A. C. Pegis, *Introduction to St. Thomas Aquinas*, xiii–xxx.

12. St. Thomas, *Expositio super librum Boethii de Trinitate*, q. 5, a. 1, ed. B. Decker, 161ff. (*The Division and Methods of the Sciences*, trans. A. Maurer, 3 ff).

13. Aristotle, *Metaphysics*, VI, 2 (1028b 20); XII, 1 (1076a 20).

14. Appropriation of form for species.

15. Aristotle, *Metaphysics*, I, 6 (987b 14–18).

16. Plato, *Republic*, VI, 508C; Aristotle, *Ethics*, 1, 6 (1096a 22–23; 1096a 35–1096b 3); St. Augustine, *De Civitate Dei*, VIII, 8 (PL 41, 233); cf. Proclus,

instituebat in substantiis a materia separatis, quos quidem ordines deos secundos esse dicebat quasi quasdam unitates secundas post primam simplicem unitatem.

Rursus quia sicut omnes aliae species participant uno, ita etiam oportet quod intellectus ad hoc quod intelligat participet entium speciebus; ideo sicut sub summo deo qui est unitas prima simplex et imparticipata sunt aliae rerum species quasi unitates secundae et dii secundi, ita sub ordine harum specierum sive unitatum ponebat ordinem intellectuum separatorum qui participant supradictas species ad hoc quod sint intelligentes in actu: inter quos tanto unusquisque est superior quanto propinquior est primo intellectui qui plenam habet participationem specierum, sicut et in diis sive unitatibus tanto unusquisque est superior quanto perfectius participat unitate prima. Separando autem intellectus a diis non excludebat quin dii essent intelligentes, sed volebat quod superintellectualiter intelligerent, non quidem quasi participantes aliquas species sed per se ipsos, ita tamen quod nullus eorum esset bonus et unum nisi per participationem primi unius et boni.

Rursus quia animas quasdam intelligentes videmus, non autem convenit hoc animae ex eo quod est anima, alioquin sequeretur quod omnis anima esset intelligens et quod anima secundum totum id quod est esset intelligens, ponebat ulterius quod sub ordine intellectuum separatorum esset ordo animarum, quarum quaedam, superiores videlicet, participant intellectuali virtute, infimae vero ab hac virtute deficiunt.

Rursus quia corpora videntur non per se moveri nisi sint animata, hoc ipsum quod est per se moveri ponebat corporibus accidere in quantum participabant animam; nam illa corpora quae ab animae participatione deficiunt non moventur nisi ab alio: unde ponebat animabus proprium esse quod se ipsas moverent secundum se ipsas. Sic igitur sub ordine animarum ponebat ordinem corporum, ita tamen quod supremum corporum, scilicet primum caelum quod primo motu movetur, participat motum a suprema anima, et sic deinceps usque ad infimum caelestium corporum.

substances separate from matter[17] diverse orders of participating and participated beings, all of which orders he called secondary gods,[18] as being certain unities below the first simple unity.[19]

Again, inasmuch as all forms participate in the one, the intellect likewise must participate in the forms of things in order to have understanding.[20] Therefore, just as under the highest god, who is the prime unity, simple and unparticipated, other forms of things exist as secondary unities and gods; so, under the order of these forms or unities, he posited an order of separate intellects, which participate in the above-mentioned forms in order to have actual understanding.[21] Among these intellects, an intellect is higher according as it is nearer to the first intellect which has full participation in the forms; just as among the gods or unities, that one is higher which shares more perfectly in the first unity. Although Plato distinguished between the gods and the intellects, he did not mean to imply that the gods could not have understanding. It was his desire, rather, that they should understand in a supra-intellectual manner: that is, instead of understanding by participating in certain forms, they should have understanding through themselves, with the proviso that every one of them was good and one only through participating in the first one and good.

Again, because we see that certain souls possess understanding, which, however, does not befit a soul by the fact that it is a soul (otherwise it would follow that every soul is an intellect and that it would he intelligent in its whole nature), he further posited that under the order of the separate intellects there was an order of souls, the nobler of which participate in intellectual power, while the lowest of them are lacking in it.[22]

Again, because bodies do not seem to be capable of moving themselves unless they have a soul, Plato held that self-motion belongs to bodies insofar as they participate in soul, since those bodies lacking in this participation are not moved unless they are moved by another. Thus he considered it to be an essential property of souls that they move themselves.[23] In this way, below the order of souls, Plato posited the order of bodies, but in such a manner that the highest of the bodies, namely, the first heavens, which is moved by its own motion, receives motion from the highest soul, and so on to the very lowest of the heavenly bodies.

Elem, Props. 12, 13, 20, 119 (pp. 15, 17, 23, 105).

 17. Proclus, *Elem*, Props. 63, 129, 139 (pp. 61, 115, 123).

 18. Nemesius, *De Nat. Hom.*, 44 (PG 40, 793, 706); St. Augustine, *De Civitate Dei*, XIII, 16 (PL41, 388).

 19. Proclus, *Elem*, Props, 6, 14, 21, 116 (pp. 7, 17, 25, 103).

 20. Cf. Proclus, *Elem*, Props. 114, 161 (pp. 101, 141).

 21. Plato, *Timaeus*, 33A ff.; Aristotle, *De Anima*, 1, 3 (406b 25–407b 26); cf. F. M. Cornford, *Plato's Cosmology*, 117 ff.; Proclus, *Elem*, Props. 129, 161 (pp. 115, 141).

 22. This division into gods, intellects, and souls seems to be taken directly from Proclus, *Elem*, Props. 12, 13, 20, 113, 116, 119, 121, 184, 189, 190, 196 (pp. 15, 17, 23, 101–107, 161, 165,167, 171); cf. St. Thomas, *In Librum de Causis*, Props. 2 ff., ed. H. D. Saffrey, 10 ff.

 23. Plato, Phaedrus, 246A; Proclus, *Elem*, Props. 20, 188, 201 (pp. 23, 165, 177).

Sub his autem ponebant Platonici et alia immortalia corpora quae perpetuo animas participant, scilicet aerea vel aetherea. Horum autem quaedam ponebant a terrenis corporibus esse penitus absoluta, quae dicebant esse corpora daemonum; quaedam vero terrenis corporibus indita, quod pertinet ad animas hominum. Non enim ponebant hoc corpus terrenum humanum quod palpamus et videmus immediate participare animam, sed esse aliud interius corpus animae incorruptibile et perpetuum sicut et ipsa anima incorruptibilis est; ita quod anima cum suo perpetuo invisibili corpore est in hoc corpore grossiori non sicut forma in materia sed sicut nauta in navi. Et sicut hominum quosdam dicebant esse bonos, quosdam autem malos, ita et daemonum; animas autem caelestes et intellectus separatos et deos omnes dicebant esse bonos.

Sic igitur patet quod inter nos et summum deum quatuor ordines ponebat, scilicet deorum secundorum, intellectuum separatorum, animarum caelestium et daemonum bonorum seu malorum. Quae si vera essent, omnes huiusmodi medii ordines apud nos angelorum nomine censerentur, nam et daemones in sacra Scriptura angeli nominantur; ipsae etiam animae caelestium corporum, si tamen sint animata, inter angelos sunt connumerandae, ut Augustinus definit in *Enchiridion*.

Below these, furthermore, the Platonists placed immortal bodies, namely, aëreal or ethereal bodies, which participate eternally in soul. Some of these they considered to be altogether independent of earthly bodies, and these they said to be bodies of demons; others became entombed in earthly bodies, which is the case with human souls.[24] For they did not believe that this earthly human body which we touch and see participates immediately in the soul; rather, there is another nobler body belonging to the soul, incorruptible and everlasting, even as the soul itself is incorruptible[25] in such wise that the soul with its everlasting and invisible body is in this grosser body not as a form in matter but as a sailor in a ship.[26] And just as they said that some men were good and others wicked, so too, with the demons. But they said the heavenly souls, the separate intellects, and all the gods were all good.[27]

In this way, therefore, between us and the highest god, it is clear that he posited four orders: namely, that of the secondary gods, that of the separate intellects, that of the heavenly souls, and that of the good or wicked demons. If all these things were true, then all these intermediate orders would be called by us 'angels,' for sacred Scripture refers to the demons themselves as angels.[28] The souls themselves of the heavenly bodies, on the assumption that these are animated, should also be numbered among the angels, as Augustine determines in the *Enchiridion*.[29]

CHAPTER 2

On the opinion of Aristotle

Huius autem positionis radix invenitur efficaciam non habere. Non enim necesse est ut ea quae intellectus separatim intelligit separatim esse habeant in rerum natura; unde nec universalia oportet separata ponere ut subsistentia praeter singularia, neque etiam mathematica praeter sensibilia, quia universalia sunt essentiae ipsorum particularium et mathematica sunt terminationes quaedam sensibilium corporum. Et ideo Aristoteles

But the basis of this position is found to be without foundation, for it is not necessary that what the intellect understands separately should have a separate existence in reality. Hence neither should we posit separate universals subsisting outside singulars, nor likewise mathematicals outside sensible things; for universals are the essences of particular things themselves and mathematicals are certain limits of sensible bodies.[30] That is why Aristotle pro-

---

24. Cf. St. Augustine, *De Civitate Dei*, VIII, 13, 16; IX, 8; XIII, 16 (PL 41, 237–247; 255–276; 387–389); On demons in neo-Platonic literature, cf. Proclus, *Elem*, 294–296; 313–321; St. Thomas, In Librum de Causis, Prop. 19, ed. H. Saffrey, 104–107.

25. Proclus, *Elem*, Prop. 196 (p. 171).

26. Aristotle, *De Anima*, II, 1 (413a 8); St. Thomas, In *De Anima*, II, lect. 2, ed. Pirotta, no. 243 AACTA, 178); cf. Nemesius, *De Nat. Hom.*, I, III (PG 40, 505; 593); Proclus, *Elem*, Props. 186, 187 (p. 163).

27. St. Augustine, *De Civitate Dei*, IX, 1, 2 (PL 41, 255–257).

28. Matt 22:30; 25:41.

29. St. Augustine, *Enchiridion de Fide, Spe et Caritate*, 58 (PL 40, 259–260); cf. A. C. Pegis, *Cosmogony and Knowledge*, I, 643–664; *The Dilemma of Being and Unity*, 179–183; *St. Thomas and the Problem of the Soul in the Thirteenth Century*, 147 ff.; *St. Thomas and the Greeks*, 9 ff.

30. Aristotle, *Metaphysics*, XII, 1–5 (1076a 8–1080a 11); St. Thomas, *De Spiritualibus Creaturis*, a. 3; a. 9 ad 6 (OSC, 41–55; 106–108; ST, I, 84, 1 (BW, I, 793–796); A. C. Pegis, *Introduction to St. Thomas Aquinas*, xiii–xxx.

manifestiori et certiori via processit ad investigandum substantias a materia separatas, scilicet per viam motus.

Primo quidem constituens et ratione et exemplis omne quod movetur ab alio moveri, et si aliquid a se ipso moveri dicatur hoc non est secundum idem sed secundum diversas sui partes, ita scilicet quod una pars eius sit movens et alia mota; et cum non sit procedere in infinitum in moventibus et motis, quia remoto primo movente esset consequens etiam alia removeri, oportet devenire ad aliquod primum movens immobile et ad aliquod primum mobile quod movetur a se ipso eo modo quo dictum est: semper enim quod per se ipsum est est prius et causa eius quod per aliud est.

Rursus constituere intendit motus aeternitatem; et quod nulla virtus movere potest tempore infinito nisi infinita, itemque quod nulla virtus magnitudinis sit virtus infinita. Ex quibus concludit quod virtus primi motoris non est virtus corporis alicuius; unde oportet primum motorem esse incorporeum et absque magnitudine.

Itemque cum in genere mobilium inveniatur appetibile sicut movens non motum, appetens autem sicut movens motum, concludebat ulterius quod primum movens immobile est sicut bonum quoddam appetibile; et quod primum movens se ipsum, quod est primum mobile, movetur per appetitum ipsius.

Est autem considerandum ulterius quod in ordine appetituum et appetibilium primum est quod est secundum intellectum; nam appetitus intellectivus appetit id quod est secundum se bonum, appetitus autem sensitivus non potest attingere ad appetendum quod est secundum se bonum, sed solum ad appetendum id quod videtur bonum: bonum enim simpliciter et absolute non cadit sub apprehensione sensus sed solius intellectus. Unde relinquitur quod primum mobile appetit primum movens appetitu intellectuali; ex quo potest concludi quod primum mobile sit appetens et intelligens. Et cum nihil moveatur nisi corpus, potest concludi quod primum mobile sit corpus animatum anima intellectuali.

Non autem solum primum mobile quod est primum caelum movetur motu aeterno, sed etiam omnes inferiores orbes caelestium corporum; unde et unumquodque caelestium corporum animatum est propria anima et unumquodque habet suum appetibile separatum quod

ceeded by a more manifest and surer way, namely, by way of motion, to investigate substances that are separate from matter.[31]

First, he established by both reason and examples the fact that everything moved is moved by another; and that if something is said to be self-moved, this is not true of it according to the same part but according to diverse parts of itself, so that one part is moving and another is moved.[32] Furthermore, since it is not possible to proceed to infinity among movers and things moved, because if the first mover is taken away, it would follow that the other movers as well would not be moved, we must therefore arrive at some first unmoved mover and some first movable which is moved by itself, in the manner already indicated; for that which is through itself is prior to and the cause of that which is through another.[33]

Furthermore, Aristotle aimed to establish the eternity of motion and that only an infinite power can move in an infinite time, and likewise that no power belonging to a magnitude is an infinite power.[34] From these premises he concluded that the power of the first mover is not a power belonging to any body; therefore, the first mover must be incorporeal and without magnitude.[35]

Again, since in the class of movable beings that which is desirable is present as an unmoved mover, whereas the one desiring is present as a moved mover, Aristotle further concluded that the first unmoved mover is as an appetible good and that the first self-moved mover (namely, the first movable) is moved through a desire of that unmoved mover.[36]

However, we must furthermore keep in mind that in the order of appetites and of appetible objects, the first is that which is through itself an object of understanding, for intellective appetite seeks that which is good through itself; whereas sensitive appetite cannot rise to the appetition of that which is good in itself but only that which appears good. For that which is simply and absolutely good does not fall under the apprehension of sense but only of the intellect. The first movable, therefore, seeks the first mover with an intellectual appetite, and from this it can be inferred that the first movable is appetitive and intelligent. And since only a body is moved, we may infer that the first movable is a body animated by an intellectual soul.

But the prime movable, namely, the first heavens, is not the only one moved with an eternal motion; but also all the lesser spheres of the heavenly bodies are likewise.[37] Therefore, each of the heavenly bodies is animated by its own soul and each has its own separate appetible object which is

---

31. Aristotle, *Physics*, VIII, 5–10 (256a 4–267b 26).
32. Aristotle, *Physics*, III, 1 (201a 10); VII, I (241b 24–242a 17).
33. Aristotle, *Physics*, VII, 1 (241b 24); VIII, 5 (256a 13–21; 256b3–9); cf. for this discussion, St. Thomas, SCG, 1, 13 (OCTF, 1, 85–96).
34. Aristotle, *Physics*, VIII, 10 (266b 6–24).
35. Aristotle, *Physics*, VIII, 10 (267b 17–26).
36. Aristotle, *Metaphysics*, XI, 7 (1072a 19–1073a 12).
37. Aristotle, *Physics*, VIII, 6 (259b 31–260a 10); *Metaphysics*, XI, 8 (1073a 11–37).

est proprius finis sui motus. Sic igitur sunt multae substantiae separatae nullis penitus unitae corporibus, sunt etiam multae intellectuales substantiae caelestibus corporibus unitae.

Harum autem numerum Aristoteles investigare conatur secundum numerum motuum caelestium corporum. Quidam autem de eius sectatoribus, scilicet Avicenna, numerum earum assignat non quidem secundum numerum motuum sed magis secundum numerum planetarum et aliorum superiorum corporum, scilicet orbis stellati et orbis qui est sine stellis; multi enim motus ordinari videntur ad motum unius stellae. Et sicut omnia alia corpora caelestia sub uno supremo caelo continentur cuius motu omnia alia revolvuntur, ita etiam sub prima substantia separata quae est unus deus omnes aliae substantiae separatae ordinantur, et similiter sub anima primi caeli omnes caelorum animae.

Sub corporibus autem caelestibus secundum Aristotelem ponuntur animata sola corpora animalium et plantarum. Non enim posuit quod aliquod simplex elementare corpus possit esse animatum, quia corpus simplex non potest esse conveniens organum tactus quod est de necessitate cuiuslibet animalis; unde inter nos et corpora caelestia nullum intermedium corpus animatum ponebat.

Sic igitur secundum Aristotelis positionem inter nos et summum deum non ponitur nisi duplex ordo intellectualium substantiarum, scilicet substantiae separatae quae sunt fines caelestium motuum, et animae orbium quae sunt moventes per appetitum et desiderium.

Haec autem Aristotelis positio certior quidem videtur, eo quod non multum recedit ab his quae sunt manifesta secundum sensum; tamen minus sufficiens videtur quam Platonis positio. Primo quidem quia multa secundum sensum apparent quorum ratio reddi non potest secundum ea quae ab Aristotele traduntur: apparent enim in hominibus qui a daemonibus opprimuntur et in magorum operibus aliqua quae fieri non posse videntur nisi per aliquam intellectualem substantiam. Tentaverunt igitur quidam sectatorum Aristotelis, ut patet in Epistola Porphyrii ad Anebontem Aegyptium, horum causas reducere in virtutem caelestium corporum, quasi sub quibusdam certis constellationibus magorum opera effectus quosdam insolitos et mirabiles assequantur; ex stellarum etiam impressionibus esse dicunt quod arreptitii interdum aliqua futura praenuntiant ad quorum eventum fit quaedam dispositio in natura per caelestia

the proper end of its motion. There are, accordingly, many separate substances that are in no way united to any bodies; there are, likewise, many intellectual substances united to heavenly bodies.

Aristotle attempts to find out the number of these on the basis of the number of motions of the heavenly bodies.[38] But one of his followers, Avicenna,[39] assigns the number of these substances not according to the number of motions, but rather according to the number of the planets and the other higher bodies (namely, the sphere of the fixed stars and the sphere without stars). For many motions seem to be ordered to the motion of one star, and just as all the other heavenly bodies are under one highest heaven by whose motion all the other bodies are revolving, so likewise all the other separate substances are ordered under the first separate substance, which is the one God. And in like manner, all the souls of the other heavenly bodies are ordered under the soul of the first heaven.

Under the heavenly bodies, according to Aristotle, the only animated bodies are those of animals and plants.[40] For he did not hold that any simple and elementary body could be animated, because a simple body cannot be a suitable organ of touch which of necessity belongs to every animal.[41] Between us and the heavenly bodies, Aristotle did not locate any intervening animate body.

Thus, according to the position of Aristotle, between us and the highest God there exists only a twofold order of intellectual substances: namely, the separate substances (which are the ends of the heavenly motions), and the souls of the spheres (which move through appetite and desire).

Now this position of Aristotle seems to be surer because it does not depart greatly from that which is evident according to sense; yet it seems to be less adequate than the position of Plato. In the first place, there are many things which are evident according to the senses for which an explanation cannot be given on the basis of what Aristotle teaches. For in men who are possessed by devils and in the works of sorcerers, we see certain phenomena which do not seem capable of taking place except through some intellectual substance. Certain followers of Aristotle, as is evident in Porphyry's letter to Anebontes the Egyptian,[42] tried to reduce the causes of these phenomena to the power of the heavenly bodies, as if the works of the sorcerers attained certain unusual and marvelous results under the influence of certain constellations. Furthermore, they say that it is through the influence of the stars that persons who are possessed sometimes foretell future events, for the re-

38. Aristotle, *Metaphysics*, XI, 8 (1073b–I1074a 14).

39. Avicenna, *Metaphysics*, IX, 3 (fol. 104rb).

40. Aristotle, *Metaphysics*, XI, 1 (1068a 30).

41. Aristotle, *De Anima*, II, 2 (413b 4); St. Thomas, In *De Anima*, II, lect. 3, ed. Pirotta, no. 260 (AACTA, 185).

42. All 12 mss. read variously from Anempotem (A) to Cermephontem (L); hence, the emendation according to Cap. XIX, below, where St. Thomas cites St. Augustine's *De Civitate Dei*, X, II (PL 41, 288–291) concerning Porphyry's letter.

corpora. Sed manifeste sunt in talibus quaedam opera quae nullo modo possunt in causam corporalem reduci, sicut quod arreptitii interdum de scientiis loquuntur quas ignorant, litteraliter loquuntur cum sint simplices idiotae, et qui vix villam unde nati sunt exierunt alienae gentis vulgare polite loquuntur; dicuntur etiam in magorum operibus quaedam imagines fieri responsa dantes et se moventes: quae nullo modo per aliquam causam corporalem perfici possent. Huiusmodi autem effectuum causam plane quis poterit secundum Platonicos assignare si dicantur haec per daemones procreari.

Secundo quia inconveniens videtur immateriales substantias ad numerum corporalium substantiarum coarctari. Non enim ea quae sunt superiora in entibus sunt propter ea quae in eis sunt inferiora, sed potius e converso, id enim propter quod aliquid est nobilius est; rationem autem finis non sufficienter aliquis accipere potest ex his quae sunt ad finem, sed potius e converso: unde magnitudinem et virtutem superiorum rerum non sufficienter aliquis accipere potest ex inferiorum rerum consideratione. Quod manifeste apparet in corporalium ordine: non enim posset caelestium corporum magnitudo et numerus accipi ex elementarium corporum dispositione, quae quasi nihil sunt in comparatione ad illa. Plus autem excedunt immateriales substantiae substantias corporales quam corpora caelestia excedant elementaria corpora; unde numerus et virtus et dispositio immaterialium substantiarum ex numero caelestium motuum sufficienter apprehendi non potest.

Et ut hoc specialius manifestetur, ipse processus, ipsa verba probationis Aristotilis assumantur. Assumit enim quod nullus motus potest esse in caelo nisi ordinatus ad alicuius delationem: quod satis probabilitatem habet, omnes enim substantiae orbium esse videntur propter astra, quae sunt nobiliora inter caelestia corpora et manifestiorem effectum habentia. Ulterius autem assumit quod omnes substantiae superiores impassibiles et immateriales sunt fines, cum sint secundum se optima: et hoc quidem rationabiliter dicitur, nam bonum habet rationem finis, unde illa quae sunt per se optima in entibus sunt fines aliorum. Sed quod concludit hunc esse numerum immaterialium substantiarum qui est caelestium motuum, non sequitur ex necessitate.

alization of which there is a certain disposition in nature through the heavenly bodies. But in such cases, there are manifestly certain works which cannot in any way be reduced to a corporeal cause. For example, that people in a trance should speak in a cultivated way of sciences which they do not know, since they are unlettered folk; and that those who have scarcely left the village in which they were born speak with fluency the vernacular of a foreign people. Likewise, in the works of magicians, certain images are said to be conjured up which answer questions and move about, all of which could not be accomplished by any corporeal cause. But one can clearly assign a cause of these effects if it is said these are brought about by demons, following the Platonists.

Second, because it seems unbefitting that immaterial substances should be limited to the number of corporeal substances. For those beings that are higher do not exist for the sake of those that are lower. But on the contrary, that because of which something else exists is the more noble. Now one cannot sufficiently ascertain the nature of an end from that which is for the end, but rather the other way about. Hence, one cannot adequately ascertain the magnitude and power of higher beings by a consideration of the lower ones. This truth is especially evident in the order of corporeal beings, for it is impossible to reckon the magnitude and number of heavenly bodies from the disposition of the elementary bodies, which are as nothing in comparison to them. But the immaterial substances surpass corporeal substances much more than the heavenly bodies surpass elementary ones. In view of this, the number, power, and disposition of immaterial substances cannot be adequately grasped from the number of heavenly movements.

Let us assume the procedure and even the very words of Aristotle's proof in order that this truth may be more particularly made manifest. Now Aristotle assumes that there can be no motion in the heavens unless it is ordered to the accomplishment of something.[43] This assumption is sufficiently probable. For all the substances of the spheres seem to exist for the sake of the stars, which are nobler among the heavenly bodies and have a more evident influence. Aristotle further assumes that all the higher substances, impassible and immaterial, are ends, being of themselves most excellent; and this assumption is reasonable.[44] For the good has the nature of an end, and hence among beings those that are by their very nature noblest are ends for other beings. But the conclusion of Aristotle—that the number of immaterial substances is determined by the number of heavenly movements—does not necessarily follow.[45]

---

43. Aristotle, *Metaphysics*, XI, 8 (1074a 17–30).
44. Aristotle, *Metaphysics*, XI, 8 (1073a 26).
45. Aristotle, *Metaphysics*, XI, (1073a 36; 1074a 5–15).

Est enim finis et proximus et remotus. Non est autem necessarium quod proximus finis supremi caeli sit suprema substantia immaterialis quae est summus deus; sed magis probabile est ut inter primam immaterialem substantiam et corpus caeleste sint multi ordines immaterialium substantiarum, quarum inferior ordinetur ad superiorem sicut ad finem, et ad infimam earum ordinetur corpus caeleste sicut ad finem proximum: oportet enim unamquamque rem esse proportionatam quodam modo suo proximo fini. Unde propter distantiam maximam primae immaterialis substantiae ad substantiam corpoream quamcumque, non est probabile quod corporalis substantia ordinetur ad supremam substantiam sicut ad proximum finem; unde etiam Avicenna posuit causam primam non esse immediatum finem alicuius caelestium motuum sed quamdam intelligentiam primam, et idem etiam potest dici de inferioribus motibus caelestium corporum. Et ideo non est necessarium quod non sint plures immateriales substantiae quam sit numerus caelestium motuum.

Et hoc praesentiens Aristoteles non induxit hoc quasi necessarium, sed quasi probabiliter dictum. Sic enim dixit antequam praedictam rationem assignet enumeratis caelestibus motibus *Quare substantias et principia immobilia et sensibilia tot rationabile est suscipere, necessarium enim dimittatur fortioribus dicere*; non enim reputabat se sufficientem ad hoc quod in talibus aliquid ex necessitate concluderet.

Potest etiam alicui videri praedictum Aristotilis processum ad substantias immateriales ponendas inconvenientem esse, eo quod procedit ex sempiternitate motus quae fidei veritati repugnat. Sed si quis diligenter attendat rationem eius processus, non tollitur etiam aeternitate motus sublata; nam sicut ex aeternitate motus concluditur motoris infinita potentia, ita etiam hoc idem concludi potest ex motus uniformitate. Motor enim qui non semper movere potest necesse est quod quandoque citius quandoque tardius moveat, secundum quod paulatim virtus eius deficit in movendo; in motibus autem caelestibus invenitur omnimoda uniformitas: unde concludi potest quod motori primi motus insit virtus ad semper movendum. Et sic idem sequitur.

For an end is both proximate and remote. And the proximate end of the highest heavens is not necessarily the highest immaterial substance, which is the most high God, but it is more probable that there are many orders of immaterial substances between the first immaterial substance and the heavenly body. The lower of these immaterial substances is ordered to the higher as to an end, and a heavenly body is ordered to the lowest of these as to its proximate end. For each thing must in some way be proportioned to its proximate end. Accordingly, because of the greatest possible distance between the first immaterial substance and any corporeal substance, it is not probable[46] that a corporeal substance should be ordered to the highest substance as to its proximate end. Hence even Avicenna[47] posited that the immediate end of any of the heavenly movements was not the first cause but a certain first intelligence; and the same can likewise be said of the lower motions of the heavenly bodies. Hence that there should not be more immaterial substances than the number of heavenly motions is not a necessary fact.

And Aristotle himself, suspecting this fact, did not advance this position as necessary but only as probable. For when he had enumerated the heavenly movements and before he offered the aforementioned explanation, he states: *Accordingly, it is reasonable to posit so many substances and immovable principles; but why it should be necessary, we shall leave to more capable individuals to pronounce.*[48] Aristotle therefore did not consider himself equal to the task of reaching a necessary conclusion in such matters.

Furthermore, it may seem to someone that Aristotle's aforesaid reasoning for positing immaterial substances is improper because it is based on the everlastingness of motion, which is contrary to the truth of faith. But if we follow his reason carefully, we can see that his argumentation still holds even if the eternity of motion is denied. For, just as the infinite power of a mover can be proved from the eternity of motion, so too, the same can be proved from the uniformity of motion. For a mover that cannot always be in motion must necessarily move at one time faster and at another time more slowly, according as his power gradually slows down in motion. But in the domain of heavenly movements there is a complete uniformity. We may therefore conclude that the mover of the first motion has the power to move everlastingly and we would thus arrive at the same conclusion.[49]

---

46. That is, it does not stand to reason.
47. Avicenna, *Metaphysics*, IX, 3 (fol. 104rb).
48. Aristotle, *Metaphysics*, XI, 8 (1074a 15).
49. Cf. St Thomas, SCG, I, 13 (OTCF, I, 85 ff.).

CHAPTER 3

How the positions of Aristotle and Plato agree

His igitur visis, de facili accipere possumus in quo conveniant et in quo differant positiones Aristotelis et Platonis circa immateriales substantias.

Primo quidem conveniunt in modo existendi ipsarum. Posuit enim Plato omnes inferiores substantias immateriales esse unum et bonum per participationem primi quod est secundum se unum et bonum; omne autem participans aliquid accipit id quod participat ab eo a quo participat, et quantum ad hoc id a quo participat est causa ipsius: sicut aer habet lumen participatum a sole, quae est causa illuminationis ipsius. Sic igitur secundum Platonem summus deus causa est omnibus immaterialibus substantiis quod unaquaeque earum et unum sit et bonum. Et hoc etiam Aristoteles posuit, quia, ut ipse dicit, necesse est ut id quod est maxime ens et maxime verum sit causa essendi et veritatis omnibus aliis.

Secundo autem conveniunt quantum ad conditionem naturae ipsarum: quia uterque posuit omnes huiusmodi substantias penitus esse a materia immunes, non tamen esse eas immunes a compositione potentiae et actus. Nam omne participans oportet esse compositum ex potentia et actu, id enim quod recipitur ut participatum oportet esse actum ipsius substantiae participantis; et sic, cum omnes substantiae praeter supremam quae est per se unum et per se bonum sint participantes secundum Platonem, necesse est quod omnes sint compositae ex potentia et actu. Quod etiam necesse est dicere secundum sententiam Aristotelis. Ponit enim quod ratio veri et boni attribuitur actui; unde illud quod est primum verum et primum bonum oportet esse actum purum, quaecumque vero ab hoc deficiunt oportet aliquam permixtionem potentiae habere.

Tertio vero conveniunt in ratione providentiae. Posuit enim Plato quod summus deus, qui hoc quod est ipsum unum est et ipsum bonum, ex primaeva ratione bonitatis proprium habet ut inferioribus omnibus provideat; et unumquodque inferiorum in quantum participat bonitate primi boni etiam providet his quae post se sunt, non solum eiusdem ordinis sed etiam diversorum. Et secundum hoc primus intellectus separatus providet toti ordini separatorum intellectuum, et quilibet superior suo inferiori; totusque ordo se-

After having examined these points, we can easily determine wherein Plato's and Aristotle's positions on the immaterial substances agree and wherein they differ.

In the first place, Plato and Aristotle agree on the manner of their existence. For Plato[50] held that all lower immaterial substances are one and good by participation in the first, which is essentially one and good. Now whatever participates in something receives that which it participates from the one from whom it participates; and to this extent that from which it participates is its cause, just as air has light, which it participates from the sun, which is the cause of its illumination. Therefore, according to Plato, the highest God is the reason why all immaterial substances are each one of them one and good.[51] Aristotle, too, held this opinion because, as he himself says, that which is most being and most truth is the cause of being and truth for all other things.[52]

Second, Plato and Aristotle agree as to the condition of their nature, for both held that all such substances are completely free of matter, although not free from the composition of potency and act, for every participating being must be composed of potency and act. For that which is received as participated must be the act of the participating substance itself. And thus, since Plato held that all substances below the highest, which is by itself one and good, are participants, they are of necessity composed of potency and act.[53] This must likewise be said according to Aristotle's position, for he maintained that the nature of the true and the good is attributed to act.[54] Hence that which is the first truth and the first good must be pure act. And whatever beings fall short of it must have a certain admixture of potency.

Third, Plato and Aristotle agree on the nature of providence. Plato held that the highest God, from the fact that he is the one itself and the good itself, has as his property to have providence over all lower things, from the root nature of goodness; and every lower thing insofar as it participates in the goodness of the first good likewise acts as a providence over the things which come after it, and not only of the same order but of diverse orders as well. Accordingly, the first separate intellect is a providence over the whole order of separate intellects, and each higher intellect over a

---

50. See above, Cap. I; cf. Proclus, *Elem*, Props. 12, 13 (pp. 15–16).

51. Aristotle, *Ethics*, 1, 6 (1096a 22–23; 1096a 35–1096b 3); St. Augustine, *De Civitate Dei*, VIII, 6, 8 (PL 41, 231–233); cf. St. Thomas, ST, I, 2, 3 (BW, I, 21).

52. Aristotle, *Metaphysics*, I, 1 (993b 24–31; transl. Ross).

53. Proclus, *Elem*, Props. 3,4, 8, 12, 13 (pp. 5, 9–11, 15–16); St. Augustine, *De Civitate Dei*, VIII, 6, 8 (PL 41, 231–233).

54. Cf. Aristotle, *Metaphysics*, XI, 7 (1072a 24–28).

paratorum intellectuum providet ordini animarum et inferioribus ordinibus. Rursumque idem observari putat in ipsis animalibus, ut supremae quidem caelorum animae provideant omnibus inferioribus animabus et toti generationi inferiorum corporum; itemque superiores animae inferioribus, scilicet animae daemonum animabus hominum: ponebant enim Platonici daemones esse mediatores inter nos et superiores substantias.

Ab hac etiam providentiae ratione Aristoteles non discordat. Ponit enim unum bonum separatum omnibus providentem sicut unum imperatorem vel dominum sub quo sunt diversi rerum ordines: ita scilicet quod superiores ordines rerum perfecte providentiae ordinem consequuntur, unde nullus defectus in eis invenitur, inferiora vero entium quae minus perfecte providentiae ordinem recipere possunt multis defectibus subiacent; sicut etiam in domo liberi qui perfecte participant regimen patrisfamilias in paucis vel nullis deficiunt, servorum autem actiones in pluribus inveniuntur inordinatae. Unde in inferioribus corporibus defectus proveniunt naturalis ordinis qui in superioribus corporibus nunquam deficere invenitur. Similiter etiam humanae animae plerumque deficiunt ab intelligentia veritatis et a recto appetitu veri boni, quod in superioribus animabus vel intellectibus non invenitur. Propter quod etiam Plato posuit daemonum esse quosdam bonos quosdam malos sicut et homines, deos vero et intellectus et caelorum animas omnino absque malitia esse.

Secundum igitur haec tria circa substantias separatas invenitur opinio Aristotelis cum Platonis opinione concordare.

lower intellect; and the whole order of separate intellects is a providence over the order of souls and the lower orders.[55] Furthermore, Plato thought that this same fact could be observed among souls themselves: namely, that the highest souls of the heavens exercise a providence over all the lower souls and over the whole generation of lower bodies; and in the same way, that the higher souls exercise a providence over the lower ones,[56] (that is, the souls of the demons over the souls of men). For the Platonists held that demons acted as mediators between us and the higher substances.[57]

With this view of providence, Aristotle likewise does not disagree. For he posits one separate good, acting as a providence over all things in the manner of a single commander or master under whom are diverse orders of things in such a way that the higher orders of things achieve the order of perfect providence,[58] and hence no defect is found in them. But lower beings which are able to receive the order of a less perfect providence are open to many defects: just as in a home, the children who perfectly share in the rule of the father fall short either in few things or in none; whereas the actions of slaves are found to lack order in many respects.[59] Hence among inferior bodies, failings arise in the natural order, which is never found to be lacking among higher bodies. In the same way, human souls themselves frequently fall short of the understanding of the truth and of the right appetite of the true good, but this is not found among the higher souls or intellects. For this reason, Plato himself posited that certain demons were good and others were wicked, as were men; whereas the gods, the intellects, and the souls of the heavens were completely without wickedness.[60]

These are the three points on which the opinion of Plato concerning the separate substances is found to be in agreement with that of Aristotle.

55. Proclus, *Elem*, Props. 119, 120, 122, 134, 141, 145, 204 (pp. 105, 109, 119, 125, 129, 179).
56. Nemesius, *De Nat. Hom.*, 44 (PG 40, 793, 796).
57. St. Augustine, *De Civitate Dei*, VIII, 14 (PL 41, 328).
58. Aristotle, *Metaphysics*, XI, 10 (1075a 11–25); On providence in Aristotle, cf. E. Gilson, *Spirit of Mediaeval Philosophy*, 148, 167, 457–458; God and Philosophy, 32 ff.
59. Aristotle, *Politics*, 1, 3 (1253b1 ff.).
60. Cf. above, Cap. I; St. Augustine, *De Civitate Dei*, VIII, 13; IX, 2 (PL 41, 237–238, 257).

CHAPTER 4

How the positions of Aristotle and Plato differ

Sunt autem alia in quibus differunt. Primo quidem, ut supra dictum est, Plato supra caelorum animas duplicem ordinem immaterialium substantiarum posuit, scilicet intellectus et deos, quos deos dicebat esse species intelligibiles separatas quarum participatione intellectus intelligunt. Aristoteles vero universalia separata non ponens, unum solum ordinem rerum posuit supra caelorum animas; in quorum etiam ordine primum esse posuit summum deum, sicut et Plato summum deum primum esse posuit in ordine specierum, quasi summus deus sit ipsa idea unius et boni.

Hunc autem ordinem Aristoteles posuit utrumque habere, ut scilicet esset intelligens et intellectum: ita scilicet quod summus deus intelligeret non participatione alicuius superioris quod esset eius perfectio, sed per essentiam suam. Et idem aestimavit esse dicendum in ceteris substantiis separatis sub summo deo ordinatis; nisi quod in quantum a simplicitate primi deficiunt et summa perfectione ipsius, eorum intelligere perfici potest per superiorum substantiarum participationem. Sic igitur secundum Aristotelem huiusmodi substantiae quae sunt fines caelestium motuum sunt et intellectus intelligentes et intelligibiles species, non autem ita quod sint species vel naturae sensibilium substantiarum sicut Platonici posuerunt, sed omnino altiores.

Secundo vero quia Plato non coarctavit numerum intellectuum separatorum numero caelestium motuum; non enim ex hac causa movebatur ad ponendum intellectus separatos, sed ipsam naturam rerum secundum se considerans. Aristoteles vero a sensibilibus recedere nolens, ex sola consideratione motuum, ut supra dictum est, pervenit ad ponendum intellectuales substantias separatas; et ideo earum numerum coarctavit caelestibus motibus.

Tertio autem quia Aristoteles non posuit aliquas animas medias inter caelorum animas et animas hominum

There are other respects in which Plato and Aristotle differ. First, as has been said above,[61] Plato posited a twofold order of immaterial substances above the souls of the heavens: namely, the intellects and the gods. He declared these gods were the separate intelligible forms,[62] by participation in which the intellects have understanding.[63] But Aristotle, since he did not posit any separate universals, posited only a single order of things above the souls of the heavens. He held, moreover, that the first among these was the highest God, just as Plato held that the highest God was first in the order of forms, among which the highest God is the very idea of the one and the good.

But Aristotle held that this order comprised both, namely, so that it was both understanding and understood, so that thus the highest God would understand not by participation in something higher that would be his perfection, but through his own essence.[64] And Aristotle likewise held the same opinion as to the other separate substances ordered below the highest God,[65] except that as they fall short of the simplicity of the first and of his highest perfection, their understanding can be perfected by participation in the higher substances.[66] Thus, according to Aristotle, such substances, which are the ends of the heavenly motions, are both understanding intellects and intelligible forms.[67] But this is not to be understood in the sense that they are the forms or natures of sensible substances, as the Platonists asserted,[68] but altogether higher forms.

They differ, second, because Plato did not restrict the number of separate intellects to the number of heavenly movements. It was not on this account that Plato was moved to posit separate intellects, but rather by considering the very nature of things in themselves. Aristotle, on the other hand, not wishing to be diverted from sensible things, came to posit separate intellectual substances as a result of the sole consideration of motion, as we have said above,[69] and for this reason, limited the number of the substances to the number of heavenly motions.[70]

Third, they differ because Aristotle did not posit any souls intermediate between the souls of the heavens and

---

61. Cf. above, Cap. I.
62. Cf. St. Thomas, *In Librum de Causis*, Prop. 3 (ed. H. Saffrey, 18): "Ideo omnes hujusmodi formas sic subsistentes 'deos' vocabat."
63. Proclus, *Elem*, Props. 101, 161, 163 (pp. 91, 141, 143).
64. Aristotle, *Metaphysics*, XI, 9 (1074b 33–35).
65. Aristotle, *Metaphysics*, XI, 9 (1074a 10–16).
66. Aristotle, *Metaphysics*, XI, 9 (1074b 26).
67. Aristotle, *Metaphysics*, XI, 9 (1074b 35–1075a 5).
68. Aristotle, *Metaphysics*, I, 6 (987b 1–10).
69. Cf. above, Cap. II.
70. Cf. above, Cap. II.

sicut posuit Plato; unde de daemonibus nullam invenitur nec ipse nec eius sequaces fecisse mentionem.

Haec igitur sunt quae de opinionibus Platonis et Aristotelis circa substantias separatas ex diversis scripturis collegimus.

the souls of men, as did Plato.[71] Hence, we find that neither Aristotle nor any of his followers has made mention of demons.

This, then, is what we have gathered from various writings concerning the opinions of Plato and Aristotle on the separate substances.[72]

CHAPTER 5

On the opinion of Avicebron and his arguments for it

Eorum vero qui post secuti sunt aliqui ab eorum positionibus recedentes in deterius erraverunt. Primo namque Avicebron in libro *Fontis vitae* alterius conditionis substantias separatas posuit esse; aestimavit enim omnes substantias sub Deo constitutas ex materia et forma compositas esse, quod tam ab opinione Platonis quam Aristotelis discordat. Qui quidem dupliciter deceptus fuisse videtur: primo quidem quia aestimavit quod secundum intelligibilem compositionem quae in rerum generibus invenitur, prout scilicet ex genere et differentia constituitur species, esset etiam in rebus ipsis compositio realis intelligenda, ut scilicet uniuscuiusque rei in genere exsistentis genus sit materia differentia vero forma. Secundo quia aestimavit quod esse in potentia et esse subiectum et esse recipiens secundum unam rationem in omnibus diceretur; quibus duabus positionibus innixus quadam resolutoria via processit investigando compositiones rerum usque ad intellectuales substantias.

Primo enim inspexit in artificialibus quod componuntur ex forma artificiali et materia quae est aliqua res naturalis, puta ferrum aut lignum, quae se habet ad formam artificialem ut potentia ad actum. Rursus consideravit quod huiusmodi naturalia corpora particularia composita erant ex elementis; unde posuit quod quatuor elementa comparantur ad formas particulares naturales, puta lapidis aut ferri, sicut materia ad formam

Among those who came after Plato and Aristotle, some departed from their positions and fell into error. First among these was Avicebron who held that separate substances were of a different state, in the book *The Fount of Life*.[73] For he held that all substances established below God are composed of matter and form,[74] an opinion that disagrees both with the view of Plato and the view of Aristotle.[75] Avicebron seems to have been twice deceived: first, because he thought that according to the intelligible composition found in the genera of things (namely, inasmuch as a species is composed of genus and difference), there would likewise be understood such a composition in things themselves, so that in the case of each and every thing existing in a genus, the genus is matter and the difference is form.[76] Second, because he thought that to be in potency, to be a subject, and to be a recipient would in all cases be said according to one notion. Therefore, basing himself upon these two positions, he proceeded in a certain reductive way in investigating the composition of all things up to intellectual substances.

In the first place, he noticed in the case of artificial things that they are composed of an artificial form and of matter, which is a certain natural thing (for example, iron or wood), which is disposed to the artificial form as potency to act.[77] Furthermore, he observed that such particular natural bodies were composed of elements.[78] Hence he asserted that the four elements are related to the particular natural forms (for example, of stone or iron) as matter to

71. Cf. above, Cap. I; Cap. III; St. Augustine, *De Civitate Dei*, VIII, 13, 14, 16; IX, 2, 8, 12; X, 1 (PL 41, 237–239, 241–242, 257, 263, 265–266, 267–279).

72. This composite doctrine of Plato and Aristotle which St. Thomas uses in his critique of other philosophical positions in Cap. V–XVI has been advanced by C. Fabro, *La nozione metafisica di Partecipazione secondo S. Tommaso d'Aquino*, Turin, 2nd edit. 1950, as an argument for a real assimilation of the metaphysical content of the Platonic notion of participation within Aristotelian thought by the Angelic Doctor (pp. 58–64). R. Henle, on the other band, in A Note on Certain Textual Evidence in Fabro's 'La Nozione Metafisica di Partecipazione', 265–282 and in Saint Thomas' Methodology in the Treatment of 'Positiones', 391–409, thoroughly disagrees with Fabro's thesis.

73. Avicebron, (Ibn Gabirol) Fons Vitae, 1, 2–4, ed. C. Baeumker, 3–6; cf. E. Gilson, *Pourquoi saint Thomas a critiqué saint Augustin*, 25–35, 108–116, 217–219; HCP, 226–229 and notes 27–35 (pp. 647–649); J. Collins, *The Thomistic Philosophy of the Angels*, 44–74; E. Kleineidam, *Das Problem der hylomorphen Zusammensetzung der geistigen Substanzen im 13 Jahrhundert, behandelt bis Thomas von Aquin*, 9–15.

74. Avicebron, *op. cit.*, I, 8 (p. 11); IV, 7 (p. 226).

75. Aristotle, *Metaphysics*, I, 6 (987b I–18).

76. Avicebron, *op. cit.*, IV, 6 (p. 223).

77. Avicebron, *op. cit.*, I, 14 (p. 17).

78. *Ibid.*, (p. 18).

et potentia ad actum. Iterum consideravit quod quatuor elementa conveniunt in hoc quod quodlibet eorum est corpus, differunt autem secundum contrarias qualitates: unde tertio posuit quod ipsum corpus est materia elementorum, quam vocavit naturalem materiam universalem, et quod formae huius materiae sunt qualitates elementorum. Sed quia videbat quod corpus caeleste convenit cum elementis in corporeitate, differt vero ab eis in hoc quod non est susceptivum contrariarum qualitatum, posuit quarto ordine materiam corporis caelestis quae etiam comparatur ad formam caelestis corporis sicut potentia ad actum. Et sic posuit quatuor ordines materiae corporalis.

Rursus, quia vidit quod omne corpus significat substantiam quamdam longam latam et spissam, aestimavit quod corporis in quantum est corpus huiusmodi tres dimensiones sunt sicut forma, et substantia quae subiicitur quantitati et aliis generibus accidentium est materia corporis in quantum est corpus. Sic igitur substantia quae sustinet novem praedicamenta, ut ipse dicit, est prima spiritualis materia. Et sicut posuit in materia universali corporali, quam dixit esse corpus, quiddam superius quod non est susceptivum contrariarum qualitatum, scilicet materiam caelestis corporis, et aliquid inferius quod est susceptivum contrariarum qualitatum, quam credidit esse materiam quatuor elementorum: ita etiam in ipsa substantia posuit quiddam superius quod non est susceptivum quantitatis, et hoc posuit substantiam separatam, et quiddam inferius quod est susceptivum quantitatis quod posuit esse materiam incorpoream corporum.

Rursus, ipsas substantias separatas vel spirituales componi posuit ex materia et forma; et hoc probavit pluribus rationibus. Primo quidem quia aestimavit quod nisi substantiae spirituales essent compositae ex materia et forma, nulla posset inter eas esse diversitas. Si enim non sunt compositae ex materia et forma, aut sunt materia tantum aut sunt forma tantum. Si sunt materia tantum, non potest esse quod sint multae substantiae spirituales, quia materia est una de se et diversificatur per formas; similiter etiam si substantia spiritualis sit forma tantum, non poterit assignari unde substantiae spirituales sint diversae. Quia si dicas quod sunt diversae secundum perfectionem et imperfectionem, sequetur quod substantia spiritualis sit subiectum perfectionis et imperfectionis; sed esse subiectum pertinet ad rationem

form and potency to act. Moreover, he noted that the four elements agree in that each one of them is a body and they differ according to contrary qualities.[79] Hence in the third place he held that body itself is the matter of the elements, which matter he named 'universal natural matter,' and that the forms of this matter are the qualities of the elements. But because he observed that a heavenly body agrees with the elements in corporeity but differs from them in not being receptive of contrary qualities,[80] he placed the matter of a heavenly body in a fourth order, which likewise is related to the form of heavenly body as potency is to act. Avicebron thus posited four orders of corporeal matter.[81]

Again, because he saw that every body signifies a certain substance with length, width, and thickness, he thought that the body, insofar as it is such a body, has three dimensions which are as form; and substance, which is the subject of quantity and the other genera of accidents, is matter of the body so far as it is a body.[82] Thus, therefore, the substance which supports the nine predicaments is the prime spiritual matter, as he himself says.[83] And just, as he posited in universal corporeal matter, which he called a body, something higher which was not receptive of contrary qualities (namely, the matter of the body of the heavens), and something lower which is receptive of contrary qualities, which he believed to be the matter of the four elements[84]—so likewise he posited in substance itself something higher which is not receptive of quantity (and which he considered to be a separate substance), and something lower, which is receptive of quantity (which he posited as the incorporeal matter of bodies).[85]

Furthermore, he asserted that the separate or spiritual substances themselves are composed of matter and form. This he proved by several arguments.[86] First, because he held that there would be no diversity among spiritual substances unless they were composed of matter and form.[87] For if they are not composed of matter and form, they are either matter alone or form alone. If they are matter alone, then spiritual substances cannot be many because matter of itself is one and is diversified through forms. In like manner, if a spiritual substance is form alone, no cause of the diversification of spiritual substances can be assigned. For if you say that they are diverse according to perfection and imperfection, it would then follow that spiritual substance is the subject of perfection and imperfection. But to be a subject belongs to the nature of matter, and not to the na-

---

79. *Ibid.*, I, 15 (p. 19).
80. *Ibid.*, I, 17 (p. 20).
81. *Ibid.*, I, 16–17 (pp. 19–21).
82. Avicebron, *op. cit.*, IV, 6 (p. 226).
83. *Ibid.*, II, 6 (p. 35); IV; 34 (p. 320).
84. *Ibid.*, V, 42 (p. 333).
85. *Ibid.*, II, 22 (p. 64).
86. Avicebron, *op. cit.*, II, 24 (p. 69); IV, I (p. 211); IV, 2 (p. 213).
87. *Ibid.*, IV, 2, 3 (pp. 215 ff.).

materiae, non autem ad rationem formae: unde relinquitur quod vel non sunt plures substantiae spirituales, vel sunt compositae ex materia et forma.

Secunda ratio eius est quia intellectus spiritualitatis est praeter intellectum corporeitatis, et ita substantia corporalis et spiritualis habent aliquid in quo differunt; habent etiam aliquid in quo conveniunt, quia utrumque est substantia. Ergo sicut in substantia corporali substantia est tanquam materia sustentans corporeitatem, ita in substantia spirituali substantia est quasi materia sustentans spiritualitatem; et secundum quod materia plus vel minus participat de forma spiritualitatis, secundum hoc substantiae spirituales sunt superiores vel inferiores, sicut etiam aer quanto est subtilior tanto plus participat de claritate.

Tertia ratio eius est quia esse communiter invenitur in substantiis spiritualibus quasi superioribus et corporalibus quasi inferioribus; illud ergo quod est consequens ad esse in substantiis corporalibus erit consequens ad esse in substantiis spiritualibus. Sed in substantiis corporalibus invenitur triplex ordo, scilicet corpus spissum quod est corpus elementorum, et corpus subtile quod est corpus caeleste, et iterum materia et forma corporis; ergo etiam in substantia spirituali invenitur substantia spiritualis inferior, puta quae coniungitur corpori, et superior quae non est coniuncta corpori, et iterum materia et forma ex quibus substantia spiritualis componitur.

Quarta ratio eius est quia omnis substantia creata oportet quod distinguatur a creatore; sed creator est unum tantum: oportet igitur quod omnis substantia creata non sit unum tantum sed composita ex duobus, quorum necesse est ut unum sit forma et aliud materia, quia ex duabus materiis non potest aliquid fieri nec ex duabus formis.

Quinta ratio eius est quia omnis substantia spiritualis creata est finita; res autem non est finita nisi per suam formam, quia res quae non habet formam per quam fiat unum est infinita: omnis igitur substantia spiritualis creata est composita ex materia et forma.

ture of form. Therefore, it remains either that spiritual substances are not many or that they are composed of matter and form.[88]

His second reason is that the concept of spirituality is outside the concept of corporeity. And thus corporeal spiritual substances have something in which they differ, and likewise in which they agree, since each is a substance. Hence, just as in the case of corporeal substance, substance is as matter upholding corporeity, so in the case of spiritual substance, substance is as matter upholding spirituality. And according as matter participates more or less in the form of spirituality, spiritual substances are accordingly higher or lower, just as the finer the air is, the more it participates in clarity.[89]

His third reason is that existence is found in common among spiritual substances as in higher beings, and in corporeal substances as in lower beings. Therefore, that which follows upon existence in corporeal substances will also follow upon existence in spiritual ones. But a three-fold order is found in corporeal substances: namely, a gross body which is the body of the elements, a refined body which is the heavenly body, and finally, the matter and form of body. Therefore, in a spiritual substance there is found a lower spiritual substance, namely, one which is joined to a body, and a more excellent one which is not joined to a body, and again, matter and form from which a spiritual substance is composed.[90]

His fourth reason is that every created substance must be distinguished from the creator. But the creator is one only. Therefore, every created substance cannot be one only but must be composed of two constituents, of which one must necessarily be form and the other matter, because it cannot be composed of two matters or of two forms.[91]

His fifth reason is that every created spiritual substance is finite. But a thing is finite only through its form, because a thing which does not have a form through which to become one is infinite. Therefore, every created spiritual substance is composed of matter and form.[92]

88. *Ibid.*, IV, 2 (pp. 212–213).
89. *Ibid.*, IV, 2 (pp. 214–215).
90. Avicebron, *op. cit.*, IV, 4 (p. 217).
91. *Ibid.*, IV, 6 (p. 222).
92. *Ibid.*, IV, 6 (pp. 223–224).

CHAPTER 6

Refutation of Avicebron's position

Haec autem quae dicta sunt in pluribus manifestam improbabilitatem continent. Primo namque quia ab inferioribus ad suprema entium ascendit resolvendo in principia materialia: quod omnino rationi repugnat. Comparatur enim materia ad formam sicut potentia ad actum; manifestum est autem quod potentia est minus ens quam actusm, non enim dicitur potentia ens nisi secundum ordinem ad actum, unde neque simpliciter dicimus esse quae sunt in potentia sed solum quae sunt in actu: quanto igitur magis resolvendo descenditur ad principia materialia, tanto minus invenitur de ratione entis. Suprema autem in entibus oportet esse maxime entia, nam et in unoquoque genere suprema quae sunt aliorum principia esse maxime dicuntur, sicut ignis est calidus maxime; unde et Plato investigando suprema entium processit resolvendo in principia formalia, sicut supra dictum est. Inconvenientissime igitur hic per contrariam viam processit in principia materialia resolvendo.

Secundo quia, quantum ex suis dictis apparet, in antiquam quodam modo Naturalium opinionem rediit qui posuerunt omnia esse unum ens, dum ponebant substantiam rerum omnium non esse aliud quam materiam; quam non ponebant esse aliquid in potentia tantum sicut Plato et Aristoteles, sed esse aliquid ens actu. Nisi quod antiqui Naturales, nihil aliud praeter corpora esse aestimantes, hanc materiam communem et substantiam omnium aliquod corpus esse dicebant, puta aut ignem aut aerem aut aquam aut aliquid medium; sed iste non solum in corporibus naturam rerum aestimans comprehendi, illud unum quod posuit esse primam materiam et communem substantiam omnium dixit esse substantiam non corpoream.

Et quod simili modo posuerit hanc universalem materiam, ut dicit, esse substantiam omnium sicut Naturales hoc ponebant de aliquo uno corporum, manifestum est ex hoc quod eorum quae conveniunt in genere ponit genus esse materiam, differentias vero

These arguments which we have set forth[93] are plainly improbable in many respects. The first argument is unacceptable because Avicebron proceeds upward from the lower beings to the highest ones by resolving[94] them into material principles, which is an argument absolutely contrary to reason. For matter is compared to form as potency to act. Now it is clear that potency is less a being than is act, for potency is said to be a being only according to its order to act. Hence neither do we say without qualification that the things which are in potency exist: we say this only of things which are in act. Therefore, the lower one descends by resolving to material principles, the less does one find of the character of being. On the other hand, among beings the highest ones must be preeminently beings, for the highest in every genus (which are the principles of all the rest) are eminently said to exist in the highest degree, just as fire is most hot.[95] Accordingly, Plato, while investigating the highest beings, proceeded by resolving them into formal principles, as has been said above.[96] Most unfittingly, therefore, did Avicebron proceed in the opposite direction by resolving beings into material principles.

Second, because at least so far as appears from his own words, Avicebron in a way returned to the opinion of the ancient naturalists who held that all things were one being, by positing that the substance of all things was nothing other than matter.[97] This matter they did not consider as something only in potency, as Plato and Aristotle did, but as some actual being. There was this difference, however, that the ancient naturalists, believing that only bodies existed, said that this common matter and substance of all things was some body, as (for example) fire or air or water or something in between.[98] Avicebron, on the other hand, thinking that the nature of things was not contained in bodies alone, said that that one principle which he held to be the first matter and common substance of all things was a non-corporeal substance.[99]

And that he posited this universal matter, which he says is the substance of all things, in the same way in which the naturalists posited this of some one body, is clear from the fact that, according to Avicebron, matter is the genus of those things which agree in genus, while the differences by

---

93. Cf. above, Cap. V; for a shorter refutation of Avicebron, see St. Thomas, *De ente et essentia*, IV, ed. M.-D. Roland-Gosselin, 29–37 (OBE, 43 ff.); *De spiritualibus creaturis*, a. 1, a. 3, (ed. L. Keeler, 1–19; 33–50 (CISC, 15–29; 41–55); ST, I, 50, 2 (BW, I, 482); In II *Sent.*, d. 3, q. 1, a. 1, (pp. 85–89).

94. Cf. Louis-M. Régis, O.P., *Analyse et synthèse dons l'oeuvre de saint Thomas*, 313–328.

95. Aristotle, *Metaphysics*, I, 1 (993b 24–31); St. Thomas, SCG, 1, 13 (OTCF, I, 95).

96. Cf. above, Cap. 1; Aristotle, *Metaphysics*, I, 7 (988a 34–988b 6); Proclus, *Elem*, Prop. 18 (p. 21).

97. Cf. above, Cap. 1.

98. *Ibid.*

99. Cf. above, Cap. V.

quibus species differunt ponit esse formas. Dicit enim quod omnium corporalium est materia communis ipsum corpus; rursumque omnium substantiarum tam corporalium quam spiritualium est communis materia ipsa substantia. Unde apparet quod est similis habitudo generis ad differentias sicut subiecti ad proprias passiones; ut scilicet substantia hoc modo dividatur per spiritualem et corporalem, et corpus per caeleste et elementare, sicut numerus per par et impar aut animal per sanum et aegrum—quorum numerus est subiectum paris et imparis sicut propriarum passionum, et animal sani et aegri, tam subiecto quam passionibus de speciebus omnibus praedicatis.

Sic igitur si substantia quae praedicatur de omnibus comparetur ad spirituale et corporale sicut materia et subiectum eorum, sequetur quod haec duo adveniant substantiae per modum accidentalium passionum, et similiter in omnibus aliis consequentibus. Quod ipse expresse concedit ponens omnes formas secundum se consideratas accidentia esse; dicuntur tamen substantiales per comparationem ad aliquas res in quarum definitionibus cadunt, sicut albedo est de ratione hominis albi.

Sic haec positio tollit quidem veritatem materiae primae, quia si de ratione materiae est quod sit in potentia, oportet quod prima materia sit omnino in potentia; unde nec de aliquo exsistentium actu praedicatur, sicut nec pars de toto. Tollit etiam logicae principia, auferens veram rationem generis et speciei et substantialis differentiae dum omnia in modum accidentalis praedicationis convertit.

Tollit etiam naturalis philosophiae fundamenta, auferens veram generationem et corruptionem a rebus, sicut et antiqui Naturales ponentes unum materiale principium; neque enim simpliciter aliquid generari dicitur nisi quia simpliciter fit ens, nihil autem fit quod prius erat: si igitur aliquid prius erat in actu—quod est simpliciter esse, sequetur quod non simpliciter fiat ens sed fiat ens hoc quod prius non erat, unde secundum quid generabitur et non simpliciter.

Tollit demum, et ut finaliter concludam, praedicta positio etiam philosophiae primae principia, auferens unitatem a singulis rebus et per consequens veram entitatem simul et rerum diversitatem. Si enim alicui existenti in actu superveniat alius actus, non erit totum unum per se sed solum per accidens, eo quod duo

which the species differ are forms.[100] For he says that the common matter of all material things is body itself. And again, the common matter of all substances, both corporeal and spiritual, is substance itself. Therefore, it is clear that there is the same relation of the genus to its differences as of a subject to its proper attributes. In other words, substance is divided into spiritual and corporeal, and body into heavenly and elemental, just as number is divided into odd and even, and animal into healthy and sick. Of these, number is the subject of the even and of the odd as of its proper attributes, and animal is the subject of the healthy and the sick, with the subject and the attributes being predicated of all the species.

Thus, therefore, if the substance that is predicated of all things should be compared to spiritual and corporeal as the matter which is their subject, it will follow that these two[101] come to substance in the manner of accidental attributes. The same applies in all subsequent cases, as he himself expressly admits by positing that all forms considered in themselves are accidents. But they are said to be substantial in comparison with certain things in whose definitions they are included, as whiteness belongs to the definition of a white man.

But this position destroys the true nature of prime matter. For if it is of the nature of matter that it be in potency, then prime matter must be completely in potency.[102] As a consequence, it is not predicated of any actually existing thing, just as a part is not predicated of the whole. This position likewise destroys the principles of logic by doing away with the true nature of genus, species, and substantial difference, inasmuch as it reduces them all to the mode of accidental predication.[103]

Moreover, it destroys the foundations of natural philosophy by removing a true generation and corruption from things, as did the ancient naturalists, in positing one material principle. For a thing is said without qualification to be generated only because it becomes a being without qualification.[104] For nothing which previously existed comes to be. Therefore, if it existed previously in act—which is for it without qualification to exist—it will follow that it will not unqualifiedly become a being, but rather a being which previously was not. Therefore, it will be generated in a certain respect and not in an unqualified manner.

Finally, and to reach a last conclusion, the aforementioned position also destroys the principles of first philosophy by taking away unity from each thing and, as a consequence, the true being and the diversity of things. For if to some being existing in act, another act is added, the whole will not be one essentially but only accidentally, be-

---

100. Cf. above, Cap. V.
101. I.e., the spiritual and the corporeal.
102. Aristotle, *Metaphysics*, VI, 3 (1029a 20).
103. Aristotle, *Metaphysics*, VI, 12 (1038a 9).
104. Aristotle, *Phys.*, V, 1 (225a 12–20); *De Gen. et Corrup.*, 1, 2 (317a 17–3 1); *Metaphysics*, X, 11 (1067b 22).

actus vel formae secundum se diversae sunt, conveniunt autem solum in subiecto. Esse autem unum per unitatem subiecti est esse unum per accidens, sive duae formae sint non ordinatae ad invicem ut album et musicum: dicimus enim quod album et musicum sunt unum per accidens quia insunt uni subiecto; sive etiam formae vel actus sint ad invicem ordinatae sicut color et superficies: non enim est simpliciter unum superficiatum et coloratum, etsi quodam modo coloratum per se de superficiato praedicetur, non quia superficiatum significet essentiam colorati sicut genus significat essentiam speciei, sed ea ratione qua subiectum ponitur in definitione accidentis, alioquin non praedicaretur coloratum de superficiato per se sed hoc de illo.

Solo autem hoc modo species est unum simpliciter in quantum vere id quod est homo animal est; non quia animal subiiciatur formae, sed quia ipsa forma animalis est forma hominis, non differens nisi sicut determinatum ab indeterminato. Si enim aliud sit animal et aliud bipes, non erit per se unum animal bipes quod est homo, unde nec erit per se ens; et per consequens sequetur quod quaecumque in genere conveniunt non different nisi accidentali differentia, et omnia erunt unum secundum substantiam quae est genus et subiectum omnium substantiarum, sicut si superficiei una pars sit alba et alia nigra totum est una superficies. Propter quod et antiqui, ponentes unam materiam quae erat substantia omnium de omnibus praedicata, ponebant omnia esse unum. Et haec etiam inconvenientia sequuntur ponentes ordinem diversarum formarum substantialium in uno et eodem.

Tertio secundum praedictae positionis processum necesse est procedere in causis materialibus in infinitum, ita quod nunquam sit devenire ad primam materiam. In omnibus enim quae in aliquo conveniunt et in aliquo differunt, id in quo conveniunt accipit ut materiam id vero in quo differunt accipit ut formam, ut ex praemissis patet; si ergo sit una materia communis omnium, ad hoc quod diversas formas recipiat oportet quod nobiliorem formam in subtiliori et altiori materia recipiat, ignobiliorem vero in inferiori materia et grossiori: puta formam spiritualitatis in subtiliori materia, formam vero corporeitatis in inferiori, ut ipse dicit. Praeexistit ergo in

cause two acts or forms are essentially diverse and agree only in subject.[105] But to be one through the unity of the subject is to be one accidentally, whether the two forms are not ordered to each other, as the white and the musical, (for we say that the white and the musical are one accidentally because they inhere in one subject), or whether the forms or the acts are ordered to one another, as color and surface. For that which is colored and has a surface is not absolutely one, though the colored is in a way essentially predicated of the surfaced thing, not indeed because 'surfaced' signifies the essence of the colored, as 'genus' signifies the essence of a species, but because the subject is included in the definition of an accident: or otherwise the colored would not be predicated of the surfaced thing essentially, but the surfaced of the colored.[106]

Now in this way alone is a species one without qualification: namely, insofar as that which is man is truly animal, not because 'animal' is the subject of the form 'man' but because the very form 'animal' is the form 'man,' differing only as the indeterminate from the determinate. For if 'animal' be one thing and 'biped' something else, the biped animal that is man will not be essentially one, and hence will not be essentially a being.[107] As a consequence, it follows that whatever things agree in the genus will differ only by an accidental difference, and all things will be one in substance which is the genus and the subject of all substances; just as the one part of a surface is white and the other part black, yet the whole is one surface. For this reason, the ancients themselves who posited one matter, which was the substance of all things and predicated of all of them, asserted that all things were one. These difficulties likewise beset those who posit an order of diverse substantial forms in one and the same being.

Third, following the method of the aforementioned position,[108] it is necessary to proceed to infinity among material causes, with the result that a first matter is never reached. For in all things which agree in some point and differ in another, that in which they agree, they have as their matter; and that in which they differ, they have as their form, as is clear from what has been said.[109] If, therefore, there is one common matter for all things, for it to receive diverse forms it is then necessary that the more noble form should be received in a finer and more excellent matter; the less noble form should be received in an inferior and coarser matter. For example, the form of spirituality should

105. Aristotle, *Metaphysics*, VI, 12 (1037b 12).
106. I.e., this means to be one by being in the same subject. Cf. Aristotle, *Metaphysics*, VI, 4 (1029b16).
107. Aristotle, *Metaphysics*, II 4 (999b 25); VII, 6 (1045b 16); cf. St. Thomas, *De Spiritualibus Creaturis*, a.3, ed. L. Keeler, 33–50 (OSC, 41–55).
108. Cf. above, Cap. V.
109. Cf. above, Cap. V.

materia differentia subtilitatis et grossitiei ante formam spiritualitatis et corporeitatis.

Oportet igitur quod iterum ante grossitiem et subtilitatem praeexistat in materia aliqua alia differentia per quam una materia sit receptiva unius et alia alterius: et eadem quaestio redibit de illis aliis praeexistentibus, et sic in infinitum. Quandocumque enim deveniretur ad materiam totaliter informem, secundum principia positionis praedictae oporteret quod non reciperet nisi unam formam et aequaliter per totum; et iterum materia illi formae substrata non reciperet consequenter nisi unam formam et uniformiter per totum. Et ita descendendo usque ad infima nulla diversitas in rebus inveniri posset.

Quarto quia antiquis Naturalibus ponentibus primam materiam communem substantiam omnium possibile erat ex ea diversas res instituere attribuendo diversis partibus eius formas diversas; poterat enim in illa communi materia, cum corporalis esset, intelligi divisio secundum quantitatem. Remota autem divisione quae est secundum quantitatem, non remanet nisi divisio secundum formam vel secundum materiam; si igitur ponatur universalis materia quae est communis omnium substantia non habens in sui ratione quantitatem, eius divisio non potest intelligi nisi vel secundum formam vel secundum materiam ipsam. Cum autem dicitur quod materia incorporea communis partim recipit formam hanc et partim recipit formam illam, divisio materiae praesupponitur diversitati formarum in materia receptarum; non ergo illa divisio potest secundum has formas intelligi. Si ergo intelligatur secundum formas aliquas, oportet quod intelligatur secundum formas priores quarum neutram materia per totum recipit; unde oportet iterum in materia praeintelligere divisionem vel distinctionem quamcumque. Erit igitur et haec secundum alias formas in infinitum, vel oportet devenire ad hoc quod prima divisio sit secundum ipsam materiam.

Non est autem divisio secundum materiam nisi quia materia secundum se ipsam distinguitur, non propter diversam dispositionem vel formam aut quantitatem, quia hoc esset distingui materiam secundum quantitatem aut formam seu dispositionem; oportet igitur quod finaliter deveniatur ad hoc quod non sit una omnium materia, sed quod materiae sint multae et distinctae secundum

be received in a more refined matter, whereas the form of corporeity should be received in an inferior matter, as he himself says.[110] Prior to the form of spirituality and of corporeity, there is therefore required in matter a difference of fineness and coarseness.

It is therefore again necessary that prior to the coarseness and fineness, there preexist in matter some other difference through which one matter is receptive of the one and the other receptive of the other. The same question will reappear concerning those other preexistent differences, and so on to infinity. For as often as one arrived at one completely uniform matter, according to the principles of the aforementioned position it would be necessary that this matter should receive only one form and this equally throughout the whole. And again the matter underlying that form would, as a consequence, receive only one form and this uniformly throughout the whole; and thus by descending even to the lowest of beings, no diversity could be found in things.

Fourth, given the position of the ancient naturalists that there was a prime matter as the common substance of all things, it was possible to produce diverse things from it by attributing diverse forms to diverse parts of this common substance.[111] For, since that common matter was corporeal, there could be understood in it a division according to quantity. But if we remove quantitative division, there remains only a division according to form or according to matter. If, therefore, we posit a universal matter which is common to every substance and which has no quantity in its nature, the division of this matter can be understood only according to form or only according to the matter itself. When, however, it is said that common incorporeal matter in part receives this form and in part that form, a division of matter is presupposed to the diversity of the forms received in the matter. That division, therefore, cannot be understood according to some other forms. If, therefore, it should be understood according to some forms, it must be understood according to prior forms of which matter receives neither one through the whole of itself. Accordingly, it is necessary again that we presuppose in matter some sort of division or distinction. This distinction or division, too, will therefore be according to other forms to infinity, or we must come to this, that the first division is according to the matter itself.

Now, there cannot be a division according to matter unless because the matter is distinguished through itself, and not through a diverse disposition or form or quantity (for this would mean that the matter is distinguished according to the quantity or form or disposition). Therefore, we must finally reach the conclusion that there is not one matter for all things but that matters are many and dis-

110. Cf. above, Cap. V.
111. Cf. above, Cap. I.

se ipsas. Materiae autem proprium est in potentia esse; hanc igitur materiae distinctionem accipere oportet non secundum quod est vestita diversis formis aut dispositionibus, hoc enim est praeter essentiam materiae, sed secundum distinctionem potentiae respectu diversitatis formarum: cum enim potentia id quod est ad actum dicatur, necesse est ut potentia distinguatur secundum id ad quod primo potentia dicitur. Dico autem ad aliquid primo potentiam dici sicut potentiam visivam ad colorem, non autem ad album aut nigrum, quia eadem est susceptiva utriusque; et similiter superficies est susceptiva albi et nigri secundum unam potentiam quae primo dicitur respectu coloris. Unde patet falsum esse principium quod supponebat dicens potentiam et receptionem in omnibus eodem modo inveniri.

tinct in themselves. Now it is proper for matter to be in potency. This distinction of matter must therefore not be understood according as matter contains its diverse forms or dispositions, for this is outside the essence of matter, but according to the distinctions of potency with respect to the diversity of forms. For, since potency is called that which is said relatively to act, it is necessary that potency be distinguished with respect to that of which potency is primarily predicated.[112] I say potency is primarily said in relation to something in the manner in which the potency to see is said in relation to color, but not to white and black, since the same potency can receive both. In the same way, a surface can receive white and black according to one potency which is primarily predicated with respect to color. Avicebron, therefore, presupposed a clearly false principle when he said that potency and reception are found in all in the same way.

CHAPTER 7

That of spiritual and corporeal substances there cannot be one matter

Ex hac autem ratione ulterius concludi potest quod spiritualis et corporalis substantiae non potest esse una materia. Nam si est materia una et communis utrorumque, oportet in ipsa distinctionem praeintelligi ante differentiam formarum, scilicet spiritualitatis et corporeitatis. Quae quidem non potest esse secundum quantitatis divisionem, quia in substantiis spiritualibus quantitatis dimensiones non inveniuntur; unde relinquitur quod ista distinctio sit vel secundum formas seu dispositiones, vel secundum ipsam materiam: et cum non possit esse secundum formas et dispositiones in infinitum, oportet tandem redire ad hoc quod sit distinctio in materia secundum se ipsam. Erit igitur omnino alia materia spiritualium et corporalium substantiarum.

Item, cum recipere sit proprium materiae in quantum huiusmodi, si sit eadem materia spiritualium et corporalium substantiarum, oportet quod in utrisque sit idem receptionis modus. Materia autem corporalium rerum suscipit formam particulariter, id est non secundum communem rationem formae; nec hoc habet materia corporalis in quantum dimensionibus subiicitur aut formae corporali, quia etiam ipsam formam corporalem individualiter materia corporalis recipit: unde manifestum fit quod hoc convenit tali materiae ex ipsa natura materiae, quae quia est infima debilissimo modo recipit

We may further conclude from this argument that there cannot be one matter for both spiritual and corporeal substances. For if both have a single and common matter, there must be understood in it a distinction prior to the difference of forms: namely, a distinction of spirituality and corporeity. This disposition cannot be according to a division of quantity, because the dimensions of quantity are not found in spiritual substances.[113] Accordingly, it remains that this distinction is either according to forms (or dispositions) or according to matter itself; and since it cannot be according to forms and dispositions to infinity, we must finally come back to this, that the distinction is present in matter according to matter itself. Therefore, the matter of spiritual substances will be absolutely other than the matter of corporeal substances.

Again, since it is the property of matter as such to receive, if the matter of spiritual and corporeal substances is the same, then it is necessary that the mode of reception be the same in both. The matter of corporeal things, however, receives the form in a particular way: that is, not according to the common nature of form.[114] Nor does corporeal matter act in this way insofar as it is subject to dimensions or to a corporeal form, since corporeal matter receives the corporeal form itself in an individual way. Accordingly, it becomes clear that this befits such a matter from the very nature of the matter: which, since it is the lowest reality,

---

112. Aristotle, *Metaphysics*, VIII, 4–6 (1047b 2–1048b 34); VIII, 8 (1049b 14).
113. St. Thomas, ST, I, 50, 2 (BW I, 482).
114. Aristotle, *Metaphysics*, VI, 9 (1034b 7–19).

formam—fit enim receptio secundum modum recipientis; et per hoc maxime deficit a completa receptione formae quae est secundum totalitatem ipsius, particulariter ipsam recipiens. Manifestum est autem quod omnis substantia intellectualis recipit formam intellectam secundum suam totalitatem, alioquin eam in sua totalitate intelligere non valeret; sic enim intellectus intelligit rem secundum quod forma eius in ipso existit. Relinquitur igitur quod materia, si qua sit in spiritualibus substantiis, non est eadem cum materia corporalium rerum sed multo altior et sublimior, utpote recipiens formam secundum eius totalitatem.

Adhuc, ultra procedentibus manifestum fit quod tanto aliquid in entibus est altius quanto magis habet de ratione essendi. Manifestum est autem quod cum ens per potentiam et actum dividatur, quod actus est potentia perfectior et magis habet de ratione essendi; non enim simpliciter esse dicimus quod est in potentia, sed solum quod est actu; oportet igitur id quod est superius in entibus magis accedere ad actum, quod autem est in entibus infimum propinquius esse potentiae. Quia igitur materia spiritualium substantiarum non potest esse eadem cum corporalium materia sed longe altior, ut ostensum est, necesse est ut longe distet a corporalium materia secundum differentiam potentiae et actus; corporalium autem materia est potentia pura secundum sententiam Aristotelis et Platonis: relinquitur igitur quod materia substantiarum spiritualium non sit potentia pura sed sit aliquid ens actu in potentia existens.

Non autem sic dico ens actu quasi ex potentia et actu compositum; quia vel esset procedere in infinitum, vel oporteret venire ad aliquid quod esset ens in potentia tantum, quod cum sit ultimum in entibus et per consequens non potens recipere nisi debiliter et particulariter, non potest esse prima materia spiritualis et intellectualis substantiae. Relinquitur ergo quod spiritualis substantiae materia ita sit ens actu quod sit actus vel forma subsistens, sicut et materia corporalium rerum ita dicitur ens in potentia quia est ipsa potentia formis subiecta.

Ubicumque autem ponitur materia ens actu, nihil differt dicere materiam et substantiam rei: sic enim antiqui Naturales, qui ponebant primam materiam corporalium rerum esse aliquid ens actu, dicebant materiam esse omnium rerum substantiam per modum quo artificialium substantia nihil est aliud quam eorum

receives form in the weakest manner (for reception takes place according to the mode of the receiver). Thereby matter, by receiving that form in a particular way, falls short in the greatest degree of that complete reception of form which is according to the totality of the form. Now it is clear that every intellectual substance receives the intellected form according to its totality, or otherwise it would not be able to know it in its totality. For it is thus that the intellect understands a thing: insofar as the form of that thing exists in it.[115] It remains, therefore, that if there be a matter in spiritual substances, it is not the same as the matter of corporeal things, but much nobler and finer, since it receives form according to its totality.

Again, as we consider the matter further, it becomes clear that a given being has a higher place among beings according as it has a greater share in being. It is clear, however, that since being is divided by potency and act, act is more perfect than potency and has a greater share in being.[116] For we do not say without qualification that what is in potency, is; we say this only of what is in act. It is therefore necessary that that which is higher among beings approach more closely to act, and that which is lowest among beings be nearer to potency. And since the matter of spiritual substances cannot be the same as the matter of corporeal substances, but is much higher, as has been shown,[117] it must be separated from the matter of corporeal substances according to the difference of potency and act. Now, according to the opinion of Aristotle and Plato, the matter of corporeal things is pure potency. It remains, therefore, that the matter of spiritual substances is not pure potency, but is something actual existing in potency.

I am not saying 'something actual existing in potency' as though I meant some thing composed of act and potency, because either we should have to proceed to infinity or we should have to arrive at something which was a being only in potency; and since this being is the lowest among beings and consequently can receive existence in a way which is weak and particularized, it cannot be the prime matter of a spiritual and intellectual substance. It remains, therefore, that the matter of a spiritual substance is in this manner a being in act so that it be a subsisting act or form, just as the matter of corporeal things is said to be a being in potency for the reason that it is the very potency which is subject to forms.

Furthermore, whenever matter is posited as an actual being, it makes no difference whether we call it the matter or the substance of a thing. For thus the ancient natural philosophers, who held that the first matter of corporeal things was some actual being, said that matter was the substance of all things in the same way that the substance of

---

115. Cf. St. Thomas, ST, I, 84, 1 (BW, I, 793).
116. Aristotle, *Metaphysics*, VIII, 8 (1049b 3).
117. Cf. above, Cap. V–VI.

materia. Sic igitur si materia spiritualium substantiarum non potest esse aliquid ens in potentia tantum sed est aliquid ens actu, ipsa spiritualium rerum materia est eorum substantia; et secundum hoc nihil differt ponere materiam in substantiis spiritualibus et ponere substantias spirituales simplices non compositas ex materia et forma.

Amplius, cum actus naturaliter sit prior potentia et forma quam materia, potentia quidem dependet in suo esse ab actu et materia a forma, forma autem in suo esse non dependet a materia secundum propriam rationem, vel actus (a potentia); non enim priora naturaliter a posterioribus dependent. Si igitur aliquae formae sint quae sine materia esse non possunt, hoc non convenit eis ex hoc quod sunt formae sed ex hoc quod sunt tales formae, scilicet imperfectae, quae per se sustentari non possunt sed indigent materiae fundamento. Sed ante omne imperfectum invenitur aliquid perfectum in omnibus generibus; puta si est ignis in materia aliena a qua ignis secundum suam rationem non dependet, necesse est esse ignem non sustentatum in materia aliena: sunt igitur supra formas in materiis receptas aliquae formae per se subsistentes, quae sunt spirituales substantiae ex materia et forma non compositae.

Hoc etiam apparet in infimis substantiarum spiritualium, scilicet animabus, si quis eas ponat corporibus uniri ut formas. Impossibile est enim id quod est ex materia et forma compositum esse alicuius corporis formam, nam esse formam alicuius est esse actum eiusdem; nulla igitur pars eius quod est alicuius forma potest esse materia, quae est potentia pura.

artificial things is nothing other than their matter.[118] Therefore, if the matter of spiritual substances cannot be only some potential being but is some actual being, then the matter itself of spiritual beings is their substance. And in this case, there is no difference whether we posit matter in spiritual substances or whether we hold that simple spiritual substances are not composed of matter and form.

Furthermore, act is by nature prior to potency, and form prior to matter, and since potency depends in its existence on act and matter depends on form, whereas form according to its proper nature does not depend on matter for its existence, neither does act depend on potency. For that which is by nature prior does not depend upon that which is by nature subsequent. Since this is the case, if there are some forms which cannot exist without matter, this befits them not because they are forms, but because they are such forms: namely, imperfect forms, which cannot exist through themselves of their own accord but need the foundation of matter. Now in all classes of being, prior to everything imperfect, there is found something perfect. For example, if there is fire in a foreign matter upon which the fire according to its nature does not depend, then it follows that the fire is not supported in the foreign matter. Therefore, above the forms received in matter, there are certain self-subsisting forms, which are spiritual substances not composed of matter and form.

This fact also appears among the lowest of the spiritual substances (namely, souls) on the assumption that they are united to bodies as forms. For it is impossible that that which is composed of matter and form be the form of some body. For to be the form of some being is to be the act of that being. Hence no part of that which is the form of some being can be matter, which is pure potency.

CHAPTER 8

Refutation of Avicebron's arguments

His igitur visis, facile est rationes dissolvere in contrarium adductas.

Prima enim ratio concludere videbatur quod non posset esse diversitas in spiritualibus substantiis si non essent ex materia et forma compositae. Quae quidem ratio in utraque parte suae deductionis deficiebat: neque enim oportet quod ea quae sunt materiae tantum sint absque diversitate, neque etiam hoc oportet de substantiis quae sunt formae tantum.

On this basis, it is easy to answer arguments advanced to the contrary.

For the first argument seemed to infer that there could not be diversity among spiritual substances if they were not composed of matter and form.[119] This argument was deficient in both parts of its reasoning. For it is not necessary that those things which are only matter be without diversity, just as it is likewise not necessary of those substances which are forms only.

118. Cf. above, Cap. I.
119. Cf. above, Cap. V.

Dictum est enim quod, quia materia secundum id quod est est in potentia ens, necesse est ut secundum potentiae diversitatem sint diversae materiae; nec aliud dicimus materiae substantiam quam ipsam potentiam quae est in genere substantiae, nam genus substantiae sicut et alia genera dividitur per potentiam et actum. Et secundum hoc nihil prohibet aliquas substantias quae sunt in potentia tantum esse diversas secundum quod ad diversa genera actuum ordinantur: per quem modum caelestium corporum materia a materia elementorum distinguitur. Nam materia caelestium corporum est in potentia ad actum perfectum, id est ad formam quae complet totam potentialitatem materiae ut iam non remaneat potentia ad alias formas; materia autem elementorum est in potentia ad formam incompletam quae totam potentiam materiae terminare non potest. Sed supra has materias est spiritualis materia, id est ipsa substantia spiritualis, quae recipit formam secundum suam totalitatem, inferioribus materiis formam particulariter recipientibus.

Similiter etiam non tenet deductio ex parte formarum. Manifestum est enim quod si res compositae ex materia et forma secundum formas differunt, quod ipsae formae secundum se ipsas diversae sunt. Sed si dicatur quod diversarum rerum formae non sunt diversae nisi propter materiae diversitatem, sicut diversi colores ex una solis illustratione causantur in aere secundum differentiam spissitudinis et diversitatis illius, necesse est quod ante colorum diversitatem praeintelligatur in aere diversitas puritatis et spissitudinis: et sic etiam necesse erit quod in materia ante unam formam intelligatur alia forma, sicut etiam in corporibus ante colorem intelligitur superficies. Invenitur igitur in formis diversitas secundum quemdam ordinem perfectionis et imperfectionis, nam quae materiae est propinquior imperfectior est et quasi in potentia respectu supervenientis formae. Sic igitur nihil prohibet in spiritualibus substantiis ponere multitudinem, quamvis sint formae tantum, ex hoc quod una earum est alia perfectior; ita quod imperfectior est in potentia respectu perfectioris, usque ad primam earum quae est actu tantum, quae Deus est: ut sic omnes inferiores spirituales substantiae et materiae possint dici secundum hoc quod sunt in potentia, et formae secundum hoc quod sunt actu.

Unde patet frivolum esse quod contra hoc obiicit concludens, si spiritualis substantia secundum perfectionem et imperfectionem differt, quod oportet ipsam esse perfectionis et imperfectionis subiectum: et sic, cum subiectum pertineat ad rationem materiae, oportebit substantiam spiritualem habere materiam. In quo

For we have said[120] that since matter according to its nature is a being in potency, there must be diverse matters according to the diversity of potency. Nor do we mean anything else by the substance of matter than that very potency which is in the genus of substance. For the genus of substance, like other genera, is divided by potency and act, and hence nothing prevents certain substances, which are only potential, to be diverse according as they are ordered to diverse genera of acts; in which sense the matter of the heavenly bodies is distinguished from the matter of the elements. For the matter of the heavenly bodies is in potency to perfect act (that is, to a form which completes the whole potentiality of matter), so that there no longer remains any potentiality to other forms. But the matter of the elements is in potency to incomplete forms, which cannot exhaust the whole potency of matter. But above these matters, there is spiritual matter (that is, a spiritual substance), which receives a form according to its totality, while the lower matters receive their form in a particular way.

In the same way, the inference based on the forms is also deficient.[121] For it is clear that if things composed of matter and form differ according to their forms, the forms themselves are diverse through themselves. But if it be said that the forms of diverse things are not diverse except because of the diversity of matter, just as diverse colors are caused by one illumination of the sun in the air according to the diversity of the difference of density and rarity in it, it is necessary that prior to the diversity of the colors, there be understood in the air a diversity of clearness and density. So, likewise, it is necessary that in matter, prior to one form, another form be understood, just as in the case of bodies, prior to color, a surface is understood. Therefore, among forms there is found a diversity according to a certain order of perfection and imperfection. For that form which is nearer to matter is more imperfect and as in potency with reference to a later form. Thus, although they are only forms, nothing prevents us from positing a multiplicity among spiritual substances, on the basis that one is more imperfect than the other, provided we do so in such wise that the more imperfect is in potency in relation to the more perfect and so on upward to the first form, which is act only, namely, God: so that in this way lower spiritual substances can be called 'matters' according as they are in potency and 'forms' according as they are in act.

Therefore, it is a clearly inconsequential objection that he brings forth against this view. He concludes that if a spiritual substance differs according to perfection and imperfection, it must be the subject of perfection and imperfection; and therefore since 'subject' belongs to the nature of matter, a spiritual substance must possess matter. In this

---

120. Cf. above, Cap. VI.
121. Cf. above, Cap. V.

quidem dupliciter fallitur. Primo quidem quia aestimat perfectionem et imperfectionem esse quasdam formas supervenientes vel accidentia quae subiecto indigeant: quod quidem manifeste falsum est. Est enim quaedam rei perfectio secundum suam speciem et substantiam, quae non comparatur ad rem sicut accidens ad subiectum vel sicut forma ad materiam sed ipsam propriam speciem rei designat. Sicut enim in numeris unus est maior alio secundum propriam speciem, unde inaequales numeri specie differunt, ita in formis tam materialibus quam a materia separatis una est perfectior alia secundum rationem propriae naturae, in quantum scilicet propria ratio speciei in tali gradu perfectionis consistit.

Secundo quia esse subiectum non consequitur solum materiam quae est pars substantiae, sed universaliter consequitur omnem potentiam; omne enim quod se habet ad alterum ut potentia ad actum ei natum est subiici: et per hunc etiam modum spiritualis substantia, quamvis non habeat materiam partem sui, ipsa tamen prout est ens secundum aliquid in potentia potest subiici intelligibilibus speciebus.

Ex hoc etiam solutio secundae rationis apparet. Cum enim dicimus aliquam substantiam corporalem esse vel spiritualem, non comparamus spiritualitatem vel corporeitatem ad substantiam sicut formas ad materiam vel accidentia ad subiectum, sed sicut differentias ad genus; ita quod substantia spiritualis non propter aliquid additum substantiae est spiritualis sed secundum suam substantiam, sicut et substantia corporalis non per aliquid additum substantiae est corporalis sed per suam substantiam. Non enim est alia forma per quam species differentiae praedicationem suscipit ab ea per quam suscipit praedicationem generis, ut supra dictum est; unde non oportet quod spiritualitati spiritualis substantiae subiiciatur aliquid sicut materia vel subiectum.

Tertia vero ratio efficaciam non habet. Cum enim ens non univoce de omnibus praedicetur, non est requirendus idem modus essendi in omnibus quae esse dicuntur; sed quaedam perfectius quaedam imperfectius esse participant: accidentia enim entia dicuntur non quia in se ipsis esse habeant, sed quia esse eorum est in hoc quod insunt substantiae. Rursumque in substantiis omnibus non est idem modus essendi. Illae enim substantiae quae perfectissime esse participant non habent in se ipsis aliquid quod sit ens in potentia solum, unde immateriales substantiae dicuntur.

argument, he is deceived in two ways. He is deceived, first, because he thinks that perfection and imperfection are certain supervening forms or accidents that a subject needs—which is clearly false. For there is a certain perfection which a thing has according to its species and substance, which is not compared to that thing as an accident to a subject or a form to matter, but designates the proper species itself of the thing. For just as one number is greater than another according to its own species, which is why unequal numbers differ in species, so, among material forms and forms separated from matter, one is more perfect than another according to the character of its own nature: namely, insofar as the proper character of its species consists in a given grade of perfection.

Second, because to be a subject not only follows upon the matter which is a part of substance but in general belongs to all potency. For everything that is related to another as potency to act is naturally subject to it, and in this way, likewise, a spiritual substance, although it does not have matter as a part of itself, nevertheless can be subject to intelligible forms insofar as it is in potency in some respect.

From this, the solution of the second argument is likewise clear.[122] For when we say that a certain substance is corporeal or spiritual, we do not compare spirituality or corporeity to a substance as forms to matter or accidents to a subject, but as differences to a genus, in such a way that a spiritual substance is spiritual not because of something added to substance, but according to its proper substance, just as a corporeal substance is corporeal not because of something added to substance but according to its own substance. For the form through which the species receives the predication of the difference is not a form other than the one through which it receives the predication of genus, as we have said before.[123] Hence, it is not necessary that something should underlie the spirituality of substance as matter or subject.

The third argument has no validity.[124] For, since being is not predicated of all things univocally, the same mode of being is not required in all things that are said to be; rather, some share in being more perfectly, and some less perfectly.[125] For accidents are called beings not because they have being in themselves but because their being lies in the fact that they are in a substance.[126] Again, there is not the same mode of being in all substances. For those substances which share in being most perfectly do not have in themselves something which is a being only in potency. That is why they are called immaterial substances.

---

122. Cf. above, Cap. V.
123. Cf. above, Cap. VI.
124. Cf. above, Cap. V.
125. Aristotle, *Metaphysics*, III, 1 (1003a 20–1003b 18); X, 3 (1060b 30–1061a 10).
126. Aristotle, *Metaphysics*, VI, 1 (1028a 18); XI, 1 (1069a 21).

Sub his vero sunt substantiae quae, etsi in se ipsis huiusmodi materiam habeant quae secundum sui essentiam est ens in potentia tantum, tota tamen earum potentialitas completur per formam ut in eis non remaneat potentia ad aliam formam, unde et incorruptibiles sunt, sicut caelestia corpora; quae necesse est ex materia et forma composita esse. Manifestum est enim ea actu existere, alioquin motus subiecta esse non possent aut sensui subiacere aut alicuius actionis esse principium; nullum autem eorum est forma tantum quia, si essent formae absque materia, essent substantiae intelligibiles actu simul et intelligentes secundum se ipsas: quod esse non potest, cum intelligere actus corporis esse non possit, ut probatur in libro *de Anima*. Relinquitur ergo quod sunt quidem ex materia et forma composita; sed sicut illud corpus ita est huic magnitudini et figurae determinatae subiectum quod tamen non est in potentia ad aliam magnitudinem vel figuram, ita caelestium corporum materia ita est huic formae subiecta quod non est in potentia ad aliam formam.

Sub his vero substantiis est tertius substantiarum gradus, scilicet corruptibilium corporum quae in se ipsis huiusmodi materiam habent quae est ens in potentia tantum; nec tamen tota potentialitas huiusmodi materiae completur per formam unam cui subiicitur quin remanet adhuc in potentia ad alias formas. Et secundum hanc diversitatem materiae invenitur in corporibus subtilius et grossius, prout caelestia corpora sunt subtiliora et magis formalia quam elementaria; et quia forma proportionatur materiae, consequens est quod etiam caelestia corpora habeant nobiliorem formam et magis perfectam, utpote totam potentialitatem materiae adimplentem.

In substantiis igitur superioribus, a quibus est omnino potentia materiae aliena, invenitur quidem differentia maioris et minoris subtilitatis secundum differentiam perfectionis formarum; non tamen in eis est compositio materiae et formae.

Quarta vero ratio efficaciam non habet. Non enim oportet ut si substantiae spirituales materia careant, quod a Deo non distinguantur: sublata omni potentialitate materiae, remanet in eis potentia quaedam in quantum non sunt ipsum esse sed esse participant. Nihil autem per se subsistens quod sit ipsum esse potest inveniri nisi unum solum, sicut nec aliqua forma si separata consideretur potest esse nisi una; inde est enim quod ea quae sunt diversa numero sunt unum specie quia natura speciei secundum se considerata est una: sicut igitur est una secundum considerationem dum per se consideratur, ita esset una secundum esse si per se exi-

Below these are those substances which, although they contain within themselves a matter which according to its essence is a being in potency, yet they have a potentiality that is entirely completed through form so that there remains in them no potentiality to another form. They are therefore also incorruptible. Such is the case of the heavenly bodies, which are necessarily composed of matter and form. In fact, they must exist in act, otherwise they could not underlie any motion or be subject to sense, nor could they be the principle of any action. No one of them is form only, because if they were forms without matter, they would be substances that are actually intelligible and having understanding through themselves. This is impossible, since 'to understand' cannot be an act of a body, as is proved in the *De Anima*.[127] It remains, therefore, that they are composed of matter and form. But just as 'that' particular body underlies this particular magnitude and determinate figure so that it is not in potency to another magnitude or figure; so, the matter of the heavenly bodies is so subject to 'this' form that it is not in potency to another form.

Below these substances, there is a third grade of substances: namely, that of corruptible bodies, which in themselves have a matter that is a being only in potency. Yet the whole potentiality of such a matter is not realized through the one form to which it is subject, so that there does not remain in it a potency to other forms. And according to this diversity of matter, this potentiality in bodies is found the more finely and the more grossly according as the heavenly bodies are finer and more formal than the bodies of the elements. And since form is proportioned to matter, it follows that the heavenly bodies likewise have a nobler and more perfect form, inasmuch as it realizes the full potentiality of matter.

Therefore, among the higher substances to which the potency of matter is completely foreign, there is found a difference of greater or lesser refinement according to the difference in the perfection of the form; but there is in them no composition of matter and form.

The fourth argument has no validity.[128] For, given that spiritual substances have no matter, it does not follow that they are not distinguished from God. For if we take away the potentiality of matter, there remains in them a certain potentiality insofar as they are not being itself but they share in being.[129] For there can be only one being which is being itself; just as some form, if it should be considered by itself, can be only one. That is why the things which are diverse in number are one in species, because the nature of the species considered in itself is one. Just as, therefore, it is one according to the consideration of it while it is being considered, so it would be one in being if it existed through

---

127. Aristotle, *De Anima*, III, 4 (429b 5); St. Thomas, In *De Anima*, III, lect. 7, ed. Pirotta, no. 699 (AACTA, 410).

128. Cf. above, Cap. V.

129. St. Thomas, ST, I, 50, 1–2 (BW I, 480–485); *Expositio super librum Boethii de Trinitate*, q. 5, a. 4 ed. B. Decker, 197–199 (*The Division and Methods of the Sciences*, trans. A. Maurer, 44–45).

steret. Eademque ratio est de genere per comparationem ad species, quousque perveniatur ad ipsum esse quod est communissimum; ipsum igitur esse per se subsistens est unum tantum: impossibile est igitur quod praeter ipsum sit aliquid subsistens quod sit esse tantum. Omne autem quod est esse habet; est igitur in quocumque praeter primum et ipsum esse tanquam actus, et substantia rei habens esse tanquam potentia receptiva huius actus quod est esse.

Potest autem quis dicere quod id quod participat (aliquid) est secundum se carens illo, sicut superficies quae nata est participare colorem secundum se considerata est non color et non colorata; similiter igitur id quod participat esse oportet esse non ens. Quod autem est in potentia ens et participativum ipsius, non autem secundum se est ens, materia est, ut supra dictum est; sic igitur omne quod est post primum ens, quod est ipsum esse, cum sit participative ens habet materiam.

Sed considerandum est quod ea quae a primo ente esse participant non participant esse secundum universalem modum essendi, secundum quod est in primo principio, sed particulariter secundum quemdam determinatum essendi modum qui convenit vel huic generi vel huic speciei. Unaquaeque autem res adaptatur ad unum determinatum modum essendi secundum modum suae substantiae; modus autem uniuscuiusque substantiae compositae ex materia et forma est secundum formam per quam pertinet ad determinatam speciem: sic igitur res composita ex materia et forma per suam formam fit participativa ipsius esse a Deo secundum quemdam proprium modum. Invenitur igitur in substantia composita ex materia et forma duplex ordo: unus quidem ipsius materiae ad formam, alius autem ipsius rei iam compositae ad esse participatum; non enim est esse rei neque forma eius neque materia ipsius, sed aliquid adveniens rei per formam.

Sic igitur in rebus ex materia et forma compositis materia quidem secundum se considerata secundum modum suae essentiae habet esse in potentia, et hoc ipsum est ei ex aliqua participatione primi entis, caret vero secundum se considerata forma per quam participat esse in actu secundum proprium modum; ipsa vero res composita in sui essentia considerata iam habet formam, sed participat esse proprium sibi per formam suam. Quia igitur materia recipit esse determinatum actuale per formam, et non e converso, nihil prohibet

itself. The same argument applies to the genus in relation to species, until we reach being itself which is most common. There is therefore only one being subsisting through itself.[130] Hence it is impossible that there should be something other than it which is being alone. Now everything that is, has being. Therefore, in every being other than the first, there is present both being itself as the act, and the substance having being as a potency receptive of the act of being.[131]

Now, someone could say that that which participates in something lacks that thing of itself, just as a surface which has the nature to participate in color is not color and not colored, considered in itself. In the same way, accordingly, that which participates in being must itself be non-being. That which is a being in potency and participative of being, but is not of itself being, is matter, as was said above.[132] Thus, therefore, since every being that is after the first being, which is being itself, is a being by participation, it has matter.

But it must be observed that the beings which share in being from the first being do not share in it according to a universal mode of being, as it is found in the first principle, but they participate in it in a particular way according to a certain determinate mode of being, which belongs to this given genus or this given species. Now, each thing is adapted to one determinate mode of being according to the mode of its substance. But the mode of every substance composed of matter and form is according to the form through which it belongs to a determinate species. Thus, a thing composed of matter and form is made through its form to receive a share in being itself from God according to a mode proper to it. A twofold order, therefore, is found in a substance composed of matter and form. One is the order of the matter to form, and the other is the order of the composite thing itself to the participated being.[133] For the being of a thing is neither its form nor its matter but something coming to the thing through the form.[134]

Consequently, in things composed of matter and form, the matter considered in itself, according to the mode of its essence, has being in potency, and this it has as a result of a certain participation in the first being;[135] but, considered in itself, it lacks the form through which it participates actually in being according to the mode proper to it.[136] Now a composite being, considered in its essence, already has a form, but it participates in its own being through its own form. Therefore, because matter receives an actual determinate being through a form and not conversely, there is

130. Cf. St. Thomas, ST, I, 3, 4; 7, 1 ad 3 (BW I, 30–31, 57, 58).
131. Cf. St. Thomas, SCG, 11, 52 (OTCF IT, 152).
132. Cf. above, Cap. VI.
133. St. Thomas, *De Ente et Essentia*, IV, V, ed. Roland-Gosselin, 29–42 (OBE, IV, V, pp. 41–54); cf. E. Gilson, *Being And Some Philosophers*, 173 ff.
134. St. Thomas, In *Metaphysics*, VII, lect. 7, ed. Cathala, no. 1419.
135. I.e., *from* the first being.
136. St. Thomas, In *Metaphysics*, VII, lect. 2, ed. Cathala, no. 1292.

esse aliquam formam quae recipiat esse in se ipsa, non in aliquo subiecto; non enim causa dependet ab effectu, sed potius e converso. Ipsa igitur forma sic per se subsistens esse participat in se ipsa, sicut forma materialis in subiecto.

Si igitur per hoc quod dico 'non ens' removeatur solum esse in actu, ipsa forma secundum se considerata est non ens sed esse participans. Si autem 'non ens' removeat non solum ipsum esse in actu sed etiam actum seu formam per quam aliquid participat esse, sic materia est non ens; forma vero subsistens non est non ens, sed est actus qui est forma participativus ultimi actus qui est esse. Patet igitur in quo differt potentia quae est in substantiis spiritualibus a potentia quae est in materia: nam potentia substantiae spiritualis attenditur solum secundum ordinem ipsius ad esse, potentia vero materiae secundum ordinem et ad formam et ad esse. Si quis autem utramque potentiam materiam esse dicat, manifestum est quod aequivoce materiam nominabit.

Quintae vero rationis solutio iam ex dictis apparet. Quia enim substantia spiritualis esse participat, non secundum suae communitatis infinitatem sicut est in primo principio, sed secundum proprium modum suae essentiae, manifestum est quod esse eius non est infinitum sed finitum; quia tamen ipsa forma non est participata in materia, ex hac parte non finitur per modum quo finiuntur formae in materia existentes.

Sic igitur apparet gradus quidam infinitatis in rebus. Nam materiales substantiae finitae quidem sunt dupliciter, scilicet ex parte formae quae in materia recipitur et ex parte ipsius esse quod participat secundum proprium modum, quasi superius et inferius finita existens; substantia vero spiritualis est quidem finita superius in quantum a primo principio participat esse secundum proprium modum, est autem infinita inferius in quantum non participatur in subiecto. Primum vero principium, quod Deus est, est modis omnibus infinitum.

nothing to prevent the existence of a form which receives the being in itself, not in some subject. For a cause does not depend on the effect, but rather conversely. In this way, therefore, a form subsisting through itself participates in being in itself just as a material form participates in its subject.

If, therefore, when I say 'non-being,' the effect is to remove only the being in act, the form, considered in itself, is non-being but sharing in being. But if 'non-being' removes not only the being in act but also the act or the form through which something shares in being, then matter is non-being in this sense, whereas a subsistent form is not non-being but an act, which is a form that can participate in the ultimate act, which is being. It is clear, therefore, in what the potency which is found in spiritual substances differs from the potency found in matter. For the potency of a spiritual substance is measured only according to its order to being, whereas the potency of matter is measured according to its order both to a form and to being. If someone were to say that both potencies are matter, it is clear that he is using the word 'matter' equivocally.

The solution of the fifth argument[137] is already apparent from what we have said.[138] For since a spiritual substance participates in being not according to the infinity of its community, as is the case in the first principle, but according to the mode proper to its essence, it is clear that its being is not infinite but finite. Nevertheless, since the form itself is not participated in matter, it is not limited in this respect by the mode through which forms found in matter are limited.

Thus, therefore, we see a certain gradation of infinity in things. For a material substance is finite in a twofold manner: namely, on the part of the form which is received in matter, and on the part of being itself, in which it shares according to its own mode, as being finite from below and from above. A spiritual substance, however, is finite from above inasmuch as it receives being from the first principle according to its proper mode; it is infinite from below, insofar as it is not received in a subject. But the first principle, God, is infinite in every way.

137. Cf. above, Cap. V.
138. Cf. above, Cap. VIII.

CHAPTER 9

On the opinion of those who say that spiritual substances are not created

Sicut autem praedicta positio circa conditionem spiritualium substantiarum a sententia Platonis et Aristotelis deviavit, eis immaterialitatis simplicitatem auferens, ita et circa modum existendi ipsarum aliqui a veritate deviasse inveniuntur auferentes earum originem a primo et summo auctore. In quo inveniuntur diversi homines tripliciter errasse. Quidam enim posuerunt praedictas substantias omnino causam sui esse non habere; quidam autem posuerunt eas quidem essendi causam habere, non tamen immediate eas omnes procedere a summo et primo principio, sed quadam serie ordinis inferiores earum a superioribus essendi originem habere; alii vero confitentur omnes quidem huiusmodi substantias immediate essendi habere originem a primo principio, sed in ceteris quae de eis dicuntur—puta quod sunt viventes intelligentes et alia huiusmodi—superiores inferioribus causas existere.

Primi quidem igitur spirituales substantias omnino increatas esse existimant, huiusmodi opinionem sumentes ex his quae secundum naturam causantur, utentes communi suppositione naturali philosophorum pro principio: ex nihilo nihil fieri. Hoc autem videtur fieri quod habet causam sui esse; quidquid igitur sui esse causam habet, oportet illud ex alio fieri. Hoc autem ex quo aliquid fit est materia; si igitur spirituales substantiae materiam non habent, consequens videtur eas omnino causam sui esse non habere.

Rursus, fieri moveri quoddam est vel mutari. Mutationis autem omnis et motus subiectum aliquod esse oportet, est enim motus actus existentis in potentia; oportet igitur omni ei quod fit subiectum aliquod praeexistere: spirituales igitur substantiae si immateriales sunt, factae esse non possunt.

Item, in qualibet factione cum pervenitur ad factum esse ultimum non remanet aliquid fieri, sicut nec post

Just as the aforementioned position[139] on the condition of spiritual substances strayed from the opinion of Plato and Aristotle[140] by taking away the simplicity of immateriality from those substances, so we find that certain people have strayed from the truth concerning their mode of being by taking away from spiritual substances an origin in a first and highest author. On this point there was a three-fold error among different thinkers. For, in the first place, some of them said that the aforementioned substances had absolutely no cause of their being.[141] Others held that these substances had indeed a cause of being but they did not proceed immediately from the highest and first principle, but the lower ones among them derived their being from the higher ones according to a certain orderly succession.[142] Still others admit that all these substances have the origin of their being immediately from the first principle; but in the case of their other attributes (for example, in that they are living, intelligent, and the like), the higher substances are as causes for the lower ones.[143]

In the first place, then, they hold that spiritual substances are completely uncreated. They derive this opinion from the things which are caused according to nature, and they base themselves on the common physical assumption of the philosophers as their principle, namely, that from nothing nothing comes.[144] That thing seems 'to become' which has a cause of its being. Whatever, therefore, has a cause for its being must come from another. Now that from which another becomes is matter. If, therefore, spiritual substances have no matter, it seems to follow that they have absolutely no cause of their being.[145]

Again, 'to become' is a certain kind of 'to be moved' or 'to be changed.' Now there must be some subject for all change and motion, since motion is the act of something existing in potency.[146] Therefore, some subject must preexist for everything that becomes. Hence, if spiritual substances are immaterial, they cannot have been made.[147]

Again, in any given making, when we arrive at the final 'having been made,' there remains nothing to be made, just

---

139. Cf. above, Caps. V–VIII.

140. Aristotle, *Metaphysics*, I, 6 (987b 1–18).

141. In all likelihood the Averroists in Paris; cf. H. Denifle et E.Chatelain, *Chartularium Universitatis Parisiensis*, I, Props. 46, 47 (p. 546), also printed in Mandonnet, *Siger de Brabant et l'Averroisme latin au XIIIème siècle*, II, 179, 184.4

142. Avicenna, *Metaphysics*, IX, 4 (fol. 104va); cf. A. Forest, *La structure métaphysique du concret selon Saint Thomas d'Aquin*, 331, 360, for a list of references to Avicenna in St. Thomas' works. Siger of Brabant likewise teaches the doctrine of cascade creation; cf. *De Necessitate et contingentia causarum*, II in Mandonnet, *op. cit.*, 112; Denifle-Chatelain, *Chartularium*, 1, Props. 55, 64 (pp. 546, 547).

143. This is definitely from the *Liber de causis*: cf. O. Bardenhewer, *Die pseudo-aristotelische Schrift über das reine Gute bekannt unter dem Namen de causis*, no. 1 (pp. 163–164); Proclus, *Elem*, Props. 55, 56, 70 (pp. 53, 55, 67).

144. Aristotle, *Phys.*, I, 4 (187a 28).

145. Cf. above, Cap. IX.

146. Aristotle, *Phys.*, III, 1 (201a 15).

147. Condemnation of 1277, cf. *Chartularium*, I, Prop. 70 (p. 547), P Mandonnet, *op. cit.*, II, 179; St. Thomas, ST, I, 61, 1 (BW, II, 565).

ultimum motum esse remanet moveri. Videmus autem in his quae generantur quod unumquodque eorum tunc factum esse dicitur quasi terminata factione quando accipit formam, est enim forma generationis terminus; adepta igitur forma, nihil restat fiendum: habens igitur formam non fit ens, sed est ens secundum suam formam. Si igitur aliquid sit secundum se forma, hoc non fit ens; spirituales autem substantiae sunt quaedam formae subsistentes, ut ex praemissis manifestum est: non igitur spirituales substantiae sui esse causam habent quasi ab alio factae.

Posset etiam aliquis ad hoc argumentari ex opinionibus Aristotelis et Platonis qui huiusmodi substantias ponunt esse sempiternas. Nullum autem sempiternum videtur esse factum, quia ens fit ex non ente sicut album ex non albo; unde videtur consequens ut quod fit prius non fuerit. Sic igitur consequens est, si spirituales substantiae sunt sempiternae, quod non sint factae nec habeant sui esse principium et causam.

Sed si quis diligenter consideret, ab eadem radice inveniet hanc opinionem procedere et praedictam quae materiam spiritualibus substantiis adhibet. Processit enim supradicta opinio ex hoc quod spirituales substantias eiusdem rationis esse existimavit cum materialibus substantiis quae sensu percipiuntur, imaginationem transcendere non valens; sic et ista opinio ex hoc videtur procedere quod elevari non potest intellectus ad intuendum alium modum causandi quam iste qui convenit materialibus rebus. Paulatim enim humana ingenia processisse videntur ad investigandam rerum originem.

Primo namque in sola exteriori mutatione rerum originem consistere homines aestimaverunt: dico autem exteriorem originem, quae fit secundum accidentales transmutationes. Primi enim philosophantes de naturis rerum fieri statuerunt nihil esse aliud quam alterari, ita quod id quod est rerum substantia—quam materiam nominabant—sit principium primum penitus non causatum; non enim distinctionem substantiae et accidentis intellectu transcendere poterant. Alii vero aliquantulum ulterius procedentes etiam ipsarum substantiarum originem investigaverunt, ponentes aliquas substantias causam sui esse habere; sed quia nihil praeter corpora mente percipere poterant, resolvebant quidem

as after the last 'having been moved,' there remains no 'to be moved.' But in the case of those things that are generated, we see that each one of them is then said to have been made, as meaning that the making is finished when it receives its form. For the form is the term of generation. Therefore, when the form is acquired, nothing remains to be made. Therefore, that which has a form does not become a being; it is a being according to its form. If, then, something is in itself a form, this does not become a being. Now spiritual substances are certain subsistent forms, as is clear from what has already been said. Therefore, spiritual substances do not have a cause of their being in the sense of having been made by another.

One could likewise argue to the same effect from the opinion of Aristotle and Plato who hold that such substances are everlasting.[148] But nothing everlasting seems to be something made, since a being comes to be from non-being, as white comes to be from non-white. It seems to follow, then, that what comes to be previously did not exist. Consequently, if spiritual substances are everlasting, it follows that they are neither made nor do they have a principle and cause of their being.[149]

But if one were to consider the matter correctly, he will find that this opinion and the previous opinion which attributes matter to spiritual substances proceed from the same source. For the previous opinion proceeded from the fact that Avicebron, unable to transcend the imagination, considered that spiritual substances were of the same nature as the material substances which are perceived by sense.[150] So, too, the present opinion seems to proceed from the fact that the intellect cannot be raised to see a mode of causing other than the one which is suited to material things. For human ability seems to have progressed slowly in investigating the origin of things.

In the beginning, men thought that the origin of things consisted only in an external change, by which I mean an external origin that takes place according to accidental changes.[151] For those who were first to philosophize about the natures of things held that to become is nothing other than to be altered, so that the substance of things—which they called matter—is a completely uncaused first principle.[152] For they were not able by their intellect to hurdle the distinction between substance and accident. Others, proceeding a little further, likewise investigated the origin of the substances themselves, asserting that certain substances had a cause of their being. But because they were not able by their minds to see anything beyond bodies, they did in-

148. St. Augustine, *De Civitate Dei*, IX, 8 (PL 41, 263); Proclus, *Elem*, Prop. 169 (pp. 147–149).

149. Cf. *Chartularium*, I, Prop. 70 (p. 547). Siger of Brabant cites Aristotle in support of the position that nothing prevents an eternal and necessary being from having a cause of its eternity and necessity. Cf. Quaestiones *De Anima Intellectiva*, q. 5 in Mandonnet, *op. cit.*, II, 159.

150. Cf. above, Caps. V–VIII; Aristotle, *De Anima*, III, 3 (427a 21); St. Thomas, In *De Anima*, III, lect. 4, ed. Pirotta, nos. 616–623 (AACTA 378–380).

151. Cf. Aristotle, *Metaphysics*, I, 3, 4 (985b 6–985b 22); *Phys.*, 1, 4 (187a 30); *De Gen. et Corrup.*, II, 9 (335b 24); St. Thomas, ST, I, 44, 2 (BW, I, 428); A. C. Pegis, A Note on St. Thomas' Summa Theologica, I, 44, 1–2, 159–168.

152. Cf. Aristotle, *Phys.*, IV, 6 (213a 29); *Metaphysics*, II, 5 (1002a 8); St. Augustine, *De Civitate Dei*, VIII, 2 (PL 41, 225).

corporales substantias in aliqua principia sed corporalia, ponentes ex quibusdam corporibus congregatis alia fieri, ac si rerum origo in sola congregatione et segregatione consisteret. Posteriores vero philosophi ulterius processerunt, resolventes sensibiles substantias in partes essentiae quae sunt materia et forma; et sic fieri rerum naturalium in quadam transmutatione posuerunt, secundum quod materia alternatim diversis formis subiicitur.

Sed ultra hunc modum fiendi necesse est secundum sententiam Platonis et Aristotelis ponere alium altiorem. Cum enim necesse sit primum principium simplicissimum esse, necesse est quod non hoc modo esse ponatur quasi esse participans, sed quasi ipsum esse existens; quia vero esse subsistens non potest esse nisi unum, sicut supra habitum est, necesse est omnia alia quae sub ipso sunt sic esse quasi esse participantia. Oportet igitur communem quamdam resolutionem in omnibus huiusmodi fieri, secundum quod unumquodque eorum intellectu resolvitur in id quod est et in suum esse; oportet igitur supra modum fiendi quo aliquid fit forma materiae adveniente, praeintelligere aliam rerum originem, secundum quod esse attribuitur toti universitati rerum a primo ente quod est suum esse.

Rursus, in omni causarum ordine necesse est universalem causam particulari praeexistere, nam causae particulares non agunt nisi in universalium causarum virtute. Manifestum est autem quod omnis causa per motum aliquid faciens particularis causa est, habet enim particularem effectum: est enim omnis motus ex hoc determinato in illud determinatum; omnisque mutatio motus cuiusdam terminus est. Oportet igitur supra modum fiendi quo aliquid fit per mutationem vel motum, esse aliquem modum fiendi sive originis rerum absque omni mutatione vel motu per influentiam essendi.

Item, necesse est quod per accidens est in id reduci quod per se est. In omni autem quod fit per mutationem vel motum, fit quidem hoc vel illud ens per se, ens autem communiter sumptum per accidens fit; non enim fit ex non ente sed ex non ente hoc: ut si canis ex equo fiat — ut Aristotelis exemplo utamur — fit quidem canis per se, non autem fit animal per se sed per accidens, quia animal erat prius. Oportet igitur originem quamdam in rebus considerari secundum quam ipsum esse communiter sumptum per se attribuitur rebus, quod omnem mutationem et motum transcendat.

deed reduce corporeal substances to certain principles, but corporeal principles, and they posited that other substances come to be through the combining of certain bodies, as though the origin of things consisted solely in combining and separating.[153] Later philosophers proceeded by reducing sensible substances into their essential parts, which are matter and form. Thus they made the becoming of physical things to consist in a certain change, according as matter is successively made subject to different forms.[154]

But beyond this mode of becoming, it is necessary to posit a higher one, according to the teaching of Plato and Aristotle.[155] For, since it is necessary that the first principle be most simple, this must of necessity be said to be, not as participating in being but as being itself existing. But because subsistent being can be only one, as was pointed out above,[156] then necessarily all other things under it must be as participating in being. Therefore, there must take place a certain common resolution in all such things according as each of them is reduced by the intellect into that which is and its being. Therefore, above the mode of coming to be by which something becomes when form comes to matter, we must presuppose another origin for things, according as being is bestowed upon the whole universe of things by the first being that is its own being.

Again, in every order of causes, a universal cause must exist prior to the particular cause, since particular causes act only in the power of universal causes. Now it is clear that every cause that makes something through motion is a particular cause, since it has a particular effect. For every motion is from this determinate point to that determinate point, and every change is the terminus of some motion. Therefore, over and above the mode of becoming by which something comes to be through change or motion, there must be a mode of becoming or origin of things, without any mutation or motion through the influx of being.

Further, that which exists by accident must be reduced to that which exists through itself. Now in every thing that comes to be through change or motion, there comes to be that which is in itself this or that being. But 'being,' taken generally, comes to be accidentally, for it does not arise from non-being but from not being this (as if dog were to arise from horse). To use the example of Aristotle, if a dog were to come to be from a horse, that which is essentially a dog comes to be, but an animal does not come to be essentially, but only accidentally, since animal existed previously.[157] It is therefore necessary to consider in things a certain origin according to which being, taken generally, is granted essentially to things—which transcends all change and motion.

---

153. Empedocles, according to Aristotle, *Metaphysics*, I, 4 (985a 8); *Phys.*, I, 5 (188b 34).
154. Cf. Aristotle, *Metaphysics*, XI, 2 (1069b 5 ff.).
155. Proclus, *Elem*, Prop. 26 (p. 31).
156. Cf. above, Cap. VIII.
157. Aristotle, *Phys.*, I, 8 (191b 16–23).

Adhuc, si quis ordinem rerum consideret, semper inveniet id quod est maximum causam esse eorum quae sunt post ipsum, sicut ignis qui est calidissimus causa est caliditatis in ceteris elementatis corporibus. Primum autem principium quod Deum dicimus est maxime ens; non enim est in infinitum procedere in rerum ordine, sed ad aliquid summum devenire quod melius est esse unum quam plura. Quod autem in universo melius est, necesse est esse, quia universum dependet ex essentia bonitatis; necesse est igitur primum ens esse causam essendi omnibus.

His autem visis, facile est solvere rationes inductas. Quod enim antiqui Naturales quasi principium supposuerunt ex nihilo nihil fieri, ex hoc processit quia solum ad particularem fiendi modum pervenire potuerunt qui est per mutationem vel motum.

De quo etiam fiendi modo secunda ratio procedebat. In his enim quae fiunt per mutationem vel motum, subiectum factioni praesupponitur; sed in supremo modo fiendi qui est per essendi influxum nullum subiectum factioni praesupponitur, quia hoc ipsum est subiectum fieri secundum hunc factionis modum: quod est subiectum esse participare per influentiam superioris entis.

Similiter etiam tertia ratio de hoc modo fiendi procedit qui est per mutationem et motum. Cum enim ad formam perventum fuerit, nihil de motu restabit; oportet tamen intelligere quod per formam res generata esse participet ab universali essendi principio: non enim causae agentes ad determinatas formas sunt causae essendi nisi in quantum agunt in virtute primi et universalis principii essendi.

Quarta etiam ratio eodem modo procedit de his quae fiunt per motum vel mutationem; in quibus necesse est ut non esse praecedat esse eorum quae fiunt, quia eorum esse est terminus mutationis vel motus. In his autem quae fiunt absque mutatione vel motu per simplicem emanationem sive influxum, potest intelligi aliquid esse factum praeter hoc quod quandoque non fuerit; sublata enim mutatione vel motu, non invenitur in actione influentis principii prioris et posterioris successio.

Unde necesse est ut sic se habeat effectus per influxum causatus ad causam influentem quamdiu agit, sicut in rebus quae per motum fiunt se habet ad causam agentem in termino actionis cum motu existentis. Tunc autem effectus iam est; necesse est igitur ut in his quae

And if one should consider the order of things, he will always find that that which is most such is always the cause of those things that come after it. For example, fire, which is hottest, is the cause of heat in other elementary bodies.[158] Now the first principle, which we call God, is most being. For we cannot proceed to infinity in the order of things, but we must come to something highest, because it is better to be one than to be many. But that which is better in the universe must necessarily be because the universe depends on the essence of God's goodness. Therefore, the first being must of necessity be the cause of being for all things.

Having seen these points,[159] we can easily solve the arguments brought forth. That the ancient naturalists assumed as a first principle that nothing comes to be from nothing was due to the fact that they were able to reach only a particular mode of coming to be: namely, that which is through change and motion.

The second argument likewise was based on this mode of coming to be. For among things which come to be through change or motion, a subject is presupposed to the making, but in the highest mode of coming to be, which takes place through the influx of being, no subject is presupposed to the making; for according to this kind of making, for a subject to come to be is for the subject to participate in being through the influence of a higher being.

So, too, the third argument is likewise based on the coming to be, which is through change or motion. For when the form is reached, there will be no further motion. Nevertheless, we must understand that through its form, a generated thing receives its being from the universal cause of being. For the causes that are acting towards the production of determinate forms are causes of being only insofar as they act in the power of the first and universal principle of being.

The fourth argument likewise applies in the same way to those things which come to be through change or motion, in which it is necessary that non-existence precede the existence of things that come to be, for their being is the terminus of a change or motion. But in those things which come to be without change or motion through a simple emanation or influx, we are able to understand that something has been made without including that it did not exist at some time. For when change or motion has been removed, there is not found in the action of the causal principle the succession of before and after.

It is therefore necessary that the effect which is produced through the influence of a cause be so related to that influencing cause while it is acting in the same way that things which come to be through motion are related to their acting cause at the terminus of the action that ex-

---

158. I.e., as common denominator and basis belonging to elements; cf. Aristotle, *Metaphysics*, I,1 (993b 23).
159. Cf. above, Cap. IX.

absque motu fiunt, simul cum agentis influxu sit ipse effectus productus.

Si autem actio influentis sine motu extiterit, non accedit agenti dispositio ut postmodum possit agere cum prius non potuerit, quia iam haec mutatio quaedam esset; potuit igitur semper agere influendo: unde et effectus productus intelligi potest semper fuisse.

Et hoc quidem aliqualiter apparet in corporalibus rebus. Ad praesentiam enim corporis illuminantis producitur lumen in aere absque aliqua aeris transmutatione praecedente; unde si semper corpus illuminans aeri praesens fuisset, semper ab ipso aer lumen haberet. Sed expressius hoc videtur in intellectualibus rebus quae sunt magis remotae a motu. Est enim principiorum veritas causa veritatis in conclusionibus semper veris; sunt enim quaedam necessaria quae suae necessitatis causam habent, ut etiam Aristoteles dicit in V *Metaphysicae* et in VIII *Physicorum*. Non ergo aestimandum est quod Plato et Aristoteles, propter hoc quod posuerunt substantias immateriales seu etiam caelestia corpora semper fuisse, eis subtraxerunt causam essendi; non enim in hoc a sententia catholicae fidei deviarunt quod huiusmodi posuerunt increata, sed quia posuerunt ea semper fuisse: cuius contrarium fides catholica tenet.

Non enim est necessarium, quamvis origo sit ab immobili principio absque motu, quod eorum esse sit sempiternum. A quolibet enim agente procedit effectus secundum modum sui esse; esse autem primi principii est eius intelligere et velle: procedit igitur universitas rerum a primo principio sicut ab intelligente et volente. Intelligentis autem et volentis est producere aliquid, non quidem ex necessitate sicut ipsum est, sed sicut vult et intelligit; in intellectu autem primi intelligentis comprehenditur omnis modus essendi et omnis mensura quantitatis et durationis: sicut igitur non eumdem modum essendi rebus indidit quo ipsum existit corporumque quantitatem sub determinata mensura conclusit, cum in eius potestate sicut et in intellectu omnes mensurae contineantur, ita etiam dedit rebus talem durationis mensuram qualem voluit, non qualem habet.

Sicut igitur corporum quantitas sub tali determinata mensura concluditur, non quia actio primi principii ad hanc mensuram quantitatis determinetur, sed quia talis mensura quantitatis sequitur in effectu qualem intellec-

ists through motion; for at that time, the effect then exists. Therefore, in the case of those things that come to be without motion, it is necessary that the produced effect be simultaneous with the influence of the acting cause.

If, however, the action of the acting cause be without motion, no disposition will come to the agent so that he might be able to act afterwards when previously he could not do so, because this disposition would already be a certain change. Hence he could always act by an influx. Therefore, the effect produced can be understood to have always existed.

And this appears somewhat among corporeal things themselves. For in the presence of an illuminating body, light is produced in the air without any preceding change of the air. Accordingly, if the illuminating body had always been present to the air, the air would always have light from it. But this appears more clearly in the case of intellectual beings which are more removed from motion. For the truth of the principles is the cause of the truth in conclusions that are always true. For there are certain necessary things which have a cause of their necessity, as Aristotle himself says in *Metaphysics* V:[160] and in *Physics* VIII.[161] Therefore, although Plato and Aristotle did posit that immaterial substances or even heavenly bodies always existed, we must not suppose on that account that they denied to them a cause of their being. For they did not depart from the position of the Catholic faith by holding such substances to be uncreated, but because they held them to have always existed—of which the Catholic faith holds the contrary.

For, although the origin of certain things may be from an unmoved principle without motion, it is not necessary that their being be everlasting. For an effect proceeds from any given agent according to the mode of the being of the agent. Now the being of the first principle is his understanding and his willing. Therefore, the universe of things proceeds from the first principle as from a being that understands and wills. But it belongs to one understanding and willing to produce something not of necessity as it itself is, but as it wills and understands. Now, in the intellect of the first understanding being, there is included every mode of being and every measure of quantity and duration. Therefore, just as the first principle did not give to things the same mode of being by which he exists, and enclosed the quantity of bodies under a determinate measure—since all measures are contained in his power as well as in his intellect—so he gave to things such a measure of duration as he willed, not as he has.

Accordingly, just as the quantity of bodies is enclosed under a given measure not because the action of the first principle is determined to this measure of quantity, but because a measure of quantity actually follows as the intellect

---

160. Aristotle, *Metaphysics*, IV, 5 (1015b 9).
161. Aristotle, *Phys.*, VIII, 1 (252b 3), 3. Cf. St. Augustine, *De Civitate Dei*, X, 31 (PL 41, 311–312).

tus causae praescripsit: ita etiam ex actione primi agentis consequitur determinata durationis mensura ex intellectu divino eam praescribente, non quasi ipse subiaceat successivae durationi ut nunc velit aut agat aliquid quod prius noluerit, sed quia tota rerum duratio sub eius intellectu et virtute concluditur ut determinet rebus ab aeterno mensuram durationis quam velit.

of the cause has prescribed: so, too, from the action of the first cause, there follows a determinate measure of duration because the divine intellect so prescribed. Not, indeed, in the sense that God is subject to successive duration, so that he now wills or does something which he previously did not will, but because the whole duration of things is included under his intellect, so that he determines from eternity the measure of duration that he wills for things.

CHAPTER 10

Against those who posit that not all spiritual substances are immediately from God

Haec igitur et huiusmodi alii considerantes asserunt quidem omnia essendi originem trahere a primo et summo rerum principio quem dicimus Deum, non tamen immediate sed ordine quodam. Cum enim primum rerum principium sit penitus unum et simplex, non aestimaverunt quod ab eo procederet nisi unum; quod quidem, etsi ceteris rebus inferioribus simplicius sit et magis unum, deficit tamen a primi simplicitate in quantum ipsum non est suum esse sed est substantia habens esse: et hanc nominant intelligentiam primam, a qua quidem iam dicunt plura posse procedere. Nam secundum quod convertitur ad intelligendum suum simplex et primum principium, dicunt quod ab ea procedit intelligentia secunda; prout vero se ipsam intelligit secundum id quod est intellectualitatis in ea, producit animam primi orbis; prout vero intelligit se ipsam quantum ad id quod est in ea de potentia, procedit ab ea corpus primum. Et sic per ordinem usque ad ultima corporum, rerum processum a primo principio determinant: et haec est positio Avicennae, quae etiam videtur supponi in *Libro de causis*.

Haec autem positio etiam in primo aspectu reprobabilis videtur. Bonum enim universi potius quam bonum cuiuscumque particularis naturae invenitur; destruit autem rationem boni in particularibus effectibus naturae vel artis, si quis perfectionem effectus non attribuat intentioni agentis, cum eadem sit ratio boni et finis. Et ideo Aristoteles reprobavit antiquorum Naturalium opinionem, qui posuerunt formas rerum quae naturaliter generantur et alia naturalia bona non esse intenta a natura sed provenire ex necessitate materiae; multo igitur magis inconveniens est ut bonum universi non proveniat

Therefore, other thinkers, considering these and similar points, assert that all things do indeed derive the origin of their being from the first and highest principle of things whom we call God, yet they do not do so immediately but in a certain order. Since the first principle of things is absolutely one and simple, they thought that only that which is one proceeded from him. And although this effect be more simple and more one than all the other lesser things, it falls short of the simplicity of the first principle, insofar as it is not its own being but is a substance having being. This substance they call the first intelligence, from which they say that it is possible for a plurality of beings to proceed. For, according as the first intelligence is turned to the understanding of its simple and first principle, they say that the second intelligence proceeds from it. Then, according as it understands itself in terms of the intellectuality in it, it produces the soul of the first sphere; but according as it understands itself in terms of that which is potential within it, the first body proceeds from it.[162] And thus, according to a certain order down to the lowest bodies, they determine the procession of things from the first principle. This is the position of Avicenna[163] which seems to be presupposed in the *Book of Causes*.[164]

But it is immediately evident that this position is open to criticism. For the good of the universe is stronger than the good of any particular nature. Since the nature of the good and of the end is the same, if anyone withdraws the perfection of the effect from the intention of the agent, he destroys the nature of the good in the particular effects of nature or art. For this reason, Aristotle criticized the opinion of the ancient naturalists, who posited that the forms of the things that are generated by nature and other natural goods are not intended by nature but come about from the necessity of matter. All the more unbefitting is it therefore that the

---

162. For the reference, see above, Cap. IX; cf. also, Algazel, *Metaphysics*, V, ed. J. Muckle (p. 119).

163. Avicenna, *Metaphysics*, IX, 4 (fol. 104va); cf. Plotinus, *Enneads*, V, 2, 4, ed. Bréhier, vol. V, 33, 80 (The *Enneads*, trans. S. MacKenna, 380–400); E. Gilson, HCP, 187–216; A.-M. Goichon, *La distinction de l'essence et de l'existence d'après Ibn Sina (Avicenne)*, Bk. II, Cap. II, A, B (pp. 201–243); *Lexique de la langue philosophique d'Ibn Sina (Avicenne)*, 421, par. 754; 20, par. 45; 327, par 604; 228–231, par. 439, nos. 3, 8; 239, par. 450; 41, par. 91.

164. On the *Liber de Causis*, cf. E. Gilson, HCP, 235–237, 367, note 3.

ex intentione universalis agentis sed quadam necessitate ordinis rerum.

Si autem bonum universi quod in distinctione et ordine consistit partium ex intentione primi et universalis agentis procedit, necesse est quod ipsa distinctio et ordo partium universi in intellectu primi principii praeexistat. Et quia res procedunt ab eo sicut ab intellectivo principio quod agit secundum formas conceptas, non oportet ponere quod a primo principio, etsi in essentia sua sit simplex, procedat unum tantum; et quod ab illo secundum modum suae compositionis et virtutis procedant plura, et sic inde: hoc enim esset distinctionem et ordinem talem in rebus esse non ex intentione primi agentis sed ex quadam rerum necessitate.

Potest tamen dici quod rerum distinctio et ordo procedit quidem ex intentione primi principii, cuius intentio est non solum ad producendum primum causatum sed ad producendum totum universum: hoc tamen ordine ut ipse immediate producat primum causatum, quo mediante alia per ordinem producat in esse.

Sed cum sit duplex modus productionis rerum, unus quidem secundum mutationem et motum, alius autem absque mutatione et motu, ut supra iam diximus: in eo quidem productionis modo qui per motum est, hoc manifeste videmus accidere quod a primo principio alia procedunt mediantibus causis secundis; videmus enim et plantas et animalia produci in esse per motum secundum virtutes superiorum causarum ordinate usque ad primum principium. Sed in eo modo producendi qui est absque motu per simplicem influxum ipsius esse, hoc accidere impossibile est; secundum enim hunc productionis modum, quod in esse producitur non solum fit per se hoc ens, sed etiam per se fit ens simpliciter, ut dictum est.

Oportet autem effectus proportionaliter causis respondere, ut scilicet effectus particularis causae particulari respondeat, effectus autem universalis universali causae. Sicut igitur cum per motum aliquid fit per se hoc ens, effectus huiusmodi in particularem causam reducitur quae ad determinatam formam movet, ita etiam cum simpliciter fit ens per se et non per accidens, oportet hunc effectum reduci in universalem essendi causam: hoc autem est primum principium quod Deus est. Possunt igitur per mutationem vel motum aliqua produci in esse a primo principio mediantibus causis secundis; sed eo productionis modo qui fit absque motu

good of the universe proceed not from the intention of the universal agent but by a certain necessity in the order of things.

Moreover, if the good of the universe (which consists in the distinction and order of its parts) does come from the intention of the first and universal agent, then it is necessary that the very distinction and order of the parts of the universe preexist in the intellect of the first principle. And because things proceed from him as from a principle with an intellect, which acts in accordance with conceived forms, we may not posit that from the first principle—even though it is simple in its essence—there proceeds only one effect; and that it is from another being, according to the mode of its composition and power, there proceeds a multitude, and so on. This would mean that such a distinction and order in things proceeded from a certain necessity in things and not from the intention of the first agent.

Now it can be replied that the distinction and order of things does indeed proceed from the intention of the first principle, which intends to produce not only the first effect but also the whole universe; yet this happens according to a certain order, so that the first principle produces the first effect immediately, and, through the mediation of the first effect, he brings things into being in a certain order.

But since there is a twofold mode of producing things, namely, one according to change and motion, and the other without change and motion—as we have already said above[165]—in the mode of production which takes place through motion, we clearly see that some things come to be from the first principle through the mediation of second causes. For thus we see plants and animals brought into being through motion according to the powers of higher causes, in an orderly way extending to the first principle. But in the mode of production that takes place without motion through a simple influx of being itself, this cannot take place. But in the mode of production according to which a thing is brought into being, not only does it itself come to be this thing, but it itself comes to be a being absolutely, as we have said.[166]

But there must be a proportion between effect and causes, namely, so that a particular effect corresponds to a particular cause and a universal effect to a universal cause. Therefore, just as when some thing itself comes to be this being through motion, an effect of this sort is reduced to a particular cause that moves towards a determinate form, so too, when some thing comes to be absolutely and not by accident a being, this effect must be reduced to the universal cause of being. This, however, is the first principle: namely, God. By way of change and motion, certain effects can be brought into being by the first principle through the mediation of second causes; but according to that mode of pro-

165. Cf. above, Cap. IX.
166. *Ibid.*

— qui creatio nominatur — in solum Deum refertur auctorem. Solo autem hoc modo produci possunt in esse immateriales substantiae, et quorumcumque corporum materia ante formam esse non potuit, sicut dictum est de materia caelestium corporum quae non est in potentia ad aliam formam. Relinquitur igitur quod omnes immateriales substantiae et caelestia corpora quae per motum produci non possunt in esse, solum Deum sui esse habent auctorem; non ergo id quod est prius in eis est posterioribus causa essendi.

Adhuc, quanto aliqua causa est superior, tanto est universalior et virtus eius ad plura se extendit. Sed id quod primum invenitur in unoquoque ente maxime commune est omnibus; quaecumque enim superadduntur contrahunt id quod prius inveniunt, nam quod posterius in re intelligitur comparatur ad prius ut actus ad potentiam: per actum autem potentia determinatur. Sic igitur oportet ut id quod primum subsistit in unoquoque sit effectus supremae virtutis, quanto autem aliquid est posterius tanto reducatur ad inferioris causae virtutem; oportet igitur quod id quod primum subsistit in unoquoque, sicut in corporibus materia et in immaterialibus substantiis quod proportionale est, sit proprius effectus primae virtutis universalis agentis. Impossibile est igitur quod ab aliquibus causis secundis aliqua producantur in esse non praesupposito aliquo effectu superioris agentis; et sic nullum agens post primum totam rem in esse producit quasi producens ens simpliciter per se et non per accidens — quod est creare, ut dictum est.

Item, alicuius naturae vel formae duplex causa invenitur: una quidem quae est per se et simpliciter causa talis naturae vel formae, alia vero quae est causa huius naturae vel formae in hoc; cuius quidem distinctionis necessitas apparet, si quis causas consideret eorum quae generantur. Cum enim equus generatur, equus generans est quidem causa quod natura equi in hoc esse incipiat, non tamen est per se causa naturae equinae; quod enim per se est causa alicuius naturae secundum speciem, oportet quod sit eius causa in omnibus habentibus speciem illam. Cum igitur equus generans habeat eamdem naturam secundum speciem, oporteret quod esset sui ipsius causa; quod esse non potest; relinquitur igitur quod oportet super omnes participantes naturam equinam esse aliquam universalem causam totius speciei. Quam quidem causam Platonici posuerunt speciem separatam a materia, ad modum quo omnium artificialium principium est forma artis non in materia existens; secundum Aristotilis autem sententiam hanc universalem causam

duction which takes place without motion, called creation, an effect[167] is reduced to God alone as its author. In this way alone can immaterial substances be brought into being, as well as the matter of such bodies as could not exist prior to form, as we have said concerning the matter of the heavenly bodies which is not in potency to other forms.[168] It remains, therefore, that all immaterial substances and the heavenly bodies, which cannot be brought into being through motion, have God alone as the author of their being. And, therefore, that which is prior among them is not the cause of being for those that come later.

Moreover, the higher a cause, by so much is it more universal and by so much does its power extend to more things. But that which is found to be first in each and every being is especially common to all beings, for whatever is added contracts that which is given as prior, for that which is understood in a thing as subsequent in reality is related to the prior as act is to potency. But potency is determined through act. Thus, therefore, that which is first in each and every thing must be the effect of the highest power. But the later the effect is, the more it is reduced to the power of a lower cause. Therefore, that which is found to be in each and every being—as matter in bodies and what is proportional to immaterial substances—is the proper effect of the prime power of the universal agent. Consequently, it is impossible that certain things should be brought into being by second causes, without presupposing the effect of a higher agent; and thus, no agent after the first brings a thing as a whole into being, in the sense of producing a being absolutely in itself and not accidentally—which is to create, as we have said.[169]

Again, a given nature or form has a twofold cause: one, which is essentially and absolutely the cause of such a nature or form; the other, which is the cause that such a nature or form is in such a being. The necessity of this distinction is apparent to any one considering the causes of the things which are generated. For when a horse is generated, the generating horse is indeed the reason why the nature of horse begins to exist in this being, but it is not the essential cause of equinity. For that which is essentially the cause of a certain specific nature must be the cause of that nature of all the beings that have that species. Since, then, the generating horse has the same nature, it would have to be its own cause, which is impossible. It remains, therefore, that above all those participating in equinity, there must be some universal cause of the whole species. This cause the Platonists posited as a form separate from matter in the manner in which the principle of all artifacts is the artistic form that does not exist in matter.[170] According to Aristotle's opinion, however, this universal cause must be located in some

167. "Aliqua" understood subject of "refertur."
168. Cf. above, Cap. VIII.
169. Cf. above, Cap. IX.
170. Aristotle, *Metaphysics*, I, 6; 9 (987b 1–14; 991a 20–991b 1); II, 2 (997b 8); VI, 8 (1033b 19–1034a 8); XI, 5 (1071a 17–30).

oportet ponere in aliquo caelestium corporum, unde et ipse has duas causas distinguens dixit quod homo generat hominem et sol.

Cum autem aliquid per motum causatur, natura communis alicui praeexistenti advenit per formam materiae advenientem vel subiecto; potest igitur sic per motum esse alicuius causa id quod particulariter naturam illam habet, ut homo hominis aut equus equi. Cum vero non per motum causatur, talis productio est ipsius naturae secundum se ipsam; oportet igitur quod reducatur in id quod est per se causa illius naturae, non autem in aliquid quod particulariter illam naturam participet. Assimilatur enim talis productio processui vel causalitati qui in intelligibilibus invenitur, in quibus natura rei secundum se ipsam non dependet nisi a primo; sicut natura senarii et eius ratio non dependet a ternario vel binario sed ab ipsa unitate: non enim sex secundum primam rationem speciei sunt bis tria sed sex solum, alioquin oporteret unius rei multas substantias esse. Sic igitur cum esse alicuius causatur absque motu, eius causalitas attribui non potest alicui particularium entium quod participat esse: sed oportet quod reducatur in ipsam universalem et primam causam essendi, scilicet in Deum qui est ipsum esse.

Amplius, quanto aliqua potentia magis distat ab actu, tanto maiori virtute indiget ad hoc quod in actum reducatur; maiori enim virtute ignis opus est ad resolvendum lapidem quam ceram. Sed nullius potentiae ad aliquam potentiam quantumcumque indispositam et remotam est comparatio absque proportione, non entis enim ad ens nulla est proportio; virtus igitur quae ex nulla potentia praeexistente aliquem effectum producit, in infinitum excedit virtutem quae producit effectum ex aliqua potentia quantumcumque remota. Infinita autem virtus aliorum quidem potest esse secundum quid; sed simpliciter respectu totius esse infinita virtus non est nisi primi agentis quod est suum esse et per hoc est modis omnibus infinitum, ut supra dictum est: sola igitur virtus primi agentis potest effectum producere nulla potentia praesupposita. Talem autem oportet esse productionem omnium ingenerabilium et incorruptibilium quae absque motu producuntur; oportet igitur omnia huiusmodi a solo Deo esse producta. Sic igitur impossibile est ut immateriales substantiae a Deo procedant in esse secundum ordinem quem dicta positio assignabat.

one of the heavenly bodies and therefore he himself, distinguishing between these two causes, said that man and the sun generate man.[171]

But when something is caused through motion, the common nature comes to some preexisting being through the coming of a form to matter or to a substance. For in this way, something that has that nature in a particular way can be through motion the cause of some being, as man is the cause of man or a horse the cause of horse. When a thing is not caused through motion, then such a making refers to the nature itself, according to itself. Therefore, it must be reduced to that which is essentially the cause of that nature, but not to something which participates in that nature in a particular way. For such a making is compared to the procession or causality which is found in intelligibles, in which the nature of a thing according to itself depends only on a first principle, just as the nature and essence of six do not depend on three or two but on unity itself. For, according to the very nature of its species six is not twice three but once six; otherwise, there would have to be many substances of one thing. Consequently, when the being of some thing is caused without motion, the causality involved cannot be attributed to any one of the particular beings that participate in being; it must be reduced to the universal and first cause of being: namely, God, who is being itself.

Further, the more distant a potency is from act, the greater the power it needs to be reduced to act. For a fire of a greater strength is needed to melt stone than to melt wax. But as between no potency and some potency in whatever way undisposed[172] and removed[173] there is no proportion; for between non-being and a being there is no proportion, for the power which produces an effect from no preceding potency infinitely exceeds the power which produces an effect from some potency, however remote it might be. Now an infinite power can belong to other things in a qualified sense, but an infinite power with respect to all of being can belong only to the first agent, which is its own being, and is thereby in all ways infinite, as we said above.[174] Therefore, only the power of the first agent can produce an effect without the presupposition of any potency.[175] Such, however, must be the production of all ingenerable and incorruptible things, which are produced without motion. Such things, therefore, must be produced by God alone. Hence, it is impossible that immaterial substances should come into being from God according to the order which the aforementioned position laid down.

---

171. Aristotle, *Phys.*, II, 2 (194b 13).
172. I.e., lacking form.
173. I.e., from act.
174. Cf. above, Cap. IX-X.
175. Cf. C. L. Sweeney, *Divine Infinity in the Writings of St. Thomas Aquinas*, II, Caps. 2, 3 (pp. 283–300).

CHAPTER 11

Against the Platonists, who posit that certain essential perfections of spiritual substances are not immediately from God

His autem rationibus moti Platonici posuerunt quidem omnium immaterialium substantiarum et universaliter omnium existentium Deum esse immediate causam essendi secundum praedictum productionis modum, qui est absque mutatione vel motu; posuerunt tamen secundum alias participationes bonitatis divinae ordinem quemdam causalitatis in praedictis substantiis. Ut enim supra dictum est, posuerunt abstracta principia secundum ordinem intelligibilium conceptionum, ut scilicet sicut unum et ens sunt communissima et primo cadunt in intellectu, sub hoc autem est vita, sub qua iterum est intellectus, et sic inde: ita etiam primum et supremum inter separata est id quod est ipsum ens et ipsum unum, et hoc est primum principium quod est Deus — de quo iam dictum est quod est suum esse —; sub hoc autem posuerunt aliud principium separatum quod est vita, et iterum aliud quod est intellectus.

Si igitur sit aliqua immaterialis substantia quae sit intelligens vivens et ens, erit quidem ens per participationem primi principii quod est ipsum esse; erit autem vivens per participationem alterius principii separati quod est vita, erit autem intelligens per participationem alterius separati principii quod est ipse intellectus: sicut si ponatur quod homo sit animal per participationem huius principii separati quod est animal, sit autem bipes per participationem secundi principii quod est bipes.

Haec autem positio quantum ad aliquid quidem veritatem habere potest, simpliciter autem vera esse non potest. Eorum enim quae accidentaliter alicui adveniunt nihil prohibet id quidem quod est prius ab aliqua universaliori causa procedere, quod vero est posterius ab aliquo posteriori principio; sicut animalia et plantae calidum quidem et frigidum ab elementis participant, sed determinatum complexionis modum ad speciem propriam pertinentem obtinent ex virtute seminali per quam generantur. Nec est inconveniens quod ab alio principio aliquid sit quantum et album seu calidum, sed in his quae substantialiter praedicantur hoc contingere penitus impossibile est. Nam omnia quae substantialiter de aliquo praedicantur sunt per se et simpliciter unum; unus autem effectus non reducitur in plura prima principia secundum eamdem rationem principii, quia effectus

Influenced by these reasons, the Platonists held that in the case of all immaterial substances and all existing things in general, God is immediately the cause of being according to the aforementioned mode of production which is without change or motion.[176] But they posited a certain order of causality in the aforementioned substances according to other participations in the divine goodness. For, as we said above,[177] the Platonists posited abstract principles according to the order of our intelligible conceptions. This would mean that just as unity and being are most common and are the first to come in the intellect, after which comes life, then intellect, and so forth, so likewise the first and highest among these separate principles is that which is being itself, and this is the first principle, God, of whom we have said that he is his own being.[178] Under this principle, they posited another separate principle, life, and yet another: intellect.

If, therefore, there be some immaterial substance which is intelligent, living, and being, it will be a being through participation in the first principle which is being itself; it will be living through participation in the second separate principle which is life; and it will be intelligent through a participation in another separate principle which is the intellect itself.[179] This would be the same as if it were posited that man is an animal through participation in the separate principle which is animal; and a biped through participation in a second principle which is biped.[180]

Now this position can be true in a certain way but, absolutely speaking, it cannot be true. For among those qualities which come accidentally to some being, nothing prevents that which is prior from coming from a more universal cause and that which is subsequent from coming from some subsequent principle. For example, animals and plants participate in heat and cold from the elements, but they obtain the determinate mode of complexion which pertains to their own species from the seminal power through which they are generated. Nor is it unsuitable that a thing have quantity or be white or hot from different principles. But this is absolutely impossible in the case of substantial attributes. For all attributes which are predicated of some thing substantially are essentially and absolutely one. Now a single effect is not reduced to several first principles according to the same notion of principle

---

176. Proclus, *Elem*, Prop. 26 (p. 31).
177. Cf. above, Cap. I.
178. Cf. above, Cap. IX.
179. Cf. above, Cap. IX.
180. Aristotle, *Metaphysics*, VI, 14; 15 (1039a 30–32; 1040b 32–34); *Ethics*, 1, 6 (1096a 35–1096b 3).

non potest esse causa simplicior. Unde et Aristoteles hac ratione utitur contra Platonicos quod si esset aliud animal et aliud bipes in principiis separatis, non esset simpliciter unum animal bipes.

Si igitur in immaterialibus substantiis aliud esset id quod est esse et aliud quod est vivere et aliud quod est intellectivum esse, ita quod vivens adveniret enti vel intelligens viventi sicut accidens subiecto vel forma materiae, haberet rationem quod dicitur; videmus enim aliquid esse causam accidentis quod non est causa subiecti, et aliquid esse causam substantialis formae quod non est causa materiae. Sed in immaterialibus substantiis id ipsum esse eorum est ipsum vivere eorum, nec est in eis aliud vivere quam intellectivum esse; unde a nullo alio habent quod vivant et intellectiva sint quam a quo habent quod sint.

Si igitur omnes immateriales substantiae a Deo habent immediate quod sint, ab eo immediate habent quod vivant et intellectivae sint. Si quid autem advenit eis supra eorum essentiam, puta intelligibiles species vel aliquid huiusmodi, quantum ad talia potest Platonicorum opinio procedere, ut scilicet huiusmodi in inferioribus immaterialium substantiarum inveniantur ordine quodam a superioribus derivata.

because an effect cannot be simpler than its cause. Whence, Aristotle himself uses this argument against the Platonists, namely, that if animal were one thing and biped another thing in separate principles, then there would not be 'one two-footed animal' without qualification.[181]

If, therefore, among immaterial substances, that which is the 'being' were different from the 'living' and from the 'being intelligent' in such a way that 'living' would come to an existing being or 'being intelligent' would come to a living being as an accident to a subject or form to matter, then what is said would be correct. For we see that something is the cause of the accident which is not the cause of the subject, and something is the cause of the substantial form that is not the cause of matter. But in immaterial substances, their 'being' itself is their 'living,' and their 'living' is not other than their 'being intelligent.' Therefore, they are living and understanding from the same principle that they are beings.

Therefore, if all immaterial substances have their being immediately from God, then they have their life and intelligence immediately from him. And if anything comes to them over and above their essence (for example, intelligible species or the like), in this respect, the position of the Platonists can hold, namely, that such qualities among lower immaterial substances may have been derived according to a certain order from higher ones.

CHAPTER 12

Against Origen, who posited that all spiritual substances are created equal

Sicut autem praedictae positiones immaterialium substantiarum ordinem considerantes non immediate sed ordine quodam earum processum a primo principio tradiderunt, ita aliqui e converso volentes salvare immediatum earum processum a primo principio totaliter ab eis naturae ordinem sustulerunt; cuius positionis auctor invenitur Origenes fuisse.

Consideravit enim quod ab uno iusto auctore res diversae et inaequales non possent procedere nisi aliqua diversitate praecedente; nulla autem diversitas praecedere potuit primam productionem rerum a Deo quae nihil praesupponit: unde ponebat omnes res a Deo primo productas esse aequales. Unde quia corpora incorporalibus substantiis aequari non possunt, posuit in prima rerum productione corpora non fuisse; sed postmodum rebus a Deo productis diversitas intervenit ex diversitate

Just as the aforementioned positions,[182] considering the order of immaterial substances, taught that they proceeded from the first principle not immediately but according to a certain order, so, contrarily, some thinkers completely took away an order of nature among them, wishing to save their immediate procession from the first principle. The author of this position is recognized to have been Origen.[183]

For it was his opinion that diverse and unequal things could not proceed from an author who is one and just unless some diversity were presupposed. But no diversity could precede the first production of things by God, which presupposes nothing at all. Whence he posits that all the things which were first produced by God were equal. Hence, because bodies cannot be made equal to non-bodily substances, he posited that there were no bodies in the first production of things. Afterwards, when the things had

---

181. Aristotle, *Metaphysics*, VI, 12, 15 (1037b 21–24; 1040a 8–29).
182. Cf. above, cap. IX.
183. Origen, *Peri Archon*, I, c. 8 (PG 11, 177A-B).

motuum voluntatis immaterialium substantiarum quae ex sua natura habent arbitrii libertatem.

Quaedam igitur earum in suum principium ordinato motu voluntatis conversae in melius profecerunt, et hoc diversimode secundum voluntarii motus diversitatem, unde et inter eas quaedam sunt aliis superiores effectae; aliae vero inordinato motu voluntatis a suo principio sunt aversae, et haec in deterius defecerunt quaedam plus quaedam minus: ita ut haec fuerit corporum producendorum occasio ut eis immateriales substantiae ab ordine boni aversae alligarentur, quasi usque ad inferiorem naturam prolapsae. Unde et totam diversitatem corporum dicebat procedere ex diversitate inordinationis voluntarii motus immaterialis substantiae, ut quae minus a Deo aversae fuerant nobilioribus corporibus alligarentur, quae autem magis ignobilioribus.

Huius autem positionis ratio vana est et ipsa positio impossibilis; cuius quidem impossibilitatis ratio accipi potest ex his quae supra iam diximus. Dictum enim est supra spirituales substantias immateriales esse; si igitur in eis sit aliqua diversitas, oportet quod hoc sit secundum formalem differentiam. In his autem quae formali differentia differunt aequalitas inveniri non potest, oportet enim omnem formalem differentiam ad primam oppositionem reduci quae est privationis ad formam; unde omnium formaliter differentium natura unius imperfecta existens respectu alterius se habet ad ipsam habitudine privationis ad formam. Hoc autem in diversitate specierum nobis notarum apparet. Sic enim specierum differentiam in animalibus et plantis et metallis et elementis invenimus secundum ordinem naturae procedere, ut paulatim ab imperfectiori ad perfectissimum natura consurgat; quod etiam apparet in speciebus colorum et saporum et aliarum sensibilium qualitatum. In his vero quae materialiter differunt eamdem formam habentibus, nihil prohibet aequalitatem inveniri; possunt enim subiecta diversa eamdem formam participare aut secundum aequalitatem aut secundum excessum et defectum. Sic igitur possibile esset spirituales substantias omnes aequales esse si solum secundum materiam differrent eamdem formam specie habentes: et forte tales eas esse Origenes opinabatur, non multum discernens naturas spirituales et corporales; quia vero spirituales substantiae immateriales sunt, necesse est in eis ordinem naturae esse.

been produced by God, a diversity entered creation as a result of the diversity in the motions of the will of the non-bodily substances which, of their nature, have freedom of choice.

According to this view, some of them, turning to their principle[184] by an orderly motion of their will, advanced in goodness, and this diversely, according to the diversity of their voluntary motion. Hence some among them were made superior to others. Some others, however, were turned away from their principle by a disorderly motion of the will and these deteriorated in goodness, some more and some less; so that this was the occasion for the production of bodies, namely, that non-bodily substances, having turned away from the order of the good, might be bound to them as having fallen down to the level of a lower nature. Hence Origen kept saying that the whole diversity of bodies was based on the diversity in the disorderliness of the voluntary motion of non-bodily substance, so that those that had turned in a lesser way from God were bound to nobler bodies, and those that were turned away more were bound to less noble bodies.

The principle of this position is groundless and the position itself is impossible. The ground of this impossibility can be gathered from what we have already said. For we said above that spiritual substances are immaterial.[185] If, therefore, there is any diversity in them, this must be according to a formal difference. Now, no equality can be found among those beings which differ by a formal difference, for every formal difference must be reduced to the first opposition which is the opposition of privation to form.[186] Therefore, among all beings that differ formally, the nature of one that is imperfect with respect to another is related to that other in the disposition of privation to form. And this is apparent to us in the diversity of the species known to us. Thus among animals and plants and metals and elements, we find that a difference of species proceeds according to the order of nature so that, little by little, nature rises from the lower to the most perfect. This is likewise apparent in the species of colors and flavors and other sensible qualities. But in things which differ materially, nothing prevents things that have the same form from being equal. For diverse subjects can participate in the same form either equally or by excess and defect. Consequently, it would be possible for all spiritual substances to be equal, if, having specifically the same form, they differed only in matter. And perhaps this is what Origen thought them to be by not distinguishing noticeably between spiritual and corporeal natures. But because spiritual substances are immaterial, there must be an order of nature among them.

---

184. I.e., originating cause. Cf. St. Thomas, *In Evangel. S. Joannis*, I, (Vivès XX, 679–680).
185. Cf. above, Cap. VII, VIII.
186. St. Thomas, *Expositio super librum Boethii de Trinitate*, q. 4, a. 2, ed. B. Decker, 137–145.

Adhuc, secundum hanc positionem necesse est spirituales substantias aut imperfectas aut superfluas esse. Non enim inveniuntur multa aequalia in uno gradu naturae nisi propter imperfectionem cuiuslibet eorum: vel propter permanendi necessitatem, ut quae eadem numero permanere non possunt multiplicata permaneant, sicut inveniuntur in corruptibilibus rebus multa individua et aequalia secundum naturam speciei; aut propter necessitatem alicuius operationis ad quam virtus unius non sufficit, sed oportet aggregari virtutem multorum quasi ad unam perfectam virtutem constituendam, ut patet in multitudine bellatorum et in multitudine trahentium navim. Illa vero quorum est virtus perfecta et permanentia in ordine suae naturae, non multiplicantur secundum numerum in aequalitate eiusdem speciei: est enim unus sol tantum qui sufficit ad semper permanendum et ad omnes effectus producendos qui sibi conveniunt secundum gradum suae naturae; et idem apparet in ceteris caelestibus corporibus. Substantiae autem spirituales sunt multo perfectiores corporibus etiam caelestibus; non igitur in eis inveniuntur multae in eodem gradu naturae, una enim sufficiente aliae superfluerent.

Item, praedicta positio universitati rerum productarum a Deo subtrahit boni perfectionem. Uniuscuiusque enim effectus perfectio in hoc consistit quod suae causae assimiletur; quod enim secundum naturam generatur tunc perfectum est quando pertingit ad similitudinem generantis, artificialia etiam per hoc perfecta redduntur quod artis formam consequuntur. In primo autem principio non solum consideratur quod ipsum est bonum et ens et unum, sed quod hoc eminentius prae ceteris habet et alia ad sui bonitatem participandam adducit; requirit igitur assimilatio perfecta universitatis a Deo productae ut non solum unumquodque sit bonum et ens, sed quod unum supereminem alteri et unum moveat alterum ad suum finem: unde et bonum universi est bonum ordinis sicut bonum exercitus. Hoc igitur bonum universitati rerum subtraxit praedicta positio omnimodam aequalitatem in rerum productione constituens.

Amplius, inconveniens est id quod est optimum in universo attribuere casui, nam id quod est optimum maxime habet rationem finis intenti; optimum autem in rerum universitate est bonum ordinis, hoc enim est bonum commune, cetera vero sunt singularia bona. Hunc autem ordinem qui in rebus nunc invenitur praedicta positio attribuit casui, secundum scilicet quod accidit unam spiritualium substantiarum sic moveri secundum

Further, according to this position, it is necessary that spiritual substances be either imperfect or superfluous. For we do not find a multitude of beings on the same grade of nature except through some imperfection of any one of them or because of the necessity of continuing in existence, so that those things that cannot endure in numerical sameness might endure through multiplication; just as among corruptible things, we find many individuals equal according to the nature of the species; or through the necessity of some operation for which the power of one is not sufficient but the power of many must be joined together as constituting one complete power, as is evident in a number of warriors and in a multitude of persons pulling a boat. But those things whose power is complete and which are enduring in the order of their nature are not multiplied numerically in the equality of the same species. For there is only one sun which suffices for permanent endurance and to produce all the effects which belong to it according to the grade of its nature; the same is clear in the case of the other heavenly bodies. But spiritual substances are much more perfect than even the heavenly bodies. Therefore, there is not among them a multitude in the same grade of nature, for, since one of them is sufficient, others would be superfluous.

Again, the aforementioned position takes away the perfection of goodness from the universe of things produced by God. For the perfection of each and every effect consists in that it is likened to its cause,[187] for that which, according to its nature, is something generated is then perfect when it reaches the likeness of its generator. Artifacts are likewise made perfect when they achieve the form of the art. But in the case of the first principle, we recognize not only that he is good, and being, and one, but also that he possesses this perfection above and beyond all other things and that he leads other things to a participation in his own goodness. Therefore, the perfect assimilation of the universe produced by God requires not only that each thing be good and be a being, but also that one thing should excel another and that one thing should move the other to its end. Hence the good of the universe, like the good of an army, is the good of an order.[188] Accordingly, the aforementioned position, by establishing a complete equality in the production of things, takes away the good of order from the universe of things.[189]

Moreover, it is unfitting to attribute that which is best in the universe to chance. For that which is best has most especially the nature of the intended end. Now the good of order is that which is best in the universe of things, for this is the common good; while other goods are singular goods. This order, which is now found in things, the aforementioned position attributes to chance: that is, according as it happens that one spiritual substance is moved in a certain

---

187. Cf. St. Thomas, SCG, I, 29 (OTCF, 1, 139).
188. Cf. *Ibid.*, I, 1 (p. 59).
189. All this concerning order is what Origen is discussing in *Peri Archon*, I, c. 8 (PG 11, 177A- B).

voluntatem et aliam aliter; est igitur praedicta positio omnino abiicienda.

Ratio etiam positionis manifeste continet vanitatem: non enim est eadem ratio iustitiae in constitutione alicuius totius ex pluribus partibus et diversis, et in distributione alicuius communis per singula. Qui enim aliquod totum constituere intendit ad hoc respicit quod totum perfectum sit, et secundum hoc diversas partes et inaequales ad eius compositionem conducit: si enim omnes essent aequales iam non esset totum perfectum. Quod patet tam in toto naturali quam in toto civili: non enim esset corpus hominis perfectum nisi membra diversa et inaequalis dignitatis haberet, neque esset civitas perfecta nisi inaequales conditiones et officia diversa in civitate existerent. In distributione vero attenditur bonum uniuscuiusque, et ideo diversis diversa assignantur secundum diversitatem in eis praecedentem, secundum quam competunt eis diversa. In prima igitur rerum productione Deus diversa et inaequalia in esse produxit, attendens ad id quod requirit perfectio universi, non ad aliquam diversitatem in rebus praeexistentem; sed hoc attendit in remuneratione finalis iudicii, unicuique retribuens secundum quod meruit.

way according to its will, and another spiritual substance in another way. Therefore, the above opinion must be completely rejected.

Furthermore, the basis of this position is clearly absurd. For the same notion of justice is not involved in the constitution of some whole out of several and diverse parts and in the distribution of some thing common among singulars. For he who intends to make a given whole aims that the whole be perfect, and accordingly brings together diverse and unequal parts to its constitution. For if all the parts were equal, then the whole would not be perfect, which is evident both in a physical whole and in a civil whole.[190] For the body of man would not be perfect unless it had members that are diverse and of unequal importance, nor would the body politic be perfect unless there were found in it unequal conditions and diverse offices. But in the distribution of something common, the concern is with the good of each singular; and therefore diverse things are assigned to diverse beings according to a preexisting diversity in them, in accordance with which diverse things befit them. Therefore, in the first production of things God brought forth diverse and unequal things in being, looking to that which the perfection of the universe requires and not to any preexisting diversity in things. But he will look to this point in the rewarding of final judgment by giving to each according to his merit.

CHAPTER 13

On the error of some concerning the knowledge and providence of spiritual substances

Non solum autem in substantia et ordine spiritualium substantiarum aliqui erraverunt ad modum inferiorum rerum de eis aestimantes, sed hoc etiam quibusdam accidit circa cognitionem et providentiam earumdem; dum enim spiritualium substantiarum intelligentiam et operationem ad modum humanae intelligentiae et operationis diiudicare voluerunt, posuerunt Deum et alias substantias immateriales singularium cognitionem non habere nec inferiorum et praecipue humanorum actuum providentiam gerere. Quia enim in nobis singularium quidem sensus est, intellectus autem propter sui immaterialitatem non singularium sed universalium est, consequens esse aestimaverunt ut intellectus substantiarum spiritualium, qui sunt multo simpliciores nostro intellectu, singularia cognoscere non possint; non est autem in substantiis spiritualibus, cum

But not only did some thinkers err concerning the substance and the order of spiritual substances, judging of them after the manner of lower beings, but some of them also fell into error concerning the knowledge and the providence of these substances. For in wanting to judge of the intelligence and the operation of spiritual substances after the manner of human intelligence and operation, they held that God and the other immaterial substances did not have a knowledge of singulars, nor did they exercise a providence over any lower beings and especially human acts.[191] For, since in our own case it is the sense that deals with singulars, but the intellect deals not with singulars but with universals (because of its immateriality), as a consequence they thought that the intellects of spiritual substances, which are much more simple than our intellect, could not grasp singulars. Now, since they are completely incorporeal, there is

---

190. Aristotle, *Politics*, II, 2 (1061a 20–b 15).

191. Very likely certain Averroists at Paris whose doctrines are given in the Condemnations of 1270 and 1277. St. Thomas follows the same order and cites almost verbatim Props. 10, 11, 12 of the Condemnation of 1270. Cf. above, Introduction; also *Chartularium*, I, 487; Mandonnet, *op. cit.*, I, III; 11, 175. For Averroist doctrine of angels, cf. A. Vacant, *Angélologie parmi les averroistes latins* in *Dictionnaire de théologie catholique*, Vol. I, coll. 1260–1264, esp. col. 1262.

sint omnino incorporeae, aliquis sensus (cuius operatio sine corpore esse non potest): unde videtur eis impossibile quod spirituales substantiae aliquam de singularibus notitiam habeant.

Adhuc, in maiorem insaniam procedentes, aestimant Deum nihil nisi se ipsum intellectu cognoscere. Sic enim videmus in nobis quod intellectum est intelligentis perfectio et actus, per hoc enim intellectus fit actu intelligens; nihil autem aliud a Deo est eo nobilius quod possit esse eius perfectio: unde ex necessitate consequi arbitrantur quod nihil aliud sit a Deo intellectum nisi eius essentia.

Amplius, ea quae ex alicuius providentia procedunt casualia esse non possunt; si igitur omnia quae in hoc mundo accidunt ex divina providentia procedunt, nihil in rebus erit fortuitum et casuale.

Item, utuntur ratione Aristotelis in VI *Metaphysicae* probantis quod, si omnem effectum ponamus habere causam per se et quod qualibet causa posita necesse sit effectum poni, sequetur quod omnia futura ex necessitate contingent, quia erit reducere quemlibet futurum effectum in aliquam praecedentem causam et illam in aliam et sic inde, quousque veniatur ad causam quae iam est vel quae fuit; haec autem iam posita est ex quo in praesenti est vel in praeterito fuit: si igitur posita causa necesse est effectum poni, ex necessitate consequuntur omnes futuri effectus. Sed si omnia quae in mundo sunt divinae providentiae subduntur, omnium causa non solum est praesens vel praeterita sed ab aeterno praecessit: non est autem possibile quin ea posita effectus sequantur, non enim cassatur divina providentia neque per ignorantiam neque per impotentiam providentis in quem nullus cadit defectus: sequetur igitur omnia ex necessitate procedere.

Adhuc, si Deus est ipsum bonum, oportet quod ordo providentiae eius secundum rationem boni procedat: aut igitur inefficax est divina providentia, aut universaliter malum a rebus excludit. Videmus autem in singularibus generabilium et corruptibilium multa mala contingere, et praecipue inter homines in quibus, praeter naturalia mala quae sunt naturales defectus et corruptiones communes eis et aliis corruptibilibus rebus, superadduntur insuper mala vitiorum et inordinatorum eventuum, puta cum iustis multotiens mala eveniunt, iniustis autem bona. Propter hoc igitur aliqui aestimaverunt divinam providentiam se extendere usque ad substantias imma-

in spiritual substances no sense, whose operation cannot take place without a body. Accordingly, they thought that it was impossible for spiritual substances to have any knowledge of singulars.[192]

Further, proceeding to a greater folly, they thought that God knew only himself by his intellect. For thus in our own case, we see that to understand is the perfection and the act of the one understanding, for it is thus that the intellect becomes actively understanding. Now, nothing other than God is nobler than he, so that it can be his perfection. Therefore, they hold that it necessarily follows that God understands only his own essence.[193]

Further, that which proceeds from the providence of any one cannot be by chance. If, therefore, all things that happen in this world proceed from the divine providence, there is no fortune or chance in things.[194]

They likewise use an argument of Aristotle in *Metaphysics* VI,[195] where he proves that if we posit that every effect has an essential cause and that, given any cause whatsoever, its effect must necessarily be posited, it will follow that all futures will happen of necessity, since any future effect will be reduced to some preceding cause, and that to another and so on, until we come to the cause which already is or already was. But this cause is now posited because it is in the present or it was in the past. If, therefore, to posit the cause means necessarily for the effect to be posited, then all future effects will follow of necessity. But if all things that are in the world are subject to the divine providence, the cause of all things is not only present or past but has preceded them from eternity. But it is not possible that when this cause is posited, its effect will not follow. For the divine providence, on which no defect falls, is not thwarted either through ignorance or through the impotence of the one providing. Therefore, it follows that all things come about of necessity.[196]

Further, if God is the good itself, the order of his providence must necessarily proceed according to the nature of the good. Therefore, either divine providence is inefficacious or it completely excludes evil from things. We see, however, many evils occurring among singular, generable, and corruptible things, and especially among men in whom, in addition to physical evils (which are natural defects) and corruptions common to them and to other corruptible things, there are added also the evils of vices and of disorderly happenings, as when numerous evils befall the just, and good things happen to the unjust. On this account, therefore, some people have thought that divine providence

---

192. Cf. *Chartularium*, I, Props. 76, 85, (pp. 547–548); Mandonnet, *op. cit.*, II, 180.

193. Cf. *Chartularium*, I, Prop. 3, 544; Mandonnet, *op. cit.*, II, 177.

194. Cf. *Chartularium*, I, Props. 21, 42, 545–546; Mandonnet, *op. cit.*, II, 177–178,183.

195. Aristotle, *Metaphysics*, V, 3 (1027a 29–1027b 16); cf. Siger of Brabant, De Necessitate et contingentia causarum in Mandonnet, *op. cit.*, Part II, 111–114; A. Maurer, Siger of Brabant's *De Necessitate et Contingentia Causarum* and Ms. Peterhouse 152 in *Mediaeval Studies* 14 (1952): 48–60; F. Van Steenberghen, *Siger de Brabant d'après ses oeuvres inédites*, Vol. II, 606–607.

196. Cf. *Chartularium*, Prop. 21, 545; Mandonnet, *op. cit.*, II, 183.

teriales et incorruptibilia et caelestia corpora, in quibus nullum malum videbant; inferiora vero providentiae subdi dicebant vel divinae vel aliarum spiritualium substantiarum quantum ad genera, non autem quantum ad individua.

extends only to immaterial substances and the incorruptible and heavenly bodies, in which they saw no evil. But the lower beings, according to them, were subject to the providence of God in genus, but not individually, nor to other spiritual substances.

CHAPTER 14

In which it is shown that God has knowledge of everything

Et quia ea quae praedicta sunt communi opinioni hominum repugnant, non solum plurium sed etiam sapientum, certis rationibus ostendendum est praedicta veritatem non habere et rationes praemissas non hoc concludere quod intendunt. Et primo quidem quantum ad divinam cognitionem, secundo quantum ad eius providentiam.

Oportet autem ex necessitate hoc firmiter tenere quod Deus omnium cognoscibilium quocumque tempore vel a quocumque cognoscente certissimam cognitionem habeat. Ut enim supra habitum est, Dei substantia est ipsum eius esse; non est autem in eo aliud esse atque aliud intelligere, sic enim non esset perfecte simplex, unde nec simpliciter primum: oportet igitur quod sicut eius substantia est suum esse, ita etiam eius substantia sit suum intelligere sive intelligentia, ut etiam Philosophus concludit in XII *Metaphysicae*. Sicut igitur eius substantia est ipsum esse separatum, ita etiam eius substantia est ipsum intelligere separatum. Si autem sit aliqua forma separata, nihil quod ad rationem illius formae pertinere posset ei deesset, sicut si albedo separata esset nihil quod sub ratione albedinis comprehenditur ei deficeret; cuiuslibet autem cognoscibilis cognitio sub universali ratione cognitionis continetur: oportet igitur Deo nullius cognoscibilis cognitionem deesse. Cognitio autem cuiuslibet cognoscentis est secundum modum substantiae eius, sicut et quaelibet operatio est secundum modum operantis; multo igitur magis divina cognitio quae est eius substantia est secundum modum esse ipsius: esse autem eius est unum simplex fixum et aeternum, sequitur ergo quod Deus uno simplici intuitu aeternam et fixam de omnibus notitiam habeat.

Adhuc, id quod abstractum est non potest esse nisi unum in unaquaque natura. Si enim albedo posset esse abstracta, sola una esset albedo quae abstracta esset, omnes autem albedines aliae essent participatae; sic igitur sicut sola Dei substantia est ipsum esse ab-

And because the things which have been said above are opposed to the common opinion of mankind and this not only of men in general but also of the wise, we must show by certain arguments that the above positions have no truth and that the above arguments do not establish the conclusion they intend. This applies first to the knowledge of God, and second to his providence.

Now we must, of necessity, hold firmly this point: namely, that God has a most certain knowledge of all things that are knowable at any time or by any knower whatsoever. For, as we have maintained above,[197] the substance of God is his very act of being. Furthermore, his being and his understanding are one and the same; otherwise, he would not be a perfectly simple being nor the absolutely prime being. Therefore, just as his substance is his act of being, so is his substance his understanding or his intelligence, as likewise the Philosopher concludes in *Metaphysics* XII.[198] Therefore, just as his substance is his separate act of being, so likewise is his substance his separate understanding. But if there should be some separate form, nothing that could belong to the nature of that form would be lacking to it, just as if there were a separate whiteness, nothing understood under the nature of whiteness would be lacking to it. Now, the knowledge of any knowable is included under the universal nature of knowing. Therefore, God cannot be lacking in the knowledge of any knowable. But the knowledge of any knower is according to the mode of his substance, just as any operation is according to the mode of the one operating. All the more so, divine knowledge (which is God's substance) is according to the mode of his being. Now his being is one, simple, abiding, and eternal. It follows, therefore, that God has an eternal and fixed knowledge of all things by one simple glance.

Further, that which is abstract[199] can be only one in each nature. For if whiteness could exist as abstracted, the only whiteness would be the one that is separate and all the others would be white by participation. Now, just as the sole substance of God is his separate existence, so his sub-

---

197. Cf. above, Cap. VIII; Cap. IX; Cap. X.

198. Aristotle, *Metaphysics*, XI, 7 (1072b 26–30).

199. "Abstract" as "separate" or "separate from matter."

stractum, ita sola eius substantia est ipsum intelligere omnino abstractum: omnia igitur alia sicut habent esse participatum, ita participative intelligunt sive qualitercumque cognoscunt. Omne autem quod convenit alicui per participationem perfectius invenitur in eo quod per essentiam est, a quo in alia derivatur: oportet igitur Deum omnium quae a quibuscumque cognoscuntur cognitionem habere; unde et Philosophus pro inconvenienti habet ut aliquid a nobis cognitum sit Deo ignotum, ut patet in I *de Anima* et in III *Metaphysicae*.

Item, si Deus se ipsum cognoscit oportet quod perfecte se cognoscat, praesertim quia si eius intelligere est eius substantia, necesse est ut quidquid est in eius substantia ipsius cognitione comprehendatur. Cuiuscumque autem rei substantia perfecte cognoscitur, necesse est ut etiam virtus perfecte cognoscatur; cognoscit igitur Deus perfecte suam virtutem: oportet igitur quod cognoscat omnia ad quae sua virtus extenditur. Sua autem virtus extenditur ad omne quod est quocumque modo in rebus vel esse potest, sive sit proprium sive commune, sive immediate ab eo productum sive mediantibus causis secundis, quia causae primae virtus magis imprimit in effectum quam virtus causae secundae; oportet igitur Deum cognitionem habere de omnibus quae sunt quocumque modo in rebus.

Amplius, sicut causa est quodam modo in effectu per sui similitudinem participatam, ita omnis effectus est in sua causa excellentiori modo secundum virtutem ipsius; in causa igitur prima omnium quae Deus est oportet omnia eminentius existere quam etiam in se ipsis. Quod autem est in aliquo oportet quod in eo sit secundum modum substantiae eius; substantia autem Dei est ipsum eius intelligere: oportet igitur omnia quae quocumque modo sunt in rebus, in Deo intelligibiliter existere secundum eminentiam substantiae eius. Necesse est igitur Deum perfectissime omnia cognoscere.

Sed quia occasionem errandi sumpserunt ex demonstratione Aristotelis in XII Metaphysicae, oportet ostendere quod Philosophi intentionem non assequuntur. Sciendum est igitur quod secundum Platonicos ordo intelligibilium praeexistebat ordini intellectuum, ita quod intellectus participando intelligibile fieret intelligens actu, ut supra iam diximus; et per hunc modum etiam Aristoteles ostendit prius in eodem libro quod supra intellectum et appetitum intellectualem quo caelum movetur est quoddam intelligibile participatum ab ipso intellectu caelum movente, sic dicens *Susceptivum intel-*

stance is his absolutely separate understanding. All other things consequently understand or know by participation, just as they exist by participation. But that which befits a being by participation is found more perfectly in that in which it is essentially and from which it is derived to others.[200] Therefore, God must have a knowledge of all things which are known by any being whatsoever. And therefore the Philosopher considers it unfitting that something which is known by us should be unknown to God, as is clear in *On the Soul* I[201] and in *Metaphysics* III.[202]

Likewise, if God knows himself, he must know himself perfectly, for if his understanding is his substance, then whatever is in his substance must be included in his knowledge. But when the substance of anything is known perfectly, its power must likewise be known perfectly. God therefore knows his power perfectly, and consequently he must know all the things to which his power extends. But his power extends to everything that in any way is in reality or can be—whether it be proper or common, immediately produced by him or through the mediation of second causes—since the power of the first cause acts on the effect more than does the power of a second cause.[203] Therefore, God must have a knowledge of all things that in any way are found in things.

Furthermore, just as the cause is in a manner present in its effect through a participated likeness of itself, so every effect is in its cause in a more excellent way according to the power of the cause. Therefore, all things must exist more eminently in their first cause, which is God, than in themselves. But whatever is in a thing must be in it according to the substance of that thing. But the substance of God is his understanding. Therefore, however things may be in reality, they must exist in God in an intelligible way according to the eminence of his substance. Therefore, God must know all things most perfectly.

But because they[204] have found an occasion to err in the demonstration of Aristotle in *Metaphysics* XII,[205] we must show that they do not attain to the Philosopher's intention. Therefore, it must be known that, according to the Platonists, an order of intelligibles existed prior to the order of intellect, so that an intellect became actually understanding by participating in an intelligible, as we have already said.[206] And in the same way Aristotle showed earlier in the same book that above the intellect and the intellectual appetite by which the heavens are moved, there is a certain intelligible, participated by the intellect moving the heavens. His

---

200. Cf. above, Cap. VI; Cap. VIII.
201. Aristotle, *De Anima*, 1, 5 (410b 4–7); St. Thomas, In *De Anima*, I, lect. 12, ed. Pirotta, no. 186 (AACTA, 146–147).
202. Aristotle, *Metaphysics*, II, 4 (1000b 4–6).
203. St. Thomas, *In Librum de Causis*, Prop. 1, ed. H. d. Saffrey, (pp. 4–10).
204. I.e., the Averroists.
205. Aristotle, *Metaphysics*, XI, 7 (1072b 22–23); 9 (1074b 15–1075a 10).
206. Cf. above, Cap. I.

ligibilis et substantiae intellectus agit autem habens, id est actu intelligit secundum quod habet iam participatum suum intelligibile superius: et ex hoc ulterius concludit quod illud intelligibile sit magis divinum.

Et interpositis quibusdam, movet quaestionem de intellectu huius divinissimi cuius participatione motor caeli est intelligens actu. Quia si istud divinissimum non intelligit, non erit insigne aliquid sed se habebit ut dormiens.

Si autem intelligit, erit primo dubitatio quomodo intelligat: quia si intelligit participando aliquid aliud superius sicut per participationem eius inferior intellectus intelligit, sequetur quod erit aliquid aliud principale respectu ipsius; quia ex quo per participationem alterius intelligit non est intelligens per suam essentiam ita quod sua substantia sit suum intelligere, sed magis sua substantia erit in potentia respectu intelligentiae — sic enim se habet substantia cuiuslibet participantis ad id quod per participationem obtinet. Et ita ulterius sequetur quod illud divinissimum *non erit optima substantia*: quod est contra positum.

Movet etiam consequenter aliam dubitationem de eo quod intelligitur ab optima substantia: sive enim detur quod substantia primi sit ipsum eius intelligere, sive substantia eius sit intellectus qui comparatur ad intelligere ut potentia, dubium erit quid sit illud quod intelligit prima substantia; aut enim intelligit se ipsam, aut aliquid diversum a se. Et si detur quod aliquid diversum a se intelligat, erit ulterius dubitabile utrum semper idem intelligat aut quandoque unum quandoque aliud.

Et quia posset aliquis dicere quod nihil differt quid intelligat, movet super hoc dubitationem utrum aliquid differat vel nihil in quocumque intelligente intelligere aliquid bonum, vel intelligere quodcumque contingens; et respondet satisfaciens huic dubitationi quod *de quibusdam absurdum est intelligi*. Cuius sensus potest esse duplex: vel quia absurdum est dubitare de quibusdam utrum ea intelligere sit ita bonum sicut quaedam alia vel multo minora vel multo meliora; alius autem sensus est quia videmus quod intelligere quaedam in actu apud nos videtur esse absurdum, unde et alia littera habet *aut inconveniens meditari de quibusdam*.

words are: *The receiver of the intelligible substance and of the intellect acts as possessing them*;[207] as if to say it actually understands as it already possesses its participated intelligible from above. And from this, he further concludes that this intelligible is more divine.

And after he has interposed certain matters, he raises the question concerning the intellect of this most divine being by participation in which the mover of the heavens is actually understanding.[208] For if that most divine being does not understand, he will not be something outstanding but will act as one who is asleep.

But if he understands, the first query will then be how he understands. For if he understands by participating in something else above him—just as a lower intellect understands by participating in him—it will follow that there will be something else which will be a principle with respect to it, because by the fact that he understands by participating in another, he is not understanding through his own essence; so that his substance is not his understanding, but rather, his substance will be in potency in relation to understanding.[209] For this is the condition of the substance of any participating being in relation to what it obtains by participation. And thus, it further follows that that divine being will *not be the most excellent substance*—which is contrary to the position.

As a result, he advances another query concerning that which is understood about the noblest substance. Whether it be granted that the first substance is its very understanding or whether its substance is an intellect that is compared as potency to understanding, there will be a question as to what it is that the first substance understands.[210] For it understands either itself or something other than itself. If it be granted that it understands something other than itself, there will arise the further query whether it always understands the same thing, or at one time one thing and at another time another.

And because some one could say that it makes no difference what it understands, Aristotle raises on this point the query whether it makes some difference or none in any being to understand something good or to understand something contingent.[211] And he answers in reply to this query that *to know certain things is trivial*. The meaning of this statement can be twofold: either that it is trivial to know concerning certain things whether to understand them is as good as to understand certain other things, whether much lesser or much greater. The other meaning is that in our own case it seems trivial for us to have an actual understanding of certain things. Whence another reading has *or it is unfitting to meditate about certain things*.

207. Aristotle, *Metaphysics*, X1, 7 (1072b 22).
208. S. Aristotle, *Metaphysics*, XI, 9 (1074b 1S).
209. *Ibid.* (1074b 18).
210. Aristotle, *Metaphysics*, XI, 9 (1074b 20).
211. *Ibid.*, (1074b 25).

Habito igitur quod melius est intelligere aliquod bonum quam intelligere minus bonum, concludit quod id quod intelligit prima substantia est optimum, et quod intelligendo non mutatur ut nunc intelligat unum nunc aliud; et hoc probat dupliciter. Primo quidem quia, cum intelligat id quod est nobilissimum, ut dictum est, sequeretur si mutaretur ad aliud intelligibile quod mutatio esset in aliquid indignius; secundo quia talis vicissitudo intelligibilium iam est motus quidam, primum autem oportet esse omnibus modis immobile.

Deinde redit ad determinandum primam quaestionem, an scilicet sua substantia sit suum intelligere: quod sic dupliciter probat. Primo quidem quia si sua substantia non est suum intelligere sed est sicut potentia ad hoc, probabile est quod continue intelligere esset ei laboriosum. Hoc autem dicit esse probabile ex eo quod in nobis sic accidit; sed quia in nobis potest accidere non ex natura intellectus sed ex viribus inferioribus quibus utimur in intelligendo, ideo non dixit hoc esse necessarium in omnibus. Si tamen hoc probabile accipiatur ut verum, sequetur quod continue intelligere sit laboriosum primae substantiae, et ita non poterit semper intelligere: quod est contra praemissa.

Secundo probat per hoc quod, si substantia sua non esset suum intelligere, sequetur quod *aliquid aliud erit dignius quam intellectus, scilicet* res intellecta per cuius participationem fit intelligens. Quandocumque enim substantia intelligentis non est suum intelligere, oportet quod substantia intellectus nobilitetur et perficiatur per hoc quod actu intelligit aliquod intelligibile, etiam si illud sit indignissimum; omne autem quo aliquid fit actu nobilius est: unde sequetur quod aliquod indignissimum intelligibile sit dignius quam intellectus qui non est intelligens per suam essentiam. *Quare fugiendum est hoc,* scilicet quod aliquid intellectum aliud ab ipso sit perfectio intellectus divini, quia ad perfectionem ipsius intelligere pertinet nobilitas ipsius intellecti: quod patet ex hoc quod in nobis, in quibus differt substantia cognoscentis a cognitione actuali, dignius est quaedam non videre quam videre. Et ita si sit sic in Deo quod suus intellectus non sit sua intelligentia et aliquid aliud intelligat, non erit sua intelligentia optima quia non

Having determined that it is better to understand something good than to understand something less good, he concludes that what the first substance understands is the best; and that in understanding, it is not changed so that it understands now one thing and now another. He proves this in a twofold way. First, since it understands that which is noblest, it would follow, as has been said,[212] that if it were changed to some intelligible object, then there would be change to something less noble. Second, because such a change of intelligibles is already a certain motion.[213] The first being, however, must be in every way immobile.

He then returns to the resolution of the first question: namely, whether God's substance is his understanding. This he proves in a twofold way as follows. First, because if his substance is not his understanding but is as potency to it, it is probable that to understand without stop would be laborious to him.[214] He says that it is probable because that is how it happens in our own case. But since this can happen in our case not because of the nature of the intellect but because of the lower powers that we use in understanding, he therefore did not say that this is necessary in all cases. If, however, this probability is accepted as true, it will follow that it might be laborious for the first substance to understand without stop and therefore it will not be able to understand everlastingly, which is contrary to what has been accepted.

Second, he proves it by the fact that if his substance were not his understanding, it would follow that *something else would be nobler than his intellect, namely,* the known thing, through participation in which it becomes understanding.[215] For whenever a substance is not its own understanding, the substance of the intellect must be ennobled and perfected by the fact that it understands some intelligible actually, even if this object be a most humble one. For every thing by which some thing becomes actual is more noble than it. Hence it would follow that some most humble intelligible is nobler than the intellect which is not understanding through its essence. *Hence this must be denied,* namely, that something else understood by him is the perfection of the divine intellect, because the nobility of the thing itself understood belongs to the perfection of his act of understanding. This point is manifest from the fact that in our case, among whom the substance of the knower differs from actual knowledge, it is more worthy for certain things not to be seen than to be seen. And so, if in the

---

212. Cf. above, Cap. XIII.
213. Aristotle, *Metaphysics*, XI, 9 (1074b 28–30).
214. Aristotle, *Metaphysics*, XI, 9 (1074b 28).
215. *Ibid.*, (1074b 30).

erit optimi intelligibilis; relinquitur ergo quod se ipsum intelligat, cum ipse sit nobilissimum entium.

Patet igitur praedicta verba Philosophi diligenter consideranti, quod non est intentio eius excludere a Deo simpliciter aliarum rerum cognitionem, sed quod non intelligit alia a se quasi participando ea ut per ea fiat intelligens, sicut fit in quocumque intellectu cuius substantia non est suum intelligere. Intelligit autem omnia alia a se intelligendo se ipsum, in quantum ipsius esse est universale et fontale principium omnis esse, et suum intelligere quaedam universalis radix intelligendi omnem intelligentiam comprehendens.

Inferiores vero intellectus separati quos angelos dicimus intelligunt quidem se ipsos singuli per suam essentiam: alia vero intelligunt secundum quidem platonicas positiones per participationem formarum intelligibilium separatarum quas deos vocabant, ut supra dictum est; secundum Aristotilis vero principia partim quidem per suam essentiam, partim vero per participationem ipsius primi intelligibilis quod est Deus, a quo et esse et intelligere participant.

case of God his intellect is not his understanding, and he understands something else, then his understanding will not be the best, because it will not have the best intelligible object.[216] It remains, therefore, since he is the noblest of things, that he understands himself.

It is therefore apparent to anyone who considers carefully the above words of the Philosopher that it is not his intention to exclude absolutely from God a knowledge of other things, but rather that God does not understand other things through themselves as participating in them, in order that he then may become understanding through them; as happens in the case of any intellect whose substance is not its understanding. He rather understands all things other than himself by understanding himself, inasmuch as his being is the universal and fontal source of all being, and his understanding is the universal root of understanding encompassing all understanding.[217]

The lower separate intellects, however, that we call angels, understand themselves in each case through their essence, but according to the Platonists' position, they understand other things by participating in the separate intelligible forms that they call gods, as we have said.[218] According to Aristotle's principles, they understand other things partly through their essence and partly through a participation in the first intelligible, who is God, from whom they participate in both being and understanding.

CHAPTER 15

That the care of divine providence extends to all things

Sicut autem divinam cognitionem necesse est secundum praemissa usque ad minima rerum extendere, ita necesse est divinae providentiae curam universa concludere. Invenitur enim in rebus omnibus bonum esse in ordine quodam secundum quod res sibi invicem subserviunt et ordinantur ad finem; necesse est autem sicut omne esse derivatur a primo ente quod est ipsum esse, ita omne bonum derivari a primo quod est ipsa bonitas: oportet igitur singulorum ordinem a prima et pura veritate derivari. A qua quidem aliquid derivatur secundum quod in eo est, per intelligibilem scilicet modum; in hoc autem ratio providentiae consistit quod ab aliquo intelligente statuatur ordo in rebus quae eius providentiae subsunt: necesse est igitur omnia divinae providentiae subiacere.

Furthermore, just as divine knowledge must extend to the least of things, according to what has been set down,[219] so the care of divine providence must enfold all things. For in all things the good is to be found in a certain order, according as things help one another and are ordered to an end.[220] Just as every being is derived from the first being, who is his own act of being, so it is necessary that every good be derived from the first good, who is goodness itself. Therefore, the order of individuals is derived from the first and pure truth, from which, however, something is derived according to its manner (namely, in an intelligible way). And the nature of providence consists in this, that an order be established by an understanding being in the things that are subject to its providence. Therefore, all things must be subject to the divine providence.

216. *Ibid.*, (1074b 30); cf. St. Thomas, SCG, 1, 45 (OTCF, 1, 173).
217. Cf. St. Thomas, ST, I, 14, 6, 8 (BW, 1, 143, 147).
218. Cf. above, Cap. I; Proclus, *Elem*, Prop. 117 (pp. 103–105).
219. Cf. above, Cap. XIII.
220. Aristotle, *Metaphysics*, XII 10 (1075a 11–23).

Adhuc, primum movens immobile quod Deus est omnium motionum principium est, sicut et primum ens est omnis esse principium; in causis autem per se ordinatis tanto aliquid magis est causa quanto in ordine causarum prior est, cum ipsa aliis conferat quod causae sint: Deus igitur omnium motionum vehementius causa est quam etiam singulares causae moventes. Non est autem alicuius causa Deus nisi sicut intelligens, cum sua substantia sit suum intelligere, ut per supra posita Aristotelis verba patet; unumquodque autem agit per modum suae substantiae: Deus igitur per suum intellectum omnia movet ad proprios fines. Hoc autem est providere: omnia igitur divinae providentiae subsunt.

Amplius, sic sunt res in universo dispositae sicut optimum est eas esse, eo quod omnia ex summa bonitate dependent; melius est autem aliqua esse ordinata per se quam quod per accidens ordinentur: est igitur totius universi ordo non per accidens sed per se. Hoc autem requiritur ad hoc quod aliqua per se ordinentur, quod primi intentio feratur usque ad ultimum; si enim primum intendat secundum movere et eius intentio ulterius non feratur, secundum vero moveat tertium, hoc erit praeter intentionem primi moventis: erit igitur talis ordo per accidens. Oportet igitur quod primi moventis et ordinantis intentio, scilicet Dei, non solum usque ad quaedam entium procedat sed usque ad ultima; omnia igitur eius providentiae subsunt.

Item, quod causae et effectui convenit eminentius invenitur in causa quam in effectu, a causa enim in effectum derivatur; quidquid igitur in inferioribus causis existens primae omnium causae attribuitur excellentissime convenit ei. Oportet autem aliquam providentiam Deo attribuere, alioquin universum casu ageretur; oportet igitur divinam providentiam perfectissimam esse. Sunt autem in providentia duo consideranda, scilicet dispositio et dispositorum executio, in quibus quodam modo diversa ratio perfectionis invenitur: nam in dispositione tanto perfectior est providentia quanto providens magis singula mente considerare et ordinare potest, unde et omnes operativae artes tanto perfectius habentur quanto quisque singula potest magis coniectare; circa executionem vero tanto videtur esse providentia perfectior quanto providens per plura media et instrumenta agens universalius movet. Divina igitur providentia habet dispositionem intelligibilem omnium et singulorum, exequitur vero disposita per plurimas et varias causas. Inter quas spirituales substantiae quas angelos dicimus primae causae propinquiores existentes

Further, the first unmoved mover, who is God, is the source of all motions, just as the first being is the source of all beings. In essentially ordered causes, something is more a cause by so much as it is prior in the order of causes, since it confers on others that they be causes. Therefore, according to this, God is more strongly the cause of all motions than are the individual moving causes themselves. Now God is the cause of something only as understanding, since his substance is his understanding, as is clear from the words of Aristotle mentioned above.[221] Each thing, however, acts according to the mode of its substance. Therefore, God moves all things to their proper ends through his intellect: and this is providence. Therefore, all things are subject to divine providence.

Moreover, things are arranged in the universe in the best way because all of them depend on the highest goodness. But it is better for certain things to be ordered essentially rather than accidentally. Therefore, the order of the whole universe is not accidental but essential. But in order for certain things be ordered essentially, it is required that the intention of the first cause be directed even to the last. For if the first cause intends to move the second, and its intention goes no further, if the second then moves the third, this will be outside the intention of the first mover; therefore, such an order will be accidental. Consequently, the intention of the first mover and orderer, namely God, must extend not only to certain beings but even to the very last ones. Therefore, all things are subject to his providence.

Likewise, that which befits a cause and an effect is found more eminently in the cause than in the effect, for it flows into the effect from the cause. Accordingly, anything that is found in lower causes and is attributed to the first cause of all belongs to it in a most excellent way. But some providence must be attributed to God, or otherwise the universe would be moved by chance. Therefore, divine providence must be most perfect. Two things, however, must be considered in providence. These are disposition and the execution of what has been disposed: in which, in a way, a different kind of perfection is found. For in disposition, providence is the more perfect as the one providing is more able with his mind to consider and order individual things. Accordingly, all operative arts are considered the more perfect as each one of them is more able to join together singulars. With respect to execution, however, providence seems to be the more perfect according as the one providing moves as a more universal agent through more intermediaries and instruments. Therefore, divine providence has an intelligible disposition of each and every thing, but it executes what it disposes through many and varied causes. Among these,

---

221. Cf. above, Cap. XIII.

universalius divinam providentiam exequuntur; sunt igitur angeli universales executores providentiae divinae; unde signanter 'angeli' id est nuntii nominantur, nuntiorum enim est (exequi) quae a domino disponuntur.

the spiritual substances whom we call angels, because they are closer to the first cause, carry out the divine providence in a more universal way. Accordingly, the angels are the universal executors of the divine providence; whence they are pointedly called 'angels,' that is, 'messengers', for it belongs to messengers to carry out what God has disposed.

CHAPTER 16

Resolution of the aforementioned positions

His igitur visis, facile est iam ad obiectiones supra positas respondere.

Non est enim necessarium quod prima ratio praetendebat, intellectum Dei et angelorum singularia non posse cognoscere si intellectus humanus ea cognoscere non potest. Et ut huius differentiae evidentius appareat ratio, considerandum est quod cognitionis ordo est secundum proportionem ordinis qui invenitur in rebus secundum esse ipsarum; in hoc enim perfectio et veritas cognitionis consistit quod rerum cognitarum similitudinem habeat. In rebus autem talis ordo invenitur quod superiora in entibus universalius esse et bonitatem habent, non quidem ita quod obtineant esse et bonitatem solum secundum rationem communem prout universale dicitur quod de pluribus praedicatur, sed quia quicquid in inferioribus invenitur in superioribus eminentius existit.

Et hoc ex virtute operativa quae est in rebus apparet: nam inferiora in entibus habent virtutes contractas ad determinatos effectus, superiora vero habent virtutes universaliter ad multos effectus se extendentes; et tamen virtus superior etiam in particularibus effectibus plus operatur quam virtus inferior. Et hoc maxime in corporibus apparet; nam in inferioribus corporibus ignis quidem per suum calorem calefacit, et semen huius animalis vel plantae ita determinate producit individuum huius speciei quod non producit alterius speciei individuum. Ex quo patet quod virtus universalis in superioribus entibus dicitur non ex hoc quod non se extendat ad particulares effectus, sed quia se extendit ad plures effectus quam virtus inferior et in singulis eorum vehementius operatur.

Per hunc igitur modum quanto virtus cognoscitiva est altior tanto est universalior: non quidem sic quod cognoscat solum universalem naturam, sic enim quanto esset superior tanto esset imperfectior—cognoscere enim aliquid solum in universali est cognoscere imper-

With these points in mind, we may easily reply to the objections set down above.

For it is not necessary, as the first argument[222] alleged, that the intellect of God and the angels cannot know singulars if the human intellect cannot know them. And so that the nature of this difference might appear more clearly, we must consider that the order of knowledge follows the proportion of the order found in things according to their being. For the perfection and truth of knowledge consists in this: that it has the likeness of the things known. In things, however, the order that is found is that the higher among beings have being and goodness more universally; not indeed, that they should come to have being and goodness only according to their common nature—insofar as the universal is said to be that which is predicated of many— but because whatever is found in lower beings is found more eminently in the higher. And this is seen from the operative power that is found in things.

For lower beings have powers which are restricted to determinate effects, whereas higher beings have powers that extend universally to many effects; and yet a higher power among particular effects is more effectual than a lower power. And this is especially evident among bodies. For in lower bodies, fire heats through its own heat, and the seed of this animal or plant so determinately produces an individual of this species that it does not produce an individual of another species.[223] It is clear from this that among higher beings a power is called universal not because it does not extend to particular effects, but because it extends to more effects than does a lower power and acts more strongly on singulars among them.

In this way, therefore, the higher the knowing power, the more universal it is; not indeed in such a way that it knows only a universal nature, for thus the higher it would be, the more imperfect it would be. For to know something universally is to know it imperfectly, and, in a manner, mid-

---

222. Cf. above, Cap. XIII.
223. Aristotle, *De Anima*, II, 4 (415a 27); St. Thomas, In *De Anima*, II, lect. 7, ed. Pirotta, nos. 311–314 (AACTA, 213–214).

fecte et medio modo inter potentiam et actum; sed ob hoc superior cognitio universalior dicitur quia ad plura se extendit et singula magis cognoscit. In ordine autem cognoscitivarum virtutum est virtus sensitiva inferior, et ideo non potest cognoscere singula nisi per species proprias singulorum; et quia individuationis principium est materia in rebus materialibus, inde est quod per species individuales in organis corporeis receptas vis sensitiva singularia cognoscit. Inter cognitiones autem intellectuales cognitio intellectus humani est infima, unde species intelligibiles in intellectu humano recipiuntur secundum debilissimum modum intellectualis cognitionis: ita quod earum virtute intellectus humanus cognoscere non potest res nisi secundum universalem naturam generis vel speciei, ad quam repraesentandam in sola sui universalitate sunt determinatae et quodam modo contractae ex hoc ipso quod a singularium phantasmatibus abstrahuntur; et sic homo singularia quidem cognoscit per sensum, universalia vero per intellectum. Sed superiores intellectus sunt universalioris virtutis in cognoscendo, ut scilicet per intelligibilem speciem utrumque cognoscant, et universale et singulare.

Secunda etiam ratio efficaciam non habet. Cum enim dicitur quod intellectum est perfectio intelligentis, hoc quidem veritatem habet secundum speciem intelligibilem quae est forma intellectus in quantum est actu intelligens: non enim natura lapidis quae est in materia est perfectio intellectus humani, sed species intelligibilis abstracta a phantasmatibus per quam intellectus intelligit lapidis naturam.

Unde oportet quod, cum omnis forma derivata ab aliquo agente procedat, agens autem sit honorabilius patiente seu recipiente, quod illud agens a quo intellectus speciem intelligibilem habet sit perfectius intellectu: sicut in intellectu humano apparet quod intellectus agens est nobilior intellectu possibili qui recipit species intelligibiles actu ab intellectu agente factas, non autem ipsae res naturales cognitae sunt intellectu possibili nobiliores; superiores autem intellectus angelorum species intelligibiles participant vel ab ideis secundum Platonicos, vel a prima substantia quae Deus est, secundum quod est consequens ad positiones Aristotelis et sicut se rei veritas habet.

Species autem intelligibilis intellectus divini per quam omnia cognoscit non est aliud quam eius substantia, quae est etiam suum intelligere ut supra probatum est per verba Philosophi: unde relinquitur quod intellectu divino nihil aliud sit altius per quod perficiatur,

way between potency and act. But a higher knowledge is called more universal on this account, that it extends to more individuals and knows singulars better. In the order of knowing powers, however, the sensitive power is lower and thus it can know singulars only through the proper species of singulars. And because matter is the principle of individuation among material things, hence it is that the sensitive power knows singulars through individual species received in corporeal organs. Among intellectual cognitions, however, that of the human intellect is the lowest. Therefore, intelligible species are received in the human intellect according to the weakest mode of intellectual knowledge, so that through them, the human intellect can know things only according to the universal nature of genus or species; to the representation of which, in its sole universality, the species are determined and in a manner limited by the fact that they are abstracted from the phantasms of singulars. And thus man knows singulars through the sense, but universals through the intellect. But the higher intellects are of a more universal power in knowing: namely, so that they are able to know both the universal and the singular through an intelligible species.

The second argument has no force.[224] For when it is said that the thing understood is a perfection of the one understanding, this indeed is true according to the intelligible species which is the form of the intellect so far as it is actually understanding. For it is not the nature of the stone in matter that is the perfection of the human intellect, but the intelligible species abstracted from the phantasms through which species the intellect understands the nature of the stone.

Accordingly, since every form that is by derivation in some being must proceed from an agent, and since an agent is more noble than the patient or recipient, it is necessary that the agent from which the intellect has an intelligible species is more perfect than the intellect; just as in the case of the human intellect, we see that the agent intellect is nobler than the possible intellect, which receives species made actually intelligible by the agent intellect. But the physical things themselves that are known are not nobler than the possible intellect. The higher intellects of the angels, however, receive intelligible species either from the ideas—according to the Platonists[225]—or from the first substance, which is God—according to that which follows from Aristotle's position and what is in reality true.[226]

The intelligible species of the divine intellect, however, through which it knows all things, is nothing other than his substance, which is likewise his understanding, as was proved above through the words of the Philosopher.[227] Hence it remains that in the case of the divine intellect there

224. Cf. above, Cap. XIII.
225. Cf. above, Cap. I; Produs, *Elem*, Prop. 117 (pp. 103–105).
226. Cf. above, Cap. I.
227. Cf. above, Cap. XIII.

sed ab ipso intellectu divino tanquam ab altiori proveniunt species intelligibiles ad intellectus angelorum, ad intellectum autem humanum a sensibilibus rebus per actionem intellectus agentis.

Tertiam vero rationem solvere facile est. Nihil enim prohibet aliquid esse fortuitum et casuale dum refertur ad inferioris agentis intentionem, quod tamen secundum superioris agentis intentionem est ordinatum: sicut patet si aliquis insidiose aliquem mittat ad locum ubi sciat esse latrones vel hostes, quorum occursus est casualis ei qui mittitur utpote praeter intentionem eius existens, non est autem casualis mittenti qui hoc praecogitavit. Sic igitur nihil prohibet aliqua fortuito vel casualiter agi secundum ea quae pertinent ad humanam cognitionem, quae tamen sunt secundum divinam providentiam ordinata.

Quartae vero rationis solutionem ex hoc accipere possumus quod necessarius consecutionis ordo effectus ad causam accipiendus est secundum rationem causae. Non enim omnis causa eadem ratione producit effectum, sed causa naturalis per formam naturalem per quam est actu, unde oportet quod agens naturale quale ipsum est tale producat et alterum; causa autem rationalis producit effectum secundum rationem formae intellectae quam intendit in esse deducere, et ideo agens per intellectum tale aliquid producit quale intelligit esse producendum, nisi virtus activa deficiat. Necesse est autem ut cuiuscumque virtuti subiicitur productio generis alicuius, ad illius etiam virtutem pertineat producere illius generis differentias proprias: sicut si ad aliquem pertineat constituere triangulum, ad eum etiam pertinet constituere triangulum aequilaterum vel isoscelem. Necessarium autem et possibile sunt propriae differentiae entis; unde ad Deum cuius virtus est proprie productiva entis pertinet secundum suam praecognitionem attribuere rebus a se productis vel necessitatem vel possibilitatem essendi. Concedendum est igitur quod divina providentia ab aeterno praeexistens causa est omnium effectuum qui secundum ipsam fiunt; qui immutabili dispositione ab ipsa procedunt, nec tamen sic omnes procedunt ut necessarii sint: sed sicut eius providentia disponit ut tales effectus fiant, ita etiam disponit ut horum effectus quidam sint necessarii ad quos causas proprias ex necessitate agentes ordinavit, quidam vero contingentes ad quos causas proprias contingentes ordinavit.

Ex his autem apparet quintae rationis solutio. Sicut enim a Deo, cuius esse est per se et summe necessarium,

is nothing nobler through which it is perfected; but from the divine intellect itself as from a higher source, intelligible species come to the intellects of the angels; whereas to the human intellect, intelligible species come from sensible things through the action of the agent intellect.

It is easy to solve the third argument.[228] For nothing prevents something from being fortuitous and by chance when it is referred to the intention of a lower agent, which yet is ordered according to the intention of a higher agent. This is evident if some person treacherously sends someone else to a certain place where he knows that there are robbers or enemies. For the one who is sent, the meeting with these persons is fortuitous, being beyond his intention. But it is not by chance to the sender, who knew this in advance. Consequently, nothing prevents certain things from taking place fortuitously or by chance so far as pertains to human knowledge, which yet are ordered according to divine providence.

We can derive the answer to the fourth argument[229] from the fact that the necessary order of consecution of an effect to cause must be understood according to the nature of the cause. For not every cause produces an effect in the same way. A natural cause does it through a natural form, through which it is in act. Therefore, a natural agent must produce an effect like unto itself. A rational cause, however, produces an effect according to the nature of an understood form which it intends to bring into being; and thus an intellectual agent produces such an effect as it understands should be produced, unless the producing power fail. Furthermore, whatsoever power is concerned with the production of any genus, must be concerned with the production of the proper differences of that genus. For example, if it pertains to some one to make a triangle, it likewise pertains to him to make an equilateral or isosceles triangle. For the necessary and the possible are proper differences of being. Therefore it pertains to God, to whom the power to produce being properly belongs, to give to things produced by him according to his foreknowledge either the necessity or possibility of being. Therefore, it must be conceded that divine providence, preexisting from eternity, is the cause of all the effects which are made in accordance with it and which proceed from it by an immutable disposition. Nevertheless, all do not so proceed as to be necessary. But just as the providence of God disposes that such effects be, so it likewise disposes that certain of these effects be necessary, for which it has ordained necessarily acting proper causes, while certain others should be contingent, for which it has ordained proper contingent causes.

The answer to the fifth argument[230] is evident from these points. For just as from God, whose being is essen-

---

228. Cf. above, Cap. XIII.
229. Cf. above, Cap. XIII.
230. Cf. above, Cap. XIII.

procedunt contingentes effectus propter propriarum causarum conditionem; ita etiam ab eo qui est summum bonum procedunt aliqui effectus, qui quidem in eo quod sunt et a Deo sunt boni sunt, incidunt tamen in eis aliqui defectus propter conditionem secundarum causarum, propter quos mali dicuntur. Sed et hoc ipsum bonum est quod a Deo tales defectus permittantur evenire in rebus, tum quia hoc est conveniens rerum ordini in quo bonum universi consistit ut effectus sequantur secundum conditionem causarum; tum etiam quia ex malo unius provenit bonum alterius: sicut in rebus naturalibus corruptio unius est alterius generatio, et in moralibus ex persecutione tyranni consequitur patientia iusti. Unde per divinam providentiam non decuit totaliter mala impediri.

tially and supremely necessary, there proceed contingent effects because of the condition of their proper causes, so likewise from him who is the highest good there proceed certain effects which, to be sure, are good in that they exist and are from God; and yet they are affected by certain defects of secondary causes, because of which they are called evil. But this, too, is a good, namely, that such effects are allowed by God to take place in reality, both because it befits the order of things (in which the good of the universe consists) that effects follow according to the condition of their causes. Also because from the evil of one, the good of another arises: just as in natural things the corruption of one thing is the generation of another, and in the case of moral realities, from the persecution of the tyrant there follows the patience of the just person. Accordingly, it was not fitting that evils should be completely prevented through divine providence.

CHAPTER 17

On the error of the Manicheans concerning spiritual substances

Omnes autem praedictos errores Manichaeorum error transcendit, qui in omnibus praedictis articulis graviter erraverunt. Primo namque rerum originem non in unum sed in duo creationis principia reduxerunt, quorum unum dicebant esse auctorem bonorum, alium vero auctorem malorum. Secundo erraverunt circa conditionem naturae ipsorum: posuerunt enim utrumque principium corporale, auctorem quidem bonorum dicentes esse quamdam lucem corpoream infinitam vim intelligendi habentem, auctorem vero malorum dixerunt esse quasdam corporales tenebras infinitas. Tertio vero erraverant per consequens in rerum gubernatione, non constituentes omnia sub uno principatu sed sub contrariis. Haec autem quae praedicta sunt expressam continent falsitatem, ut potest videri per singula.

Primo namque penitus irrationale est ut malorum ponatur esse aliquod primum principium quasi contrarium summo bono. Nihil enim potest esse activum nisi in quantum est ens actu, quia unumquodque tale alterum agit quale ipsum est; rursumque ex hoc aliquid agitur quod actu fit. Unumquodque autem ex hoc bonum dicimus quod actum et perfectionem propriam consequitur, malum autem ex hoc quod debito actu et perfectione privatur: sicut vita est corporis bonum,

All the preceding errors were surpassed by the error of the Manicheans,[231] who erred gravely in all the aforementioned points of doctrine. First of all, they reduced the origin of things not to one, but to two, principles of creation.[232] They said that one of these was the author of good, while the other was the author of evils. Second, they erred concerning the condition of the nature of these principles.[233] For they posited both principles to be corporeal, saying that the author of good things was a certain infinite corporeal light with a power of understanding. But they said that certain infinite corporeal darknesses were the author of evils. Third, they erred as a consequence in the government of things, establishing all things not under one dominion but under contraries, in a manner.[234] These notions which we have just set down contain a manifest falsity, as can be seen if we take them up one by one.

In the first place, it is completely irrational that something should be posited as the first principle of evils, as contrary to the highest good. For nothing can be active except insofar as it is a being in act, because each being produces something else like itself; and furthermore, a thing is produced in order to be actually. Now we call each thing good because it achieves act and its proper perfection; and it is evil because it is deprived of its due act and perfection. For example, life is a good of the body, for the body lives accord-

---

231. St. Thomas' source is most likely St. Augustine's *De Natura Boni Contra Manichaeos*.

232. Cf. St. Augustine, *De Natura Boni Contra Manichaeos*, 41 (PL 42, 563, 564); *Confessions*, V, 10, 20 (PL 32, 715).

233. St. Augustine, *De Natura Boni Contra Manichaeos*, 42 (PL 42, 565).

234. *Ibid.* (PL 42, 566).

vivit enim corpus secundum animam quae est perfectio et actus ipsius, unde et mors malum corporis dicitur per quam corpus anima privatur. Nihil igitur agit neque agitur nisi in quantum bonum est, in quantum vero unumquodque malum est in tantum deficit in hoc quod perfecte agatur vel agat: sicut domum malam fieri dicimus si ad debitam perfectionem non perducatur, et aedificatorem malum dicimus si in arte aedificandi deficiat. Neque igitur malum in quantum huiusmodi principium activum habet, neque principium activum esse potest; sed consequitur ex defectu alicuius agentis.

Secundo vero impossibile est corpus aliquod intellectum esse aut vim intellectivam habere. Intellectus enim neque corpus est neque corporis actus, alioquin non esset omnium cognoscitivus, ut probat Philosophus in III De anima; si igitur primum principium confitentur vim intellectivam habere — quod sentiunt omnes qui de Deo loquuntur —, impossibile est primum principium esse aliquid corporale.

Tertio vero manifestum est quod bonum habet finis rationem; hoc enim bonum dicimus in quod appetitus tendit. Omnis autem gubernatio est secundum ordinem in aliquem finem, secundum cuius rationem ea quae sunt ad finem ordinantur in ipsum; omnis igitur gubernatio est secundum rationem boni: non potest igitur esse nec gubernatio nec principatus aliquis seu regnum mali in quantum est malum. Frustra igitur ponunt duo regna vel principatus, unum bonorum aliud autem malorum.

Videtur autem hic error provenisse, sicut et alii supradicti, ex eo quod ea quae circa particulares causas consideraverunt conati sunt in universalem rerum causam transferre. Viderunt enim particulares effectus contrarios ex contrariis particularibus causis procedere, sicut quod ignis calefacit aqua vero infrigidat: unde crediderunt quod hic processus a contrariis effectibus in contrarias causas non deficiat usque ad prima rerum principia; et quia omnia contraria contineri videntur sub bono et malo in quantum contrariorum semper unum est deficiens ut nigrum et amarum, aliud vero perfectum ut dulce et album, ideo aestimaverunt quod prima omnium activa principia sint bonum et malum.

Sed manifeste defecerunt in considerando contrariorum naturam. Non enim contraria omnino diversa sunt, sed secundum aliquid quidem conveniunt, secundum aliquid autem differunt: conveniunt enim in genere, differunt autem secundum specificas differentias. Sicut igitur contrariorum sunt contrariae causae propriae secundum quod specificis differentiis differunt, ita eorum oportet esse unam causam communem totius generis in quo conveniunt; causa autem communis prior est et

ing to the soul, which is its perfection and its act. Hence, death, through which the body is deprived of the soul, is called an evil of the body. Nothing therefore acts or is done except insofar as it is good. However, insofar as anything is evil, to that extent it falls short of being done perfectly or of acting perfectly. For example, we say that a house is badly built if it is not brought through to its due perfection, and we call a builder bad if he falls short in the art of building. Therefore, evil as such neither has an active principle nor can it be an active principle, but follows from a defect of some agent.

In the second place, it is impossible for any body to be intellective or to have an intellective power. For the intellect is neither a body nor is it the act of a body; otherwise, it would not know all things, as the Philosopher proves in the third book of *On the Soul*.[235] Therefore, if they admit that the first principle has intellective power—which is held by all who speak of God—it is impossible for the first principle to be something corporeal.

Third, it is clear that the good has the nature of an end, for we call that thing good towards which the appetite tends. All government, however, follows an order to some end, and, according to the nature of this order, the things that are directed to the end are ordered to it. Now all government is according to the nature of good. Therefore, evil as evil cannot have a government or a dominion or rulership. In vain, therefore, do they posit two kingdoms or governments, one of the good and the other of the evil.

This error, like those mentioned above,[236] seems to have come about because the Manicheans tried to transfer to the universal cause of things what we find among particular causes. They saw particular contrary effects proceed from particular contrary causes, for example, that fire heats and water causes cold. Hence they believed that this process from contrary effects to contrary causes holds right up to the first principles of things. And because all contraries are seen to be contained under good and evil, insofar as one of two contraries is always deficient (for example, the black and the bitter), and the other is realized (like the sweet and the white), for this reason they thought that good and evil are the first active principles of all things.

But they manifestly failed in considering the nature of contraries. For contraries are not altogether diverse, but they agree in one respect and differ in another. For they agree in genus and they differ according to specific differences. Therefore, just as there are contrary proximate causes of contraries insofar as they differ by their specific differences, so they have one common cause of the whole genus in which they agree. A common cause, however, is prior to and higher than the proper causes. For the higher a cause

---

235. Aristotle, *De Anima*, III, 4 (429a 18–25), St. Thomas, In *De Anima*, III, lect. 7, ed. Pirotta, nos. 677–683 (AACTA, 404–406).
236. Cf. above, Cap. XVI.

superior propriis causis, quanto enim est aliqua causa superior tanto virtus eius maior et ad plura se extendens: relinquitur igitur contraria non esse prima rerum activa principia, sed omnium esse unam primam causam activam.

is, by so much is its power greater and reaching out to more effects. It remains, therefore, that contraries are not the first active principles of things but that there is one active cause of all things.

CHAPTER 18

On the origin of spiritual substances according to the Catholic faith

Quia igitur ostensum est quid de substantiis spiritualibus praecipui philosophi Plato et Aristoteles senserunt quantum ad earum originem, conditionem naturae, distinctionem et gubernationis ordinem, et in quo ab eis alii errantes dissenserunt: restat ostendere quid de singulis habeat christianae religionis assertio. Ad quod utemur praecipue Dionysii documentis, qui super alios ea quae ad spirituales substantias pertinent excellentius tradidit.

Primum quidem igitur circa spiritualium substantiarum originem firmissime docet christiana traditio omnes spirituales substantias sicut et ceteras creaturas a Deo esse productas; et hoc quidem canonicae Scripturae auctoritate probatur. In Psalmo enim dicitur *Laudate eum omnes angeli eius, laudate eum omnes virtutes eius*; et enumeratis aliis creaturis subditur *Quia ipse dixit et facta sunt, mandavit, et creata sunt.*

Sed et Dionysius IV cap. Caelestis hierarchiae hanc originem subtiliter explicat dicens *Primum illud dicere verum est quod bonitate universali superessentialis divinitas eorum quae sunt essentias substituens ad esse adduxit*; et post pauca subdit quod *ipsae — caelestes substantiae — sunt primo et multipliciter in participatione Dei factae*. Et in IV cap. De divinis nominibus dicit quod *propter divinae bonitatis radios substiterunt intelligibiles et intellectuales omnes et substantiae et virtutes et operationes; propter istos sunt et vivunt et vitam habent indeficientem.*

Quod autem a Deo immediate productae sint omnes spirituales substantiae et non solum supremae, expresse in V cap. De divinis nominibus *Sanctissimae*, inquit, *et provectissimae virtutes existentes et sicut in vestibulis*

Since, therefore, it has been shown what the foremost philosophers, Plato[237] and Aristotle,[238] believed about the spiritual substances as to their origin, the condition of their nature, their distinction and order of government, and in what respect others[239] disagreed with them through error, it remains to show what the teaching of the Christian religion holds about each individual point. For this purpose, we shall use especially the writings of Dionysius, who excelled all others in teaching what pertains to spiritual substances.

First, as to the origin of the spiritual substances, Christian tradition[240] teaches most firmly that all spiritual substances—like all other creatures—were made by God, and this is proved by the authority of the canonical Scriptures. For it is said in the Psalms: *Praise him, all his angels, praise him, all his host* (Ps 148:2). And after all the other creatures have been enumerated, it is added: *For he spoke and they were made; he commanded and they were created* (Ps 148:5).

And Dionysius explains this origin finely in the fourth chapter of the *Celestial Hierarchy* when he says: *In the first place, it is true to say that the super-essential dignity, by its universal goodness, in establishing the essences of all the things that are, brought them to being.*[241] And after a few words he adds that *the celestial substances are first and in many ways made in the participation of God.*[242] And in the fourth chapter of *On the Divine Names*, he says that *because of the rays of divine goodness, all intelligible and intellectual substances and powers and operations were established. Because of these rays, they are and live and have an inexhaustible life.*[243]

Furthermore, he expressly states that all spiritual substances and not only the highest were immediately produced, in the fifth chapter of *On the Divine Names*:[244] *The most holy and exalted existing powers (as if on the threshold*

---

237. Cf. above, Cap. I; Cap. III; Cap. XI.
238. Cf. above, Cap. II – Cap. IV.
239. Cf. above, Cap. V – Cap. X; Cap. XII – Cap. XVI.
240. Cf. Conc. Lateran. IV, anno 1215 (Denziger, 428).
241. Pseudo-Dionysius, *De Coelesti Hierarchia*, IV, no. I (PG 3, 177C); *Dionysiaca*, II, c. IV, sec. 60 (pp. 800–801).
242. *Ibid.*, IV, no. 2 (PG 3, 180A-B); *Dionysiaca*, II, c. IV, sec. 61 (p. 826).
243. Pseudo-Dionysius, *De Divinis Nominibus*, IV, 1 (PG 3, 693B-C) *Dionysiaca*, I, c. IV, sec. 16 (pp. 146, 147).
244. Pseudo-Dionysius, *De Divinis Nominibus*, V, 8 (PG 3, 821C); *Dionysiaca*, I, c. V, sec. 21 (pp. 350–351).

supersubstantialis Trinitatis collocatae ab ipsa et in ipsa et esse et deiformiter esse habent; et post illas subiectae, id est inferiores supremis, *subiecte* id est inferiori modo esse habent a Deo; *et extremae* id est infimae, *extreme* id est infimo modo, *sicut ad angelos, sicut ad nos autem supermundane.* Per quod dat intelligere quod omnes spiritualium substantiarum ordines ex divina dispositione instituuntur, non ex hoc quod una earum causetur ab alia. Et hoc expressius dicitur in IV cap. Caelestis hierarchiae: *Est,* inquit, *omnium causae et super omnia bonitatis proprium ad communionem suam ea quae sunt vocare ut unicuique eorum quae sunt ex propria definitur analogia*; unamquamque enim rem constituit in ordine qui competit suae naturae.

Similiter etiam christianae doctrinae repugnat quod spirituales substantiae ab alio et alio principio habeant bonitatem et esse et vitam et alia huiusmodi quae pertinent ad earum perfectionem. Nam in canonica Scriptura uni et eidem Deo attribuitur quod sit ipsa essentia bonitatis, unde dicitur Matth. XIX, 17 *Unus est bonus Deus*; et quod sit ipsum esse, unde Ex. III, 14 Moysi quaerenti quod esset nomen Dei respondit Dominus *Ego sum qui sum*; et quod sit ipsa viventium vita, unde dicitur Deut. XXX, 20 *Ipse est viventium vita.*

Et hanc quidem veritatem expressissime Dionysius tradit V cap. De divinis nominibus dicens quod sacra doctrina *non aliud dicit esse bonum et aliud existens et aliud vitam aut sapientiam, neque multas causas et aliorum alias productivas deitates excedentes subiectas*; in quo removet opinionem Platonicorum qui ponebant quod ipsa essentia bonitatis erat summus deus, sub quo erat alius deus qui est ipsum esse et sic de aliis, ut supra dictum est. Subdit autem *Sed unius,* scilicet deitatis, dicit *esse omnes bonos processus,* quia scilicet et esse et vivere et omnia alia huiusmodi a summa deitate procedunt in res.

Hoc etiam diffusius explicat in XI cap. De divinis nominibus dicens *Non enim substantiam quamdam divinam aut angelicam esse dicimus per se esse quod est causa quod sint omnia: solum enim quod sint existentia omnia ipsum esse supersubstantiale,* scilicet summi Dei, *est principium et substantia et causa,* 'principium' quidem effectivum, 'substantia' autem quasi forma exemplaris,

of the super-substantial Trinity) *have been established by it and in it they have both being and godlike being; and after those they are subjected,* that is, the lower to the higher; *subjected,* that is, they have being from God in a lower way; *and the lowest,* that is, at the bottom; *extremely,* that is, in the lowest manner, *with respect to the angels but the highest, however, with respect to us.* Through this statement, he gives us to understand that all the orders of spiritual substances are established by divine disposition and not from the fact that one of them is caused by another. And this is said more expressly in the fourth chapter of the *Celestial Hierarchy*:[245] *It is fitting,* he says, *for the cause of all things and of the goodness which is above all to call to its communion all those things which are, so that each being which is should be determined by a proper analogy.* For he established each thing in the order which befits its nature.

Likewise, it is repugnant to Christian teaching that spiritual substances should have goodness, being, and life, and other such attributes that pertain to their perfection, from different principles. For in the canonical Scriptures, it is attributed to the one and the same God that he is the very essence of goodness. Accordingly, it is said in Matthew 19:17, *One is good, God*; and that he is being itself—hence in Exodus 3:14, God answers Moses, who asks what is God's name: *I am who am*; and that he himself is the life of living beings—hence it is said in Deuteronomy 30:20: *He is the life of the living.*

And Dionysius most expressly teaches this truth in the fifth chapter of *On the Divine Names*,[246] when he says that sacred doctrine *does not say that to be good is one thing and to be a being is another and that life or wisdom is something else, nor that there are many causes and lesser productive deities of whom some extended to some things and others to others.* In this statement he removes the opinion of the Platonists who posited that the very essence of goodness was the highest God,[247] under whom there was another god who is being itself[248] and so forth, with the rest as has been said above.[249] And he adds: *But the opinion says that all the good processions belong to one,* that is, one deity: namely, because both being and life and all other such characteristics proceed to things from the highest deity.

This point he explains at greater length in the eleventh chapter of *On the Divine Names*,[250] saying: *For we do not say that a certain divine or angelic substance is through itself the being which is the cause of all things that are; for only the super-substantial being itself* (namely, of the highest God) *is the principle and substance and cause that all things are by nature*—a *principle* which is indeed productive, a *substance*

---

245. Pseudo-Dionysius, *De Coelesti Hierarchia*, IV, 1 (PG 3, 177C) *Dionysiaca*, II, c. IV, sec. 60 (pp. 800–802).

246. Pseudo-Dionysius, *De Divinis Nominibus*, V, 2 (PG 3, 816D–817A); *Dionysiaca*, I, c. V. sec. 21 (pp. 325–326).

247. Proclus, *Elem.* Props. 8, 13 (pp. 9–11; 15–17).

248. Proclus, *Elem*, Prop. 138 (p. 123).

249. Cf. above, Cap. XI.

250. Pseudo-Dionysius, *De Divinis Nominibus*, XI, 6 (PG 3, 9531D); *Dionysiaca*, I, c. IX, sec. 38 (pp. 519–521).

'causa' autem finalis. Subdit autem *Neque vitae genera-tivam aliam deitatem dicimus praeter superdeam vitam, causam omnium quaecumque vivunt et ipsius per se vi-tae*, quae scilicet formaliter viventibus inhaeret; *neque, ut colligendo dicamus, dicimus principales existentium et creativas substantias et personas quas et deos existentium et creatores per se facientes dixerunt.*

Ad hanc etiam positionem excludendam signan-ter Dionysius ab essentiali bonitate, quam Platonici summum deum esse ponebant, dicit in substantiis spi-ritualibus procedere quod sunt et vivunt et intelligunt, et omnia alia huiusmodi ad earum perfectionem pertinen-tia sortiuntur. Et idem etiam replicat in singulis capitulis ostendens quod ab esse divino habent quod sint, et a vita divina habent quod vivunt, et sic de ceteris.

Est autem christianae doctrinae contrarium ut sic dicantur spirituales substantiae a summa deitate origi-nem trahere quod fuerint ab aeterno, sicut Platonici et Peripatetici posuerunt; sed hoc habet assertio catholicae fidei quod coeperunt esse postquam prius non fuerant. Unde dicitur Is. XL, 26 *Levate in excelsum oculos vestros et videte quis creavit haec* scilicet superiora omnia; et ne intelligeretur de corporalibus solum subdit *Qui educit in numero militiam eorum.* Solet autem sacra Scriptu-ra nominare 'militiam caeli' spiritualium substantiarum caelestem exercitum propter earum ordinem et virtu-tem in exequendo voluntatem divinam, unde dicitur Luc. II, 13 quod *facta est cum angelo multitudo caelestis militiae*; datur igitur intelligi non solum corpora sed etiam spirituales substantias per creationem de non esse in esse fuisse eductas, secundum illud Rom. IV, 17 *Qui vocat ea quae non sunt tanquam ea quae sunt.* Unde et Dionysius dicit X cap. De divinis nominibus quod *non omnino et absolute ingenita et vere aeterna ubique* sacra Scriptura *nominat aeterna; sed incorruptibilia et immortalia et invariabilia et existentia eodem modo*, scili-cet nominat aeterna, *sicut quando dicit: Elevamini portae aeternales, et similia*; quod maxime videtur de spiritua-libus substantiis dictum. Et postea subdit *Oportet igitur non simpliciter coaeterna Deo qui est ante aevum arbitrari aeterna dicta.*

Sed quia sacra Scriptura in Gen. I in serie creatio-nis rerum de spiritualium substantiarum productione expressam mentionem non facit, ne populo rudi qui-bus lex proponebatur idolatriae daretur occasio si plures spirituales substantias super omnes corporeas creatu-ras introduceret sermo divinus, non potest ex Scripturis

in the manner of an exemplary form, and a *cause* which is final. And he adds: *Nor do we say that there is any other deity that generates life besides the super-divine life, which is the cause of all things whatsoever that live, and of life it-self in its essence, that life*, namely, which formally inheres in living things; *nor, to say in conclusion, do we call causes the principles of existing things and the creative substances and persons, whom they have called both the gods of existing things and the self-acting creators.*[251]

To exclude this position, moreover, under the essential goodness, which the Platonists said was the highest god, Dionysius pointedly says that spiritual substances have be-ing, and life, and intelligence and all other such attributes pertaining to their perfection. He likewise repeats the same point in the individual chapters, showing that they owe to the divine being that they are, and to the divine life that they are living, and so forth.

Furthermore, it is contrary to Christian teaching that spiritual substances should be said to derive their origin from the highest deity in such a way that they should have been from eternity—as the Platonists and the Peripatetics held. But, on the contrary, the declaration of the Catholic faith has it that they began to be after they had previously not existed. Accordingly, it is said in Isaiah 40:26: *Lift up your eyes on high and see who created these*—namely, all the higher beings. And lest it be understood about the bodies alone, he adds, *Who brings out their host by number.* Now sacred Scripture is in the habit of calling the heavenly host of spiritual substances 'the heavenly army,' because of their order and power in carrying out the divine will. Therefore, it is said in Luke 2:13 that *there was with the angel a mul-titude of the heavenly army.* It is, therefore, given to be un-derstood that not only bodies but also spiritual substances were brought into being from non-being by creation. Ac-cordingly, it is said in Romans 4:17: *He calls into existence the things that do not exist.* Therefore, Dionysius says in the tenth chapter of *On the Divine Names*[252] that sacred Scripture *does not exclusively apply the name 'eternal' to that which is absolutely ungenerated and truly eternal, but the incorruptible and immortal and invariable and unchanging, it calls 'eternal,' as when it says, Lift up, O eternal gates*, and the like, which seems especially to be said concerning spiritual substances. And afterwards he adds: *Therefore, the eternal beings cannot be thought to be absolutely coeternal with God, who is before eternity.*

But because in the succession of the creation of things, sacred Scripture, in Genesis 1, makes no explicit mention of the production of spiritual substances—lest an occasion of idolatry be given to an unlettered people, to whom the law was proposed, if the divine work should bring in many spir-itual substances above all corporeal creatures—it cannot be

---

251. Cf. above, Cap. IX; St. Augustine, *De Civitate Dei*, IX, 8, 12, 13, 23; X, 31 (PL 41, 261–262; 265–268; 275–276; 311–312).

252. Pseudo-Dionysius, *De Divinis Nominibus*, X, 3 (PG 3, 937C); *Dionysiaca*, I, c. X, sec. 36 (p. 489).

canonicis expresse haberi quando creati fuerunt angeli. Quod enim post corporalia creati non fuerint, et ratio manifestat quia non fuit decens ut perfectiora posterius crearentur; et ex auctoritate sacrae Scripturae expresse colligitur: dicitur enim Iob XXXVIII, 7 *Cum me laudarent simul astra matutina et iubilarent omnes filii Dei*, per quos spirituales substantiae intelliguntur.

Arguit autem Augustinus XI De civitate Dei *Iam ergo erant angeli quando facta sunt sidera; facta sunt autem quarto die: numquidnam ergo die tertio factos esse dicimus? Absit. In promptu est enim quid illo die factum sit, ab aquis utique terra discreta. Numquidnam secundo? Nec hoc quidem, tunc enim firmamentum factum est.* Et postea subicit *Nimirum ergo si ad istorum opera Dei pertinent angeli, ipsi sunt illa lux quae diei nomen accepit.* Sic igitur secundum sententiam Augustini simul cum corporalibus creata est spiritualis creatura quae significatur nomine caeli cum in Genesi dicitur *In principio fecit Deus caelum et terram*; formatio autem eius et perfectio significatur in lucis productione, ut multipliciter prosequitur in libro Super Genesim ad litteram.

Sed, ut Damascenus dicit in secundo libro, *Quidam aiunt quod ante omnem creationem* scilicet corporalis creaturae, *geniti sunt angeli, ut Gregorius theologus dicit: Primum quidem excogitavit angelicas virtutes et caelestes et excogitatio eius opus fuit*; et huic sententiae ipse Damascenus consentit. Sed et Hieronymus praedicti Gregorii Nazianzeni discipulus eamdem sententiam sequitur; dicit enim Super Epist. ad Titum *Sex millia necdum nostri temporis implentur annorum, et quantas prius aeternitates quanta tempora quantas saeculorum origines fuisse arbitrandum est in quibus angeli throni et dominationes ceterique ordines servierunt Deo absque temporum vicibus atque mensuris et Deo iubente substiterunt?*

Neutrum autem horum aestimo esse sanae doctrinae contrarium, quia nimis praesumptuosum videretur asserere tantos Ecclesiae doctores a sana doctrina pietatis deviasse. Sententia tamen Augustini magis videtur competere suae positioni qua ponit in rerum productione non fuisse temporis ordinem secundum dierum senarium quem Scriptura commemorat, sed illos sex dies refert ad intelligentiam angelicam sex rerum generibus praesentatam; sententia vero Gregorii Nazianzeni

expressly ascertained from the canonical Scriptures when the angels were created. That they indeed should not have been created after the corporeal beings, reason itself makes clear, for it was not fitting that the more perfect should be created later. This point is also expressly gathered from the authority of sacred Scripture, for it is said in Job 38:7: *When the morning stars sang together, and all the sons of God shouted for joy*; through which are understood the spiritual substances.

Furthermore, Augustine argues in *On the City of God*:[253] *Therefore, the angels already existed when the skies were made. The latter, however, were created on the fourth day. Do we therefore say that the angels were created on the third day? No. For it is well known what was made on that day: the earth was separated from the waters. Perhaps on the second day? Indeed not, for the firmament was made then.* And afterwards he adds, *No wonder, therefore, if the very angels pertain to these works of God, just as that light which receives the name of day.* Therefore, according to Augustine's opinion,[254] the spiritual creature, which is signified by the name 'heaven,' was created along with the corporeal beings, when it is said: *In the beginning God created heaven and earth* (Gen 1:1). But the formation and perfection of this spiritual creature is signified in the production of light, as is described many times at length in the second book of *A Literal Commentary on Genesis*.[255]

But as Damascene says in the second book,[256] *Certain thinkers say that the angels were begotten before all creation*—namely, of corporeal creatures—*as Gregory the Theologian says: First, indeed, he thought out the angelic and celestial powers, and his thinking was the deed.* And Damascene himself agreed with this opinion. And Jerome, a pupil of the aforementioned Gregory Nazianzen, follows the same opinion, for he says in commenting on the Epistle to Titus,[257] *Six thousand years of our time are not yet completed and how many eternities, how many times, how many origins of ages are we to think first existed in which the angels, thrones, and dominations and the other orders served God without the succession and measurement of time and did God's bidding.*

But I do not consider either one of these positions to be contrary to sound teaching because it seems too presumptuous to assert that such great doctors of the Church had strayed from the sound teaching of faith. Nevertheless, Augustine's opinion seems to agree more with his position according to which he posits that in the production of things, there was no order of time according to the six days which Scripture recounts; but on the contrary, he refers those six days to the understanding of the angels brought face to

253. St. Augustine, *De Civitate Dei*, XI, 9 (PL 41, 324).

254. *Ibid.*, (PL 41, 323).

255. St. Augustine, *De Gen. ad Litt.*, II, 8 (PL 34, 269–270).

256. St. John Damascene, *De Fide Orthodoxa*, II, 3 (PG 94, 873AB).

257. St. Jerome, *Commentarium in Epistola ad Titum*, I (PL 26, 560A).

Hieronymi et Damasceni convenientior est secundum eorum positionem, qui ponunt in rerum productione successionem temporis secundum sex dies praedictos: si enim creaturae non fuerunt omnes simul productae, satis probabile est creaturas spirituales omnia corpora praecessisse.

Si vero quaeratur ubi creati sunt angeli, manifestum est quod quaestio ista locum non habet si sunt creati ante omnem corpoream creaturam, cum locus sit aliquid corporale, nisi forte pro loco accipiamus spiritualem claritatem qua illustrantur a Deo; unde Basilius dicit in II Hexaemeron *Arbitramur quia si fuit quidpiam ante institutionem sensibilis huius et corruptibilis mundi, profecto in luce fuit; neque enim dignitas angelorum nec omnium caelestium militiae vel si quid est nominatum aut inappellabile aut aliqua rationalis virtus vel ministrator spiritus degere posset in tenebris, sed in luce et laetitia decentem sibi habitum possidebat: de qua re neminem puto contradicturum.*

Si vero simul cum corporali creatura creati fuerint angeli, quaestio locum potest habere, eo tamen modo quo angelis competit esse in loco: de quo infra dicetur. Et secundum hoc quidam dixerunt in quodam supremo caelo splendido angelos esse creatos quod empyreum nominant, id est igneum, non ab ardore sed a splendore; et de hoc caelo Strabus et Beda exponunt quod dicitur *In principio creavit Deus caelum et terram*, quamvis haec expositio ab Augustino et aliis antiquioribus Ecclesiae doctoribus non tangatur.

face with the six kinds of things. The opinion of Gregory Nazianzen, of Jerome, and of Damascene, however, is more fitting according to the position of those who posit in the production of things a succession of time according to the aforesaid six days. For if all the creatures were not made at the same time, it is quite probable that spiritual creatures preceded all bodies.

If, however, it should be asked where the angels were created, it is clear that such a question has no place if they were created before all corporeal creatures, since place is something corporeal, unless perhaps we should take for place a spiritual clarity, by which the angels are illumined by God. Accordingly, Basil says in *Hexaemeron* II:[258] *We believe that if anything did exist before the establishment of this sensible and corruptible world, it was effected in light. For neither the dignity of the angels nor the armies of all the heavenly beings, whether named or unnamed, whether some rational power or ministration of the spirit, could have endured in darkness, but it was fittingly clothed in light and joy. No one, I think, will contradict this point.*

If, however, the angels had been created at the same time as the corporeal creature, the question can have a place only in that way in which it befits the angels to be in a place—about which we shall speak below.[259] And according to this position, certain individuals said that the angels were created in a certain highest, brilliant heaven which they call the empyrean (that is, fiery) heavens—not from the heat but from the brilliance. And it is of this heaven that Strabo and Bede interpret the words, *In the beginning God created heaven and earth*, though this interpretation is not touched upon by Augustine and the other more ancient doctors of the Church.

CHAPTER 19

On the condition of spiritual substances

Deinde considerare oportet quid de conditione spiritualium substantiarum secundum catholicae doctrinae sententiam sit tenendum.

Fuerunt igitur quidam qui angelos putaverunt corporeos esse vel ex materia et forma esse compositos: quod quidem sensisse videtur Origenes in primo Peri archon ubi dicit *Solius Dei, id est Patris et Filii et Spiritus Sancti, naturae id proprium est ut sine materiali substantia et absque ulla corporeae adiectionis societate intelligatur existere.* Et ad hoc quidem quod angelos corporeos ponerent, movere potuerunt eos verba Scripturae

Next, we must consider what must be held concerning the condition of spiritual substances according to the opinion of Catholic teaching.

There were certain thinkers who thought that the angels were corporeal or composed of matter and form. Origen seems to have held this opinion in the *Peri Archon*[260] where he says, *It is proper to the nature of God alone (that is, of the Father and of the Son and of the Holy Spirit) that it be understood to exist without material substance and without any association of a corporeal adjunct.* The words of sacred Scripture, which seems to attribute certain corporeal char-

---

258. St. Basil, *In Hexaemeron, Hom.* II, 5 (PG 29, 40C–41A).
259. Cf. below, Cap. XVIII.
260. Origen, *Peri Archon*, I, 1 (PG 11, 129).

quae quaedam corporalia angelis attribuere videtur, cum eos et in loco corporali esse pronuntiet secundum illud Matth. XVIII, 10 *Angeli eorum in caelis semper vident faciem Patris mei qui in caelis est*, et eos moveri asserat secundum illud Is. VI, 6 *Volavit ad me unus de Seraphim.*

Et quod est amplius, eos figura corporali describat sicut ibidem de Seraphim dicitur *Sex alae uni et sex alae alteri*, et de Gabriele dicitur Dan. VI *Ecce vir unus vestitus lineis et renes eius accincti auro obrizo et corpus eius quasi chrysolitus*, et cetera quae ad haec pertinentia ibidem subduntur.

Quod autem in angelis, etsi non sint corporei, sit tamen in eis compositio formae et materiae, ex quibus rationibus accipere volunt supra iam diximus; sed quod angeli incorporei sint, canonicae Scripturae auctoritate probatur quae eos spiritus nominat. Dicitur enim in Psalmo *Qui facit angelos suos spiritus*, et Apostolus dicit ad Hebraeos I, 14 de angelis loquens *Omnes sunt administratorii spiritus in ministerium missi propter eos qui hereditatem capiunt salutis*; consuevit autem Scriptura nomine spiritus aliquid incorporeum designare, secundum illud Io. IV, 24 *Spiritus est Deus et eos qui adorant eum in spiritu et veritate adorare oportet*, et Is. XXXI, 3 *Aegyptus homo et non deus, et equi eorum caro et non spiritus.* Sic igitur consequens est secundum sacrae Scripturae sententiam angelos incorporeos esse.

Si quis autem diligenter velit verba sacrae Scripturae inspicere, ex eisdem accipere poterit eos immateriales esse. Nominat enim eos sacra Scriptura quasdam virtutes: dicitur enim in Psalmo *Benedicite Domino omnes angeli*, et postea subditur *Benedicite Domino omnes virtutes eius*; et Luc. XXI, 26 dicitur *Virtutes caelorum movebuntur*, quod de sanctis angelis omnes doctores exponunt. Quod autem materiale est non est virtus sed habet virtutem, sicut non est essentia sed habens essentiam, sequitur enim virtus essentiam; non est autem homo sua humanitas neque sua virtus, similiter autem neque aliquid aliud ex materia et forma compositum: relinquitur igitur secundum intentionem Scripturae angelos immateriales esse.

Utrumque autem horum expresse Dionysii verbis astruitur, qui in IV cap. De divinis nominibus de angelis loquens dicit quod *intellectuales substantiae ab universis corruptione et morte et materia et generatione mundae existunt, et sicut incorporales et immateriales intelligun-*

acteristics to angels and which pronounces the angels as being with corporeal things in a corporeal place, could have moved these thinkers to posit the angels as being corporeal, according to the words of Matthew 18:10: *Their angels in heaven always behold the face of my Father who is in heaven.* And Scripture asserts them to be moved, according to the words of Isaiah 6:6, *Then flew one of the seraphim to me.*

And what is more, that it should describe them as having a corporeal form, just as is said in the same place of the seraphim, *The one had six wings and the other had six wings* (Isa 6:2). And it is said about Gabriel in Daniel: *Behold, a man clothed in linen, and his loins were girded with the finest gold, and his body was like the chrysolite* (Dan 10:5–6), and other points which are pertinent to these are described in the same place.

Furthermore, we have already stated above,[261] on the basis of arguments they may wish to hold, that there is in the angels a composition of form and matter, even though they are not corporeal. But that the angels are incorporeal is proved from the authority of sacred Scripture, which calls them 'spirits.' For it is said in the Psalm: *You make your angels spirit* (Ps 103:4). And the Apostle, in speaking of the angels, says in Hebrews 1:14: *Are they not all ministering spirits sent forth to serve, for the sake of those who are to obtain salvation?* Scripture, however, was accustomed to designate something incorporeal by the name of 'spirit,' according to the words of John 4:24: *God is spirit, and those who worship him must worship in spirit and truth*; and according to the words of Isaiah 31:3: *The Egyptians are men, and not God; and their horses are flesh, and not spirit.* Therefore, according to the sense of sacred Scripture, it follows that the angels are incorporeal.

If, however, one should wish to examine diligently the words of sacred Scripture, he will be able to gather from them that the angels are immaterial, for sacred Scripture calls them certain powers. For it is said in the Psalm: *Bless the Lord, all you angels* (Ps 102:20), and later it is added: *Bless the Lord, all his powers* (Ps 102:21). And it is said in Luke 21:26: *The powers of the heavens will be shaken*, which all the doctors apply to the holy angels. Furthermore, that which is material is not a power but it has power, just as it is not an essence but it has essence, for power follows upon essence. For neither is man his humanity nor is he his power; and the same is the case with every other composite of matter and form. It remains, therefore, that according to the intention of the Scriptures, angels are immaterial.

Furthermore, both of these points are expressly ascribed to the words of Dionysius who, speaking of the angels, says in the fourth chapter of *On the Divine Names*[262] that *the intellectual substances exist free from all corruption and death and matter and generation and are understood to be incorpo-*

---

261. Cf. above, Cap. V; Cap. VIII.

262. Pseudo-Dionysius, *De Divinis Nominibus*, IV, I (PG 3, 693C); *Dionysiaca*, I, c. IV, sec. 16 (pp. 147–148).

tur. In primo etiam capitulo *Caelestis hierarchiae* dicit quod divina *dispositio immateriales angelorum hierarchias materialibus figuris varias tradidit*; et in secundo capitulo eiusdem libri quaerit quare sacri doctores *ad corporalem formationem incorporalium — scilicet angelorum — venientes*, non figuraverunt ea pretiosissimis figuris sed *immaterialibus substantiis et deiformibus simplicitatibus terrenas* figuras circumposuerunt. Ex quibus omnibus patet hanc fuisse Dionysii sententiam quod angeli sunt immateriales et simplices substantiae; quod etiam ex hoc patet quod frequenter eos nominat caelestes intellectus seu divinas mentes: intellectus autem et mens aliquid incorporeum et immateriale est, ut Philosophus probat in III *De anima*.

Augustinus etiam dicit in II *Super Genesim ad litteram* quod *primo die quo lux facta est conditio spiritualis et intellectualis creaturae lucis appellatione intimatur, in qua natura intelliguntur omnes sancti angeli atque virtutes*. Damascenus etiam dicit quod *angelus est substantia intellectualis et incorporea*; sed dubitationem facit quod postea subdit *Incorporeus autem et immaterialis dicitur quantum ad nos, omne enim comparatum ad Deum grossum et materiale invenitur*. Quod ad hoc inducitur ne aestimetur angelus propter suam incorporeitatem et immaterialitatem divinam simplicitatem aequare.

Corporales vero figurae seu formae quae in Scriptura sacra interdum angelis attribuuntur per quamdam similitudinem sunt intelligenda, quia sicut dicit Dionysius primo capitulo *Caelestis hierarchiae Non est possibile nostrae menti ad immaterialem illam sursum excitari caelestium hierarchiarum et imitationem et contemplationem nisi secundum se materiali manuductione utatur*; sicut et de ipso (Deo) multa corporalia in Scripturis per quamdam similitudinem dicuntur. Unde in XV cap. *Caelestis hierarchiae* Dionysius exponit quid spirituale significetur in angelis per omnes huiusmodi corporales figuras.

Nec solum huiusmodi formas corporeas per similitudinem de angelis asserit dici, sed etiam ea quae pertinent ad affectionem sensitivi appetitus, ut per hoc detur intelligi quod non solum angeli non sunt corpora, sed etiam non sunt spiritus corporibus uniti quae sensificando perficiant ut sic in eis inveniantur operationes animae sensitivae. Dicit enim in secundo capitulo *Caelestis hierarchiae* quod *furor irrationabilibus ex passibili motu ingignitur*, sed in angelis *furibundum demonstrat*

real and immaterial. He likewise says, in the first chapter of the *Celestial Hierarchy*,[263] that the divine *government made certain material figures to stand for the various immaterial hierarchies of angels.* And in the second chapter of the same book[264] he asks why the sacred doctors, *coming to the corporeal representation of incorporeal beings, that is, the angels,* did not picture them with the most resplendent figures but *gave earthly figures to immaterial and godlike simple beings.* It is clear from all these words that Dionysius' opinion was that the angels are immaterial and simple substances. This is likewise clear from the fact that he frequently calls them celestial intellects or divine minds. The intellect or the mind, however, is something incorporeal and immaterial, as the Philosopher proves in *On the Soul* III.[265]

Augustine likewise says in the second book of the *Literal Commentary on Genesis*[266] that *on the first day when the light was made, the condition of the spiritual and intellectual creature is announced by the name of 'light,' in which nature are understood all the holy angels and powers.* Damascene[267] likewise says that *the angel is an intellectual and incorporeal substance.* But what he later adds creates a doubt: *It is called an incorporeal and immaterial nature with reference to us, for everything compared to God is found to be coarse and material.* This point is introduced so that the angel, because of his incorporeity and immateriality, would not be considered to be equal to the simplicity of the divine substance.

The corporeal shapes or forms, however, which are sometimes attributed to the angels in sacred Scripture must be understood in the manner of a likeness, because, as Dionysius says in the first chapter of the *Celestial Hierarchy*:[268] *It is not possible for our mind to be raised up to the immaterial imitation and contemplation of the celestial hierarchies, unless, in accord with its nature, it makes use of some material guidance*—just as many corporeal things are said about God in the Scriptures through a certain likeness. Accordingly, Dionysius expounds in the fifteenth chapter of the *Celestial Hierarchy*[269] what spiritual thing might be signified in the angels through all such corporeal figures.

He asserts that not only corporeal forms of such a kind are predicated of the angels by likeness, but also these things which pertain to the affection of the sensitive appetite, so that thereby we might be given to understand not only that angels are not bodies, but likewise that they are not spirits united to bodies which they perfect with sense life, so that, thus, there maybe found in them operations of the sensitive soul. For he says in the second chapter of the *Celestial Hierarchy*[270] that *rage is begotten in irrational*

263. Pseudo-Dionysius, *De Coelesti Hierarchia*, I, 3 (PG 3, 121C); *Dionysiaca*, II, c. I, sec. 56 (pp. 733–736).

264. *Ibid.*, in its entirety (PG 3, 136–145); *Dionysiaca*, II, c. II, secs. 57–58 (pp. 740–784).

265. Aristotle, *De Anima*, III, 4 (429a 10–b 5); St. Thomas, In *De Anima*, III, lect. 7, ed. Pirotta, nos. 671–699 (AACTA, 402–410).

266. St. Augustine, *De Gen. ad Litt.*, II, 8 (PL 34, 269).

267. St. John Damascene, *De Fide Orthodoxa*, II, 3 (PG 94, 865B 868A).

268. Pseudo-Dionysius, *De Coelesti Hierarchia*, I, 3 (PG 3, 121C D); *Dionysiaca*, II, c. I sec. 56 (pp. 735–736).

269. *Ibid.*, XV in its entirety (PG 3, 328–340); *Ibid.*, II, c. XV, sec. 71 (pp. 983–1071).

270. *Ibid.*, II, 4 (PG 3, 141D); *Ibid.*, II, c. 11, sec. 58 (pp. 765–766).

virilem ipsorum rationabilitatem; et similiter dicit quod concupiscentia in eis significat amorem divinum. Cui convenienter Augustinus dicit in IX De civitate Dei quod sancti angeli sine ira puniunt quos accipiunt aeterna Dei lege puniendos, et miseris sine miseriae compassione subveniunt, et periclitantibus eis quos diligunt sine timore opitulantur; et tamen istarum nomina passionum consuetudine locutionis humanae etiam in eos usurpantur propter quamdam operum similitudinem, non propter affectionum infirmitatem.

Quod autem angeli dicuntur esse in caelis aut in aliquibus aliis corporalibus locis, non est intelligendum quod sint in eis corporali modo, scilicet per contactum dimensivae quantitatis, sed modo spirituali per quemdam contactum virtutis. Proprius autem locus angelorum est spiritualis, secundum quod Dionysius dicit V cap. De divinis nominibus quod supremae spirituales substantiae sunt *in vestibulis Trinitatis collocatae.* Et Basilius dicit in II Hexaemeron quod sunt *in luce et laetitia spirituali.* Et Gregorius Nyssenus dicit in libro De homine quod *intelligibilia existentia in intelligibilibus locis sunt; aut enim in se ipsis sunt aut in superiacentibus intelligibilibus: cum igitur in corpore dicatur intellectuale aliquid localiter esse, non ut in loco in corpore dicitur esse sed ut in habitudine et in eo quod adest, ut dicimus Deum esse in nobis;* et post pauca subdit *Cum igitur in habitudine fuerit intelligibile aliquod vel loci alicuius vel rei ut in loco existentis, abusivius dicimus illic id esse propter actum eius qui est illic, locum pro habitudine suscipientes; cum enim deberemus dicere 'illic agit', dicimus 'illic est'.* Et hoc sequens Damascenus dixit quod angelus ubi operatur ibi est. Augustinus etiam VIII Super Genesim ad litteram dicit quod *Spiritus creator movet conditum spiritum per tempus sine loco, movet autem corpus per tempus et locum.*

Ex quibus omnibus datur intelligi quod angeli non sunt in loco corporali modo, sed quodam modo spirituali. Et quia eodem modo competit alicui moveri in loco et esse in loco, per consequens neque corporali modo angeli moventur in loco; sed motus eorum qui exprimitur in Scripturis, si referatur ad locum corporalem, est accipiendus secundum successionem virtualis contactus ad loca diversa; vel est accipiendus secundum mysti-

beings from a passible movement, but in angels, *the irascible must be understood in a different way, namely, as showing— as I believe—their strength and reason.* And in like manner, he says that concupiscence in the angels signifies a divine love. Agreeing with this, Augustine says in the ninth book of *On the City of God* that *the holy angels punish without anger those whom they receive for punishment by the eternal law of God; they help the suffering without the compassion of pity; and when those whom they love fall in danger, they minister without fear; and yet, the names of these passions are applied to them from a habit of human speech because of a kind of likeness in works and not because of a weakness in affections.*[271]

Furthermore, that angels are said to be in the heavens or in some other corporeal place must not be understood that they might be in them in a corporeal manner—namely, through a contact of measurable quantity—but in a spiritual manner, through a certain contact of power. Now the proper place of the angels is spiritual, according to what Dionysius says in the fifth chapter of *On the Divine Names,*[272] that the highest spiritual substances are *stationed on the threshold of the Trinity.* And Basil says in II *Hexaemeron*[273] that they are *in spiritual light and joy.* And Gregory of Nyssa says in the book *On Man*[274] that *the existing intelligibles are in intelligible places, for either they are in themselves or in superior intelligibles. Since, therefore, something intellectual is said to be locally in a body, it is said to be in a body not as in a place but in disposition, and in the sense of being present, as we say that God is in us.* And after a few words, he adds: *Since, therefore, there was something understandable in the disposition either of place or of some thing as existing in a place, we say by improper use, taking the place for the condition, that that is there because of the act of that which is there; for when we should say, 'it acts there,' we say 'it is there.'* And following this, Damascene[275] says that where the angel acts, there he is. Augustine likewise says in Book VIII of the *Literal Commentary on Genesis*[276] that *the creator Spirit moves the created spirit through time and without place; he moves the body, however, through time and place.*

From all these arguments, we may understand that angels are in a place not in a corporeal but in a kind of spiritual manner. And because it befits a thing to be moved and to be in a place in the same way, as a consequence, neither are angels moved in place in a corporeal manner; but rather, their movement, which is described in the Scriptures—if it is referred to a corporeal place—must be understood as a succession of contacts of power at diverse places; or it

271. St. Augustine, *De Civitate Dei,* IX, 5 (PL 41, 261).

272. Pseudo-Dionysius, *De Divinis Nominibus,* V, 8 (PG 3, 821C); *Dionysiaca,* I, c. V, sec. 21 (p. 350). Cf. St. Thomas, *In Librum de Causis,* Prop. 19, ed. H. d. Saffrey, 104–107.

273. St. Basil, *In Hexaemeron, Hom.* II, 5 (PG 29, 41A).

274. Nemesius, *De Nat. Hom.,* 3 (PG 40, 600A).

275. St. John Damascene, *De Fide Orthodoxa,* II, 3 (PG 94, 869B-C).

276. St. Augustine, *Super Gen. ad Litt.,* VIII, 20 (PL 34, 388).

cam intelligentiam, sicut Dionysius IV cap. De divinis nominibus dicit quod *moveri dicuntur divinae mentes circulariter quidem unitae illuminationibus pulchri et boni, in directum autem quando procedunt ad subiectorum providentiam, oblique autem quando providentes minus habentibus inegressibiliter manent* circa Deum.

Ex his igitur manifestum est quid circa conditionem spiritualium substantiarum, id est angelorum, sacri doctores tradiderint asserentes eos incorporeos et immateriales esse.

must be understood according to a mystical meaning, just as in the fourth chapter of *On the Divine Names*,[277] Dionysius says that *the divine minds are said to be moved in a circular manner when they are united to the illuminations of the beautiful and the good; they are moved in a straight line, however, when they proceed to the providence of what is subject to them; then, they are moved obliquely, however, when in their providence over lesser beings, they remain fixed before God.*[278]

Therefore, it is clear from these statements what the sacred doctors taught concerning the condition of the spiritual substances—that is, of the angels—when they asserted that the angels are incorporeal and immaterial.

CHAPTER 20

On the distinction of angelic spirits

Oportet autem consequenter considerare quid secundum sacram doctrinam de distinctione spirituum sit tenendum: ubi et primum considerationi occurrit differentia boni et mali, est enim apud multos receptum esse quosdam spiritus bonos, quosdam vero malos. Quod et auctoritate sacrae Scripturae comprobatur: de bonis enim spiritibus dicitur Hebr. I, 14 *Omnes sunt administratorii spiritus in ministerium missi propter eos qui hereditatem capiunt salutis*; de malis autem spiritibus dicitur, Matth. XII, 43 *Cum immundus spiritus exierit ab homine ambulat per loca arida quaerens requiem et non invenit*, et postea subditur *Tunc vadit et assumit septem alios spiritus nequiores se.* Et quamvis, ut Augustinus narrat in IX De civitate Dei, quidam posuerunt et bonos et malos spiritus deos esse, et similiter bonos et malos daemones nominari, quidam tamen melius deos non nisi bonos asserunt, quos nos angelos dicimus, daemones autem secundum communem usum loquendi non nisi in malo accipitur: quod, ut dicit, rationabiliter accidit, daemones enim in graeco a scientia nominantur, quae sine caritate secundum sententiam Apostoli per superbiam inflat.

Sed causa malitiae daemonum non eadem ab omnibus assignatur. Quidam enim eos asserunt naturaliter malos, tanquam a malo productos principio sic etiam ut ipsorum natura sit mala: quod ad Manichaeorum errorem pertinet, ut patet ex dictis. Sed hunc errorem

Furthermore, we consequently consider next what we must hold according to sacred doctrine concerning the distinction of spirits. Our first consideration is the difference between good and evil. For it has been accepted among many thinkers that certain spirits are good and certain others evil. This is likewise proved by the authority of sacred Scripture. For it is said about the good spirits in Hebrews 1:14: *Are they not all ministering spirits sent forth to serve for the sake of those who are to obtain salvation?* About the evil spirits, however, it is said in Matthew 12:43: *When the unclean spirit has gone out of a man, he passes through waterless places seeking rest, but he finds none.* And afterwards it is added, *Then he goes and brings with him seven other spirits more evil than himself* (Matt 12:45). And although, as Augustine narrates in the ninth book of *On the City of God*,[279] certain thinkers posited both good and evil spirits to be gods, and likewise good and evil spirits to be called demons, nevertheless, others more correctly assert only the good spirits to be gods. These we call 'angels,' whereas according to the received manner of speaking, 'demons' are accepted only as evil. This distinction, as he says, is reasonable.[280] For the demons are named from the word 'science' in Greek, which, without charity, according to the opinion of the Apostle, puffs up through pride.

But the cause of the wickedness of the demons is not assigned by all thinkers in the same way. For some of them assert that demons are naturally evil as having been produced by an evil principle, and thus their nature must be evil—which is part and parcel of the error of the Manicheans, as is

---

277. Pseudo-Dionysius, *De Divinis Nominibus*, IV, 8 (PG 3, 704D) *Dionysiaca*, I, c. IV, see. 18 (pp. 189–190).
278. Cf. St. Thomas, ST, II-IIae, 180, 6.
279. St. Augustine, *De Civitate Dei*, IX, 1 ff. (PL 41, 255).
280. *Ibid.*, IX, 20 (PL 41, 273).

efficacissime Dionysius improbat IV cap. De divinis nominibus dicens *Sed neque daemones natura mali sunt.* Quod probat primo quidem quia si naturaliter mali essent, simul oporteret dicere quod neque essent producti ex bono principio neque inter existentia computarentur, quia malum non est aliquid existens nec si esset natura aliqua causaretur a bono principio.

Secundo, quia si sunt naturaliter mali, aut sibi ipsis aut aliis: si sibi ipsis, se ipsos corrumperent, quod est impossibile (malum enim rationem corruptivi habet). Si vero sunt mali aliis, oporteret quod ea quibus sunt mali corrumperent; quod autem est naturaliter tale est omnibus tale et omnino tale, sequeretur ergo quod omnia et omnino corrumperent: quod est impossibile, tum quia quaedam sunt incorruptibilia quae corrumpi non possunt, tum quia ea etiam quae corrumpuntur non totaliter corrumpuntur. Non igitur ipsa natura daemonum est mala.

Tertio, quia si essent naturaliter mali non essent a Deo facti, quia *bonum bona producit et subsistere facit*; et hoc est impossibile secundum id quod supra probatum est <quod> oportet omnium Deum esse principium.

Quarto, quia *si daemones semper eodem modo se habent non sunt mali, quod enim est semper idem boni est proprium; si autem non semper mali, non natura mali.*

Quinto, quia *non sunt omnino expertes boni secundum quod sunt et vivunt et intelligunt et* aliquod bonum desiderant.

Fuerunt autem alii ponentes daemones naturaliter malos non quia eorum natura sit mala, sed quia habent quandam inclinationem naturalem ad malum; sicut Augustinus X De civitate Dei introducit Porphyrium dicentem in Epistola ad Anebontem quosdam *opinari esse quoddam spirituum genus cui exaudire sit proprium, natura fallax omniforme multimodum, simulans deos et daemones et ipsas animas defunctorum.*

Quae quidem opinio veritatem habere non potest, si ponatur daemones incorporeos esse et intellectus quosdam separatos. Cum enim omnis natura bona sit, impossibile est quod natura aliqua habeat inclinationem ad malum nisi sub ratione particularis boni; nihil enim prohibet aliquid quod est particulariter bonum alicui naturae, in tantum dici malum in quantum repugnat

clear from what has been said.[281] But Dionysius refutes this error most effectively in the fourth chapter of *On the Divine Names*[282] when he says: *But neither are the demons evil by nature.* He proves this first because if they were naturally evil, it would be necessary to say at one and the same time that neither had they been produced by a good principle nor should they be numbered among existing beings, since evil is not something existing, nor if there existed an evil nature, was it caused by a good principle.

In the second place, because if they are evil by nature, they are evil to themselves or to others: if to themselves, they would destroy themselves (for evil has the nature of something corruptive), which is impossible. But if they are evil to others, then they would have to destroy those things to which they are evil. However, what is such by nature must be completely such with respect to all. It would follow therefore that they would destroy all things, and this completely. This is impossible, both because certain beings are incorruptible and cannot be destroyed, and also because those which are destroyed are not destroyed completely. Therefore, the nature itself of the demons is not evil.

In the third place, if they were naturally evil, they would not have been made by God because *good produces good effects and makes them subsist.*[283] This is impossible according to that which has been proved above,[284] namely, that God must be the source of all things.

In the fourth place, because *if the demons are always disposed in the same way, they are not evil, for that which is always the same belongs to the good. If, however, they are not always evil, they are not evil by nature.*

In the fifth place, *they are not completely devoid of good, for according as they are and live and have understanding, they desire some good.*

Now there were others who held that the demons were naturally evil, not because their nature is evil, but because they have a certain natural inclination to evil, as Augustine advances in the tenth book of *On the City of God*[285] through Porphyry, who says in the *Epistle to Anebontes* that some men *thought that there is a certain class of spirits which it is proper to obey and which is deceitful by nature in all forms and in many ways, imitating the gods and demons and the very souls of the dead.*

This opinion cannot have any truth if it be posited that demons are incorporeal and certain separate intellects. For, since every nature is good, it is impossible that some nature should have an inclination to evil, except under the character of some particular good. For nothing prevents some thing which is good in a particular manner to be called 'bad' with respect to a certain nature, insofar as it is opposed

281. Cf. above, Caps. XVI.
282. Pseudo-Dionysius, *De Divinis Nominibus*, IV, 23 (PG 3, 724C); *Dionysiaca*, I, c. IV, sec. 20 (pp. 271–272).
283. Dionysius, *de Divinis Nominibus*, IV.
284. Cf. above, Cap. IX; Cap. X.
285. St. Augustine, *De Civitate Dei*, X, 11 (PL 41, 289).

perfectioni nobilioris naturae, sicut furiosum esse quoddam bonum est cani, quod tamen malum est homini rationem habenti: possibile tamen est in homine secundum sensibilem et corporalem naturam in qua cum brutis communicat, esse quamdam inclinationem ad furorem qui est homini malum. Sed hoc de intellectuali natura dici non potest, quia intellectus ordinem habet ad bonum commune: unde impossibile est in daemonibus inveniri naturalem inclinationem ad malum, si essent pure intellectuales non habentes admixtionem naturae corporeae.

Sciendum est ergo quod Platonici posuerunt, ut etiam supra dictum est, daemones esse animalia quaedam corporea habentia intellectum. Et in quantum habent corpoream et sensitivam naturam sunt variis animae passionibus subiecti sicut et homines, ex quibus inclinantur ad malum: unde Apuleius in libro De deo Socratis definiens daemones dixit eos *esse genere animalia, animo passiva, mente rationalia, corpore aerea, tempore aeterna*; et sicut ipse dicit, subiecta est mens daemonum passionibus libidinum formidinum irarum atque huiusmodi ceteris. Sic ergo daemones etiam loco discernunt a diis — quos angelos dicimus —, aerea loca daemonibus attribuentes, aetherea vero angelis sive diis.

Hanc autem positionem quantum ad aliquid aliqui Ecclesiae doctores sequuntur. Augustinus enim III Super Genesim ad litteram videtur dicere vel sub dubio relinquere quod *daemones aerea sunt animalia, quoniam corporum aereorum natura vigent et propterea morte non dissolvuntur, quia praevalet in eis elementum quod ad faciendum quam ad patiendum est aptius*, scilicet aer; et hoc idem in pluribus aliis locis dicit. Sed et Dionysius videtur in daemonibus ponere ea quae ad sensibilem animam pertinent; dicit enim IV cap. De divinis nominibus quod *est in daemonibus malum furor irrationabilis, demens concupiscentia et phantasia proterva*: manifestum est autem phantasiam et concupiscentiam et iram sive furorem non ad intellectum sed ad sensitivae partem animae pertinere. Sed et quantum ad locum quidam cum eis consenserunt putantes daemones non caelestes vel supercaelestes angelos fuisse, ut Augustinus narrat in III Super Genesim ad litteram; sed et Damascenus (dicit) in secundo libro daemones *ex his angelicis virtutibus*

to the perfection of a higher nature; just as to be raging is a certain good with respect to a dog, is nevertheless an evil with respect to man, who has reason. Yet it is possible that there should be in man, according to his sensible and corporeal nature which he shares with brutes, a certain inclination to raging, which is evil for man. But this cannot be said of an intellectual nature because the intellect has an order to the good in general. Accordingly, it is impossible for a natural inclination to evil to be found in demons, if they are purely intellectual[286] and have no admixture of a corporeal nature.

It must be known, therefore, that the Platonists posited, as has likewise been said above,[287] that the demons are certain corporeal animals which have an intellect. And inasmuch as they have a corporeal and sensible nature, they are subject to various passions of the soul, just as men are subject to passions which incline them towards evil. Accordingly, when Apuleius was defining the demons in the book, *On the god of Socrates*,[288] he said that they are *animals in genus, passible in soul, rational in mind, airy in body, eternal in time*. And just as he himself says, the mind of the demons is subject to the passions of lusts, fears, and angers and all other such things. Therefore, the demons are likewise locally separated from the gods—whom we call angels—attributing the airy places to the demons but the ethereal ones to the angels or gods.

Certain of the doctors of the Church follow this position in some respect. For in the third book of the *Literal Commentary on Genesis*,[289] Augustine seems to say or to leave unsettled that *the demons are airy animals because they have the nature of airy bodies; and, for that reason, they are not destroyed by death, because there prevails in them an element*, namely air, *which is quite suitable both for acting as well as being acted upon*—and he says the same thing in several other places. And Dionysius seems to posit in demons those attributes which belong to a sensible soul; for he says in the fourth chapter of *On the Divine Names*[290] that *there is in demons an evil—an irrational rage, a mad concupiscence, and wanton fancy*. And it is clear that fancy and concupiscence and anger or rage pertain not to the intellect but to a part of the sensitive soul. And with respect to place, certain doctors agreed with these thinkers because they did not consider the demons to be either celestial or super-celestial angels, as Augustine relates in the third book of the *Literal Commentary on Genesis*.[291] And Damascene

---

286. As in the case of Cap. I, there seems to be no palaeographical justification for the reading which we give. Eleven manuscripts used in the preparation of this text (METZ, Bibl. de la Ville 1158 comprises only folios 12v and 13r, i.e., Cap. I to Cap. II, read "essent." We have preferred the reading "sunt" which is found in the 1488 *Soncinas*, the 1490, 1498, and 1508 *Pizzamanus* printed editions. Concerning the value of these incunabula with respect to the establishing of a truly critical text, cf. above, Introduction, and F. Lescoe, *op. cit.*, Introduction: Literary Problems).

287. Cf. above, Cap. I.

288. Cf. St. Augustine, *De Civitate Dei*, IX, 8 (PL 41, 263).

289. St. Augustine, *De Gen. ad Litt.*, II, 10 (PL 34, 284).

290. Pseudo-Dionysius, *De Divinis Nominibus*, IV, 23, (PG 3, 725C); *Dionysiaca*, I, c. IV, sec. 20 (p. 280).

291. St. Augustine, *De Gen. ad Litt.*, III, 10 (PL 34, 285).

fuisse qui terrestri ordini praeerant; sed et Apostolus ad Ephes. II, 2 nominat diabolum *principem potestatis aeris huius.*

Sed occurrit hic aliud consideratione dignum. Cum enim unicuique speciei sit attributa materia secundum convenientiam suae formae, non videtur esse possibile quod in tota aliqua specie sit naturalis inclinatio ad id quod est malum illi speciei secundum rationem propriae formae, sicut non omnibus hominibus inest naturalis inclinatio ad immoderantiam concupiscentiae sive irae. Sic igitur non est possibile omnes daemones habere naturalem inclinationem ad fallacia et ad alia mala, etiam si omnes essent unius speciei; multo minus ergo si singuli essent in singulis speciebus. Quamvis, si sint corporei, nihil impedire videatur plures sub una specie contineri, poterit enim secundum diversitatem materiae diversitas individuorum unius speciei causari. Oportebit igitur dicere quod non omnes nec semper fuerunt mali, sed aliqui eorum mali esse inceperunt proprio arbitrio passionum inclinationem sequentes.

Unde et Dionysius dicit quod *aversio*, scilicet a Deo, *est ipsis* daemonibus *malum et convenientium ipsis excessus*, quia per superbiam ultra se ipsos sunt elati; et postea subdit quaedam ad poenam pertinentia, sicut *non consecutio* finis ultimi, *et imperfectio* per carentiam debitae perfectionis, *et impotentia* consequendi quod naturaliter desiderant, *et infirmitas virtutis* conservantis naturalem in eis ordinem revocantem a malo. Augustinus etiam dicit in III Super Genesim ad litteram quod *transgressores angeli ante transgressionem suam fuerunt in superiori parte aeris propinqua caelo cum principe suo nunc diabolo tunc archangelo*, manifeste exprimens per transgressionem quamdam eos esse malos factos. Sed et Damascenus dicit in secundo libro quod diabolus *non natura malus factus est, sed bonus existens et in bono genitus liberi sui arbitrii electione versus est.*

Hoc insuper et Origenes in I Peri archon et Augustinus in XI De civitate Dei auctoritatibus sacrae Scripturae confirmant inducentes id quod habetur Is. XIV, 12 dictum diabolo sub similitudine regis Babylonis *Quomodo cecidisti, Lucifer, qui mane oriebaris?* Et Ez. XXVIII, 12 ad eum dicitur in persona regis Tyri *Tu signaculum similitudinis, plenus sapientia, perfectus decore in deliciis paradisi*

says in the second book[292] that the demons *were among the angelic powers which were in command of the earthly order.* And the Apostle in Ephesians 2:2 calls the devil *the prince of the power of the air.*

But something presents itself here which is worthy of consideration. For, since matter is attributed to each species according to the suitability of its form, it does not seem possible that there should be in a whole of a given species a natural inclination to that which is evil for that species according to the nature of its proper form; just as there is not present in all men a natural inclination to the immoderation of concupiscence or anger. Therefore, it is not possible that all demons should have a natural inclination to deception and to other evils, even if they were all of one species. Much less, therefore, if there should be individuals in individual species—although if they are corporeal, nothing seems to prevent many of them from being contained under one species, for a diversity of individuals of one species could be caused according to a diversity of matter. Therefore, we shall have to say that the demons were not always evil but some of them began to be evil when, by their own choice, they followed the inclination of the passions.

And accordingly, Dionysius says in the fourth chapter of *On the Divine Names*[293] that *aversion*, namely, from God, *is an evil* for the demons *themselves, and it is a forsaking of those things which are fitting to them* because they were carried away by pride beyond themselves. And later on, he adds certain remarks pertaining to punishment as *not reaching* the ultimate end, *and imperfection*, through a lack of a due perfection, *and impotence* of pursuing that which they desire by nature, *and an infirmity of the power* conserving in them a natural order, calling them back from evil. Augustine likewise says in the third book of the *Literal Commentary on Genesis*[294] that *the transgressing angels were before their transgression, along with their leader, now a devil and formerly an archangel*, in the higher part of the air near the heaven. He gives us clearly to understand that some of the angels were made evil through their transgression. And Damascene says in the second book[295] that the devil *was not created evil in nature but, existing as good and begotten in the good, he used the election of his own choice.*

In addition, both Origen in I *Peri Archon*[296] and Augustine in Book XI of *On the City of God*[297] confirm this with texts of the sacred Scriptures, when they introduce what is contained in Isaiah 14:12 about the devil under the likeness of the king of Babylon: *How have you fallen, O Lucifer, who rose in the morning?* And in Ezechiel 28:12–13 it is said to him in the person of the king of Tyre: *You were the signet*

292. St. John Damascene, *De Fide Orthodoxa*, II, 4 (PG 94, 873C–876A).

293. Pseudo-Dionysius, *De Divinis Nominibus*, IV, 23 (PG 3, 735B) *Dionysiaca*, I, c. IV, sec. 20 (p. 279).

294. St. Augustine, *De Gen. ad Litt.*, III, 10 (PL 34, 285).

295. St. John Damascene, *De Fide Orthodoxa*, II, 4 (PG 94, 876A).

296. Origen, *Peri Archon*, I, 5 (PG 11, 160C ff., 163A-C).

297. St. Augustine, *De Civitate Dei*, XI, 15 (PL 41, 330).

Dei fuisti; et postea subditur *Perfectus in viis tuis a die conditionis tuae, donec inventa est iniquitas in te.* Solvit Augustinus ibidem quod dicitur Io. VIII, 44 *Ille homicida erat ab initio et in veritate non stetit,* et quod in Canonica Ioannis dicitur quod *diabolus ab initio peccat,* referens hoc ad initium quo incepit peccare, vel ad initium conditionis humanae, quod deceptum hominem spiritualiter occidit.

Huic autem sententiae consonare videtur Platonicorum opinio qui daemonum quosdam bonos quosdam malos dicunt, quasi eos proprio arbitrio bonos vel malos factos. Unde et Plotinus ulterius procedens dixit *animas hominum daemones esse et ex hominibus fieri lares si meriti boni sunt, lemures autem si mali seu larvas, manes autem deos dici si incertum est bonorum eos seu malorum esse meritorum,* sicut Augustinus introducit IX De civitate Dei. Quod quidem quantum ad hoc praemissae sanctorum assertioni concordat quod pro meritis bonis vel malis aliquos daemones bonos vel malos esse asserunt, quamvis non sit nostrae consuetudinis quod bonos spiritus daemones, sed angelos nominemus.

Quantum vero ad hoc quod dixit animas hominum mortuorum fieri daemones, est erronea eius positio; unde Chrysostomus dicit, exponens id quod habetur Matth. VIII, 28 quod duo habentes daemonia exibant de monumentis, *Per hoc, inquit, quod de monumentis exibant perniciosum dogma imponere volebant quod animae morientium daemones fiunt; unde et multi aruspicum occiderunt pueros ut animam eorum cooperantem haberent. Propter quod et daemoniaci clamant: Quoniam anima illius ego sum. Non est autem anima defuncti quae clamat, sed daemon effingit ut decipiat audientes; si enim in alterius corpus animam mortui possibile esset intrare, multo magis in corpus suum. Sed neque habet rationem iniqua passam animam cooperari iniqua sibi facienti; neque etiam rationabile est animam a corpore separatam hic iam oberrare, iustorum enim animae in manu Dei sunt: sed et quae peccatorum sunt confestim hinc abducuntur, ut manifestum est ex Lazaro et divite.*

Nec tamen putandum est Plotinum in hoc a Platonicorum opinione deviasse ponentium daemones esse aerea corpora, quod animas hominum post mortem fieri (daemones) aestimabat; quia etiam animae homi-

of perfection, full of wisdom and perfect in beauty; you were in Eden, the garden of God. And afterwards, it is added: *You were blameless in your ways from the day you were created, till iniquity was found in you* (Ezek 28:15). In the same place, Augustine[298] resolves what is said in John 8:44: *He was a murderer from the beginning, and did not stand in the truth,* and what is said in 1 John 3:8, that *the devil has sinned from the beginning,* referring this to the beginning when he began to sin, or to the beginning of the human state when he killed man spiritually after having deceived him.

Furthermore, the opinion of the Platonists, who say that certain demons are good and others are evil—as if having been made good or evil by their own free choice—seems to agree with this opinion.[299] Accordingly, Plotinus, proceeding further, says that *the souls of men become demons and the lares are made of men if the latter are of good merit; the lemures or larvae, however, if they are of evil merit; and they are called manes if it is uncertain whether they are of good or evil merit,* as Augustine sets forth in *On the City of God.*[300] This opinion agrees with the aforementioned position[301] of the saints in this, that the latter assert some demons to be good and others evil because of good or evil merits, although it is not customary for us to call the good spirits 'demons' but rather 'angels.'

As to what he says (namely, that the souls of the dead become demons), his position is in error. Accordingly, Chrysostom,[302] expounding on what is contained in Matthew 8:28, that two men possessed with devils came out of the sepulchres, says: *Through this fact, namely that they were going out of the sepulchres, they wanted to impose a pernicious doctrine, that the souls of the dying become demons. Accordingly, many soothsayers killed children so that they might have their cooperating soul. And because of this, many demoniacs shout: I am that one's soul. However, it is not the dead person's soul which shouts, but the demon pretends so that he might deceive the hearers. For if it were possible for the soul of one dead to enter the body of another, it would be much more possible for it to enter its own body. Nor is it reasonable for a soul suffering iniquities to cooperate with the one that brings iniquities on it. Nor likewise is it reasonable that a soul separated from the body should still be wandering here. For the souls of the just are in the hand of God.*[303] *But those which are of sinners are led away from here at once, as is evident from Lazarus and Dives.*

Nevertheless, we must not think that in this respect, Plotinus deviated from the opinion of the Platonists who posited the demons to be airy bodies—namely, because Plotinus thought that the souls of men become demons af-

---

298. St. Augustine, *De Civitate Dei*, XI, 14–15 (PL 41, 330–331).
299. St. Augustine, *De Civitate Dei*, IX, 1–2 (PL 41, 255–257).
300. *Ibid.*, IX, 11 (PL 41, 265).
301. Cf. above, Cap. XIX; Cap. I.
302. St. John Chrysostom, *Homilia in Matt.*, XXVIII (PG 57, 353).
303. Wis 3:1.

num secundum Platonicorum opinionem praeter ista corpora corruptibilia habent quaedam aetherea corpora quibus semper, etiam post horum sensibilium corporum dissolutionem, quasi incorruptibilibus uniuntur. Unde Proclus dicit in Libro divinarum coelementationum *Omnis anima participabilis corpore utitur primo perpetuo et habente hypostasim ingenerabilem et incorruptibilem;* et sic animae a corporibus separatae secundum eos aerea animalia esse non desinunt.

Sed secundum aliorum sanctorum sententiam daemones, quos malos angelos dicimus, non solum fuerunt de inferiori angelorum ordine, sed etiam de superioribus ordinibus quos incorporeos et immateriales esse ostendimus, ita quod inter eos unus est qui summus omnium fuit. Unde Gregorius in quadam homilia exponens illud Ez. XXVIII, 13 *Omnis lapis pretiosus operimentum eius,* dicit quod princeps malorum angelorum in aliorum angelorum comparatione ceteris clarior fuit; et in hoc consentire videtur illis qui deorum quosdam bonos quosdam malos esse asserebant, secundum quod dii angeli nominantur. Unde et Iob IV, 18 dicitur *Ecce qui serviunt ei non sunt stabiles et in angelis suis reperit pravitatem.*

Sed hoc multas difficultates habet. In substantia enim incorporea et intellectuali nullus appetitus esse videtur nisi intellectivus, qui quidem est simpliciter boni, ut per Philosophum patet in XII Metaphysicae; nullus autem efficitur malus ex hoc quod eius intellectus tendit in hoc quod est simpliciter bonum, sed ex hoc quod tendit in aliquid quod est secundum quid bonum ac si esset simpliciter bonum: non ergo videtur esse possibile quod proprio appetitu aliqua incorporea et intellectualis substantia mala efficiatur.

Rursus, appetitus esse non potest nisi boni vel apparentis boni, bonum enim est quod omnia appetunt; ex hoc autem quod aliquis verum bonum appetit non efficitur malus: oportet igitur in omni eo qui per proprium appetitum malus efficitur, quod appetat apparens bonum tanquam vere bonum. Hoc autem non potest esse nisi in suo iudicio fallatur: quod non videtur posse contingere in substantia incorporea intellectuali quae falsae apprehensionis capax, ut videtur, esse non potest; nam et in nobis quando in quantum intelligimus aliquid falsitas esse non potest. Unde Augustinus dicit in Libro LXXXIII Quaestionum quod *omnis qui fallitur, id in quo fallitur non intelligit;* unde et circa ea quae proprie intellectu capimus, sicut circa prima principia, nullus decipi potest. Impossibile igitur videtur quod aliqua incorporea

ter death—for according to the Platonists' opinion, even the souls of men have, over and above these corruptible bodies, certain ethereal bodies to which they are always joined as to something incorruptible, even after the dissolution of these sensible bodies. Accordingly, Proclus says in the *Book of the Divine Elementations:*[304] *Every soul capable of participating uses the first and perpetual body and one having an ungenerated and incorruptible hypostasis.* And thus, according to them, the souls separated from the bodies do not cease to be airy animals.

But, according to the opinion of other saints, the demons (whom we call evil angels) not only came from a lower order of angels but also from the higher orders, whom we have shown to be incorporeal and immaterial,[305] so that among them, there was one who was the highest of all. Accordingly, Gregory[306] explaining in a certain homily the words of Ezechiel 28:13, *Every precious stone was his covering,* says that the leader of the evil angels was, in comparison with the other angels, more brilliant than the rest. And in this respect, he seems to agree with those who asserted some demons to be good and others to be evil, according to which demons are called angels. And therefore it is said in Job 4:18: *Behold, they who serve him are not steadfast, and in his angels he found wickedness.*

But this presents many difficulties. For in an incorporeal and intellectual substance, there seems to be no appetite except the intellectual, which is of that which is absolutely good, as appears through the Philosopher in XII *Metaphysics.*[307] Now no one is made evil from the fact that his intellect tends toward that which is good absolutely, but from the fact that it tends toward a qualifiedly good thing as though it were absolutely good. Therefore, it does not seem possible that an incorporeal and intellectual substance should be made evil by its own appetite.

Again, appetite can be only of the good or of the seeming good, for the good is that which all beings seek, and one is not rendered evil because he seeks the true good. Therefore, every individual who is made evil through his own appetite must seek a seeming good as though it were truly good. This, however, cannot be unless he is deceived in his judgment, which does not seem capable of happening in an incorporeal and intellectual substance, which, as it seems, cannot have a false apprehension. For even in our case, insofar as we understand something, there can be no falsity. Accordingly, Augustine says in the *Book of Eighty-Three Questions,*[308] that *everyone who is deceived, that, indeed, in which he is deceived, he does not understand.* And accordingly, no one can be deceived concerning those things which we grasp properly by our intellect, as well as concern-

---

304. Proclus, *Elem*, Prop. 196 (p. 171).
305. Cf. above, Cap. VII.
306. St. Gregory the Great, *Moral. in Job*, XXXII, 23 (PL 76, 665C).
307. Aristotle, *Metaphysics*, XI, 7 (1072b 18–19); 9 (1074b 23–24).
308. St. Augustine, Liber LXXXIII *Quaestionum*, q. 32 (PL 40, 22).

et intellectualis substantia per proprium appetitum mala fiat.

Adhuc, substantia quae est intellectualis naturae a corpore separata necesse est quod sit omnino a tempore absoluta. Natura enim uniuscuiusque rei ex eius operatione deprehenditur, operationis vero ratio cognoscitur ex obiecto; intelligibile autem in quantum huiusmodi neque est hic neque nunc sed abstractum sicut a loci dimensionibus ita et a temporum successione: ipsa igitur intellectualis operatio si per se consideretur, oportet quod sicut est abstracta ab omni corporali dimensione ita etiam excedat omnem successionem temporalem. Et si alicui intellectuali operationi continuum vel tempus adiungatur, hoc non est nisi per accidens, sicut in nobis accidit in quantum intellectus noster a phantasmatibus abstrahit intelligibiles species, quas etiam in eis considerat; quod in substantia incorporea et intellectuali locum habere non potest: relinquitur igitur quod huiusmodi substantiae operatio et per consequens substantia omnino sit extra omnem temporalem successionem. Unde et Proclus dicit quod *omnis intellectus in aeternitate substantiam habet et potentiam et operationem*; et in Libro de causis dicitur quod *intelligentia parificatur aeternitati*. Quidquid igitur substantiis illis incorporeis et intellectualibus convenit, semper et absque successione convenit illis; aut igitur semper fuerunt malae, quod est contra praemissa, aut nequaquam malae fieri potuerunt.

Amplius, cum Deus sit ipsa essentia bonitatis ut Dionysius dicit in primo capitulo De divinis nominibus, necesse est quod tanto aliqua sint perfectius in participatione bonitatis firmata quanto sunt Deo propinquiora. Manifestum est autem substantias intellectuales incorporeas supra omnia corpora esse; si igitur suprema corpora, scilicet caelestia, non sunt susceptiva alicuius inordinationis vel mali, multo minus illae supercaelestes substantiae inordinationis et mali capaces esse non potuerunt. Unde et Dionysius dicit IV cap. Caelestis hierarchiae quod *sancti caelestium substantiarum ornatus super solum existentia et irrationabiliter viventia et ea quae secundum nos sunt rationalia in participatione divinae traditionis sunt facti, et copiosiores habent ad Deum communiones, attenti manentes et semper ad superius sicut est fas in fortitudine divini et indeclinabilis amoris extenti*. Hoc igitur videtur ordo rerum habere ut, sicut inferiora corpora inordinationi et malo possunt esse subiecta, non autem caelestia corpora, ita etiam intellectus corporibus inferioribus uniti possunt subiici

ing the first principles. Therefore, it seems impossible that some incorporeal and intellectual substance should become evil through its own appetite.

Furthermore, a substance which is of an intellectual nature and separate from a body must be absolutely free of time. For the nature of a thing is grasped from its operation, while the character of an operation is known from its object. However, the intelligible, precisely as such, is neither here nor now; but it is rather something abstracted both from the dimensions of place as well as from the succession of time. Therefore, the intellectual operation itself, if it be considered by itself, must likewise rise above all temporal succession, just as it is abstracted from all corporeal dimension. And if a magnitude or time be joined to any intellectual operation, this happens only accidentally, just as it happens in our case insofar as our intellect abstracts intelligible species from phantasms which it likewise considers in them—which can have no place in an incorporeal and intellectual substance. It remains, therefore, that the operation of such a substance (and consequently the substance itself) should be altogether outside all temporal succession. And Proclus says accordingly that *every intellect has substance, and power, and operation, in eternity.*[309] And in the *Book on Causes*[310] it is said that *understanding is on a par with eternity.* Therefore, whatever befits those incorporeal and intellectual substances befits them always and without succession. Therefore, either they were always evil—which is against what has been set down—or they could in no way have been made evil.

Moreover, since God is the very essence of goodness, as Dionysius says in the first chapter of *On the Divine Names*,[311] it is necessary that the closer they are to God, the more firmly are certain beings strengthened in the participation of goodness. But it is evident that intellectual, incorporeal substances are above all bodies. If, therefore, the highest bodies, (namely, the heavenly bodies) are not receptive of any disorder or evil, much less could those super-celestial substances be capable of disorder and evil. Accordingly, Dionysius says in the fourth chapter of the *Celestial Hierarchy*,[312] that *the holy ornaments of the celestial substances participated in the divine teaching in greater measure than those beings that only exist, those that live with an irrational life, and those that we call rational; and they have more abundant communications with God, with their minds fixed and, as is befitting, stretched towards what is above them in the power of a love that is divine and unswerving.* The order of things then seems to have this: that just as the lower bodies can be subject to disorder and evil, but not the heavenly bodies, so likewise the intellects joined to

---

309. Proclus, *Elem.*, Prop. 169 (pp. 147–149).

310. *Liber de Causis*, II, ed. O. Bardenhewer, 165, 14.

311. Pseudo-Dionysius, *De Divinis Nominibus*, I, 5 (PG 3, 593D); *Dionysiaca*, I, c. 1, sec. 4 (pp. 39–41).

312. Pseudo-Dionysius, *De Coelesti Hierarchia*, IV, 2 (PG 3, 180A); *Dionysiaca*, II, c. 4 sec. 60 (pp. 803–805).

malo, non autem illae supercaelestes substantiae. Et hoc secuti esse videntur qui posuerunt daemones, quos malos angelos dicimus, ex inferiori ordine et corporeos esse.

the lower bodies can be subject to evil, but not those super-celestial substances. And this view those thinkers seemed to follow who posited that the demons, who for us are the bad angels, are from a lower order and corporeal.

ON KINGSHIP

PROLOGUE

Cogitanti mihi quid offerrem regiae celsitudini dignum meaeque professioni et officio congruum, id occurrit potissime offerendum ut regi librum de regno conscriberem, in quo et regni originem et ea quae ad regis officium pertinent secundum Scripturae divinae auctoritatem, philosophorum dogmata et exempla laudatorum principum, diligenter depromerem iuxta ingenii proprii facultatem, principium, progressum et consummationem operis ex illius expectans auxilio qui est Rex regum et Dominus dominantium, per quem reges regnant, Deus magnus Dominus, et rex magnus super omnes deos.

As I was turning over in my mind what I might present to your majesty as a gift, at once worthy of your royal highness and befitting my profession and office, it seemed to me a highly appropriate offering that, for a king, I should write a book on kingship, in which, so far as my ability permits, I should carefully expound, according to the authority of Scripture and the teachings of the philosophers, as well as the practice of worthy princes, both the origin of kingly government and the things which pertain to the office of a king, relying for the beginning, progress and accomplishment of this work on the help of him who is King of kings and Lord of lords, through whom kings rule, God the mighty Lord, the great king above all gods.

Book I

Kingship

Chapter 1

What is signified by the name of king

Principium autem intentionis nostrae hinc sumere oportet ut quid nomine regis intelligendum sit, exponatur. In omnibus autem quae ad finem aliquem ordinantur, in quibus contingit sic et aliter procedere, opus est aliquo dirigente per quod directe debitum perveniatur ad finem. Non enim navis, quam secundum diversorum ventorum impulsum in diversa moveri contingit, ad destinatum finem perveniret nisi per gubernatoris industriam dirigeretur ad portum. Hominis autem est aliquis finis ad quem tota eius vita et actio ordinatur, cum sit agens per intellectum cuius est manifeste propter finem operari. Contingit autem diversimode homines ad finem intentum procedere, quod ipsa diversitas humanorum studiorum et actionum declarat; indiget igitur homo aliquo dirigente ad finem.

Est autem unicuique hominum naturaliter insitum rationis lumen, quo in suis actibus dirigatur ad finem. Et si quidem homini conveniret singulariter vivere sicut multis animalium, nullo alio dirigente indigeret ad finem, sed ipse sibi unusquisque esset rex sub Deo summo rege, inquantum per lumen rationis divinitus sibi datum in suis actibus se ipsum dirigeret. Naturale autem est homini ut sit animal sociale et politicum, in multitudine vivens, magis etiam quam omnia alia animalia; quod quidem naturalis necessitas declarat. Aliis enim animalibus natura praeparavit cibum, tegumenta pilorum, defensionem, ut dentes, cornua, ungues, vel saltem velocitatem ad fugam; homo autem institutus est nullo horum sibi a natura praeparato, sed loco omnium data est ei ratio per quam sibi haec omnia officio manuum posset praeparare. Ad quae omnia praeparanda unus homo non sufficit, nam unus homo per se sufficienter vitam transigere non posset; est igitur homini naturale quod in societate multorum vivat.

Amplius, aliis animalibus insita est naturalis industria ad omnia ea quae sunt eis utilia vel nociva, sicut ovis naturaliter existimat lupum inimicum; quaedam etiam animalia ex naturali industria cognoscunt aliquas herbas medicinales et alia eorum vitae necessaria. Homo autem horum quae sunt suae vitae necessaria naturalem

The first step in our undertaking must be to set forth what the name 'king' means. In all things which are ordered towards an end, in which this or that course may be adopted, some directive principle is needed through which the due end may be reached by the most direct route. A ship, for example, which moves in different directions according to the impulse of the changing winds, would never reach its destination were it not brought to port by the skill of the pilot. Now, man has an end to which his whole life and all his actions are ordered; for man is an intelligent agent, and it is clearly the part of an intelligent agent to act in view of an end. Men also adopt different methods in proceeding towards their proposed end, as the diversity of men's pursuits and actions clearly indicates. Consequently, man needs some directive principle to guide him towards his end.

Now the light of reason is placed by nature in every man to guide him in his acts towards his end. And if man were intended to live alone, as many animals do, he would require no other guide to his end. Each man would be a king unto himself, under God the highest king, inasmuch as he would direct himself in his acts by the light of reason given him from on high. Yet it is natural for man, more than for any other animal, to be a social and political animal living in a group. This is clearly a necessity of man's nature. For all other animals, nature has prepared food, a covering of hair, and means of defense such as teeth, horns, claws, or at least speed in flight. Man alone was made without any natural provisions for these things, yet in their place he was given reason, through which he could procure all these things for himself by the work of his hands. Now, one man alone is not able to procure them all for himself, for one man could not sufficiently provide for life, unassisted. It is therefore natural that man should live in the society of many.

Moreover, all other animals are able to discern, by inborn skill, what is useful and what is injurious (as the sheep naturally regards the wolf as his enemy). Some animals also recognize by natural skill certain medicinal herbs and other things necessary for their life. Man, on the contrary, has a natural knowledge of the things which are essential for his

cognitionem habet solum in communi, quasi eo per rationem valente ex naturalibus principiis ad cognitionem singulorum quae necessaria sunt humanae vitae pervenire. Non est autem possibile quod unus homo ad omnia huiusmodi per suam rationem pertingat; est igitur necessarium homini quod in multitudine vivat, ut unus ab alio adiuvetur, ut diversi in diversis inveniendis per rationem occupentur, puta unus in medicina, alius in hoc alius in alio.

Hoc etiam evidentissime declaratur per hoc quod est proprium hominis locutione uti, per quam unus homo aliis suum conceptum totaliter exprimere potest. Alia quidem animalia exprimunt mutuo suas passiones in communi, ut canis iram per latratum, et alia animalia passiones alias diversis modis; magis igitur homo est communicativus alteri quam quodcumque aliud animal quod gregale videtur, ut grus et formica et apis. Hoc ergo considerans Salomon ait *Melius est duos esse quam unum; habent enim emolumentum mutuae societatis.*

Si igitur naturale est homini quod in societate multorum vivat, necesse est in omnibus esse aliquid per quod multitudo regatur. Multis enim existentibus hominibus et unoquoque id quod est sibi congruum providente, multitudo in diversa dispergeretur nisi etiam esset aliquid de eo quod ad bonum multitudinis pertinet curam habens, sicut et corpus hominis et cuiuslibet animalis deflueret nisi esset aliqua vis regitiva communis in corpore, quae ad bonum commune omnium membrorum intenderet. Quod considerans Salomon dixit *Ubi non est gubernator, dissipabitur populus.*

Hoc autem rationabiliter accidit. Non enim idem est quod proprium et quod commune est; secundum propria quidem differunt, secundum commune autem uniuntur. Diversorum autem diversae sunt causae; oportet igitur, praeter id quod movet ad proprium bonum uniuscuiusque, esse aliquid quod movet ad bonum commune multorum. Propter quod et in omnibus quae in unum ordinantur, aliquid invenitur alterius regitivum: in universitate enim corporum per primum corpus, scilicet caeleste, alia corpora ordine quodam divinae providentiae reguntur, omniaque corpora per creaturam rationalem. In uno etiam homine anima regit corpus, atque inter animae partes irascibilis et concupiscibilis ratione reguntur. Itemque inter membra corporis unum est principale quod omnia movet, aut cor aut caput. Oportet igitur esse in omni multitudine aliquod regitivum.

Contingit autem in quibusdam quae ordinantur ad finem et recte et non recte procedere; quare et in regimine multitudinis et rectum et non rectum invenitur.

life only in a general fashion, inasmuch as he is able to attain knowledge of the particular things necessary for human life by reasoning from natural principles. But it is not possible for one man to arrive at a knowledge of all these things by his own individual reason. It is therefore necessary for man to live in a multitude so that each one may assist his fellows, and different men may be occupied in seeking to make different discoveries by reason—one, for example, in medicine, one in this and another in that.

This point is further and most plainly evidenced by the fact that the use of speech is proper to man, through which one man is able to fully express his conceptions to others. Other animals, it is true, express their feelings to one another in a general way, as a dog may express anger by barking and other animals give vent to other feelings in various fashions. But man communicates with his kind more completely than any other animal known to be gregarious, such as the crane, the ant or the bee. Considering this, Solomon says: *It is better that there be two than one; for they have the advantage of their company* (Eccl 4:9).

If, then, it is natural for man to live in the society of many, there must exist among men some means by which the group may be governed. For where there are many men together and each one is looking after his own interest, the multitude would be broken up and scattered unless there were also an agency to take care of what appertains to the commonweal. In like manner, the body of a man or any other animal would disintegrate unless there were a general ruling force within the body which watches over the common good of all members. With this in mind, Solomon says: *Where there is no governor, the people shall fall* (Prov 11:14).

Indeed, it is reasonable that this should happen, for what is proper and what is common are not identical. Things differ by what is proper to each: they are united by what they have in common. But diversity of effects is due to diversity of causes. Consequently, beyond that which moves toward the proper good of each individual, there must exist something which moves toward the common good of the many. Also on account of this, in all things that are ordained towards one end, one thing is found to rule the rest. Thus, in the corporeal universe, corporeal things are regulated according to the order of Divine Providence by the first body (namely, the celestial body); and all physical creation is ruled by a rational creature. Likewise, in the individual man the soul rules the body, and, among the parts of the soul, the irascible and the concupiscible parts are ruled by reason. Likewise, among the members of a body, one (such as the heart or the head) is the principal and moves all the others. Therefore, in every multitude there must be some governing power.

Now, it happens in certain things which are ordained towards an end that there is both a right and a wrong way to proceed: and for this reason, in the government of a mul-

Recte autem dirigitur unumquodque quando ad finem convenientem deducitur, non recte autem quando ad finem non convenientem. Alius autem est finis conveniens multitudini liberorum et servorum; nam liber est qui sui causa est, servus autem est qui id quod est alterius est. Si igitur liberorum multitudo a regente ad bonum commune multitudinis ordinetur, erit regimen rectum et iustum quale convenit liberis. Si vero non ad bonum commune multitudinis sed ad bonum privatum regentis regimen ordinetur, erit regimen iniustum atque perversum; unde et Dominus talibus rectoribus comminatur per Ezechielem dicens *Vae pastoribus qui pascebant se ipsos*, quasi sua propria commoda quaerentes, *nonne greges pascuntur a pastoribus?* Bonum siquidem gregis pastores quaerere debent, et rectores quique bonum multitudinis sibi subiectae.

Si igitur regimen iniustum per unum tantum fiat qui sua commoda ex regimine quaerat, non autem bonum multitudinis sibi subiectae, talis rector tyrannus vocatur nomine a fortitudine derivato, quia scilicet per potentiam opprimit, non per iustitiam regit; unde et apud antiquos potentes quique tyranni vocabantur. Si vero iniustum regimen non per unum fiat sed per plures, si quidem per paucos oligarchia vocatur, id est principatus paucorum, quando scilicet pauci propter divitias opprimunt plebem, sola pluralitate a tyranno differentes. Si vero iniquum regimen exerceatur per multos, democratia nominatur, id est potentatus populi, quando scilicet populus plebeiorum per potentiam multitudinis opprimit divites: sic enim populus totus erit quasi unus tyrannus.

Similiter autem et iustum regimen distingui oportet. Si enim administretur per aliquam multitudinem, communi nomine politia vocatur, utpote cum multitudo bellatorum in civitate vel provincia dominatur. Si vero administretur per paucos, virtuosos autem, huiusmodi regimen aristocratia vocatur, id est potentatus optimus, vel optimorum, qui propterea optimates dicuntur. Si vero iustum regimen ad unum tantum pertineat, ille proprie rex vocatur: unde Dominus per Ezechielem dicit *Servus meus David rex super eos erit et pastor unus erit omnium eorum.* Ex quo manifeste ostenditur quod de ratione regis est quod sit unus qui praesit, et quod sit pastor bonum commune multitudinis et non suum quaerens.

Cum autem homini competat in multitudine vivere, quia sibi non sufficit ad necessaria vitae si solitarius maneat, oportet quod tanto sit perfectior multitudinis societas quanto magis per se sufficiens erit ad necessaria vitae. Habetur siquidem aliqua vitae sufficientia in una familia domus unius, quantum scilicet ad natu-

titude there is a distinction between right and wrong. A thing is rightly directed when it is led towards a fitting end; wrongly, when it is led towards an unfitting end. Now the end which befits a multitude of free men is different from that which befits a multitude of slaves, for the free man is one who exists for his own sake, while the slave, as such, exists for the sake of another. If, therefore, a multitude of free men is ordered by the ruler towards the common good of the multitude, that rulership will be right and just, as is suitable to free men. If, on the other hand, a rulership aims not at the common good of the multitude, but at the private good of the ruler, it will be an unjust and perverted rulership. And hence the Lord threatens such rulers, saying by the mouth of Ezekiel: *Woe to the shepherds that feed themselves*, as seeking their own interest, *should not the flocks be fed by the shepherd?* (Ezek 34:2). Shepherds indeed should seek the good of their flocks, and every ruler the good of the multitude subject to him.

If an unjust government is carried on by one man alone, who seeks his own benefit from his rule and not the good of the multitude subject to him, such a ruler is called a 'tyrant'—a word derived from strength—because he oppresses by might instead of ruling by justice. Thus, among the ancients, all powerful men were called tyrants. If an unjust government is carried on not by one but by several, and if they be few, it is called an 'oligarchy'—that is, the rule of a few. This occurs when a few, who differ from the tyrant only by the fact that they are more than one, oppress the people by means of their wealth. If the bad government is carried on by the multitude, it is called a 'democracy'—that is, control by the populace—which comes about when the plebeian people by force of numbers oppress the rich. In this way the whole people will be as one tyrant.

In like manner we must divide just governments. If the government is administered by many, it is given the name 'polity,' common to all forms of government: as, for instance, when a group of warriors exercise dominion over a city or province. If it is administered by a few men of virtue, this kind of government is called an 'aristocracy,' that is, the best governance, or governance by the best men, who for this reason are called the 'Optimates.' And if a just government is in the hands of one man alone, he is properly called a 'king.' Wherefore the Lord says by the mouth of Ezekiel: *My servant, David, shall be king over them and all of them shall have one shepherd* (Ezek 37:24). From this it is clearly shown that the idea of king implies that there be one man who is chief, and that he be a shepherd, seeking the common good of the multitude and not his own.

Now, since man must live in a group, because he is not sufficient unto himself to procure the necessities of life if he were to remain solitary, it follows that a society will be the more perfect the more it is sufficient unto itself to procure the necessities of life. There is, to some extent, sufficiency for life in one family of one household: namely, in-

rales actus nutritionis et generandae prolis et aliorum huiusmodi; in uno autem vico, quantum ad ea quae ad unum artificium pertinent; in civitate vero, quae est perfecta communitas, quantum ad omnia necessaria vitae; sed adhuc magis in provincia una, propter necessitatem compugnationis et mutui auxilii contra hostes. Unde qui perfectam communitatem regit, id est civitatem vel provinciam, antonomastice rex vocatur; qui autem domum regit, non rex sed paterfamilias dicitur, habet tamen aliquam similitudinem regis, propter quam aliquando reges patres populorum nominantur.

Ex dictis igitur patet quod rex est qui unus multitudinem civitatis vel provinciae et propter bonum commune regit: unde Salomon dicit *Universae terrae rex imperat servienti*.

sofar as pertains to the natural acts of nourishment, and the begetting of offspring, and other things of this kind. Self-sufficiency exists, furthermore, in one street with regard to those things which belong to one trade. In a city, which is the perfect community, it exists with regard to all the necessities of life. Still more self-sufficiency is found in a province because of the need of fighting together and of mutual help against enemies. Hence the man ruling a perfect community (which is a city or a province), is antonomastically called the 'king.' The ruler of a household is called 'father,' not 'king,' although he bears a certain resemblance to the king, for which reason kings are sometimes called the fathers of their peoples.

It is plain, therefore, from what has been said, that a king is one who rules the people of one city or province, and rules them for the common good. Hence Solomon says: *The king rules over all the land subject to him* (Eccl 5:8).

CHAPTER 2

Whether it is more expedient for a city or province to be ruled by one man or by many

His autem praemissis inquirere oportet quid provinciae vel civitati magis expedit, utrum pluribus regi vel uno.

Hoc autem considerari potest ex ipso fine regiminis. Ad hoc cuiuslibet regentis ferri debet intentio ut eius quod regendum suscepit salutem procuret: gubernatoris enim est navem contra maris pericula servando illaesam perducere ad portum salutis. Bonum autem et salus consociatae multitudinis est ut eius unitas conservetur, quae dicitur pax; qua remota socialis vitae perit utilitas, quinimmo multitudo dissentiens sibi ipsi fit onerosa.

Hoc igitur est ad quod maxime rector multitudinis intendere debet, ut pacis unitatem procuret; nec recte consiliatur an pacem faciat in multitudine sibi subiecta, sicut nec medicus an sanet infirmum sibi commissum: nullus enim consiliari debet de fine quem intendere debet, sed de his quae sunt ad finem. Propterea quod Apostolus, commendata fidelis populi unitate, *Solliciti*, inquit, *sitis servare unitatem spiritus in vinculo pacis*. Quanto igitur regimen efficacius fuerit ad unitatem pacis servandam, tanto erit utilius; hoc enim utilius dicimus quod magis perducit ad finem. Manifestum est autem quod unitatem magis efficere potest quod est per se unum quam plures, sicut efficacissima causa calefactio-

Having set forth these preliminary points we must now inquire whether it is better for a province or a city to be ruled by one man or by many.

This question may be considered first from the viewpoint of the purpose of government. The aim of any ruler should be directed towards securing the welfare of that which he undertakes to rule. The duty of the pilot, for instance, is to preserve his ship amidst the perils of the sea, and to bring it unharmed to the port of safety. Now the welfare and safety of a multitude formed into a society lies in the preservation of its unity, which is called peace. If this is removed, the benefit of social life is lost; moreover, a dissenting multitude becomes a burden to itself.

The chief concern of the ruler of a multitude, therefore, is to procure the unity of peace. It is not even legitimate for him to deliberate whether he shall establish peace in the multitude subject to him, just as a physician does not deliberate whether he shall heal the sick man encharged to him, for no one should deliberate about an end which he is obliged to seek, but only about the means to attain that end. Therefore, the Apostle, having commended the unity of the faithful people, says: *Be eager to maintain the unity of the Spirit in the bond of peace* (Eph 4:3). Thus, the more efficacious a government is in keeping the unity of peace, the more useful it will be. For we call that more useful which leads more directly to the end. Now it is manifest that what

nis est quod est per se calidum. Utilius igitur est regimen unius quam plurium.

Amplius, manifestum est quod plures multitudinem nullo modo regerent si omnino dissentirent; requiritur igitur in pluribus quaedam unio ad hoc quod quoquo modo regere possint, quia nec multi navem in unam partem traherent nisi aliquo modo coniuncti. Uniri autem dicuntur plura per appropinquationem ad unum; melius igitur regit unus quam plures ex eo quod appropinquant ad unum.

Adhuc, ea quae sunt ad naturam sunt optime se habent, in singulis enim operatur natura quod optimum est. Omne autem naturale regimen ab uno est: in membrorum enim multitudine est unum quod principaliter movet, scilicet cor; et in partibus animae una vis principaliter praesidet, scilicet ratio; et in apibus unus rex, et in toto universo unus Deus omnium factor et rector. Et hoc rationabiliter: omnis enim multitudo derivatur ab uno. Quare, si ea quae sunt secundum artem imitantur ea quae sunt secundum naturam, et tanto magis opus artis melius est quanto magis assequitur similitudinem eius quod est in natura, necesse est quod in humana multitudine optimum sit quod per unum regatur.

Hoc etiam experimentis apparet. Nam provinciae vel civitates quae non reguntur ab uno dissensionibus laborant et absque pace fluctuant, ut videatur impleri quod Dominus per prophetam conqueritur dicens *Pastores multi demoliti sunt vineam.* E contrario vero provinciae et civitates quae sub rege uno reguntur pace gaudent, iustitia florent et affluentia rerum laetantur: unde Dominus pro magno munere per prophetas populo suo promittit quod ponet sibi caput unum et quod *princeps unus erit in medio eorum.*

is itself one can more efficaciously bring about unity than several—just as the most efficacious cause of heat is that which is by its nature hot. Therefore, the rule of one man is more useful than the rule of many.

Furthermore, it is evident that several persons could by no means preserve the stability of the community if they totally disagreed. For union is necessary among them if they are to rule at all: several men, for instance, could not pull a ship in one direction unless joined together in some fashion. Now, several are said to be 'united' according as they come closer to being one. So one man rules better than several who come near being one.

Again, whatever is in accord with nature is best, for nature does what is best in each thing. Now, every natural governance is governance by one. In the multitude of bodily members there is one which is the principal mover (namely, the heart); and among the powers of the soul one power presides as chief (namely, the reason). Among bees there is one king bee, and in the whole universe there is one God, Maker and Ruler of all. And this is reasonable, for every multitude is derived from unity. Therefore, if artificial things are an imitation of natural things, and a work of art is better according as it attains a closer likeness to what is in nature, it follows that it is best for a human multitude to be ruled by one person.

This is also evident from experience. For provinces or cities which are not ruled by one person are torn with dissensions and tossed about without peace, so that the complaint seems to be fulfilled which the Lord uttered through the prophet: *Many pastors have destroyed my vineyard* (Jer 12:10). On the other hand, provinces and cities which are ruled under one king enjoy peace, flourish in justice, and delight in prosperity. Hence, the Lord by his prophets promises to his people as a great reward that he will give them one head and that *one prince will be in the midst of them* (Ezek 34:24; Jer 30:21).

CHAPTER 3

That the dominion of a tyrant is the worst

Sicut autem regimen regis est optimum, ita regimen tyranni est pessimum. Opponitur enim politiae quidem democratia, utrumque enim, sicut ex dictis apparet, est regimen quod per plures exercetur; aristocratiae vero oligarchia, utrumque enim exercetur per paucos; regnum autem tyranno, utrumque enim per unum exercetur. Quod autem regnum sit optimum regimen,

Just as the government of a king is the best, so the government of a tyrant is the worst. For democracy is the opposite of polity, since both are governments carried on by many persons, as is clear from what has already been said; while oligarchy is the opposite of aristocracy, since both are governments carried on by a few persons; and kingship is the opposite of tyranny, since both are carried on by one

ostensum est prius; si igitur *optimo opponitur pessimum*, necesse est quod tyrannis sit pessimum.

Adhuc, virtus unita magis est efficax ad effectum inducendum quam dispersa vel divisa: multi enim congregati simul trahunt illud quod divisim per partes singulariter a singulis trahi non posset. Sicut igitur utilius est virtutem operantem ad bonum esse magis unam, ut sit virtuosior ad operandum bonum, ita magis est noxium si virtus operans malum sit una quam divisa. Virtus autem iniuste praesidentis operatur ad malum multitudinis, dum commune bonum multitudinis in sui ipsius bonum tantum retorquet. Sicut igitur in regimine iusto quanto regens est magis unum, tanto est utilius regimen, ut regnum utilius est quam aristocratia, aristocratia vero quam politia: ita e converso erit et in iniusto regimine, ut videlicet quanto regens est magis unum, tanto magis sit noxium. Magis igitur est noxia tyrannis quam oligarchia, oligarchia autem quam democratia.

Amplius, per hoc regimen fit iniustum quod, spreto bono communi multitudinis, quaeritur bonum privatum regentis; quanto igitur magis receditur a bono communi, tanto est regimen magis iniustum. Plus autem receditur a bono communi in oligarchia, in qua quaeritur bonum paucorum, quam in democratia in qua quaeritur bonum multorum; et adhuc plus receditur a bono communi in tyrannide, in qua quaeritur bonum unius tantum: omni enim universitati propinquius est multum quam paucum, et paucum quam unum solum; regimen igitur tyranni est iniustissimum.

Simul autem hoc manifestum fit considerantibus divinae providentiae ordinem, quae optime universa disponit. Nam bonum provenit in rebus ex una causa perfecta, quasi omnibus adunatis quae ad bonum iuvare possunt, malum autem singillatim ex singularibus defectibus. Non enim est pulchritudo in corpore nisi omnia membra fuerint decenter disposita; turpitudo autem contingit quodcumque membrum inconvenienter se habeat. Et sic turpitudo ex pluribus causis diversimode provenit, pulchritudo autem uno modo ex una causa perfecta; et sic est in omnibus bonis et malis, tanquam hoc Deo providente ut bonum ex una causa sit fortius, malum autem ex pluribus causis sit debilius. Expedit igitur ut regimen iustum sit unius tantum ad hoc quod sit fortius; quod si a iustitia declinat regimen, expedit magis quod sit multorum, ut sit debilius et se invicem

person. Now, as has been shown above, monarchy is the best government. If, therefore, *the best is the opposite of the worst*,[1] it follows that tyranny is the worst kind of government.

Further, a united force is more efficacious in producing its effect than a force which is scattered or divided. Many persons together can pull a load which could not be pulled by each one taking his part separately and acting individually. Therefore, just as it is more useful for a force operating for a good to be more united, in order that it may work good more effectively, so a force operating for evil is more harmful when it is one than when it is divided. Now, the power of one who rules unjustly works to the detriment of the multitude in that he diverts the common good of the multitude to his own benefit. Therefore, for the same reason that, in a just government, the government is better in proportion as the ruling power is one—thus monarchy is better than aristocracy, and aristocracy better than polity—so the contrary will be true of an unjust government: namely, the ruling power will be more harmful in proportion as it is more one. Consequently, tyranny is more harmful than oligarchy, and oligarchy more harmful than democracy.

Moreover, a government becomes unjust by the fact that the ruler, paying no heed to the common good, seeks his own private good. Therefore, the further he departs from the common good, the more unjust will his government be. But there is a greater departure from the common good in an oligarchy, in which the advantage of a few is sought, than in a democracy, in which the advantage of many is sought; and there is a still greater departure from the common good in a tyranny, where the advantage of only one man is sought. For a large number is closer to the totality than a small number, and a small number than only one. Thus, the government of a tyrant is the most unjust.

The same conclusion is made clear to those who consider the order of divine providence, which disposes everything in the best way. In all things, good ensues from one perfect cause (as from the totality of the conditions favorable to the production of the effect), while evil results from any one partial defect. There is beauty in a body when all its members are fittingly disposed; ugliness, on the other hand, arises when any one member is not fittingly disposed. Thus ugliness results in different ways from many causes; beauty in one way from one perfect cause. It is thus with all good and evil things, as if God so provided that good, arising from one cause, be stronger, and evil, arising from many causes, be weaker. It is expedient, therefore, that a just government be that of one man only in order that it may be stronger. However, if the government should turn away from justice, it is more expedient that it be a government by

---

1. Aristotle, *Ethics* VIII, 10.

impediant. Inter iniusta igitur regimina tolerabilius est democratia, pessimum vero tyrannis.

Idem etiam maxime apparet si quis consideret mala quae ex tyrannis proveniunt; quia cum tyrannus contempto communi bono quaerit privatum, consequens est ut subditos diversimode gravet secundum quod diversis passionibus subiacet ad bona aliqua affectanda. Qui enim passione cupiditatis detinetur, bona subditorum rapit; unde Salomon *Rex iustus erigit terram, vir avarus destruet eam*. Si vero iracundiae passioni subiaceat, pro nihilo sanguinem fundit, unde dicitur per Ezechielem *Principes eius in medio eius quasi lupi rapientes praedam ad effundendum sanguinem*. Hoc igitur regimen fugiendum esse sapiens monet dicens *Longe esto ab homine potestatem habente occidendi*, quasi scilicet non pro iustitia sed per potestatem occidit pro libidine voluntatis. Sic igitur nulla potest esse securitas, sed omnia sunt incerta cum a iure disceditur; nec firmari quidquam potest *quale sit* quod positum est in alterius voluntate, ne dicam libidine.

Nec solum in corporalibus subditos gravat, sed etiam spiritualia eorum bona impedit. Quia enim plus praeesse appetunt quam prodesse, omnem profectum subditorum impediunt, suspicantes omnem subditorum excellentiam suae iniquae dominationis praeiudicium esse: tyrannis enim magis boni quam mali suspecti sunt, semperque his aliena virtus formidolosa est. Conantur igitur praedicti tyranni ne ipsorum subditi virtuosi effecti magnanimitatis concipiant spiritum et eorum iniquam dominationem non ferant. Conantur etiam ne inter subditos amicitiae foedus firmetur et pacis emolumento ad invicem gaudeant, ut sic, dum unus de altero non confidit, contra eorum dominium aliquid moliri non possint. Propter quod inter ipsos discordias seminant, exortas nutriunt, et ea quae ad confoederationes hominum pertinent ut connubia et convivia prohibent, et caetera huiusmodi per quae inter homines solet familiaritas et fiducia generari. Conantur etiam ne potentes aut divites fiant, quia de subditis secundum suae malitiae conscientiam suspicantes, sicut ipsi potentia et divitiis ad nocendum utuntur, ita timent ne potentia et divitiae subditorum eis nocivae reddantur. Unde in Iob de tyranno dicitur *Sonitus terroris semper in auribus illius, et cum pax sit*, nullo scilicet ei malum intentante, *ille semper insidias suspicatur*.

Ex hoc autem contingit ut, dum praesidentes, qui subditos ad virtutes inducere deberent, virtuti subditorum nequiter invident et eam pro posse impediunt, sub tyrannis pauci virtuosi inveniantur. Nam, iuxta senten-

many, so that it may be weaker, and the many may mutually hinder one another. Among unjust governments, therefore, democracy is the most tolerable, but the worst is tyranny.

This same conclusion is also apparent if one considers the evils which come from tyrants. Since a tyrant, despising the common good, seeks his private interest, it follows that he will oppress his subjects in different ways according as he is dominated by different passions to acquire certain goods. The one who is enthralled by the passion of cupidity seizes the goods of his subjects; hence Solomon says: *A just king sets up the land; a covetous man shall destroy it* (Prov 29:4). If he is dominated by the passion of anger, he sheds blood for nothing; whence it is said by Ezekiel: *Her princes in the midst of her are like wolves tearing the prey, shedding blood* (Ezek 22:27). Therefore, this kind of government is to be avoided, as the wise man admonishes: *Keep far from a man who has the power to kill* (Sir 9:13), because he kills not for justice's sake but by his power, for the lust of his will. Thus there can be no safety. Everything is uncertain when there is a departure from justice. Nobody will be able firmly to state, *this thing is such and such*, when it depends upon the will of another, not to say upon his caprice.

Nor does the tyrant merely oppress his subjects in corporal things but he also hinders their spiritual good. Those who seek more to use, than to be of use to, their subjects prevent all progress, suspecting all excellence in their subjects to be prejudicial to their own evil domination. For tyrants hold the good in greater suspicion than the wicked, and to them the valour of others is always fraught with danger. So, the above-mentioned tyrants strive to prevent those of their subjects who have become virtuous from acquiring valour and high spirit in order that they may not want to cast off their iniquitous domination. They also see to it that there be no friendly relations among these so that they may not enjoy the benefits resulting from being on good terms with one another, for as long as one has no confidence in the other, no plot will be set up against the tyrant's domination. Wherefore they sow discords among the people, foster any that have arisen, and forbid anything which furthers society and co-operation among men, such as marriage, banquets, and anything of like character, through which familiarity and confidence are engendered among men. They moreover strive to prevent their subjects from becoming powerful and rich, since, suspecting these to be as wicked as themselves, they fear their power and wealth; for the subjects might become harmful to them even as they are accustomed to use power and wealth to harm others. Hence Job 15:21 says of the tyrant: *The sound of dread is always in his ears and when there is peace*, that is, when there is no one to harm him, *he always suspects treason*.

It thus results that when rulers, who ought to induce their subjects to virtue, are wickedly jealous of the virtue of their subjects and hinder it as much as they can, few virtuous men are found under the rule of tyrants. For, ac-

tiam Aristotelis, apud illos inveniuntur fortes viri apud quos fortissimi quique honorantur; et ut Tullius dicit *Iacent semper et parum vigent quae apud quosque improbantur.* Naturale etiam est ut homines sub timore nutriti in servilem degenerent animum et pusillanimes fiant ad omne virile opus et strenuum: quod experimento patet in provinciis quae diu sub tyrannis fuerunt; unde Apostolus ad Colossenses dicit *Patres, nolite ad indignationem provocare filios vestros ut non pusillo animo fiant.*

Haec igitur nocumenta tyrannidis rex Salomon considerans dicit *Regnantibus impiis ruinae hominum,* quia scilicet per nequitiam tyrannorum subiecti a virtutum perfectione deficiunt. Et iterum dicit *Cum impii sumpserint principatum gemet populus,* quasi sub servitute redactus; et iterum *Cum surrexerint impii abscondentur homines,* ut tyrannorum crudelitatem evadant. Nec est mirum, quia homo absque ratione secundum animi sui libidinem praesidens nihil differt a bestia; unde Salomon dicit *Leo rugiens et ursus esuriens, princeps impius super populum pauperem*; et ideo a tyrannis se abscondunt homines sicut a crudelibus bestiis, idemque videtur tyranno subiici et bestiae saevienti substerni.

cording to Aristotle's sentence,[2] brave men are found where brave men are honoured. And as Cicero says: *Those who are despised by everybody are disheartened and flourish but little.*[3] It is also natural that men, brought up in fear, should become small-spirited and discouraged in the face of any strenuous and manly task. This is shown by experience in provinces that have long been under tyrants. Hence the Apostle says to the Colossians: *Fathers, do not provoke your children to indignation, lest they become discouraged* (Col 3:21).

So, considering these evil effects of tyranny, King Solomon says: *When the wicked reign, men are ruined* (Prov 28:12), because, through the wickedness of tyrants, subjects fall away from the perfection of virtue. And again he says: *When the wicked rule, the people groan* (Prov 29:2), as though led into slavery. And again: *When the wicked rise, men hide themselves* (Prov 28:28), that they may escape the cruelty of the tyrant. It is no wonder, for a man governing without reason, following the lust of his soul, differs in no way from the beast. Hence Solomon says: *Like a roaring lion or a charging bear is a wicked ruler over a poor people* (Prov 28:15). Therefore, men hide from tyrants as from cruel beasts, and it seems that to be subject to a tyrant is the same thing as to lie prostrate beneath a raging beast.

CHAPTER 4

Why the royal dignity is rendered hateful to the subjects

Quia igitur optimum et pessimum regimen existit in monarchia, id est in principatu unius, multis quidem propter tyrannorum malitiam redditur regia dignitas odiosa; quidam vero dum regimen regni desiderant, incidunt in saevitias tyrannorum, rectoresque quam plures tyrannidem exercent sub praetextu regis dignitatis.

Horum quidem exemplum evidenter apparet in Romana republica. Regibus enim a populo Romano expulsis, dum regium vel potius tyrannicum fastum ferre non possent, instituerant sibi consules et alios magistratus per quos regi coeperunt et dirigi, regnum in aristocratiam commutare volentes; et, sicut refert Salustius, *incredibile est memoratu quantum adepta libertate in brevi Romana civitas creverit.* Plerumque namque contingit ut homines sub rege viventes segnius ad bonum commune nitantur, utpote aestimantes id quod ad commune bonum impendunt non sibi ipsis conferre, sed alteri sub cuius potestate vident esse bona communia. Cum vero

Because both the best and the worst government are latent in monarchy (that is, in the rule of one man), the royal dignity is rendered hateful to many people on account of the wickedness of tyrants. Some men, indeed, while they desire to be ruled by a king, fall under the cruelty of tyrants, and not a few rulers exercise tyranny under the cloak of royal dignity.

A clear example of this is found in the Roman Republic. When the kings had been driven out by the Roman people, because they could not bear the royal, or rather tyrannical, arrogance, they instituted consuls and other magistrates by whom they began to be ruled and guided. They changed the kingdom into an aristocracy, and, as Sallust relates: *The Roman city, once liberty was won, waxed incredibly strong and great in a remarkably short time.*[4] For it frequently happens that men living under a king strive more sluggishly for the common good, since they consider that what they devote to the common good they do not confer upon themselves, but upon another, under whose power they see the common

2. *Eth.* III, 11 (1116a 20).
3. *Tuscul. Disp.* I, 2, 4.
4. *Bellum Catilinae* VI, 7.

bonum commune non vident esse in potestate unius, non attendunt ad bonum commune quasi ad id quod est alterius, sed quilibet attendit ad illud sicut ad suum; unde experimento videtur quod una civitas per annuos rectores administrata plus potest interdum quam rex aliquis si haberet tales tres vel quatuor civitates, parvaque servitia exacta a regibus gravius ferunt quam magna onera si a communitate civium imponantur. Quod in promotione Romanae reipublicae servatum fuit. Nam plebs et ad militiam scribebatur et pro militantibus stipendia exsolvebant; et cum stipendiis exsolvendis non sufficeret commune aerarium, *in usus publicos opes venere privatos, adeo ut praeter singulos annulos aureos singulasque bullas, quae erant dignitatis insignia, nihil sibi auri etiam senatus ipse reliquerit.*

Sed tamen dissensionibus fatigarentur continuis, quae usque ad bella civilia excreverunt; quibus bellis civilibus eis libertas ad quam multum studuerant de manibus erepta est, et sub potestate imperatorum esse coeperunt, qui se reges appellari a principio noluerunt quia Romanis fuerat nomen regium odiosum. Horum autem quidam more regio bonum commune fideliter procuraverunt, per quorum studium Romana respublica et aucta et conservata est; plurimi vero eorum in subditos quidem tyranni, ad hostes vero effecti desides et imbecilles, Romanam rempublicam ad nihilum redegerunt.

Similis etiam processus fuit in populo Hebraeorum. Primo quidem dum sub iudicibus regebantur, undique diripiebantur ab hostibus; *unusquisque quod bonum erat in oculis suis faciebat.* Regibus vero eis divinitus datis ad eorum instantiam, propter regum malitiam a cultu unius Dei recesserunt et finaliter in captivitatem sunt ducti.

Utrinque igitur pericula imminent, sive dum timetur tyrannus evitetur regis optimum regimen, sive dum hoc desideratur potestas regia in malitiam tyrannicam convertatur.

goods to be. But when they see that the common good is not under the power of one man, they do not attend to it as if it belonged to another, but each one attends to it as if it were his own. Experience thus teaches that one city administered by rulers, changing annually, is sometimes able to do more than some kings having three or four such cities; and small taxes exacted by kings weigh more heavily than great burdens imposed by the community of citizens. This held good in the history of the Roman Republic. The plebs were enrolled in the army and were paid wages for military service; and when the common treasury was failing, *private riches came forth for public uses, to such an extent that not even the senators retained any gold for themselves save one ring and the one bulla, which were the insignia of their dignity.*

On the other hand, when the Romans were worn out by continual dissensions taking on the proportion of civil wars, and when by these wars the freedom for which they had greatly striven was snatched from their hands, they began to find themselves under the power of emperors who, from the beginning, were unwilling to be called kings, for the royal name was hateful to the Romans. Some emperors, it is true, faithfully cared for the common good in a kingly manner, and by their zeal the commonwealth was increased and preserved. But most of them became tyrants towards their subjects while indolent and vacillating before their enemies, and brought the Roman Republic to nothing.

A similar process also took place among the Hebrew people. At first, while they were ruled by judges, they were ravished by their enemies on every hand, for each one *did what was good in his sight* (1 Sam 3:18). Yet when God gave them kings at their insistence, they departed from the worship of the one God and were finally led into bondage on account of the wickedness of their kings.

Danger thus lurks on either side. Either men are held by the fear of a tyrant and they miss the opportunity of having kingship, the best government, or they want a king, and the kingly power turns into tyrannical wickedness.

CHAPTER 5

That it is a lesser evil when a monarchy turns into tyranny
than when an aristocracy becomes corrupt

Cum autem inter duo ex quorum utroque periculum imminet eligere oportet, illud videtur potissime eligendum ex quo sequitur minus malum. Ex monarchia autem, si in tyrannidem convertatur, minus malum sequitur quam ex regimine plurium optimatum quando corrumpitur. Dissensio enim quae plurimumque sequitur ex regimine plurium contrariatur bono pacis, quod est praecipuum in multitudine sociali; quod quidem bonum per tyrannidem non tollitur, sed aliqua particularium hominum bona impediuntur, nisi fuerit excessus tyrannidis quod in totam communitatem desaeviat. Magis igitur praeoptandum est unius regimen quam multorum, quamvis in utroque sequantur pericula.

Adhuc, illud magis fugiendum videtur ex quo pluries sequi possunt magna pericula; frequentius autem sequuntur maxima pericula multitudinis ex multorum regimine quam ex regimine unius. Plerumque enim contingit ut ex pluribus aliquis ab intentione communis boni deficiat, quam quod unus tantum. Quicumque autem ex pluribus praesidentibus divertat ab intentione boni communis, dissensionis periculum multitudini subditorum imminet, quia dissentientibus principibus consequens est ut in multitudine sequatur dissensio. Si vero unus praesit, plerumque quidem ad bonum commune respicit; aut si a bono communi intentionem avertat, non statim sequitur ut totaliter ad subditorum oppressionem intendat, quod est excessus tyrannidis et in malitia regiminis maximum gradum tenens, ut supra ostensum est. Magis igitur sunt fugienda pericula quae proveniunt ex regimine plurium quam ea quae proveniunt ex gubernatione unius.

Amplius, non minus contingit in tyrannidem verti regimen multorum quam unius, sed forte frequentius. Exorta namque dissensione per regimen plurium, contingit saepe unum alios superare et sibi soli multitudinis dominium usurpare: quod quidem ex his quae pro tempore fiunt manifeste inspici potest. Nam fere omne multorum regimen est in tyrannidem terminatum, ut in Romana republica manifeste apparet. Quae cum diu per plures magistratus administrata fuisset, exortis simultatibus, dissensionibus et bellis civilibus, in crudelissimos tyrannos inciderunt.

Et universaliter si quis praeterita facta et quae nunc fiunt diligenter consideret, plures inveniet exercuisse tyrannidem in terris quae per multos reguntur, quam in

When a choice is to be made between two things, from both of which danger impends, surely that one should be chosen from which the lesser evil follows. Now, lesser evil follows from the corruption of a monarchy (which is tyranny) than from the corruption of an aristocracy. Group government (polyarchy) most frequently breeds dissension. This dissension runs counter to the good of peace, which is the principal social good. A tyrant, on the other hand, does not destroy this good: rather, he obstructs one or the other individual interests of his subjects—unless, of course, there be an excess of tyranny, and the tyrant rages against the whole community. Monarchy is therefore to be preferred to polyarchy, although either form of government might become dangerous.

Further, it seems that from which great dangers may follow is to be avoided more frequently. Now, considerable dangers to the multitude follow more frequently from polyarchy than from monarchy. There is a greater chance that, where there are many rulers, one of them will abandon the intention of the common good than that it will be abandoned when there is but one ruler. When any one among several rulers turns aside from the pursuit of the common good, danger of internal strife threatens the group because, when the chiefs quarrel, dissension will follow in the people. When, on the other hand, one man is in command, he more often keeps to governing for the sake of the common good. Should he not do so, it does not immediately follow that he also proceeds to the total oppression of his subjects. This, of course, would be the excess of tyranny and the worst wickedness in government, as has been shown above. The dangers, then, arising from a polyarchy are more to be guarded against than those arising from a monarchy.

Moreover, in point of fact, a polyarchy deviates into tyranny not less but perhaps more frequently than a monarchy. When dissensions arise in such a government on account of there being many rulers, it often happens that the power of one preponderates and he then usurps the government of the multitude for himself. This indeed may be clearly seen from history. There has hardly ever been a polyarchy that did not end in tyranny. The best illustration of this fact is the history of the Roman Republic. It was for a long time administered by the magistrates but then animosities, dissensions, and civil wars arose, and it fell into the power of the most cruel tyrants.

In general, if one carefully considers what has happened in the past and what is happening in the present, he will discover that more men have held tyrannical sway in lands

illis quae gubernantur ab uno. Si igitur regium, quod est optimum regimen, maxime vitandum videatur propter tyrannidem, tyrannis autem non minus, sed magis contingere solet in regimine plurium quam unius: relinquitur simpliciter magis esse expediens sub rege uno vivere quam sub regimine plurium.

previously ruled by many rulers than in those ruled by one. The strongest objection why monarchy, although it is the best form of government, is not agreeable to the people is that, in fact, it may deviate into tyranny. Yet tyranny tends to occur not less but more frequently on the basis of a polyarchy than on the basis of a monarchy. It follows that it is, in any case, more expedient to live under one king than under the rule of several men.

CHAPTER 6

How to make provision lest the king fall into tyranny

Quia ergo unius regimen praeeligendum est, quod est optimum, et contingit ipsum in tyrannidem converti, quod est pessimum, ut ex dictis patet, diligenti studio laborandum est ut sic multitudini provideatur de rege ut non incidant in tyrannum.

Primum autem est necessarium ut talis conditionis homo, ab illis ad quos hoc spectat officium, promoveatur in regem, quem non sit probabile in tyrannidem declinare; unde Samuel Dei providentiam erga institutionem regis commendans ait *Quaesivit sibi Dominus virum secundum cor suum, et praecepit ei Dominus ut esset dux super populum suum.* Deinde sic disponenda est regni gubernatio ut regi iam instituto tyrannidis subtrahatur occasio. Simul etiam sic eius temperetur potestas ut in tyrannidem de facili declinare non possit; quae quidem quomodo fiant, in sequentibus considerandum erit. Demum vero curandum est, si rex in tyrannidem diverteret, qualiter posset occurri.

Et quidem si non fuerit excessus tyrannidis, utilius est remissam tyrannidem tolerare ad tempus, quam contra tyrannum agendo multis implicari periculis quae sunt graviora ipsa tyrannide. Potest enim contingere ut qui contra tyrannum agunt praevalere non possint, et sic provocatus tyrannus magis desaeviat. Quod si praevalere quis possit adversus tyrannum, ex hoc multotiens proveniunt gravissimae dissensiones in populo, sive dum in tyrannum insurgitur, sive post deiectionem tyranni dum erga ordinationem regiminis multitudo separatur in partes. Contingit etiam interdum ut, dum alicuius auxilio multitudo expellit tyrannum, ille potestate accepta tyrannidem arripit, et timens pati ab alio quod ipse in alium fecit, graviori servitute subditos opprimat.

Therefore, since the rule of one man (which is the best) is to be preferred, and since it may happen to be changed into a tyranny (which is the worst), as is clear from what has been said, a scheme should be carefully worked out which would prevent the multitude ruled by a king from falling into the hands of a tyrant.

First, it is necessary that the man who is raised up to be king by those whom it concerns should be of such condition that it is improbable that he should become a tyrant. Thus Samuel, commending the providence of God with respect to the institution of the king, says: *The Lord sought a man according to his own heart, and the Lord appointed him to be prince over his people* (1 Sam 13:14). Then, once the king is established, the government of the kingdom must be so arranged that opportunity to tyrannize is removed. At the same time his power should be so tempered that he cannot easily fall into tyranny. How these things may be done we must consider in what follows. Finally, provision must be made for facing the situation should the king stray into tyranny.

Indeed, if there be not an excess of tyranny, it is more expedient to tolerate the milder tyranny for a while than to become involved in many perils more grievous than the tyranny itself by acting against the tyrant. For it may happen that those who act against the tyrant are unable to prevail and the tyrant then will rage the more. Yet if one can prevail against the tyrant, the gravest dissensions frequently ensue among the people from this very fact: the multitude may be broken up into factions either during their revolt against the tyrant, or in process of the organization of the government, after the tyrant has been overthrown. Moreover, it sometimes happens that while the multitude is driving out the tyrant by the help of some man, the latter, having received the power, thereupon seizes the tyranny. Then, fearing to suffer from another what he did to his predecessor, he oppresses his subjects with an even more grievous slavery.

Sic enim in tyrannide solet contingere ut posterior gravior fiat quam praecedens, dum praecedentia gravamina non deserit et etiam ipse ex sui cordis malitia nova excogitat. Unde Syracusis quondam Dionysii mortem omnibus desiderantibus, anus quaedam ut incolumis et sibi superstes esset continue orabat; quod ut tyrannus cognovit, cur hoc faceret interrogavit. Tum illa *Puella, inquit, existens cum gravem tyrannum haberemus, alium cupiebam; quo interfecto aliquantulum durior successit, eius quoque finiri dominationem magnum existimabam. Tertium te importuniorem habere coepimus rectorem; itaque si tu fueris absumptus, deterior in locum tuum succedet.*

Et si sit intolerabilis excessus tyrannidis, quibusdam visum fuit ut ad fortium virorum virtutem pertineat tyrannum interimere, seque pro liberatione multitudinis exponere periculis mortis; cuius rei exemplum etiam in Veteri testamento habetur. Nam Aioth quidam Eglon regem Moab, qui gravi servitute populum Dei premebat, sica infixa in eius femore interemit, et factus est populi iudex. Sed hoc apostolicae doctrinae non congruit. Docet enim nos Petrus *non solum bonis et modestis, verum etiam dyscolis dominis reverenter subditos esse: haec est enim gratia, si propter conscientiam Dei sustineat quis tristitias patiens iniuste.* Unde cum multi Romanorum imperatores fidem Christi persequerentur tyrannice, magnaque multitudo tam nobilium quam populi esset ad fidem conversa, non resistendo sed mortem patienter et armati sustinentes pro Christo laudantur, ut in sacra Thebaeorum legione manifeste apparet. Magisque Aioth iudicandus est hostem interemisse quam populi rectorem, licet tyrannum; unde et in Veteri testamento leguntur occisi fuisse hi qui occiderunt Ioas regem Iuda, quamvis a cultu Dei recedentem, eorumque filiis reservatis secundum legis praeceptum.

Esset autem hoc multitudini periculosum et eius rectoribus, si privata praesumptione aliqui attentarent praesidentium necem, etiam tyrannorum: plerumque enim huiusmodi periculis magis exponunt se mali quam boni; malis autem solet esse grave dominium non minus regum quam tyrannorum, quia, secundum sententiam Salomonis, *dissipat impios rex sapiens.* Magis igitur ex huiusmodi praesumptione immineret periculum multitudini de amissione boni regis, quam remedium de subtractione tyranni.

This tends to happen in tyranny: the second becomes more grievous than the one preceding, inasmuch as, without abandoning the previous oppressions, he himself thinks up fresh ones from the malice of his heart. Thus, in Syracuse, when everyone desired the death of Dionysius, a certain old woman kept constantly praying that he might be unharmed and that he might survive her. When the tyrant learned this he asked why she did it. Then she said: *When I was a girl we had a harsh tyrant and I wished for his death; when he was killed, there succeeded him one who was a little harsher. I was very eager to see the end of his dominion also, and we began to have a third ruler still more harsh—that was you. So if you should be taken away, a worse would succeed in your place.*

If the excess of tyranny is unbearable, some have been of the opinion that it would be an act of virtue for strong men to slay the tyrant and to expose themselves to the danger of death in order to set the multitude free. An example of this even occurs in the Old Testament, for a certain Aioth slew Eglon, King of Moab, who was oppressing the people of God under harsh slavery, thrusting a dagger into his thigh; and he was made a judge of the people.[5] But this opinion is not in accord with apostolic teaching. For Peter admonishes us *to be submissive to your masters with all respect, not only to the kind and gentle but also to the overbearing. For one is approved if, mindful of God, he endures pain while suffering unjustly* (1 Pet 2:18–19). Wherefore, when many emperors of the Romans tyrannically persecuted the faith of Christ, a great number both of the nobility and the common people were converted to the faith and were praised for patiently bearing death for Christ. They did not resist although they were armed, and this is plainly manifested in the case of the holy Theban legion. Aioth, then, must be considered rather as having slain a foe than assassinated a ruler, however tyrannical, of the people. Hence in the Old Testament we also read that they who killed Joas, the king of Judah, who had fallen away from the worship of God, were slain and their children spared according to the precept of the law.[6]

Should private persons attempt on their own private presumption to kill the rulers, even though tyrants, this would be dangerous for the multitude as well as for their rulers. This is because the wicked usually expose themselves to dangers of this kind more than the good, for the rule of a king, no less than that of a tyrant, is burdensome to them since, according to the words of Solomon: *A wise king winnows the wicked* (Prov 20:26). Consequently, by presumption of this kind, danger to the people from the loss of a good king would be more probable than relief through the removal of a tyrant.

---

5. Judges 3:14–30.
6. 2 Sam 14:5–6.

Videtur autem magis contra tyrannorum saevitiam non privata praesumptione aliquorum, sed auctoritate publica procedendum. Primo quidem, si ad ius alicuius multitudinis pertineat sibi providere de rege, non iniuste ab eadem rex institutus potest destitui, vel refrenari eius potestas, si potestate regia tyrannice abutatur. Nec putanda est talis multitudo infideliter agere tyrannum destituens, etiam si ei se in perpetuum ante subiecerat; quia hoc ipse meruit in multitudinis regimine se non fideliter gerens ut exigit regis officium, quod ei pactum a subditis non servetur. Sic Romani Tarquinium Superbum, quem in regem susceperant, propter eius et filiorum tyrannidem a regno eiecerunt, substituta minori, scilicet consulari, potestate. Sic etiam Domitianus, qui modestissimis imperatoribus Vespasiano patri et Tito fratri eius successerat, dum tyrannidem exercet a senatu Romano interemptus est, omnibus quae idem perverse fecerat per senatusconsultum iuste et salubriter in irritum revocatis. Quo factum est ut beatus Ioannes evangelista, dilectus Dei discipulus, qui per ipsum Domitianum in Patmos insulam fuerat exilio relegatus, ad Ephesum per senatusconsultum remitteretur.

Si vero ad ius alicuius superioris pertineat multitudini providere de rege, expectandum est ab eo remedium contra tyranni nequitiam. Sic Archelai, qui in Iudaea pro Herode patre suo regnare iam coeperat, paternam malitiam imitantis, Iudaeis contra eum querimoniam ad Caesarem Augustum deferentibus, primo quidem potestas diminuitur, ablato sibi regio nomine et medietate regni sui inter duos fratres eius divisa; demum cum nec sic a tyrannide compesceretur, a Tiberio Caesare relegatus est in exilium apud Lugdunum Galliae civitatem.

Quod si omnino contra tyrannum auxilium humanum haberi non possit, recurrendum est ad regem omnium Deum qui est *adiutor in opportunitatibus, in tribulatione.* Eius enim potentiae subest ut cor tyranni crudele convertat in mansuetudinem, secundum Salomonem *Cor regis in manu Dei, quocumque voluerit inclinabit illud*; ipse enim regis Assueri crudelitatem, qui Iudaeis mortem parabat, in mansuetudinem vertit; ipse est qui ita Nabuchodonosor crudelem regem in tantam devotionem convertit, quod factus est divinae potentiae praedicator: *Nunc igitur*, inquit, *ego Nabuchodonosor laudo et magnifico et glorifico regem caeli, quia opera eius vera et viae eius iudicia, et gradientes in superbia potest humiliare.*

Tyrannos vero quos reputat conversione indignos, potest auferre de medio vel ad infimum statum reducere, secundum illud Sapientis *Sedes ducum superborum*

Furthermore, it seems that to proceed against the cruelty of tyrants is an action to be undertaken not through the private presumption of a few, but rather by public authority. If to provide itself with a king belongs to the right of a given multitude, it is not unjust that the king be deposed or have his power restricted by that same multitude if, becoming a tyrant, he abuses the royal power. It must not be thought that such a multitude is acting unfaithfully in deposing the tyrant, even though it had previously subjected itself to him in perpetuity, because he himself has deserved that the covenant with his subjects should not be kept, since, in ruling the multitude, he did not act faithfully as the office of a king demands. Thus did the Romans, who had accepted Tarquin the Proud as their king, cast him out from the kingship on account of his tyranny and the tyranny of his sons; and they set up in their place a lesser power: namely, the consular power. Similarly Domitian, who had succeeded those most moderate emperors, Vespasian, his father, and Titus, his brother, was slain by the Roman senate when he exercised tyranny, and all his wicked deeds were justly, and profitably, declared null and void by a decree of the senate. Thus it came about that Blessed John the Evangelist, the beloved disciple of God, who had been exiled to the island of Patmos by that very Domitian, was sent back to Ephesus by a decree of the senate.

If, on the other hand, it pertains to the right of a higher authority to provide a king for a certain multitude, a remedy against the wickedness of a tyrant is to be looked for from him. Thus when Archelaus, who had already begun to reign in Judaea in the place of Herod his father, was imitating his father's wickedness, a complaint against him having been laid before Caesar Augustus by the Jews, his power was at first diminished by depriving him of his title of king and by dividing one-half of his kingdom between his two brothers. Later, since he was not restrained from tyranny even by this means, Tiberius Caesar sent him into exile to Lugdunum, a city in Gaul.

Should no human aid whatsoever against a tyrant be forthcoming, recourse must be had to God, the King of all, who is *a helper in due time in tribulation* (Ps 9:10). For it lies in his power to turn the cruel heart of the tyrant to mildness. According to Solomon: *The heart of the king is in the hand of the Lord; he turns it wherever he will* (Prov 21:1). It was he who turned into mildness the cruelty of King Assuerus, who was preparing death for the Jews. It was he who so filled the cruel king Nebuchadnezzar with piety that he became a proclaimer of the divine power. *Therefore*, he said, *I, Nabuchodonosor do now praise and magnify and glorify the King of Heaven; because all his works are true and his ways judgments, and they that walk in pride he is able to abase* (Dan 4:34).

Those tyrants, however, whom he deems unworthy of conversion, he is able to put out of the way or to degrade, according to the words of the wise man: *The Lord has cast*

destruxit Deus et sedere fecit mites pro eis. Ipse est qui videns afflictionem populi sui in Aegypto et audiens eorum clamorem, Pharaonem tyrannum deiecit cum exercitu suo in mare. Ipse est qui memoratum Nabuchodonosor prius superbientem, eiectum non solum de regni solio sed etiam de hominum consortio, in similitudinem bestiae commutavit. Nec est abbreviata manus eius, ut populum suum a tyrannis liberare non possit: promittit enim per Isaiam populo suo requiem se daturum *a labore et concussione et servitute dura* qua ante servierat; et per Ezechielem dicit *Liberabo meum gregem de ore eorum*, scilicet pastorum qui pascunt se ipsos. Sed ut hoc beneficium populus a Deo consequi mereatur, debet a peccatis cessare, quia in ultionem peccati divina permissione impii accipiunt principatum, dicente Domino per Oseam *Dabo tibi regem in furore meo*; et in Iob dicitur quod *regnare facit hominem hypocritam propter peccata populi*. Tollenda est igitur culpa ut cesset tyrannorum plaga.

down the thrones of rulers, and has seated the lowly in their place (Sir 10:14). He it was who, seeing the affliction of his people in Egypt and hearing their cry, hurled Pharaoh, a tyrant over God's people, with all his army into the sea. He it was who not only banished from his kingly throne the above-mentioned Nabuchodonosor because of his former pride, but also cast him from the fellowship of men and changed him into the likeness of a beast. Indeed, his hand is not shortened so that he cannot free his people from tyrants. For by Isaiah he promised to give his people rest *from pain and turmoil and hard service* (Isa 14:3) in which they had formerly served; and by Ezekiel he says: *I will rescue my sheep from their mouths* (Ezek 34:10), that is, from the mouth of shepherds who feed themselves. But to deserve to secure this benefit from God, the people must desist from sin, for it is by divine permission that wicked men receive power to rule as a punishment for sin, as the Lord says by the Prophet Hosea: *I will give you a king in my wrath* (Hos 13:11) and it is said in Job that he *makes a man who is a hypocrite to reign for the sins of the people* (Job 34:30). Sin must therefore be done away with in order that the scourge of tyrants may cease.

CHAPTER 7

That worldly honor and glory are not an adequate reward for a king

Quoniam autem secundum praedicta regis est bonum multitudinis quaerere, nimis videretur onerosum regis officium nisi ei aliquod proprium bonum ex hoc proveniret. Oportet igitur considerare quale sit boni regis conveniens praemium.

Quibusdam igitur visum est regis praemium non esse aliud quam honorem et gloriam, unde et Tullius in libro *de Republica* definit *principem civitatis esse alendum gloria*; cuius rationem Aristoteles in libro *Ethicorum* assignare videtur, *quia princeps cui non sufficit honor et gloria consequenter tyrannus efficitur*. Inest enim animis omnium ut proprium bonum quaerant; si ergo contentus non sit princeps gloria et honore, quaeret voluptates et divitias, et sic ad rapinas et subditorum iniurias convertitur.

Sed si hanc sententiam receperimus, plurima sequuntur inconvenientia. Primo namque hoc esset regibus dispendiosum, si tot labores et sollicitudines paterentur pro mercede tam fragili: nihil enim videtur in rebus humanis fragilius gloria et honore favoris hominum, cum dependeat ex opinionibus hominum et verbis eorum, quibus nihil mutabilius in vita ho-

Since, according to what has been said thus far, it is the king's duty to seek the good of the multitude, the task of a king may seem too burdensome unless some advantage to himself should result from it. Therefore, we must consider what a suitable reward for a good king is.

Some men considered this reward to be nothing other than honor and glory. Hence Cicero says in the book *On the Republic*: *The prince of the city should be nourished by glory*,[7] and Aristotle seems to assign the reason for this in the *Ethics*: *Because the prince for whom honor and glory is not sufficient consequently turns into a tyrant.*[8] For it is in the hearts of all men to seek their proper good. Therefore, if the prince is not content with glory and honor, he will seek pleasures and riches, and so will resort to plundering and injuring his subjects.

However, if we accept this opinion, a great many incongruous results follow. In the first place, it would be costly to kings if so many labors and anxieties were to be endured for a reward so perishable: for nothing, it seems, is more perishable among human things than the glory and honor of men's favor, since it depends upon the report of men and their opinions, which nothing in human life is more fickle

7. *De Republica* V, 7, 9.
8. *Ethics* V, 10, 1134b 7.

minibus; et inde est quod Isaias propheta huiusmodi gloriam nominat *florem foeni.* Deinde humanae gloriae cupido animi magnitudinem aufert: qui enim favorem hominum quaerit, necesse est ut in omni quod dicit aut facit eorum voluntati deserviat; et sic dum placere omnibus studet, fit servus singulorum. Propter quod et idem Tullius, in libro *de Officiis,* cavendam dicit esse gloriae cupidinem: *Eripit enim animi libertatem, pro qua magnanimis viris omnis debet esse contentio.* Nihil autem principem qui ad magna peragenda instituitur, magis decet quam animi magnitudo; est igitur incompetens regis officio humanae gloriae praemium.

Simul etiam est multitudini noxium si tale praemium statuatur principibus. Pertinet enim ad boni viri officium ut contemnat gloriam sicut et alia temporalia bona: virtuosi enim et fortis animi est pro iustitia contemnere gloriam sicut et vitam. Unde fit quiddam mirabile, ut quia virtuosos actus consequitur gloria ipsaque gloria virtuose contemnatur, ex contemptu gloriae homo gloriosus reddatur, secundum sententiam Fabii dicentis *Gloriam qui spreverit, veram habuit.* Et de Catone dixit Salustius *Quo minus petebat gloriam, tanto magis assequebatur illam*; ipsique Christi discipuli se sicut Dei ministros exhibebant *per gloriam et ignobilitatem, per infamiam et bonam famam.* Non est igitur boni viri conveniens praemium gloria quam contemnunt boni. Si igitur hoc solum praemium statuatur principibus, sequetur bonos viros non assumere principatum, aut si assumpserint impraemiatos esse.

Amplius, ex cupidine gloriae periculosa mala proveniunt. Multi enim dum immoderate gloriam in rebus bellicis quaerunt, se ac suos exercitus perdiderunt, libertate patriae sub hostium servitute redacta: unde Torquatus Romanus princeps, in exemplo huius vitandi discriminis, filium, qui contra imperium suum ab hoste provocatus iuvenili ardore pugnavit, licet vicisset occidit, ne plus mali esset in praesumptionis exemplo quam utilitatis in gloria hostis occisi.

Habet etiam cupido gloriae aliud sibi familiare vitium, simulationem videlicet. Quia enim difficile est paucisque contingit veras virtutes assequi, quibus solis honor debetur et gloria, multi gloriam cupientes virtutum simulatores fiunt; propter quod, sicut Salustius dicit, *ambitio multos mortales falsos fieri coegit: aliud clausum in pectore, aliud promptum habere in lingua, magisque*

than. And this is why the Prophet Isaiah calls such glory *the flower of grass* (Isa 40:6). Moreover, the desire for human glory takes away greatness of soul. For he who seeks the favor of men must serve their will in all he says and does, and thus, while striving to please all, he becomes a slave to each one. Therefore, the same Cicero says in his book *On Duties* that the inordinate desire for glory is to be guarded against: *It takes away freedom of soul, for the sake of which high-minded men should put forth all their efforts.*[9] Indeed, there is nothing more becoming to a prince who has been set up for the doing of good works than greatness of soul. Thus, the reward of human glory is not enough for the services of a king.

At the same time it also hurts the multitude if such a reward be set up for princes, for it is the duty of a good man to take no account of glory, just as he should take no account of other temporal goods. It is the mark of a virtuous and brave soul to despise glory as he despises life, for justice's sake. From this comes a wonder: glory ensues from virtuous acts, and out of virtue glory itself is despised. And therefore, through his very contempt for glory, a man is made glorious—according to the sentence of Fabius: *He who scorns glory shall have true glory*, and as Sallust says of Cato: *The less he sought glory the more he achieved it.*[10] Even the disciples of Christ exhibited themselves as the ministers of God *in honor and dishonor, in ill repute and good repute* (2 Cor 6:8). Therefore, it is not fitting for glory, spurned by good men, to be the reward of a good man. And, if it alone be set up as the reward for princes, it will follow that good men will not take upon themselves the chief office of the city, or if they take it, they will go unrewarded.

Furthermore, dangerous evils come from the desire for glory. Many have been led unrestrainedly to seek glory in warfare, and have sent their armies and themselves to destruction, while the freedom of their country was turned into servitude under an enemy. Consider Torquatus, the Roman chief: in order to impress upon the people how imperative it is to avoid such danger, he slew his own son who had acted against his orders (he had been challenged by an enemy whom he had fought and vanquished). Torquatus acted thus lest more harm should accrue from the example of his son's presumption than advantage from the glory of slaying the enemy.[11]

Moreover, the desire for glory has another vice akin to it: namely, hypocrisy. Since it is difficult to acquire true virtues, to which alone honor and glory are due, and it is therefore the lot of but a few to attain them, many who desire glory become simulators of virtue. On this account, as Sallust says: *Ambition drives many mortals to become false. They keep one thing shut up in their heart, another ready on*

9. *De officiis,* I, 20, 68.
10. *Bellum Catilinae* 54, 6.
11. Cf. Augustine, *De civ. Dei,* V, 18.

vultum quam ingenium bonum habere. Sed et Salvator noster eos qui bona opera faciunt ut ab hominibus videantur, hypocritas, id est simulatores, vocat. Sicut igitur periculosum est multitudini si princeps voluptates et divitias quaerat pro praemio, ne raptor contumeliosus fiat, ita periculosum est si ei determinetur gloriae praemium, ne praesumptuosus et simulator existat.

Sed quantum ex dictorum sapientium intentione apparet, non ea ratione honorem et gloriam pro praemio principi decreverunt tanquam ad hoc principaliter ferri debeat boni regis intentio, sed quia tolerabilius est si gloriam quaerat quam si pecuniam cupiat aut voluptatem sequatur. Hoc enim vitium virtuti propinquius est, cum gloria quam homines cupiunt nihil aliud sit, ut Augustinus definit, quam *iudicium hominum bene de hominibus opinantium.* Cupido enim gloriae aliquod habet virtutis vestigium, dum saltem bonorum approbationem quaerit et eis displicere recusat. Paucis igitur ad veram virtutem pervenientibus, tolerabilius videtur si praeferatur ad regimen qui, vel iudicium hominum metuens, saltem a malis manifestis retrahitur. Qui enim gloriam cupit, aut vera via, id est per virtutis opera, nititur ut ab hominibus approbetur, vel saltem dolis ad hoc contendit atque fallaciis. Qui vero dominari desiderat, si cupiditate gloriae carens non timeat bene iudicantibus displicere, *etiam per apertissima scelera quaerit plerumque obtinere quod diligit,* unde bestias superat sive crudelitatis sive luxuriae vitiis, sicut in Nerone Caesare patet, cuius, ut Augustinus dicit, *fuit tanta luxuria ut nihil putaretur ab eo virile metuendum, tanta crudelitas ut nihil molle habere putaretur.* Hoc autem satis exprimitur per id quod Aristoteles de magnanimo in *Ethicis* dicit, quod non quaerit honorem et gloriam quasi aliquid magnum quod sit virtutis sufficiens praemium, sed nihil ultra hoc ab hominibus exigit. Hoc enim inter omnia terrena videtur esse praecipuum, ut homini ab hominibus testimonium de virtute reddatur.

the tongue, and they have more countenance than character.[12] But our Savior also calls those persons 'hypocrites,' or simulators, who do good works to be seen by men. Therefore, just as there is danger for the multitude that the prince may become abusive and a plunderer if he seeks pleasures and riches as his reward, so there is danger that he may become presumptuous and a hypocrite if glory is assigned to him as reward.

Looking at what the above-mentioned wise men intended to say, they do not seem to have decided upon honor and glory as the reward of a prince because they judged that the king's intention should be principally directed to that object, but because it is more tolerable for him to seek glory than to desire money or pursue pleasure. For this vice is akin to virtue inasmuch as the glory which men desire, as Augustine says, is nothing else than *the judgment of men who think well of men.*[13] So the desire for glory has some trace of virtue in it, at least so long as it seeks the approval of good men and is reluctant to displease them. Therefore, since few men reach true virtue, it seems more tolerable if one be set up to rule who, fearing the judgment of men, is restrained from manifest evils. For the man who desires glory either endeavors to win the approval of men in the true way, by deeds of virtue, or at least strives for this by fraud and deceit. But if the one who desires to domineer lacks the desire for glory, he will have no fear of offending men of good judgment *and will commonly strive to obtain what he chooses by the most open crimes.*[14] Thus he will surpass the beasts in the vices of cruelty and lust, as is evidenced in the case of the Emperor Nero, of whom Augustine says: *He was so lustful that he despised everything virile, and yet so cruel that nobody would have thought him to be effeminate.*[15] Indeed all this is quite clearly contained in what Aristotle says in his *Ethics*[16] regarding the magnanimous man: true, he does seek honor and glory, but not as something great which could be a sufficient reward of virtue. And beyond this he demands nothing more of men, for among all earthly goods the chief good, it seems, is this, that men bear testimony to the virtue of a man.

---

12. *Bellum Catilinae* 10, 5.
13. *de Civitate Dei* V, 12.
14. Augustine, *de Civitate Dei* V, 19.
15. *Loc. cit.*
16. *Ethics* IV, 7:1124a 16.

CHAPTER 8

That the king should look to God for adequate reward

Quoniam ergo mundanus honor et hominum gloria regiae sollicitudini non est sufficiens praemium, inquirendum restat quale sit eius sufficiens praemium.

Est autem conveniens ut rex praemium expectet a Deo. Minister enim pro suo ministerio praemium expectat a domino; rex autem populum gubernando minister Dei est, dicente Apostolo quod *omnis potestas a Domino Deo est*, et quod est *Dei minister vindex in iram ei qui male agit*; et in libro Sapientiae reges regni Dei esse ministri describuntur. Debent igitur reges pro suo regimine praemium expectare a Deo.

Remunerat autem Deus pro suo ministerio interdum temporalibus bonis, sed talia praemia sunt bonis malisque communia; unde Dominus ad Ezechielem dicit *Nabuchodonosor rex Babylonis servire fecit exercitum suum servitute magna adversus Tyrum, et merces non est reddita ei neque exercitui eius de Tyro pro servitute qua servivit mihi adversus eam*, ea scilicet servitute qua potestas, secundum Apostolum, *Dei minister est, vindex in iram ei qui male agit*. Et postea de praemio subdidit *Propterea haec dicit Dominus Deus: Ecce ego dabo Nabuchodonosor regem Babylonis in terra Aegypti, et diripiet spolia eius et erit merces exercitui eius*.

Si ergo reges iniquos contra Dei hostes pugnantes, licet non intentione serviendi Deo sed sua odia et cupiditates exequendi, tanta mercede Dominus remunerat ut eis de hostibus victoriam tribuat, regna subiiciat et spolia diripienda proponat, quid faciet bonis regibus qui pia intentione populum Dei regunt et hostes impugnant? Non quidem terrenam sed aeternam eis mercedem promittit, nec in alio quam in se ipso, dicente Petro pastoribus populi Dei *Pascite qui in vobis est gregem Domini, ut cum venerit Princeps pastorum*, id est Rex regum Christus, *percipiatis immarcescibilem gloriae coronam*; de qua dicit Isaias *Erit Dominus sertum exultationis et diadema gloriae populo suo*.

Hoc autem ratione manifestatur. Est enim mentibus omnium ratione utentium inditum virtutis praemium beatitudinem esse; virtus enim uniuscuiusque rei esse describitur *quae bonum facit habentem et opus eius bonum reddit*. Ad hoc autem quisque bene operando

Therefore, since worldly honor and human glory are not a sufficient reward for royal cares, it remains to inquire what sort of reward is sufficient.

It is proper that a king look to God for his reward, for a servant looks to his master for the reward of his service. The king is indeed the minister of God in governing the people, as the Apostle says: *There is no authority except from God* (Rom 13:1) and God's minister is *the servant of God to execute his wrath on the wrongdoer* (Rom 13:4). And in the Book of Wisdom, kings are described as being ministers of God (Wis 6:5). Consequently, kings ought to look to God for the reward of their ruling.

Now God sometimes rewards kings for their service by temporal goods, but such rewards are common to both the good and the wicked. Hence the Lord says to Ezechiel: *Nabuchodonosor king of Babylon made his army labor hard against Tyre; every head was made bald and every shoulder was rubbed bare; yet neither he nor his army got anything from Tyre to pay for the labor that he had performed for me against it* (Ezek 29:18), namely, for that service by which power is *the minister of God and the avenger to execute wrath upon him who does evil* (Rom 13:4). Afterwards he adds, regarding the reward: *Therefore, thus says the Lord God: Behold, I will give the land of Egypt to Nabuchodonosor king of Babylon; and he shall carry off its wealth and despoil it and plunder it; and it shall be the wages for his army* (Ezek 29:19).

Therefore, if God recompenses wicked kings who fight against the enemies of God, though not with the intention of serving him but to execute their own hatred and cupidity, by giving them such great rewards as to yield them victory over their foes, subject kingdoms to their sway, and grant them spoils to rifle, what will he do for kings who rule the people of God and assail his enemies from a holy motive? Indeed, he promises them not an earthly reward, but an everlasting one, and in none other than in himself. As Peter says to the shepherds of the people: *Tend the flock of God that is your charge . . . and when the chief Shepherd is manifested*, that is, Christ the King of kings, *you will obtain the unfading crown of glory* (1 Pet 5:2, 4). Concerning this, Isaiah says: *The Lord of hosts will be a crown of glory and a diadem of beauty to his people* (Isa 28:5).

This is also clearly shown by reason. It is implanted in the minds of all who have the use of reason that the reward of virtue is happiness. The virtue of anything whatsoever is explained to be *that which makes its possessor good and renders his deed good*.[17] Moreover, everyone strives by

---

17. Aristotle, *Ethics* II, 6.

375

nititur pervenire quod est maxime desiderio inditum; hoc autem est esse felicem, quod nullus potest non velle: hoc igitur praemium virtutis convenienter expectatur quod hominem facit beatum. Si autem bene operari virtutis est opus, regis autem opus est bene regere subditos, hoc etiam erit praemium regis quod eum faciat beatum. Quid autem hoc sit, hinc considerandum est.

Beatitudinem quidem dicimus ultimum desideriorum finem; neque enim desiderii motus usque in infinitum procedit, esset enim inane naturale desiderium, cum infinita pertransiri non possint. Cum autem desiderium intellectualis naturae sit universalis boni, hoc solum bonum vere beatum facere poterit, quo adepto nullum bonum restat quod amplius desiderari possit; unde et beatitudo dicitur bonum perfectum, quasi omnia desiderabilia in se comprehendens. Tale autem non est aliquod bonum terrenum; nam qui divitias habent amplius habere desiderant, qui voluptatibus perfruuntur amplius perfrui desiderant, et simile patet in caeteris. Et si ampliora non quaerunt, desiderant tamen ut ea permaneant, vel alia in locum eorum succedant: nihil enim permanens invenitur in rebus terrenis; nihil igitur terrenum est quod quietare desiderium possit. Neque igitur terrenum aliquod beatum facere potest, ut possit esse regis conveniens praemium.

Adhuc, cuiuslibet rei finalis perfectio et bonum completum ab aliquo superiore dependet, quia et ipsa corporalia meliora redduntur ex adiunctione meliorum, peiora vero si deterioribus misceantur; sicut argento si misceatur aurum, argentum fit melius, quod ex plumbi admixtione impurum efficitur. Constat autem terrena omnia esse infra mentem humanam; beatitudo autem est hominis finalis perfectio et bonum completum ad quod omnes pervenire desiderant: nihil igitur terrenum est quod hominem possit beatum facere, neque igitur terrenum aliquod est praemium regis sufficiens. *Non enim, ut Augustinus dicit, christianos principes felices dicimus quia diutius imperarunt, vel imperatores filios morte placida reliquerunt, vel hostes reipublicae domuerunt, vel cives adversum se insurgentes et cavere et opprimere potuerunt; sed felices eos dicimus si iuste imperant, si malunt cupiditatibus potius quam gentibus quibuslibet imperare, si omnia faciunt non propter ardorem inanis gloriae, sed propter caritatem felicitatis aeternae. Tales imperatores christianos dicimus esse felices, interim spe, postea re ipsa futuros cum id quod expectamus advenerit.* Sed nec aliud aliquod creatum est quod hominem beatum faciat et possit regi decerni pro praemio. Tendit enim uniuscuiusque rei desiderium in suum principium a quo suum esse causatur; causa vero mentis humanae non est aliud quam Deus qui eam ad suam imaginem facit:

working well to attain what is most deeply implanted in desire: namely, to be happy. No one is able not to wish this. It is therefore fitting to expect as a reward for virtue that which makes man happy. Now, if to work well is a virtuous deed, and the king's work is to rule his people well, then that which makes him happy will be the king's reward. What this is has now to be considered.

Happiness, we say, is the ultimate end of our desires. Now the movement of desire does not go on to infinity, else natural desire would be vain, for infinity cannot be traversed. Since, then, the desire of an intellectual nature is for universal good, that good alone can make it truly happy which, when attained, leaves no further good to be desired. Hence happiness is called the perfect good inasmuch as it comprises in itself all things desirable. But no earthly good is such a good. They who have riches desire to have more, they who enjoy pleasure desire to enjoy more, and the like is clear for the rest: and if they do not seek more, they at least desire that those they have should abide or that others should follow in their stead. For nothing permanent is found in earthly things. Consequently, there is nothing earthly which can calm desire. Thus, nothing earthly can make man happy, so that it may be a fitting reward for a king.

Again, the last perfection and perfect good of anything one chooses depends upon something higher, for even bodily things are made better by the addition of better things and worse by being mixed with baser things. If gold is mingled with silver, the silver is made better, while by an admixture of lead it is rendered impure. Now all earthly things are beneath the human mind; but happiness is the last perfection and the perfect good of man, which all men desire to reach. Therefore, there is no earthly thing which could make man happy, nor is any earthly thing a sufficient reward for a king. For, as Augustine says, *We do not call Christian princes happy merely because they have reigned a long time, or because after a peaceful death they have left their sons to rule, or because they subdued the enemies of the state, or because they were able to guard against or to suppress citizens who rose up against them. Rather, we call them happy if they rule justly, if they prefer to rule their passions rather than nations, and if they do all things not for the love of vainglory but for the love of eternal happiness. Such Christian emperors we say are happy, now in hope, afterwards in very fact when that which we await shall come to pass.*[18] But neither is there any other created thing which would make a man happy and which could be set up as the reward for a king. For the desire of each thing tends towards its source which causes its being. But the cause of the human soul is none other than God, who made it to his own image. Therefore, it is

---

18. Augustine, *de Civitate Dei*, V, 24.

solus igitur Deus est qui hominis desiderium quietare potest et facere hominem beatum et esse regi conveniens praemium.

Amplius, mens humana universalis boni cognoscitiva est per intellectum et desiderativa per voluntatem; bonum autem universale non invenitur nisi in Deo, nihil igitur est quod possit hominem beatum facere eius implendo desiderium nisi Deus, de quo dicitur in Psalmo *Qui replet in bonis desiderium tuum*; in hoc ergo rex suum praemium statuere debet. Hoc igitur considerans David rex dicebat *Quid mihi est in caelo et a te quid volui super terram?*; cui quaestioni postea respondens subdit *Mihi adhaerere Deo bonum est et ponere in Deo spem meam*. Ipse enim est qui dat salutem regibus, non solum temporalem qua communiter salvat homines et iumenta, sed eam de qua per Isaiam dicit *Salus autem mea in sempiternum erit*, qua homines salvat eos ad aequalitatem angelorum perducens.

Sic igitur verificari potest quod regis praemium sit honor et gloria. Quis enim mundanus et caducus honor huic honori similis esse potest, ut homo sit *civis sanctorum et domesticus Dei*, et inter Dei filios computatus haereditatem regni caelestis assequatur cum Christo? Hic est honor quem concupiscens et admirans rex David dicebat *Nimis honorati sunt amici tui, Deus*. Quae insuper humanae laudis gloria huic gloriae comparari potest, quam non fallax blandientium lingua, non decepta hominum opinio profert, sed ex interioris conscientiae testimonio prodit et Dei testimonio confirmatur qui suis confessoribus repromittit quod confiteatur eos in gloria Patris coram angelis Dei? Qui autem hanc gloriam quaerunt eam inveniunt, et quam non quaerunt gloriam hominum consequuntur, exemplo Salomonis qui non solum sapientiam quam quaesivit accepit a Domino, sed factus est super reges alios gloriosus.

God alone who can still the desires of man, and make him happy, and be the fitting reward for a king.

Furthermore, the human mind knows the universal good through the intellect, and desires it through the will: but the universal good is not found except in God. Therefore, there is nothing which could make man happy, fulfilling his every desire, but God, of whom it is said in the Psalm: *Who satisfies your desire with good* (Ps 103 [102]:5). In this, therefore, should the king place his reward. Thus King David, with this in mind, said: *Whom have I in heaven but you? And there is nothing upon earth that I desire besides you* (Ps 73 [72]:25) and he afterwards adds in answer to this question: *It is good for me to adhere to my God and to put my hope in the Lord God* (Ps 73 [72]:28). For it is he who gives salvation to kings, not merely temporal salvation by which he saves both men and beasts together, but also that salvation of which he says by the mouth of Isaiah: *But my salvation shall be forever* (Isa 51:6), that salvation by which he saves man and makes them equal to the angels.

It can thus also be verified that the reward of the king is honor and glory. What worldly and frail honor can indeed be likened to this honor, that a man be made a *fellow citizen with the saints and member of the household of God* (Eph 2:19), numbered among the sons of God, and that he obtain the inheritance of the heavenly kingdom with Christ? This is the honor of which King David, in desire and wonder, says: *Your friends, O God, are made exceedingly honorable* (Ps 138:17). And further, what glory of human praise can be compared to this, not uttered by the false tongue of flatterers nor the fallacious opinion of men, but issuing from the witness of our inmost conscience and confirmed by the testimony of God, who promises to those who confess him that he will confess them before the angels of God in the glory of the Father? They who seek this glory will find it and they will win the glory of men which they do not seek: witness Solomon, who not only received from the Lord wisdom which he sought, but was made glorious above other kings.

CHAPTER 9

What degree of heavenly beatitude the king may obtain

Considerandum autem restat ulterius, quod sublimen et eminentem obtinebunt caelestis beatitudinis gradum qui officium regium digne et laudabiliter exequuntur. Si enim beatitudo virtutis est praemium, consequens est ut maiori virtuti maior gradus beatitudinis debeatur. Est autem virtus praecipua qua homo aliquis non solum se ipsum, sed etiam alios dirigere potest, et tanto magis quanto plurium est regitiva, quia et secundum virtutem corporalem tanto aliquis virtuosior reputatur, quanto plures vincere potest aut pondera plura levare. Sic igitur maior virtus requiritur ad regendum domesticam familiam quam ad regendum se ipsum, multoque maior ad regimen civitatis et regni. Est igitur excellentis virtutis bene regium officium exercere: debetur igitur ei excellens in beatitudine praemium.

Adhuc, in omnibus artibus et potentiis laudabiliores sunt qui alios bene dirigunt, quam qui secundum aliorum directionem bene se habent. In speculativis enim maius est veritatem docendo aliis tradere, quam ab alio traditam capere posse; in artificiis etiam maius existimatur maiorique conducitur praemio architector qui aedificium disponit, quam artifex qui secundum eius dispositionem manualiter operatur; et in rebus bellicis maiorem gloriam de victoria consequitur prudentia ducis quam militis fortitudo. Sic autem se habet rector multitudinis in his quae sunt a singulis secundum virtutem agenda, sicut doctor in disciplinis et architector in aedificiis et dux in bellis. Est igitur rex maiori praemio dignus si bene subiectos gubernaverit, quam aliquis subditorum si sub rege bene se habuerit.

Amplius, si virtutis est ut per eam opus hominis bonum reddatur, maioris virtutis esse videtur quod maius bonum aliquis operetur. Maius autem et divinius est bonum multitudinis quam unius; unde et interdum malum unius sustinetur si in bonum multitudinis cedat, sicut occiditur latro ut pax multitudini detur. Et ipse Deus mala esse in mundo non sineret, nisi ex eis bona eliceret ad utilitatem et pulchritudinem universi. Pertinet autem ad regis officium ut bonum multitudinis studiose procuret; maius igitur praemium debetur regi pro bono regimine, quam subdito pro recta actione.

Hoc autem manifestius fiet si quis magis in speciali consideret. Laudatur enim ab hominibus quaevis privata persona et ei a Deo computatur in praemium, si egenti subveniat, si discordantes pacificet, si oppressum a potentiore eripiat, denique si alicui qualitercumque opem vel consilium conferat ad salutem. Quanto igitur

Now it remains further to consider that they who discharge the kingly office worthily and laudably will obtain an elevated and outstanding degree of heavenly happiness. For if happiness is the reward of virtue, it follows that a higher degree of happiness is due to greater virtue. Now, that virtue is eminent by which a man can guide not only himself but others, and the more persons he rules, the greater his virtue. Similarly, in regard to bodily strength, a man is reputed to be more powerful the more adversaries he can beat or the more weights he can lift. Thus, greater virtue is required to rule a household than to rule one's self, and much greater to rule a city and a kingdom. To discharge well the office of a king is therefore a work of extraordinary virtue. To it, therefore, is due an extraordinary reward of happiness.

Again, those who rule others well are more worthy of praise than those who act well under others' direction. This applies to the field of all arts and sciences. In the speculative sciences, for instance, it is nobler to impart truth to others by teaching than to be able to grasp what is taught by others. So, too, in matters of the crafts, an architect who plans a building is more highly esteemed and paid a higher wage than is the builder who does the manual labor under his direction; and in warfare the strategy of the general wins greater glory from victory than the bravery of the soldier. Now, the ruler of a multitude stands in the same relation to the virtuous deeds performed by each individual as the teacher to the matters taught, the architect to the buildings, and the general to the wars. Consequently, the king is worthy of a greater reward if he governs his subjects well than any of his subjects who act well under him.

Further, if it is the part of virtue to render a man's work good, it seems that one does greater good from greater virtue. But the good of the multitude is greater and more divine than the good of one man. Hence the evil of one man is sometimes endured if it redounds to the good of the multitude, as when a robber is killed to bring peace to the multitude. God himself would not allow evils to be in the world unless he brings good out of them for the advantage and beauty of the universe. Now, it belongs to the office of the king to have zealous concern for the good of the multitude. Therefore, a greater reward is due to the king for good ruling than to the subject for acting according to rule.

This will become clearer if considered in greater detail. For a private person is praised by men, and his deed reckoned for reward by God, if he helps the needy, brings peace to those in discord, rescues one oppressed by a mightier—in a word, if in any way he gives to another assistance or advice for his welfare. How much the more, then, is he to be

magis laudandus est ab hominibus et praemiandus a Deo, qui totam provinciam facit pace gaudere, violentias cohibet, iustitiam servat, et disponit quid sit agendum ab hominibus suis legibus et praeceptis.

Hinc etiam magnitudo regiae virtutis apparet quod praecipue Dei similitudinem gerit, dum hoc agit in regno quod Deus in mundo: unde et in Exodo iudices multitudinis dii vocantur; imperatores etiam apud Romanos divi vocantur. Tanto autem est aliquid magis Deo acceptum, quanto magis ad eius imitationem accedit; unde et Apostolus monet: *Estote imitatores Dei sicut filii charissimi.* Sed si secundum Sapientis sententiam, *omne animal diligit simile sibi,* secundum quod causae similitudinem aliqualiter habent causata, consequens igitur est bonos reges Deo esse acceptissimos et ab eo maxime praemiandos.

Simul etiam, ut Gregorii verbis utar, *quid est [potestas culminis] nisi tempestas mentis? Quieto autem mari recte navem etiam imperitus dirigit, turbato autem tempestatis fluctibus etiam peritus se nauta confundit; unde plerumque in occupatione regiminis ipse quoque boni operis usus perditur, qui in tranquillitate tenebatur.* Valde enim difficile est si, ut Augustinus dicit, *inter linguas sublimiter honorantium et obsequia nimis humiliter salutantium non extollantur, sed se homines esse meminerint.* Et in Ecclesiastico beatus dicitur *dives qui post aurum non abiit, nec speravit in pecuniae thesauris; qui potuit impune transgredi et non est transgressus, facere mala et non fecit*: ex quo quasi in virtutis opere probatus, invenitur fidelis. Unde secundum Biantis proverbium *principatus virum ostendit*: multi enim ad principatus culmen pervenientes a virtute deficiunt, qui dum in statu essent infimo virtuosi videbantur. Ipsa igitur difficultas quae principibus imminet ad bene agendum, eos facit maiori praemio dignos, et si aliquando per infirmitatem peccaverint, apud homines excusabiliores redduntur et facilius a Deo veniam promerentur, si tamen, ut Augustinus dicit, *pro suis peccatis humilitatis et miserationis et orationis sacrificium Deo suo vero immolare non negligunt.* In cuius rei exemplum de Achab rege Israel, qui multum peccaverat, Dominus ad Heliam dixit *Quia humiliatus est mei causa, non inducam malum in diebus euis.*

Non solum autem ratione ostenditur quod regibus excellens praemium debeatur, sed etiam auctoritate divina firmatur. Dicitur enim in Zacharia quod in illa beatitudinis die qua erit Dominus protector habitantium

praised by men and rewarded by God who makes a whole province rejoice in peace, who restrains violence, preserves justice, and arranges by his laws and precepts what is to be done by men?

The greatness of kingly virtue also appears in this, that he bears a special likeness to God, since he does in his kingdom what God does in the world; wherefore in Exodus the judges of the people are called gods,[19] and also among the Romans the emperors were called 'divine.' Now the more a thing approaches to the likeness of God, the more acceptable it is to him. Hence, also, the Apostle urges: *Be imitators of God, as beloved children* (Eph 5:1). But if, according to the saying of the wise man, *every creature loves its like* (Sir 13:15) inasmuch as causes bear some likeness to the caused, it follows that good kings are most pleasing to God and are to be most highly rewarded by him.

Likewise, if I may use the words of Gregory: *What else is it for a king to be at the pinnacle of power if not to find himself in a mental storm? When the sea is calm even an inexperienced man can steer a ship straight; when the sea is troubled by stormy waves, even an experienced sailor is bewildered. Hence it frequently happens that in the business of government the practice of good works is lost which in tranquil times was maintained.*[20] For, as Augustine says, it is very difficult for rulers *not to be puffed up amid flattering and honoring tongues and the obsequiousness of those who bow too humbly, but to remember that they are men.*[21] It is said also in Sirach: *Blessed is the rich man who has not gone after gold, nor put his trust in money, nor in treasures, who could have transgressed with impunity and did not transgress, who could do evil and did not do it* (Sir 31:8, 10). Hence, having been tried in the work of virtue, he is found faithful, and so according to the proverb of Bias: *Authority shows the man.*[22] For many who seemed virtuous while they were in lowly state fall from virtue when they reach the pinnacle of power. The very difficulty, then, of acting well, which besets kings, makes them worthy of greater reward; and if through weakness they sometimes do amiss, they are rendered more excusable before men and more easily obtain forgiveness from God: provided, as Augustine says,[23] *they do not neglect to offer up to their true God the sacrifice of humility, mercy, and prayer for their sins.* As an example of this, the Lord said to Elias concerning Achab, king of Israel, who had sinned a great deal: *Because he has humbled himself before me, I will not bring the evil in his days* (1 Kgs 21:29).

That a very high reward is due to kings is not only demonstrated by reason but is also confirmed by divine authority. It is said in Zachariah 12:8 that, in that day of blessedness wherein God will be the protector of the inhab-

---

19. Exod 22:9.
20. *Regula Pastoralis* I, 9.
21. *de Civitate Dei* V, 24.
22. Aristotle, *Eth. Nic.* V, 3: 1130a 1.
23. *De civ. Dei*, V, 24.

in Ierusalem, id est in visione pacis aeternae, aliorum domus erunt sicut domus David, quia scilicet omnes reges erunt et regnabunt cum Christo sicut membra cum capite; sed domus David erit sicut domus Dei, quia sicut regendo fideliter Dei officium gessit in populo, ita in praemio Deo propinquius inhaerebit. Hoc etiam fuit apud Gentiles aliqualiter somniatum, dum civitatum rectores atque servatores in deos transformari putabant.

itants of Jerusalem (that is, in the vision of eternal peace), the houses of others will be as the house of David, because all will then be kings and reign with Christ as the members with their head. But the house of David will be as the house of God, because just as he carried out the work of God among the people by ruling faithfully, so in his reward he will adhere more closely to God. Likewise, among the Gentiles this was dimly realized, as in a dream, for they thought to transform into gods the rulers and preservers of their cities.

CHAPTER 10

What advantages which are rendered to kings are lost by the tyrant

Cum igitur regibus tam grande in caelesti beatitudine praemium proponatur si bene se in regendo habuerint, diligenti cura se ipsos observare debent ne in tyrannidem convertantur. Nihil enim eis acceptabilius esse potest quam quod, ex honore regio quo sublimantur in terris, in caelestis regni gloriam transferantur. E contra vero tyranni, quia propter quaedam terrena commoda iustitiam deserunt, tanto privantur praemio quod adipisci poterant iuste regendo. Quod autem stultum sit pro huiusmodi parvis et temporalibus bonis maxima et sempiterna perdere bona, nullus nisi stultus aut infidelis ignorat.

Addendum est autem quod etiam haec temporalia commoda, propter quae tyranni iustitiam deserunt, magis ad lucrum proveniunt regibus dum iustitiam servant. Primo namque inter mundana omnia nihil est quod amicitiae dignae praeferendum videatur. Ipsa enim est quae virtuosos in unum conciliat, virtutem conservat atque promovet. Ipsa est qua omnes indigent in quibuscumque negotiis exequendis, quae nec prosperis importune se ingerit, nec deserit in adversis. Ipsa est quae maximas delectationes affert, in tantum ut quaecumque delectabilia in taedium sine amicis vertantur; quaelibet autem aspera, facilia et prope nulla facit amor. Nec est alicuius tyranni tanta crudelitas ut amicitia non delectetur. Dionysius enim quondam Syracusanorum tyrannus cum duorum amicorum, qui Damon et Pythias dicebantur, alterum occidere vellet, is qui occidendus erat inducias impetravit ut domum profectus res suas ordinaret; alter vero amicorum obsidem se tyranno pro eius reditu dedit. Appropinquante autem praefixo die, nec illo redeunte, unusquisque fideiussorem stultitiae arguebat; at ille nihil se de amici constantia metuere praedicabat. Eadem autem hora qua fuerat praefixa, occidendus rediit. Admirans autem amborum animum, tyrannus supplicium propter fidem amicitiae remisit,

Since such a magnificent reward in heavenly blessedness is in store for kings who have acted well in ruling, they ought to keep careful watch over themselves in order not to turn to tyranny. Nothing, indeed, can be more acceptable to them than to be transferred from the royal honor, to which they are raised on earth, into the glory of the heavenly kingdom. Tyrants, on the contrary, who desert justice for a few earthly advantages, are deprived of such a great reward which they could have obtained by ruling justly. How foolish it is to sacrifice the greatest and eternal goods for trifling, temporal goods is clear to everyone but a fool or an infidel.

It is to be added further, however, that the very temporal advantages for which tyrants abandon justice work to the greater profit of kings when they observe justice. First of all, among all worldly things there is nothing which seems worthy to be preferred to friendship. Friendship unites good men and preserves and promotes virtue. Friendship is needed by all men in whatsoever occupations they engage. In prosperity it does not thrust itself unwanted upon us, nor does it desert us in adversity. It is what brings with it the greatest delight, to such an extent that all that pleases is changed to weariness when friends are absent, and all difficult things are made easy and as nothing by love. There is no tyrant so cruel that friendship does not bring him pleasure. When Dionysius, sometime tyrant of Syracuse, wanted to kill one of two friends, Damon and Pythias, the one who was to be killed asked leave to go home and set his affairs in order, and the other friend surrendered himself to the tyrant as security for his return. When the appointed day was approaching and he had not yet returned, everyone said that his hostage was a fool, but he declared he had no fear whatever regarding his friend's loyalty. The very hour when he was to be put to death, his friend returned. Admiring the courage of both, the tyrant remitted the sentence on account of the loyalty of their friendship, and asked in

insuper rogans ut eum tertium reciperent in amicitiae gradu.

Hoc tamen amicitiae bonum quamvis desiderent tyranni, consequi non possunt. Dum enim commune bonum non quaerunt sed proprium, fit parva vel nulla communio eorum ad subditos; omnis autem amicitia super aliqua communione firmatur: eos enim qui conveniunt vel per naturae originem vel per morum similitudinem vel per cuiuscumque societatis communionem, videmus amicitia coniungi; parva igitur vel potius nulla est amicitia tyranni et subditi. Simulque dum subditi per tyrannicam iniustitiam opprimuntur et se amari non sentiunt sed contemni, nequaquam amant. Est enim maioris virtutis inimicos diligere et persequentibus benefacere quam quod a multitudine observatur; nec habent unde de subditis conquerantur si ab eis non diliguntur, quia nec ipsi se tales eis exhibent ut diligi debeant.

At boni reges dum communi profectui studiose intendunt et eorum studio subditi plurima commoda se consequi sentiunt, diliguntur a plurimis, dum subditos se amare demonstrant; quia et hoc etiam est maioris malitiae quam quod in multitudine cadat, ut odio habeantur amici et benefactoribus rependatur malum pro bono. Ex hoc amore provenit quod bonorum regum regimen sit stabile, dum pro ipsis se subditi quibuscumque periculis exponere non recusant. Cuius exemplum in Iulio Caesare apparet, de quo Suetonius refert quod milites suos usque adeo diligebat ut, audita quorumdam caede, *capillos et barbam ante non dempserit quam vindicasset*; quibus rebus devotissimos sibi et fortissimos milites reddidit, ita quod plerique eorum capti concessam sibi sub ea conditione vitam, si militare adversus Caesarem vellent, recusarent. Octavianus etiam Augustus, qui modestissime imperio usus est, in tantum diligebatur a subditis, ut plerique *morientes victimas quas devoverant immolari mandarent quia eum superstitem reliquissent*. Non est ergo facile ut principis perturbetur dominium quem tanto consensu populus amat; propter quod Salomon dicit *Rex qui iudicat in iustitia pauperes, thronus eius in aeternum firmabitur*.

Tyrannorum vero dominium diuturnum esse non potest, cum sit multitudini odiosum; non potest enim diu conservari quod votis multorum repugnat. Vix enim a quoquam praesens vita transigitur quin aliquas adversitates patiatur; adversitatis autem tempore occasio

addition that they should receive him as a third member in their bond of friendship.[24]

Yet, although tyrants desire this very benefit of friendship, they cannot obtain it, for when they seek their own good instead of the common good there is little or no communion between them and their subjects. Now, all friendship is based upon something common among those who are to be friends, for we see that those are united in friendship who have in common either their natural origin, or some similarity in habits of life, or any kind of social interests. Consequently, there can be little or no friendship between tyrants and their subjects. When the latter are oppressed by tyrannical injustice and feel they are not loved but despised, they certainly do not conceive any love, for it is too great a virtue for the common man to love his enemies and to do good to his persecutors (cf. Matt 5:44). Nor have tyrants any reason to complain of their subjects if they are not loved by them, since they do not act towards them in such a way that they ought to be loved by them.

Good kings, on the contrary, are loved by many when they show that they love their subjects and are studiously intent on the common welfare, and when their subjects can see that they derive many benefits from this zealous care. For to hate their friends and return evil for good to their benefactors—this, surely, would be too great a malice to ascribe fittingly to the generality of men. The consequence of this love is that the government of good kings is stable, because their subjects do not refuse to expose themselves to any danger whatsoever on behalf of such kings. An example of this is to be seen in Julius Caesar who, as Suetonius relates, loved his soldiers to such an extent that when he heard that some of them were slaughtered, *he refused to cut either hair or beard until he had taken vengeance*.[25] In this way, he made his soldiers most loyal to himself as well as most valiant, so that many, on being taken prisoner, refused to accept their lives when offered them on the condition that they serve against Caesar. Likewise, Octavianus Augustus, who was most moderate in his use of power, was so loved by his subjects that some of them *on their deathbeds provided in their wills a thank-offering to be paid by the immolation of animals, so grateful were they that the emperor's life outlasted their own*.[26] Therefore, it is no easy task to shake the government of a prince whom the people so unanimously love. This is why Solomon says: *The king that judges the poor in justice, his throne shall be established forever* (Prov 29:14).

The government of tyrants, on the other hand, cannot last long because it is hateful to the multitude, and what is against the wishes of the multitude cannot be long preserved. For a man can hardly pass through this present life without suffering some adversities, and in the time of

---

24. Cf. Valerius Maximus IV, 7, Ext. 1; Vincent of Beauvais, *Specul. Doctrinale* V, 84.
25. *Divus Iulius* 67.
26. Suetonius, *Divus Augustus* 59.

deesse non potest contra tyrannum insurgendi, et si adsit occasio, non deerit ex multis vel unus qui occasione non utatur. Insurgentem autem populus votive prosequitur, nec de facili carebit effectu quod cum favore multitudinis attentatur. Vix ergo potest contingere quod tyranni dominium protendatur in longum.

Hoc etiam manifeste patet, si quis consideret unde tyranni dominium conservatur. Non enim conservatur amore, cum parva vel nulla sit amicitia subiectae multitudinis ad tyrannum, ut ex praehabitis patet. De subditorum autem fide tyrannis confidendum non est: non enim invenitur tanta virtus in multis, ut fidelitatis virtute comprimantur ne indebitae servitutis iugum si possunt excutiant. Fortassis autem nec fidelitati contrarium reputabitur secundum opinionem multorum, si tyrannicae nequitiae qualitercumque obvietur. Restat ergo ut solo timore tyranni regimen sustentetur, unde et timeri se a subditis tota intentione procurant. Timor autem est debile fundamentum; nam qui timore subduntur, si occurrat occasio qua possint impunitatem sperare, contra praesidentes insurgunt eo ardentius quo magis contra voluntatem ex solo timore cohibebantur, sicut si aqua per violentiam includatur, cum aditum invenerit impetuosius fluit. Sed nec ipse timor caret periculo, cum ex nimio timore plerique in desperationem inciderint; salutis autem desperatio audacter ad quaelibet attendenda praecipitat. Non potest igitur tyranni dominium esse diuturnum.

Hoc etiam non minus exemplis quam rationibus apparet. Si quis enim antiquorum gesta et modernorum eventus consideret, vix inveniet tyranni alicuius dominium diuturnum fuisse. Unde Aristoteles in sua Politica multis tyrannis enumeratis, omnium monstrat dominium brevi tempore fuisse finitum; quorum tamen aliqui diutius praefuerunt, quia non multum in tyrannide excedebant sed quantum ad multa imitabantur regalem modestiam.

Adhuc autem, hoc magis fit manifestum ex consideratione divini iudicii. Ut enim in Iob dicitur, *regnare facit hominem hypocritam propter peccata populi*. Nullus autem verius hypocrita dici potest quam qui regis assumit officium et exhibet se tyrannum; nam hypocrita dicitur qui alterius repraesentat personam, sicut in spectaculis fieri consuevit. Sic igitur Deus praefici permittit tyrannos ad puniendum subditorum peccata. Talis autem punitio in Scripturis ira Dei consuevit nominari; unde per Oseae Dominus dicit *Dabo tibi regem in furore meo*. Infelix autem rex qui populo in furore Dei conce-

his adversity occasion cannot be lacking to rise against the tyrant; and when there is an opportunity there will not be lacking at least one of the multitude to use it. Then the people will fervently favor the insurgent, and what is attempted with the sympathy of the multitude will not easily fail of its effects. It can thus scarcely come to pass that the government of a tyrant will endure for a long time.

This is very clear, too, if we consider the means by which a tyrannical government is upheld. It is not upheld by love, since there is little or no bond of friendship between the subject multitude and the tyrant, as is evident from what we have said. On the other hand, tyrants cannot rely on the loyalty of their subjects, for such a degree of virtue is not found among the generality of men that they should be restrained by the virtue of fidelity from throwing off the yoke of unmerited servitude, if they are able to do so. Nor would it perhaps be a violation of fidelity at all, according to the opinion of many, to frustrate the wickedness of tyrants by any means whatsoever. It remains, then, that the government of a tyrant is maintained by fear alone, and consequently they strive with all their might to be feared by their subjects. Fear, however, is a weak support. Those who are kept down by fear will rise against their rulers if the opportunity ever occurs when they can hope to do it with impunity, and they will rebel against their rulers all the more furiously the more they have been kept in subjection against their will by fear alone, just as water confined under pressure flows with greater impetus when it finds an outlet. That very fear itself is not without danger, because many become desperate from excessive fear, and despair of safety impels a man boldly to dare anything. Therefore, the government of a tyrant cannot be of long duration.

This appears clearly from examples no less than from reason. If we scan the history of antiquity and the events of modern times, we shall scarcely find one government of a tyrant which lasted a long time. So Aristotle, in his *Politics*,[27] after enumerating many tyrants, shows that all their governments were of short duration; although some of them reigned a fairly long time because they were not very tyrannical, but in many things imitated the moderation of kings.

All this becomes still more evident if we consider the divine judgment, for, as we read in Job, *He makes a man who is a hypocrite to reign for the sins of the people* (Job 24:30). No one, indeed, can be more truly called a hypocrite than the man who assumes the office of king and acts like a tyrant, for a hypocrite is one who mimics the person of another, as is done on the stage. Hence God permits tyrants to get into power to punish the sins of the subjects. In Sacred Scripture it is customary to call such punishment 'the anger of God.' Thus in Hosea the Lord says: *I will give you a king in my anger* (Hos 13:11). Unhappy is a king who is given to

---

27. V, 12: 1315b 11–39.

ditur: non enim eius stabile potest esse dominium, quia *non obliviscetur misereri Deus, nec continebit in ira sua misericordias suas*; quinimmo, ut per Ioelem dicitur, *est patiens, multae misericordiae et praestabilis super malitia*. Non igitur diu permittit Deus regnare tyrannos, sed post tempestatem per eos inductam populo, per eorum deiectionem tranquillitatem inducet; unde Sapiens dicit *Sedes ducum superborum destruxit Dominus et sedere fecit mites pro eis*.

Experimento etiam apparet quod reges per iustitiam magis adipiscuntur divitias, quam per rapinam tyranni. Quia enim tyrannorum dominium subiectae multitudini displicet, opus habent tyranni multos habere satellites per quos contra subditos tuti reddantur, in quibus necesse est plura expendere quam a subditis rapiant. Regum autem dominium quia subditis placet, omnes subditos pro satellitibus ad custodiam habent, in quibus expendere opus non habent, sed interdum in necessitatibus plura regibus sponte donant quam tyranni diripere possint: et sic impletur quod Salomon dicit *Alii*, scilicet reges, *dividunt propria benefaciendo subiectiset divitiores fiunt; alii*, scilicet tyranni, *rapiunt non sua et semper in egestate sunt*. Similiter etiam iusto Dei contingit iudicio, ut qui divitias iniuste congregant inutiliter eas dispergant, aut etiam iuste auferantur ab eis. Ut enim Salomon dicit, *avarus non implebitur pecunia, et qui amat divitias fructum non capiet ex eis*; quinimmo, ut alibi dicit, *conturbat domum suam qui sectatur avaritiam*. Reges vero dum iustitiam quaerunt, divitiae ipsis adduntur a Deo, sicut Salomoni qui, dum sapientiam quaesivit ad faciendum iudicium, promissionem de abundantia divitiarum accepit.

De fama vero superfluum videtur dicere. Quis dubitet bonos reges non solum in vita, sed magis post mortem quodammodo laudibus hominum vivere, in desiderio haberi, malorum vero nomen aut statim deficere, vel, si excellentes in malitia fuerint, cum detestatione ipsorum rememoratur. Unde Salomon dicit *Memoria iusti cum laudibus, nomen autem impiorum putrescet*, quia vel deficit, vel remanet cum foetore.

the people in God's wrath, for his power cannot be stable, because *God does not forget to show mercy nor does he shut up his mercies in his anger* (Ps 77 [76]:10). On the contrary, as we read in Joel: *He is patient and rich in mercy and ready to repent of the evil* (Joel 2:13). So God does not permit tyrants to reign a long time, but after the storm brought on the people through these tyrants, he restores tranquillity by casting them down. Therefore, the wise man says: *The Lord has cast down the thrones of rulers, and has seated the lowly in their place* (Sir 10:17).

Experience further shows that kings acquire more wealth through justice than tyrants do through rapine. Because the government of tyrants is displeasing to the multitude subject to it, tyrants must have a great many guards to safeguard themselves against their subjects. On these it is necessary to spend more than they can rob from their subjects. On the contrary, the government of kings, since it is pleasing to their subjects, has for its protection all the subjects instead of guards. And they demand no pay but, in time of need, freely give to their kings more than the tyrants can take. Thus the words of Solomon are fulfilled: *Some*, namely, the kings, *distribute their own goods*, doing good to their subjects, *and grow richer; others*, namely, the tyrants, *take away what is not their own and are always in want* (Prov 11:24). In the same way it comes to pass, by the just judgment of God, that those who unjustly heap up riches uselessly scatter them, or are justly deprived of them. For as Solomon says: *He who loves money will not be satisfied with money; nor he who loves wealth, with gain* (Eccl 5:9). Rather, we read in Proverbs: *He who is greedy for unjust gain makes trouble for his household* (Prov 15:27). But to kings who seek justice, God gives wealth, as he did to Solomon who, when he sought wisdom to do justice, received a promise of an abundance of wealth.

It seems superfluous to speak about fame, for who can doubt that good kings live in a sense in the praises of men, not only in this life, but still more after their death, and that men yearn for them? But the name of wicked kings straightway vanishes, or, if they have been excessive in their wickedness, they are remembered with detestation. Thus Solomon says: *The memory of the righteous is a blessing, but the name of the wicked will rot* (Prov 10:7), because it either vanishes or remains with stench.

CHAPTER 11

What punishments are in store for a tyrant

Ex his ergo manifestum est quod stabilitas potestatis, divitiae, honor et fama magis regibus quam tyrannis ad votum proveniunt, propter quae tamen indebite adipiscenda declinant in tyrannidem princeps: nullus enim a iustitia declinat nisi cupiditate alicuius commodi tractus. Privatur insuper tyrannus excellentissima beatitudine quae regibus debetur pro praemio et, quod est gravius, maximum tormentum sibi acquirit in poenis: si enim qui unum hominem spoliat vel in servitutem redigit vel occidit maximam poenam meretur, quantum quidem ad iudicium hominum mortem, quantum vero ad iudicium Dei damnationem aeternam, quanto magis putandum est tyrannum deteriora mereri supplicia, qui undique ab omnibus rapit, contra omnium communem libertatem laborat, pro libito voluntatis quoscumque interficit. Tales insuper raro poenitent, vento inflati superbiae, merito peccatorum a Deo deserti et adulationibus hominum delibuti, et rarius digne satisfacere possunt. Quando enim restituent omnia quae praeter iustitiae debitum abstulerunt, ad quae tamen restituenda nullus dubitat eos teneri? Quando recompensabunt eis quos oppresserunt et iniuste qualitercumque laeserunt?

Adiicitur autem ad eorum impoenitentiam quod omnia sibi licita existimant quae impune sine resistentia facere potuerunt; unde non solum emendare non satagunt quae male fecerunt, sed sua consuetudine pro auctoritate utentes, peccandi audaciam transmittunt ad posteros, et sic non solum suorum facinorum apud Deum rei tenentur, sed etiam eorum quibus peccandi occasionem reliquerunt.

Aggravatur etiam eorum peccatum ex dignitate suscepti officii. Sicut enim terrenus rex gravius punit suos ministros si invenit eos sibi contrarios, ita Deus magis puniet eos quos sui regiminis executores et ministros facit, si nequiter agant Dei iudicium in amaritudinem convertentes. Unde et in libro Sapientiae ad reges iniquos dicitur *Quoniam cum essetis ministri regni illius non iuste iudicastis, neque custodistis legem iustitiae, neque secundum voluntatem Dei ambulastis, horrende et cito apparebit vobis, quoniam iudicium durissimum his qui praesunt fiet. Exiguo enim conceditur misericordia, potentes autem potenter tormenta patientur*. Et Nabuchodonosor per Isaiam dicitur *Ad infernum detraheris in profundum laci. Qui te viderint, ad te inclinabuntur teque prospicient*, quasi profundius in poenis submersum.

From the above arguments it is evident that stability of power, wealth, honor and fame come to fulfill the desires of kings rather than tyrants, and it is in seeking to acquire these things unduly that princes turn to tyranny. For no one falls away from justice except through a desire for some temporal advantage. The tyrant, moreover, loses the surpassing beatitude which is due as a reward to kings and, which is still more serious, brings upon himself great suffering as a punishment. For if the man who despoils a single man, or casts him into slavery, or kills him, deserves the greatest punishment (death in the judgment of men, and in the judgment of God eternal damnation), how much worse tortures must we consider a tyrant deserves, who on all sides robs everybody, works against the common liberty of all, and kills whom he will at his merest whim? Again, such men rarely repent; but puffed up by the wind of pride, deservedly abandoned by God for their sins, and besmirched by the flattery of men, they can rarely make worthy satisfaction. When will they ever restore all those things which they have received beyond their just due? Yet no one doubts that they are bound to restore those ill-gotten goods. When will they make amends to those whom they have oppressed and unjustly injured in their many ways?

The malice of their impenitence is increased by the fact that they consider everything licit which they can do unresisted and with impunity. Hence they not only make no effort to repair the evil they have done, but, taking their customary way of acting as their authority, they hand on their boldness in sinning to posterity. Consequently, they are held guilty before God not only for their own sins, but also for the crimes of those to whom they gave the occasion of sin.

Their sin is made greater also from the dignity of the office they have assumed. Just as an earthly king inflicts a heavier punishment upon his ministers if he finds them traitors to him, so God will punish more severely those whom he made the executors and ministers of his government if they act wickedly, turning God's judgment into bitterness. Hence, in the Book of Wisdom, the following words are addressed to wicked kings: *Because as servants of his kingdom you did not rule rightly, nor keep the law, nor walk according to the purpose of God, he will come upon you terribly and swiftly, because severe judgment falls on those in high places. For the lowliest man may be pardoned in mercy, but mighty men will be mightily tested* (Wis 6:4–6). And to Nabuchodonosor it is said by Isaiah: *You are brought down to hell, to the depths of the pit. Those who see you will stare at you, and ponder over you* (Isa 14:15–16), as one more deeply buried in punishments.

CHAPTER 12

Recapitulation of this first book

Si igitur regibus abundanter temporalia bona proveniunt et excellens beatitudinis gradus praeparatur a Deo, tyranni autem a temporalibus bonis quae cupiunt plerumque frustrantur, multis insuper periculis temporalibus subiacentes et, quod est amplius, bonis aeternis privantur ad poenas gravissimas reservati, vehementer studendum est his qui regendi suscipiunt officium ut reges se subditis praebeant, non tyrannos.

De rege autem quid sit, et quod expediat multitudini regem habere, adhuc autem quod praesidenti expediat se regem multitudini exhibere subiectae, non tyrannum, tanta a nobis dicta sint.

So, then, if an abundance of temporal goods is given to kings and an eminent degree of beatitude prepared for them by God, while tyrants are often prevented from obtaining even the temporal goods which they covet, subjected also to many dangers and, worse still, deprived of eternal happiness and destined for most grievous punishment, surely those who undertake the office of ruling must earnestly strive to act as kings towards their subjects, and not as tyrants.

We have said enough to show what a king is, and that it is good for the multitude to have a king, and also that it is expedient for a ruler to conduct himself towards the multitude of his subjects as a king, not as a tyrant.

Book II

Chapter 1

On the duties of a king

Consequens autem est dictis considerare quid sit regis officium et qualem oporteat esse regem.

Quoniam vero ea quae sunt secundum artem imitantur ea quae sunt secundum naturam, ex quibus accipimus ut secundum rationem operari possimus, optimum videtur regis officium a forma regiminis naturalis assumere. Invenitur autem in rerum natura regimen et universale et particulare: universale quidem, secundum quod omnia sub Dei regimine continentur quia sua providentia universa gubernat; particulare autem regimen, maxime quidem divino regimini simile, invenitur in homine, qui ob hoc minor mundus appellatur, quia in eo invenitur forma universalis regiminis. Nam sicut universa creatura corporea et omnes spirituales virtutes sub divino regimine continentur, sic et corporis membra et caeterae vires animae a ratione reguntur; et sic quodammodo se habet ratio in homine sicut Deus in mundo.

Sed quia, sicut supra ostendimus, homo est animal naturaliter sociale in multitudine vivens, similitudo divini regiminis invenitur in homine non solum quantum ad hoc quod ratio regit ceteras hominis partes, sed ulterius quantum ad hoc quod per rationem unius hominis regitur multitudo; quod maxime pertinet ad officium regis, dum et in quibusdam animalibus quae socialiter vivunt quaedam similitudo invenitur huius regiminis, sicut in apibus in quibus et reges esse dicuntur, non quod in eis per rationem sit regimen, sed per instinctum naturae inditum a summo regente qui est auctor naturae.

Hoc igitur officium rex suscepisse cognoscat ut sit in regno sicut in corpore anima et sicut Deus in mundo; quae si diligenter recogitet, ex altero iustitiae in eo zelus accenditur dum considerat ad hoc se positum ut loco Dei iudicium in regno exerceat, ex altero vero mansuetudinis et clementiae lenitatem acquirit dum reputat singulos qui suo subsunt regimini sicut propria membra.

The next point to be considered is what the kingly office is and what qualities the king should have.

Since things which are in accordance with art are an imitation of the things which are in accordance with nature (from which we accept the rules to act according to reason), it seems best that we learn about the kingly office from the pattern of nature's regime. In things of nature there is both a universal and a particular government. The former is God's government, whose rule embraces all things and whose providence governs them all. The latter is found in man and it is much like the divine government. Hence man is called a 'microcosm.' Indeed, there is a similitude between both governments in regard to their form: for just as the universe of corporeal creatures and all spiritual powers come under the divine government, in like manner the members of the human body and all the powers of the soul are governed by reason. Thus, in a proportionate manner, reason is to man what God is to the world.

Since, however, man is by nature a social animal living in a multitude, as we have pointed out above, the analogy with the divine government is found in him not only in this way that one man governs himself by reason, but also in that the multitude of men is governed by the reason of one man. This is what first of all constitutes the office of a king. True, among certain animals that live socially there is a likeness to the king's rulership; so we say that there are kings among bees. Yet animals exercise rulership not through reason, but through their natural instinct which is implanted in them by the Great Ruler, the Author of nature.

Therefore, let the king recognize that this is the office which he undertakes: namely, to be in the kingdom like the soul is in the body, and like God is in the world. If he reflect seriously upon this, a zeal for justice will be enkindled in him when he contemplates that he has been appointed to this position in place of God, to exercise judgment in his kingdom; further, he will acquire the gentleness of clemency and mildness when he considers as his own members those individuals who are subject to his rule.

CHAPTER 2

What it is incumbent upon a king to do and how he should go about doing it

Oportet igitur considerare quid Deus in mundo faciat, sic enim manifestum erit quid immineat regi faciendum.

Sunt autem universaliter consideranda duo opera Dei in mundo: unum quo mundum instituit, alterum quo mundum institutum gubernat. Haec etiam duo opera anima habet in corpus: nam primo quidem virtute animae formatur corpus, deinde vero per animam corpus regitur et movetur. Horum autem secundum quidem magis proprie pertinet ad regis officium; unde ad omnes reges pertinet gubernatio, et a gubernationis regimine regis nomen accipitur. Primum autem opus non omnibus regibus convenit: non enim omnes regnum aut civitatem instituunt in quo regnant, sed regno aut civitati iam institutis regiminis curam impendunt.

Est tamen considerandum quod nisi praecessisset qui institueret civitatem aut regnum, locum non haberet gubernatio regni; sub regis enim officio comprehenditur etiam institutio civitatis et regni: nonnulli enim civitates instituerunt in quibus regnarent, ut Ninus Ninivem, et Romulus Romam. Similiter etiam ad gubernationis officium pertinet ut gubernata conservet ac eis utatur ad quod sunt constituta; non igitur gubernationis officium plene cognosci poterit si institutionis ratio ignoretur.

Ratio autem institutionis regni ab exemplo institutionis mundi sumenda est: in quo primo consideratur ipsarum rerum productio, deinde partium mundi ordinata distinctio. Ulterius autem singulis mundi partibus diversae rerum species distributae videntur, ut stellae caelo, volucres aeri, pisces aquae, animalia terrae; deinde singulis ea quibus indigent abundanter divinitus provisa videntur. Hanc autem institutionis rationem Moyses subtiliter et diligenter expressit. Primo enim rerum productionem proponit dicens *In principio creavit Deus caelum et terram*; deinde secundum convenientem ordinem omnia divinitus distincta esse denuntiat, videlicet diem a nocte, a superioribus inferiora, mare ab arida. Hinc caelum luminaribus, avibus aerem, mare piscibus, animalibus terram ornatam refert, ultimo assignatum hominibus animalium terraeque dominium; usum vero plantarum tam ipsis quam animalibus caeteris ex providentia divina denuntiat.

Institutor autem civitatis et regni de novo producere homines et loca ad inhabitandum et caetera vitae

Let us then examine what God does in the world, for in this way we shall be able to see what it is incumbent upon a king to do.

Looking at the world as a whole, there are two works of God to be considered: the first is creation; the second, God's government of the things created. These two works are, in like manner, performed by the soul in the body since, first, by the virtue of the soul the body is formed, and then the latter is governed and moved by the soul. Of these works, the second more properly pertains to the office of kingship. Therefore, government belongs to all kings (the very name *rex, regis* is derived from the fact that they regulate the government), while the first work does not fall to all kings, for not all kings establish the kingdom or city in which they rule, but bestow their regal care upon a kingdom or city already established.

We must remember, however, that if there were no one to establish the city or kingdom, there would be no question of governing the kingdom. The very notion of kingly office, then, comprises the establishment of a city and kingdom, and some kings have indeed established cities in which to rule; for example, Ninus founded Ninevah, and Romulus, Rome. It pertains also to the governing office to preserve the things governed, and to use them for the purpose for which they were established. If, therefore, one does not know how a kingdom is established, one cannot fully understand the task of its government.

Now, one may learn how a kingdom is established by the example of the creation of the world, in which we may first consider the production of things, and then the orderly distinction of the parts of the world. Further, we observe that different species of things are distributed in different parts of the world: stars in the heavens, fowls in the air, fishes in the water, and animals on land. We notice further that, for each species, the things it needs are abundantly provided by the divine power. Moses has minutely and carefully set forth this plan of how the world was made. First of all, he sets forth the production of things in these words: *In the beginning God created the heavens and the earth* (Gen 1:1). Next, he declares that all things were distinguished from one another by God according to a suitable order: day from night, higher things from lower, the sea from the dry land. He next relates that the sky was adorned with luminaries, the air with birds, the sea with fishes, the earth with animals; finally, dominion over earth and animals was given to men. He further states that, by divine providence, plants were made for the use of men and the other animals.

Now, the founder of a city and kingdom cannot newly produce men, dwelling places, and the other necessities of

subsidia non potest, sed necesse habet his uti quae in natura praeexistunt; sicut et caeterae artes operationis suae materiam a natura accipiunt, ut faber ferrum, aedificator autem ligna et lapides in artis usum assumunt. Necesse est igitur institutori civitatis et regni primum quidem congruum locum eligere qui salubritate habitatores conservet, ubertate ad victum sufficiat, amoenitate delectet, munitione ab hostibus tutos reddat. Quod si aliquid de dicta opportunitate deficiat, tanto locus erit convenientior quanto plura vel magis necessaria de praemissis habebit. Deinde necesse est ut locum electum institutioni civitatis aut regni distinguat secundum exigentiam eorum quae perfectio civitatis aut regni requirit: puta si regnum instituendum sit, oportet providere quis locus sit aptus urbibus constituendis, quis villis, quis castris, ubi constituenda sint studia litterarum, ubi exercitia militum, ubi negotiatorum conventus, et sic de aliis quae perfectio regni requirit. Si autem institutioni civitatis opera detur, providere oportet quis locus sit sacris, quis iuri reddendo, quis artificibus singulis deputandus. Ulterius autem oportet homines congregare, qui sunt congruis locis secundum sua officia deputandi. Demum vero providendus est ut singulis necessaria suppetant secundum uniuscuiusque condicionem et statum: aliter enim nequaquam posset regnum vel civitas commanere.

life, but must use those which preexist in nature, just as the other arts derive the material for their work from nature: for example, as the smith takes iron, the builder wood and stone, to use in their respective arts. Therefore, the founder of a city and kingdom must first choose a suitable place which will preserve the inhabitants by its healthfulness, provide the necessities of life by its fruitfulness, please them with its beauty, and render them safe from their enemies by its natural protection. If any of these advantages be lacking, the place will be more or less convenient in proportion as it offers more or less of the said advantages, or the more essential of them. Next, the founder of a city and kingdom must mark out the chosen place according to the exigencies of things necessary for the perfection of the city and kingdom. For example, when a kingdom is to be founded, he will have to determine which place is suitable for establishing cities, and which is best for villages and hamlets, where to locate the places of learning, the military training camps, the markets—and so on with other things which the perfection of the kingdom requires. And if it is a question of founding a city, he will have to determine what site is to be assigned to the churches, the law courts, and the various trades. Furthermore, he will have to gather together the men, who must be apportioned suitable locations according to their respective occupations. Finally, he must provide for each one what is necessary for his particular condition and state in life; otherwise, the kingdom or city could never endure.

Haec igitur sunt, ut summarie dicatur, quae ad regis officium pertinent in institutione civitatis aut regni, ex similitudine institutionis mundi assumpta.

These are, briefly, the duties that pertain to the office of king in founding a city and kingdom, as derived from a comparison with the creation of the world.

CHAPTER 3

That the manner of governing the kingdom is taken from the divine government

Sicut autem institutio civitatis aut regni ex forma institutionis mundi convenienter accipitur, sic et gubernationis ratio ex divina gubernatione sumenda est.

Est tamen praeconsiderandum quod gubernare est id quod gubernatur convenienter ad debitum finem perducere: sic enim navis gubernari dicitur, dum per nautae industriam recto itinere ad portum illaesa perducitur. Si igitur aliquid ad finem extra se ordinetur ut navis ad portum, ad gubernationis officium pertinebit non solum ut rem in se conservet illaesam, sed quod ulterius ad finem perducat. Si vero aliquid esset cuius finis non esset extra ipsum, ad hoc solum tenderet gubernatoris intentio ut rem illam in sua perfectione conservaret illaesam. Et quamvis nihil tale esse inveniatur in rebus praeter

Just as the founding of a city or kingdom may suitably be learned from the way in which the world was created, so too the way to govern may be learned from the divine government of the world.

Before going into that, however, we should consider that 'to govern' is to lead the thing governed in a suitable way towards its proper end. Thus a ship is said to be governed when, through the skill of the pilot, it is brought unharmed and by a direct route to harbor. Consequently, if a thing be directed to an end outside itself (as a ship to the harbor), it is the governor's duty, not only to preserve the thing unharmed, but further to guide it towards this end. If, on the contrary, there be a thing whose end is not outside itself, then the governor's endeavors will merely tend to preserve the thing undamaged in its proper perfection. Nothing of

ipsum Deum qui est omnibus finis, erga id tamen quod ad extrinsecum ordinatur multipliciter cura impenditur a diversis. Nam forte alius erit qui curam gerit ut res in suo esse conservetur, alius autem ut ad ulteriorem perfectionem perveniat, ut in ipsa navi, unde gubernationis nomen assumitur, manifeste apparet. Faber enim lignarius curam habet restaurandi si quid fuerit collapsum in navi, sed nauta sollicitudinem gerit ut navim perducat ad portum. Sic etiam contingit in homine: nam medicus curam gerit ut hominis vita conservetur, oeconomus ut suppetant necessaria vitae, doctor autem curam gerit ut veritatem cognoscat, institutor autem morum ut secundum rationem vivat.

Quod si homo non ordinaretur ad aliud exterius bonum, sufficerent homini curae praedictae; sed est quoddam bonum extraneum homini quamdiu mortaliter vivit, scilicet ultima beatitudo quae in fruitione Dei expectatur post mortem, quia, ut Apostolus dicit, *quamdiu sumus in corpore peregrinamur a Domino*. Unde homo christianus, cui beatitudo illa est per Christi sanguinem acquisita et qui pro ea consequenda Spiritus Sancti arrham accepit, indiget alia spirituali cura per quam dirigatur ad portum salutis aeternae; haec autem cura per ministros Ecclesiae Christi fidelibus exhibetur.

Idem autem oportet esse iudicium de fine totius multitudinis et unius. Si igitur finis ultimus hominis esset bonum quodcumque in ipso existens, et regendae multitudinis ultimus finis esset ut tale bonum multitudo acquireret et in eo permaneret. Et si quidem ultimus sive unius hominis sive multitudinis finis esset corporalis vita et sanitas corporis, medici esset officium; si vero ultimus finis esset divitiarum affluentia, oeconomus rex quidam multitudinis esset; si vero bonum veritatis cognoscendae tale quid esset ad quod posset multitudo pertingere, rex haberet doctoris officium.

Videtur autem ultimus finis esse multitudinis congregatae vivere secundum virtutem: ad hoc enim homines congregantur ut simul bene vivant, quod consequi non posset unusquisque singulariter vivens; bona autem vita est quae est secundum virtutem, virtuosa igitur vita finis est congregationis humanae. Huius autem signum est, quia hi soli partes sunt multitudinis congregatae qui sibi invicem communicant in bene vivendo. Si enim propter solum vivere homines convenirent, animalia et servi essent pars aliqua congregationis civilis; si vero propter acquirendas divitias, omnes simul negotiantes ad unam civitatem pertinerent. Nunc autem videmus eos

this kind is to be found in reality, except God himself, who is the end of all. However, as concerns the thing which is directed to an end outside itself, care is exercised by different providers in different ways. One might have the task of preserving a thing in its being, another of bringing it to a further perfection. Such is clearly the case in the example of the ship: the first meaning of the word 'governor' is a pilot. It is the carpenter's business to repair anything which might be broken, while the pilot bears the responsibility of bringing the ship to port. It is the same with man. The doctor sees to it that a man's life is preserved, the tradesman supplies the necessities of life, the teacher takes care that man may learn the truth: but the founder sees that he lives according to reason.

Now if man were not ordained to another end outside himself, the above-mentioned cares would be sufficient for him. But as long as man's mortal life endures, there is an extrinsic good for him: namely, final beatitude which is looked for after death in the enjoyment of God. As the Apostle says: *While we are at home in the body we are away from the Lord* (2 Cor 5:6). Consequently, the Christian man, for whom that beatitude has been purchased by the blood of Christ, and who, in order to attain it, has received the earnest of the Holy Spirit, needs another and spiritual care to direct him to the harbor of eternal salvation, and this care is provided for the faithful by the ministers of the Church of Christ.

Now the same judgment is to be formed about the end of society as a whole as about the end of one man. If, therefore, the ultimate end of man were some good that existed in himself, then the ultimate end of the multitude to be governed would likewise be for the multitude to acquire such good, and persevere in its possession. If such an ultimate end either of an individual man or a multitude were corporeal life and health of body, it would be the physician's job to govern. If that ultimate end were an abundance of wealth, then the economist would be the king of the multitude. If the good of the knowledge of truth were of such a kind that the multitude might attain to it, the king would have to be a teacher.

It is, however, clear that the end of a multitude gathered together is to live virtuously. For men form a group for the purpose of living well together, a thing which the individual man living alone could not attain. Now, the good life is a virtuous life; therefore, virtuous life is the end for which men gather together. The evidence for this lies in the fact that only those who render mutual assistance to one another in living well form a genuine part of an assembled multitude. If men assembled merely to live, then animals and slaves would form a part of the civil community. Or, if men assembled only to accrue wealth, then all those who traded together would belong to one city. Yet we see that

solos sub una multitudine computari qui sub eisdem legibus et eodem regimine diriguntur ad bene vivendum.

Sed quia homo vivendo secundum virtutem ad ulteriorem finem ordinatur, qui consistit in fruitione divina ut supra iam diximus, oportet autem eumdem finem esse multitudinis humanae qui est hominis unius, non est ultimus finis multitudinis congregatae vivere secundum virtutem, sed per virtuosam vitam pervenire ad fruitionem divinam.

Siquidem igitur ad hunc finem perveniri posset virtute humanae naturae, necesse esset ut ad officium regis pertineret dirigere homines in hunc finem: hunc enim regem dici supponimus cui summa regiminis in rebus humanis committitur. Tanto autem est regimen sublimius quanto ad finem altiorem ordinatur: semper enim invenitur ille ad quem pertinet ultimus finis imperare operantibus ea quae in finem ultimum ordinantur; sicut gubernator, ad quem pertinet navigationem disponere, imperat ei qui navem constituit qualem navem navigationi aptam facere debeat; civilis qui debet uti armis, imperat fabro qualia fabricet arma. Sed quia finem fruitionis divinae non consequitur homo per virtutem humanam sed virtute divina, secundum illud Apostoli *Gratia Dei vita aeterna*, perducere ad illum ultimum finem non est humani regiminis sed divini.

Ad illum igitur regem huiusmodi regimen pertinet qui non est solum homo sed etiam Deus, scilicet ad Dominum Iesum Christum, qui homines filios Dei faciens in caelestem gloriam introduxit. Hoc igitur est regimen ei traditum quod *non corrumpetur*, propter quod non solum sacerdos sed rex in Scripturis sacris nominatur, dicente Ieremia *Regnabit rex et sapiens erit*; unde ab eo regale sacerdotium derivatur, et quod est amplius, omnes Christi fideles in quantum sunt membra eius reges et sacerdotes dicuntur.

Huius ergo regni ministerium, ut a terrenis spiritualia essent discreta, non terrenis regibus sed sacerdotibus est commissum, et praecipue summo sacerdoti successori Petri, Christi vicario Romano Pontifici, cui omnes reges populi Christiani oportet esse subiectos sicut ipsi Domino Iesu Christo. Sic enim, ut dictum est, ei ad quem ultimi finis pertinet cura subdi debent illi ad quos pertinet cura antecedentium finium, et eius imperio dirigi.

Quia igitur sacerdotium gentium et totus divinorum cultus erat propter temporalia bona conquirenda, quae omnia ordinantur ad multitudinis bonum commune cuius regi cura incumbit, convenienter sacerdotes gentilium regibus subdebantur. Sed et in Veteri lege promittebantur bona terrena, non a daemonibus sed a Deo

only such are regarded as forming one multitude as are directed to live well by the same laws and the same government.

Yet through virtuous living man is further ordained to a higher end, which consists in the enjoyment of God, as we have said above. Consequently, since society must have the same end as the individual man, it is not the ultimate end of an assembled multitude to live virtuously, but through virtuous living to attain to the possession of God.

If this end could be attained by the power of human nature, then the duty of a king would have to include the direction of men to it. We are supposing, of course, that he is called king to whom the supreme power of governing in human affairs is entrusted. Now, the higher the end to which a government is ordained, the loftier that government is. Indeed, we always find that the one to whom it pertains to achieve the final end commands those who execute the things that are ordained to that end. For example, the captain, whose business it is to regulate navigation, tells the shipbuilder what kind of ship he must construct to be suitable for navigation; and the ruler of a city, who makes use of arms, tells the blacksmith what kind of arms to make. But because a man does not attain his end, which is the possession of God, by human power but by divine, according to the words of the Apostle: *By the grace of God, life everlasting* (Rom 6:23)—therefore, the task of leading him to that last end does not pertain to human but to divine government.

Consequently, government of this kind pertains to that king who is not only a man, but also God, namely, our Lord Jesus Christ, who by making men sons of God brought them to the glory of Heaven. This, then, is the government which has been delivered to him and which *shall not be destroyed* (Dan 7:14), on account of which Sacred Scripture calls him not only Priest, but King. As Jeremiah says: *He shall reign as king and deal wisely* (Jer 23:5). Hence a royal priesthood is derived from him, and what is more, all those who believe in Christ, in so far as they are his members, are called kings and priests.

Thus, so that spiritual things might be distinguished from earthly things, the ministry of this kingdom has been entrusted not to earthly kings but to priests, and most of all to the chief priest, the successor of St. Peter, the Vicar of Christ, the Roman Pontiff. To him all the kings of the Christian people are to be subject as to our Lord Jesus Christ himself. For those to whom pertains the care of intermediate ends should be subject to him to whom pertains the care of the ultimate end, and be directed by his rule.

Because the priesthood of the gentiles and the whole worship of their gods existed merely for the acquisition of temporal goods (which were all ordained to the common good of the multitude, whose care devolved upon the king), the priests of the gentiles were very properly subject to the kings. Similarly, since in the Old Law earthly goods were

vero, religioso populo exhibenda; unde et in Veteri lege sacerdotes regibus leguntur fuisse subiecti. Sed in Nova lege est sacerdotium altius, per quod homines traducuntur ad bona caelestia; unde in lege Christi reges debent sacerdotibus esse subiecti.

Unde mirabiliter ex divina providentia factum est ut in Romana urbe, quam Deus praeviderat christiani sacerdotii principalem sedem futuram, hic mos paulatim inolesceret ut civitatis rectores sacerdotibus subderentur. Sicut enim Maximus Valerius refert, *omnia post religionem ponenda semper nostra civitas duxit, etiam in quibus summae maiestatis conspici decus voluit. Quapropter non dubitaverunt sacris imperia servire, ita se humanarum rerum habitura regimen existimantia, si divinae potentiae bene atque constanter fuissent famulata.* Quia etiam futurum erat ut in Gallia christiani sacerdotii plurimum vigeret religio, divinitus est provisum ut etiam apud Gallos gentiles sacerdotes, quos druidas nominabant, totius Galliae ius definirent, ut refert Iulius Caesar in libro quem *de Bello gallico* scripsit.

promised to the religious people (not indeed by demons but by the true God), the priests of the Old Law, we read, were also subject to the kings. But in the New Law there is a higher priesthood by which men are guided to heavenly goods. Consequently, in the law of Christ, kings must be subject to priests.

It was therefore also a marvelous disposition of divine providence that, in the city of Rome, which God had foreseen would be the principal seat of the Christian priesthood, the custom was gradually established that the rulers of the city should be subject to the priests, for as Valerius Maximus relates: *Our city has always considered that everything should yield precedence to religion, even those things in which it aimed to display the splendor of supreme majesty. We therefore unhesitatingly made the imperial dignity minister to religion, considering that the empire would thus hold control of human affairs if, faithfully and constantly, it were submissive to the divine power.*[28] And because it was to come to pass that the religion of the Christian priesthood should especially thrive in France, God also provided that among the Gauls their tribal priests, called druids, should lay down the law of all Gaul, as Julius Caesar relates in the book which he wrote *On the Gallic War.*

CHAPTER 4

That regal government should be ordained principally to eternal beatitude

Sicut autem ad vitam quam in caelo speramus beatam ordinatur sicut ad finem vita qua hic homines bene vivunt, ita ad bonam multitudinis vitam ordinantur sicut ad finem quaecumque particularia bona per hominem procurantur, sive divitiae, sive lucra, sive sanitas, sive facundia vel eruditio. Si igitur, ut dictum est, qui de ultimo fine curam habet praeesse debet his qui curam habent de ordinatis ad finem, et eos dirigere suo imperio, manifestum ex dictis fit quod rex, sicut divino regimini quod administratur per sacerdotum officium subdi debet, ita praeesse debet omnibus humanis officiis et ea imperio sui regiminis ordinare.

Cuicumque autem incumbit aliquid perficere quod ordinatur in aliud sicut in finem, hoc debet attendere ut suum opus sit congruum fini: sicut faber sic facit gladium ut pugnae conveniat, et aedificator sic debet domum disponere ut ad inhabitandum sit apta. Quia igitur vitae qua in praesenti bene vivimus finis est beatitudo caelestis, ad regis officium pertinet ea ratione bonam vitam multitudinis procurare secundum quod congruit ad caelestem beatitudinem consequendam, ut scilicet ea praecipiat quae ad caelestem beatitudinem ducunt, et

As the life by which men live well here on earth is ordered, as to its end, to that blessed life which we hope for in heaven, so too whatever particular goods are procured by man's agency—whether wealth, profits, health, eloquence, or learning—are ordained to the good life of the multitude. If, then, as we have said, the person who is charged with the care of our ultimate end ought to be over those who have charge of things ordained to that end, and to direct them by his rule, it clearly follows that, just as the king ought to be subject to the divine government administered by the office of priesthood, so he ought to preside over all human offices, and regulate them by the rule of his government.

Now anyone on whom it devolves to do something which is ordained to another thing as to its end is bound to see that his work is suitable to that end; thus, for example, the armorer so fashions the sword that it is suitable for fighting, and the builder should so lay out the house that it is suitable for habitation. Therefore, since the beatitude of heaven is the end of that virtuous life which we live at present, it pertains to the king's office to promote the good life of the multitude in such a way as to make it suitable for the attainment of heavenly happiness. That is to say, he

---

28. *De Bello Gallico* VI, 13, 5.

eorum contraria secundum quod fuerit possibile interdicat.

Quae autem sit ad veram beatitudinem via et quae sint impedimenta ipsius, ex lege divina cognoscitur, cuius doctrina pertinet ad sacerdotum officium, secundum illud Malachiae *Labia sacerdotum custodiunt scientiam et legem requirent ex ore eius*. Et ideo in Deuteronomio Dominus praecipit *Postquam sederit rex in solio regni sui, describet sibi Deuteronomium legis huius in volumine, accipiens exemplar a sacerdotibus Leviticae tribus; et habebit secum, legetque illud omnibus diebus vitae suae, ut discat timere Dominum Deum suum et custodire verba et caeremonias eius quae in lege praecepta sunt.*

Per legem igitur divinam edoctus, ad hoc praecipuum studium oportet intendere qualiter multitudo sibi subdita bene vivat. Quod quidem studium in tria dividitur: ut primo quidem in subiecta multitudine bonam vitam instituat, secundo ut institutam conservet, tertio ut conservatam ad meliora promoveat.

Ad bonam autem unius hominis vitam duo requiruntur: unum principale quod est operatio secundum virtutem, virtus enim est qua bene vivitur; aliud vero secundarium et quasi instrumentale, scilicet corporalium bonorum sufficientia quorum usus est necessarius ad actum virtutum. Ipsa tamen hominis unitas per naturam causatur, multitudinis autem unitas quae pax dicitur est per regentis industriam procuranda. Sic igitur ad bonam vitam multitudinis instituendam tria requiruntur. Primo quidem ut multitudo in unitate pacis constituatur; secundo ut multitudo vinculo pacis unita dirigatur ad bene agendum: sicut enim homo nihil bene agere potest nisi praesupposita suarum partium unitate, ita hominum multitudo pacis unitate carens, dum se ipsam impugnat, impeditur a bene agendo; tertio vero requiritur ut per regentis industriam necessariorum ad bene vivendum adsit sufficiens copia.

Sic igitur bona vita per regis officium in multitudine constituta, consequens est ut ad eius conservationem intendat. Sunt autem tria quibus bonum publicum permanere non sinitur, quorum unum quidem est a natura proveniens: non enim bonum multitudinis ad unum tantum tempus institui debet, sed ut sit quodammodo perpetuum; homines autem cum sint mortales in perpetuum durare non possunt, neque dum vivunt semper sunt in eodem vigore, quia multis variationibus humana vita subiicitur, et sic non sunt homines ad eadem officia peragenda aequaliter per totam vitam idonei. Aliud autem impedimentum boni publici conservandi ab interiori proveniens in perversitate voluntatum consistit, dum vel desides ad ea peragenda quae requirit res publica, vel insuper sunt paci multitudinis noxii, dum transgrediendo iustitiam aliorum pacem perturbant.

should command those things which lead to the happiness of Heaven and, as far as possible, forbid the contrary.

What conduces to true beatitude and what hinders it are learned from the law of God, the teaching of which belongs to the office of the priest, according to the words of Malachi: *The lips of a priest should guard knowledge, and men should seek law from his mouth* (Mal 2:7). Therefore, the Lord prescribes in the Book of Deuteronomy that *when the king sits on the throne of his kingdom, he shall write for himself in a book a copy of this law, from that which is in charge of the Levitical priests; and it shall be with him, and he shall read in it all the days of his life, that he may learn to fear the Lord his God, by keeping all the words of this law and these statutes* (Deut 7:18–19).

Thus the king, taught the law of God, should have for his principal concern the means by which the multitude subject to him may live well. This concern is threefold: first of all, to establish a virtuous life in the multitude subject to him; second, to preserve it once established; and third, having preserved it, to promote its greater perfection.

For an individual man to lead a good life two things are required. The first and most important is to act in a virtuous manner (for virtue is that by which one lives well); the other, which is secondary and instrumental, is a sufficiency of those bodily goods whose use is necessary for virtuous life. Yet the unity of man is brought about by nature, while the unity of the multitude, which we call peace, must be procured through the efforts of the ruler. Therefore, to establish virtuous living in a multitude three things are necessary. First of all, that the multitude be established in the unity of peace. Second, that the multitude thus united in the bond of peace be directed to acting well. For just as a man can do nothing well unless unity within his members be presupposed, so a multitude of men lacking the unity of peace will be hindered from virtuous action by the fact that it is fighting against itself. In the third place, it is necessary that there be at hand a sufficient supply of the things required for proper living, procured by the ruler's efforts.

When virtuous living is set up in the multitude by the efforts of the king, it then remains for him to look to its conservation. Now there are three things which prevent the permanence of the public good. One of these arises from nature. The good of the multitude should not be established for one time only; it should be in a sense perpetual. Men, on the other hand, cannot abide forever, because they are mortal. Even while they are alive they do not always preserve the same vigor, for the life of man is subject to many changes, and thus a man is not equally suited to the performance of the same duties throughout the whole span of his life. A second impediment to the preservation of the public good, which comes from within, consists in the perversity of the wills of men, inasmuch as they are either too lazy to perform what the commonweal demands, or, still further, they are harmful to the peace of the multitude because,

Tertium autem impedimentum rei publicae conservandae ab exteriori causatur, dum per incursum hostium pax dissolvitur et interdum regnum aut civitas funditus dissipatur.

Igitur contra tria praedicta triplex cura imminet regi. Primo quidem de successione hominum et substitutione illorum qui diversis officiis praesunt; ut sicut per divinum regimen in rebus corruptibilibus, quia semper eadem durare non possunt, provisum est ut per generationem alia in locum aliorum succedant, ut vel sic conservetur integritas universi, ita per regis studium conservetur subiectae multitudinis bonum, dum sollicite curat qualiter alii in deficientium locum succedant.

Secundo autem ut suis legibus et praeceptis, poenis et praemiis homines sibi subiectos ab iniquitate coerceat et ad opera virtuosa inducat, exemplum a Deo accipiens qui hominibus legem dedit, observantibus quidem mercedem, transgredientibus vero poenas retribuens. Tertio imminet regi cura ut multitudo sibi subiecta contra hostes tuta reddatur: nihil enim prodesset interiora vitare pericula, si ab exterioribus defendi non posset.

Sic igitur bonae multitudinis institutioni tertium restat ad regis officium pertinens, ut sit de promotione sollicitus: quod fit dum in singulis quae praemissa sunt si quid inordinatum est corrigere, si quid deest supplere, si quid melius fieri potest studet perficere. Unde et Apostolus monet fideles ut semper *aemulentur charismata meliora.*

Haec igitur sunt quae ad regis officium pertinent, de quibus per singula diligentius tractare oportet.

by transgressing justice, they disturb the peace of others. The third hindrance to the preservation of the commonweal comes from without: namely, when peace is destroyed through the attacks of enemies and, as it sometimes happens, the kingdom or city is completely blotted out.

In regard to these three dangers, a triple charge is laid upon the king. First of all, he must take care of the appointment of men to succeed or replace others in charge of the various offices. Just as in regard to corruptible things (which cannot remain the same forever) the government of God made provision that through generation one would take the place of another so the integrity of the universe might be maintained in this way, so too the good of the multitude subject to the king will be preserved through his care when he sets himself to attend to the appointment of new men to fill the place of those who drop out.

In the second place, by his laws and orders, punishments and rewards, he should restrain the men subject to him from wickedness and induce them to virtuous deeds, following the example of God who gave his law to man and requites those who observe it with rewards, and those who transgress it with punishments. The king's third charge is to keep the multitude entrusted to him safe from the enemy, for it would be useless to prevent internal dangers if the multitude could not be defended against external dangers.

Finally, for the proper direction of the multitude there remains the third duty of the kingly office: namely, that he be solicitous for its improvement. He performs this duty when, in each of the things we have mentioned, he corrects what is out of order and supplies what is lacking, and if any of them can be done better he tries to do so. This is why the Apostle exhorts the faithful to always *earnestly desire the higher gifts* (1 Cor 12:31).

These then are the duties of the kingly office, each of which must now be treated in greater detail.

CHAPTER 5

That it belongs to the office of a king to found the city

Primum igitur incipere oportet exponere regis officium ab institutione civitatis aut regni. Nam, sicut Vegetius dicit, *potentissimae nationes et principes commendati nullam maiorem gloriam putaverunt quam aut fundare novas civitates, aut ab aliis conditas in nomen suum sub quadam amplificatione transferre*; quod quidem documentis sacrae Scripturae concordat: dicit enim Sapiens in Ecclesiastico quod *aedificatio civitatis confir-*

We must begin by explaining the duties of a king with regard to the founding of a city or kingdom. For, as Vegetius declares, *The mightiest nations and most commended kings thought it their greatest glory either to found new cities or have their names made part of, and in some way added to, the names of cities already founded by others.*[29] This, indeed, is in accord with Sacred Scripture, for the wise man says in Sirach: *The building of a city establishes a man's name*

---

29. *De Re Militari* IV, prol.

mabit nomen. Hodie namque nomen Romuli nesciretur nisi quia condidit Romam.

In institutione autem civitatis aut regni, si copia detur, primo quidem est regio eligenda, quam temperatam esse oportet: ex regionis enim temperie habitatores multa commoda consequuntur. Primo namque consequuntur homines ex temperie regionis incolumitatem corporis et longitudinem vitae. Cum enim sanitas in quadam temperie humorum consistat, in loco temperato conservabitur sanitas: simile namque suo simili conservatur. Si vero fuerit excessus caloris vel frigoris, necesse est quod secundum qualitatem aeris corporis qualitas immutetur; unde quadam naturali industria animalia quaedam tempore frigido ad calida loca se transferunt, rursum tempore calido loca frigida repetentes, ut ex contraria dispositione loci et temporis temperiem consequantur.

Rursus, cum animal vivat per calidum et humidum, si fuerit calor intensus, cito naturale humidum exsiccatur et deficit vita, sicut lucerna cito extinguitur si humor infusus cito propter ignis magnitudinem consumatur. Unde in quibusdam calidissimis Aethiopum regionibus homines ultra triginta annos non vivere perhibentur; in regionibus vero frigidis in excessu, naturale humidum de facili congelatur et calor naturalis extinguitur. Deinde ad opportunitates bellorum quibus tuta redditur humana societas, regionis temperies plurimum valet. Nam, sicut Vegetius refert, *omnes nationes quae vicinae sunt soli, nimio calore siccatae, amplius quidem sapere sed minus sanguinem habere dicuntur, ac propterea constantiam atque fiduciam de propinquo pugnandi non habent, quia metuunt vulnera qui modicum sanguinem se habere noverunt. Contra, septentrionales populi remoti a solis ardoribus inconsultiores quidem, sed tamen largo sanguine redundantes, sunt ad bella promptissimi. His autem qui in temperatioribus habitant plagis, et copia sanguinis suppetit ad vulnerum mortisque contemptum, nec prudentia deficit quae modestiam servet in castris et non parum prodest in dimicatione consiliis.*

Demum temperata regio ad politicam vitam non modicum valet. Ut enim Aristoteles dicit in sua *Politica, Quae in frigidis locis habitant gentes sunt quidem plenae animositate, intellectu autem et arte magis deficientes, propter quod libere perseverant magis: non vivunt autem politice et vicinis propter imprudentiam principari non possunt. Quae autem in calidis locis sunt, intellectivae quidem sunt et artificiosae secundum animam, sine animositate autem, propter quod subiectae quidem et servientes perseverant. Quae autem in mediis locis habitant*

(Sir 40:19). The name of Romulus, for instance, would be unknown today had he not founded the city of Rome.

Now in founding a city or kingdom, the first step is the choice of its location, if plenty are available. A temperate region should be chosen, for the inhabitants derive many advantages from a temperate climate. In the first place, it ensures them health of body and length of life; for, since good health consists in the right temperature of the vital fluids, it follows that health will be best preserved in a temperate clime, because like is preserved by like. Should, however, heat or cold be excessive, the condition of the body will necessarily be affected by the condition of the atmosphere. Thus some animals instinctively migrate in cold weather to warmer regions, and in warm weather return to the colder places, in order to obtain, through the contrary dispositions of both locality and weather, the due temperature of their humors.

Again, since it is warmth and moisture that preserve animal life, if the heat is intense the natural moisture of the body is dried up and life fails, just as a lantern is extinguished if the liquid poured into it be quickly consumed by too great a flame. Thus it is said that in certain very torrid parts of Ethiopia a man cannot live longer than thirty years. On the other hand, in extremely cold regions the natural moisture is easily frozen and the natural heat soon lost. Then, too, a temperate climate is most conducive to fitness for war, by which human society is kept in security. As Vegetius tells us, *All peoples that live near the sun and are dried up by the excessive heat have keener wits but less blood, so that they possess no constancy or self-reliance in hand-to-hand fighting; for, knowing they have but little blood, they have great fear of wounds. On the other hand, Northern tribes, far removed from the burning rays of the sun, are more dull-witted indeed, but because they have an ample flow of blood, they are ever ready for war. Those who dwell in temperate climes have, on the one hand, an abundance of blood and thus make light of wounds or death, and, on the other hand, no lack of prudence, which puts a proper restraint on them in camp and is of great advantage in war and peace as well.*[30]

Finally, a temperate climate is of no little value for political life. As Aristotle says in his *Politics: Peoples that dwell in cold countries are full of spirit but have little intelligence and little skill. Consequently, they maintain their liberty better but have no political life and (through lack of prudence) show no capacity for governing others. Those who live in hot regions are keen-witted and skillful in the things of the mind but possess little spirit, and so are in continuous subjection and servitude. But those who live between these extremes of climate are both spirited and intelligent; hence they are con-*

---

30. *De Re Militari* 1, 2.

et animositatem et intellectum habent, propter quod et liberi perseverant et maxime politice vivere possunt, et sciunt aliis principari.

Est igitur eligenda regio temperata ad institutionem civitatis vel regni.

tinuously free, their political life is very much developed, and they are capable of ruling others.[31]

Therefore, a temperate region should be chosen for the foundation of a city or a kingdom.

Chapter 6

That the city should have wholesome air

Post electionem autem regionis, oportet civitati construendae idoneum locum eligere, in quo primo videtur aeris salubritas requirenda. Conversationi namque civili praeiacet naturalis vita, quae per salubritatem aeris conservatur illaesa. Locus autem saluberrimus erit, ut Vitruvius tradit, *excelsus, non nebulosus, non pruinosus, regionesque caeli spectans neque aestuosus neque frigidus, demum paludibus non vicinus.* Eminentia quidem loci solet ad aeris salubritatem conferre, quia locus eminens ventorum perflationibus patet quibus redditur aer purus; vapores etiam, qui virtute radii solaris resolvuntur a terra et aquis, multiplicantur magis in convallibus et in locis demissis quam in altis. Unde in locis altis aer subtilior invenitur.

Huiusmodi autem subtilitas aeris quae ad liberam et sinceram respirationem plurimum valet, impeditur per nebulas et pruinas quae solent in locis multum humidis abundare; unde loca huiusmodi salubritati inveniuntur esse contraria. Et quia loca paludosa nimia humiditate abundant, oportet locum construendae urbi electum a paludibus esse remotum. *Cum enim aurae matutinae sole oriente ad locum ipsum pervenient, et eis ortae a paludibus nebulae adiungentur, flatus bestiarum palustrium venenatarum cum nebula mixtos spargent et locum facient pestilentem. Si tamen moenia constructa fuerint in paludibus quae fuerint prope mare spectentque ad septentrionem vel circa, haeque paludes excelsiores fuerint quam littus marinum, rationabiliter videbuntur esse constructa. Fossis enim ductis exitus aquae patebit ad littus, et mare tempestatibus auctum in paludes redundando non patietur animalia palestria nasci. Et si aliqua animalia de superioribus locis advenerint, inconsueta salsedine occidentur.*

Oportet etiam locum urbi destinatum ad calorem et frigus temperate disponi secundum aspectum ad plagas caeli diversas. *Si enim moenia maxime prope mare constituta spectabunt ad meridiem, non erunt salubria: nam huiusmodi loca mane quidem erunt frigida quia non re-*

After deciding on the locality of the kingdom, the king must select a site suitable for building a city. Now the first requisite would seem to be wholesome air, for civil life presupposes natural life, whose health in turn depends on the wholesomeness of the air. According to Vitruvius, the most healthful spot is *a high place, troubled neither by mists nor frosts and facing neither the sultry nor the chilly parts of the sky. Also, it should not lie near marsh country.*[32] The altitude of the place contributes to the wholesomeness of the atmosphere because highlands are open to all the breezes which purify the air; besides, the vapors, which the strength of the sun's rays causes to rise from the earth and waters, are more dense in valleys and in low-lying places than in highlands. For this reason the air on mountains is rarer.

Now this rarified air, which is the best for easy and natural breathing, is vitiated by mists and frosts which are frequent in very damp places; as a consequence, such places are found to be inimical to health. Since marshy districts have an excess of humidity, the place chosen for the building of a city must be far from any marshes. *For when the morning breezes come at sunrise to such a place, and the mists that rise from the swamps join them, they will scatter through the town the breath of the poisonous beasts of the marshes mingled with the mist, and will render the site pestilential. Should, however, the walls be built in marshes that lie along the coast and face the north (or thereabouts) and if these marshes be higher than the seashore, they would seem to be quite reasonably built, since, by digging ditches, a way will be opened to drain the water of the marshes into the sea, and when storms swell the sea it will flow back into the marshes and thus prevent the propagation of the animals there. And if any animals come down from higher places, the unwonted saltiness of the water will destroy them.*[33]

When laying out the city, further provision for the proper proportion of heat and cold must be made by having it face the correct part of the sky. *If the walls, particularly of a town built on the coast, face the south, it will not be healthy, since such a locality will be cold in the morning, for*

---

31. *Politics*, VII, 7: 1327b 23–32.
32. *De Architectura* I, 4.
33. Ibid.

spiciuntur a sole, meridie vero erunt ferventia propter solis respectum. Quae autem ad occidentem spectant, orto sole tepescunt vel etiam frigent, meridie calent, vespere fervent propter caloris continuitatem et solis aspectum. Si vero ad orientem spectabunt moenia, mane quidem propter solis oppositionem directam temperate calescent; nec multum in meridie calor augebitur, sole non directe spectante ad locum, vespere vero totaliter radiis solis adversis loca frigescent. Eademque vel similis temperies erit si ad aquilonem locus urbis respiciat. Experimento autem cognoscere possumus quod in maiorem calorem minus salubriter aliquis transmutatur: *quae enim a frigidis regionibus corpora traducuntur in calidas non possunt durare sed dissolvuntur,* quia calor sugendo vaporem naturales virtutes dissolvit; unde etiam in salubribus locis corpora aestate infirma redduntur.

Quia vero ad corporum sanitatem convenientium ciborum usus plurimum confert, oportet loci salubritatem qui constituendae urbi eligitur, etiam ex conditione ciborum discernere qui nascuntur in terra; quod quidem explorare solebant antiqui ex animalibus ibidem ·nutritis. Cum enim hominibus aliisque animalibus commune sit uti ad nutrimentum his quae nascuntur in terra, consequens est ut, si occisorum animalium viscera inveniuntur bene valentia, quod homines etiam in loco eodem salubriter possint nutriri. Si vero animalium occisorum appareant morbida membra, rationabiliter accipi potest quod nec etiam hominibus illius loci habitatio sit salubris.

Sicut autem aer temperatus, ita et aqua salubris est requirenda: ex his enim maxime dependet sanitas corporum quae saepius in usum hominis assumuntur. Et de aere quidem manifestum est quod continue ipsum respirando introrsum attrahimus usque ad ipsa vitalia; unde principaliter eius salubritas ad incolumitatem hominum confert. Inter alia vero quae assumuntur per modum nutrimenti, aqua saepissime utimur tam in potibus quam in cibis, unde nihil post aeris puritatem magis pertinet ad loci sanitatem quam aquarum salubritas.

Est et aliud signum ex quo considerari potest loci salubritas, si videlicet hominum in loco commorantium facies bene coloratae apparent, robusta corpora et membra bene disposita, si pueri multi et vivaces, si senes multi reperiantur ibidem. E contrario vero, si facies hominum deformes apparent, debilia corpora, exinanita membra vel inordinate tumentia, si pauci et morbidi pueri et adhuc pauciores senes, dubitari non potest locum fore mortiferum.

the rays of the sun do not reach it, but at noon will be baked in the full glare of the sun. *As to places that face the west, at sunrise they are cool or even cold, at noon quite warm, and in the evening unpleasantly hot,*[34] both on account of the long-continued heat and the exposure to the sun. On the other hand, if it has an eastern exposure, in the morning, with the sun directly opposite, it will be moderately warm, at noon it will not be much warmer since the sun does not reach it directly, but in the evening it will be cold, as the rays of the sun will be entirely on the other side. And there will be the same or a similar proportion of heat and cold if the town faces the north. By experience we may learn that the change from cold to heat is unhealthy: *Animals which are transferred from cold to warm regions cannot endure but are dissolved,*[35] since the heat sucks up their moisture and weakens their natural strength; whence even in salubrious districts all bodies become weak from the heat.

Again, since suitable food is very helpful for preserving health, we must further judge of the salubrity of a place which has been chosen as a town-site by the condition of the food which grows upon its soil. The ancients were wont to explore this condition by examining the animals raised on the spot. For man, like other animals, finds nourishment in the products of the earth. Hence, if in a given place we kill some animals and find their entrails to be sound, the conclusion will be justified that man also will get good food in the same place. If, however, the members of these animals should be found diseased, we may reasonably infer that that country is no healthy place for men either.

Just as temperate air is required, so is good water, for the body depends for its health on those things which men more frequently put to their use. With regard to the air it is clear that, breathing it continuously, we draw it down into our very vitals; as a result, purity of air is what conduces most to the preservation of men. But of all things put to use as nourishment, water is used most frequently both as drink and food. Nothing, therefore, so much helps to make a district healthy as does pure water (except good air).

There is still another means of judging the healthfulness of a place: by the ruddy complexion of the inhabitants, their sturdy, well-shaped limbs, the presence of many and vivacious children, and of many old people. On the other hand, there can be no doubt about the deadliness of a climate where people are misshapen and weak, their limbs either withering or swollen beyond proportion, where children are few and sickly, and old people rather scarce.

---

34. Ibid.
35. Ibid.

Chapter 7

That the city should have an abundant supply of food

Oportet autem ut locus construendae urbi electus non solum talis sit qui salubritate habitatores conservet, sed etiam ubertate ad victum sufficiat: non enim est possibile multitudinem hominum habitare ubi victualium non suppetit copia. Unde Vitruvius refert, cum Dinocrates architector peritissimus Alexandro Macedoni demonstraret in quodam monte civitatem egregiae formae construi posse, interrogasse Alexandrum si essent agri qui civitati possent frumentorum copiam ministrare. Quod cum deficere inveniret, respondit vituperandum esse si quis in tali loco civitatem construeret; sicut enim natus infans sine nutricis lacte non potest ali nec ad incrementum perduci, sic civitas sine ciborum abundantia frequentiam populi habere non potest.

Duo tamen sunt modi quibus alicui civitati potest affluentia rerum suppetere: unus qui dictus est, propter regionis fertilitatem abunde omnia producentis quae humanae vitae requirit necessitas; alius autem per mercationis usum, ex quo fit ut necessaria vitae ad civitatem ex diversis partibus adducantur. Primus autem modus convenientior esse manifeste convincitur: tanto enim aliquid dignius est quanto per se sufficientius invenitur, quia quod alio indiget deficiens esse monstratur. Sufficientiam autem plenius possidet civitas cui circumiacens regio sufficit ad necessaria vitae, quam illa quae indiget ab aliis per mercationes accipere. Dignior igitur est civitas si abundantiam rerum habeat ex territorio proprio, quam si per mercationes abundet. Cum hoc etiam videtur esse securius, quia propter bellorum eventus et diversa viarum discrimina de facili potest impediri deportatio victualium et accessus mercatorum ad locum, et sic civitas per defectum victualium opprimetur.

Est etiam hoc utilius ad conversationem civilem. Nam civitas quae ad sui sustentationem mercatorum multitudine indiget, necesse est ut continuum extraneorum convictum patiatur; extraneorum autem conversatio corrumpit plurimum civium mores, secundum Aristotelis doctrinam in sua *Politica*, quia necesse est evenire ut homines extranei, aliis legibus et consuetudinibus enutriti, in multis aliter agant quam sint civium mores; et sic dum cives eorum exemplo ad agenda similia provocantur, civilis conversatio perturbatur.

Rursus, si cives ipsi mercationibus fuerint dediti, pandetur pluribus vitiis aditus. Nam cum negotiatorum studium maxime ad lucrum tendat, per negotiationis usum cupiditas in cordibus civium radicatur; ex quo

It is not enough, however, that the place chosen for the site of a city be such as to preserve the health of the inhabitants; it must also be sufficiently fertile to provide food. A multitude of men cannot live where there is not a sufficient supply of food. Thus Vitruvius[36] narrates that when Dinocrates, a brilliant architect, was explaining to Alexander of Macedon that a beautifully laid out city could be built upon a certain mountain, Alexander asked whether there were fields that could supply the city with sufficient grain. Finding out that there were not, he said that an architect who would build a city on such a site would be blameworthy. For just as a newborn infant cannot be fed nor made to grow as it should except on the nurse's milk, so a city cannot have a large population without a large supply of food.

Now there are two ways in which an abundance of food can be supplied to a city. The first we have already mentioned, where the soil is so fertile that it amply provides for all the necessities of human life. The second is by trade, through which the necessaries of life are brought to the town in sufficient quantity from different places. It is quite clear that the first means is better. The more dignified a thing is, the more self-sufficient it is, since whatever needs another's help is by that fact proven to be deficient. Now the city which is supplied by the surrounding country with all its vital needs is more self-sufficient than another which must obtain those supplies by trade. A city, therefore, which has an abundance of food from its own territory is more dignified than one which is provisioned through trade. It seems that self-sufficiency is also safer, for the import of supplies and the access of merchants can easily be prevented, whether owing to wars or to the many hazards of the sea, and thus the city may be overcome through lack of food.

Moreover, this first method of supply is more conducive to the preservation of civic life. A city which must engage in much trade in order to supply its needs also has to put up with the continuous presence of foreigners. But association with foreigners, according to Aristotle's *Politics*, is particularly harmful to civic customs. For it is inevitable that strangers, brought up under other laws and customs, will in many cases act contrary to the citizens' customs, and thus, since the citizens are drawn by their example to act likewise, their own civic life is upset.

Again, if the citizens themselves devote their lives to matters of trade, the way will be opened to many vices. Since the foremost tendency of tradesmen is to make money, greed is awakened in the hearts of the citizens

36. I, 5.

398

contingit ut in civitate omnia fiant venalia, et fide subtracta locus fraudibus aperitur, publicoque bono contempto proprio commodo quisque deserviet; deficiet virtutis studium, dum honor virtutis divitibus deferetur: unde necesse erit in tali civitate civilem conversationem corrumpi.

Est autem negotiationis usus nociuus quam plurimum exercitio militari: negotiatores namque, dum umbram colunt, a laboribus vacant et fruuntur deliciis, mollescunt animi et corpora redduntur debilia et ad labores militares inepta; unde secundum iura civilia negotiatio est militibus interdicta. Denique civitas illa solet esse magis pacifica, cuius populus rarius congregatur minusque intra urbis moenia resident: ex frequenti namque hominum concursu datur occasio litibus, et seditionibus materia ministratur. Unde, secundum Aristotelis doctrinam, utilius est quod populus civitates exerceatur in agris quam quod intra civitatis moenia iugiter commoretur. Si autem civitas sit mercationibus dedita, maxime necesse est ut intra urbem cives resideant ibique mercationes exerceant. Melius igitur est quod civitati victualium copia suppetat ex propriis agris, quam quod civitas sit totaliter negotiationi exposita.

Nec tamen negotiatores omnino a civitate oportet excludi, quia non facili potest inveniri locus qui sic omnibus vitae necessariis abundet, quod non indigeat aliquibus aliunde allatis. Eorumque quae in loco superabundant eodem redderetur inutilis copia, si per mercatorum officium ad alia loca deferri non posset. Unde oportet quod perfecta civitas mercationibus moderate utatur.

through the pursuit of trade. The result is that everything in the city will become venal; good faith will be destroyed and the way opened to all kinds of trickery; each one will work only for his own profit, despising the public good; the cultivation of virtue will fail since honor, virtue's reward, will be bestowed upon the rich. Thus, in such a city, civic life will necessarily be corrupted.

The pursuit of trade is also very unfavorable to military activity. Tradesmen, not being used to the open air and not doing any hard work, but enjoying all pleasures, grow soft in spirit and their bodies are weakened and rendered unsuited to military labors. In accordance with this view, civil law forbids soldiers to engage in business. Finally, that city enjoys a greater measure of peace whose people are more sparsely assembled together and dwell in smaller proportion within the walls of the town, for when men are crowded together it is an occasion for quarrels and all the elements for seditious plots are provided. Hence, according to Aristotle's doctrine, it is more profitable to have the people engaged outside the cities than for them to dwell constantly within the walls. But if a city is dependent on trade, it is extremely necessary for the citizens to stay within the town and engage in trade there. It is better, therefore, that the supplies of food be furnished to the city from its own fields than that it be wholly dependent on trade.

Still, trade must not be entirely kept out of a city, since one cannot easily find any place so overflowing with the necessaries of life as not to need some commodities from other parts. Also, when there is an over-abundance of some commodities in one place, these goods would serve no purpose if they could not be carried elsewhere by professional traders. Consequently, the perfect city will make a moderate use of merchants.

CHAPTER 8

That the city should have a pleasant site

Est etiam locus construendis urbibus eligendus qui amoenitate habitatores delectet. Non enim facile deseritur locus in quo delectabiliter vivitur, neque de facili ad locum illum confluit habitantium multitudo cui deest amoenitas, eo quod absque delectatione hominum vita diu durare non possit. Ad hanc autem amoenitatem pertinet ut sit locus camporum planitie distentus, arborum ferax, montium propinquitate conspicuus, nemoribus gratus et aquis irriguus.

Verum nimia loci amoenitas superflue ad delicias allicit homines, quod civitati plurimum nocet. Primo namque homines vacantes deliciis sensu hebetantur: immergit enim earum suavitas sensibus animam, ita

When choosing a site for the founding of a city, it should also charm its inhabitants by its beauty. A spot where life is pleasant will not easily be abandoned, nor will men commonly be ready to flock to unpleasant places, since the life of man cannot endure without enjoyment. A beautiful place has a broad expanse of meadows, fruitful trees, mountains to be seen close at hand, pleasant groves, and overflowing waters.

However, if a country is too beautiful, it will draw men to indulge in pleasures, and this is most harmful to a city. In the first place, when men give themselves up to pleasure their senses are dulled, since this sweetness immerses the

quod de rebus delectabilibus liberum iudicium habere non possunt; unde secundum Aristotelis sententiam, prudentiae iudicium per delectationem corrumpitur. Deinde delectationes superfluae ab honestate virtutis homines deficere faciunt: nihil enim facilius perducit ad immoderatum augmentum per quod medium virtutis corrumpitur, quam delectatio; tum quia natura delectationis est avida, et sic modica occasione sumpta praecipitatur homo in turpium delectationum illecebras, sicut ligna sicca ex modico igne accenduntur; tum etiam quia delectatio appetitum non satiat, sed gustata sitim sui magis inducit. Unde ad virtutis officium pertinet ut homines se a delectationibus abstrahant: sic enim superfluitate vitata facilius ad medium virtutis pervenitur.

Consequenter etiam deliciis superflue dediti mollescunt animo et ad ardua quaeque attentanda necnon ad tolerandos labores et pericula subeunda pusillanimes fiunt; unde et ad bellicum usum deliciae plurimum nocent, quia, ut Vegetius dicit in libro *de Re militari*, *minus timet mortem qui minus deliciarum se novit habuisse in vita*. Demum deliciis resoluti plerumque pigrescunt et, praetermissis necessariis studiis et negotiis debitis, solis deliciis adhibent curam, in quas quae prius ab aliis fuerant congregata profusae dispergunt; unde ad paupertatem deducti, dum consuetis deliciis carere non possunt, se furtis et rapinis exponunt ut habeant unde possint suas voluptates explere. Est igitur nocivum civitati, vel ex loci dispositione vel ex quibuscumque aliis rebus, deliciis superfluis abundare.

Opportunum est autem in conversatione humana modicum delectationis quasi pro condimento habere, ut animi hominum recreentur.

soul in the senses so that man cannot pass free judgment on the things which cause delight. Hence, according to Aristotle's sentence,[37] the judgment of prudence is corrupted by pleasure. Again, indulgence in superfluous pleasure leads from the path of virtue, for nothing conduces more easily to immoderate increase, which upsets the mean of virtue, than pleasure. Pleasure is greedy by its very nature, and thus a slight occasion precipitates a man into the seductions of shameful pleasures, just as a little spark is sufficient to kindle dry wood. Moreover, indulgence does not satisfy the appetite, for the first sip only makes the thirst all the keener. Consequently, it is part of virtue's task to lead men to refrain from pleasures. By thus avoiding any excess, the mean of virtue will be more easily attained.

Also, they who give themselves up to pleasures grow soft in spirit and become weak-minded when it is a question of tackling some difficult enterprise, enduring toil, and facing dangers. Thus, likewise, indulgence in pleasures is detrimental to warfare, as Vegetius puts it in his *On the Art of Knighthood*: *He fears death less who knows that he has had little pleasure in life.*[38] Finally, men who have become dissolute through pleasures usually grow lazy, and, neglecting necessary matters and all the pursuits that duty lays upon them, devote themselves wholly to the quest of pleasure, on which they squander all that others had so carefully amassed. Thus, reduced to poverty and yet unable to deprive themselves of their accustomed pleasures, they do not shrink from stealing and robbing in order to have the means to indulge their craving for pleasure. It is therefore harmful to a city to superabound in delightful things, whether it be on account of its situation or from whatever other cause.

However, in human community it is best to have a moderate share of pleasure as a spice of life, so to speak, so that man's mind may find some recreation.

---

37. *Eth. Nic.* VI, 5: 1140b 11–21.
38. *De re militari* I, 3.